Lecture Notes of the Institute for Computer Sciences, Social Informatics and Telecommunications Engineering 483

The LNICST series publishes ICST's conferences, symposia and workshops.

LNICST reports state-of-the-art results in areas related to the scope of the Institute.

The type of material published includes

- Proceedings (published in time for the respective event)
- Other edited monographs (such as project reports or invited volumes)

LNICST topics span the following areas:

- General Computer Science
- E-Economy
- E-Medicine
- Knowledge Management
- Multimedia
- Operations, Management and Policy
- Social Informatics
- Systems

Hongming Yang · Jiang Fei · Tang Qiang
Editors

Smart Grid and Innovative Frontiers in Telecommunications

7th EAI International Conference, SmartGIFT 2022
Changsha, China, December 10–12, 2022
Proceedings

Editors
Hongming Yang
Changsha University of Science and Technology
Changsha, China

Jiang Fei
Changsha University of Science and Technology
Changsha, China

Tang Qiang
Changsha University of Science and Technology
Changsha, China

ISSN 1867-8211 ISSN 1867-822X (electronic)
Lecture Notes of the Institute for Computer Sciences, Social Informatics and Telecommunications Engineering
ISBN 978-3-031-31732-3 ISBN 978-3-031-31733-0 (eBook)
https://doi.org/10.1007/978-3-031-31733-0

This Springer imprint is published by the registered company Springer Nature Switzerland AG
The registered company address is: Gewerbestrasse 11, 6330 Cham, Switzerland

Preface

We are pleased to present the proceedings of the 7th EAI International Conference on Smart Grid and Innovative Frontiers in Telecommunications (SmartGIFT 2022) hosted by the European Innovation Alliance (EAI). This conference, which was held in Changsha, Hunan Province, China on December 10–11, 2022, brought together researchers, developers, and practitioners from around the world who are leveraging and developing smart grid technology for a smarter and more resilient grid. The theme of SmartGIFT 2022 was *Challenges and Opportunities of Intelligent Technologies in New Energy Systems.*

The technical program of SmartGIFT 2022 consisted of 44 full papers belonging to six technical paper sessions. Aside from the high-quality technical paper presentations, the technical program also featured two keynote speeches. The two keynote speeches were from Archie Johnston and from the University of Sydney, Australia, Hongming Yang and Sheng Xiang from Changsha University of Science & Technology, China, and Chenye Wu from the Chinese University of Hong Kong, China. The topics of their presentations were *Innovation and Strategic Role of Smart Grid Technology* and *Learning for the Future Power Grid*. The six paper sessions organized were *Simulation and analysis of the integrated energy system, Disaster prevention and reduction for power grid, Industry 4.0 applications, Flexible planning and regulation techniques in smart grids, Smart control and diagnosis of distributed power system*, and *Control and operation of UAV*. These sessions aimed to address and gain insights into key challenges, understanding, and criteria of new technologies to develop and implement future industry-related services and applications.

Coordination with the steering chairs, Prof. Kun Yang, Yijia Cao, and Xiangjun Zeng was essential for the success of the conference. We sincerely appreciate their constant support and guidance. It was also a great pleasure to work with such an excellent organizing committee team for their hard work in organizing and supporting the conference. In particular, the Technical Program Committee, led by our TPC Co-Chairs, Prof. Wen Wang, and Fei Jiang, completed the peer-review process of technical papers and made a high-quality technical program. We are also grateful to the Conference Manager, Veronika Kissova, for her support and to all the authors who submitted their papers to the SmartGIFT 2022 conference.

We strongly believe that the SmartGIFT conference provides an international platform for scholars and engineers engaged in electrical engineering, information technology, electronic technology, and control technology aspects that are relevant to smart grids. We also expect that the future SmartGIFT conferences will be as successful and stimulating, as indicated by the contributions presented in this volume.

Hongming Yang
Jiang Fei
Tang Qiang

Organization

Steering Committee

Kun Yang	University of Essex, UK
Yijia Cao	Changsha University of Science and Technology, China
Xiangjun Zeng	Changsha University of Science and Technology, China

Organizing Committee

General Chair

Hongming Yang	Changsha University of Science and Technology, China

General Co-chairs

Andrew Rae	University of the Highlands and Islands, UK
Archie Johnston	University of Sydney, Australia
Zhaoyang Dong	Nanyang Technological University, Singapore

TPC Chair and Co-chair

Wen Wang	Changsha University of Science and Technology, China
Fei Jiang	Changsha University of Science and Technology, China

Local Chair

Jiechao Wu	Changsha University of Science and Technology, China

Workshops Chair

Junhua Zhao	Chinese University of Hong Kong (Shenzhen), China

Publicity and Social Media Chair

Gengfeng Ren	Changsha University of Science and Technology, China

Publications Chair

Ci Tang	Changsha University of Science and Technology, China

Sponsorship and Exhibit Chair

Xiafei Tang	Changsha University of Science and Technology, China

Web Chair

Angela Yingjun Zhang	The Chinese University of Hong Kong, China

Posters and PhD Track Chair

Yan Xu	Nanyang Technological University, Singapore

Panels Chair

Zhuoqun Xia	Changsha University of Science and Technology, China

Demos Chair

Zhao Xu	Hong Kong Polytechnic University, China

Tutorials Chair

Chenye Wu	Chinese University of Hong Kong (Shenzhen), China

Technical Program Committee

Ling Li	Changsha University of Science and Technology, China
Jingjie Huang	Changsha University of Science and Technology, China
Qiang Tang	Changsha University of Science and Technology, China

Contents

Industry 4.0 Applications

Control and Operation of UAV

Simulation and Analysis of the Integrated Energy System

Optimized Operation of Integrated Electricity-Heat-Gas Energy System Considering the Optimal Consumption of Wind and Photovoltaic Power Generation

Wenye Wang[1], Fengzhe Dai[1](✉), Fei Jiang[1], and Zhichang Li[2]

[1] School of Electrical and Information Engineering, Changsha University of Science and Technology, Changsha 410076, Hunan, China
2420193033@qq.com

[2] State Grid Information and Telecommunication Accenture Information Technology Co., Ltd., Haidian, Beijing 100095, China

Abstract. The continuous expansion of installed capacity and grid-connected scale of new energy sources such as wind power and photovoltaic power generation will affect the stability and economic operation of the integrated energy system. Aiming at this problem, an optimized operation method of the electric-heat-gas interconnected Integrated Energy System considering the optimal wind and light absorption is proposed. The constraints of electric heating and gas systems, coupling constraints, wind-photovoltaic energy abandonment penalties, operating costs and environmental costs have been considered to construct an optimal energy abandonment cost model; with the goal of minimizing the total system cost in the dispatch period, the optimal operation of each unit is decided, including the optimal wind, light absorption, and the model is solved with the help of the commercial optimization software CPLEX.Finally, the example uses the improved IEEE-39-node electric power system, the Belgian 20-node natural gas system, and the 6-node thermal system for simulation analysis.The results show that the proposed model can effectively improve the stability and economy of system scheduling in the IES with electric heating and gas interconnection, and realize the optimal consumption of wind and photovoltaic power.

Keywords: Optimal Energy Consumption · Integrated Power · Heat and Natural Gas · Integrated Energy System · Mixed Integer Linear Programming

1 Introduction

Under the background of the "carbon peaking and carbon neutrality", Integrated Energy System (IES) has the high efficiency of energy supply and the strong flexibility of coordinated operation, which is one of the important ways to improve the consumption of renewable energy. However, there is a strong uncertainty of clean energy generation, resulting in its grid-connected operation facing many challenges.

H. Yang et al. (Eds.): SmartGIFT 2022, LNICST 483, pp. 3–13, 2023.
https://doi.org/10.1007/978-3-031-31733-0_1

Domestic and foreign scholars have carried out some research on the optimal operation of IES with clean energy. Reference [1] regulated high energy load and conventional power supply to participate in power grid dispatching to improve wind power utilization. References [2, 3] proposed the IES optimal scheduling model considering the rational utilization of curtailed wind power, which reduced the operation cost of the system. In references [4–6], a coordinated optimal scheduling model of integrated electric heating system considering source-load uncertainty was proposed, and the improvement effect of the model on wind power consumption was verified. In reference [7], an electric heating and gas interconnection IES considering demand response was proposed to realize the environmental and economic optimal scheduling of the system. Reference [8] took the minimum sum of deterministic cost and random cost as the objective function to improve the reliability of power supply. In references [9, 10], the output of each device was optimized and the fluctuation of clean energy output was reduced by considering the prediction error of wind and light. However, the above literature did not cover the case of optimal renewable energy consumption rate in each period of time, and was less applied in Electro-Thermal-Gas coupled IES.

In summary, this paper constructs an optimization model of the integrated energy system considering the optimal wind and solar consumption. Considering the constraints and coupling constraints of the electric heating and gas system, the operation model of the electric heating and gas interconnection IES is constructed, and the minimum operating cost of the system is taken as the objective function. The IEEE-39 node power system, Belgium 20 node natural gas system and 6 node thermal system are used for example analysis to prove the effectiveness of the model.

2 IES Considering Optimal Accommodation of Wind Power and Photovoltaic Power

Wind power and photovoltaic power have anti-peak shaving characteristics, and their output fluctuation characteristics are opposite to the fluctuation of grid load. When the load decreases, wind farms and photovoltaic power stations compete for power generation; When the load increases, the wind power output may decrease. Based on this feature, on the basis of satisfying the operating constraints of the electric-heat-gas integrated energy system and the constraints of wind abandonment and photovoltaic abandonment rate, the conditions of wind and photovoltaic abandonment in different periods are optimized, so as to alleviate the phenomenon of wind and photovoltaic reverse peak shaving and improve the system. Overall operation stability and optimal economy are realized.

2.1 The Model of Wind Power and Photovoltaic Power

In order to avoid unreasonable wind abandonment and abandonment of light due to the search for minimum economy during the solution process, the optimization results are inconsistent with the goal of using renewable energy, the minimum allowable wind and light consumption must meet the following constraints respectively:

$$\mathrm{con_{PW}}\sum_{t=1}^{T}P_{\mathrm{PW},t}\leq\sum_{t=1}^{T}con_{\mathrm{PW},t}P_{\mathrm{PW},t}\leq\sum_{t=1}^{T}P_{\mathrm{PW},t} \tag{1}$$

$$\mathrm{con_{PV}}\sum_{t=1}^{T}P_{\mathrm{PV},t}\leq\sum_{t=1}^{T}\mathrm{con}_{\mathrm{PV},t}P_{\mathrm{PV},t}\leq\sum_{t=1}^{T}P_{\mathrm{PV},t} \tag{2}$$

where $con_{\mathrm{PW},t}$ and $con_{\mathrm{PV},t}$ denote the absorption rate of wind power and photovoltaic power during t period, $P_{\mathrm{PW},t}$ and $P_{\mathrm{PV},t}$ denote the output power of wind farm and photovoltaic power plant during t period, $P_{\mathrm{PWcon},t}$ and $P_{\mathrm{PVcon},t}$ denote the consumption of wind power and photovoltaic power plants in t period, $\mathrm{con_{PW}}$ and $\mathrm{con_{PV}}$ denote the minimum consumption rates of wind power and photovoltaic total output in the dispatch period.

In order to further refine the optimization model of wind power and photovoltaics, in addition to introducing penalty factors to restrict energy consumption behavior, and comprehensively considering the operating cost and environmental cost of the unit, the objective function can be expressed as:

$$C_{\mathrm{PW}}=\sum_{t=1}^{T}[(\lambda_{\mathrm{p}}+\lambda_{\mathrm{r}}-\lambda_{\mathrm{b}})\times\sum_{i=1}^{N_{\mathrm{PW}}}P_{\mathrm{PW},t}^{i}] \tag{3}$$

$$C_{\mathrm{PV}}=\sum_{t=1}^{T}[(\omega_{\mathrm{p}}+\omega_{\mathrm{r}}-\omega_{\mathrm{b}})\times\sum_{i=1}^{N_{\mathrm{PV}}}P_{\mathrm{PV},t}^{i}] \tag{4}$$

where C_{PW} and C_{PV} are respectively the total cost of optimized dispatch of wind and photovoltaic models, λ_{p} and ω_{p} are the penalty factors for wind abandonment and photovoltaic abandonment respectively, λ_{r} and ω_{r} are the operating costs of wind power and photovoltaics respectively, λ_{b} and ω_{b} are the environmental costs of wind power and photovoltaics respectively, N_{PW} and N_{PV} are the number of wind turbines and photovoltaic power plants respectively.

2.2 Optimization of IES Based on Electricity-Heat-Gas Considering the Optimal Accommodation of Wind Power and Photovoltaic Power

The schematic diagram of the IES considering optimal wind power and photovoltaic power is shown in Fig. 1. The system includes three types of networks with different energy attributes: electric power system, natural gas system, and thermal system. Among them, Gas Turbine (GT) and Power to Gas (P2G) realize the coupling of electric and gas systems. The Heat Recovery Steam Generator (HRSG) is connected to the gas turbine to realize the coupling of gas and heat systems. The Electric Boiler (EB) completes the energy conversion between heat and electricity systems [11].

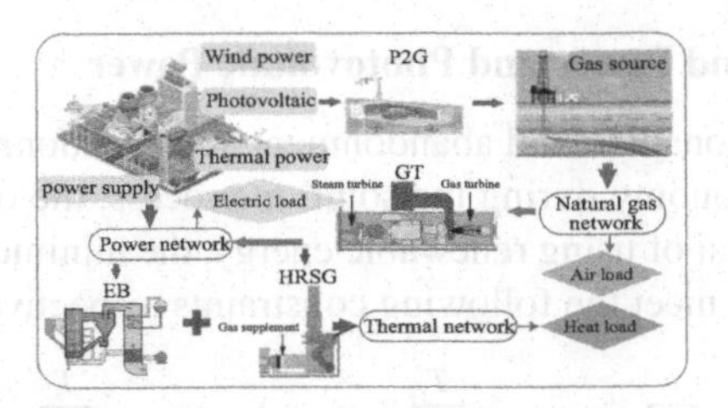

Fig. 1. Schematic Diagram of the IES

3 Optimal Scheduling Model of IES for Electric Heating Gas Interconnection

The optimization of the IES of electric heating and gas interconnection aims at minimizing the economic dispatch cost in the cycle. Dispatching costs mainly include the power generation cost of traditional thermal power units, the cost of gas source output in the natural gas system, the operating cost of wind power and photovoltaics, which can be calculated as:

$$\min F = \min(C_e + C_g + C_{PW} + C_{PV}) \tag{5}$$

where C_e and C_g respectively denote the operating costs of the power system and natural gas system.

3.1 Coupling Device Model

In the P2G realization of the electric-gas system coupling process, the relationship between the consumed electric energy and the natural gas produced can be described as:

$$V_{P2G,t} = \frac{\eta_{P2G} \times P_{P2G,t}}{HHV_{gas}} \tag{6}$$

where $V_{P2G,t}$ and $P_{P2G,t}$ are the volume value of natural gas and the electric energy consumed during the process of converting electricity to gas in t period, respectively; η_{P2G} is the energy conversion efficiency; HHV_{gas} is the high calorific value of natural gas.

As the coupling node of the gas-electric system, the gas turbine has the relationship between its power generation and natural gas consumption can be cacluated as:

$$V_{GT,t} = \frac{P_{GT,t}}{\eta_{GT} \times LHV_{gas}} \tag{7}$$

where $V_{GT,t}$ denotes the gas consumption during the operation of the gas turbine during t period, $P_{GT,t}$ denotes the output electric power, η_{GT} denotes the power generation efficiency of the gas turbine, LHV_{gas} denotes the low heating value of natural gas.

The energy conversion of waste heat boiler can be cacluated as

$$Q_{HR,t} = \eta_{HR} \times \frac{P_{GT,t}(1 - \eta_{GT} - \eta_L)}{\eta_{GT}} \tag{8}$$

where $Q_{\mathrm{HR},t}$ denotes the output heat power during the operation of HRSG in t period, η_{HR} denotes the waste heat recovery efficiency of HRSG, η_{L} denotes the loss rate.

The output model of EB can be cacluated as:

$$Q_{\mathrm{EB},t} = \eta_{\mathrm{EB}} \times P_{\mathrm{EB},t} \tag{9}$$

where $Q_{\mathrm{EB},t}$ and $P_{\mathrm{EB},t}$ respectively denote the thermal power and input electric power during the operation of EB during t period, $\eta_{\mathrm{EB,h}}$ denotes the thermal efficiency of EB.

3.2 Power System Optimization Model

The operating cost of a thermal power unit can be expressed as:

$$C_{\mathrm{e}} = \sum_{t=1}^{T} F_{i,t} \tag{10}$$

$$F_{i,t} = \mathrm{a}_i (P^i_{\mathrm{PU},t})^2 + \mathrm{b}_i P^i_{\mathrm{PU},t} + \mathrm{c}_i \tag{11}$$

where a_i, b_i, c_i respectively denote the cost coefficients of unit i, $P^i_{\mathrm{PU},t}$ denotes the output of thermal power unit i in period t.

The operation constraints of the power system include power balance constraints, generator output constraints, phase angle constraints and line power flow constraints when using DC power flow method.

The power consumption of the gas turbine is included in the node as the load of the power network.

$$P_{\mathrm{PU},t} + P_{\mathrm{GT},t} + P_{\mathrm{PW},t} + P_{\mathrm{PV},t} = P_{\mathrm{LD},t} + P_{\mathrm{L},t} \tag{12}$$

where $P_{\mathrm{LD},t}$, $_{\mathrm{L},t}$ respectively denote the electric load and line power flow during t period.

3.3 Natural Gas System Optimization Model

The optimization of natural gas network mainly considers natural gas sources, natural gas pipelines, pressurizing stations to supplement pressure loss, and natural gas loads. Among them, the coupling device P2G converts the excess electric energy of the system into natural gas and injects it into the natural gas system, acting as the gas source of the natural gas system; The natural gas consumed by the gas turbine is included in the gas load of the node.

Natural gas source cost can be calculated as:

$$C_{\mathrm{g}} = \sum_{t=1}^{T} c_{\mathrm{g}} V_{\mathrm{s},t} \tag{13}$$

where C_{g} denotes the cost of gas source output, c_{g} is the unit price of natural gas, $V_{\mathrm{s},t}$ denotes the gas source output during t period.

The node energy balance constraint of the natural gas system can be calculated as:

$$V_{s,t} + V_{P2G,t} = V_{LD,t} + V_{L,t} \tag{14}$$

where $V_{LD,t}$ denotes the gas load at time period t, $V_{L,t}$ denotes the natural gas pipeline tidal current.

Natural gas pipelines will produce losses and pressure drops due to pipe wall friction and external factors during the transmission process. At this time, compressors are installed along the pipeline to alleviate this problem. The compressor model can be calculated as:

$$p_{out} = \Gamma_c p_{in} \tag{15}$$

where p_{out} and p_{in} respectively denote the pressure at the outlet and inlet of the compressor respectively, Γ_c is the compression ratio of the compressor, ignoring its own loss, the compression ratio is constant.

3.4 Thermodynamic System Optimization Model

Thermal network equilibrium constraints.

$$Q_{EB,t} + Q_{HB,t} = Q_{LD,t} + Q_{loss,t} \tag{16}$$

where $Q_{EB,t}$, $Q_{HB,t}$, $Q_{LD,t}$ respectively denote the heat production and heat load of electric heating boiler and waste heat boiler in t period.

The thermal power of each heat source node and load node is related to the water supply temperature, return water temperature and heat medium flow in the pipeline, which can be expressed as

$$\mathrm{H}_i = \mathrm{C}_p m_i (T_s^i - T_r^i) \tag{17}$$

where H_i is the thermal power flowing into node i, and it is specified that the inflow is positive and the outflow is negative, C_p is the specific heat capacity of water, m_i is the water flow out of node i, T_s^i, T_r^i respectively denote the node i heating temperature and regenerative temperature respectively.

$$\mathrm{H}_{ij} = \mathrm{C}_p m_j (T_r^i - T_r^j) \tag{18}$$

where H_{ij} denotes the heat loss of the heat pipe ij, m_j is the water flow out of node j, T_r^i, T_r^j respectively denote the heating temperature of nodes i and j.

4 Case Studies

Based on the optimal wind and light absorption model, the mathematical model of IES optimal scheduling including electric thermal gas is established. Under the MATLAB environment, the Yalmip toolbox is used to call the CPLEX solver for simulation analysis.

4.1 Introduction to the Example

For the optimal accommodation of wind power and photovoltaic power model proposed above, the improved IEEE-39 node power system, Belgium 20 node natural gas system, and 6-node thermal system are used for simulation in the calculation example. The specific structure of the IES for the electric-heat-gas interconnection is shown in the Fig. 2. Among them, the generators of the power system network nodes 30, 33, and 37 are set as gas turbines, which are connected to the natural gas network nodes 3, 6, and 19 respectively; nodes 6, 12 are connected to wind farms, and nodes 1, 17 are respectively equipped with photovoltaic power plants. The output of the unit is shown in Fig. 3. It is assumed that the gas source of the natural gas system network node 13 is an electric-to-gas device, which is connected to the power system network node 15. Node 1 of the thermal system network is the heat source. The electric boiler installed at this node is connected to node 24 of the power system network, and the waste heat boiler is connected to the gas turbine at node 30 of the power system network.

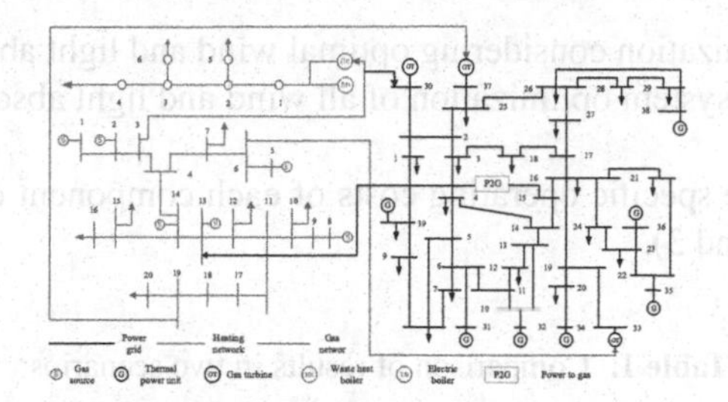

Fig. 2. Structure diagram of the integrated power, heat and natural gas energy system

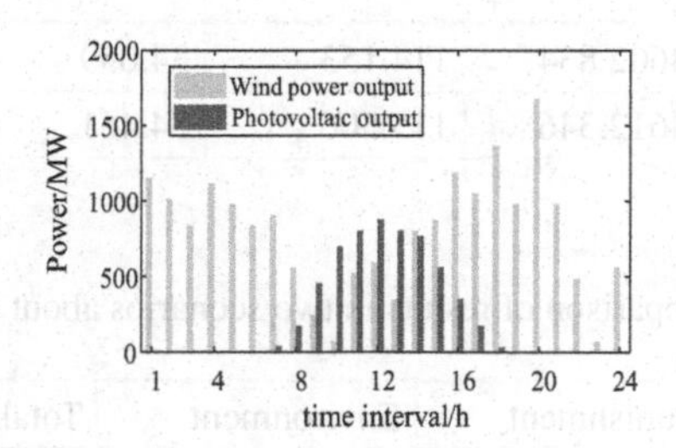

Fig. 3. The output of wind power and photovoltaic

The curves of the optimized electrical load, gas load and thermal load of the system on a typical day are shown in Fig. 4. The size of the system node load is distributed according to the node load ratio.

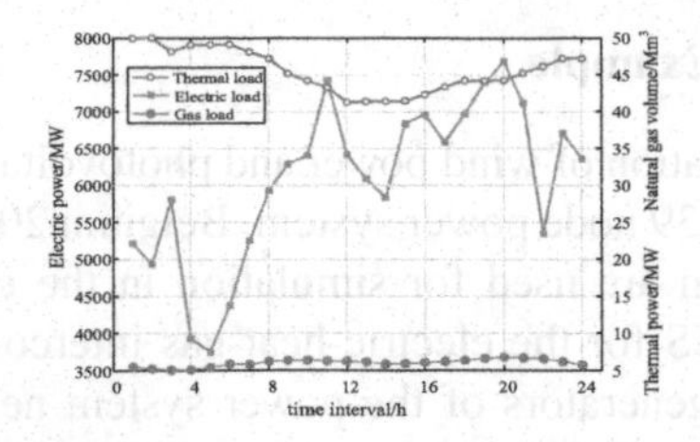

Fig. 4. The daily load curve of integrated power, heat and natural gas energy system

4.2 The Running Result Analys

In order to propose the optimal accommodation of wind power and photovoltaic power model for the research on the impact of the operation of the electric-heat-gas interconnected integrated energy system, two cases were set up for comparative analysis, respectively as follows:

Case 1: System optimization considering optimal wind and light absorption;
Case 2: Consider the system optimization of all wind and light absorption.

Table 1 shows the specific operating costs of each component of the system in the two cases (Tables 2 and 3).

Table 1. Comparison of results in two scenarios

case	Thermal power	Gas source	Wind power	photovoltaic	Total(/ten thousand dollars)
1	2377.522	4602.834	114.153	34.059	7133.567
2	2367.423	4612.346	115.500	34.461	7134.731

Table 2. Comparison of results in two scenarios about wind power

case	Function	Punishment	Environment	Total/ten thousand dollars
1	188.650	0.963	75.460	114.153
2	192.500	–	77.000	115.500

Table 3. Comparison of results in two scenarios about PV

case	Function	Punishment	Environment	Total(/ten thousand dollars)
1	56.286	0.287	22.515	34.059
2	57.435	–	22.974	34.461

The wind abandonment rate and the abandonment rate in each period under the optimal wind and light absorption are shown in Fig. 5.

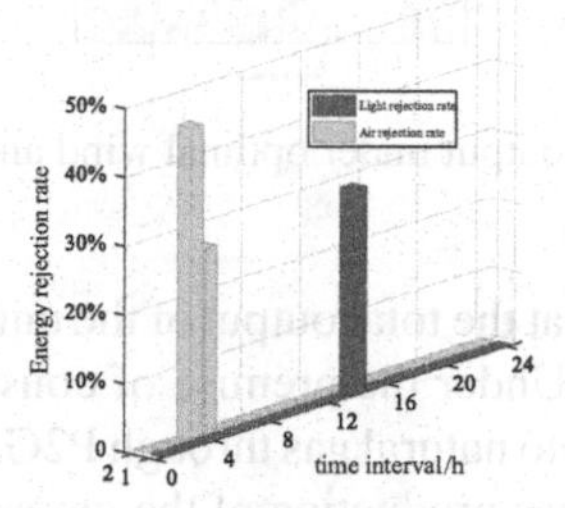

Fig. 5. The optimal abandonment rate in different time

Comparing the wind abandonment situation in Fig. 5 with the electric load curve in Fig. 5, it can be seen that the wind abandonment rate in the period 4–5 is significantly higher than that in other periods, and the electric load in the corresponding period is in a low state, which can explain the scenario The model applied in 1 has a positive effect on improving the anti-peaking characteristics of wind power.

It can be seen from Fig. 3 that the time period of photovoltaic output is concentrated in time period 7–18, which happens to be during the peak energy consumption period, which is only generated by the abandonment of light in time period 14, while the electrical load of time period 14 is at the lowest in time period 7–18. Therefore, it can be explained that the model applied in scenario 1 can improve the anti-peaking phenomenon of photovoltaic.

At the same time, wind power and photovoltaic anti-peaking characteristics will also affect the output of thermal power units. The output change curves of thermal power units under the two models are shown in Fig. 6.

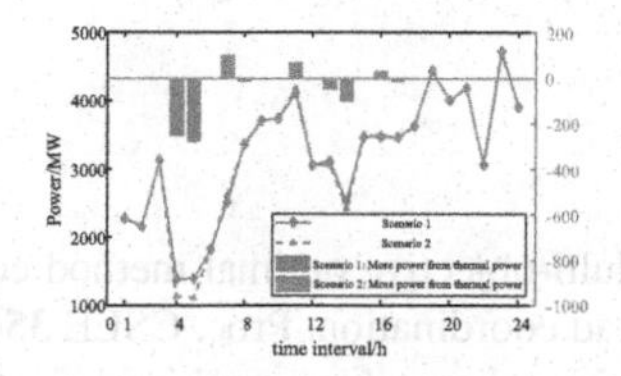

Fig. 6. Comparison of the output of thermal power units in two scenarios

Combined with the electric load curve in Fig. 4, when the reverse peak shaving phenomenon occurs, wind and light may compete for power generation during the trough periods of power consumption 4–5, 13–14, etc., and abandonment may occur during the peak period of power consumption 11, etc. The wind phenomenon increases the difficulty of peak shaving of the power grid.

The output of other units of the power system in scenario 1 is shown in Fig. 7.

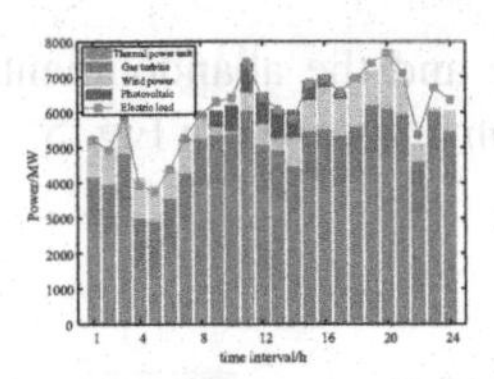

Fig. 7. Power system unit output under optimal wind and photovoltaic absorption

It can be seen from Fig. 6 that the total output of the units in each period of case 1 will be greater than that in case 2. Under the premise of constant electrical load, excessive electrical energy is converted into natural gas through P2G. In order to ensure the balance of the natural gas system, the gas production of the gas source will be reduced, and the cost of the gas source will be higher, leading to a significant reduction in the operating cost of the gas source. According to the data in Table 1, the gas source cost under case 1 is reduced by $951200 compared with case 2, and the proposed optimization model is effective.

5 Conclusion

With the objective of minimizing the economic operation cost of the two cases, this paper establishes a scheduling model for the IES of electric heating gas interconnection considering the optimal wind and light consumption, and calls CPLEX to solve the model. The main conclusions are as follows:The traditional wind power and photovoltaic full consumption method will put pressure on the operation of the grid and affect the economics of the dispatch of the integrated energy system of electric heating and gas interconnection; the optimal wind and light absorption model proposed in this paper comprehensively considers the power generation cost, gas source output cost, wind and photovoltaic operation and maintenance, and environmental cost of thermal power units, which improves the stability of system scheduling while ensuring the economics of IES.

References

1. Liu, W., Wen, J., Xie, C.: Multi-objective optimal method considering wind power accommodation based on source-load coordination. Proc. CSEE **35**(5), 1079–1088 (2015)
2. Li, Y., Liu, W., Zhao, J.: Optimal dispatch of combined electricity-gas-heat energy systems with power-to-gas devices and benefit analysis of wind power accommodation. Power Syst. Technol. **40**(12), 3680–3689 (2016)

3. Zhang, R., Jiang, T., Li, G.: Bi-level optimization dispatch of integrated electricity-natural Gas systems considering P2G for wind power accommodation. Proc. CSEE **38**(19), 5668–5678 (2018)
4. Shui, Y., Liu, J., Gao, H.: A distributionally robust coordinated dispatch model for integrated electricity and heating systems considering uncertainty of wind power. Proc. CSEE **38**(24), 7235–7247, 7450 (2018)
5. Pan, G., Gu, W., Zhang, H.: Electricity and hydrogen energy system towards accomodation of high proportion of renewable energy. Autom. Electr. Power Syst. **44**(23), 1–10 (2020)
6. Tian, B., He, F., Chang, X.: Environmental economic optimal dispatch of electricity-heat-gas integrated energy system considering integrated demand response. Power Demand Side Manage. **23**(1), 18–24 (2021)
7. Li, X., Sui, Q., Lin, X.: A flexible load control strategy for power grid considering fully consumption of surplus wind power and global benefits. Proc. CSEE **40**(18) (2020)
8. Tian, D., Chen, Z., Deng, Y.: Integrated energy system optimal dispatching model considering prediction errors. Acta Energiae Photovolt. Sinica **40**(7), 1890–1896 (2019)
9. Wang, J., Xu, J., Liao, S.: Coordinated optimization of integrated electricity-gas energy system considering uncertainty of renewable energy output. Autom. Electr. Power Syst. **43**(15), 2–9 (2019)
10. Deng, J., Jiang, F., Tu, C.: Study of NIST's interoperable smart grid technology architecture. Power Syst. Protect. Control **48**(3), 9–21 (2020)
11. Jiang, F., Peng, X., Tu, C.: An improved hybrid parallel compensator for enhancing PV power transfer capability. IEEE Trans. Industr. Electron. **69**(11), 11132–11143 (2022)

Carbon Emission Accounting of Typical Megacities Based on Electricity Statistics

Qiaoqian Lan[1(✉)] and Bin Zhong[2]

[1] State Grid Shanghai Jiading Power Supply Company, Shanghai, China
735286417@qq.com

[2] State Grid Shanghai Electric Power Company, Shanghai, China

Abstract. With the continuous improvement of the urbanization rate, the pressure on my country's cities to reduce emissions is increasing. In the context of emission peak and carboon neutrality, the quantification of urban carbon emissions is of great significance. Considering producer responsibility and consumer responsibility comprehensively, starting from the shared responsibility sharing accounting method, and taking electricity equivalent value and electricity equivalent value as important indicators, a power carbon emission accounting model based on the principle of shared responsibility is constructed. Select urban characteristic factors closely related to urban carbon emissions to construct an extended STIRPAT equation; use XGBoost to score the importance of multiple features to complete important feature selection; take carbon emissions as the dependent variable, night lights, electricity carbon emissions data, other Significant influencing factors are independent variables, and urban carbon emissions are calculated with the help of the spatial Durbin model.

Keywords: Shared Responsibility · Electricity Carbon Emissions · Urban Carbon Emissions · Carbon Emissions Accounting

1 Introduction

At present, domestic and foreign scholars use the input-output model to calculate carbon emission data more. Ref. [1] used the input-output model to calculate the carbon emissions of 13 cities in China from the perspective of consumption, and found that there were significant differences in the levels of carbon emissions obtained from the perspectives of consumption and production. Ref. [2] builds an estimation model for China's urban carbon emissions data based on the energy balance sheet, which includes 47 socio-economic sectors, 17 fossil fuels and 9 basic production sectors. Some scholars have used night light data to study the related issues of regional carbon emissions. Ref. [3] built a model to explore the relationship between the carbon emissions of provincial residents and night lights, and found that the goodness of fit between the two was as high

Project: State Grid Shanghai Electric Power Company Science and Technology Project (52090021N00U).

H. Yang et al. (Eds.): SmartGIFT 2022, LNICST 483, pp. 14–19, 2023.
https://doi.org/10.1007/978-3-031-31733-0_2

as 0.94. Ref. [4] uses a variety of socioeconomic factors to correct nighttime lights. The study found that after the nighttime light data is corrected, it can effectively alleviate the carbon emission estimation problem caused by the lack of statistical data in county-level areas. Ref. [5] found that there is a one-way causal relationship between urbanization, economic growth and carbon emission intensity by testing the causal relationship, and the study showed that economic growth is the main determinant of carbon emission intensity. Ref. [6] uses the symbolic regression method and the data from 1995 to 2014 to the influencing factors of carbon emission intensity in 34 OECD member countries, and finds that there are differences in the influencing factors of carbon emission intensity in each country. In 17 of these countries, the most common and important factor in carbon intensity is GDP; in 4 of these countries, the most prominent factor is industrialization and technological innovation; in 3 of these countries, urbanization, population and foreign direct investment play a positive role effect.

Through the above related literature, it can be obtained that the factors affecting urban carbon emissions in the current related research include: population, urbanization, industrialization, economic level, GDP, affluence, industrial structure, technological progress and innovation, climate difference, foreign investment, etc. Among them, factors such as population, GDP, economic level and affluence are closely related to urbanization.

In order to avoid the drawbacks of carbon emission accounting from the perspective of production and consumption, and considering that most of the carbon emissions in municipal areas come from energy consumption, this paper will adopt the principle of carbon emission accounting shared by producers and consumers, comprehensively consider night lights, Influencing factors such as electricity carbon emissions are independent variables, and urban carbon emissions are calculated with the help of the spatial Durbin model.

2 Shared Responsibility Principle

The principle of shared responsibility, that is, the responsibility for carbon emissions is shared by producers and consumers. This accounting principle can incorporate all links and consumers in the industrial chain into the emission accounting system, so that all parties involved bear the corresponding emission responsibilities. The core issue of the shared responsibility principle accounting method is to determine the share of emissions between producers and consumers. The share ratio proposed in this subject is the urban power generation efficiency, which is determined according to the equivalent value and equivalent value of urban power. Taking the power generation efficiency of each city as the shared proportion, on the one hand, it can reflect the differences in the power generation efficiency of cities, and effectively encourage cities to adopt more efficient and low-carbon power generation methods and power generation technologies to reduce their emission responsibilities; Consumers take more measures to reduce electricity consumption, thereby reducing their emission responsibilities.

$$EEV_y = \frac{\sum_i FC_{i,y} R_i}{TP_y} + \frac{\sum_j FQ_{j,y} S_j}{TQ_y} \tag{1}$$

$$K_y = \frac{ECV}{EEV_y} \tag{2}$$

$$\theta_y = 1 - K_y \tag{3}$$

where: EEV_y denotes the equivalent value of urban electricity in year *y*; $FC_{i,y}$ denotes the consumption of fossil fuel i in urban thermal power generation in year y; R_i denotes the converted standard coal coefficient of fossil fuel *i*; TP_y denotes urban thermal power in year *y* Power generation; $FQ_{j,y}$ denotes the consumption of clean energy *j* in urban clean energy power generation in year *y* (mainly refers to the carbon emissions generated by the full life cycle of clean energy power generation equipment, including manufacturing, installation, operation and maintenance, scrapping, etc.); S_j represents the standard coal coefficient converted by clean energy *j*; TQ_y refers to the urban clean energy power generation in year *y*; *i* denotes the type of fossil fuel consumed in thermal power generation; K_y denotes the thermal power generation efficiency in the *y*th year; *ECV* denotes the equivalent value of electricity; θ_y denotes the emission commitment of the power production side in the *y*th year. Since the ratio of commitment is inversely related to the thermal power generation efficiency, it is conducive to promoting the provinces to take effective measures to improve the thermal power generation efficiency and reduce the carbon emission responsibility of their electricity.

3 The Accounting Model of Urban Electricity-Related Carbon Emissions Based on the Principle of Shared Responsibility

3.1 Production-Side Carbon Emissions

$$EP_y = \theta_y EM_y \tag{4}$$

where EP_y denotes the emission borne by the urban power generation in year *y*; EM_y denotes the direct emission of urban electricity in year *y*.

$$EM = \sum_i AC_i \cdot EF_i \tag{5}$$

where AC_i denotes the consumption of fuel *i* in the electricity production process; EF_i denotes the emission factor of fuel *i*.

3.2 Consumer Carbon Emissions

The emissions borne by the power consumer are composed of two parts: the power consumption emissions in the regional power grid and the net transfer (transfer) power consumption emissions from other regional power grids [7, 8].

$$EC_{p,y} = (1 - \theta_y)EM_y + EFIC_y NEP_y \tag{6}$$

where $EC_{p,y}$ denotes the city's electricity consumption emissions in the power grid in the *y*th year; $EFIC_y NEP_y$ denotes the net transfer (transfer) to the city's electricity emissions.

3.3 Grid Carbon Emissions

The transmission loss emission of the power grid can be regarded as the emission of power consumption of the power grid. To calculate this part of the emission, the power consumption of the provincial power grid can be directly multiplied by the emission factor of the corresponding urban power consumption end. The carbon emission factor of electricity consumption can be estimated according to the carbon emission of electricity consumption and the total electricity consumption in the city.

$$EFC_y = \frac{EC_y}{CE_y} \tag{7}$$

where $EFC_{p,y}$ denotes the carbon emission factor of the city's electricity consumption in the yth year; CE_y denotes the total electricity consumption of the city in the yth year.

$$E_{grid,y} = EFC_y \cdot CE_{s,y} \tag{8}$$

where $E_{grid,y}$ denotes the carbon emission responsibility of the grid side in the yth year; $CE_{s,y}$ denotes the power transmission loss of the grid in the yth year.

4 Urban Carbon Emission Accounting Based on Electricity Statistics

Select urban characteristic factors closely related to urban carbon emissions, covering social, economic, physical geography, etc., including GDP, industry, transportation, total population, energy structure, industrial structure, technology level, foreign trade, energy consumption intensity, land Statistical data of each factor are obtained from statistical data such as China Urban Statistical Yearbook, China Statistical Yearbook and China Regional Statistical Yearbook over the years [9].

With the help of the extended STIRPAT equation, the influence of k factors on urban carbon emissions is analyzed, and *m* factors that have a significant impact on carbon emissions are obtained.

Using the extended STIRPAT equation to analyze the influence of k factors on urban carbon emissions, according to [10]:

$$\ln E = a + b_1 \ln B_1 + b_2 \ln B_2 + \ldots + b_k \ln B_k + \varepsilon_1 \tag{9}$$

where E denotes the urban carbon emission; a denotes a constant quantity; $B_1, B_2 \ldots B_k$ are the k factors that characterize the urban carbon emission characteristics; $b_1, b_2 \ldots b_k$ are the k factor coefficients respectively.

SPSS is used to process the data related to m factors that have a significant impact on urban carbon emissions over the years, and the method of ridge regression analysis is used to model the urban carbon emissions data and carry out a significance test. The constant number and k factors can be obtained. Factor coefficients. According to the obtained coefficients, the influence degrees of k independent variables on carbon emission changes are summarized, and m factors with significant influence on urban carbon emissions are obtained after sorting the influence degrees [11, 12].

Use XGBoost to calculate the feature importance of m factors, and select n factor sets for subsequent urban carbon emission accounting after scoring the importance of m features.

With the help of XGBoost, the feature importance of m factors is calculated, that is, the number of factors used in key decisions in the statistical decision tree. The more the number of times, the higher the relative importance. Then, the feature importance of m factors is scored to complete feature selection. The main steps are as follows:

1) Divide the data into training set and test set, and conduct model training on the entire training data set;
2) The feature importance calculated by using the training data set, that is, the number of factors used in the key decision-making in the statistical decision tree. The more the number of times, the higher the relative importance;
3) Wrap the training model in a Select From Model instance, repeat feature selection by setting different thresholds, and form feature subsets;
4) The model is then evaluated on the test set until the subset of the most important features is obtained.

Taking carbon emissions as the dependent variable, night lights and n significant influencing factors as independent variables, and calculating the urban carbon emissions with the help of the spatial Durbin model.

$$E_i = \omega Q_{ij} E_i + \lambda_1 C_i + \lambda_2 R_i + \gamma_1 Q_{ij} C_i + \gamma_2 Q_{ij} R_i + \varepsilon \tag{10}$$

where E_i denotes the carbon emission of city i; ω denotes the spatial regression coefficient of the carbon emission of city i; Q_{ij} denotes the spatial weight matrix, which is 1 when cities i and j are adjacent, and 0 otherwise; C_i is the night lights of carbon emission in city i; λ_1 and γ_1 are the accounting coefficients and spatial lag coefficients of night lights, respectively; R_i is the set of the aforementioned n factors in city i; λ_2 and γ_2 are the accounting coefficients and spatial lag coefficients of the set factors; ε denotes a random disturbance term that satisfies the normal independent and identical distribution.

5 Conclusion

Taking the typical megacities in my country as the research object, comprehensively considering the responsibility of producers and consumers, starting from the shared responsibility sharing accounting method, and using the equivalent value of electricity and the value of electricity as important indicators, the power carbon emission accounting model with shared responsibility for production and consumption is constructed. Select the urban characteristic factors that are strongly related to urban carbon emissions, based on the extended STIRPAT equation, and use XGBoost to score the importance of multiple features to complete the important feature selection. Taking carbon emissions as the dependent variable, night lights, electricity carbon emissions data, and other significant influencing factors as independent variables, the urban carbon emissions are calculated with the spatial Durbin model.

References

1. Mi, Z., Zhang, Y., Guan, D., et al.: Consumption-based emission accounting for Chinese cites. Appl. Energy **184**, 1073–1081 (2016)
2. Shan, Y., Guan, D., Liu, J., et al.: Methodology and applications of city level CO_2 emission accounts in China. J. Clean. Prod. **161**, 1215–1225 (2017)
3. Meng, L.N., Graus, W., Worrell, E., et al.: Estimating CO_2 (carbon dioxide) emissions at urban scales by DMSP/OLS (defense meteorological satellite program's operational linescan system) nighttime light imagery: methodological challenges and a case study for China. Energy **71**, 468–478 (2014)
4. De Bruyn, S.M., Opschoor, J.B.: Developments in the throughout-income relationship: theoretical and empirical bservations. Ecol. Econ. **20**(3), 255–268 (1997)
5. Zhang, Y., Liu, Z., Zhang, H., et al.: The impact of economic growth, Industrial structure and urbanization on carbon emission intensity in China. Nat. Hazards **73**(2), 579–595 (2014)
6. Pan, X.F., Uddin, M.K., Ai, B., et al.: Influential factors of carbon emissions intensity in OECD countries: evidence from symbolic regression. J. Clean. Prod. **220** (2019)
7. Fu, K., Qi, S.Z.: Accounting method and application of China's provincial power carbon emission responsibility. China Popul. Resour. Environ. **24**(04), 27–34 (2014)
8. Deng, J., Jiang, F., Wang, W., et al.: Low-carbon optimized operation of integrated energy system considering electric-heat flexible load and hydrogen energy refined modeling. Power Grid Technol. **46**(05), 1692–1704 (2022)
9. Jiang, Y.: Carbon emission accounting and emission reduction path of urban and rural energy systems. Sustain. Dev. Econ. Guide (04), 14–19 (2022)
10. National Bureau of Statistics: China Statistical Yearbook. China Statistics Press, Beijing (2008–2017)
11. Jiang, F., Peng, X., Tu, C., Guo, Q., Deng, J., Dai, F.: an improved hybrid parallel compensator for enhancing PV power transfer capability. IEEE Trans. Industr. Electron. **69**(11), 11132–11143 (2022)
12. Wang, X., Wu, J., Wang, Z.: Accounting and characteristic analysis of CO_2 emissions in Chinese cities. Urban Environ. Res. (01), 67–80 (2020)

Comprehensive Evaluation of Carbon Emission Reduction Maturity of Typical Megacities

Bingruo Li[1(✉)] and Bin Zhong[2]

[1] State Grid Shanghai Shibei Power Supply Company, Shanghai, China
1184358092@qq.com
[2] State Grid Shanghai Electric Power Company, Shanghai, China

Abstract. Addressing climate change by reducing carbon emissions has become the consensus of all countries in the world. Urban carbon emissions account for more than 80% of the total carbon emissions, which is a key link in reducing carbon emissions. A systematic evaluation of the maturity of low-carbon city construction can help improve the targeted reduction of carbon emissions by low-carbon measures. Select three key indicators such as output value energy consumption intensity, energy consumption carbon emission intensity and output value carbon emission intensity, use the grey correlation analysis method to calculate the grey correlation coefficient between the indicators, and further construct the development index, coordination index and coordinated development Based on the data of seven typical megacities from 2008 to 2017, a comprehensive evaluation of the urban carbon emission reduction maturity was carried out. The results show that there is inconsistency between the development index and coordination index of carbon emission reduction maturity in some years, but the overall carbon emission reduction development index, coordination index and coordination development index show a continuous growth trend, indicating that the maturity of emission reduction has been steadily improved.

Keywords: Maturity Model · Urban Carbon Emission Reduction · Grey Correlation · Relative Coordinated Development Index

1 Introduction

As the main source of greenhouse gas emissions, cities will directly affect the development of low-carbon economy and the realization of the "emission peak and carboon neutrality". Therefore, the evaluation of urban carbon emission reduction development has forward-looking significance.

Ref. [1] draws on the project management maturity model, constructs a management maturity evaluation model for college teachers' training programs abroad, and uses AHP and grey theory to evaluate project management maturity. Ref. [2] introduces the

Project: State Grid Shanghai Electric Power Company Science and Technology Project (52090021N00U).

H. Yang et al. (Eds.): SmartGIFT 2022, LNICST 483, pp. 20–29, 2023.
https://doi.org/10.1007/978-3-031-31733-0_3

maturity model into the field of industrial carbon emission reduction analysis, constructs a maturity measurement index, and conducts a comprehensive evaluation of carbon emission reduction in 30 provinces and 38 industrial sectors in China. Ref. [3] develops a digital maturity model by means of literature research and expert review, and evaluates the digital maturity of an enterprise by constructing key process areas, primary indicators, and secondary indicators. Ref. [4] aims to assess the digital maturity of MSEs, using the Brazilian context as a research model, digital maturity was shown to be statistically correlated with innovation and business revenue. Ref. [5] proposes 23 specific criteria based on triple bottom line (environmental, economic, and social aspects) to assess the maturity of carbon market, and puts forward a novel multi-criteria decision approach, which integrates subjective weights and objective weights. Ref. [6] introduces a method for assessing LCC performance by using Capability Maturity Model (CMM), this method identifies LCC maturity grade through assessing the performance of individual LCC dimensions which contributes to overall performance.

Based on the above research, this paper takes the data of seven typical megacities in China from 2008 to 2017 as examples, and selects the total carbon emission, carbon emission intensity, and output value energy consumption intensity that are closely related to carbon emission reduction as key evaluation indicators. The carbon emission reduction development degree, coordination degree, and coordinated development degree index are formed, and the carbon emission reduction maturity model is formed, and the carbon emission reduction situation of seven typical megacities and the carbon emission reduction situation of typical megacities in China are comprehensively evaluated.

2 Carbon Emission Reduction Assessment Indicators

In order to accurately complete the assessment of carbon emission reduction maturity, this paper comprehensively considers the impact of various factors on carbon emission reduction, and establishes a comprehensive index system. The key indicators reflecting urban carbon emission reduction include the following three, acoording to the [7, 8]:

The first is the total amount of carbon emissions, which refers to the total greenhouse gas emissions of a certain region in a certain period of time. Controlling the total amount of carbon emissions is the key to realizing dual control as soon as possible.

The second is carbon emission intensity, which refers to the carbon emission per unit of GDP and is mainly used to measure the relationship between the economic development level of a country, region or city and carbon emission. The factors affecting carbon emission intensity are not single factors, and different conclusions can be drawn according to different analysis angles.

The third is the energy consumption intensity of output value, which is the main indicator reflecting the level of energy consumption and the status of energy conservation and consumption reduction.

3 Construction of Carbon Emission Reduction Maturity Model

The concept of maturity mainly emphasizes the description of the degree of development of things, in addition to the comprehensive description and measurement of the degree of coordination and development of things. The degree of development is the degree of realization of things from a low-level stage to a high-level stage, reflecting the level achieved by the system in the process of changing from small to large, from simple to complex. The degree of coordination refers to the degree of integration between the internal subsystems of a thing to adapt to each other, cooperate with each other and promote each other. The degree of coordinated development can reflect the comprehensive effect of the development level of comprehensive things and the level of coordination. This paper will analyze the relative maturity and overall maturity of carbon emission reduction, and provide an empirical basis for urban development to scientifically formulate carbon emission reduction strategies.

3.1 Modelling of Carbon Emission Reduction Development Levels

The relative development index is introduced to measure the development level of carbon emission intensity to compare the final effect of carbon emission reduction. According the [9], the grey relational degree analysis method is often used to study the correlation problem, consider using the grey relational degree to analyze the relative development index of carbon emission reduction. The overall development degree is introduced to measure the average development level of carbon emission reduction to compare the overall effect of carbon emission reduction in different years.Please note that the first paragraph of a section or subsection is not indented. The first paragraphs that follows a table, figure, equation etc. does not have an indent, either.

Relative Development Index. The research object is typical megacities, and the carbon emission intensity development of different cities in m years is compared. The reference sequence of carbon emission intensity is $C_0 = (c_0(1), c_0(2), ..., c_0(m))$, and the comparison sequence of the carbon emission intensity of the jth city is $C_j = (c_j(1), c_j(2), ..., c_j(m))$, the gray correlation coefficient of carbon emission intensity in the i year can be calculated as:

$$\varepsilon(i) = \frac{\min\left|C_0(i) - C_j(i)\right| + \rho \max\left|C_0(i) - C_j(i)\right|}{\left|C_0(i) - C_j(i)\right| + \rho \max\left|C_0(i) - C_j(i)\right|} \tag{1}$$

where $\left|C_0(i) - C_j(i)\right|$ denotes the absolute difference in carbon emission intensity in year i; $\min\left|C_0(i) - C_j(i)\right|$ denotes the minimum absolute difference of carbon emission intensity in year i; $\max\left|C_0(i) - C_j(i)\right|$ denotes the maximum absolute difference of carbon emission intensity in year i; ρ represent the resolution coefficient, generally 0.5. The relative development index is positively correlated with the carbon emission reduction maturity, that is, the larger the relative development index, the better the carbon emission reduction development of the city.

Overall Development Index. The overall development index of carbon emission reduction of typical megacities in year i can be calculated by the arithmetic mean of the relative development index of carbon emission reduction:

$$\mu_i = \frac{1}{m}\sum_{i=1}^{m} \varepsilon(i) \tag{2}$$

where μ_i denotes the overall development index of carbon emission reduction of typical megacities in year i.

3.2 Modeling of Carbon Emission Reduction Coordination Levels

The relative coordination degree is introduced to measure the coordination level relationship between the energy consumption intensity of output value and the energy consumption carbon emission intensity, so as to compare the coordination among the driving factors of carbon emission reduction. The overall coordination degree is introduced to measure the coordination degree of carbon emission reduction development level to compare the overall coordination of carbon emission reduction in different years, according to [10]. In this paper, the evaluation model of the actual state and the ideal state of the Euclidean distance measurement system is used to construct the overall coordination index model in the urban carbon emission reduction maturity model.

Carbon Emission Reduction Relative Coordination Index. The geometric mean of energy consumption per unit of GDP and energy consumption emission intensity is expressed as the relative coordination degree of carbon emission reduction, it can be calculated as:

$$\varphi(i) = \sqrt{\tau(i) \times \upsilon(i)} \tag{3}$$

where $\tau(i)$ denotes the gray correlation coefficient of energy consumption per unit of GDP; $\upsilon(i)$ denotes the gray correlation coefficient of energy consumption emission intensity. Among them, the calculation method of $\tau(i)$ and $\upsilon(i)$ is calculated with the gray correlation degree of carbon emission intensity. Similarly, it can be seen that the larger the relative coordination index of carbon emission reduction, the higher the maturity of carbon emission reduction.

Overall Coordination Index of Carbon Emission Reduction. The overall coordination level can be calculated by the Euclidean distance and Chebyshev distance between the actual and ideal values of carbon emission intensity, according to [11, 12]:

$$D_i = 1 - \sqrt{(d_i)^2 / \sum_{j=1}^{n} (h_j)^2} \tag{4}$$

$$d_i = \sqrt{\sum_{j=1}^{n} \left[c_0(i) - c_j(i)\right]^2} \tag{5}$$

$$h_j = \max_{\leq i \leq m} \left\{ \left| c_0(i) - c_j(i) \right| \right\} \tag{6}$$

where d_i denotes the Euclidean distance between the actual and ideal carbon emission intensity; h_j denotes the Chebyshev distance between the actual and ideal carbon emission intensity; D_i denotes the overall coordination index of carbon emission reduction.

3.3 Modelling of Coordinated Development Level of Carbon Emission Reduction

Considering that there is a mismatch between the relative development trend of carbon emission reduction and the relative coordination trend, that is, the situation of low development level, high coordination degree or high development level and low coordination degree in economic development. The relative coordinated development degree is introduced to measure the degree of harmonious development between the relative development level of carbon emission reduction and the relative coordination level, so as to compare the comprehensive balance between the development level of carbon emission reduction and the coordination level. The degree of harmonious development between the overall development level and the coordination level is measured to compare the comprehensive balance between the overall development level and coordination level of carbon emission reduction.

Relative Coordinated Development Index. Due to the inconsistency between the relative development index and the relative coordination index of urban carbon emission reduction, it is impossible to comprehensively, objectively and effectively reflect the real situation of urban carbon emission reduction based on the relative coordination index. Index to conduct a comprehensive and objective analysis of carbon emission reduction. Using the geometric mean of the relative development index and the relative coordination index as the relative coordinated development index of carbon emission reduction, it can be calculated as:

$$\theta(i) = \sqrt{\varepsilon(i) \times \varphi(i)} \tag{7}$$

where $\theta(i)$ denotes the relative coordinated development index of carbon emission reduction in year i, which is positively correlated with carbon emission reduction maturity.

Overall Coordinated Development Index. In the same year, there may be inconsistencies between the overall development level and overall coordination level of carbon emission reduction in typical megacities, resulting in a comprehensive evaluation of the overall maturity of carbon emission reduction using the overall development index or overall coordination index alone. There is one-sidedness. Therefore, the overall coordinated development index of carbon emission reduction is constructed by the aggregate of the overall coordination index and the overall development index. The details are as follows:

$$T_i = \sqrt{\mu_i D_i} \tag{8}$$

where Ti denotes the overall coordinated development index of carbon emission reduction of typical megacities in year i, which is positively correlated with carbon emission reduction maturity.

4 Comprehensive Evaluation of Urban Carbon Emission Reduction and Electricity-Related Maturity

First, the data related to carbon emissions in typical megacities from 2008 to 2017 were sorted out, including energy consumption, GDP, carbon emissions, etc., and the carbon emission intensity, output value energy consumption intensity, and energy consumption carbon emission intensity of each city Calculate; calculate and analyze the carbon emission reduction maturity of each city from 2008 to 2017 with the help of the maturity model, and evaluate the carbon emission reduction maturity of the city.

4.1 Data Processing

Raw Data. Find the relevant data required for carbon emission reduction assessment from the China Energy Statistical Yearbook over the years, as shown in Fig. 1, according to Ref. [13, 14].

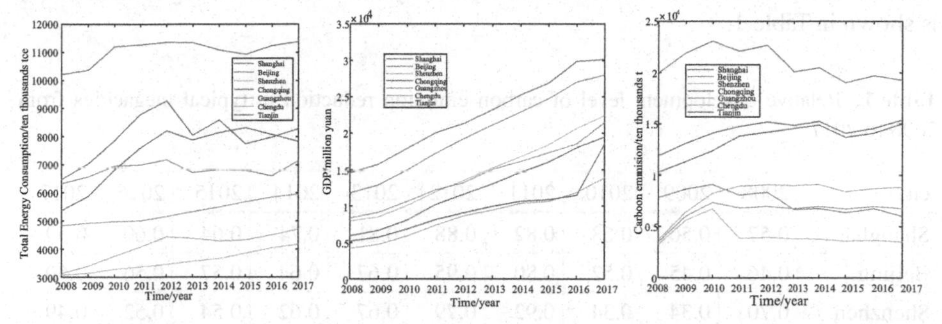

Fig. 1. Energy consumption, GDP, carbon emissions, etc. of typical megacities from 2008 to 2017.

Indicator Data. The raw data is processed according to the constructed carbon emission maturity model, and the urban carbon emission intensity, output value energy consumption intensity, and energy consumption carbon emission intensity can be further obtained. As shown in Fig. 2. Carbon emission intensity, output value energy consumption intensity, and energy consumption carbon emission intensity are calculated from the ratio of carbon emission to carbon emission intensity, the ratio of energy consumption to GDP, and the ratio of carbon emission to energy consumption in a certain period.

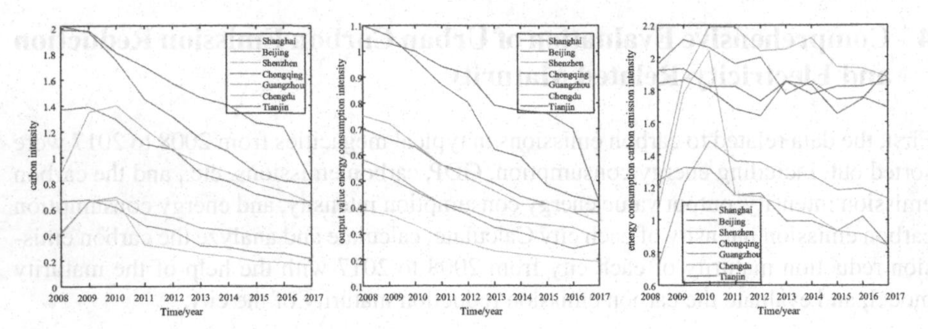

Fig. 2. Carbon emission intensity, output value energy consumption intensity, and energy consumption carbon emission intensity of typical megacities from 2008 to 2017.

4.2 Evaluation and Analysis of Urban Carbon Emission Reduction Maturity

Relative Development Level of Carbon Emission Reduction. The relative development level of carbon emission reduction of each city calculated according to formula (1) is shown in Table 1.

Table 1. Relative development level of carbon emission reduction in typical megacities from 2008 to 2017

city	2008	2009	2010	2011	2012	2013	2014	2015	2016	2017
Shanghai	0.57	0.56	0.63	0.82	0.88	0.81	0.74	0.64	0.60	0.59
Beijing	0.46	0.45	0.52	0.80	0.95	0.67	0.64	0.57	0.56	0.50
Shenzhen	0.70	0.34	0.34	0.92	0.79	0.67	0.62	0.54	0.52	0.49
Chongqing	0.49	0.50	0.61	0.84	1.00	0.79	0.71	0.60	0.57	0.56
Guangzhou	0.81	0.58	0.54	0.76	0.84	0.89	0.83	0.73	0.69	0.59
Chengdu	0.83	0.58	0.55	0.69	0.90	0.93	0.82	0.72	0.66	0.59
Tianjin	0.62	0.63	0.73	0.81	0.95	0.93	0.87	0.75	0.73	0.52

As can be seen from Table 1, since 2008, the relative development level of carbon emission reduction in each city has shown an increasing trend. Only in some years the relative development index has decreased, especially in 2012 or 2013. Significant growth occurred.

Relative Coordination Level of Carbon Emission Reduction. The relative coordination level of carbon emission reduction of each city calculated according to formula (3) is shown in Table 2.

From Table 2, it can be seen that the relative coordination index of carbon emission reduction also peaked in 2012 or 2013, and then declined in a small range. Showing an upward trend. Comparing Table 1 and Table 2, it can be seen that the relative development level of carbon emission reduction in each city is positively correlated with the relative

Table 2. Relative coordination level of carbon emission reduction in typical megacities from 2008 to 2017.

city	2008	2009	2010	2011	2012	2013	2014	2015	2016	2017
Shanghai	0.61	0.61	0.66	0.83	0.90	0.84	0.78	0.68	0.64	0.61
Beijing	0.51	0.50	0.57	0.78	0.93	0.73	0.68	0.59	0.60	0.53
Shenzhen	0.52	0.41	0.42	0.89	0.90	0.71	0.65	0.58	0.55	0.50
Chongqing	0.56	0.58	0.67	0.71	0.78	0.76	0.74	0.64	0.62	0.59
Guangzhou	0.42	0.65	0.61	0.84	0.84	0.78	0.75	0.74	0.73	0.62
Chengdu	0.42	0.61	0.62	0.75	0.91	0.78	0.67	0.75	0.69	0.63
Tianjin	0.67	0.67	0.75	0.82	0.81	0.90	0.88	0.77	0.74	0.54

coordination level, but there are still cases where the relative development level rises and the relative coordination level declines. For example, Guangzhou City From 2008 to 2010, the relative development level rose as a whole while the relative coordination level declined as a whole.

Relatively Coordinated Development Level of Carbon Emission Reduction. The relative coordinated development level of each city's carbon emission reduction calculated according to formula (7) is shown in Table 3.

Table 3. Relatively coordinated development level of carbon emission reduction in typical megacities from 2008 to 2017.

city	2008	2009	2010	2011	2012	2013	2014	2015	2016	2017
Shanghai	0.59	0.58	0.64	0.82	0.89	0.82	0.76	0.66	0.62	0.60
Beijing	0.48	0.47	0.54	0.79	0.94	0.70	0.66	0.58	0.58	0.51
Shenzhen	0.60	0.37	0.38	0.90	0.84	0.69	0.63	0.56	0.53	0.49
Chongqing	0.52	0.54	0.64	0.77	0.88	0.77	0.72	0.62	0.59	0.57
Guangzhou	0.58	0.61	0.57	0.80	0.84	0.83	0.79	0.73	0.71	0.60
Chengdu	0.59	0.59	0.58	0.72	0.90	0.85	0.74	0.73	0.67	0.61
Tianjin	0.64	0.65	0.74	0.81	0.88	0.91	0.87	0.76	0.73	0.53

As can be seen from Table 3, 2012 or 2013 was still regarded as the turning point of carbon emission reduction development from 2008 to 2017, and the relative coordinated development level reached the maximum in that year, and the overall relative coordinated development level of carbon emission reduction during the research period rise.

The Overall Maturity of Carbon Emission Reduction in Typical Megacities. The overall development level, overall coordination level, and overall coordinated development level of each city calculated according to formula (2), (4)–(6), (8) are shown in Table 4.

Table 4. The overall maturity of carbon emission reduction in typical megacities from 2008 to 2017.

year	2008	2009	2010	2011	2012	2013	2014	2015	2016	2017
level of development	0.64	0.52	0.56	0.81	0.90	0.81	0.75	0.65	0.68	0.76
level of coordination	0.37	0.07	0.13	0.76	0.87	0.73	0.65	0.49	0.42	0.47
level of coordinated development	0.49	0.19	0.27	0.78	0.88	0.77	0.70	0.56	0.51	0.63

It can be seen from Table 4 that from 2008 to 2017, the overall trend showed an increase. Although there was a slight decline from 2012, in the following years, each index began to recover as a whole, and it has never been lower than 2008.

5 Conclusion

This paper constructs the carbon emission reduction maturity model of typical megacities, and analyzes the carbon emission reduction of typical megacities from 2008 to 2017 from the three indexes of carbon emission reduction development level, coordination level and coordinated development level. It can be seen that the carbon emission reduction maturity of most cities shows an upward trend in terms of relative development, relative coordination or relative coordination. Considering that the relative development level of carbon emission reduction and the coordinated development level of carbon emission reduction are out of sync in some years, the urban carbon emission reduction maturity is further evaluated through the relative coordinated development index of carbon emission reduction. The overall maturity of carbon emission reduction The index also shows an upward trend in carbon emission reductions across typical megacities.

References

1. Hu, S.: Evaluation model of training project maturity based on multi-level grey theory. Stat. Decis. **34**(16), 177–180 (2018)
2. Wang, W., Li, F.: Research on china's industrial carbon emission reduction maturity. China Industr. Econ. **08**, 20–34 (2015)
3. Wang, H., Wang, S., Liu, R.: Research on enterprise digital maturity model. Manage. Rev. **33**(12), 152–162 (2021)

4. da Costa, L.S., PoleziMunhoz, L., Alessandra, L.P.: Assessing the digital maturity of micro and small enterprises: a focus on an emerging market. Proc. Comput. Sci. **200**, 175–184 (2022)
5. Zhang, F., Fang, H., Song, W.: Carbon market maturity analysis with an integrated multi-criteria decision making method: a case study of EU and China. J. Clean. Prod. **7**(2021), 997–1015 (2019)
6. Shen, L., Du, X., Cheng, G.: Capability Maturity Model (CMM) method for assessing the performance of low-carbon city practice. **87**(2021)
7. Cheng, J.: Research on the decomposition of total carbon emission control targets in China. China Popul. Resour. Environ. **26**(01), 23–30 (2016)
8. Teng, F., Liu, Y., Jin, F.: Decomposition of influencing factors and regional differences of energy consumption changes in Chinese megacities. Resour. Sci. **35**(02), 240–249 (2013)
9. Li, H., Wang, S., Liu, Y.: Evaluation method and demonstration of regional collaborative development based on grey relational theory and distance collaborative model. Syst. Eng. - Theory Pract. **34**(07), 1749–1755 (2014)
10. Ji, M., Zeng, X.: Research on spatiotemporal evolution prediction and driving mechanism of coordinated development of new urbanization and ecological civilization construction. Ecol. Eco. 1–19 (2022)
11. Dan, Z., Ma, X.: Evaluation of the geoeconomic relationship between China and the Eurasian Economic Union: Based on the application of the Euclidean distance-grey correlation degree two-step method. Regional Res. Dev. **40**(04), 12–17 (2021)
12. Deng, J., Jiang, F., Wang, W., et al.: Low-carbon optimized operation of integrated energy system considering electric-heat flexible load and hydrogen energy refined modeling. Power Grid Technol. **46**(05), 1692–1704 (2022)
13. Jiang, F., Peng, X., Tu, C., Guo, Q., Deng, J., Dai, F.: An improved hybrid parallel compensator for enhancing pv power transfer capability. IEEE Trans. Industr. Electron. **69**(11), 11132–11143 (2022)
14. National Bureau of Statistics: China Statistical Yearbook. China Statistics Press, Beijing (2008–2017)

Voltage Control Strategy of Power Distribution Network with Schedulable Distributed Resources

Ling Wang[1,2](✉), Bo Fu[3], Youyong Lin[3], Chunming Tu[4], Fan Xiao[4], and Qi Guo[4]

[1] Electric Power Research Institute of Guangdong Power Grid Co., Ltd., Guangzhou, China
360409837@qq.com

[2] Key Laboratory of Power Quality of Guangdong Power Grid Co., Ltd., Guangzhou, China

[3] Guangdong Power Grid Corporation Zhuhai Power Supply Bureau, Zhuhai, China

[4] College of Electrical and Information Engineering, Hunan University, Changsha, China

Abstract. Wide use of schedulable distributed resources for flexible and effective power generation, combined with the actual situation of the country, has been valued by all countries of the world. Connecting schedulable distributed resources to power grid is an effective choice to solve the current energy shortage and improve energy utilization. When high proportion of schedulable distributed resources are connected to the power distribution network, power quality problems such as voltage fluctuation, flicker and off-limit will occur. Therefore, based on the distributed resource cluster, the power distribution network voltage control with a high proportion of distributed resource access is implemented. Through the calculation of the capacity utilization ratio of the leading nodes of the distributed resource cluster to the distributed power capacity, a quantitative relationship between the node voltage and the distributed resource output is established. And the corresponding parameter setting methods are given. Finally, the effectiveness of the proposed control strategy is verified by a numerical example in the IEEE 33-node system.

Keywords: Power Distribution Network · Distributed Resource · High Permeability · Distributed Control

1 Introduction

A high proportion of renewable resource is connected to the power grid in the way of Distributed Resource (DR), which is an effective choice to solve the contradictions between energy shortage and demand growth, energy utilization and environmental protection. The use of large-scale renewable resources to generate electricity will help make full use of the abundant, clean and diverse forms of energy available everywhere. And it can also provide customers with green electricity, so it is an important measure to achieve the goals of energy conservation and emission reduction [1]. Especially in the power distribution network in remote areas, with the further strengthening of the national new energy poverty alleviation policy, a large number of distributed renewable resource

H. Yang et al. (Eds.): SmartGIFT 2022, LNICST 483, pp. 30–41, 2023.
https://doi.org/10.1007/978-3-031-31733-0_4

have been connected to the grid. And the penetration rate in some areas has been greater than 100% [2]. In the power distribution network, the power quality problems caused by the high proportion of distributed resource access are mainly reflected in voltage fluctuation, flicker and off-limit [3]. These problems not only limit the utilization rate of renewable energy, but also endanger the safe and stable operation of the system. At the same time, it brings great challenges to the planning, operation and control of the local power grid.

The control methods of power distribution network considering the access of distributed resource can be divided into two types: centralized coordinated control and decentralized autonomous control [4]. The centralized control mode is mainly based on the optimal power flow of the power distribution network, and relies on comprehensive data collection and reliable communication transmission to build and solve the optimal scheduling model [5]. Therefore, a high proportion of schedulable distributed resource connected to the power distribution network will cause a huge burden on the communication network and its computing capacity. The distributed control mode only uses local measurement information, which improves the response speed of the control system and reduces the investment cost. However, the distributed control mode uses limited information, so the utilization of adjustable resources is not sufficient [6].

In order to ensure the orderly, safe, reliable, flexible and efficient access to the power distribution network of high-proportion distributed resource, distributed control has been paid more and more attention in the power system. Compared with centralized and decentralized control, distributed control mode has better control robustness, communication flexibility and system scalability [7]. In recent years, distributed control mode has been partially studied in power system economic dispatch [8], virtual power plant [9] and the micro grid [10]. But the application in power quality control of power distribution network is less involved.

In this paper, the distributed control mode is adopted to realize the voltage control of power distribution network with a high proportion of distributed resource access based on distributed resource cluster. By calculating the dominant node of distributed resource cluster and the capacity utilization ratio of distributed resources, the quantitative relationship between the node voltage and the output of the distributed power supply is established. And the tuning method of the corresponding parameters is given. Finally, the effectiveness of the proposed control strategy is verified by an example of IEEE 33-node system.

2 Distributed Control Framework

The output of distributed resource is intermittent, volatile and uncertain under the influence of external environment. Its high proportion and large-scale access puts forward higher demand for the operation control of power distribution network. Cluster technology is an efficient technical means to achieve the security, stability and economic operation of power distribution network in the future [11, 12]. The power distribution network structure based on distributed resource cluster is shown in Fig. 1:

Several adjacent distributed resources in the dotted box form a distributed resource cluster with specific control objectives. By adopting the same distributed control strategy for each cluster, the output of distributed resource can be optimized to smooth the voltage deviation of power distribution network.

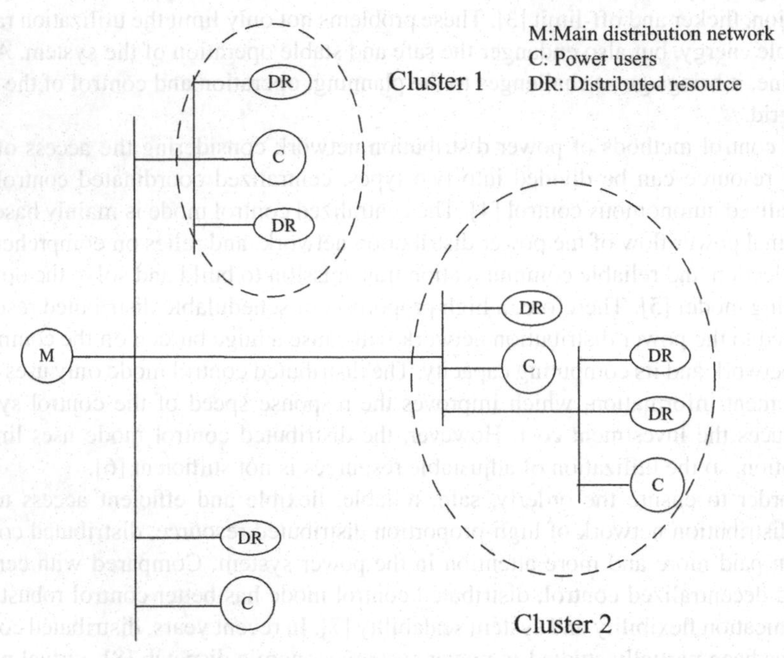

Fig. 1. Power distribution network structure based on distributed resource cluster

3 Distributed Control Strategy

3.1 Cluster Dominant Node

The selection of cluster dominant nodes is a key step in voltage control of power distribution network. The selection results have an important impact on the effect of organizing and coordinating controllable resources in power distribution network and maintaining the voltage level of power distribution network. Dominant nodes are defined as follows: there are a number of key nodes in a region, which are closely connected with other nodes in the region and can represent the voltage level of the region. By monitoring their voltage status, the voltage of other nodes nearby can be grasped [13].

The selected dominant node of the cluster should have both observability and controllability. On the one hand, the voltage of the dominant node can reflect the common voltage level in its region, which can be seen to have observability. On the other hand, when the controllable resources of the system are sufficient, the voltage control of the dominant node can effectively improve the overall voltage level of the region. But it has little influence on the neighboring region, which can be seen to have controllability [14]. Based on the observability and controllability of nodes, the comprehensive sensitivity S of all nodes in cluster i is calculated. The node with the highest comprehensive sensitivity is the dominant node:

$$\max S = \max(C + dD) \tag{1}$$

In the formula, C and D respectively represent the observability and controllability of nodes, and d is the weight coefficient.

The controllability of node l and its calculation equation can be expressed as:

$$\begin{cases} C_l = \sum_{i \in M_a} \dfrac{\Delta V_l}{\Delta V_k} \\ D_l = \sum_{h \in M_b} \dfrac{\Delta V_l}{\Delta Q_h} \end{cases} \tag{2}$$

In the formula, M_a represents the set of all nodes in the cluster; $\frac{\Delta V_l}{\Delta V_k}$ is the voltage sensitivity of node k to node l; M_b denotes the set of all controllable nodes in the cluster; $\frac{\Delta V_l}{\Delta Q_h}$ is the reactive voltage sensitivity of the voltage amplitude of node l to the reactive power injected into node h.

By locally linearizing the stable operation point of the power distribution network, the active voltage sensitivity and reactive voltage sensitivity can be obtained.

$$\begin{cases} \dfrac{\Delta V}{\Delta P} = \begin{bmatrix} (B+Q)(G-P)^{-1}(B-Q)+ \\ (G+P) \end{bmatrix}^{-1} \\ \dfrac{\Delta V}{\Delta Q} = \begin{bmatrix} (G-P)(B+Q)^{-1}(G+P)+ \\ (B-Q) \end{bmatrix}^{-1} \end{cases} \tag{3}$$

In the formula, B and G are the real and imaginary parts of the nodal admittance matrix respectively. P and Q are the diagonal matrices of the active and reactive power injected by the nodes.

3.2 Node Voltage Control

After determining the dominant node of the distributed resource cluster, the voltage of the dominant node is controlled by adjusting the output of all distributed resources in the cluster. Firstly, the evaluation function of node voltage performance is defined, and the quantitative relationship between node voltage and distributed resource output is established through the capacity utilization ratio of distributed resource. Then, the reference value of the variation of the capacity utilization ratio of distributed resource in the cluster is calculated according to the voltage deviation of dominant nodes. Finally, the active power output of each distributed resource is calculated iteratively to achieve the goal of node voltage control.

Control Objectives

Take cluster i ($i = 1, 2, \ldots, N$) as an example. The optimization control objective is to control the voltage of the corresponding leading node to a rated value:

$$V_i = 1(p.u.) \tag{4}$$

In the formula, V_i is the voltage of the dominant node corresponding to cluster i.

In cluster i, the distributed resource u is responsible for node voltage measurement and voltage control performance evaluation. The voltage control performance evaluation function $f_{v,i}$ of the leading node of the cluster is defined as:

$$f_{v,i} = \frac{1}{2}(V_i - 1)^2 \tag{5}$$

Control Variables

The calculation equation of capacity utilization ratio at the *kth* iteration of distributed resource j in cluster i can be expressed as:

$$\gamma_{i,j}(k) = \frac{P_j(k)}{S_{i,j}\varphi_{i,j}} \tag{6}$$

In the formula, $\gamma_{i,j}(k)$ and $P_j(k)$ are respectively the capacity utilization ratio and active power output at the *kth* iteration of distributed resource j. $S_{i,j}$ and $\varphi_{i,j}$ are the capacity and power factor of distributed resource j.

The reference value calculation equation defining the capacity utilization ratio at the *kth* iteration of cluster i can be expressed as:

$$\Delta\gamma_i^{ref}(k) = -\left.\frac{\partial f_{v,i}}{\partial \gamma_{i,u}}\right|_{\gamma_{i,u}(k)} \tag{7}$$

$$\begin{aligned}\frac{\partial f_{v,i}}{\partial \gamma_{i,u}} &= \frac{\partial f_{v,i}}{\partial V_i} \cdot \frac{\partial V_i}{\partial P_u} \cdot \frac{\partial P_u}{\partial \gamma_{i,u}} \\ &= (V_i - 1)\frac{\partial V_i}{\partial P_u} S_{i,u}\varphi_{i,u}\end{aligned} \tag{8}$$

In the formula, $\Delta\gamma_i^{ref}(k)$ is the reference value of capacity utilization ratio at the *kth* iteration of cluster *i*; $\frac{\partial V_i}{\partial P_u}$ is the active voltage sensitivity of the dominant node voltage of cluster *i* relative to the active power injected by the distributed resource *u*.

The updated calculation equation of capacity utilization ratio of distributed resource *j* can be expressed as:

$$\gamma_{i,j}(k+1) = \sum_{n=1}^{N_i} d_{i,jn}\gamma_{i,n}(k) + d_{i,u}\varepsilon_i\Delta\gamma_i^{ref}(k) \tag{9}$$

In the formula, $\gamma_{i,j}(k+i)$ is the capacity utilization ratio at the $k+1$ iteration of distributed resource *j* in cluster *i*; N_i is the total number of distributed resources in cluster *i*; $d_{i,jn}$ is the communication weight coefficient between distributed resource *j* and *n*; $\gamma_{i,n}(k)$ is the capacity utilization ratio at the *kth* iteration of distributed resource *j*; $d_{i,u}$ is the weight coefficient of node voltage measurement in cluster *i*; ε_i is the iteration step.

The calculation equation of the communication weight coefficient $d_{i,jn}$ can be expressed as:

$$d_{i,jn} = \frac{d_{jn}}{\sum_{n=1}^{N_i} d_{jn}} \tag{10}$$

In the formula, for the distributed resource *n* in cluster *i* that communicates with distributed resource *j*, there is $d_{jn} = 1$; For a distributed resource *n* with no communication connection, there is $d_{jn} = 0$.

For the distributed resource *u* responsible for node voltage measurement in cluster *i*, there is $d_{i,u} = 1$; For the rest of the distributed resource, there is $d_{i,u} = 0$.

According to the updated capacity of the distributed resource *j*, the active power output at the $k+1$ iteration can be deduced by using the ratio:

$$P_j(k+1) = \gamma_{i,j}(k+1)S_{i,j}\phi_{i,j} \tag{11}$$

Control Process

The voltage control flow of power distribution network with high proportion of distributed resource access based on distributed resource cluster is shown in Fig. 2:

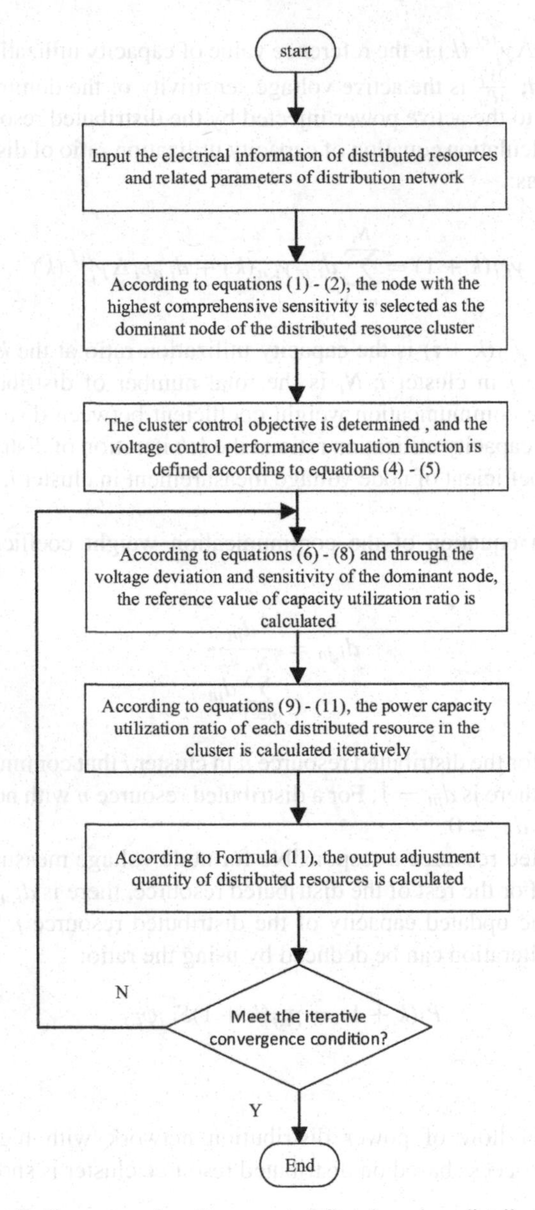

Fig. 2. Power distribution network voltage control flow based on distributed resource cluster

4 Simulation Examples

In this paper, the standard IEEE 33-node power distribution network system is used for simulation calculation, and the proposed voltage control strategy is analyzed by example. The system structure is shown in Fig. 3.

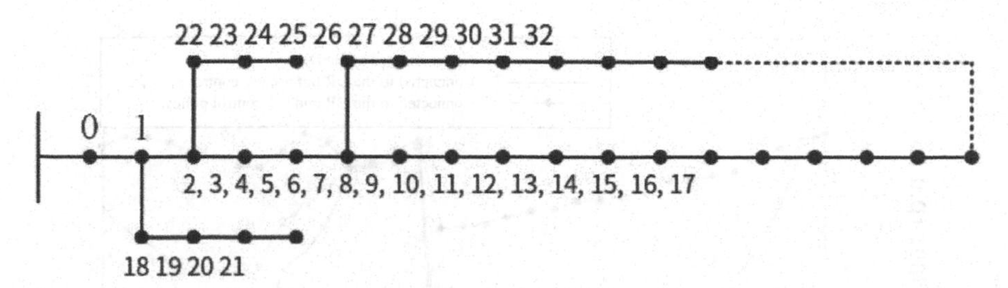

Fig. 3. IEEE 33 node network structure

The system has 32 branches, one contact switch branch, and node 0 is the balance node of the system. The reference voltage of the system is 12.66 kV. The reference power is 10 MVA. The total active load is 3715 kW. The total reactive load is 2300 kVar. The line impedance, node load and other parameters are detailed in the reference. The access capacity of the distributed resource is 1500 kVA. The minimum power factor is set as 0.9, and the maximum number of simulation iterations is 1500. In each example, the permeability of distributed resource is 50%. In other words, the total output power of distributed resource is 1857.5 kW.

In order to verify the effectiveness of the control strategy proposed in this paper, different load capacities and different wiring modes of the power distribution network system are selected. The effect of node voltage control in power distribution network is compared and analyzed.

4.1 Example 1 (Radial Connection Mode)

When the contact switch of the system is unlocked, the system is in radial connection mode. Four distributed resources are connected to the system, which are located at nodes 23, 31, 31 and 31 respectively. The three distributed resources connected to node 31 constitute a distributed resource cluster, and the dominant node is 31. The distributed resources connected to node 23 constitute the distributed resource cluster, and the dominant node is 23.

In this example, Fig. 4 shows the node voltage distribution after iteration when the system is at rated load in the radiant wiring mode. Figure 5 shows the node voltage distribution after iteration when the system is at low load (10% load rate) in the radiant wiring mode.

According to the voltage distribution under different conditions, when the system load is high and voltage control is not carried out, the lower limit of node voltage at the end of the line is prone to occur. For example, the voltage deviation of node 17 at the end of the power distribution network in Fig. 4 reaches 0.05924 (p.u.). At the same time, there are several nodes with voltage deviations ranging from 0.03 to 0.06 (p.u.), which have exceeded the lower limit of node voltage for normal operation of the power distribution network system. When the output of the distributed power supply in the system is large and voltage control is not carried out, the power distribution network will generate reverse power flow to make the node voltage exceed the upper limit. For example, the voltage deviation of node 31 in Fig. 5 reaches 0.04873 (p.u.). At the same

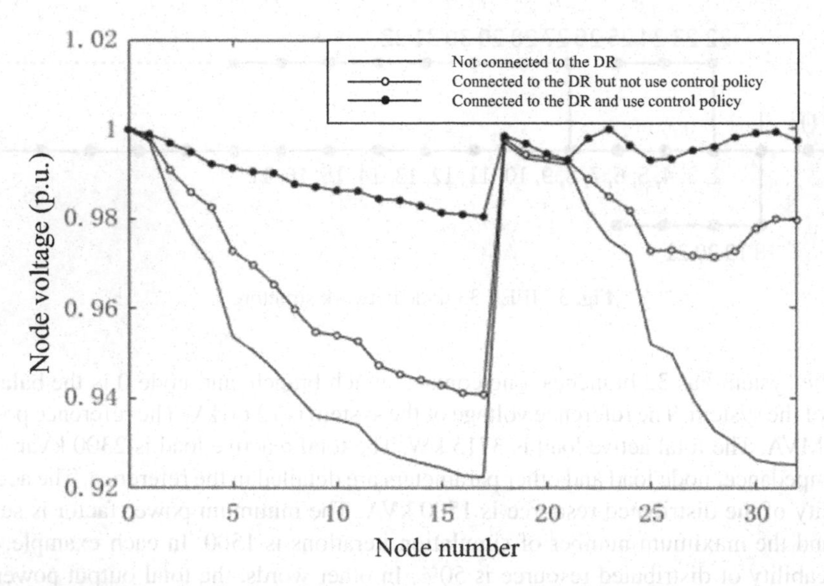

Fig. 4. The voltage distribution of the system nodes in radial wiring mode during rated load

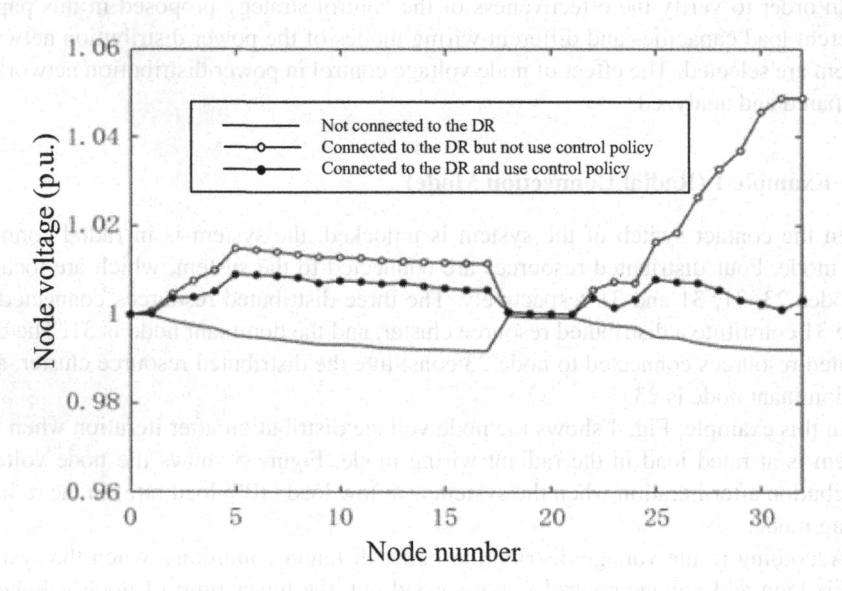

Fig. 5. The voltage distribution of the system nodes in radial wiring mode during low load

time, there are several nodes with voltage deviation in the range of 0.02–0.05 (p.u.), which has exceeded the upper limit of node voltage for normal operation of the power distribution network system.

As can be seen from Fig. 4 and Fig. 5, after accessing the distributed resource and controlling it, the voltage of leading nodes 23 and 31 converge to the rated value. The voltage offset of each node in the system is significantly reduced, and the voltage of all nodes is finally in the range of 0.98–1.02 (p.u.). Simulation results show that the proposed voltage control strategy can achieve good control of node voltage under different load conditions in power distribution network.

4.2 Example 2 (Loop Mesh Wiring Mode)

When the contact switch of the system is unlocked, the system is in ring mesh connection mode. Four distributed resources are connected to the system, which are located at nodes 29, 29, 31 and 31 respectively. The four distributed resources connected to nodes 29 and 31 constitute a distributed resource cluster, and the dominant node is 30.

In this example, Fig. 6 shows the node voltage distribution after iteration when the system is under the rated load of the loop mesh wiring mode. Figure 7 shows the node voltage distribution after iteration when the system is under the low load (10% load rate) of the loop mesh wiring mode.

Similar to the node voltage distribution in the radiant wiring mode of the system in example 1, when the system is in the ring-mesh wiring mode without voltage control, the voltage deviation of some nodes reaches 0.02–0.04 (p.u.).

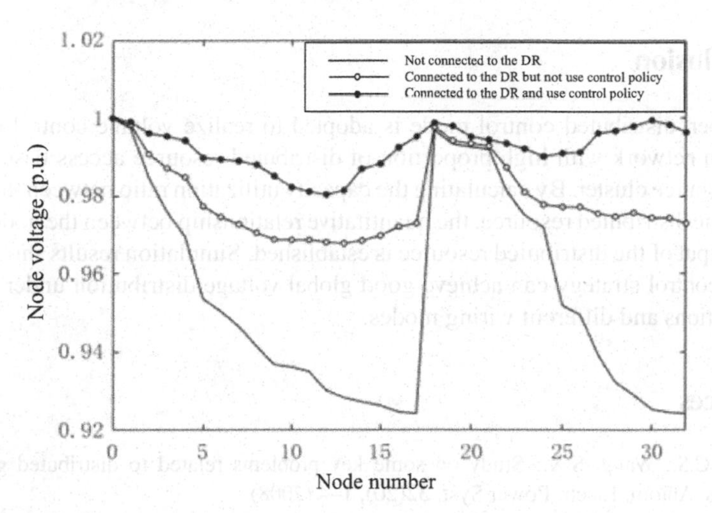

Fig. 6. The voltage distribution of the nodes in the system loop mesh wiring mode during rated load

As can be seen from Fig. 6 and Fig. 7, after the distributed resource is connected and controlled, the node voltages of the system under different loads in the ring-mesh wiring mode are finally within the normal range of the power distribution network system.

The comprehensive analysis of example 1 and example 2 shows that the voltage control strategy proposed in this paper can achieve good control of node voltage under different wiring modes of the power distribution network.

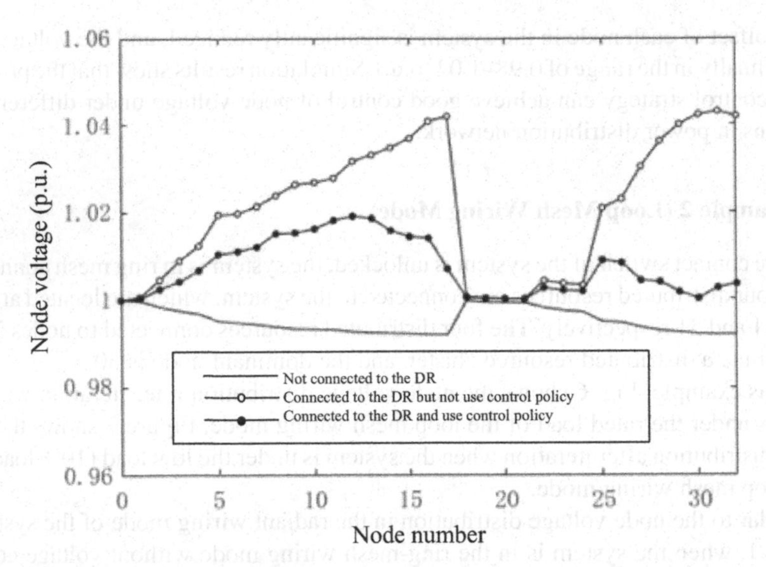

Fig. 7. The voltage distribution of the nodes in the system loop mesh wiring mode during low load

5 Conclusion

In this paper, distributed control mode is adopted to realize voltage control of power distribution network with high proportion of distributed resource access based on distributed resource cluster. By calculating the capacity utilization ratio between the leading node and the distributed resource, the quantitative relationship between the node voltage and the output of the distributed resource is established. Simulation results show that the proposed control strategy can achieve good global voltage distribution under different load conditions and different wiring modes.

References

1. Wang, C.S., Wang, S.X.: Study on some key problems related to distributed generation systems. Autom. Electr. Power Syst. **32**(20), 1–4 (2008)
2. Ding, M., Wang, W.S., Wang, X.L.: A review on the effect of large-scale PV generation on power systems. Proc. CSEE **34**(1), 1–14 (2014)
3. Pei, W., Sheng, K., Kong, L.: Impact and improvement of distributed generation on distribution network voltage quality. Proc. CSEE **28**(13), 152–157 (2008)
4. Chen, X., Zhang, Y.J., Huang, X.M.: Review of reactive power and voltage control method in the background of active distribution network. Autom. Power Syst. **40**(1), 143–151 (2016)
5. Pahwa, A., Deloach, S.A., Natarajan, B.: Goal-based holonic multiagent system for operation of power distribution systems. IEEE Trans. Smart Grid **6**(5), 2510–2518 (2017)
6. Xin, H., Zhao, R., Zhang, L.: A decentralized hierarchical control structure and self-optimizing control strategy for F-P type DGs in islanded Microgrids. IEEE Trans. Smart Grid **7**(1), 3–5 (2017)

7. Ge, X., Han, Q.L., Ding, D.: A survey on recent advances in distributed sampled-data cooperative control of multi-agent systems. Neurocomputing **275**, 1684–1701 (2017)
8. Hug, G., Kar, S., Wu, C.: Consensus innovations approach for distributed multiagent coordination in a microgrid. IEEE Trans. Smart Grid **6**(4), 1893–1903 (2017)
9. Zhao, Y.L., Chen, B., Fan, Y.L.: Convergence speed analysis and optimization for distributed control of virtual power plant. Power Grid Technol. **40**(8), 2288–2294 (2016)
10. Abessi, A., Vahidinasab, V., Ghazizadeh, M.S.: Centralized support distributed voltage control by using end-users as reactive power support. IEEE Trans. Smart Grid **7**(1), 178–188 (2015)
11. Sheng, W.X., Wu, M., Ji, Y.: Key techniques and engineering practice of distributed renewable generation clusters integration. Proc. CSEE **39**(8), 2175–2186 (2019)
12. Ding, M., Liu, X.F., Bi, R.: Method for cluster partition of high-penetration distributed generators based on comprehensive performance index. Autom. Electr. Power Syst. **42**(15), 47–52 (2018)
13. Paul, J.P., Leost, J.Y., Tesseron, J.M.: Survey of the secondary voltage control in France: present realization and investigations. IEEE Trans. Power Syst. **2**(2), 505–511 (1987)
14. Liu, H.B., Li, P., Gu, W.: Cluster monitoring system for regional distributed generators. Autom. Power Syst. **42**(8), 163–168 (2018)

The Evaluation Method of Distribution Network Operation Performance Based on Combination Weighting and Improved Grey Correlation

Kaitao Guo, Rui Yin(✉), Zutan Liu, and Fangreng Wu

College of Electrical and Information Engineering, Hunan University of Technology, Zhuzhou 412007, Hunan, China
526118658@qq.com

Abstract. Reasonable evaluation of distribution network operation performance can provide reference for distribution network planning, transformation and operation optimization. This has an important impact on the security and stability of the distribution network. Based on related indexes, a method of distribution network operation level evaluation is proposed based on combination weighting and improved grey correlation. Firstly, the correlation coefficient of each evaluation index of distribution network operation performance is introduced, and the combined weight method is used to modify the comprehensive weight of each index, and then the Comprehensive Evaluation Index of each region is obtained, thus, the weak area of distribution network operation performance is identified and the target area in urgent need of transformation is obtained. Then, the mean difference influence coefficient is introduced to improve the traditional grey correlation method, and the correlation degree between the influencing factors of distribution network operation performance and the Comprehensive Evaluation Index is obtained, so as to get the influence degree of each influencing factor on the distribution network operation performance, determine the renovation plan. Finally, the effectiveness and superiority of the proposed method are verified by an example.

Keywords: Operation Performance · Combination Of Empowerment · Improved Grey Correlation · Comprehensive Evaluation

1 Introduction

With the continuous development of smart grid and energy internet strategy, the form of power and power network are faced with different changes, and the new form puts forward higher requirements for the operation performance of distribution network [1], reasonable evaluation of the operation performance of distribution net-work can provide reference for the planning, transformation and operation optimization of distribution net-work, which has a very important impact on the security and stability of distribution network [2].

There are many indexes that affect the operation performance of distribution network, such as the common comprehensive line loss rate [3], line heavy load ratio [4],

H. Yang et al. (Eds.): SmartGIFT 2022, LNICST 483, pp. 42–55, 2023.
https://doi.org/10.1007/978-3-031-31733-0_5

distribution transformer heavy load ratio [5], etc., and the operation performance of distribution network can't be evaluated simply by a single index [6, 7]. How to use each single index to construct the Comprehensive Evaluation Index is the research emphasis of distribution network operation performance evaluation, and the key to construct the Comprehensive Evaluation Index is to determine the index weight [8].

In present research, there are two common methods of weighting: subjective weighting and objective weighting. Literature [9] uses the subjective analytic hierarchy process (AHP) to establish the multi-operator analytic hierarchy process (MAHP) fuzzy evaluation model and the corresponding weight solution method, but don't classify and analyze the objective data, it ignores the laws and influences of the data itself. Literature [10, 11] studies the objective weighting, and introduces the order Relation Analysis Method and the improved AHP method combined with the improved entropy weight method to calculate the comprehensive weight of each power quality index. The final decision-making will be influenced by the deviation between the subjective or objective weighting and the calculation of the relative degree of the influencing factors. Literature [12, 13] puts forward the optimization model which combines several typical ways of subjective and objective weights, but it fails to allocate the proportion of subjective and objective weights scientifically and reasonably, ignore the inherent law of data, and the actual situation is not consistent with the scene. Therefore, it is necessary to further study the overall and effective weighting method in order to get a more reasonable comprehensive evaluation index.

After the establishment of the Comprehensive Evaluation Indicators, it is necessary to further determine the degree of correlation between the influencing factors and them in order to obtain the degree of influence of the influencing factors on the operation performance of distribution net-work [14]. In the past, the grey correlation method [15] was used to analyze the correlation degree between each influencing factor and a single index, which can also be used to analyze the correlation degree between each influencing factor and a comprehensive evaluation index. However, the traditional grey correlation method only considers the overall similarity between the reference series and the comparative series when calculating the correlation degree, and does not consider the error coefficient between the series, it may lead to the concentration of the correlation degree between each influencing factor and the Comprehensive Evaluation Index of distribution network operation performance, while the correlation degree of individual influencing factors is too close to each other, and it is difficult to choose when the regional operation performance is improved to provide optimal selection.

In order to solve these problems, this paper proposes a method of distribution network operation performance evaluation based on combination weighting and improved grey correlation. Firstly, the combined weight analysis method, which combines the objective entropy weight method and the subjective analytic hierarchy process, is adopted to scientifically and reasonably modify the comprehensive weight of each single index by introducing the correlation related coefficient, according to the comprehensive weight, the comprehensive evaluation indexes of each region are calculated, and the weak areas of distribution network operation performance are judged, and the target areas in urgent need of transformation are obtained. Then, the traditional grey correlation method is improved by introducing the mean difference coefficient, and the correlation degree between each influencing factor and the Comprehensive Evaluation Index is calculated, so we can get more accurate influence degree of each influence factor to the distribution network operation performance, and determine the transformation plan. Finally, the effectiveness and superiority of the proposed method are verified by an example. The principle of distribution network operation performance analysis based on combination weighting and improved grey correlation is shown in Fig. 1.

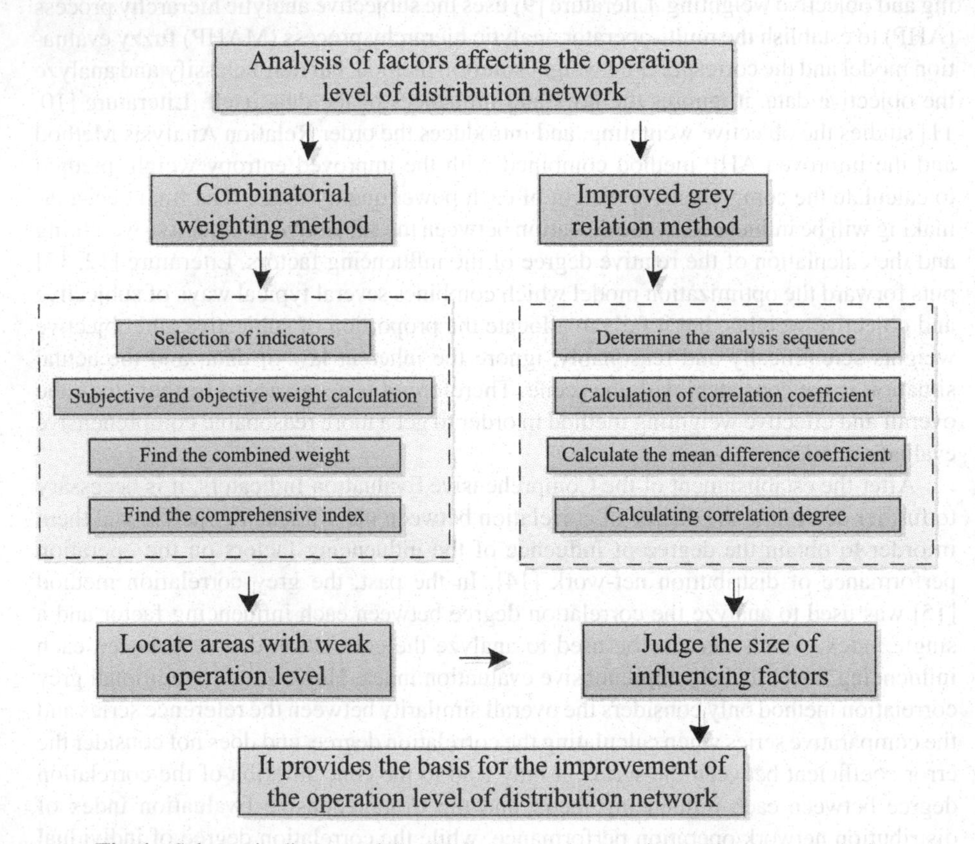

Fig. 1. Schematic diagram of distribution network operation performance analysis

2 Strives for the Comprehensive Evaluation Index

This paper uses the combination of subjective and objective weighting method to give the index reasonable weighting.

2.1 The Determination of Single Evaluation Index Weight

In this paper, three typical indexes, which are Y1) Composite line loss ratio, Y2) line heavy load ratio and Y3) distribution transformer heavy load ratio, are selected as single index to evaluate distribution network operation performance. The following single indicator of the weight of the calculation.

Subjective Weight Calculation
The analytic hierarchy process is used to calculate the weight of each index of distribution network operation performance, which can be carried out in two steps as follows:

Step 1: build the judgment matrix

$$X = \begin{bmatrix} x_{11} \dots x_{1n} \\ \vdots \quad x_{ij} \quad \vdots \\ x_{n1} \dots x_{nn} \end{bmatrix} \tag{1}$$

According to the experience of experts and decision-makers, the judgment matrix X shown in formula (1) can be obtained by using 1–9 and its reciprocal as the criterion of comparison between the two indexes. Each value represents the relative importance between the two indexes.

Step two: the AHP weights for each indicator are calculated as follows:

$$\mathrm{W_{1j}} = \frac{1}{\mathrm{n}} \sum_{i=1}^{\mathrm{n}} \frac{\mathrm{x_{ij}}}{\sum_{i=1}^{\mathrm{n}} \mathrm{x_{ij}}} \tag{2}$$

In the formula, W_{1j} indicates that the weight of single index j can be calculated by AHP.

Objective Weight Calculation
The entropy weight method can make full use of objective data to determine objective weight. The specific calculation steps are as follows:

The first step is to standardize the original evaluation index matrix.

Let m be the evaluation index and n be the evaluation object, the original data matrix Y can be obtained as follows:

$$Y = \begin{bmatrix} y_{11} \; y_{12} \cdots y_{1n} \\ y_{21} \; y_{22} \cdots y_{2n} \\ \vdots \quad \vdots \quad y_{ij} \quad \vdots \\ y_{m1} \; y_{m2} \cdots y_{mn} \end{bmatrix} \tag{3}$$

In the formula, Y_{ij} represents the value of the j single indicator in the i region.

After the normalization of the above original matrix, the resulting matrix Y'.

Step two: define the index entropy.

In the evaluation problem with m evaluation indexes and n evaluation objects, the first step is to determine the normalized value Pij, and then the entropy value e_j of the corresponding indexes can be obtained as shown in formula (4). The entropy calculation can be expressed as:

$$e_j = -k\sum_{i=1}^{m} p_{ij}\ln p_{ij} \tag{4}$$

In the formula, k = 1/lnm, and define $Pij = 0, P_{ij}lnP_{ij} = 0$.

Step three: calculate the weight of the index.

After calculating the entropy of index j, the weight of index j is calculated as follows:

$$W_{2j} = \frac{1 - e_j}{\sum_{j=1}^{n} 1 - e_j} \tag{5}$$

In the formula, W_{2J} is used to calculate the weight of single index j by entropy weight method.

2.2 The Calculation of the Combination Weight

This paper introduced the correlation coefficient, the final combination weights can be calculated more objectively by using the correlation coefficient between the weight and each index calculated by the single weighting method.

The first step is to determine the coefficient of Pirsson coefficient V_{ij}, and then the correlation coefficient L_j, as shown in formula (6).

$$L_j = \frac{\sum_{i=1}^{m}\sum_{j=1}^{n}\left|V_{ij}\right| - 3}{\sum_{j=1}^{n}\left|V_{ij}\right| - 1} \tag{6}$$

In the formula, X and Y denote the sequence of index i and Index j.

The combination weights are determined as follows:

$$W_j = \frac{\sqrt{W_{1j}\cdot W_{2j}\cdot L_j}}{\sum_{j=1}^{n}\sqrt{W_{1j}\cdot W_{2j}\cdot L_j}} \tag{7}$$

In the formula, W_j is the final combination weight of single index j.

2.3 The Establishment of Comprehensive Evaluation Index

Using the value of the combination weight and the normalized value of the index, it first needs to determine the normalized value of the group i data under the j index y''_{ij}.

The Comprehensive Evaluation Index under the power supply *i* area can be obtained as shown in formula (8).

$$Z_i = \sum_{j=1}^{n} \sqrt{W_j.y''_{ij}} \tag{8}$$

The comprehensive evaluation index, the greater the representative operation performance, the better, according to the size of the corresponding value of each area, can determine run performance relatively weak areas.

3 The Improved Grey Correlation Method is Used to Calculate the Correlation Degree

The operation performance of distribution network is mainly affected by the following nine factors: A1) high-loss distribution transformer ratio; A2) integrated voltage pass rate; A3) line N-1 pass rate; A4) power supply reliability rate; A5) low-voltage station area proportion; A6) line standardized connection rate; A7) line connection rate; A8) overall household distribution transformer capacity; A9) line frequent trip rate.

In this paper, the error influence coefficient is introduced to improve the traditional grey correlation method, so that the correlation degree between each influence factor and the Comprehensive Evaluation Index is calculated.

3.1 Determine the Analysis Matrix

The analysis matrix *B* as shown in formula (9) can be obtained by using the Comprehensive Evaluation Index as the reference sequence and the nine influencing factors as the comparison sequence.

$$B = \begin{bmatrix} b_0(1) & b_1(1) & \ldots & b_n(1) \\ b_0(2) & b_1(2) & \ldots & b_n(2) \\ \vdots & \vdots & b_i(j) & \vdots \\ b_0(m) & b_1(m) & \ldots & b_n(m) \end{bmatrix} \tag{9}$$

In the formula, b_0 represents the reference series composed of comprehensive evaluation indexes, and b_1–b_n represents the comparison series composed of influencing factors. $b_i(j)$ and $b_n(m)$ represent the *j* number of the first influencing factor and *n* influencing factors in the m-dimensional analysis matrix, respectively.

3.2 Determine the Correlation Coefficient

According to the analysis matrix after normalization, the difference sequence $C_i\ (j)$ is calculated from the absolute difference between the comparison sequence and the reference sequence, as shown in formula (10), and then the difference matrix is composed of the difference sequence.

$$C_i(j) = \left| b'_0(j) - b'_i(j) \right| \tag{10}$$

The maximum and minimum elements of the difference matrix are expressed as C_{max} and C_{min}, respectively. And the correlation coefficient $g_i(j)$ according to the data in the difference matrix is shown in formula (11):

$$g_i(j) = \frac{C_{\min} + 0.5C_{\max}}{C_i(j) + 0.5C_{\max}} \tag{11}$$

3.3 The Mean Difference Influence Coefficient is Introduced

The mean square error value can be determined according to the comparison sequence and the reference sequence, and then the distance mean difference coefficient can be obtained, as shown in formula (12):

$$w_i = \frac{1}{e^{\partial_i}} \tag{12}$$

3.4 Calculate the Correlation Degree of the Influencing Factors

The correlation degree of each influencing factor is calculated by the spatial distance coefficient and the correlation coefficient together, as follows:

$$r_i = \frac{1}{n} w_i \sum_{i=1}^{m} g_i(j) \tag{13}$$

In the formula, r_i is the correlation degree of the i influencing factor.

The correlation degree indicates the influence degree of each influence factor on the Comprehensive Evaluation Index, that is, the influence degree on the operation performance.

4 Conclusion of Actual Case Analysis

Above provides nine influencing factors for correlation analysis and three categories of single evaluation indicators for calculation of comprehensive evaluation indicators.

4.1 The Determination of Single Index Weight

The single indicator data for the performance of operation of the distribution networks in the eight regions are shown in Table 1.

Table 1. Single indicator data sheet

Area	Combined line loss rate	Proportion of line overload	Distribution transformer heavy ratio
Area 1	3.60	11.31	4.08
Area 2	4.18	7.83	3.84
Area 3	3.91	8.71	3.13
Area 4	3.38	10.04	3.81
Area 5	4.50	10.36	3.14
Area 6	5.12	6.03	3.86
Area 7	4.28	9.05	4.06
Area 8	5.33	7.83	3.65

According to the single index shown in the table above, the AHP weights, entropy weights and combination weights of line loss rate, line heavy load ratio and distribution transformer heavy load ratio are shown in Table 2.

Table 2. Each weight value data table

	Combined line loss rate	Proportion of line overload	Distribution transformer heavy ratio
Weight of AHP	0.66	0.16	0.19
Entropy weight method	0.27	0.27	0.46
Combination weight	0.58	0.24	0.19

The value of the Comprehensive Evaluation Index reflects the operation performance of the distribution network in each region. From Table 3 and Fig. 2, if the operation performance of distribution network needs to be adjusted at this stage, priority should be given to the area with the weakest performance of distribution network operation 3.

Table 3. Evaluation of comprehensive index values for region

Area	Area 1	Area 2	Area 3	Area 4	Area 5	Area 6	Area 7	Area 8
Index	0.81	0.79	0.74	0.77	0.84	0.86	0.83	0.91

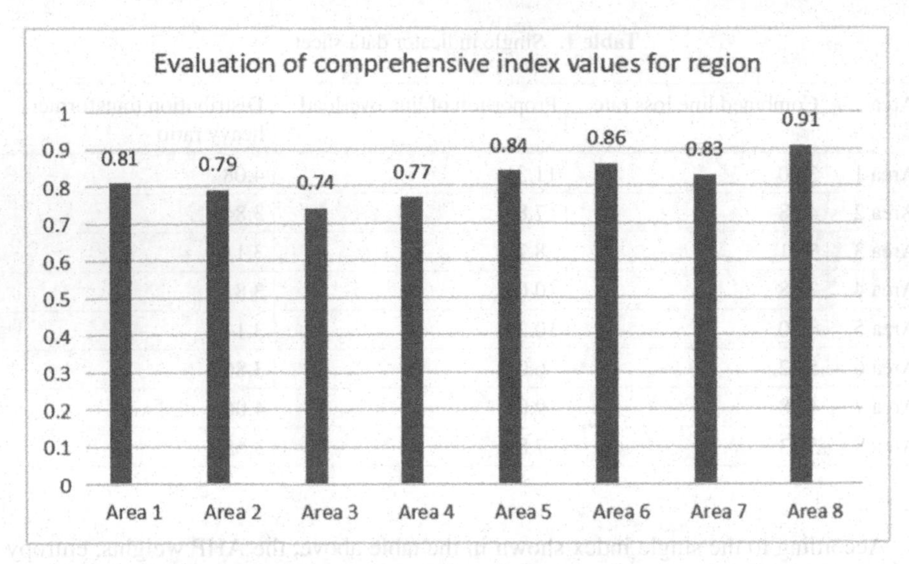

Fig. 2. Evaluation of comprehensive index values for region

4.2 The Calculation of Correlation Degree

The data of nine kinds of influencing factors on the operation performance of distribution network in different regions are shown in Table 4.

Table 4. Influencing factors data table

Area	A1	A2	A3	A4	A5
Area 1	3.23	94.54	36.65	85.64	31.72
Area 2	4.96	95.08	36.55	88.57	33.92
Area 3	4.93	95.48	37.50	94.91	32.60
Area 4	4.93	95.98	37.60	95.11	34.32
Area 5	2.86	70.02	34.55	80.41	24.08
Area 6	3.89	70.73	34.64	81.85	26.27
Area 7	4.01	72.49	35.44	88.80	28.51

(*continued*)

Table 4. (*continued*)

Area	A1	A2	A3	A4	A5
Area 8	4.09	76.52	34.83	94.93	32.08
Area	A6	A 7	A 8	A9	
Area 1	0	77.54	2.34	7.13	
Area 2	26.03	78.33	28.06	6.15	
Area 3	52.03	80.92	38.22	7.52	
Area 4	65.62	85.31	52.28	5.18	
Area 5	0.23	51.10	2.41	9.82	
Area 6	7.71	56.90	22.25	8.70	
Area 7	22.28	61.14	35.19	6.39	
Area 8	54.10	64.02	38.18	7.75	

Here set up five other groups of method correlation degree calculation results. The first group uses the traditional grey correlation method but still considers the correlation coefficient when calculating the correlation degree, and the second group uses the improved grey correlation method without considering the correlation coefficient. After that, the three groups used a single index instead of a comprehensive evaluation index to calculate the degree of association. The third group calculates the correlation degree with the comprehensive line loss rate as the comprehensive Index, the fourth group calculates the correlation degree with the line heavy load ratio as the comprehensive index, and the fifth group calculates the correlation degree with the line heavy load ratio as the distribution transformer heavy load ratio. Each group of correlation order are shown in Table 5.

Table 5. Ranking table of correlation degree results

	Group 1	Group 2	Group 3	Group 4	Group 5	This article
A1	6	7	7	7	7	6
A2	5	5	6	3	5	5
A3	2	1	3	2	2	2
A4	3	4	2	4	1	3
A5	4	8	4	5	4	4
A6	9	9	9	9	9	9
A7	7	2	1	6	6	7
A8	8	3	8	8	8	8
A9	1	6	5	1	3	1

By comparing the correlation degrees in the table above, the order of the influencing factors is as follows: A9 > A3 > A4 > A5 > A2 > A1 > A7 > A8 > A6. The third group was ranked as A7 > A4 > A3 > A5 > A9 > A2 > A1 > A8 > A6, and the fourth group was A9 > A3 > A2 > A4 > A5 > A7 > A1 > A8 > A6. The fifth group is ranked A4 > A3 > A9 > A5 > A2 > A7 > A1 > A8 > A6.

From the above, the low voltage station area ratio and the average load rate relative to other factors are the lowest correlation ranking. However, when only a single index is considered, the third group with the highest degree of correlation is the comprehensive voltage qualification rate, the fourth group with the highest degree of correlation is the frequent trip rate of the line, and the fifth group with the highest degree of correlation is the power supply reliability rate, in order to find out the influential factors in the current stage, we neglect the influence of other indicators when we judge the magnitude of the influence factors, it is easy to be out of line with the actual situation, and it is difficult to provide a more comprehensive reference method for the improvement of the operation performance of the distribution network. In this paper, the method combines three cases of considering only one index, and comprehensively considers the ranking of the degree of association under the condition of three cases of single index, which effectively avoids the error caused by individual index, it provides a more comprehensive and objective method for improving the operation performance of distribution network.

The second group is A3 > A7 > A8 > A4 > A2 > A9 > A1 > A5 > A6. The order of line contact rate and line frequent trip rate is too low, which is not in accordance with the actual situation, and the result is easy to produce error, and can't provide effective reference for the operation performance of distribution network.

The first group is ranked A9 > A3 > A4 > A5 > A2 > A1 > A7 > A8 > A6. In this case, the data of A1 and A2, A3 and A4 have little difference and poor reference, so it is difficult to decide the actual correlation degree.

The 20-year index forecast value, 20-year field data and the percentage of improvement are shown in Table 6 and Fig. 3.

Table 6. Improvement in indicators

Attribute for the indicator	Indicators	This article methods	2020 data	Increase in percentage (%)
Positive indicators	All households allocated variable capacity	4.93	4.08	20.83
	Standardized line connection rate	95.48	93.84	1.75
	Line N-1 passrate	37.50	34.13	9.87
	Reliability of power supply	94.91	93.81	1.1
	Line connection rate	32.6	30.14	8.16
	Average load rate	52.03	49.86	4.35
	Integrated voltage pass rate	80.92	78.06	3.66
Negative indicators	Low voltage station area ratio	38.22	40.65	5.98
	Frequency trip rate of line	7.52	8.97	16.16

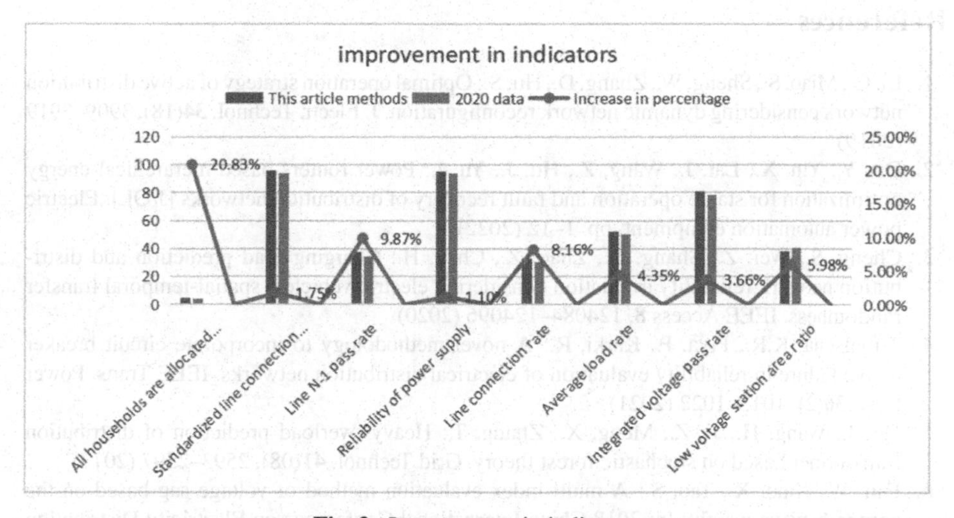

Fig. 3. Improvement in indicators

As shown in Table 6, both the positive and negative indicators, based on the method proposed in this paper to improve the distribution network has a better effect, in which, the main indexes with higher promotion range are the capacity of distributed transformer in the whole world, the passing rate of line N-1 and the frequent trip rate of line. The capacity improvement rate of the whole distribution network is 20.83%, the pass rate of line N-1 is 9.87%, and the frequent trip rate of line is 16.16%, which proves the effectiveness of the proposed method.

To sum up, compared with the existing methods, this method not only effectively avoids the error caused by only considering a single evaluation index, but also improves the calculation method of correlation degree, which greatly improves the accuracy of distribution network operation performance, at the same time can provide support for the reasonable transformation of distribution network.

5 Conclusion

In this paper, a method based on combination weighting and improved grey correlation is proposed to evaluate the operation performance of distribution network:

(1) Compared with the traditional single evaluation index method, the Integrated Evaluation Index method based on combination weighting can identify the weak areas of distribution network more accurately.
(2) Compared with the traditional grey correlation method, the improved grey correlation method is more accurate in calculating the correlation degree and more effective in evaluating the operation performance.

References

1. Li, C., Miao, S., Sheng, W., Zhang, D., Hu, S.: Optimal operation strategy of active distribution network considering dynamic network reconfiguration. J. Electr. Technol. **34**(18), 3909–3919 (2019)
2. Du, Y., Yin, X., Lai, J., Wang, Z., Hu, J., Yu, J.: Power routers-based hierarchical energy optimization for stable operation and fault recovery of distribution networks [J/OL]. Electric power automation equipment, pp. 1–12 (2022)
3. Cheng, S., Wei, Z., Shang, D., Zhao, Z., Chen, H.: Charging load prediction and distribution network reliability evaluation considering electric vehicles' spatial-temporal transfer randomness. IEEE Access **8**, 124084–124096 (2020)
4. Timalsena, K.R., Piya, P., Karki, R.: A novel methodology to incorporate circuit breaker active failure in reliability evaluation of electrical distribution networks. IEEE Trans. Power Syst. **36**(2), 1013–1022 (2021)
5. He, J., Wang, H., Ji, Z., Meng, X., Zhang, T.: Heavy overload prediction of distribution transformer based on stochastic forest theory. Grid Technol. **41**(08), 2593–2597 (2017)
6. Fan, W., Xiao, X., Tao, S.: A multi-index evaluation method of voltage sag based on the comprehensive weight. In: 2018 China International Conference on Electricity Distribution (CICED), pp. 613–617. IEEE (2018)
7. Ji, Z., Liu, J., Tian, H., Zhang, W.: ECT sensor simulation and fuzzy optimization design based on multi index orthogonal experiment. IEEE Access **8**, 190039–190048 (2020)
8. Mu, G., Chen, Q., Liu, H., An, J., Wang, C.: Inverse information entropy causal reasoning method for Revealing causality in power system operation data. Proc. CSEE 1–14 (2022)
9. Mu, Y., et al.: Comprehensive evaluation index system of power grid safety and efficiency based on multi-operator AHP fuzzy evaluation. Power Grid Technol. **39**(01), 23–28 (2015)

10. Liu, X., Wei, J., Zhang, W., et al.: Investment benefits evaluation and decision for distribution network based on information entropy and fuzzy analysis method. Power Syst. Protect. Control **47**(12), 48–56 (2019)
11. Guo, X., Li, Y., Wang, S., et al.: A comprehensive weight-based severity evaluation method of voltage sag in distribution networks. Energies **14**(19), 6434 (2021)
12. Li, X., Niu, S.: Proc. CSEE **41**(S1), 178–184 (2021)
13. Ai, L., Liu, S., Ma, L., et al.: A Multi-attribute decision making method based on combination of subjective and objective weighting. In: 2019 5th International Conference on Control, Automation and Robotics (ICCAR), pp. 576–580. IEEE (2019)
14. Zhao, H., Li, J.: Energy efficiency evaluation and optimization of industrial park customers based on PSR model and improved grey-TOPSIS method. IEEE Access **9**, 76423–76432 (2021)
15. Nan, Y., Song, R.-Q., Chen, P., Hu, J., Gao, T., Han, W.: Based on the improved entropy weight-grey correlation analysis method of distribution network reliability factors. Power Syst. Protect. Control **47**(24), 101–107 (2019). https://doi.org/10.19783/j.carolcarrollnkiPSPC.190220

Multi-angle Identification of Small Target Faults in Transmission Lines Based on Improved YOLOX Algorithm

Shurong Peng, Jieni He(✉), Huixia Chen, Bin Li, Jiayi Peng, and Lijuan Guo

Changsha University of Science and Technology, Changsha 410114, China
1535133864@qq.com

Abstract. In the grid patrol work, there are some fault types with small targets in the line that needs to be detected. For the problem of partial feature loss when the target is small in UAV image recognition, CutMix is used to perform multi-angle image fusion on the line images captured by UAV, which is used to improve the accuracy of target detection. The improved YOLOX-pruning algorithm model is used for deep learning to prune and sparse the network structure, thus removing the redundant nodes of the network to improve the speed of target detection. In this experiment, manually labeled line images are fed into the model to train the features of the faulty components in the images. With a 50% reduction in channel parameter size and multi-angle feature fusion, the algorithm target detection speed is improved by 2.569 frames per second and the mAP value of the faulty data set is improved by 3.378%, reducing the amount of operation while improving the target detection accuracy.

Keywords: Transmission Line Inspection · Deep Learning · Target Detection · Multi Angle · Channel Prunning

1 Introduction

In the power system, the transmission line corridor environment is very complex, the circuit operation state will change with the line element changes, and these changes are partly caused by weather changes, partly caused by foreign body invasion. Transmission lines change more with the terrain, and the power grid personnel need to inspect before and after the peak of electricity consumption and some bad weather before and after, in this case for the personal safety of personnel has a certain adverse impact.

In the process of manual inspection of transmission lines, an infrared thermometer is usually used for local temperature measurement [1] and power robot inspection [2], etc. With the continuous application of UAV inspection in power systems, in addition to general high-voltage transmission lines, UAV inspection has also been continuously applied to the field of new energy generation, such as wind turbine hub center detection and tracking [3] and photovoltaic power generation module temperature detection using infrared thermal imaging UAV [4].

H. Yang et al. (Eds.): SmartGIFT 2022, LNICST 483, pp. 56–72, 2023.
https://doi.org/10.1007/978-3-031-31733-0_6

Traditional target detection methods include HOG gradient histogram, feature pyramid [5], and sliding window technique [6]. The path aggregation network PANet [7] improves the feature pyramid by facilitating the flow of information in an instance-based segmentation framework through bottom-up path enhancement and precise localization of low-level signals. In the context of power system inspection, for the problems of poor image quality, complex background, and poor contrast captured in complex scenes, Ref. [8] proposed a regional convolutional neural network infrared image target detection method incorporating image direction gradient histogram to solve the problem of large scale super-resolution image reconstruction task with large loss of image information, but and to solve the problem of small target fault features under conventional scale image The problem of loss, this study starts from several small target faults in the power grid, combines the fault characteristics, uses multi-angle fusion images, and optimizes the learning of small target fault features by the algorithm.

The target detection feature extraction process is affected by the location and scale of the target in the image, and the detection results will have different degrees of deviation. To address these problems and the features of large computation and high dimensionality, the spatial selection method and multilevel method are proposed to reduce the computation by eliminating regions with less information [9]; and the sliding window in the sliding scan, because it has to be repeatedly scanned under different scales of the same image, will regions overlap and cause redundancy, using a new method that can directly create very small order Markov sets can greatly improve the computational efficiency compared to existing methods [10]. For the current target detection in computer vision, the main function implemented is to identify the target object in the picture and to classify and localize it. Using neural network deep learning for target detection can be achieved based on a large amount of raw data, using a better generalization to fit the nonlinear function [11] and solve the problem of missing features in traditional target detection. In the process of image feature processing, the principal component analysis method PCA (principal component analysis) can reduce the dimensionality of the feature vector, and for the problem of its time-consuming computation of the eigenvector space, Ref. [12] proposed a 2DPCA algorithm, based on the principal component analysis of 2D image matrices, which does not need to transform the image matrix into a vector before feature extraction. In this study, we introduce the channel pruning method to optimize the modal feature extraction channel and remove the redundant nodes and parameters of the network while retaining the main feature network to reduce the computational effort to improve the algorithm running speed.

For various problems arising in transmission lines, many authors have proposed detection methods for specific features of a single fault. In Ref. [13], for aerial transmission line images, a color model conversion method based on grayscale variance normalization is proposed to highlight conductor areas and achieve accurate identification of conductor surface damage areas. For the problem of missing cotter pins in a railroad power installation, Ref. [14] proposed a fault detection method based on a deep convolutional neural network and integrated learning, using an integrated classifier composed of multiple linear SVMs to achieve cotter pin missing fault detection. For the sample class imbalance problem in transmission line insulator defect detection, Ref. [5] used ResNeXt-101 as a feature extraction network to fully extract features and applied an online hard example mining (OHEM) training strategy to solve the positive and negative sample imbalance problem. For the more difficult to identify transmission line broken strands detection problem, this study further refines the detection targets into conductor loose strands and conductor broken strands and uses multi-scale calibration to change the category imbalance problem and improve the detection effect.

In this study, CSPDarknet [15] is the backbone network algorithm to train the target detection network for several types of faults that are difficult to be detected by image recognition in overhead lines of high-voltage networks, and the model is improved and optimized by channel pruning. Faults containing broken wires, dropped cotter pins, broken insulators, and loose anti-vibration hammers are pre-processed with images, and the target detection is performed after multi-angle image fusion to enhance the input image quality using CutMix for small faults. By comparison, the improved model ensures the accuracy of target detection under the same size data set while the volume is smaller.

2 Transmission Line Fault Characteristics

Transmission lines are exposed to the natural environment for long periods and the components are susceptible to corrosion by rain, snow, high temperatures, and disturbance by strong winds. In transmission lines, cotter pin dislodgement sometimes occurs due to thermal expansion, contraction, or wind [16]. And the cotter pin installation environment is not fixed, the target is small and the background is cluttered, etc., which often leads to missed detection during the identification process.

Anti-vibration hammers are used to prevent fatigue damage to the wire and to absorb wire vibrations during wind [17]. Due to vibration over due to wind often accompanied by rain and erosion resulting in rusting of metal parts, making the anti-vibration hammer loose, fracture, and slip [18], the loss of the original damping effect; long-term operation of the line leads to a certain arc sag and the aging phenomenon of the wire, as well as the line in the air by wind disturbance when the different amplitude of vibration occurs, easily caused by the occurrence of loose strands, half broken strands, and broken strands, resulting in local Current and wire temperature abnormalities; part of the obvious wire breakage due to broken strands produce wire branching, resulting in a straight wire reduction [19], while a small part of the wire produced loose strands and not completely broken strands in the image for the increase in the radius of the wire, which can determine whether there is a wire breakage fault in the image and the extent of the broken strands.

The detection of faults such as missing open pins is a small target detection, which is one of the most time-consuming and labor-intensive parts of manual judgment and is prone to miss detection in the case of large image areas, object occlusion, and complex backgrounds. CutMix was used to achieve multi-angle image fusion, improve the problem of small target fault feature loss when the algorithm samples the image, and conduct deep learning with UAV patrol images so that the neural network is trained to learn the iconographic features of faults such as cotter pin dropped, loose anti-vibration hammer, broken insulator and broken wire in the image.

3 Deep Learning Based on the YOLOX Model

The YOLOX [20] algorithm makes many improvements based on the YOLO series, one of the more important improvements is the use of Anchor-Free detection, and the target detection framework is shown in Fig. 1.

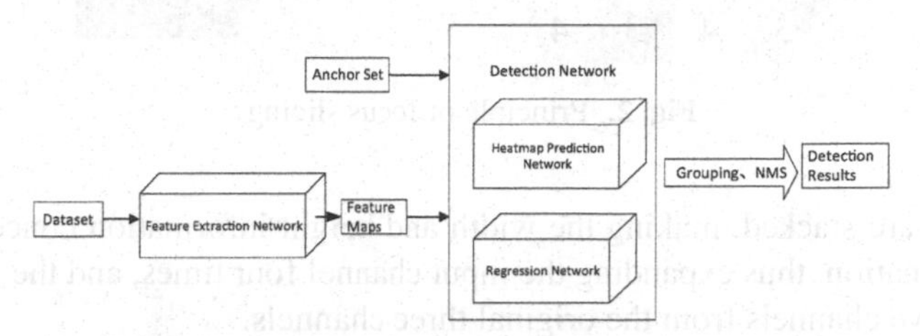

Fig. 1. Anchor-Free target detection framework

Anchor-Free detection is used to solve the problem of the high missed detection rate of objects with serious occlusion and small scale.

Anchor-Free detection is the same as Anchor-Based [21] detection in that both are based on the feature points on the training graph to construct the learned target and the construction process back-calculates the sensory field by the feature points. The difference is that Anchor-Free is an endogenous perspective, i.e., it starts from the properties of the feature points themselves to generate the prediction frame without hyperparameters, so the code complexity is relatively low, and a single feature point responds to a target object, which can directly predict the boundary of the object.

3.1 Model Analysis

The overall structure of the YOLOX model consists of four parts: the input, the backbone network, the neck network, and the prediction. In the input part, methods such as Mosaic [22] data augmentation are used. Deep learning uses the CSPDarknet feature extraction network, which contains the Residual Network, which can be used to improve the accuracy of the algorithm by increasing the number of network layers. The residual convolution is divided into two parts, the backbone part contains two convolutional layers of 1 × 1 and 3 × 3, the residual edge directly combines the input and output of the backbone, while the internal residual block uses jump links to alleviate the problem of gradient disappearance caused by increasing depth in deep neural networks with. The SPP structure is used to improve the perceptual field of the network by maximizing the pooling of the same pooling kernel size for feature extraction.

The backbone of the algorithm uses the Focus network structure as shown in Fig. 2.

Compared with the normal convolutional approach of neural networks, Focus sampling does not cause information loss and replaces three normal down-sampling convolutional layers at a time, reducing the number of parameters, Cuda memory, and increasing the speed of forward and backward propagation. In the training process, Focus sampling first slices the image, i.e., every other pixel in a picture is taken, similar to proximity down-sampling, to obtain four independent feature layers, and then the four independent

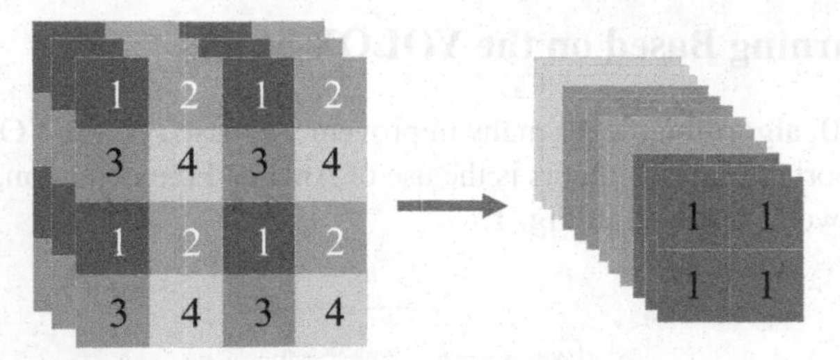

Fig. 2. Principle of focus slicing

feature layers are stacked, making the width and height information concentrated into channel information, thus expanding the input channel four times, and the feature layer becomes twelve channels from the original three channels.

The improvement of the main function of the model, the ReLU activation function, is shown in Fig. 3, by the transformation of Eq. (1).

$$f(x) = x \cdot sigmoid(x) \tag{1}$$

where is the ReLU function. The Sigmoid activation function is combined with the ReLU function to produce the SiLU function, as shown in Fig. 3(b), with no upper bound with a lower bound, smooth, and non-monotonic, i.e., the ReLU function is smoothed.

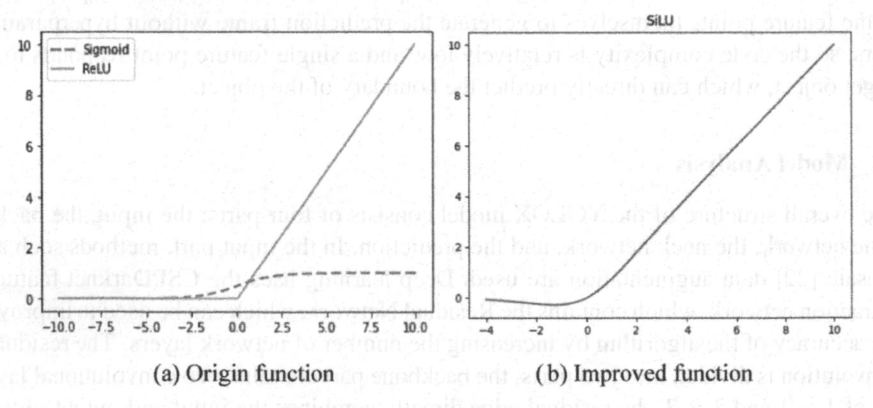

Fig. 3. Function image of SiLU

The YOLOX algorithm extracts three feature layers for target detection in the feature utilization part, which are located in the middle, lower middle, and bottom layers of CSPDarknet. After obtaining the three effective feature layers, a new enhanced feature layer is obtained by stacking after convolution, up-sampling, and down-sampling.

Since the output channel classification task and regression task are put together, there is a conflict between the two tasks, YOLOX adopts decoupled head to replace the coupled head, which has a better expression effect and the model accuracy will be improved, while the convergence speed of the network is accelerated. The decoupled head network decomposition is shown in Fig. 4.

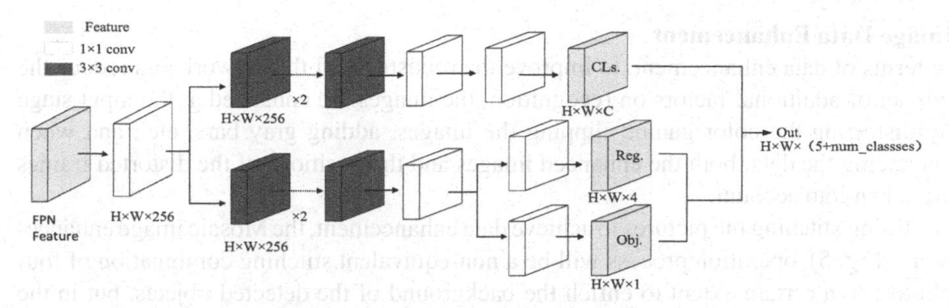

Fig. 4. Decoupled head network decomposition.

FPN Feature denotes the FPN feature layer, and H and W in the figure represent the height (height) and width (width) of the feature map; Reg(H, W, 4) is used to judge the regression parameters of each feature point, and the regression parameters are adjusted to obtain the prediction frame; Obj(H, W, 1) is used to judge whether each feature point contains objects; Cls(H, W, 4 + 1 + num_classes) the first four parameters of the third item are used to judge the regression parameters of each feature point, and the prediction box is obtained after adjustment, the fifth parameter is used to judge whether each feature point contains objects, and finally num_classes is used to judge the kinds of objects contained in the feature points.

The two parallel branches of the decoupling head have two 3 × 3 convolutional layers for classification and regression tasks respectively. The FPN feature layer extracts better features by fusing feature layers of different morphologies, after which these features are passed into the Yolo Head to obtain prediction results.

3.2 Data Enhancement with Model-Based Channel Cropping Improvements

To improve the accuracy of small target fault recognition and enhance the speed and efficiency of model recognition, we can enhance the learning of target features in images and reduce the redundancy of the network by enhancing the data and optimizing the model channels to obtain a lightweight model while enhancing the target weight mapping.

Image Data Enhancement

In terms of data enhancement, to improve the robustness of the network and reduce the impact of additional factors on recognition, the images are enhanced at the input stage by distorting the color gamut, flipping the images, adding gray bars, etc., and when enhancing the data, both the enhanced images and the positions of the distorted frames are taken into account.

Using stitching the pictures to achieve data enhancement, the Mosaic image enhancement (Fig. 5), operation process will be a non-equivalent stitching combination of four photos, to a certain extent to enrich the background of the detected objects, but in the process of use, Mosaic data enhancement part of the operation will bring the inaccurate annotation box. Therefore, to reduce the redundant boxes generated by the data enhancement operation, this experiment performs mosaic data enhancement on the first 90% of epochs for image data.

Fig. 5. Mosaic picture enhancement effect

Channel Pruning

To obtain a lightweight model suitable for fast detection, this study uses channel pruning to structurally simplify the convolution module of the algorithm. The structural simplification mainly involves tensor decomposition, sparse connectivity, and channel pruning. The parameters of the YOLOX convolutional module are shown in Table 1.

Table 1. Structural parameters of the YOLOX multilayer convolution module.

Convolution	Number	Output feature map	Parameters
Convolution Module	Number of layers	Output feature map size number of channels × length × width	Parameters (convolutional layer size)
Conv2d	1	32, 320, 320	3456
	2	64, 160, 160	22528
	4	32, 160, 160	14336
	8	128, 80, 80	729088
	12	64, 80, 80	212992
	4	256, 40, 40	491520
	23	128, 40, 40	1884160
	4	512, 20, 20	2228224
	11	256, 20, 20	2686976
BatchNorm2d	1	32, 320, 320	64
	2	64,160, 160	256
	4	32, 160, 160	256
	8	128, 80, 80	2048
	12	128, 40, 40	1536
	5	128, 20, 20	1280
	4	64, 80, 80	2048
	23	256, 40, 40	5888
	4	512, 20, 20	4096
	11	256, 20, 20	5632

For pruning the feature map with c channels, a convolutional filter W of $n \times c \times k_h \times k_u$ is considered to be applied to the mapping X with an input volume of $N \times c \times k_h \times k_w$, resulting in an output matrix Y of $N \times n$. Where N is the number of samples, n is the number of output channels, and k_h, k_w is the size of the convolutional kernel. When performing the pruning of the input channel c to the desired $c_0 (0 \leqslant c_0 \leqslant c)$ value, the bias term is discarded to make the representation simpler while minimizing the reconstruction error, and the representation is shown in Eq. (2).

$$l_0 = \begin{matrix} arg\min \\ \beta, W \end{matrix} \frac{1}{2N} \left\| \sum_{i=1}^{c} \beta_i X_i W_i^T - Y \right\|_F^2 \quad (2)$$

where $\|\beta\|_0 \leqslant c'$; $\|\cdot\|_F$ is the Frobenius norm, X_i is the $N \times k_h k_w$ matrix of the channel slice of the ith input mapping X, $i = 1, \cdots, c$; W_i is the $N \times k_h k_w$ filter weight cut from the ith channel of W; β is a coefficient vector of length c for channel selection, and β_i (the ith element of β) is the scalar mask of the ith channel (i.e., whether to discard the entire channel), when $\beta_i = 0$, X_i and W_i can be safely clipped from the feature map. c' is the number of reserved channels, which can be calculated from the desired acceleration ratio and set manually. For overall model acceleration, the acceleration ratio is first assigned to each layer and then calculated for each c'.

To solve the NP puzzle in the optimization equation, the relaxation from to is regularized as shown in Eq. (3).

$$l_1 = arg \min_{\beta, W} \frac{1}{2N} \left\| \sum_{i=1}^{c} \beta_i X_i W_i^\top - Y \right\|_F^2 + \lambda \|\beta\|_1, \|\beta\|_0 \leqslant c', \quad \forall_i \|W_i\|_F = 1 \quad (3)$$

where λ is the penalty factor, by increasing the value of λ, there will be more zero terms in β and a higher acceleration ratio can be obtained. Adding the constraint $\forall_i \|W_i\|_F = 1$ to Eq. (3) reduces the computational redundancy caused by the F-parameter of the over-range W_i.

Now perform the channel selection by fixing W and solving for it; secondly, fix the value of and solve for W to reconstruct the error.

Step 1: Fix the W solution, and solve the channel selection problem using LASSO regression as shown in Eq. (4).

$$\hat{\beta}^{LASSO}(\lambda) = arg \min_{\beta} \frac{1}{2N} \left\| \sum_{i=1}^{c} \beta_i Z_i - Y \right\|_F^2 + \lambda \|\beta\|_1, \|\beta\|_0 \leqslant c' \quad (4)$$

where $Z_i = X_i W_i^\top$, the ith channel that makes $\beta_i = 0$ is ignored.

Step 2: Fix the solution W and use the selected minimum channel solution W to reconstruct the error as shown in Eq. (5).

$$arg \min_{W'} \left\| Y - X'(W')^\top \right\|_F^2 \quad (5)$$

where $X' = [\beta_1 X_1 \beta_2 X_2 \cdots \beta_i X_i \cdots \beta_c X_c]_{N \times ck_h k_w}$, W' is the W that has been reconstructed by $n \times ck_h k_w$, $W' = [W_1 W_2 \cdots W_i \cdots W_c]$. After deriving W', reformulate it to W and then specify $\beta_i \leftarrow \beta_i \|W_i\|_F$, $W_i \leftarrow W_i / \|W_i\|_F$ so that it satisfies the constraint $\forall_i \|W_i\|_F = 1$.

In practice, the repetition of the two steps is time-consuming, and multiple iterations of step one are used until step two is used once after $\|\beta\|_0 \leqslant c'$ is satisfied to obtain the final result.

For channel pruning of the overall model, the above steps are used sequentially, layer by layer. For each layer, the input volume is obtained from the current input feature map and the output volume is obtained from the output feature map of the unpruned model as shown in Eq. (6).

$$arg \min_{\beta, W} \frac{1}{2N} \left\| \sum_{i=1}^{c} \beta_i X_i, W_i^\top - Y' \right\|_F^2, \|\beta\|_0 \leq c' \quad (6)$$

Considering the cumulative error during sequential pruning, Y' of the feature map from the source model is used instead of Y in Eq. (6).

3.3 Multi-angle Image Fusion

To address the problem of feature loss in the recognition of small target faults in images, this experiment uses CutMix for image fusion of multi-angle images with different kinds of faults to enhance the learning of fault features by neural networks. CutMix uses the complete target detection object as a classification label and selectively combines blocks between training images to maintain the regularization effect of region loss by effectively using training pixels. The merging operation of CutMix is Eq. (7) and Eq. (8).

$$\overline{x} = M \odot x_A + (1 - M) \odot x_B \tag{7}$$

$$\overline{y} = \lambda y_A + (1 - \lambda) y_B \tag{8}$$

where $M \in \{0, 1\}W \times H$, denotes the binary mask representing the locations of deletion and fill in the two images, sampled from the bounding box coordinates of the image cropping region; and $\lambda \in (0, 1)$, sampled uniformly from the range of values. A new training sample $(\overline{x}, \overline{y})$ is generated by combining two training samples (x_A, y_A), (x_B, y_B) for training the model of the original loss function.

After the open pin image is fused by CutMix, the areas of different parts are proportionally blended as shown in Fig. 6, and the open pin image is fused with the side image to form a new training image.

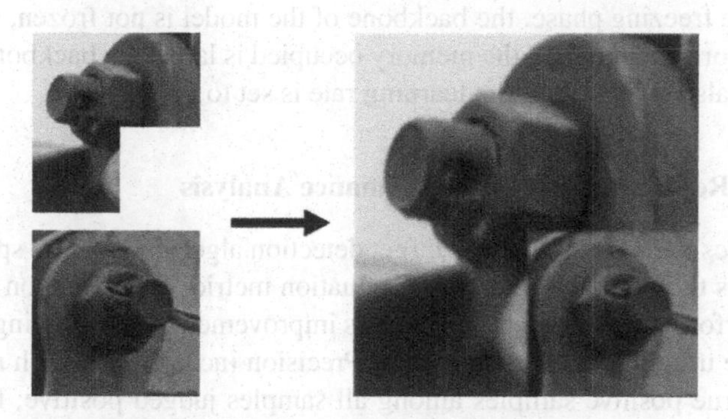

Fig. 6. CutMix Multi-Angle Image Fusion

4 Training Results and Prediction Analysis

The hardware platform used for training this model is Intel Xeon Gold 5217 CPU and NVIDIA Quadro P2200 GPU. The simulation environment is a deep learning virtual environment based on Anaconda with python version 3.6.

4.1 Data Pre-processing and Training Parameters Setting

Before the training, the UAV inspection video of transmission lines in an area of Changsha was selected for the extraction of training images, with a total of 2550 photos, and the data set contained “cotter pin”, “cotter pin off”, “insulator broken” To reduce the large loss value caused by the unbalanced category, some of the higher quality images in each fault image were filtered out to maintain a balanced number of samples. The labelImg is used to calibrate the images, and the calibrated images will generate a file in XML format, which contains the fault categories as well as the coordinates of the calibration box. The training set and validation set are generated by the code. To improve the training effect and network learning efficiency, the ratio of the training set and validation set is set to 9:1, and the input images are uniformly processed to 640 × 640 pixels to complete the placement of the dataset.

The data set was increased and supplemented during the second training, with the addition of broken wires and anti-vibration hammers, and the data set contained 3190 UAV patrol images, with some of the new images containing 2 or more types of faults within one image. When training the new dataset, the initial training weight file was used to train on the original architecture to optimize the network weight parameters for the fault features.

Training on the dataset is divided into two phases, the freezing phase, and the thawing phase. Freezing the training can speed up the training due to the common features of the backbone feature extraction network, and also prevent the weights from being destroyed in the early stage of training. In the freezing phase, the backbone of the model is frozen so that the feature extraction network does not change, so that the memory occupied during training is small and only the network is fine-tuned, and the learning rate is set to $1e^{-3}$. For the freezing phase, the backbone of the model is not frozen, so the feature extraction network changes and the memory occupied is large, the backbone parameters of the network also change, and the learning rate is set to $1e^{-4}$.

4.2 Training Results and Model Performance Analysis

The main metrics used to evaluate the target detection algorithm are the speed of recognition as well as the accuracy, and other evaluation metrics developed on this basis. To evaluate the performance of the model after its improvement, the following target detection metrics are used to evaluate the model: Precision (accuracy), which represents the proportion of true positive samples among all samples judged positive; Recall, which represents the proportion of all actual positive samples correctly judged by the algorithm; AP (area under the P-R curve for each category of targets), mAP (Mean Average Precision) is the average value of AP for each category. The formulas for precision and recall are shown in Eq. (9) and Eq. (10).

$$Precision = \frac{TP}{TP + FP} \tag{9}$$

$$Recall = \frac{TP}{TP + FN} \tag{10}$$

where TP (True Positives) are positive samples correctly classified; FP (False Positives) are negative samples incorrectly classified; FN (False Negatives) are positive samples incorrectly assigned, and the sample distribution is as shown in Fig. 7.

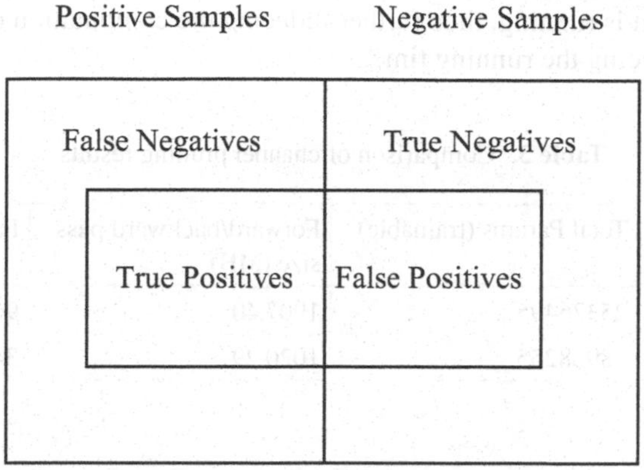

Positive Samples Negative Samples

False Negatives True Negatives

True Positives False Positives

Fig. 7. Sample distribution diagram

Image Data Enhancement

To test the effectiveness of CutMix on the VOC dataset, the YOLOX algorithm in this experiment and the SSD and Faster RCNN target detection algorithms using the backbone network changed to ResNet-50 were considered as controls. The UAV patrol dataset in Pascal VOC format was tested and used mAP values as model evaluation metrics as shown in Table 2. From the table, it can be seen that Mixup and Cutout differ greatly from each model fusion, and both have insignificant and decreasing mAP improvement when combined with YOLOX model, and CutMix performs better in the algorithm adaptation. The combination of CutMix image fusion with the YOLOX algorithm for UAV patrol dataset images can bring greater improvement in target detection performance, with a 1.3% increase in mAP value.

Table 2. Comparison of the effect of CutMix applied to different models

Models	Base (mAP)	Cutout (mAP)	Mixup (mAP)	CutMix (mAP)
SSD	76.7	76.8 (+0.1)	76.6 (−0.1)	77.6 (+0.9)
FasterRCNN	75.6	75.0 (−0.6)	73.9 (−1.7)	76.7 (+1.1)
YOLOX	77.4	77.1 (−0.3)	77.6 (+0.2)	78.7 (+1.3)

Comparison of Channel Pruning Results

In this experiment, the model is channel pruned to achieve structural simplification, and the number of channels is pruned using 1×1 convolution. The parameters of the convolution module after feature channel pruning are shown in Table 3, and the channel reduction rate reaches 50%. Through channel pruning, the redundant nodes in the channels are removed to sparse the weights of the model, and the size of the neural network parameters of the algorithm decreases significantly, saving the memory when the algorithm is running, thus further reducing the computation during the model operation and reducing the running time.

Table 3. Comparison of channel pruning results

Models	Total Params (trainable)	Forward/backward pass size (MB)	Params size (MB)
YOLOX	25326495	1907.40	96.61
YOLOX+pruning	8968255	1020.29	34.21

Improved YOLOX Evaluation Comparison

The different types of accuracy values output by the evaluation code after training are shown in Fig. 8. The figure shows the accuracies obtained for the prediction frames with a suppression probability of 0.5 or less when the confidence value is set to 0.5. The target detection accuracies are 94.44% for anti-vibration hammer, 95.24% for the cotter pin, 100% for insulator breakage cotter pin drop, 82.05% for wire breakage, and 72% for wire loose strand.

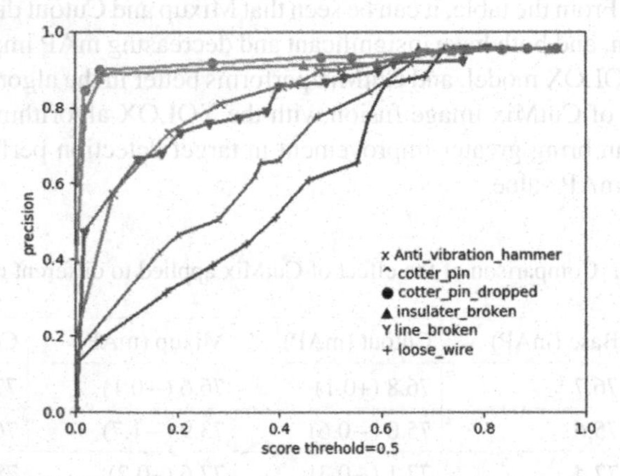

Fig. 8. Different target characteristics recognition accuracy

In the experiments, the loss value images trained with the modified YOLOX model are shown in Fig. 9. Loss represents the loss value of the training set, which is used in the network to update the network parameters; val_loss represents the loss value of the validation set, which is only used for validation, and the output prediction frames of different feature layers are mapped back to the original image for loss calculation.

A generic weight file was added as a pre-training model at the beginning of training, and the backbone network was frozen to prevent the phenomenon that the feature extraction was not effective due to too few random weights during training. In the training to about the 50th time, due to the unfrozen backbone network can be found that the loss

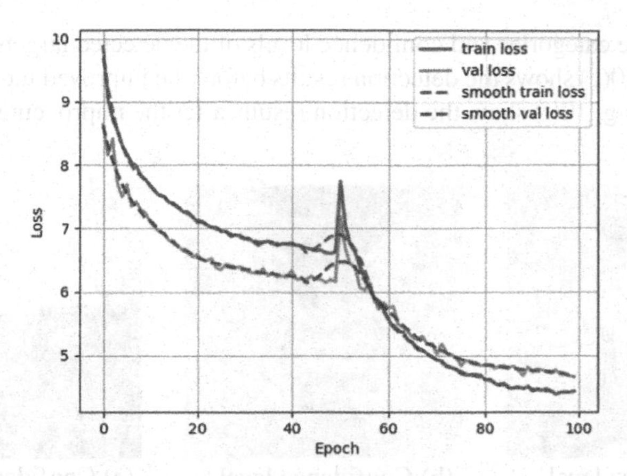

Fig. 9. Training loss value iterative image

function image after the oscillation, the loss value further reduced until convergence, the improved network loss value and val_loss.

This experiment uses CutMix for multi-angle image fusion for data enhancement for grid UAV patrol images, and YOLOX+pruning uses channel pruning to improve the feature channels based on the original model with the same network backbone part.

Table 4 lists the AP enhancement values in, letters in the table correspond to the following target types and models: A: Line broken, B: Insulater broken, C: Cotter pin dropped, D: Cotter pin, E: Anti vibration hammer, F: Loose wire, X: YOLOX, Y: YOLOX+Channel pruning, Z: YOLOX+Channel pruning+Cutmix. It can be seen that the overall decrease in detection accuracy of the algorithm after adding channel pruning is 0.86%, which is due to the temporary decrease in generalization performance caused by channel pruning, and after adding CutMix, the AP of different fault types detection results of the enhanced model are improved to different degrees.

Table 4. Comparison of AP after algorithm improvement

Models	AP/%					
	A	B	C	D	E	F
X	59	71.5	94.82	96.2	89.52	97.83
Y	58.8	70.35 (−1.15)	93.64 (−1.28)	94.87	88.51 (−1.01)	97.73 (−0.1)
Z	62.3	81.47 (+9.97)	96.4 (+1.58)	100	90.89 (+1.47)	98.11 (+0.28)

4.3 Detection Results

The comparison of the results of the improved YOLOX algorithm and the improved target detection model for UAV patrol image detection is shown in Fig. 10, and the labels contain the categories and confidence levels of the detected targets. Figure 10(a), Fig. 10(b), Fig. 10(c) shows the detection results before the improved model; Fig. 10(d), Fig. 10(e), and Fig. 10(f) show the detection results after the improvement.

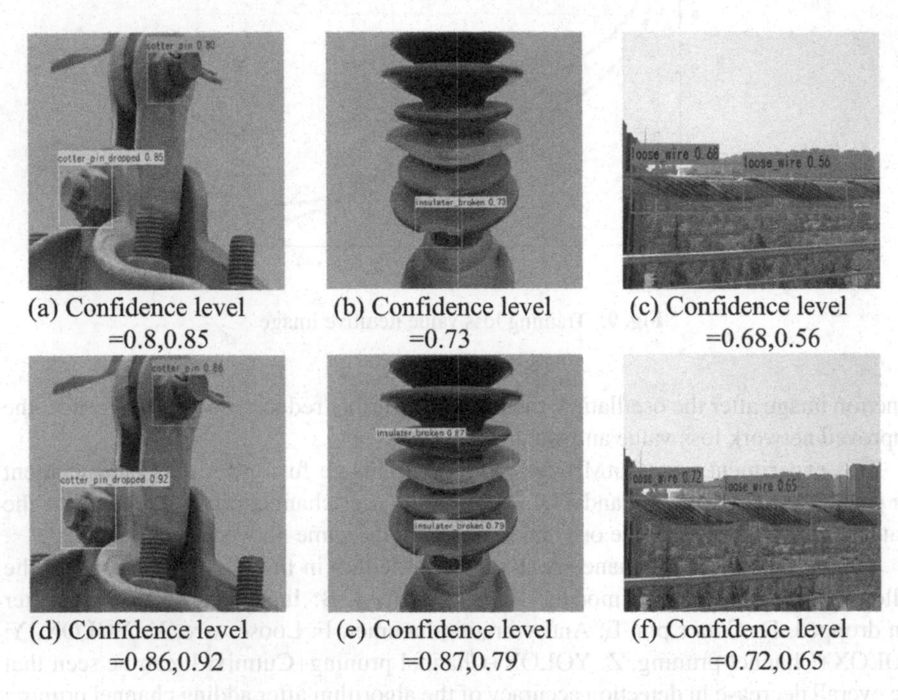

(a) Confidence level =0.8,0.85 (b) Confidence level =0.73 (c) Confidence level =0.68,0.56

(d) Confidence level =0.86,0.92 (e) Confidence level =0.87,0.79 (f) Confidence level =0.72,0.65

Fig. 10. Comparison of model target detection results.

Table 5 lists the comparison of the target detection results, it can be seen that compared with the YOLOX algorithm before the improvement, the improved input and channel pruning improved the target detection accuracy in complex backgrounds with a 3.31% increase in accuracy, a 1.106% decrease in the missed detection rate, and a 2.569 increase in the FPS value of the number of images detected per second by the network.

Table 5. Comparison of algorithm

Models	Precision/%	Recall/%	Miss Rate/%	mAP/%	FPS
YOLOX	87.52	87.4	5.327	84.817	39.978
YOLOX+Channel pruning	88.746	85.7	5.365	85.772	42.323
YOLOX+Channel pruning+CutMix	90.83	89.3	4.221	88.195	42.547

5 Conclusions

1. In this study, an improved YOLOX target detection network is used to solve the problems of low recognition rate, slow speed, and large leakage rate of some fault types in power grid inspection images. Based on the feature loss characteristics of small and medium target faults in transmission lines, multi-scale sampling and feature fusion are used to improve; for the fault type data imbalance problem, the wire breakage is further refined into wire scattering and wire breakage faults, and the labels are increased proportionally to solve the data set category imbalance problem.
2. The improved form of channel pruning is used for the algorithm feature acquisition channel, and the experimental results show that the improved YOLOX algorithm reduces the feature channel parameter scale by 50% and increases the FPS by 2.569. The improved algorithm uses CutMix for data improvement and enhancement, which fuses the images of different angles of small target faults while having some improvement in accuracy, and the mAP value increases by 3.378%.
3. The experimental results show that the improved model can improve the target detection speed in small target fault detection in power system, and can be better applied in target detection and power robot overhaul in power system.

References

1. Chen, Z., Bo, W., Le, D., et al.: Application of infrared temperature measurement technology in power system. Electr. Eng. (2017)
2. Tang, L., Fang, L., Wang, H.: Development of an inspection robot control system for 500KV extra-high voltage power transmission lines. In: SICE Conference. IEEE (2005)
3. Dobakhshari, A.S., Ranjbar, A.M.: A circuit approach to fault diagnosis in power systems by wide area measurement system. Int. Trans. Electr. Energ. Syst. **23**, 1272–1288 (2013)
4. Xiang, D.: Application of infrared thermal imaging UAV on board in new energy generation equipment. Heilongjiang Sci. **13**(04), 68–69 (2022)
5. Li, X., Su, H., Liu, G.: Insulator defect recognition based on global detection and local segmentation. IEEE Access **PP**(99), 1 (2020)
6. Zhou, J.Y., Wu, X.P., Zhang, C., et al.: A moving object detection method based on sliding window Gaussian mixture model. J. Electron. Inf. Technol. **35**(7), 1650–1656 (2013)
7. Liu, S., Qi, L., Qin, H., et al.: Path aggregation network for in-stance segmentation. IEEE (2018)
8. Wei, H., Zhang, K., Zheng, L.: Infrared image object detection of power inspection based on HOG-RCNN. Infrared Laser Eng. **49**(S2), 242–247(2020)
9. Dang, L., Bui, B., Vo, P.D., et al.: Improved HOG descriptors. In: Third International Conference on Knowledge & Systems Engineering. IEEE Computer Society (2011)
10. Zhao, K., Zhu, M., Yang, X., et al.: A new method of creating minimal-order Markov set and transition states of M/N sliding window. IEEE Access **PP**(99) 1 (2019)
11. Pan, R., Sun, W.: Deep learning target detection based on pre-segmentation and regression. Opt. Precis. Eng. **25**, 221–227 (2017)
12. Jian, Y., David, Z., Frangi, A.F., et al.: Two-dimensional PCA: a new approach to appearance-based face representation and recognition. IEEE Trans. Pattern Anal. Mach. Intell. **26**(1(1)), 131–137 (2004)

13. Liu, X.: Research on image recognition algorithm for broken strands and damage faults of transmission conductor. Xi'an Polytechnic University (2018)
14. Kang, G., Gao, S., Yu, L., et al.: Fault detection of missing split pins in swivel with clevis in high-speed railway catenary based on deep learning. J. China Rail. Soc. **42**(10), 45–51 (2020)
15. Bochkovskiy, A., Wang, C.Y., Liao, H.: YOLOv4: optimal speed and accuracy of object detection (2020)
16. Wang, H., Shao, Y., Zou, S., Ma, Z., Zhao, S.: Detection of cotter pins missing of connection fittings on transmission lines of power system. In: 2021 40th Chinese Control Conference (CCC), pp. 6873–6879 (2021). https://doi.org/10.23919/CCC52363.2021.9550162
17. Heng, Y., Tao, G., Ping, S., et al.: Anti-vibration hammer detection in UAV image, pp. 204–207 (2017)
18. Zhang, B., Xue, D., Liu, H.: Analysis of the effect of wind loads on the dynamic response of the suspended crossing-tower auxiliary system. IOP Conf. Ser. Earth Environ. Sci. **621**, 012020 (2021)
19. Ai, Z.: Research on overhead transmission lines abnormal detection algorithm based on UAV aerial image. Northeast Electric Power University (2021). https://doi.org/10.27008/d.cnki.gdbdc.2021.000046
20. Ge, Z., Liu, S., Wang, F., et al.: YOLOX: exceeding YOLO series in 2021 (2021)
21. Ma, W., Li, K., Wang, G.: Location-aware box reasoning for anchor-based single-shot object detection. IEEE Access **PP**(99),1 (2020)
22. Lv, H., Zhang, H., Zhao, C., et al.: An improved SURF in image mosaic based on deep learning. In: 2019 IEEE 4th International Conference on Image, Vision, and Computing (ICIVC). IEEE (2019)

Fault Protection Method of Single-Phase Break for Distribution Network Based on Current Ratio Between Negative and Zero Sequence Current

Xiaohan Li(✉), Tao Tang, Yu Zhou, and Zhongyi Yang

College of Electrical and Information Engineering, Changsha University of Science and Technology, Hunan, China
1357746897@qq.com

Abstract. To solve the identification problem of single-phase break fault with power-side grounding (SPBF-PG) and single-phase break fault with load-side grounding (SPBF-LG), a protection method of single-phase break for distribution network is proposed, which is based on current ratio between negative and zero sequence current. The variation characteristics of sequence current of SPBF-PG and SPBF-LG are analyzed by using compound sequence network. Then the protection criterion of negative-zero sequence current amplitude ratio is constructed. This paper presents a new protection method for single-phase break fault (SPBF) which is not affected by line break location, load variation and transition resistance. The method is verified to be correct by simulation.

Keywords: Distribution network · Zero sequence current · Negative sequence current · Single-phase break fault

1 Introduction

Low-current grounding system is commonly used in medium-voltage distribution network. Interphases short-circuit fault, single line-to-ground fault (SLGF) and SPBF are common faults in low-current grounding system [1]. However, the treatment of SLGF in distribution network has been widely concerned for a long time, but there are few methods to identify and deal with SPBF [2]. Along with the expansion of overhead insulation line laying area and the improvement of lead insulation rate in China's distribution network, overhead insulation line break fault occurs frequently due to lightning strike and other reasons [3]. When the overhead line is struck by lightning, SLGF is caused. The single-phase fault arc continues to burn in the overhead insulated line, and the line at the fault point will be severely oxidized and embrittlement, which will then develop into SPBF, which is easy to affect state of the distribution network and damage the safety of

This work was supported by the National Natural Science Foundation of China (52207075).

H. Yang et al. (Eds.): SmartGIFT 2022, LNICST 483, pp. 73–83, 2023.
https://doi.org/10.1007/978-3-031-31733-0_7

people and property [4]. Therefore, accurate identification and treatment of SPBF helps to enhance the stability of power grid operation.

SPBF usually include single-phase break and ungrounded fault (SPBUF), SPBF-PG and SPBF-LG. Due to the essential difference between SLGF and SPBF, the existing method of line selection cannot be directly applied to SPBF. The existing methods can detect and isolate faults only one hour after the line falls to the ground, which has some problems, such as delayed information acquisition, low accuracy, and long time for fault resection. Literature [5–7] comprehensively considered the influence of neutral grounding mode, load impedance, transition resistance, line break position and the fault line to earth capacitance and analyzed the neutral voltage migration rules of SPBF. The voltage variation of the three phases before and after the fracture was obtained. Literature [8, 9] puts forward the detection method of SPBF based on artificial intelligence algorithm, which requires large sample data to train the algorithm and depends on the completeness of the information acquisition system. Literature [10] analyzes the law of negative sequence voltage and current and puts forward a method to detect SPBF by using the correlation coefficient of waveform. However, this method is difficult to implement because negative sequence voltages are difficult to measure. Literature [11] deduced the sequence currents of break fault with power side or load side grounding and analyzed the change characteristics and correlation of the sequence current. This method is suitable for small resistance grounding system, but not for small current grounding system because the zero-sequence current does not change obviously.

In this paper, a protection method is proposed which is based on current ratio between negative and zero sequence current. Based on compound sequence network diagram, the expressions of sequence current of SPBF-PG and SPBF-LG are derived. Then the law of the negative and zero sequence current at the head of the fault line and the non-fault line with the transition resistance are analyzed. Thus, the protection criterion of current amplitude ratio between negative and zero sequence current is constructed. Finally, a simulation example is given to verify that the proposed method is not affected by load impedance, line break location and transition resistance value.

2 Analysis of SPGF

10 kV distribution network typical structure as shown in Fig. 1. $\dot{E}_A$, $\dot{E}_B$, $\dot{E}_C$ are the three-phase power. C_{Aj}, C_{Bj}, C_{Cj} are the capacitances to ground of the line j. R_f is transition resistance. L_P is the inductance of arc suppression coil. When the switch K is open, system is the neutral ungrounded system. When it closed, system is a resonant grounding system.

2.1 Sequence Current Analysis of SPBF-PG

As shown in Fig. 1, when switch K_1 is closed and K_2 is disconnected, SPBF-PG occurs in the system. Point M on the power side of line L_i is grounded by the transition resistance R_f, and a fracture is formed between point M and point N.

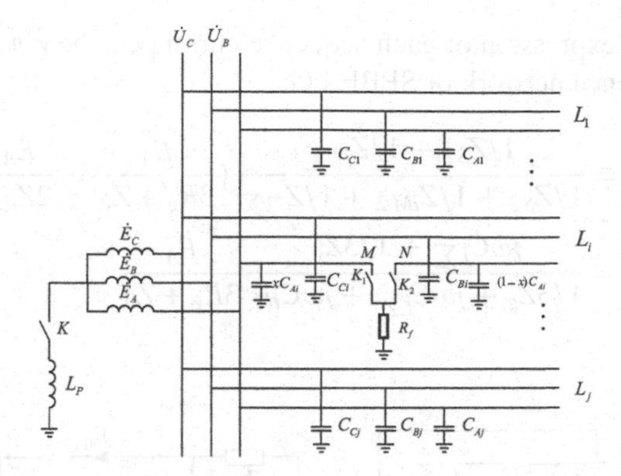

Fig. 1. Equivalent model of 10 kV distribution network.

The voltage at the ground point is transition resistance voltage. The boundary conditions of point M are:

$$\begin{cases} \dot{I}'_{ig1} = \dot{I}'_{ig2} = \dot{I}'_{ig0} \\ \dot{U}'_{iA1} + \dot{U}'_{iA2} + \dot{U}'_{iA0} = 3\dot{I}'_{ig0}R_f \end{cases} \tag{1}$$

where, $\dot{I}'_{ig1}, \dot{I}'_{ig2}, \dot{I}'_{ig0}$ are the positive, negative and zero sequence currents of ground point in SPBF-PG. $\dot{U}'_{iA1}, \dot{U}'_{iA2}, \dot{U}'_{iA0}$ are the positive, negative and zero sequence voltage of ground point.

The current of fault line at the break point is 0. The boundary conditions of point N are:

$$\begin{cases} \dot{I}'_{il1} + \dot{I}'_{il2} + \dot{I}'_{il0} = 0 \\ \Delta\dot{U}'_{iA1} = \Delta\dot{U}'_{iA2} = \Delta\dot{U}'_{iA0} \end{cases} \tag{2}$$

where, $\dot{I}'_{il1}, \dot{I}'_{il2}, \dot{I}'_{il0}$ are the positive, negative and zero sequence currents at the breakpoint of SPBF-PG. $\Delta\dot{U}'_{iA1}, \Delta\dot{U}'_{iA2}, \Delta\dot{U}'_{iA0}$ are the positive, negative and zero sequence voltage at the breakpoint.

According to Eqs. (1) and (2), the compound sequence network of SPBF-PG can be obtained, as shown in Fig. 2(a). In urban distribution network, the load impedance is large, so the line impedance can be ignored. Where, Z_{S1}, Z_{S2} are the equivalent impedance of positive and negative sequence of the system. Z_{iM1}, Z_{iM2} are the positive and negative sequence impedances upstream of the breakpoint. Z_{iL1}, Z_{iL2} are the load impedances from fault line end to breakpoint. In urban distribution network, $Z_{iL1} = Z_{iL2}$. $Z_{j1\Sigma}, Z_{j2\Sigma}$ are positive and negative sequence equivalent load impedances of non-fault lines. C_{0M} is the capacitance upstream of the breakpoint. C_{iL} is the capacitance downstream of the breakpoint. $C_{j1\Sigma}$ is all of the capacitors of all non-fault lines.

In fault line, the expression of each sequence current can be obtained according to the compound sequence network of SPBF-PG:

$$\begin{cases} \dot{I}'_{i2} = \dfrac{1/Z_{S2} + 1/Z_{j2\sum}}{1/Z_{S2} + 1/Z_{iM2} + 1/Z_{j2\sum}} \left(\dfrac{\dot{E}_A}{3R_g + Z_0} - \dfrac{\dot{E}_A}{2Z_{iL2}}\right) \\ \dot{I}'_{i0} = \dfrac{j\omega C_{j\sum} + 1/3Z_g}{1/3Z_g + j\omega C_{j\sum} + j\omega C_{iM}} \dfrac{\dot{E}_A}{3R_g + Z_0} \end{cases} \quad (3)$$

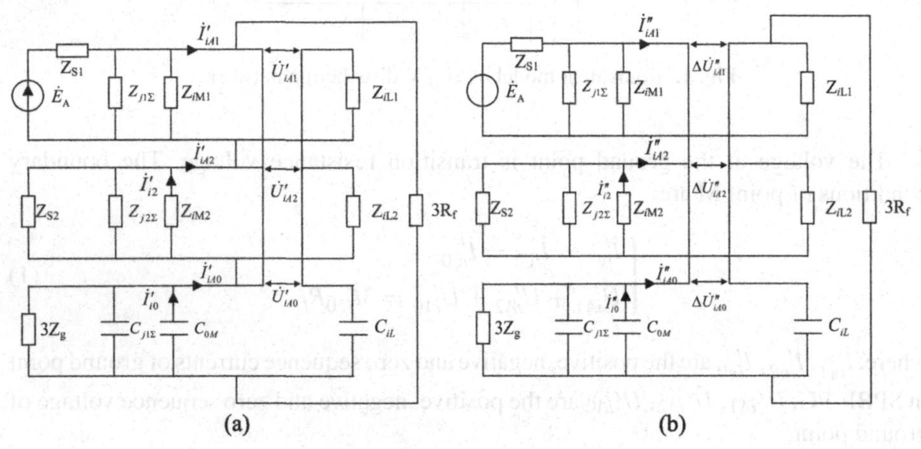

Fig. 2. The compound sequence network of SPBF-PG and SPBF-LG. (a) SPBF-PG.(b) SPBF-LG.

Assuming that $\dot{I}'_2$ and $\dot{I}'_0$ are two components of negative sequence current, the expressions of $\dot{I}'_2$ and $\dot{I}'_0$ are as follows:

$$\begin{cases} \dot{I}'_2 = \dfrac{\dot{E}_A}{2Z_{iL2}} \\ \dot{I}'_0 = \dfrac{\dot{E}_A}{3R_f + Z_0} \end{cases} \quad (4)$$

According to the formula, the change of $\dot{I}'_2$ mainly depends on Z_{iL2}. Taking the direction of $\dot{E}_A$ as a reference, the phase angle of $\dot{I}'_2$ is equal to the load negative sequence impedance angle, that is, $\alpha < 26°$. The change of $\dot{I}'_2$ is shown in Fig. 3. Its amplitude is about half of the load current before the break. The change of $\dot{I}'_0$ mainly depends on R_f. In a neutral ungrounded system, the phase angle of $\dot{I}'_0$ is:

$$\beta = \arctan\left(\frac{1}{3R_f \omega C_0}\right) \quad (5)$$

where, $C_0 = \sum_{j=1, j\neq i}^{n} C_j + C_{iM}$.

In an arc suppression coil grounding system, the phase angle of $\dot{I}'_0$ is:

$$\beta = \arctan(\frac{3\omega^3 C_0 L^2 - \omega L}{R_f(1 + 9\omega^4 C_0^2 L - 6\omega^3 C_0 L)}) \tag{6}$$

Combined with Eqs. (5) and (6), with the increase of transition resistance R_f, the phase angle and amplitude of $\dot{I}'_0$ decrease. The change in $\dot{I}'_0$ is shown in Fig. 3.

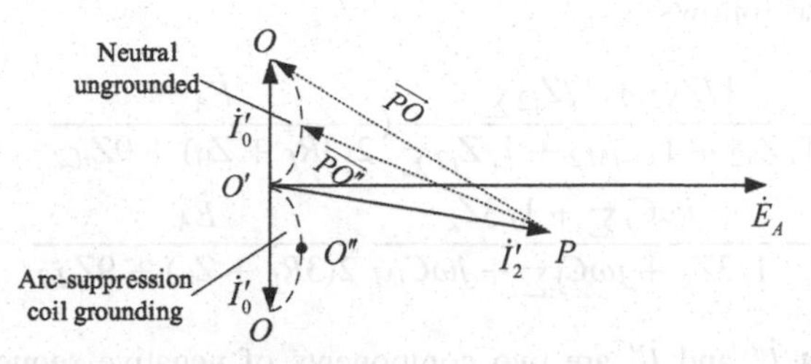

Fig. 3. The change of the negative sequence current in SPBF-PG.

When the transition resistance R_f is 0, the amplitude of $\dot{I}'_0$ reaches the maximum value $|\dot{E}_A/Z_0|$. The phase Angle β is also at its maximum, and $\dot{I}'_0$ points to O. When the transition resistance R_f approaches infinity, the amplitude and the phase angle approach zero.

Therefore, as the transition resistance increases, $\dot{I}'_0$ changes from point O to O', and the negative sequence current $\dot{I}'_{i2}$ changes from $\overrightarrow{PO}$ to $\overrightarrow{PO'}$. The negative sequence current amplitude decreases first and then increases.

K_m is defined as the current amplitude ratio between negative and zero sequence current. When $\dot{I}'_{i2}$ is $\overrightarrow{PO}$, the amplitude reaches the maximum value. In this case, K_m is:

$$K_m = \frac{|\dot{I}'_{i2}|}{|\dot{I}'_0|} > 1 \tag{7}$$

When $\dot{I}'_{i2}$ is $\overrightarrow{PO''}$, the negative sequence current value decreases. In this case, K_m is:

$$K_m = \frac{|\dot{I}'_{i2}|}{|\dot{I}'_0|} > 1 \tag{8}$$

When $\dot{I}'_{i2}$ is $\overrightarrow{PO'}$, the amplitude and phase angle of $\dot{I}'_0$ both tend to zero. In this case, K_m is:

$$K_m = \frac{|\dot{I}'_{i2}|}{|\dot{I}'_0|} \approx \infty \tag{9}$$

2.2 Sequence Current Analysis of SPBF-LG

As shown in Fig. 1, when switch K_2 is closed and K_1 is disconnected, SPBF-LG occurs in the system. Point N on the load side of line L_i is grounded by the transition resistance R_f, and a fracture is formed between point M. The boundary conditions of M and N points are opposite to those of SPBF-PG.

The compound sequence network of SPBF-LG can be obtained, as shown in Fig. 2(b). According to the compound sequence network, the negative and zero sequence current can be expressed as follows:

$$\begin{cases} \dot{I}''_{i2} = \dfrac{1/Z_{S2} + 1/Z_{j2\sum}}{1/Z_{S2} + 1/Z_{iM2} + 1/Z_{j2\sum}} \left(\dfrac{\dot{E}_A}{2(3R_f + Z_0) + 9Z_{iL2}} - \dfrac{\dot{E}_A}{2Z_{iL2}} \right) \\ \dot{I}''_{i0} = -\dfrac{j\omega C_{j\sum} + 1/3Z_g}{1/3Z_g + j\omega C_{j\sum} + j\omega C_{iM}} \dfrac{\dot{E}_A}{2(3R_f + Z_0) + 9Z_{iL2}} \end{cases} \tag{10}$$

Assuming that $\dot{I}''_2$ and $\dot{I}''_0$ are two components of negative sequence current, the expressions of $\dot{I}''_2$ and $\dot{I}''_0$ are as follows:

$$\begin{cases} \dot{I}''_2 = \dfrac{\dot{E}_A}{2Z_{iL2}} \\ \dot{I}''_0 = \dfrac{\dot{E}_A}{2(3R_f + Z_0) + 9Z_{iL2}} \end{cases} \tag{11}$$

Combining the two equations, at the head of the fault line, $\dot{I}''_{i2}$ is related to the negative sequence impedance and transition resistance. Whatever the ground resistance is, there's always $\dot{I}''_2 \gg \dot{I}''_0$.As the transition resistance increases, $\dot{I}''_0$ decreases. When SPBF-LG occurs, as the transition resistance increases, $\dot{I}''_{i2}$ increases. While the zero-sequence current $\dot{I}''_{i0}$ decreases.

If the transition resistance goes to zero, the negative sequence current is the minimum, and K_m is the minimum. In this case, K_m is:

$$K_m = \frac{|\dot{I}''_{i2}|}{|\dot{I}''_0|} = \frac{|7\dot{E}_A/18Z_{iL2}|}{|\dot{E}_A/9Z_{iL2}|} = 3.5 \tag{12}$$

When the transition resistance approaches infinity, the negative sequence current value reaches the maximum, and zero-sequence current is largest. In this case, K_m is:

$$K_m = \frac{|\dot{I}''_{i2}|}{|\dot{I}''_0|} \approx \frac{|\dot{E}_A/2Z_{iL2}|}{0} \approx \infty \tag{13}$$

3 Fault Identification Method Based on Current Ratio Between Negative and Zero Sequence

In the break line of SPBF-PG,. as the increase of transition resistance, the negative sequence current shows a trend of first small and then large decreases. While the zero-sequence current decreases. In the break line of SPBF-LG, as the transition resistance increases, negative sequence current decreases while zero sequence current changes in reverse the zero-sequence current decreases. In two kinds of fault, compared with the zero-sequence current, negative sequence current value is larger.

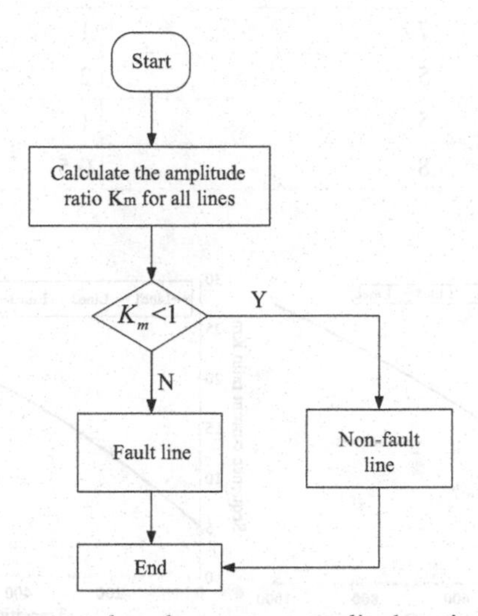

Fig. 4. Fault line selection process based on current amplitude ratio between negative and zero sequence current.

Most of the distribution networks are radiation networks, and the load impedance is nearly 100 times the system impedance. That is, most of the negative sequence current flows from break point to source. In the break line, the negative sequence current is at least one magnitude larger than that in the non-break line. The zero-sequence impedance of each component of the system is generally greater than negative sequence impedance numerically. In the non-break line, the zero-sequence current is several times the negative sequence current.

When SPBF-PG or SPBF-LG faults occur, K_m in the break line is greater than 1. In the non-break line, K_m is less than 1. The specific line selection process is shown in Fig. 4.

4 Simulation and Verification

To verify that the method is correct, the typical structure of 10kV distribution network as shown in Fig. 1 was established based on Matlab/Simulink. It has 6 lines, which adopt neutral ungrounded system. The line length and load are shown in Table 1. Positive sequence and zero sequence parameters of the line are: $R_1 = 0.031\ \Omega/km$, $L_1 = 0.096$ mH/km, $C_1 = 0.338\ \mu F/km$ $R_0 = 0.234\ \Omega/km$, $L_0 = 0.355$ mH/km, $C_0 = 0.265\ \mu F/km$.

Table 1. Line and load parameters.

Line number	Length (km)	Load size (MW)
1	10	1
2	10	2
3	7	1
4	5	2
5	5	1
6	8	0.5

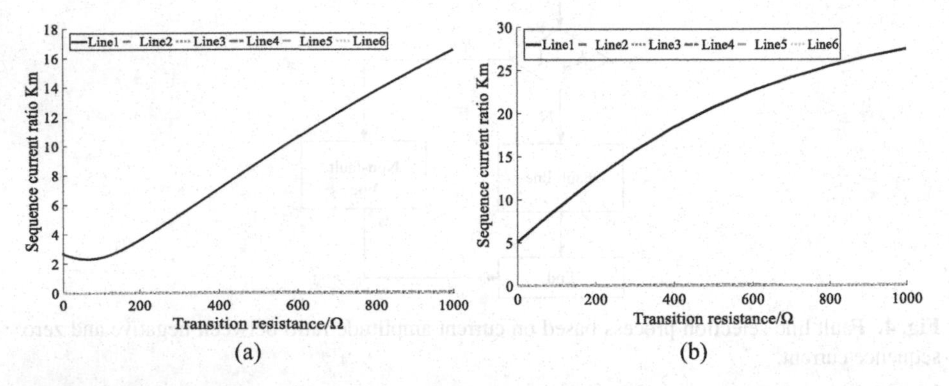

Fig. 5. Km of each line varies with the transition resistance. (a)SPBF-PG. (b)SPBF-LG.

SPBF-PG and SPBF-LG are respectively set at 5km of line L1. K_m of each line with the change of transition resistance is shown in Fig. 5. With the change of transition resistance, the K_m of the break line is always much larger than that of the non- break line in the two faults. In non-fault line, K_m is always less than 0.1. In SPBF-PG, the K_m of the fault line decreases first and then increases, and the minimum K_m value is 2.3. In SPBF-LG, K_m increases continuously from 5.

In the case of 0, 100, 300 and 500 Ω transition resistance respectively, change the fault position of line L_1. The variation of K_m of the break line L_1 and non-break line L_2 can be obtained as shown in Fig. 6. At different fault locations, K_m of the fault line changes little, and Km is always greater than 1. In non-fault line, K_m is less than 1.

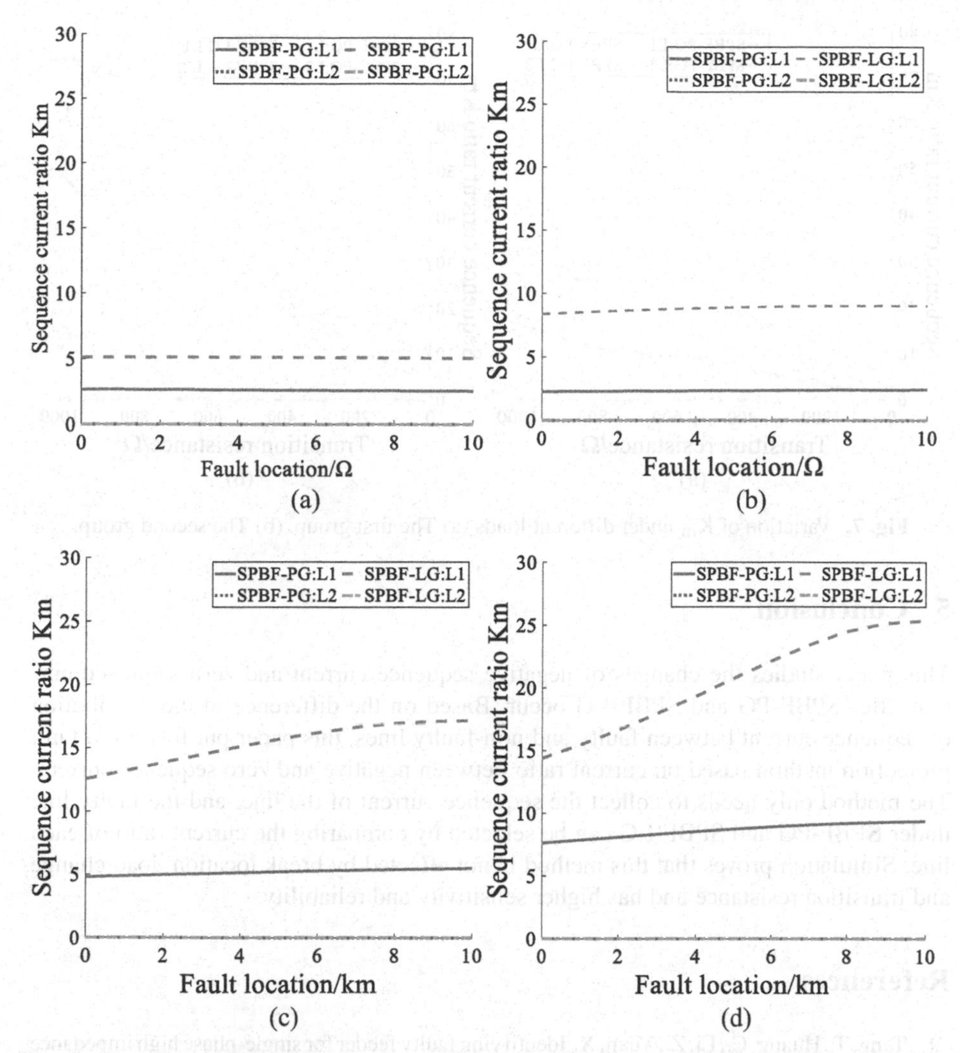

Fig. 6. The influence of position change on K_m under different transition resistance (a) 0Ω. (b) 100Ω. (c)300Ω. (d) 500Ω.

To explore the influence of load distribution on K_m, two groups of different loads were connected to the system respectively. In the first group, 1 WM load is set at 2 km of line L1; 2 WM Load is set at 5 km of line L2; 2 WM Load is set at 6 km of line L5. In the second group, 1 WM load is set at 7 km of line L1; 0.5WM Load is set at 4 km of line L3; 1 WM Load is set at 1 km of line L4. SPBF-PG and SPBF-LG occurred at 5km of line L_1, and K_m of the fault line L_1 and non-fault line L_2 changes with transition resistance as shown in Fig. 7. Increasing load behind breakpoint has great influence on the K_m of the fault line. As the load increases, the negative sequence current of increases, so does the K_m. No matter how the load changes, the method can still distinguish the fault line accurately.

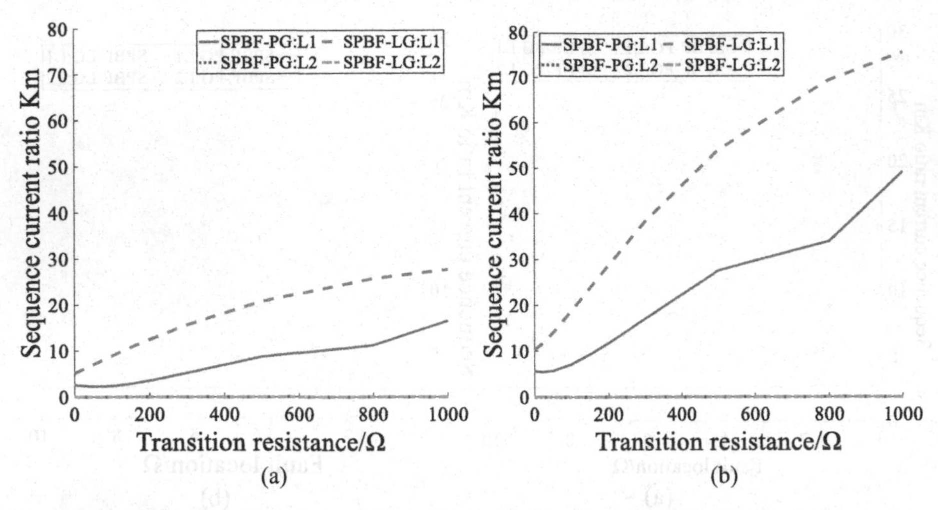

Fig. 7. Variation of K_m under different loads (a) The first group. (b) The second group.

5 Conclusion

This paper studies the changes of negative sequence current and zero sequence current after SPBF-PG and SPBF-LG occur. Based on the difference in the distribution of sequence current between faulty and non-faulty lines, this paper put forward a fault protection method based on current ratio between negative and zero sequence current. The method only needs to collect the sequence current of the line, and the faulty line under SPBF-PG and SPBF-LG can be selected by comparing the current ratio of each line. Simulation proves that this method is not affected by break location, load change and transition resistance and has higher sensitivity and reliability.

References

1. Tang, T., Huang, C., Li, Z., Yuan, X.:Identifying faulty feeder for single-phase high impedance fault in resonant grounding distribution system. Energies **12**, 598 (2019)
2. Wang, S., Zhang, H., Xu, B.: Diagnosis of the type of single-phase disconnection and ground fault in the small current grounding system. Electr. Power Autom. Equipment **38**(7), 134–139+147 (2018)
3. Wang, M., Lv, Y., Zou, H.: Analysis of lightning-caused break mechanism of 10 kV insulation-covered conductors and its countermeasures. High Voltage Eng. **33**(1), 102–105 (2007)
4. Shen, H., Chen, W., Wang, S.: Simulation tests on lightning stroke-caused wire-breakage of 10 kV overhead transmission line. Power Syst. Technol. **35**(01), 117–121 (2011)
5. Xue, Y., Chen, M., Cao, L.: Analysis of voltage characteristics of single-phase disconnection fault in ungrounded distribution system. Proc. CSEE **41**(4), 1322–1333 (2021)
6. Zhang, L., Cao, L., Li, L.: Analysis and fault section location of single-phase open fault for ungrounding system. Power Syst. Prot. Control **46**(16), 1–7 (2018)
7. Zhang, H., Cao, L., Feng, G.: Analysis of single-phase open fault for resonant grounded system. Proc. CSU-EPSA **31**(2), 58–65 (2019)

8. Suwo, W., Zhang, Y., Yun, S.: Open-line fault diagnosis based on data association of MV distribution network. Electr. Power Autom. Equipment **37**(7), 101–109 (2017)
9. Guo, N., Yun, S., Tian, Y.: Disconnected unground fault detection in medium voltage distribution network based on FC-AdaBoost. Electr. Meas. Instrum. **56**(16), 1–6 (2019)
10. Chang, Z., Song, G., Zhang, W.: Characteristic analysis and fault segment location on negative sequence voltage and current of single-phase line breakage fault in distribution network. Power Syst. Technol. **44**(8), 3065–3072 (2020)
11. Xiao, Y., Ouyang, J., Xiong, X.: Protection method of compound break fault with grounding for distribution network considering influence of fault resistance. Power Syst. Technol. **45**(11), 4296–4307 (2021)

Disaster Prevention and Reduction for Power Grid

Forecast of the Ice Disaster in Hunan Power Grid in Late January 2022 Using a High Resolution Global NWP Model

Lei Wang(✉), Tao Feng, Zelin Cai, Xunjian Xu, Li Li, and Jinhai Huang

State Key Laboratory of Disaster Prevention and Reduction for Power Grid Transmission and Distribution Equipment, Changsha, China
wangleiapple@126.com

Abstract. The icing of power grid has great influence on the safe and stable operation of power grid. Under the background of global warming, the frequency and duration of grid line icing events have increased. Under the influence of warm and humid air flow and special terrain in winter, it is very easy to have ice cover in Hunan Province. From the winter of 2021 to the spring of 2022, Hunan experienced five rounds of grid line icing, and the icing event lasted for more than three days totally. In this study, a global numeric weather forecast model with a resolution of 10 km is used to explore its prediction performance for the ice events at the end of January 2022 (27–29th January). The results show that it has a good prediction performance for the ice cover in Hunan, and the spatial distribution characteristics of the ice cover can be predicted 6 days in advance, although the intensity is slightly weak. A test also shows that the ability to predict heavy icing events can be improved by fusing icing observation information at the initial time of icing prediction, which emphasizes the importance of icing observation to icing prediction.

Keywords: grid line icing · numeric weather forecast model · prediction performance

1 Introduction

The safe and stable operation of power grid is an important foundation for high-quality life and economic development. In winter, due to the influence of cold and warm air, the wire icing events often occur. The cold air affecting China is mainly controlled by the Arctic polar vortex. Under the background of global warming, the polar vortex becomes unstable making it easier for the cold air to move southward, forming a cooling rain and snow freezing event in China. Due to the special horseshoe shaped geographical characteristics of Hunan province, which is surrounded by mountains in the East, South and West, the cold air in winter is easy to drive in from the flat area of Dongting Lake, bringing about a large-scale freezing disaster process. In recent years, Hunan Province has experienced many severe rain and snow freezing events, which have brought

H. Yang et al. (Eds.): SmartGIFT 2022, LNICST 483, pp. 87–94, 2023.
https://doi.org/10.1007/978-3-031-31733-0_8

serious damage to the power grid [1, 2]. From late January to February 2022, Hunan was continuously affected by multiple rounds of grid line icing due to cold and warm air. The earliest two occurred from January 24–25th to January 27–29th.

Numerical weather forecasting model is an important tool for forecasting weather and extreme events. Numerical weather forecasting needs a lot of computing and storage resources. In recent years, with the development of supercomputers, the resolution of numerical models has increased from hundreds of kilometers to ten kilometers or even higher, and the prediction ability of numerical models has been gradually improved [3–5]. The numerical prediction model includes a variety of physical parameterization schemes that can describe the atmospheric movement process, and forecasts the temperature, precipitation, cloud water content, etc., which provides the possibility for the prediction of transmission line icing.

In this study, we evaluated the forecast performance of the ice disaster in Hunan power grid in late January 2022 using a high resolution global NWP model with a 10-km resolution. The remainder of the paper is organized as follows: Sect. 2 describes the ECMWF model used in this study. Section 3 describes the key features if grid line icing in late January 2022 in Hunan. Section 4 analysis the prediction performance for the ice disaster in Hunan power grid in late January 2022. A summary of our key findings and further discussion are provided in Sect. 5.

2 Model and Datasets

2.1 Model

The model data used in this study is from European Centre for Medium-Range Weather Forecasts (ECMWF) Integrated Forecasting System (IFS) High-Resolution Operational Forecasts [6]. The ECMWF Integrated Forecasting System (IFS) consists of several components, which include an atmospheric model, an ocean wave model, an ocean model, a land surface model, a data analysis system, and perturbation techniques for generation of the ensembles. Many studies show that ECMWF IFS has good prediction ability for some key weather systems (e.g. Arctic polar vortex and subtropical high), thus has been widely used in many Weather Forecast Department. The resolution of the ECMWF IFS datasets is about 10-km used in this study.

2.2 Datasets

To compare the model's results of the ice disaster in Hunan power grid in January 2022, the observed line icing data are collected from the intelligent analysis and control platform for power grid operation inspection of Hunan, with a daily frequency. To analysis the model's results of the precipitation and temperature, the observed precipitation data and temperature data from China Meteorological Administration (CMA) are used in our study.

3 Observed of Grid Line Icing Features in Hunan Province During Late January 2022

The grid line ice cover in Hunan province mainly began at the late of January 2022. As shown in Table 1, the line ice cover was observed at 70 stations during January 24–25th. Among them, about 59 sites (88% of total) were lightly (icing thickness less than 10 mm) covered with ice, 8 sites (12% of total) were moderately (icing thickness less than 20 mm while higher than 10 mm) covered with ice, and no sites are severe (icing thickness higher than 20 mm) icing. The icing became more severe on January 27–29th. The line ice cover was observed at 461 stations during January 27–29th. Among them, about 375 sites (81% of total) were lightly (icing thickness less than 10 mm) covered with ice, 76 sites (16% of total) were moderately (icing thickness less than 20 mm while higher than 10 mm) covered with ice, and 10 sites (3% of total) are severe (icing thickness higher than 20 mm) icing.

Table 1. The grid line icing sites in Hunan province during 24–25th and 27–29th January 2022.

Icing thickness	Number of sites (24–25th January)	Number of sites (27–29th January)
$0.1 \le x < 2$	26	133
$2 \le x < 5$	29	162
$5 \le x < 10$	4	80
$10 \le x < 20$	8	76
$20 \le x < 30$	0	10
total	67	461

Figure 1 shows geographical distribution characteristics of minimum temperature, precipitation as well as grid line icing in Hunan Province on 24–25th January and 27–29th January of 2022 in observation data. During 24–25th January, the minimum temperature is lower in the north of Hunan Province, which is about 2–4 °C, while higher in the south of Hunan Province, which is higher than 4 °C and can up to 10 °C (south of Yongzhou and Chenzhou city).One thing to keep in mind is that the meteorological observation stations are usually located in urban or suburban areas, while the grid lines prone to icing are mainly concentrated in mountainous areas, of which the temperature is often 3–4 °C lower than that in urban or suburban areas. Thus, the temperature in mountainous areas may be below 0 °C when the temperature is 2–4 °C in urban or suburban areas. A lower temperature will make it more likely to freeze in the north of Hunan Province. As is show in Fig. 1, the icing area are mainly locate in the center and northwest of Hunan province 24–25th January.

With the activity of cold air, Hunan province experienced further cooling. Compared with that on 24–25th January, the temperature in much low on 27–29th January. The minimum temperature is lower in the north of Hunan Province, which is less than 0 °C, while higher in the south of Hunan Province, which is about 2–6 °C. The icing area

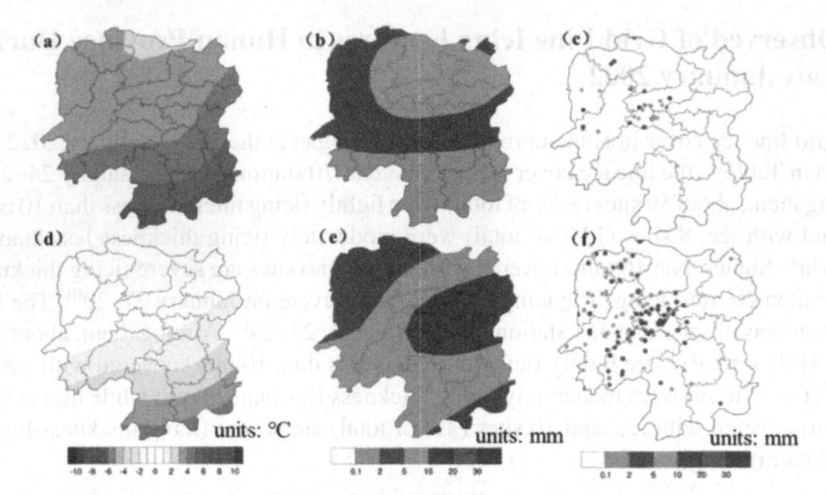

Fig. 1. Geographical distribution characteristics of minimum temperature (a and d), precipitation (b and e) as well as grid line icing (c and f) in Hunan Province on 24–25th (up row) and 27–29th (down row) January of 2022 in observation data.

extend to the southwest of Hunan province on 27–29th January. Also, some sites in the center (Yiyang city) and southwest (Hengyang city) of Hunan Province occurs severe icing.

4 Forecast of Grid Line Icing Using a 10-km NWP Model

This study is mainly aimed at the assessment of the icing process on 27–29th January, because the icing is more serious compared with that on 24–25th January. In order to comprehensively evaluate the performance of ECMWF IFS model, temperature, precipitation and icing are evaluated in this study. The temperature and precipitation are directly predicted by the model, while the icing are diagnosed by the meteorological parameters. Since ECMWF IFS can provide the forecast data of the next 10 days at the longest, we have given the results of icing process with different leading time in this study. For example, L1D is the forecast one day in advance, which means the forecast of January 29th is made on January 28th; L2D is the forecast two day in advance, which means the forecast of January 29th is made on January 27th, and the like.

Figure 2 shows the geographical distribution characteristics of minimum temperature in Hunan Province on 29th January of 2022 predicted by ECMWF IFS with different leading time. The result shows that ECMWF IFS has good simulation ability for temperature and can reproduce the characteristics of low temperature in the north and high temperature in the south, expect that the predicted temperature is lower than that in observations. The minimum temperature is lower in the north of Hunan Province, which is less than 0 °C (and less than −2 °C in northwest of Hunan Province), while higher in the south of Hunan Province, which is about 2–3 °C. Also, the temperature prediction results of the numerical model have high similarity 1–4 days in advance (the spatial correlation coefficient of which exceeds 0.83), and the similarity can be maintained 6 days in advance.

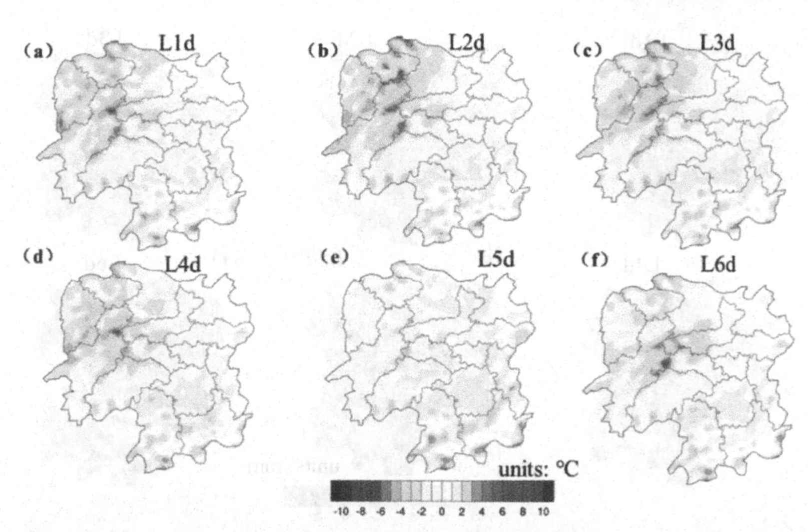

Fig. 2. Geographical distribution characteristics of minimum temperature in Hunan Province on 29th January of 2022 predicted by ECMWF IFS with different leading time.

Figure 3 shows the geographical distribution characteristics of precipitation in Hunan Province on 29th January of 2022 predicted by ECMWF IFS with different leading time. The result shows that The predicted precipitation amount in ECMWF IFS is larger southwest to northeast of Hunan province, which is larger than 20 mm, while smaller in the northwest and southeast of Hunan province, which is smaller than 10 mm. Also, the precipitation prediction results of the numerical model have high similarity 1–4 days in advance (the spatial correlation coefficient of which exceeds 0.8), and the similarity can be maintained 6 days in advance. Compared with that in observation, the intensity of precipitation is relatively strong. The maximum precipitation intensity during observation is less than 10 mm, which is about half of the predicted precipitation amount.

Figure 4 shows the geographical distribution characteristics of grid line icing in Hunan Province on 29th January of 2022 predicted by ECMWF IFS with different leading time. The result shows that ECMWF IFS has good simulation ability for grid line icing prediction and can reproduce the geographical characteristics of icing. For example, the icing is more serious in Southwest Hunan and central Hunan, of which the maximum ice thickness is more than 10 mm. While the ice thickness in southern Hunan is less than 5mm, which is consistent with the observation. Also, the grid line icing prediction results of the numerical model have high similarity 1–4 days in advance (the spatial correlation coefficient of which exceeds 0.83), and the similarity can be maintained 6 days in advance.

Compared with that in observation, the maximum icing thickness is relatively small. The maximum icing thickness is larger than 20 mm (Yiyang city and Hengyang city), which are all missed in all 6 day forecast. This is because that the precipitation in the numerical model is cumulative precipitation. At the beginning of all the forecast, the precipitation in the numerical model is zero, so the ice thickness calculated at the initial time is zero, which may be different from the actual observations. In order to improve

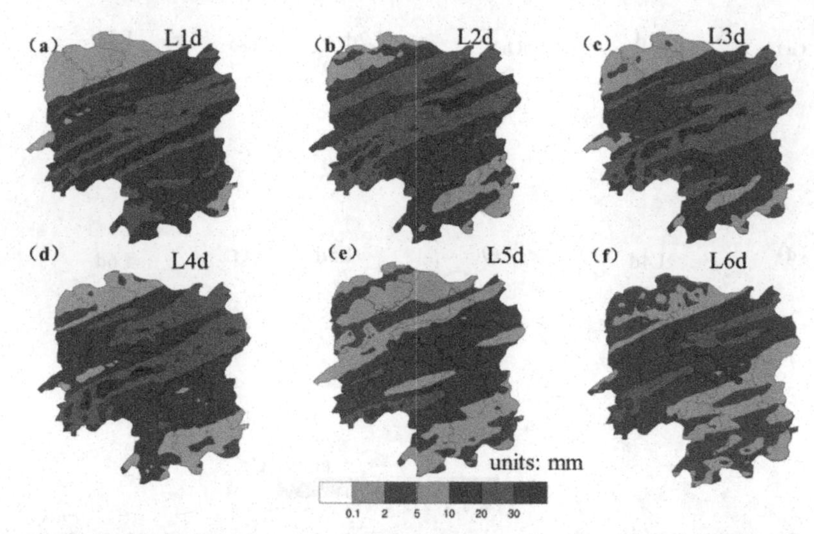

Fig. 3. Geographical distribution characteristics of precipitation in Hunan Province on 29th January of 2022 predicted by ECMWF IFS with different leading time.

the prediction performance of the model, we try to combine the observed ice thickness into the initial predicted icing value of the numerical model to make it consistent with the observation. As the icing observation on January 25th is relatively complete, we use the prediction on January 25th for analysis. As is shown in Fig. 5, the maximum icing thickness is larger than 20 mm in Yiyang city of Hunan province, which is consistent as that in observations. This indicates that the fusion of observed icing information in the prediction can help to improve the prediction of severe icing events.

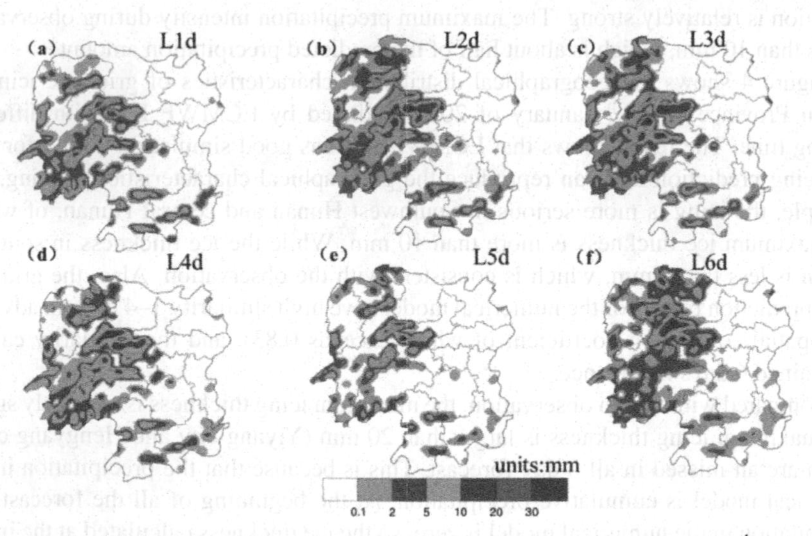

Fig. 4. Geographical distribution characteristics of icing in Hunan Province on 29th January of 2022 predicted by ECMWF IFS with different leading time.

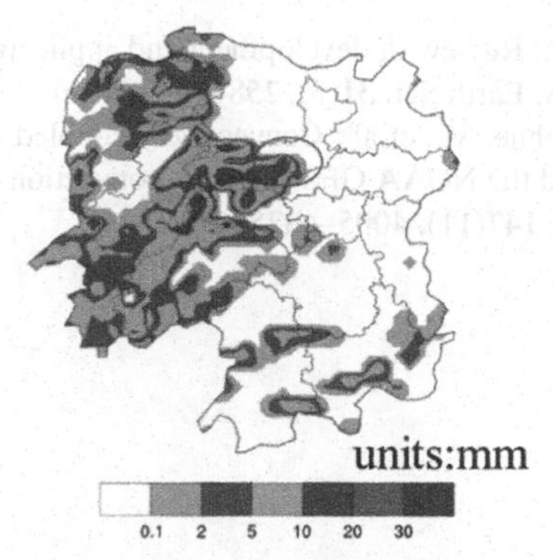

Fig. 5. Geographical distribution characteristics of icing in Hunan Province on 29th January of 2022 predicted by ECMWF IFS from 25th January of 2022 with observed icing data combined.

5 Conclusions and Discussions

In this study, ECMWF IFS data with a resolution of 10km is used to explore its prediction performance for the ice events at the end of January 2022 (27–29thJanuare). The results show that it has a good prediction performance for the ice cover in Hunan, and the spatial distribution characteristics of the ice cover can be predicted 6 days in advance, although the intensity is slightly weak. A test also shows that the ability to predict heavy icing events can be improved by fusing icing observation information at the initial time of icing prediction, which emphasizes the importance of icing observation to icing prediction. The prediction of grid line icing on a longer time scale means that we can have enough time to carry out anti-ice preparation. Therefore, we will evaluate the prediction ability of the numerical model for grid line icing on a longer time scale (such as sub-seasonal to seasonal prediction) in the future.

Acknowledgements. The present research is supported by the Science and Technology Project of the State Grid Corporation of China (Grant Number: 5216A0210040).

References

1. Lu, J, Peng, J., Zhang, H., et al.: Icing meteorological genetic analysis of Hunan power grid in 2008. Electr. Power Constr. (06), 29–32 (2009). (in Chinese)
2. Lu, J., Jiang, Z., Lei, H., et al.: analysis of Hunan power grid lee disaster accident in 2008. Autom. Electr. Power Syst. (32), 16–20 (2008). (in Chinese)
3. Haarsma, R.J., Roberts, M.J., Vidale, P.L., et al.: High resolution model intercomparison project (HighResMIP v1.0) for CMIP6. Geosci. Model Dev. **9**, 4185–4208 (2016)
4. Zhou, T., Zou, L., Wu, B., et al.: Development of earth/climate system models in China: a review from the coupled model intercomparison project perspective. Acta Meteorol. Sinica **5**, 892–907 (2014)

5. Luan, Y., Yu, Y., Zheng, W.: Review of development and application of high resolution global climate system model. Adv. Earth Sci. **31**(3), 258–268 (2016)
6. Bengtsson, L., Dias, J., Gehne, M., et al.: Convectively coupled equatorial wave simulations using the ECMWF IFS and the NOAA GFS cumulus convection schemes in the NOAA GFS model. Mon. Weather Rev. **147**(11), 4005–4025 (2019)

A Two-Step Approach for Forecasting Wind Speed at Offshore Wind Farms During Typhoons

Xuan Liu[1](✉) and Jun Guo[2]

[1] Energy and Electricity Research Center, Jinan University, Zhuhai 519070, Guangdong, China
xliu514@gmail.com

[2] State Key Laboratory of Disaster Prevention and Reduction for Power Grid Transmission and Distribution Equipment, State Grid Hunan Electric Power Company Disaster Prevention and Reduction Center, Changsha 410007, Hunan, China

Abstract. Wind power has become the leading factor in the transition from fossil fuels to renewable energy sources. The total capacity of offshore wind farms in China has increased significantly in the past decade. It's essential to understand the risk posed by typhoons to offshore wind farms. However, the impacts of typhoons are hard to predict due to the limited number of observations. In this study, a deep learning-based two-step approach is proposed for estimating the wind speed of given locations during typhoons. An LSTM-based seq2seq model is implemented in the first step to predict the typhoon track and intensity. In the second step, a linear wind field model is adopted to calculate the wind speed at specific locations. The case study results show that the proposed approach is capable of predicting the extreme wind speed at specific offshore locations during typhoons. This study demonstrates the potential of assessing wind risk with a combination of data-driven and physics-based models.

Keywords: Wind Speed Prediction · Offshore Wind Farm · Typhoon · Neural Network · LSTM · Seq2seq

1 Introduction

Due to the global climate crisis, the energy industry is transitioning from fossil fuels to renewable energy, such as wind and solar. In 2005, China introduced the Renewable Energy Law, which changed the global wind energy market significantly. By the end of 2015, China has installed one-third (33.5%) of global wind power [1]. It's worth noting that offshore wind quality is better than onshore

Supported by the Open Project Funding of State Key Laboratory of Disaster Prevention and Reduction for Power Grid Transmission and Distribution Equipment.

H. Yang et al. (Eds.): SmartGIFT 2022, LNICST 483, pp. 95–107, 2023.
https://doi.org/10.1007/978-3-031-31733-0_9

wind quality. The power output of an offshore wind turbine is expected to be 1.7 times the same onshore wind turbine [2]. The offshore wind resources are abundant in China's coastal area. By the end of 2020, China's offshore wind farm installation accounts for more than 50% of the global installed offshore wind farm capacity [3].

Unlike onshore wind farms, offshore wind farms are exposed to more natural hazards, such as extreme wave heights and Tropical Cyclones (TCs). TCs are one of the most severe natural hazards responsible for massive damage and causalities in coastal areas. TCs come with strong winds and thunderstorms and are the leading cause of floods and storm surges in coastal regions. Structures are highly vulnerable to typhoons when the wind speed exceeds the design limits, while storm surges are the deadliest effect of TCs, causing 90% of TC deaths historically [4]. TCs are referred to as Typhoons in the Western North Pacific basin. According to the State Oceanic Administration of China (SOA), the long-term average of annual direct economic losses is about $2.6 billion from 1989 to 2017. Moreover, studies show that the average typhoon intensity is increasing due to global warming [5]. Therefore, an effective tool for predicting the wind speed at critical locations during typhoons is necessary and urgent for the risk mitigation, management, and decision-making of wind farms.

Thanks to the presence of satellites, TCs can be tracked accurately anywhere in the world. TC track forecasting has improved substantially during the past few decades. According to the National Hurricane Center (NHC), the average 24h TC track forecast error has dropped from ∼130 nmi to ∼30 nmi [6]. The cyclone forecast models can be categorized into four main categories: statistical models, numerical models, ensemble models, and deep learning models.

Statistical models are based on the statistical analysis of historical cyclone information instead of explicitly considering the physics of tropical cyclones. This type of model is relatively simple to compute compared to the more complex models that consider the physics of the atmosphere but is also less accurate due to its simplicity. The climatology and persistence (CLIPER) model, first developed in 1972 [7], is a statistical regression model considering the non-linear relationship between input predictors and the predictands. Errors of the CLIPER model are often used as a baseline for other forecast models. Linear autoregressive models that only consider the current and previous translation speeds and directions are also shown to be plausible [8] for track generation. Vickery et al. [9] suggest that the translation speed and direction are interdependent and depend on the cyclone location.

Numerical models, also known as dynamical models, are highly complex and require supercomputers to process the mathematical equations governing the physics and motion of the atmosphere. Dynamical models come with different resolutions: the global models calculate the atmospheric variables of the entire earth, while the regional models only calculate the variables in a limited area. An example of a global model is the Global Environmental Multiscale Model (GEM) [10] developed by the Canadian Meteorological Centre (CMC). GEM has a variable-resolution capability so that it can also produce high-resolution regional forecasts. In operational applications, GEM runs the output for up to 10 days to provide medium-range and short-range forecasts.

Ensemble models (or consensus models) combine multiple forecasting results to produce better-quality results. The ensemble can consist of either multiple forecasts from a single base model or different models. In the single-base-model approach, a single numerical model is initialized with a set of different initial conditions to generate a set of forecasts for the ensemble. Monte Carlo Simulation [11,12] is shown to be a plausible initialization method. Krishnamurti et al. [13] suggest that a physical initialization method, which entails the assimilation of observed rain rates in a numerical model, could reduce the variance of an ensemble forecast with one single base model. However, single-model ensembles are rarely used in current operational applications since they are not as effective as multi-model ensembles. In multi-model ensembles, the forecasts of all ensemble members are usually weighted to reduce the bias in the final predictions. The multi-model ensembles are shown to be capable of providing significantly better track predictions than individual models [14].

In recent years, deep learning has been proven to be a powerful tool in cyclone behavior modeling. Alemany et al. [15] utilize Recurrent Neural Network (RNN) to predict TC trajectories and show that the performance is comparable to the NHC official forecasts in a grid-based system. However, the error of the RNN-based model increases significantly when converting the grid location to latitude and longitude coordinates. Giffard-Rosin and Yang [16] combine Convolutional Neural Network (CNN) and Multi-Layer Perceptron (MLP) to extract features from multimodal source data and feed the extracted features to a fusion network to predict the 24-forecast cyclone displacement. The results show that the proposed model has lower forecast errors on all basins than BCD5, a benchmark statistical model.

The existing forecasting models mainly focus on predicting the track or intensity of the TCs. These models can not be directly used to assess the wind speed at given offshore wind farms during typhoons. In this study, a two-step model that utilizes both the deep-learning technique and cyclone physics is proposed. The model takes the initial typhoon condition (the current and previous track location and intensity) as input and produces the wind speed predictions at given observation locations. The main contribution of this study can be described as follows:

- Feature extraction methods, including geographical representation, storm velocity, and grid transition probabilities, are used during data preprocessing to extract interpretable explicit features from raw data.
- A two-step approach is proposed to predict wind speed at given locations during typhoons. An LSTM-based seq2seq model is developed as the first step of the proposed approach. The seq2seq model predicts the future typhoon trajectory based on the initial typhoon condition. After that, a linear boundary layer wind model is employed in the second step to calculate the wind speed at given locations.

– The proposed approach is validated using measurement data gathered from a real-world offshore wind farm. The results suggest that the proposed method is capable of predicting wind speed accurately at given offshore wind farms during typhoons.

The rest of the paper is organized as follows: Sect. 2 describes the training data and the preprocessing method for the proposed model. The proposed two-step approach is presented in Sect. 3. In Sect. 4 the case study based on real-world data is discussed. Section 5 concludes.

2 Data Preprocessing

The raw track data comes from the CMA Tropical Cyclone Best Track Dataset [17,18], which covers tropical cyclones that develop over the Western North Pacific. The records in the dataset contain the storm IDs and names, date and time of the record, storm intensity category, storm location (storm center latitude and longitude), minimum pressure near the storm center, and 2-min mean maximum sustained wind speed near the storm center. However, about 10% of the entries in the dataset don't have valid 2-min mean maximum sustained wind speed records. Therefore, only the storm location and minimum pressure near the storm center data were used to construct the feature space for the track forecasting model in step 1. The dataset provides 3-hourly data for the landed typhoons since 2017, while most of the data are 6 h apart. Since the track forecasting model makes predictions in 6-h intervals, only data that are 6 h apart were used in this study.

2.1 Geographical Representation

The latitude and longitude coordinates of the storm locations are transformed into pairs of x and y coordinates using Lambert's Conic Conformal (LCC) Projection [19]. The LCC-transformed coordinates make better geographical representations of the cyclone track since the conic projections reduce the distortion associated with the spherical coordinate system at higher latitudes and maintain the geographic shapes.

2.2 Storm Velocity

The geographic coordinate sequences obtained from the raw track dataset are non-stationary. Therefore, the storm velocity is calculated to de-trend the sequences. The storm velocity is represented by the storm translation direction and speed. The translation direction (θ) and speed (c) are calculated using the Haversine formula:

$$\Delta\phi_i = \phi_i - \phi_{i-1} \tag{1}$$

$$\Delta\lambda_i = \lambda_i - \lambda_{i-1} \tag{2}$$

$$a_i = \sin^2\left(\frac{\Delta\phi_i}{2}\right) + \cos\phi_{i-1} \cdot \cos\phi_i \cdot \sin^2\left(\frac{\Delta\lambda_i}{2}\right) \tag{3}$$

$$c_i = 2 \cdot R \cdot \arctan\left(\sqrt{\frac{a_i}{1-a_i}}\right) / \Delta t \tag{4}$$

$$\theta_i = \arctan\left(\frac{\sin(\Delta\lambda_i) \cdot \cos\phi_i}{\sin\phi_i \cdot \cos\phi_{i-1} - \sin\phi_{i-1} \cdot \cos\phi_i \cdot \cos(\Delta\lambda_i)}\right) \tag{5}$$

where $R = 6371$ km is the earth radius and $\Delta t = 6\,\text{h}$ is the time difference between track records.

2.3 Grid Transition Probabilities

The cyclone track behavior is affected by many geographic-related features, such as surface roughness, height, and temperature. In order to better capture the spatial patterns influenced by geography, the grid transition probabilities are calculated based on historical data. First, a 0.7×0.7 degree grid network is created to cover all the tracks in the dataset. If a historical storm record is contained in a grid cell (i, j), the grid transition probability of the nearby $9 \times 9 = 81$ grid cells centered at grid cell (i, j) is then calculated as

$$p_{ij}(k) = \frac{n_k}{m_{ij}}, k = 1, 2, ..., 81 \tag{6}$$

where k is the index of the k_{th} associated cell centered at grid cell (i, j), n_k is the total number of records transit from cell (i, j) to the k_{th} associated cell in 6 h, and $\sum_1^m n_k = m_{ij}$.

2.4 Sliding Window

In many real-life applications (e.g., unit commitment), day-ahead forecasting is desired for forecasting models. Since each input record is 6 h from its previous record, one day is a sequence of length 4 in the track data. The training data is then generated using a sliding window of length 8 (4 for input and 4 for validation) on the original dataset.

2.5 Normalization

A min-max normalization is applied to features to make each input feature have equal scales:

$$x' = \left(\frac{x - \min(x)}{\max(x) - \min(x)}\right) \tag{7}$$

where x is the original feature value and x' is the normalized value. The range of the normalized features is $[0, 1]$.

After the data preprocessing, the final input features after preprocessing include the LCC transformed coordinates (x, y), the minimum central pressure p, the storm translation direction θ, and speed (c), and the transition probabilities.

3 Methodology

3.1 Problem Formulation

Definition 1. *Typhoon Track: A typhoon track X is composed of consecutive spatial temporal points $X = \{X_1, X_2, ..., X_T\}$. Each spatial temporal point X_i contains several parameters that essentially characterize the typhoon track: $X_i = [\lambda_i, \phi_i, p_{ci}]$, where λ_i, ϕ_i are the longitude and latitude coordinates of the typhoon center, and p_{ci} is the typhoon central pressure.*

Problem 1. Given a set of n observation locations $A = \{A_1, A_2, ..., A_n\}$ and a typhoon track $X = \{X_1, X_2, ..., X_T\}$, the goal is to predict the maximum sustained wind speed $V = \{V_1, V_2, ...V_n\}$ of each observation location in the next k time steps. The observation locations are defined by their geographic coordinates $A_i = (\lambda_i, \phi_i), i = 1, 2, 3, ..., n$, where λ_i is the longitude and ϕ_i is the latitude.

The problem is solved in two steps: First, the typhoon track information is fed into a deep neural network to generate a prediction of the typhoon track in the next k ($k = 4$ in this study) time steps. After that, a linear boundary layer wind field model is utilized to calculate the wind speed at each observation location based on the predicted track.

3.2 Seq2Seq Track Forecasting Model

The proposed approach utilizes a sequence-to-sequence (Seq2Seq) deep learning model to predict future typhoon locations based on the current typhoon track information. The techniques used in this model are described below:

Artificial Neural Network (ANN). ANNs are layered computing models inspired by the biological neural networks in human brains. A typical ANN consists of an input layer, one or more hidden layers, and an output layer. ANN is proven to be able to approximate any given function [20] and is capable of conducting time-series forecasting.

Recurrent Neural Network (RNN). RNN is a special class of ANN. The basic ANN models are not particularly good at processing sequence data since they assume that the data entries are independent. In RNNs, the output depends on not only the current input but also the output of previous data. This enables RNNs to capture the temporal dynamic behavior of time-series data.

Long Short-Term Memory (LSTM). Although RNNs work well with time-series data, they suffer from vanishing gradients and cannot catch the long-term relationships within the sequence data. LSTM is a variation of RNN that is specifically designed to solve the vanishing gradient problem. LSTM models utilize the "gate" mechanism to control the information flow. The gates are able to keep important information with a weight of 1. Therefore, long-term memory won't vanish anymore. The gates also have the ability to "forget" less important information to make the networks more efficient.

Seq2Seq Model. The Seq2Seq model is widely used in sequence-to-sequence tasks such as language translation and time-series forecasting. It utilizes the encoder-decoder architecture to process sequence data with variable lengths. The encoder-decoder architecture consists of an encoder and a decoder. The encoder transforms the input sequence into a fixed-shape state. The decoder maps the fixed shape state to a variable-length output sequence. Figure 1 shows the proposed seq2seq model architecture.

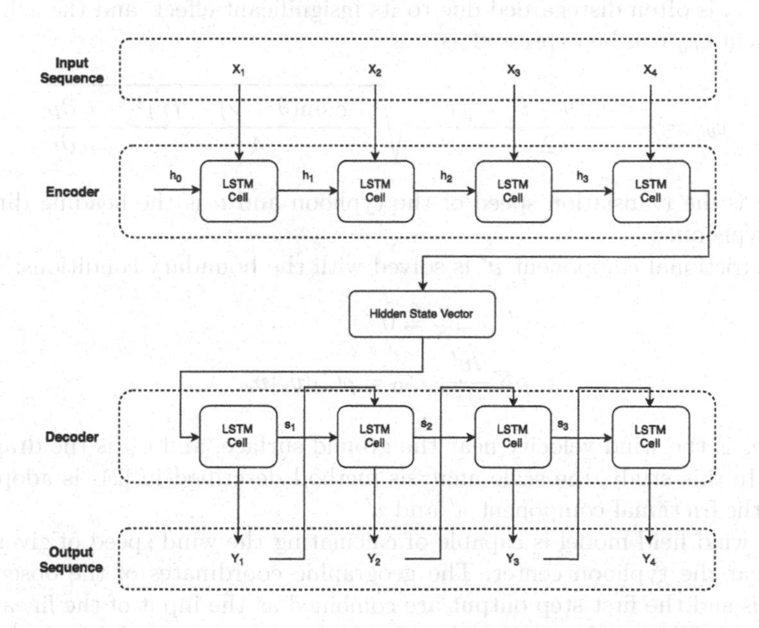

Fig. 1. Proposed Track Forecasting Model Architecture

3.3 Linear Typhoon Boundary Layer Wind Field Model

A linear height-resolving wind field model [21] is employed to generate the typhoon boundary layer wind field. The typhoon boundary layer wind fields are governed by 3D Navier-Stokes equations:

$$\frac{\partial \boldsymbol{v}}{\partial t} + \boldsymbol{v} \cdot \nabla \boldsymbol{v} = -\frac{1}{\rho}\nabla p - f\boldsymbol{k} \times \boldsymbol{v} + \boldsymbol{F} \tag{8}$$

where $\boldsymbol{v}$ is the wind velocity, f is the Coriolis parameter, $\boldsymbol{k}$ is the unit vector in the vertical direction, ρ is the air density, $\boldsymbol{F}$ is the frictional force, and p is the pressure. The pressure is calculated using the Holland pressure profile [22]:

$$p = p_c + \Delta p \exp[(-\frac{r_m}{r})^B] \tag{9}$$

where p_c, Δp, r_m, and B stand for central pressure, central pressure difference, radius to maximum winds, and Holland's B parameter, respectively.

The wind velocity $\boldsymbol{v}$ is expressed as a sum of the gradient wind velocity $\boldsymbol{v_g}$ and the frictional component $\boldsymbol{v'}$:

$$\boldsymbol{v} = \boldsymbol{v_g} + \boldsymbol{v'} \tag{10}$$

In a cylindrical coordinate system (r, θ, z), the gradient wind can be decomposed into the radial velocity v_{rg} and the azimuthal velocity $v_{\theta g}$. The radial component v_{rg} is often disregarded due to its insignificant effect, and the azimuthal component $v_{\theta g}$ can be expressed as:

$$v_{\theta g} = \frac{-c\sin(\theta - \nu) - fr}{2} + \sqrt{\frac{(-c\sin(\theta - \nu) - fr)^2}{4} + \frac{r}{\rho}\frac{\partial p}{\partial r}} \tag{11}$$

where c is the translation speed of the typhoon and ν is the heading direction of the typhoon.

The frictional component $\boldsymbol{v'}$ is solved with the boundary conditions:

$$\boldsymbol{v'}|_{z' \to \infty} = 0 \tag{12}$$

$$\rho K \frac{\partial \boldsymbol{v'}}{\partial z}|_{z'=0} = \rho C_d |\boldsymbol{v_s}| \boldsymbol{v_s} \tag{13}$$

where $\boldsymbol{v_s}$ is the wind velocity near the ground surface, and C_d is the drag coefficient. In this study, the scale analysis method described in [21] is adopted to obtain the frictional component u' and v'.

The wind field model is capable of calculating the wind speed of given locations near the typhoon center. The geographic coordinates of the observation locations and the first step output are combined as the input of the linear wind field model. The wind speed at the observation locations is then calculated as the prediction results of the proposed approach. Figure 2 illustrates the overall workflow of the proposed method.

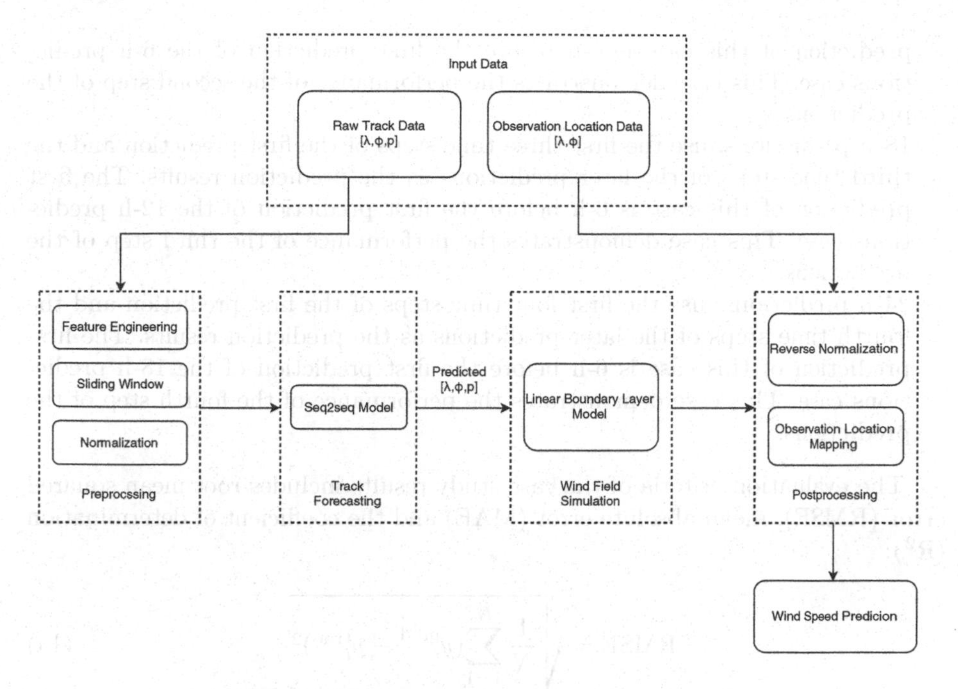

Fig. 2. Work flow of the proposed method

4 Case Study

4.1 Case Description

The case study considers the Guishan offshore wind farms (22.155N, 113.732E) as the observation locations. In this case study, the 10-min maximum sustained wind speeds observed at the Guishan offshore wind farms are used as ground truth values for the predictions. Typhoon Higos (2020) is the only typhoon that had a direct impact on the Guishan offshore wind farms after the wind farms were built. Therefore the case study only considers the wind speeds when typhoon Higos hit the Guishan offshore wind farms (2020-8-18 6:00 to 2020-8-19 12:00). The proposed model is implemented using Python [23] and Tensorflow [24] on a machine equipped with an NVIDIA GeForce RTX 3090 GPU.

The input data is derived from the CMA best track dataset using the preprocessing method described in Sect. 2. The track data of typhoon Higos is excluded from the training dataset to make fair predictions. Since the proposed model predicts the wind speed of the next four time steps, the following four different cases are implemented to test the performance of the individual prediction time steps:

- 6-h predictions: only use the first time step of each prediction as the prediction results. By doing so, the model is only able to make predictions 6-h ahead.
- 12-h predictions: use the first two time steps of the first prediction and the second time steps of the later predictions as the prediction results. The first

prediction of this case is 6-h before the first prediction of the 6-h predictions case. This case demonstrates the performance of the second step of the predictions.
- 18-h predictions: use the first three time steps of the first prediction and the third time steps of the later predictions as the prediction results. The first prediction of this case is 6-h before the first prediction of the 12-h predictions case. This case demonstrates the performance of the third step of the predictions.
- 24-h predictions: use the first four time steps of the first prediction and the fourth time steps of the later predictions as the prediction results. The first prediction of this case is 6-h before the first prediction of the 18-h predictions case. This case demonstrates the performance of the fourth step of the predictions.

The evaluation criteria of the case study results includes root mean squared error (RMSE), mean absolute error (MAE) and the coefficient of determination (R^2):

$$\mathrm{RMSE} = \sqrt{\frac{1}{N}\sum_{1=1}^{N}(y_i^{\mathrm{pred}} - y_i^{\mathrm{true}})^2} \tag{14}$$

$$\mathrm{MAE} = \frac{1}{N}\sum_{1=1}^{N}|y_i^{\mathrm{pred}} - y_i^{\mathrm{true}}| \tag{15}$$

$$\mathrm{R}^2 = 1 - \frac{\sum_{1=1}^{N}(y_i^{\mathrm{pred}} - y_i^{\mathrm{true}})^2}{\sum_{1=1}^{N}(y_i^{\mathrm{pred}} - \overline{y}_i^{\mathrm{pred}})^2} \tag{16}$$

where y_i^{pred} denotes the predicted value and y_i^{true} denotes the ground truth value.

Table 1. Approximation Error

Model	6-h	12-h	18-h	24-h
RMSE (m/s)	4.6976	**2.0232**	3.9228	6.0110
MAE (m/s)	4.4172	**1.7489**	3.1820	5.2779
R^2	0.5358	**0.8250**	−0.0869	−3.0790

4.2 Performance Comparison

The prediction results are plotted in Fig. 3. The RMSE, MAE and R^2 of the different cases are shown in Table 1. Since the hidden states are passed through time steps in the seq2seq model, the approximation error will also accumulate through the steps. Therefore the errors are expected to be larger in further time steps. However, the results show that the 12-h predictions yield the best results.

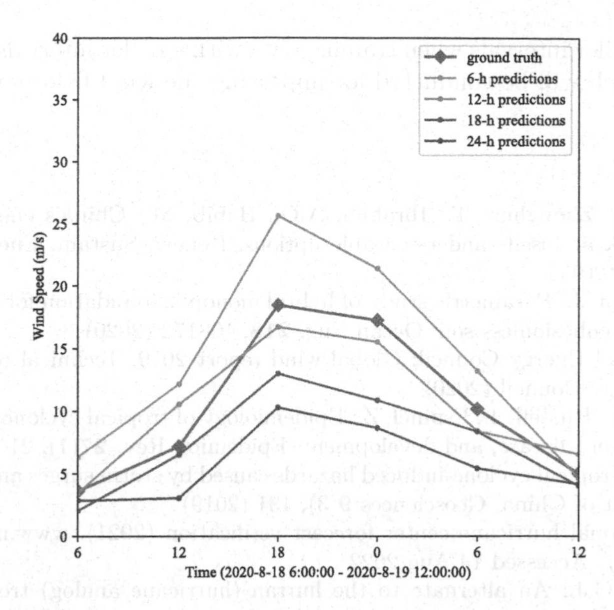

Fig. 3. Observed and simulated wind speeds at Guishan offshore windfarm during typhoon Higos (2020).

This is because the wind field model tends to overestimate the wind speed under our model configuration. The exact values of the wind field model parameters, such as the Holland B parameter and the radius of maximum winds, are hard to obtain. Thus the results may vary under different configurations of these parameters. Overall, the 12-h predictions are more reliable than the 18-h and 24-h predictions. The results suggest that the 12-h ahead predictions best suit the wind speed prediction task.

5 Conclusion

This paper presents a two-step approach for forecasting wind speed at offshore wind farms during typhoons. A feature extraction method is applied to the raw input to extract explicit information about the typhoons before the data is fed into the model in the first step. The first step utilizes an LSTM-based seq2seq model to predict the typhoon track and intensity based on the initial typhoon conditions. In the second step, the wind speed at given offshore locations is calculated using a physics-based linear wind field model. The proposed approach is tested on real-world observation data collected from Guishan Offshore Wind Farms during typhoon Higos (2020). The results show that the proposed approach is capable of predicting the wind speed 12-h ahead during typhoons accurately. Since most of the historical typhoon track datasets only provide data at 6-h intervals, the model in this work only makes reasonable predictions at 6-h intervals. Nevertheless, the proposed model can be easily trained to make predictions with smaller intervals when training data with smaller intervals is available. Further research will be conducted for improving the wind field model.

References

1. Musa, S.D., Zhonghua, T., Ibrahim, A.O., Habib, M.: China's energy status: a critical look at fossils and renewable options. Renew. Sustain. Energy Rev. **81**, 2281–2290 (2018)
2. Wang, X., Li, J.: Parametric study of hybrid monopile foundation for offshore wind turbines in cohesionless soil. Ocean Eng. **218**, 108172 (2020)
3. Global Wind Energy Council: Global wind report 2019. Technical report. Global Wind Energy Council (2020)
4. Shultz, J.M., Russell, J., Espinel, Z.: Epidemiology of tropical cyclones: the dynamics of disaster, disease, and development. Epidemiol. Rev. **27**(1), 21–35 (2005)
5. You, Z.J.: Tropical cyclone-induced hazards caused by storm surges and large waves on the coast of China. Geosciences **9**(3), 131 (2019)
6. NHC: National hurricane center forecast verification (2021). www.nhc.noaa.gov/verification/. Accessed 14 Aug 2022
7. Neumann, C.J.: An alternate to the hurran (hurricane analog) tropical cyclone forecast system. Technical report, National Hurricane Center (1972)
8. Emanuel, K., Ravela, S., Vivant, E., Risi, C.: A statistical deterministic approach to hurricane risk assessment. Bull. Am. Meteor. Soc. **87**(3), 299–314 (2006)
9. Vickery, P.J., Skerlj, P.F., Twisdale, L.A.: Simulation of hurricane risk in the U.S. using empirical track model. J. Struct. Eng. **126**(10), 1222–1237 (2000)
10. Côté, J., Gravel, S., Méthot, A., Patoine, A., Roch, M., Staniforth, A.: The operational CMC-MRB global environmental multiscale (GEM) model. Part I: Design considerations and formulation. Mon. Weather Rev. **126**(6), 1373–1395 (1998)
11. Leith, C.: Theoretical skill of Monte Carlo forecasts. Mon. Weather Rev. **102**(6), 409–418 (1974)
12. Mullen, S.L., Baumhefner, D.P.: Monte Carlo simulations of explosive cyclogenesis. Mon. Weather Rev. **122**(7), 1548–1567 (1994)
13. Krishnamurti, T., Correa-Torres, R., Rohaly, G., Oosterhof, D., Surgi, N.: Physical initialization and hurricane ensemble forecasts. Weather Forecast. **12**(3), 503–514 (1997)
14. Krishnamurti, T.N., et al.: Multimodel ensemble forecasts for weather and seasonal climate. J. Clim. **13**(23), 4196–4216 (2000)
15. Alemany, S., Beltran, J., Perez, A., Ganzfried, S.: Predicting hurricane trajectories using a recurrent neural network. In: Proceedings of the AAAI Conference on Artificial Intelligence, vol. 33, pp. 468–475 (2019)
16. Giffard-Roisin, S., Yang, M.: Deep learning for hurricane track forecasting from aligned spatio-temporal climate datasets. In: 32nd Annual Conference on Neural Information Processing Systems Workshop on Modeling and Decision-Making in the Spatiotemporal Domain (2018)
17. Ying, M., et al.: An overview of the China meteorological administration tropical cyclone database. J. Atmos. Oceanic Tech. **31**(2), 287–301 (2014)
18. Lu, X., et al.: Western north pacific tropical cyclone database created by the China meteorological administration. Adv. Atmos. Sci. **38**(4), 690–699 (2021)
19. Lambert, J.H., Tobler, W.R., Lambert, J.H.: Notes and comments on the composition of terrestrial and celestial maps. Department of Geography, University of Michigan (1972)

20. Hornik, K., Stinchcombe, M., White, H.: Multilayer feedforward networks are universal approximators. Neural Netw. **2**(5), 359–366 (1989)
21. Snaiki, R., Wu, T.: A linear height-resolving wind field model for tropical cyclone boundary layer. J. Wind Eng. Ind. Aerodyn. **171**, 248–260 (2017)
22. Holland, G.J.: An analytic model of the wind and pressure profiles in hurricanes. Mon. Weather Rev. (1980)
23. Van Rossum, G., Drake, F.L.: Python 3 Reference Manual. CreateSpace, Scotts Valley (2009)
24. Abadi, M., Agarwal, A., Barham, P., Brevdo, E., et al.: TensorFlow: large-scale machine learning on heterogeneous systems (2015). Software available from https://www.tensorflow.org/

Regional Model Simulation of the Ice Disaster in Hunan Power Grid During January 2022: Effect of Nanling Mountains on Precipitation

Tao Feng, Yihao Zhou(✉), Zelin Cai, Xunjian Xu, and Lei Wang

State Key Laboratory of Disaster Prevention and Reduction for Power Grid Transmission and Distribution Equipment, Changsha, China

zhouyhao@outlook.com

Abstract. Hunan Province is one of the regions that are mostly affected by the freezing rain and ice disaster in China, because its unique topography is conducive to the southward intrusion of cold air from the north. This hazard can cause the line icing, threaten the operation of power grid and bring great socioeconomic losses. Understanding the mechanisms related to the topography effect on precipitation near Hunan is important to improve the prediction and prevention for the ice disaster during winter. In this study, we focus on an icing event at the beginning of 2022. The frontal precipitation in central Hunan features a southwest-northeast band distribution in this event, which is caused by the strong convergence from northern cold air and southwesterly flows in the subtropics. The numerical simulations are further conducted based on WRF model to test the effect of topography near Nanling Mountains on the local precipitation in Hunan. The results show that the reduction or elimination of the Nanling Mountains has limited impact on the overall distribution and amplitude of precipitation near Hunan in this event, but the latitudinal location of precipitation band and its western range slightly change. These changes might be related to the changed local convergence caused by the enhanced southward intrusion of cold air without the blocking of the Nanling Mountains.

Keywords: Power line icing · Topography · Numerical simulation

1 Introduction

The southern region of China often suffers from persistent freezing rain events in winter, which can cause the severe icing disaster of transmission lines and significantly threaten the operation of power grid. For example, during January and February in 2008, a severe and persistent ice disaster occurred in many provinces of southern China. The thick ice accumulated on power lines led to the collapse of electricity transmission towers and caused great socioeconomic losses [1–3]. Therefore, it is significantly important to understand the factors modulating the local precipitation and temperature and mechanisms for their evolutions during winter, which can improve the ability of the power grid to predict the ice disaster and prevent or mitigate its potential damage.

H. Yang et al. (Eds.): SmartGIFT 2022, LNICST 483, pp. 108–116, 2023.
https://doi.org/10.1007/978-3-031-31733-0_10

There are many previous studies that investigated the favorable conditions and formation mechanisms for the freezing rain events [4–8]. The freezing rain generally occurs when the surface temperature below 0 degrees Celsius, and is typically associated with the southward movement of the northern cold air. Hunan Province is one of the regions that are mostly affected by the icing hazard in China, because it has a unique topographic distribution, which is surrounded by multiple mountains in the east, south and west, while the north is flat and has no barrier for the cold surge from the north. Such condition is very conducive to the southward movement of cold air and the consequent formation of freezing rain. Some authors explored the effect of topography near Hunan Province on the freezing rain [9–11], and indicated that the topography (e.g., the Nanling Mountains) can block the low-level flows and influence the local distribution of surface temperature, water vapor and characteristics of inversion layer, and thus change the precipitation feature. Understanding the role of topography in winter precipitation and temperature provides helpful insights for the mechanism of freezing rain to improve the prediction ability.

At the beginning of 2022, state grid of Hunan Province experienced several icing events due to the northern cold air activity. The present study will focus on the power line icing event during 27–29 January in Hunan Province. As shown in Fig. 1a, the icing is mainly distributed at the western and northwestern part of Hunan. Figures 1b and 1c show the mean precipitation and temperature derived from multi-stations observation during this period, respectively. The precipitation is mainly located in central Hunan with a southwest-northeast band distribution, and the precipitation and low temperature at western part of Hunan together contribute to the icing there. In this study we will show the synoptic background for this event and test the effect of Nanling Mountains (the topography in southern part of Hunan) on local precipitation using the numerical model simulation, to provide insights for the icing process related to the orographic precipitation.

The rest of this paper is organized as follows: Sect. 2 describes the model setup and datasets. Section 3 examines the large-scale circulation background for this icing event. Section 4 compares the results of observation and control experiment. Section 5 shows the differences in sensitivity experiments and discusses the possible effect of Nanling Mountains. A summary is given in Sect. 6.

2 Model and Datasets

2.1 Model

The numerical simulation in this study is based on the Weather Research and Forecasting (WRF) Model version 3.8.1 [12], which is broadly used to investigate the regional atmospheric events and related mechanisms. We used two computational domains (D01 and D02) in the model with the two-way nesting technique (Fig. 2), and the horizontal grid spacing is 9 and 3 km, respectively. D01 covers China and surrounding large-scale Asian region in the low and mid latitudes, which can capture both the cold air from Siberia and warm moist air from the tropics. D02 (red box in Fig. 2a) is located over the small region near Hunan Province. The model has 51 vertical levels with the top at 10 hPa. The Noah land surface physics scheme is used to compute the diurnal cycle of surface temperature and heat fluxes. The Rapid Radiative Transfer Model (RRTM) and the Dudhia scheme are used for longwave and shortwave radiation parameterization, respectively. The Thompson scheme is used for microphysics, and the Yonsei University (YSU) PBL scheme is used for boundary processes. No cumulus parameterization is used for both domains.

The control experiment is initialized at 1200 UTC 23 January 2022 and integrated to 1200 UTC 31 January 2022. The initial and boundary conditions for the model are obtained from 6-hourly 1 × 1 FNL reanalysis data from National Centers for Environmental Prediction (NCEP). To test the effect of Nanling Mountains, we set the terrain height in this region (red box in Fig. 2b) as half of the original values in Half-Terrain experiment, and set the terrain height to 10 m in No-Terrain experiment.

2.2 Datasets

The NCEP-FNL reanalysis is used to drive the WRF model and provide the large-scale circulation fields including geopotential, wind, and water vapor for this event. The observed line icing data are derived from the intelligent analysis and control platform for power grid operation inspection of Hunan to show the ice disaster in this event (as shown in Fig. 1a). The in-situ multi-station observation data from China Meteorological Administration (CMA) is used to show the precipitation and temperature in this event (as shown in Figs. 1b–c) and validate our model simulation.

3 Large-Scale Circulation Background

We first examine the large-scale circulation background for this precipitation event in Hunan. Figure 3 shows the large-scale geopotential height, wind and specific humidity at different pressure levels during this event. On 27 January (Fig. 3a), there is a pressure trough and ridge near Balkhash Lake (40–60°N, 60–80°E) at 500 hPa, leading the northern cold air to move southwards between them. In the subtropical region, there is a strong pressure trough at the Bay of Bengal. The southwesterly flows at the front of trough transport abundant low-level water vapor from the tropical ocean to Hunan. The northern cold air and southwestern warm moist air strongly converge in Southwest and Central China, and the evident west-east shear line at the north of Hunan can be found at 700 hPa. Therefore, the frontal precipitation develops in this region with the abundant low-level moisture. On 28 January (Fig. 3b), the trough and ridge systems in the midlatitudes propagate eastwards gradually, but the northerly cold air and southwesterly flow at 700 hPa remain active, so the quasi-stationary front in central and northern Hunan maintains for a long time, resulting in the persistent precipitation in this region. On 29 January (Fig. 3c), the northern trough and ridge systems continue to move eastwards and strengthen, which favors stronger southward intrusion of the mid-level cold air. Meanwhile, the pressure trough near the Bay of Bengal weakens and propagates into the Southeast Asian region, which leads to weaker southwestern flows and moisture near Hunan. Therefore, the precipitation in Hunan gradually decays and disappears during this period.

In general, the precipitation process in this event is due to the strong convergence from the northern cold air that moves southwards and the subtropical trough induced southwesterly flows, which is associated with a typical frontal genesis process. The maintenance of 700 hPa shear line and quasi-stationary front cause the persistent precipitation during this event, and the strong cold air from the north reduces the surface temperature in Hunan, which further favors the freezing rain and line icing.

4 Results in Control Experiment

Figure 4 shows the mean precipitation and surface air temperature from station observation and control experiment during this event, as well as their differences. The observational precipitation is mainly located at the center of Hunan with a southwest-northeast band distribution, due to the maintenance of the frontal system as mentioned above. The precipitation maximum is at the northeastern and western side of Hunan. The simulated precipitation is also characterized by the southwest-northeast distribution, with the maximum located at the central and northern Hunan. Figure 4c shows that the location of precipitation is broadly consistent between observation and simulation (the latter slightly shifts northward), but the amplitude of simulated precipitation is much stronger especially at northwestern side of Hunan. The surface air temperature features the southward intrusion of the northern cold air, and the northern and western parts of Hunan are primarily affected (Fig. 4d). The western part of Hunan was the main area suffering from the freezing rain and icing disaster in this event (Fig. 1a) because it was affected by both precipitation and low surface temperature. The model simulation broadly reproduces the activity of cold air and overall distribution of temperature, but with a greater north-south gradient of temperature at Hunan (Fig. 4f).

In general, the control experiment reasonably captures the distribution of precipitation and temperature, but has a much stronger amplitude of precipitation. The greater north-south gradient of temperature in the simulation might destabilize the vertical stratification and produce a stronger convergence of flows, and thus result in stronger frontal precipitation. One may note that the northwestern Hunan is characterized by stronger precipitation and lower temperature in the simulation, which might result in overestimated icing in the model at this region.

5 Results in Terrain Sensitivity Experiments

Figure 5 shows the mean precipitation results in Half-Terrain and No-Terrain experiments and their differences from control experiment. While the overall distribution and amplitude of precipitation in Half-Terrain are similar as control, some local differences still exist. The precipitation in Half-Terrain slightly shifts southward and extends broader at southwestern side, while the northern precipitation weakens (Fig. 5d). The precipitation in No-Terrain weakens in central and northern Hunan, and intensifies at southwestern part of the rain band (but weakens at the southern side, Fig. 5e). These changes in precipitation might cause decreased icing at north and increased icing at west of Hunan.

In general, the reduction or elimination of the Nanling topography has limited impact on the overall distribution and amplitude of Hunan precipitation in this event. This might be partly because the precipitation is mainly located in central and northern Hunan away from the Nanling Mountains, so the terrain has little influence on the upstream cold air activity and precipitation. However, there are still some local changes in precipitation in sensitivity experiments. When the Nanling topography is reduced or eliminated, the northern cold air moves southward more smoothly, and the local detouring flow around the terrain and small-scale convergence may disappear, which weakens the precipitation at the northern flank of terrain. On the other hand, part of the enhanced northerly flow moves westward at southern Hunan, which may influence the local convergence and divergence there, leading to the precipitation changes at the southwestern side of Hunan. The important effect of Nanling Mountains topography on the local flow convergence, location of quasi-stationary front is also indicated by previous studies [13], which may lead to variations of magnitude and distribution of freezing rain and ice disaster in Hunan.

6 Summary

In this study, we focus on the line icing event during 27–29 January 2022 in Hunan Province, and investigate the large-scale atmospheric background and conduct numerical simulations using WRF model to test the effect of Nanling Mountains on local precipitation. The main conclusions are as follows:

(1) The frontal precipitation is mainly located in central Hunan with a southwest-northeast band distribution, which is caused by the strong convergence from cold air induced by the northern trough and ridge systems and the southwesterly moist flows induced by the trough at the Bay of Bengal. The cold air moves southward and reduces the surface temperature in western part of Hunan, resulting in the freezing rain and line icing there.
(2) The control experiment reasonably captures the distribution of observed precipitation and temperature, but has a much stronger amplitude of precipitation. The greater north-south gradient of temperature in the simulation might contribute to the stronger flow convergence and frontal precipitation.
(3) The reduction or elimination of the Nanling topography has limited impact on the overall distribution and amplitude of Hunan precipitation in this event, but the latitudinal location of precipitation band and its western range slightly change. These changes might be related to the changed local convergence caused by the enhanced southward intrusion of cold air without the blocking of Nanling Mountains.

In this event, the location of precipitation is not exactly in the Nanling Mountains region, which might be a possible reason that the terrain has limited effect on the precipitation. Other icing cases in Hunan (e.g., at the beginning of 2022) will be further tested in the future to further understand the effect of Nanling Mountains on precipitation, which helps improve the prediction of icing disaster and prevention for it.

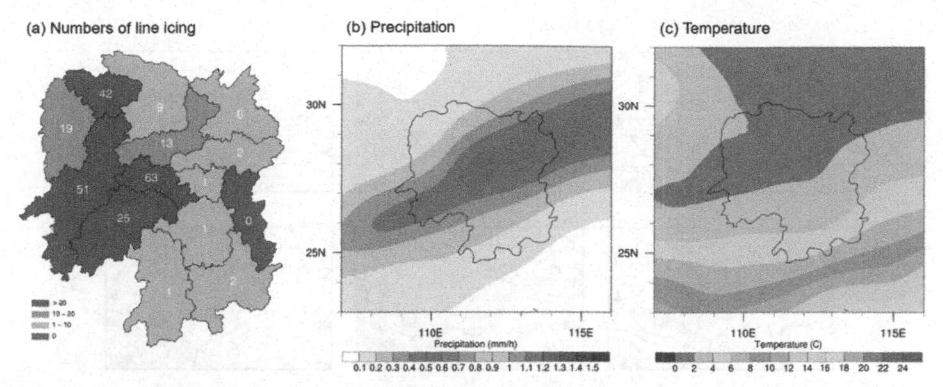

Fig. 1. The observed (a) numbers of line icing, (b) precipitation (mm/h) and (c) surface air temperature (C°) near Hunan Province during 27–29 January of 2022.

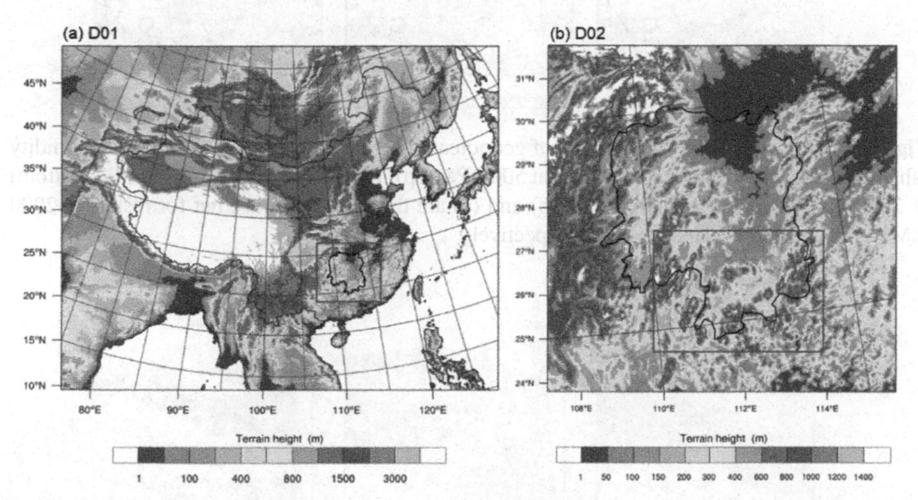

Fig. 2. (a) The WRF 9-km domain D01 and (b) 3-km domain D02 with terrain height (shading; m). Red box in (a) indicates D02, while in (b) indicates the Nanling mountain region where the terrain sensitivity experiments are performed. (Color figure online)

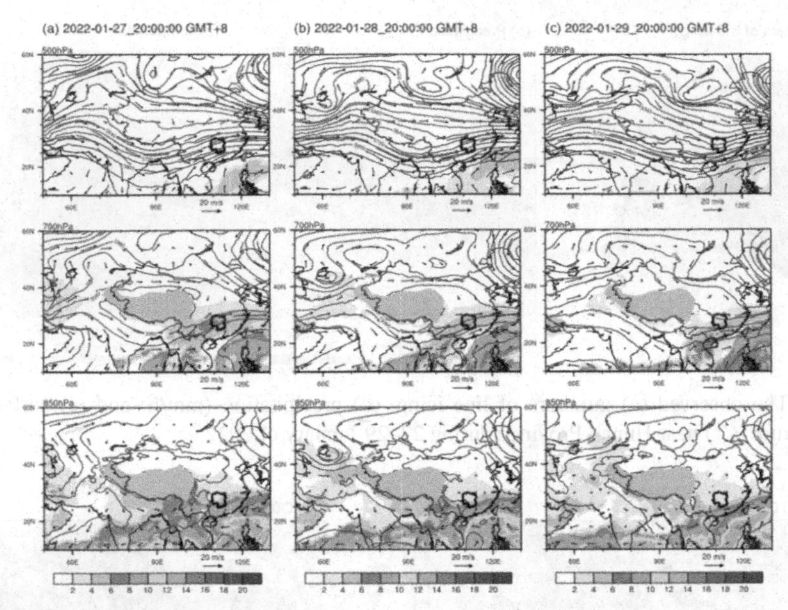

Fig. 3. (a) The large-scale background of geopotential height (contours; gpm), specific humidity (shading; g/kg), and wind (vectors; m/s) at 500-hPa (top), 700-hPa (middle) and 850-hPa (bottom) at 2000 GMT+8 on 27 January 2022. (b) and (c) are the same as in (a), but for results at 2000 GMT+8 on 28 and 29 January 2022, respectively.

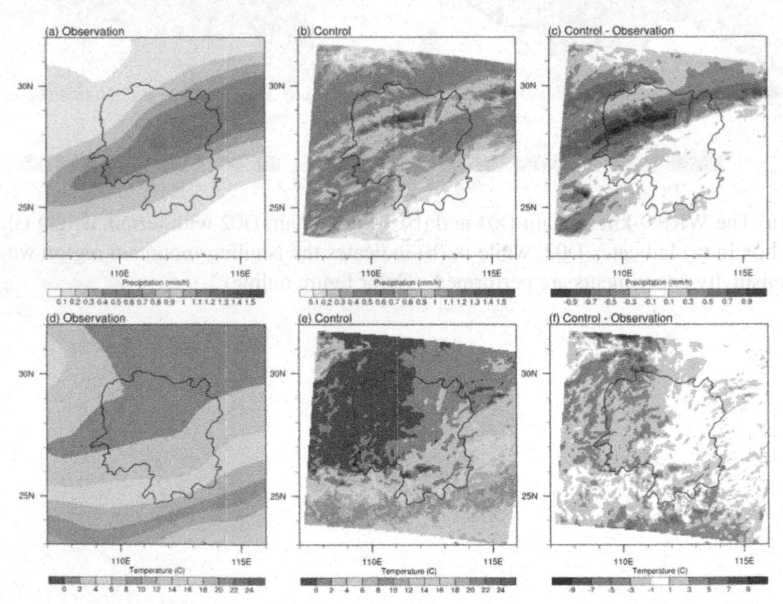

Fig. 4. Mean precipitation (mm/h) in the (a) observation, (b) control experiment and (c) their differences near Hunan Province during 27–29 January of 2022. (d)–(f) are the same as in (a)–(c), but for mean surface air temperature (C°) results.

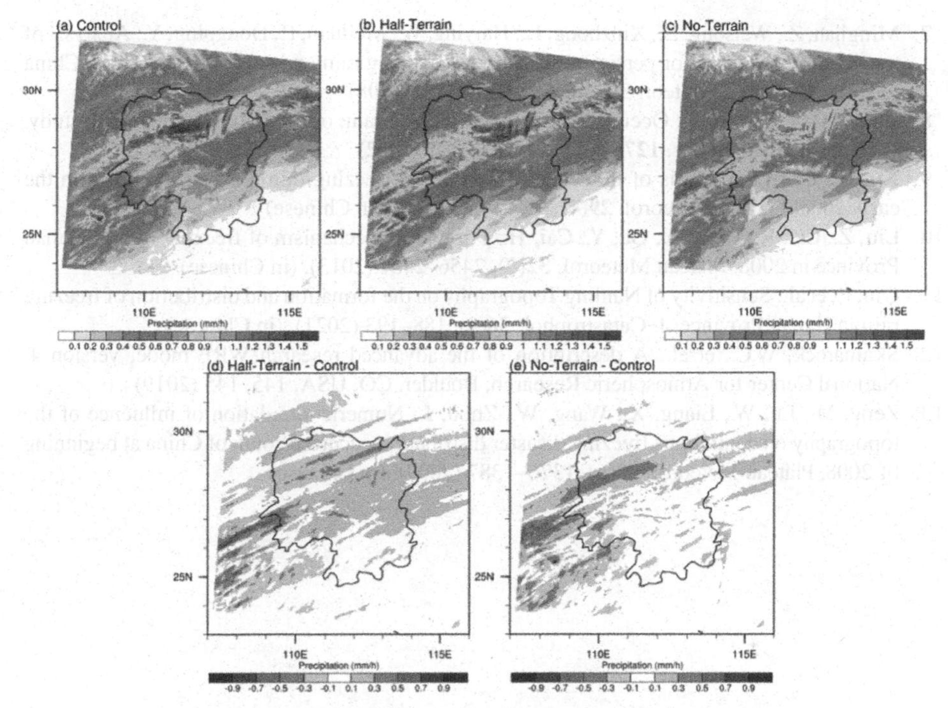

Fig. 5. Mean precipitation (mm/h) in the (a) control experiment, (b) Half-Terrain experiment and (c) No-Terrain experiment near Hunan Province during 27–29 January of 2022. Differences of precipitation between (d) Half-Terrain and control, (e) No-Terrain and control.

Acknowledgement. The present research is supported by the Science and Technology Project of the State Grid Corporation of China (Grant Number: 5216A020005D).

References

1. Zhou, B., et al.: The great 2008 Chinese ice storm: its socioeconomic–ecological impact and sustainability lessons learned. Bull. Am. Meteor. Soc. **92**(1), 47–60 (2011)
2. Zhao, L.N., et al.: The impact and the disasters of a severe snow and freezing rain over southern China in the early of 2008. Climatic Environ. Res. **14**, 556–566 (2008). (in Chinese)
3. Wang, L., et al.: Analysis of the severe cold surge, ice-snow and frozen disasters in South China during January 2008: I. Climatic features and its impact. Meteorol. Mon. **34**(4), 95–100 (2008). (in Chinese)
4. Sun, J., Zhao, S.: The impacts of multiscale weather systems on freezing rain and snowstorms over southern China. Weather Forecast. **25**(2), 388–407 (2010)
5. Gu, Z.C.: On the importance of the dynamical influence of Tibetan Plateau on the circulation over East Asia. Acta Meteor. Sin. **1**, 283–303 (1951). (in Chinese)
6. Rauber, R.M., Olthoff, L.S., Ramamurthy, M.K., Kunkel, K.E.: The relative importance of warm rain and melting processes in freezing precipitation events. J. Appl. Meteorol. **39**(7), 1185–1195 (2000)

7. Mingjian, Z., Weisong, L., Xinzhong, L., Haiying, W., Meijuan, P., Dongping, Y.: Analysis of temperature structure for persistent disasterous freezing rain and snow over southern China in early 2008. Acta Meteor. Sin. **66**(6), 1043–1052 (2008)
8. Lu, Z., Han, Y., Liu, Y.: Occurrence of warm freezing rain: observation and modeling study. J. Geophys. Res. Atmos. **127**(5), e2021JD036242 (2022)
9. Xu, H., Jin, R.: Analysis of influence of Terrain on freezing-rain weather in Hunan in the early 2008. Plateau Meteorol. **29**(4), 957–967 (2010). (in Chinese)
10. Liu, Z., Cai, R., Deng, J., Qu, Y., Cai, H.: Formation mechanism of freezing rain in Hunan Province in 2008. Plateau Meteorol. **32**(2), 2456–2467 (2013). (in Chinese)
11. Qin, P., et al.: Sensitivity of Nanling Topography on the formation and distribution of freezing rain in Hunan Province. J. Catastrophol. **36**(4), 188–193 (2021). (in Chinese)
12. Skamarock, W.C., et al.: A description of the advanced research WRF model version 4. National Center for Atmospheric Research, Boulder, CO, USA, 145, 145 (2019)
13. Zeng, M., Lu, W., Liang, X., Wang, W., Zhou, J.: Numeric simulation of influence of the topography on continuous freezing disaster distribution occurred south of China at beginning of 2008. Plateau Meteorol. **28**(6), 1376–1387 (2009). (in Chinese)

Research on Typhoon Identification of FY-4A Satellite Based on CNN-LSTM Model

Wenqing Feng[1], Xinyu Pi[1], Lifu He[1], Jing Luo[1], Ouyang Yi[1], Qiming Cao[1], Zihang Li[2], and Zhao Zhen[2](✉)

[1] State Key Laboratory of Disaster Prevention and Reduction for Power Grid Transmission and Distribution Equipment, State Grid Hunan Electric Company Limited Disaster Prevention and Reduction Center, Changsha, China
wq_feng@whu.edu.cn

[2] Department of Electrical Engineering, North China Electric Power University, Baoding, China
georgiazhz@foxmail.com

Abstract. Typhoons are one of the most serious natural disasters, which are extremely destructive and pose a great threat to the safe operation of power grids. To improve the risk warning and pre-control capability of power grid operation under typhoon weather, this paper proposes a typhoon cloud system identification method based on a two-dimensional convolutional neural network (CNN) and long short-term memory (LSTM) network. First, the spectral features are selected according to the physical characteristics of clouds, combined with the square field of point clouds as the spatial information of point clouds to construct a sample library of typhoon cloud blocks; then, the spatial features are automatically extracted by the convolutional neural network; Finally, the LSTM network extracts the spatial local difference features and the time series features of continuous changes of a typhoon cloud system to provide multi-angle features for satellite cloud map to identify typhoon cloud system. Combined with the multi-channel scanning imaging radiometer AGRI (Advanced Geostationary Radiation Imager) data in the geostationary Fengyun-4 meteorological satellite (FY-4A), the monitoring and research of typhoon weather in Guangdong Province, China, is taken as an example. The experimental results show that compared with the Faster-RCNN method of abstracting typhoon features for identification, the CNN-LSTM model-based typhoon identification method can achieve a more detailed division between typhoon and non-typhoon regions based on the multidimensional features of the cloud system in typhoon regions, and achieve better identification results.

Keywords: Typhoon Cloud System Identification · CNN-LSTM Hybrid Model · Feature Extraction · FY-4A Satellite

1 Introduction

Under the strategic background of "peak carbon dioxide emissions" and "carbon neutrality," the scale of new energy installed capacity has continued to increase, and the

H. Yang et al. (Eds.): SmartGIFT 2022, LNICST 483, pp. 117–129, 2023.
https://doi.org/10.1007/978-3-031-31733-0_11

operating characteristics of large power grids have undergone profound changes. At the same time, the impact of natural disasters such as typhoons, lightning, freezing, and mountain fires on the power grid has become increasingly prominent [1, 2]. Among them, the summer typhoon has threatened the safe and stable power grid operation in my country's southeastern coastal areas [3, 4]. Effectively improving typhoon forecasting [5–7] and real-time monitoring capabilities can enhance the ability of large power grids to resist the impact of extreme weather such as typhoons. Therefore, the development of practical typhoon identification methods is of great significance to the safe operation of power grids.

Currently, there are few conventional statistical and observation data, and it is difficult to identify typhoons' locations accurately. However, satellite remote sensing data has high spatial and temporal coverage and resolution and is an essential means of observing and studying typhoons [8, 9]. It not only makes up for the low observation height of the ground meteorological observatory, but also makes up for the limited observation range. In the research of typhoon monitoring based on satellite cloud images, the edge contour features or gray image threshold are mostly used to identify and locate the typhoon. The traditional conventional methods include the threshold method, mathematical morphology method, rotation coefficient method and least square fitting method. In 2003, Liu et al. [10] proposed a method for locating the center of a typhoon with an eye on a satellite cloud image based on the mathematical morphology method. The typhoon cloud system was extracted by using erosion and expansion edge extraction techniques, and the center and radius of the maximum inscribed circle were obtained. In 2012, Li et al. [11] extracted typhoon cloud features based on image threshold segmentation technology based on entropy, obtained typhoon eye contour based on morphology and seed filling method, and applied gravity calculation method to locate the typhoon center. Experiments show that the positioning deviation is small and the positioning algorithm is feasible. Qiao et al. [12] used gray prediction and Chan-Vese model to obtain the positioning center based on infrared sequence images. The gray prediction is to obtain the initial position of the typhoon at the next predicted time point. After the Chan-Vese model calculates the eyewall near the typhoon center, a circle is fitted to obtain the typhoon center. This method is mainly used for the position of eyeless typhoons. The positioning accuracy of typhoons in the weakening period is relatively low, which needs further improvement. Liu et al. [13] automatically identified tropical cyclone cloud systems based on Canny edge detection and contour extraction. Although there may be some errors in obtaining the image centroid, this method can automatically track tropical cyclones. In 2014, Geng et al. [14] determined the segmentation threshold of the target cloud system based on satellite images and the maximum inter-class variance method, combined with the characteristics of cloud system area and brightness temperature distribution, and used the rotation coefficient to identify tropical cyclone cloud systems automatically.

However, the traditional method has some limitations in practical application, such as the mathematical morphology method is complicated to implement and takes much time; in the process of least squares fitting circle, the texture characteristics of the cloud system are ignored. At present, machine learning is widely used in the field of image recognition.

Some scholars have also begun to apply machine learning methods to typhoon recognition. Based on cloud texture features in satellite cloud images, deep convolutional neural networks extract and learn cloud features to realize typhoon recognition. The positioning of the boundary position is more time-saving and efficient than traditional identification methods. Zhou et al. [15] proposed a GCN-LSTM model framework, which uses satellite cloud images to classify and predict t1000phoons at different levels. The experimental results show that the algorithm of the model can effectively improve classification accuracy. Shi et al. [16] conducted a study on cloud type classification. Considering the unique characteristics of clouds, it is believed that local rich texture information may be more important than global layout information, so it is recommended to use convolution-based activation-based features for terrestrial cloud classification. Some scholars [17] have converted the typhoon identification problem into a target identification problem and realized how to locate the whole typhoon cloud system on the cloud map. This method achieves identification by abstracting the features of the typhoon region's satellite cloud map without analyzing the cloud system's characteristics.

At present, there are few practical applications related to typhoon cloud system monitoring using deep learning methods, so for the traditional mathematical morphology method to achieve a complex process, it is difficult to apply to the actual typhoon cloud system monitoring as well as the current deep learning-based practices mostly abstract typhoon features on a large range of cloud maps to achieve the localization of typhoon identification, without deep excavation of typhoon cloud system features, however, based on deep learning methods to extract Typhoon cloud system features to identify typhoon cloud system is rarely studied, this paper analyzes and integrates for typhoon cloud system features, and proposes a typhoon cloud system identification method based on two-dimensional convolutional neural network (CNN) and long short-term memory (LSTM) network. The contributions of this paper are summarized as follows:

1. To improve the recognition of typhoon cloud systems, this paper constructs a sample library with square neighborhood cloud blocks based on the data of fourteen channels of the FY-4A satellite and the brightness temperature difference of cloud tops and effectively fuses the typhoon spatial-spectral information.
2. In this paper, we propose a typhoon cloud system identification method based on CNN-LSTM networks to analyze the multidimensional features of typhoon cloud systems and automatically extract spectral and spatial features from cloud maps using hybrid models, avoiding relying on human experience to manually design and extract mathematical morphological features.
3. This paper uses AGRI (Advanced Geostationary Radiation Imager) data from (FY-4A) as the data source for the study of Guangdong Province, China. The experimental results show that the proposed CNN-LSTM model-based typhoon cloud system identification method can better distinguish typhoon areas from non-typhoon areas and achieve better identification results.

2 Methodology

2.1 Convolutional Neural Network

In recent years, CNN has been widely used in the field of image processing. The network model uses the gradient descent method to minimize the loss function to reversely adjust the weight parameters in the network layer by layer and improves the accuracy of the network through frequent iterative training [18, 19]. The basic structure of CNN consists of an input layer, a convolution layer, a pooling layer, a fully connected layer, and an output layer. Generally, several convolution layers and pooling layers are used, and the convolution layers and pooling layers are alternately set. The CNN structure is shown in Fig. 1.

Convolutional layer: The convolutional layer contains many feature maps. The function of the convolutional layer is to use the convolution kernel to perform the convolution operation on each convolutional image, and then use the activation function to perform nonlinear processing on the convolution result. The formula for the convolutional layer is as follows:

$$x_j^l = f(\sum_{i \in M_j} x_j^{l-1} w_{ij}^l + b_j^l) \tag{1}$$

where l represents the number of layers; w represents the convolution kernel; b represents the bias value; M_j represents the feature map of the middle layer; f represents the activation function.

Pooling layer: After the initial feature extraction of the convolution layer, the output feature map size may be too large, which will result in too many features in the output result. After inputting to the classifier, it may lead to over-fitting. After the convolutional layer, the pooling layer is connected to reduce the features through dimensionality reduction, retain the main features, increase the receptive field of the convolution kernel, and enhance the fitting ability.

Fully connected layer: As the last layer in the hidden layer of CNN, its output will be passed to the output layer. The main function is to integrate the highly abstracted features after multiple convolutions, and then normalize them. Both output a probability, and the subsequent classifiers are classified according to the probability obtained by the full connection.

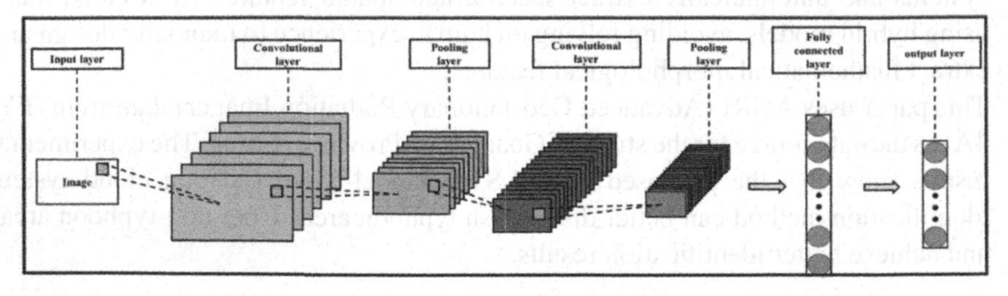

Fig. 1. Structure of the CNN (Color figure online)

2.2 Long Short Term Memory

LSTM network is an improved recurrent neural network (RNN), which can effectively overcome the gradient disappearance problem in RNN and can accurately model with short-term or long-term data [20, 21]. LSTM implements a more refined internal processing unit and adopts three gates to achieve efficient storage and update of contextual information. There are three types of gates in LSTM cells: input gates, forget gates, and output gates. The network basic unit is shown in Fig. 2. The feature information extracted by CNN is transmitted to the cell unit of LSTM, where the input x_t in the forget gate, the state memory unit C_{t-1}, and the intermediate output ht−1 jointly determine the forgetting part of the state memory unit. The x_t in the input gate is changed by the sigmoid and tanh functions to jointly determine the update information of the state memory unit. The intermediate output h_t is determined by the updated C_t and the output o_t. The calculation formula is as follows:

$$f_t = \sigma(W_f \cdot [h_{t-1}, x_t] + b_f) \tag{2}$$

$$i_t = \sigma(W_i \cdot [h_{t-1}, x_t] + b_i) \tag{3}$$

$$g_t = tanh(W_g \cdot [h_{t-1}, x_t] + b_g) \tag{4}$$

$$o_t = \sigma(W_o \cdot [h_{t-1}, x_t] + b_o) \tag{5}$$

$$C_t = g_t \odot i_t + C_{t-1} \odot f_t \tag{6}$$

$$h_t = o_t \cdot \tanh(C_t) \tag{7}$$

where f_t, i_t, g_t, o_t, h_t and C_t are the states of the forget gate, input gate, input node, output gate, intermediate output and state unit, respectively; W_f, W_i, W_g, W_o are the matrix weights of the corresponding gates; b_f, b_i, b_g, b_o are the bias terms of the corresponding gate and memory unit respectively; ⊙ represents the bitwise multiplication of elements in the vector; σ represents the change of the sigmoid function; tanh is the activation function.

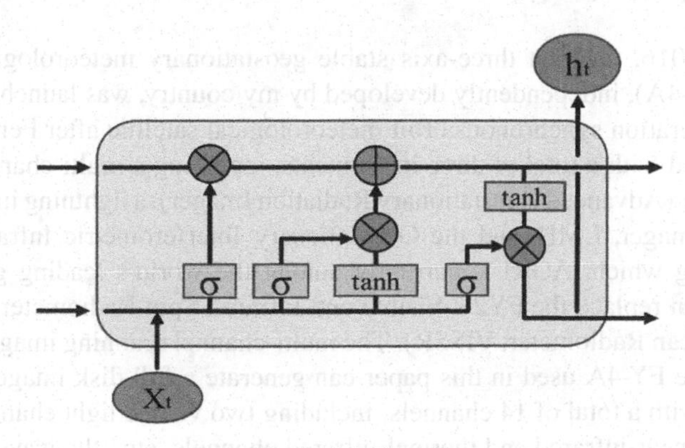

Fig. 2. LSTM cell

2.3 CNN-LSTM Combined Model

The C-LSTM (Convolutional-LSTM) combination model has been used in many fields such as text sentiment analysis [22]. Experiments have shown that CNN-LSTM performs better than CNN or LSTM alone. The overall process of the model is mainly divided into five steps: 1. Input the standardized data picture into the CNN convolution layer, and use the wide convolution kernel to extract image features adaptively. 2. The extracted features are subjected to the pooling operation of the maximum pooling layer to reduce the data dimension and retain the main feature information. 3. The standardized data images are serialized, and the time-dimensional information is extracted from the static images using long and short-term memory networks. 4. The ADD layer combines the described depth image features and spatial sequence features. 5. Use the Softmax activation function to classify Integration image features to complete image recognition. The network structure of the combined model is shown in Fig. 3 below. The detailed process is as follows:

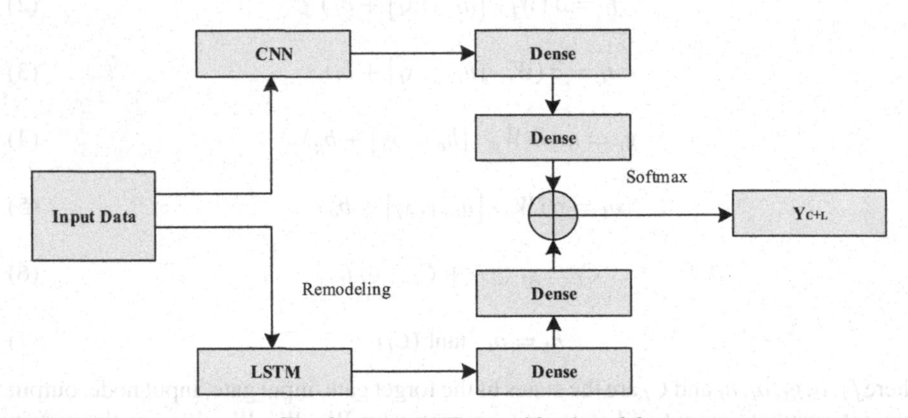

Fig. 3. CNN-LSTM combined model

3 Data Preprocessing

In December 2016, the first three-axis stable geostationary meteorological satellite, Fengyun-4 (FY-4A), independently developed by my country, was launched. FY-4A is the second-generation synchronous orbit meteorological satellite after Fengyun-2 (FY-2). It is equipped with a total of three instruments, including a multi-channel scanning radiation imager (Advanced Geostationary Radiation Imager), a lightning imager (Lighting Mapping Imager, LMI), and the Geostationary Interferometric Infrared Sounder (GIIRS), among which, AGRI is currently among the world's leading geostationary imagers, and can replace the FY2's Visible and Infrared Spin Radiometer (Visible and Infrared Spin Scan Radiometer, VISSR). The multi-channel scanning imaging radiometer AGRI on the FY-4A used in this paper can generate a full disk image observation every 15 min, with a total of 14 channels, including two visible light channels (red and blue light) and near-infrared and thermal infrared channels, etc., the wavelength range is from visible light to long-wave infrared (0.45–13.8 μm), and the spatial resolution of AGRI is 4 km, which meets the time resolution requirements of real-time dynamic monitoring of sand and dust. The data used are 4 km resolution China regional data and GEO calibration data with 14 channels in AGRI.

3.1 Cloud Feature Selection

By changing the HDF data format of FY-4 into a grayscale image format, the identification of typhoon cloud systems can usually be carried out according to the characteristics of cloud range size, shape, pixel distribution, spectral, and texture [23, 24].

The grayscale image representation information, the luminance ratio between different bands, and the color representation information in the satellite cloud image constitute the spectral characteristics of the cloud image [25, 26]. It has corresponding pixels corresponding to it in the image. Specifically, on the image of the converted infrared channel of FY-4A, since it reflects the temperature information, it essentially shows the temperature in the cloud image. Since the surface, ocean, and various cloud systems have different temperatures on the one hand, and on the other hand, and their vertical heights are also different, the absorbed light is also different. Furthermore, the emissivity of different light is also different in different objects, so the grayscale information fed back by the ocean, the surface and various cloud systems is not the same, so the spectral characteristics can be used as the main feature to distinguish the typhoon cloud system from the surface and ocean.

However, it is impossible to accurately distinguish typhoon cloud systems from other cloud systems by simply relying on spectral features. Therefore, texture and geometric features need to be introduced in the process of cloud feature selection. The texture in the satellite cloud image is composed of many indistinguishable particles in the smallest unit of the imaging resolution system, and many different cloud systems can be identified according to this feature of texture. Due to the differences in the intracloud circulation, atmospheric circulation, and water vapor content of various cloud systems, they usually have their texture structures. Visually, the texture features of cloud systems can be roughly divided into regular and irregular, smooth and rough, smooth and undulating, etc. Typhoon cloud systems have relatively smooth texture features and have a significant rotation coefficient. A rotating body, so texture features can be used as the main feature to distinguish other cloud systems. In addition, different cloud systems have different pixel distributions on satellite cloud maps. Typhoon cloud systems are expressed in the form of a very concentrated pixel distribution on meteorological satellite cloud maps.

This paper uses the 14 single spectral channel features in the FY-4A satellite cloud image data, and also selects 2 comprehensive channel spectral features Brightness Temperature Difference (BTD). BTD not only helps to improve the impact of geographical changes on cloud system identification, but also It can weaken the influence of the sun's altitude angle on the identification of cloud systems, so as to distinguish different cloud phases, thereby reducing the identification error of a single channel. Finally, the single pixel data in the channel data is converted into pixel block data that can contain texture features.

3.2 The Establishment of Sample Library

Combined with the satellite images obtained by the National Meteorological Satellite Meteorological Center in Guangdong and the early warning information of typhoon weather from the China Meteorological Administration information platform, four typical typhoon processes from 2020 to 2022 were determined, namely CHABA, Cempaka, Higos,and Nuri, of which FY-4A satellite data imaging time is 16:00 on July 2, 2022 (Beijing time), 14:00 on July 20, 2021, 8:00 on August 19, 2021, and 11:00 on June 14, 2020. In addition, referring to the classification of satellite cloud images by meteorological experts, texture features with a coverage range of 32 km * 32 km are generally selected. The coverage of a single pixel in the data used in this paper is 4 km * 4 km. To match it, an 8 * 8 square neighborhood sample (coverage range of 32 km * 32 km) is selected. Then, 16 spectral features are selected for each pixel point, the size of the cloud block sample data is 16 * 8 * 8, and finally, the sample data size is processed to 32 * 32. The flow chart of cloud block sample establishment is shown in Fig. 4 below.

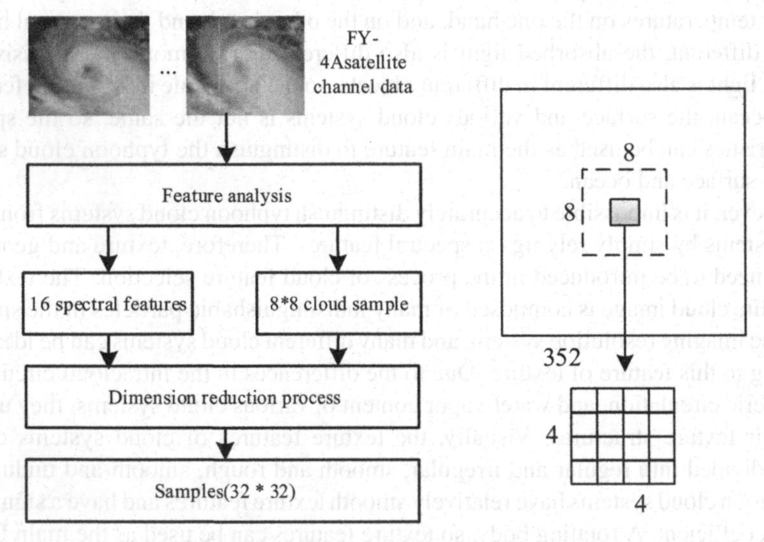

Fig. 4. The flow chart of cloud block samples

The construction of the sample library is mainly divided into three steps. The flow chart of the sample library establishment is shown in Fig. 5 below. The detailed steps are as follows:

(1) Cut out the study area and select areas with large typhoon frequency and typhoon range based on satellite images of the National Meteorological Satellite Meteorological Center and typhoon weather warning information on the China Meteorological Administration information platform, including Guangdong and adjacent sea areas.
(2) Mark the typhoon area, use the data of the first three channels of the multi-channel scanning imaging radiometer AGRI in the FY-4A to synthesize RGB images and

find the RGB images when the typhoon occurred by comparing the geographical and time information of the historical typhoon occurrence area. The satellite cloud map is split into typhoon area and non-typhoon area.

(3) Construct a data set. Using 16 satellite remote sensing data of typhoon region and non-typhoon region are integrated into multiple square neighborhood samples to obtain cloud block sample data of typhoon region and non-typhoon region and construct datasets of typhoon cloud block type and non-typhoon cloud block type for model training.

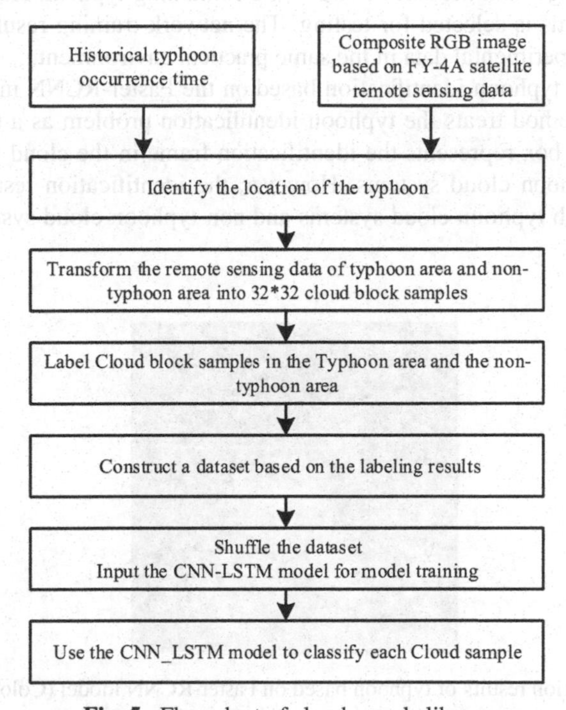

Fig. 5. Flow chart of cloud sample library

4 Analysis of Results

4.1 Experimental Data and Model Adjustment

The number of network layers, the number of filters, and the size of the filter in the CNN network require repeated experiments. The optimal hyperparameter settings of the network are selected according to the classification accuracy. By fixing the number of network layers and filters and changing the filter size step by step, the optimal filter size with the highest classification accuracy is obtained. The same fixed parameter debugging method is used to obtain other optimal hyperparameter settings. In the CNN-LSTM network model, the number of convolutional layer filters is 30, 40. The filter size is 3 * 3, the number of LSTM units is 128 parameters, the optimizer is set to Adam, the input image size is 32 * 32, the initial learning rate is 0.001, the decay rate is 0.1, the batch size is set to 64. The maximum epoch parameter is set to 200.

4.2 Comparative Experiment Analysis

To verify the recognition effect of the CNN-LSTM network model, the typhoon "Hagupit", which occurred on August 3, 2020, is selected as the test sample, and a satellite cloud image with the size of 352 * 352 containing typhoon cloud systems and other cloud systems is selected for testing. The network training results are obtained using the same experimental data in the same practical environment.

The results of typhoon identification based on the Faster-RCNN model are shown in Fig. 6. This method treats the typhoon identification problem as a target detection problem. The red box represents the identification frame in the cloud map to identify the localized typhoon cloud systems. However, the identification results are insufficient to distinguish typhoon cloud systems and non-typhoon cloud systems within the localization range.

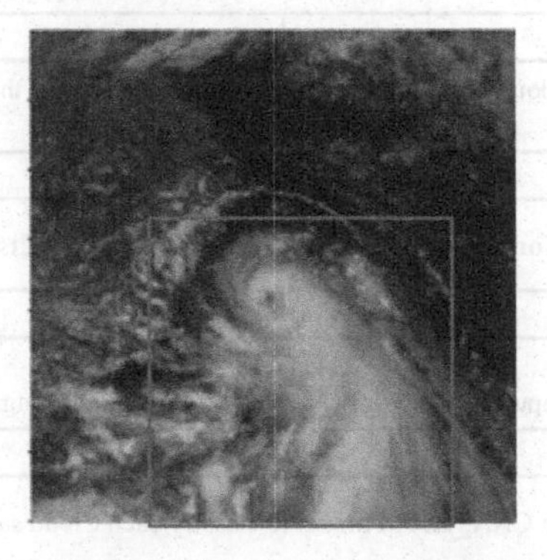

Fig. 6. Identification results of typhoon based on Faster-RCNN model (Color figure online)

The proposed method identifies typhoon cloud systems based on their spectral, textural, and pixel features, as well as the connectivity of the cloud system.

Firstly, the method of identifying typhoon cloud systems based on spectral features is used as a comparison method, using fourteen channels of FY-4A data and two integrated channels of spectral features bright temperature difference (BTD) as input data. This method identifies typhoon cloud systems and non-typhoon cloud systems based on the feature that typhoon cloud systems usually have large optical thickness and reflectivity of the cloud body and uses pixel points as the basic unit to identify typhoon cloud systems and non-typhoon cloud systems. The experimental results are shown in Fig. 1. The yellow pixel dots in the red box line are typhoon cloud systems, while the yellow pixel dots in the green box line are other cloud systems. It can be found that typhoon cloud systems can be effectively identified by using spectral features, but there is a large area of misidentified area, and the location of typhoon cloud systems cannot be accurately judged based on the characteristics of typhoon cloud system connectivity.

The proposed method introduces texture features based on spectral features and recognizes pixel blocks based on the CNN-LSTM model of the typhoon recognition method. The results are shown in Fig. 8. Compared with the method that introduces spectral information alone, the method can solve the problem of false recognition in small area regions, such as the green boxed area in the upper right corner of Fig. 7(b). It can effectively reduce the false recognition rate, such as the boxed area in the lower left corner of Fig. 7(b).

As shown in Fig. 8(a) and (b), the typhoon cloud system identification results of the CNN-LSTM network are compared with the CNN model identification results. The typhoon cloud system is determined based on RGB synthetic images, and pixel-by-pixel statistics analyze the typhoon cloud system monitored by both models. The results show that about 13% of the pixel blocks in the CNN model-based typhoon cloud system identification method are incorrectly identified. In comparison, about 9.5% of the pixel blocks in the CNN-LSTM model-based typhoon cloud system identification method are incorrectly identified. This shows that the CNN-LSTM model can better utilize the cloud system features and can effectively improve the recognition accuracy of the typhoon cloud system.

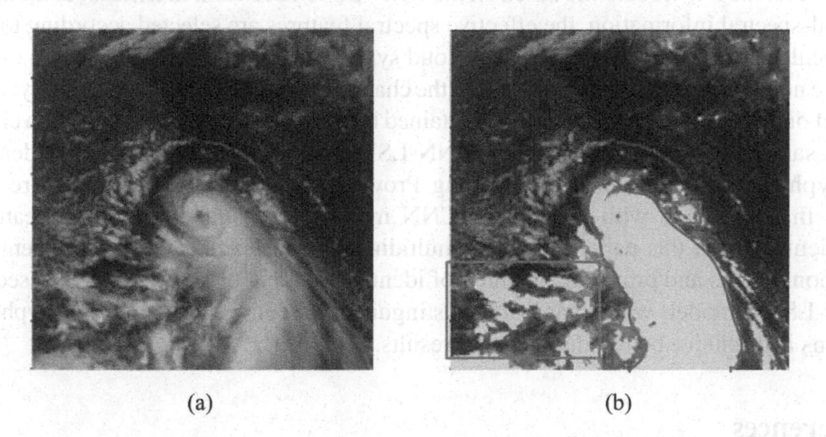

(a) (b)

Fig. 7. RGB composite image (a), Typhoon identification method based on spectral features (b)

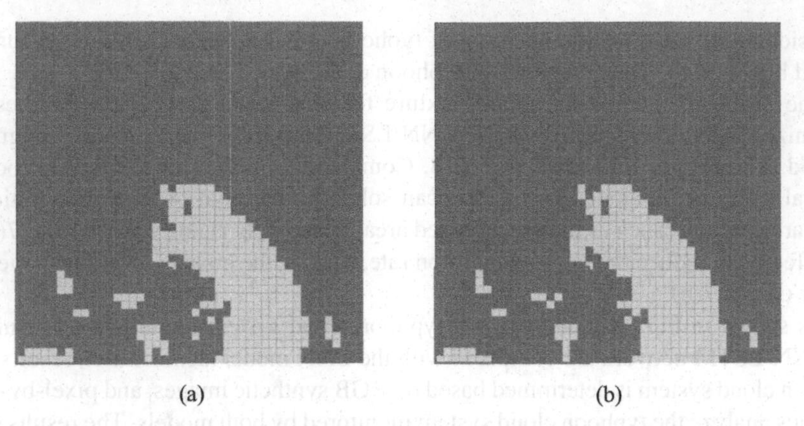

Fig. 8. Typhoon identification method based on spatial and spectral fusion features. CNN model (a), CNN-LSTM model (b)

5 Conclusion

To fully use the space-spectral information, this paper proposes a typhoon identification method for the FY-4A satellite based on the CNN-LSTM network. In terms of combining spatial-spectral information, the effective spectral features are selected according to the physical characteristics of the typhoon cloud system, and the spatial information of the square neighborhood is combined to form the characteristics of the typhoon cloud system. Based on the data of 14 bands in AGRI obtained by Fengyun-4 (FY-4A), a typhoon cloud block sample was constructed, and the CNN-LSTM network model was used to identify the typhoon cloud system in Guangdong Province, China. The experimental results show that compared with the Faster-RCNN method of abstracting typhoon features for identification, this paper mines the multidimensional features of cloud systems in typhoon regions and proposes a method of identifying typhoon cloud systems based on CNN-LSTM model, which can better distinguish typhoon regions from non-typhoon regions and achieve better identification results.

References

1. Ye, J., Lin, G., Zhang, M., Gao, L.: Hazard analysis of typhoon disaster-causing factors based on different landing paths: a case study of Fujian Province China. Nat. Hazards **100**(2), 811–828 (2020)
2. Guo, Y., Hou, Y., Liu, Z., Du, M.: Risk prediction of coastal hazards induced by Typhoon: a case study in the coastal region of Shenzhen, China. Remote Sens. **12**(11) (2020)
3. Wang, L., et al.: Special field measurement results of an onshore wind farm connected to power grid of Taiwan power system subject to Typhoon Matmo. IEEE Trans. Ind. **55**(1), 158–166 (2019)
4. Yuan, S., Quiring, S.M., Zhu, L., Huang, Y., Wang, J.: Development of a typhoon power outage model in Guangdong, China. Int. J. Electr. Power Energy Syst. **117** (2020)
5. Kossin, J.P., Olander, T.L., Knapp, K.R.: Trend analysis with a new global record of tropical cyclone intensity. J. Clim. **26**(24), 9960–9976 (2013)

6. Ruttgers, M., Jeon, S., Lee, S., You, D.: Prediction of typhoon track and intensity using a generative adversarial network with observational and meteorological data. IEEE Access **10**, 48434–48446 (2022)
7. Zhou, G., Xu, J., Qian, Q., Xu, Y.: Discriminating technique of typhoon rapid intensification trend based on artificial intelligence. Atmosphere (Basel) **13**(3) (2022)
8. Mei, W., Lien, C.C., Lin, I.I., Xie, S.P.: Tropical cyclone-induced ocean response: a comparative study of the South China Sea and tropical Northwest Pacific. J. Clim. **28**(15), 5952–5968 (2015)
9. Xingfa, G., Xudong, T.: Overview of China earth observation satellite programs. IEEE Geosci. Remote Sens. Mag. (2015)
10. Liu, Z., Zhou, L., Wu, B.: The center location of eyed typhoon in satellite cloud image. PR AI **16**(3), 334–337 (2003)
11. Li, H., Huang, X.Y., Qin, D.Y.: Research the artificial intelligent algorithm for positioning of eyed typhoon with high resolution satellite image. In: Proceedings of the 2012 5th International Joint Conference on Computational Sciences and Optimization, CSO 2012, pp. 889–891 (2012)
12. Qiao, W., Li, Y., Xu, Y., Hu, Q.: Typhoon center locating based on gray model and Chan-Vese model. Laser Infrared **42**(4), 443–447 (2012)
13. Liu, Y., Shao, L., Yang, W.: Automatic recognition tropical cyclone method based on satellite images. Mar. Forecast. **29**(1), 13–17 (2012)
14. Geng, X., Li, Z., Yang, X.: Tropical cyclone auto-recognition from stationary satellite imagery. J. Image Graph. **19**(6), 964–970 (2014)
15. Zhou, J., Xiang, J., Huang, S.: Classification and prediction of typhoon levels by satellite cloud pictures through GC–LSTM deep learning model. Sensors (Switzerland) **20**(18), 1–17 (2020)
16. Shi, C., Wang, C., Wang, Y., Xiao, B.: Deep convolutional activations-based features for ground-based cloud classification. IEEE Geosci. Remote Sens. Lett. **14**(6), 816–820 (2017)
17. Lu, X., Qian, Q., Wang, D., Zhou, G., Xu, J.: Intelligent technique of typhoon vortex detection based on object detection with deep learning of satellite. J. Trop. Meteorol. **38**(4), 492–501 (2022)
18. Yan, J., et al.: Frequency-domain decomposition and deep learning based solar PV power ultra-short-term forecasting model. IEEE Trans. Ind. Appl. **57**(4), 3282–3295 (2021)
19. Wang, F., Yu, Y., Zhang, Z., Li, J., Zhen, Z., Li, K.: Wavelet decomposition and convolutional LSTM networks based improved deep learning model for solar irradiance forecasting. Appl. Sci. **8**(8), 1–29 (2018)
20. Wang, F., Xuan, Z., Zhen, Z., Li, K., Wang, T., Shi, M.: A day-ahead PV power forecasting method based on LSTM-RNN model and time correlation modification under partial daily pattern prediction framework. Energy Convers. Manag. **212** (2020)
21. Zhen, Z., et al.: Ultra-short-term irradiance forecasting model based on ground-based cloud image and deep learning algorithm. IET Renew. Power Gener. 1–13 (2021)
22. Naqvi, U., Majid, A., Abbas, S.A.: UTSA: Urdu text sentiment analysis using deep learning methods. IEEE Access **9**, 114085–114094 (2021)
23. Liu, J., Wang, F., Zhen, Z.: Deep learning based visualized speed matrix forecasting model for wind power forecasting. In: 2020 IEEE Student Conference on Electric Machines and Systems, pp. 9–25 (2019)
24. Wang, F., et al.: A satellite image data based ultra-short-term solar PV power forecasting method considering cloud information from neighboring plant. Energy **238** (2021)
25. Si, Z., Yang, M., Yu, Y., Ding, T.: Photovoltaic power forecast based on satellite images considering effects of solar position. Appl. Energy. **302** (2021)
26. Zhao, X., Wei, H., Wang, H., Zhu, T., Zhang, K.: 3D-CNN-based feature extraction of ground-based cloud images for direct normal irradiance prediction. Sol. Energy **181**, 510–518 (2019)

Condition Assessment of Oil-Immersed Transformers Based on Fuzzy Theory and Combination Weighting of Least Squares

Wenqing Feng[1(✉)], Xinyu Pi[1], Lifu He[1], Ouyang Yi[1], Jing Luo[1], and Lingzhi Yi[2]

[1] State Key Laboratory of Disaster Prevention and Reduction for Power Grid Transmission and Distribution Equipment State Grid Hunan Electric Company Limited Disaster Prevention and Reduction Center Changsha, Changsha, China
wq_feng@whu.edu.cn

[2] School of Automation and Electronic Information of Xiangtan University, Xiangtan, China
ylzwyh@xtu.edu.cn

Abstract. Oil-immersed power transformer is the key equipment to maintain the safe and stable operation of the whole power system, it is very important to improve the accuracy of the condition assessment results to keep the power system running safely and stably. Aiming at the problems that the traditional condition evaluation model of oil immersed transformer is difficult to evaluate and the evaluation result is inaccurate. A condition assessment model of oil immersed power transformer based on fuzzy theory and combination weighting of least squares is proposed in this paper. The model combines subjective weightings with objective weightings, and uses the least square method to determine the subjective and objective weight coefficients, which reduces the error impact caused by artificial subjective determination. The final transformer condition assessment results are determined by the fuzzy theory method. Using the oil-immersed transformer test data provided by a power supply company as a sample for experimental verification and analysis. The results show that the method proposed in this paper can accurately evaluate the state of oil-immersed power transformers, which has certain practical significance in engineering.

Keywords: Analytic Hierarchy Process · Least Squares · Oil-immersed power transformer · Condition assessment

1 Introduction

Oil-immersed power transformer is the critical equipment in the whole power system. It is used to connect power transmission systems of different voltage levels. Its operation status determines whether the power system can operate safely and reliably. In domestic and foreign blackouts, regardless of natural disasters, equipment failures are the main cause of grid failures. Therefore, it is of great significance to evaluate the condition of oil immersed transformers and diagnose the faults of transformers with poor operating conditions in time to ensure the safe and stable operation of the whole power system.

H. Yang et al. (Eds.): SmartGIFT 2022, LNICST 483, pp. 130–141, 2023.
https://doi.org/10.1007/978-3-031-31733-0_12

Oil immersed power transformer is a very complex power equipment, and there are many possible problems in its operation. Therefore, there are many assessment indicators involved in its condition assessment, and some changes of each assessment indicator may have a certain impact on its healthy operation state. Therefore, when establishing the condition assessment model of oil immersed power transformer, the relationship between each evaluation indicators must be fully considered [1, 2]. In recent years, domestic and foreign researchers have done a lot of research work on state assessment. Literature [3] used AHP (Analytic Hierarchy Process, AHP) and rough set theory to establish hierarchical indicators for the condition assessment of transformers. Rough set theory data was not easy to deal with, and it was too subjective to determine the weight only by AHP method. Literature [4] used the principal component analysis weighting method to determine the weights of each assessment index, which improved the accuracy of the evaluation results to a certain extent, but only the principal component analysis method determines the weights, ignoring that some other secondary indicators also had a certain impact on the transformer state. Literature [5] used the combination of subjective weighting method and grey clustering to evaluate the transformer status, but it still did not avoid the contradiction of subjective weighting.

Due to the problems of difficult assessment and error of assessment results in the condition assessment of oil immersed power transformers, a condition assessment model of oil immersed power transformer based on fuzzy theory and combination weighting of least squares is proposed in this paper. The model combines subjective weightings with objective weightings, and uses the least square method to determine the subjective and objective weight coefficients. The final transformer condition assessment results are determined by the fuzzy theory method. The results show that the method proposed in this paper can accurately evaluate the state of oil-immersed power transformers, which has certain practical significance in engineering.

2 Establishment of Condition Assessment Model for Oil Immersed Transformer

2.1 Establishment of Condition Assessment Indicator System for Oil-Immersed Transformer

There are many indicators that affect the transformer state, so it is very important to select a comprehensive transformer state assessment indicator system. In order to meet the needs of transformer condition assessment, the assessment system of transformers established in this paper is a two-layer indicator system composed of first-level indicators and second-level indicators. And this paper divides the secondary indicators into three categories: "bigger is better", "smaller is better" and "intermediate optimal". Among them, the total hydrocarbon content, C_2H_2 content, furfural, H_2 content, relative CO rate, dielectric loss of oil, dielectric loss of winding, ground current of iron core, and service life are the smaller the better type, the working environment temperature is the intermediate optimal type, and the other indicators are the larger the better type [6–10].

By consulting relevant papers and materials on transformers [11, 12], different initial values and critical values are set according to different assessment indicators. After determining the assessment indicator system of transformer status, the classification of transformer health status is established. Transformer is an intelligent electrical equipment with a very complex structure. In order to reflect the status of the transformer in more detail, the oil-immersed power transformer condition assessment system established in this paper is shown in Table 1.

Table 1. Condition assessment system of oil-immersed power transformer.

First-level indicators	Second-level indicators	Initial values	Critical values
Test characteristic indicators (B1)	furfural, mg/l(B11)	0	0.2
	interfacial tension, Mn/m(B12)	45	19
	polymerisation degree(B13)	1000	250
DGA (B2)	H_2 content, ul/l(B21)	5.8	150
	total hydrocarbon content, l/l(B22)	5.59	150
	C_2H_2 content, ul/l(B23)	0	10
	CO relative production, %month(B24)	0	100
Inherent electrical characteristic indicators (B3)	breakdown voltage of oil, kv(B31)	60	35
	dielectric loss of oil, %(B32)	0.21	4
	dielectric loss of winding, %(B33)	0.15	0.6
	volume resistivity, 10^9 Ωm(B34)	65	5
	core earthing current, MA(B35)	10	100
Historical operating environment indicators (B4)	service years(B41)	0	30
	appearance factor(B42)	100	50
	operatingambient temperature(B43), °C	−30	40/−20

2.2 Transformer Assessment Indicator Set Data Preprocessing

Oil-immersed power transformer is a complex structure system with a large number of states and most of them are nonlinear [2, 10]. And the dimensions of different state variables are different, which makes it difficult to normalize the set of state variables. For the initial values and critical values of the condition assessment indicators of oil immersed power transformers described in Table 1, the concept of forward data normalization is introduced for each assessment indicators (The larger the normalized value, the better it is, and the smaller the value, the greater the deterioration), so as to realize the data preprocessing of the transformer condition assessment indicator.

For the larger, the better indicators:

$$x = \begin{cases} \frac{X - X_{down}}{X_{\max} - X_{down}} & X > X_{down} \\ 0 & X \leq X_{down} \end{cases} \tag{1}$$

For the intermediate optimal indicators:

$$x = \begin{cases} 1 - \frac{X_b - X}{X_b - X_{best}} & X_{best} < X < X_b \\ 1 - \frac{X - X_a}{X_{best} - X_a} & X_a < X < X_{best} \\ 0 & X \geq X_b \; or \; X \leq X_a \end{cases} \tag{2}$$

For the smaller, the better indicators:

$$x = \begin{cases} \frac{X_{up} - X}{X_{up} - 0} & 0 < X_{up} \\ 0 & X \geq X_{up} \end{cases} \tag{3}$$

where X is the actual test value of the evaluation index., X_{down} is the lower limit threshold of the larger and better type. Where X max is the maximum value of the index test data in the group, X_a and X_b are the upper and lower limit thresholds of the intermediate optimal type index, respectively, U_{best} is the optimal value of the intermediate optimal type indicator, X_{up} is the upper threshold of the smaller and better indicator. The normalization matrix can be obtained by Eqs. (1) to (3). $X = \left(x_{ij}\right)_{n \times m}$.

2.3 Establishment of Assessment Indicator Weight Matrix

Subjective Empowerment

According to the hierarchy defined by the transformer condition assessment system in Table 1, each indicator element forms a sub-domain with the lower-level indicator elements governed by that indicator element, where all elements form a judgment matrix [13, 14]. The significance of the constructs is quantified in terms of the relative importance among all sublevels of indicators governed by the upper-level indicators. In this paper, the judgment matrix D is constructed using the 1–9 scale method [15].

The weights of each dimension are the eigenvectors of the maximum characteristic root $\lambda_{\max}$ of the judgment matrix D. It is normalized and recorded as B.

$$DB = \lambda_{\max} B \tag{4}$$

The consistency validity of the matrix D is then expressed as:

$$f_{CI} = \frac{(\lambda_{\max} - n)}{(n - 1)} \tag{5}$$

Introduce of random consistency metrics f_{RI} to measure consistency metrics f_{CI}.Where f_{RI} is determined by the order of the matrix itself. RI = [0 0 0.58 0.90 1.12 1.24 1.32 1.41 1.45 1.49 1.51]. Define consistency ratio f_{CR} as the ratio of the two [16]:

$$f_{CR} = \frac{f_{CI}}{f_{RI}} \tag{6}$$

When $f_{CR} < 0.1$, it means the matrix D passes the consistency validity. After the judgment matrix D satisfies the consistency requirement, the resulting weight vector is A.

Objective Empowerment

The entropy weighting method can deeply reflect the differentiation ability of transformer condition assessment indexes and determine better weights. Empowerment is more objective, theoretically based, and credible. The entropy weighting algorithm is simple and does not require additional software analysis.

The entropy value of the j-th indicator is:

$$K_j = \frac{\sum_{i=1}^{n} v(i,j)\ln(i,j)}{\ln n} \tag{7}$$

where $v(i,j)$ is the characteristic weight of the i-th object under the j-th indicator.

$$v(i,j) = \frac{x^*(i,j)}{\sum_{i=1}^{n} x^*(i,j)} \tag{8}$$

The entropy weight of the j-th indicator is:

$$\omega_j = \frac{1 - k_j}{\sum_{j=1}^{m} \left(1 - k_j\right)} \tag{9}$$

Least Squares Combination Weighting to Determine Comprehensive Weights

Let the weights of each evaluation index obtained by the AHP method are $W_1 = [\omega_{11}, \omega_{12}, \cdots, \omega_{1m}]$. The objective weights obtained by the entropy method method are $W_2 = [\omega_{21}, \omega_{22}, \cdots, \omega_{2m}]$. Then the combined weights determined by least squares are $W = [\omega_1, \omega_2, \cdots, \omega_m]$. For the normalized standard matrix $X = \left(x_{ij}\right)_{n\times m}$. The evaluation value of the i-th sample is:

$$g_i = \sum_{j=1}^{m} \omega_j x_{ij} \text{ (i = 1, 2, } \cdots\text{, n)} \tag{10}$$

where ω_j is the combination weight of the j-th indicator of u, x_{ij} is the normalized value of the j-th indicator of the ith assessment series. In order to minimize the influence of human factors on the error in determining the subjective and objective weight coefficients.

$$\omega = diag\left[\sum_{i=1}^{n} x_{i1}^2, \sum_{i=1}^{n} x_{i2}^2, \cdots, \sum_{i=1}^{n} x_{m}^2\right] \tag{11}$$

2.4 The Realization of Condition Assessment Method of Fuzzy Comprehensive Evaluation

Step 1. Determination of index weight
The least squares method is used to determine the combination weights W. The weight vector of the first-level indicators is noted as $W = [\omega_1, \omega_2, \cdots, \omega_m]$, The weight vector of secondary indicators is noted as $W_i = [\omega_{i1}, \omega_{i2}, \cdots, \omega_{im}]$.

Step 2. The determination of the domain of judgment
The domain of the rating scale is a collection of the evaluation results of each evaluation index [17]. According to the characteristics of oil-immersed power transformers, the evaluation domain is divided into four levels: "good", "average", "warning" and "poor". Then the affiliation is determined, corresponding to $V = (V_1, V_2, V_3, V_4)$ (Table 2).

Table 2. Judging criteria description.

Judging level	Effects
V1	The transformer is operating normally. And there is no tendency of deterioration
V2	There are still a few evaluation factors outside the normal range, but the overall operation is still normal
V3	Nearly half of the transformer indicators have close to or even beyond the critical value, the transformer operating condition is poor, may not be normal operation, the need to organize maintenance as soon as possible
V4	Transformer operating condition is poor, may not be normal operation, need to immediately organize maintenance

Step 3. Fuzzy evaluation
Perform fuzzy evaluation to improve the reasonableness and accuracy of transformer condition assessment. Considering the respective characteristics of trapezoidal and triangular distributions. In this paper, we use the improved triangular trapezoidal distribution to determine the affiliation degree and obtain a reasonable distribution state.

$$r(v_1)\begin{cases} \frac{v-0.4}{0.2} & 0 \le v \le 0.4 \\ \frac{v-v_{i-1}}{v_i-v_{i-1}} & v_{i-1} \le v \le v_i \\ \frac{v-v_{i+1}}{(-1)^i(v_{i+1}-v_i)} & v_i \le v \le v_{i+1} \\ \frac{v-0.8}{0.2} & 0.8 \le v \le 1 \end{cases} \tag{12}$$

The single-factor evaluation matrix is obtained from the fuzzy relationship matrix. Based on the comprehensive weight values of the secondary index factors determined by the least squares combination assignment and the resulting evaluation level affiliation matrix, the evaluation model of the secondary index factors for transformer condition assessment is constructed.

$$B_i = W * R_I = [b_{i1}, b_{i2}, b_{i3}, b_{i4}] \tag{13}$$

where W is the set of comprehensive index weights, R_i is the fuzzy evaluation matrix of the ith scheme.

Based on the evaluation factor model of the secondary indexes and then determine the comprehensive evaluation matrix of the primary factors by Eq. (13). Then according to the principle of maximum subordination can determine the oil-immersed power transformer status evaluation results.

2.5 Establishment of Condition Assessment Model for Oil-Immersed Power Transformers

According to the above theoretical introduction, a condition assessment model of oil immersed power transformer based on fuzzy theory and combination weighting of least squares is constructed in this paper. As shown in Fig. 1.

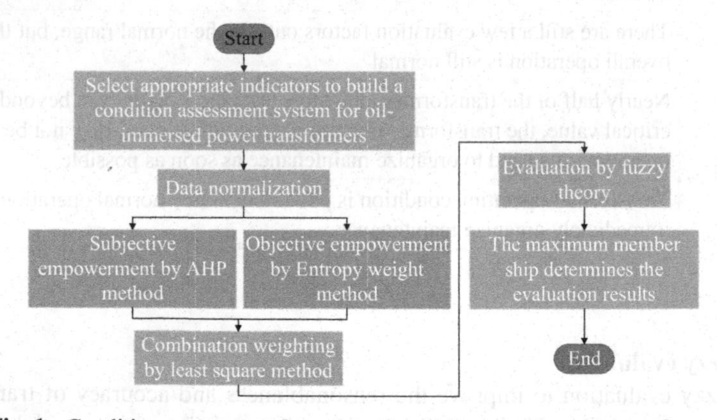

Fig. 1. Condition assessment flow chart for oil-immersed power transformers.

3 Example Analysis

3.1 Data Pre-processing

To verify the reliability and accuracy of the evaluation results of the condition assessment model of oil-immersed power transformers based on the combination of fuzzy theory method and least squares assignment. The actual test data of 3 groups of oil-immersed power transformers of 110 kV provided by a power supply station in Hubei Province is used as the test analysis. The data of each assessment index after data pre-processing in Sect. 2.2 are shown in Table 3.

Table 3. Normalized results of assessment metric.

	C1	C2	C3		C1	C2	C3		C1	C2	C3
B11	0.5	0.25	0.75	B23	0.2	0.3	0.35	B34	0.36	1	0.89
B12	1	0.76	0.85	B24	0.5	0.21	0.32	B35	0.2	0.34	0.55
B13	1	0.44	0.78	B31	1	0.98	0.25	B41	0.27	0.67	0.5
B21	0.87	0.77	0.49	B32	0.91	0.5	0.4	B42	0.53	0.87	1
B22	0.7	0.41	0.57	B33	0.67	0.6	0.17	B43	0.5	0.4	0.3

3.2 Least Squares Method to Determine the Value of Comprehensive Weights

Step 1. Subjective Empowerment
Relative ranking of importance of the 15 indicators in Table 1 based on the experience base of transformer experts. Hierarchical analysis was used to construct judgment matrices for the four first-level indicators and 15 second-level indicators according to the 1–9 scale method. The corresponding subjective weights are shown in Table 4.

Table 4. The corresponding subjective weights are shown

B11	B12	B13	B21	B22	B23	B24	B31
0.1220	0.2297	0.6483	0.1065	0.2775	0.0492	0.5668	0.4356
B32	B33	B34	B35	B41	B42	B43	
0.0986	0.2358	0.1939	0.0362	0.6144	0.1172	0.2684	

The weights of indicators B11–B15 are obtained as shown in Fig. 2. The consistency validity of the above five fuzzy judgment matrices according to the above. The corresponding compatibility indexes were 0.0064, 0.0018, 0.0340, 0.0075, 0.0368, all of which passed the consistency test.

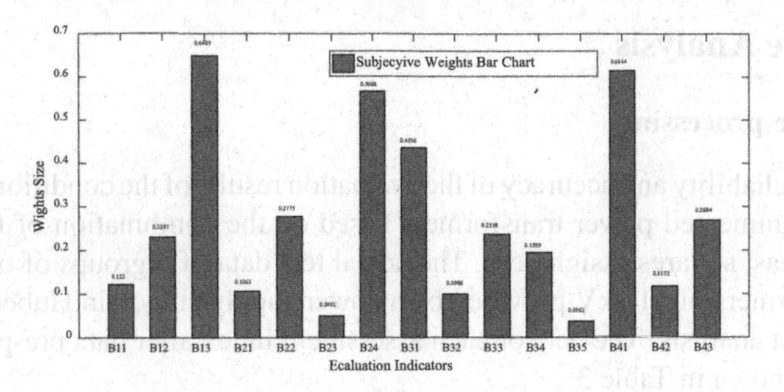

Fig. 2. Subjective weighting chart

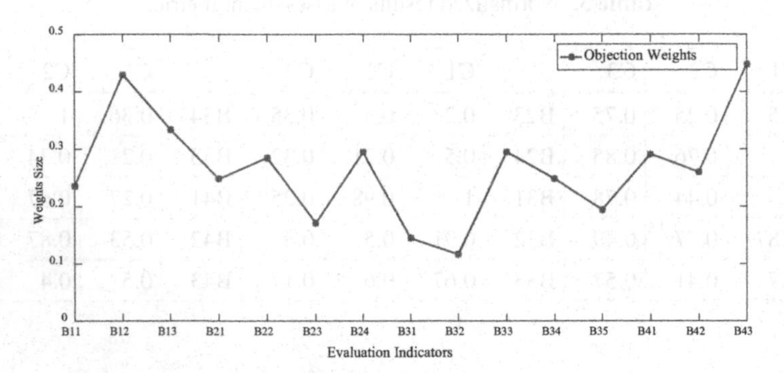

Fig. 3. Objective weighting chart

Step 2. Objective Empowerment

The entropy method can deeply reflect the differentiation ability of transformer status assessment indexes to make the assignment more objective and theoretically based. The weights obtained by applying the entropy weighting method to the 15 indicators in this paper are shown in Fig. 3.

Step 3. Least squares combination assignment

By using the least squares method to obtain the combination weights, the randomness of AHP and the one-sidedness of the entropy weight method can be eliminated as much as possible while maintaining the amount of information of subjective and objective weights. The weights obtained by the combined assignment method are shown in Table 5 (Figs. 4 and 5).

Table 5. .

Indicators	B11	B12	B13	B21	B22
Indicator weights	0.0451	0.0835	0.1237	0.0432	0.0747
Indicators	B23	B24	B31	B32	B33
Indicator weights	0.0244	0.1086	0.0667	0.0285	0.0701
Indicators	B34	B35	B41	B42	B43
Indicator weights	0.0583	0.0223	0.1124	0.0464	0.0921

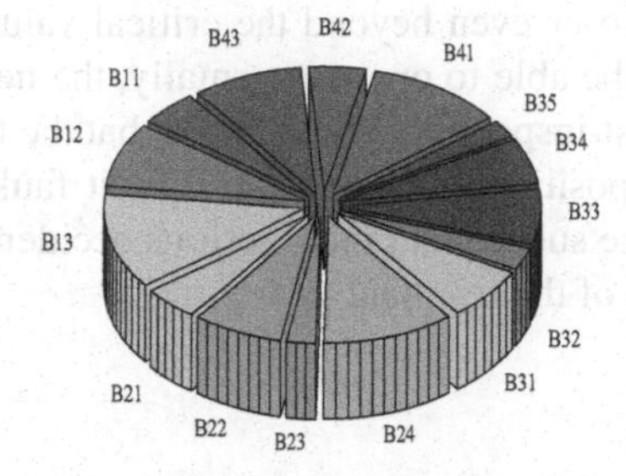

Fig. 4. Integrated weighting pie chart.

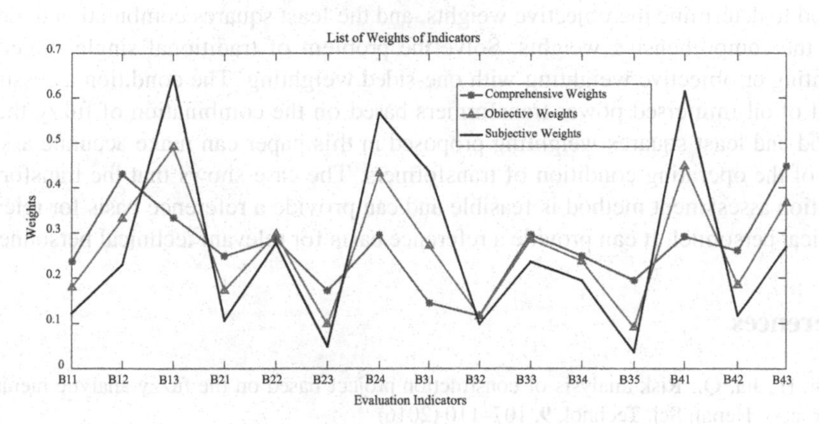

Fig. 5. Comparison of weights.

3.3 Transformer Fuzzy Theory Evaluation Results

According to Sect. 2.4 to obtain the assessment results of the three groups of transformer status, and in accordance with the principle of maximum subordination to determine the evaluation level. The results are shown in Table 6.

As can be seen from Table 6, the condition assessment result of the first transformer is "good", and the transformer is operating normally and there is no tendency of deterioration, only need to go for normal maintenance. The condition of the second transformer was assessed as "average", it shows that there are still a small number of assessment

Table 6. Status assessment results.

	Good	Average	Early Warning	Poor	Score	Results
C1	0.4406	0.3027	0.1804	0.0765	3.1078	Good
C2	0.2403	0.3564	0.2681	0.1354	2.8020	Average
C3	0.1900	0.1819	0.2398	0.3885	2.1739	Poor

factors that are outside the normal range, but the overall operation is still normal. The operating result of the third transformer is "poor", This means that many indicators of this transformer are close to or even beyond the critical value, transformer operating condition is poor, may not be able to operate normally, the need to immediately organize maintenance. After post-inspection, it was found that the transformer did have line inrush, voltage peak superposition and line short circuit faults, and there was also a certain insulation aging. The subsequent more serious accident was avoided only after the immediate organization of the overhaul.

4 Conclusion

The hierarchical analysis method is used to determine the subjective weights, the entropy method to determine the objective weights, and the least squares combination to determine the comprehensive weights. Solve the problem of traditional single subjective weighting or objective weighting with one-sided weighting. The condition assessment model of oil-immersed power transformers based on the combination of fuzzy theory method and least squares weighting proposed in this paper can make accurate assessment of the operating condition of transformers. The case shows that the transformer condition assessment method is feasible and can provide a reference basis for relevant technical personnel. It can provide a reference basis for relevant technical personnel.

References

1. Qi, H., Jia, Q.: Risk analysis of construction project based on the fuzzy analytic hierarchy process. Henan Sci. Technol. **9**, 107–110 (2016)
2. Zhou, L., Hu, T.: Multifactorial condition assessment for power transformers. IET Gener. Transm. Distrib. **14**(9), 1607–1615 (2020)
3. Peng, D.G., Chen, Y.W.: Research on assessment of transformer state using analytic hierarchy process and rough set theory. **55**(07), 150–157 (2019)
4. Borucki, S.: Diagnosis of technical condition of power transformers based on the analysis of vibroacoustic signals measured in transient operating conditions. IEEE Trans. Power Deliv. **27**(2), 670–676 (2012)
5. Liu, C.F., Luo, R.C.: Power transformer condition assessment based on AHP grey fixed-weight clustering. Electr. Power Autom. Equipment **33**(6), 104–107+133 (2013)
6. Dong, X.H., Zhang, X.M., Zheng, K.: Health status assessment of wind turbine based on combination weighting and cloud model. Acta ENERGIAE Solaris SINICA **39**(8), 2139–2146 (2018)

7. Cheng, H.B., He, Z.Y., He, H.T.: Comprehensive evaluation of health status of high-speed railway catenaries based on entropy weight. J. China Railway Soc. **36**(3), 19–24 (2014)
8. Dong, Y.X., Zhou, H.W.: Risk assessment of dam break in tailing pond based on game theory-finite cloud model. Water Resour. Power **38**(12), 75–78+168 (2020)
9. Arshad, M., Islam, S.M.: Significance of cellulose power transformer condition assessment. IEEE Trans. Dielectr. Electr. Insul. **27**(2), 1591–1598 (2011)
10. Sun, L., Ma, Z., Shang, Y., Liu, Y., Wu, G.: Research on multi-attribute decision-making in condition evaluation for power transformer using fuzzy AHP and modified weighted averaging combination. IET Gener. Transm. Distrib. **10**, 3855–3864 (2016)
11. Shi, S.W., Wang, K., Chen, L.: Power transformer status evaluation and warning based on fuzzy comprehensive evaluation and Bayes discrimination. Electr. Power Autom. Equipment **36**(09), 60–66 (2016)
12. Eschenroeder, A.Q., Faeder, E.J.: A Monte Carlo analysis of health risks from PCB-contaminated mineral oil transformer fires. Risk Anal. **8**, 291–297 (1988)
13. Yi, L.Z., Zhao, J., Yu, W., et al.: Health status evaluation of catenary based on normal fuzzy matter-element and game theory. Electron. Eng. Technol. **15**, 2373–2385 (2020)
14. Yi, C., Hui, M.: Multi-source information fusion for power transformer condition assessment. In: IEEE Power & Energy Society General Meeting, vol. 16, pp. 978–984 (2016)
15. Du, J., Sun, M.Y.: Research on multi-index evaluation method of transformer design scheme. Transformer **56**(7), 19–23 (2019)
16. Yi, L., Guo, Y., Liu, N., et al.: Health status sensing of catenary based on combination weighting and normal cloud model. Arab. J. Sci. Eng. **47**, 2835–2849 (2021)
17. Yuan, S.N., Qiang, M.S., Weng, Q.: Organizational effectiveness evaluation model for construction project based on fuzzy-analytic hierarchy process. J. Tsinghua Univ. **55**(6), 616–623 (2015)

Research Progress on On-Orbit Calibration of Infrared Sensors for Power Grid Fire Monitoring

Huyan Ziyu[1](✉), Wenqing Feng[2,3], Zhiqiang Zhang[1], Jing Luo[2,3], Xinyu Pi[2,3], Ouyang Yi[2,3], Lifu He[2,3], Qiming Cao[2,3], Fuzhou Duan[1], and Xiaoqin Luo[4]

[1] Capital Normal University, 105 West Third Ring Road North, Beijing, China
2210902162@cnu.edu.cn

[2] State Key Laboratory of Disaster Prevention and Reduction for Power Grid Transmission and Distribution Equipment, Changsha, China

[3] State Grid Hunan Electric Company Limited Disaster Prevention and Reduction Center, Changsha, China

[4] Beijing Zhongguancun Zhilian Safety Science Research Institute Co., Ltd., Beijing, China

Abstract. With the rapid development of China's economy and the increase in the value of industrial output, power consumption is increasing on a large scale. By the end of 2021, the domestic installed power generation capacity will be 2.38 billion kilowatts. With the continuous expansion of the scale of high-voltage and cross-regional power grids, transmission lines usually require passing through mountainous areas and agrarian areas, and the number of wildfires near the line corridor continues to increase. Compared with traditional observation methods such as unmanned aerial vehicles, ground online monitoring, and manual inspections, satellite remote sensing monitoring has a wider coverage and a shorter update cycle for large-scale data. Among them, the accurate targeting of satellite sensors is an important prerequisite and guarantee for the realization of wildfire detection, which can greatly enhance the ability to distinguish the accuracy of fires in remote sensing images. In this paper, based on the needs of power grid wildfire monitoring and the characteristics of satellite infrared sensors, by gathering, sorting, selecting and refining existing literature, the calibration methods of satellite infrared sensors are summarized and sorted, and the research is depicted in detail, progress.

Keywords: Power Grid · Wildfire Monitoring · Satellite · Infrared Calibration

1 Introduction

Wildfires refer to disasters that are difficult to control, spread and expand freely in forest land, and cause certain harm and loss to forests, forest ecosystems and humans. Due to the large scale of the transmission network and the fact that the transmission lines often pass through mountains, forests and other places in the fire-prone areas, the natural environment factors such as the aggravation of the global greenhouse effect and the

H. Yang et al. (Eds.): SmartGIFT 2022, LNICST 483, pp. 142–152, 2023.
https://doi.org/10.1007/978-3-031-31733-0_13

frequent occurrence of extreme weather and the human factors that people sacrifice to sacrifice and open up mountains and wastes due to customs Under the combined influence, the transmission lines are very vulnerable to fire hazards in forests, grasslands, and mountains, resulting in abnormal currents, trips and power outages. Because wildfires are difficult to control and are extremely harmful, it is a joint research of power grid managers and many scholars to find the fire source earlier, faster and more accurately, contain the fire in the "early stage", and reduce the economic losses caused by the fire subject [1].

Power grid security is related to people's lives. In order to ensure the safety and stability of power supply, it is necessary to conduct regular inspections of power transmission channels, master the operation of power grids and changes in power transmission channels, and timely discover and eliminate potential safety hazards in equipment and transmission lines. In the monitoring of mountain fires in power transmission lines, ground monitoring is a traditional detection method, mainly including ground patrol, watchtower monitoring, video monitoring, etc. [2, 3]. These methods have a small scope of application and high monitoring costs. The disadvantage of weak anti-interference.

However, satellite remote sensing technology has come into people's eyes due to its advantages of low observation cost, large observation range, diversified observation methods, and few restricted conditions [4]. With the advancement of space technology, the resolution of remote sensing satellite sensors has been greatly improved, and the combination of visible light band and non-visible light band has broken through the spectral range of human eye observation. Continuous and stable acquisition of information, wide observation range, many types of image information [5]. China's FY-3D/MERSI-II fire point observation products and the US's VNP14IMG fire point monitoring products based on VIIRS sensors play an important role in the world. When the satellite remote sensing sensor is observing the power grid fire, the high-precision geolocation accuracy is the basis for its application effectiveness and value, and the accurate calibration of the geometric parameters and radiation model of the remote sensing satellite imaging system is an essential key link [6]. In order to accurately identify mountain fire disasters in remote sensing image products, the radiation calibration and geometric calibration of satellite sensors are the basis and premise to ensure fire monitoring. Before the launch of remote sensing satellites, strict and comprehensive calibration and performance tests were carried out in the laboratory. However, due to factors such as vibration and acceleration during the launch process, on-orbit stress release and pollution, space environment, and detector decay, their performance will be affected. Different degrees of decay, calibration during orbital operation directly affects the quantitative application level of satellite remote sensing data. Therefore, after the satellite is launched, it is very important to give accurate and credible calibration coefficients through on-orbit radiation calibration and geometric calibration, which is very important for the application of various satellite products and is a key factor directly related to the application of satellite data.

2 On-Orbit Absolute Radiometric Calibration

When the user needs to calculate the spectral reflectance or spectral radiance of the ground object, or needs to compare the images obtained at different times and different sensors, the brightness gray value of the image must be converted into absolute radiance. This process is radiation. Target. The ultimate purpose of radiation calibration is to eliminate the error of the sensor itself and determine the accurate radiation value at the entrance of the sensor (Table 1).

Table 1. On-orbit absolute radiometric calibration methods.

lab calibration		
On-orbit absolute radiometric calibration method	On-board calibration	Based on on-board calibration equipment
		Based on stars and moon
	Based on the site calibration	reflectance-based method
		irradiance-based method
		radiance-based method
	intercalibration	

3 Progress in On-Orbit Absolute Radiometric Calibration

3.1 Lab Calibration

Lab calibration is the premise and guarantee of on-orbit radiation calibration. The sensor manufacturer needs to calibrate the sensor in the laboratory first, which is to verify whether the various indicators (response, signal-to-noise ratio, etc.) of the instrument meet the design requirements. Means, and also the initial data for the stability confirmation of these parameters during the sensor operation. At present, laboratory calibration equipment such as integrating sphere, standard lamp or solar light source or field calibration equipment is mainly used to calibrate the sensor to achieve radiation calibration [13]. The pre-launch calibration of SeaWiFs, FY series satellites and HJ satellites all use laboratory calibration [15].

3.2 On-Board Calibration

Based on on-board calibration equipment. The laboratory calibration environment is ideal, and the accuracy of the test instruments is high, so the calibration accuracy is high, and the basic parameters related to calibration can be provided. However, the satellite is affected by the impact of the launch and the radiation, collision, attenuation, etc. during operation, which makes the optical and electronic parameters of the remote sensor change, such as dark current [16], so many spaceborne remote sensors are equipped with calibration devices on the satellite to perform real-time calibration and long-term detection of the decay of the remote sensor response.

The EOS satellite is equipped with a medium-resolution imaging spectrometer MODIS [21], which adopts the calibration method based on "sun+diffuser reflector".

Images of targets such as land and ocean temperature, land surface cover, clouds, aerosols, water vapor, and fire are calibrated to an accuracy of about 2% in the solar reflectance spectrum. However, the disadvantage of the calibration method of the sun and the diffuse reflector is that the direct exposure of the diffuse reflector to the ultraviolet environment will cause serious attenuation of the di-directional reflectance of the diffuse reflector, that is, its performance becomes uncertain. And this calibration method is limited by the sun azimuth angle, which is not conducive to high-frequency calibration tasks [10].

TRUTHS by a research group led by Nigel Fox at NPL, UK. The plan establishes a radiation calibration system traceable to SI by performing absolute measurement of the 0.2–0.25 μm reflected solar radiation spectrum, thereby greatly improving the accuracy of remote sensing measurement. The laser diode is used as the monochromatic light source calibrated on the star, and the absolute low temperature radiometer is used as the traceable SI benchmark [17], which belongs to the method of "lamp+diffuse reflector".

The European Sentinel-2 satellite is equipped with a multi-spectral MSI imager, with a total of 13 multi-spectral spectra in the visible light to short-wave infrared spectrum, and push-broom imaging with a spatial resolution of 10–60 m and a width of 290 km. During absolute radiometric calibration, through the calibration shutter assembly CSM before the entrance pupil of the optical system of the remote sensor, the solar diffuse reflector and the rotating mechanism are used to switch to the calibration mode for full-aperture absolute radiometric calibration. The absolute radiometric calibration accuracy of the spectral band is about 3% [18, 19].

FY series meteorological satellite FY-3A was successfully launched on May 27, 2008. MERSI is a main instrument carried on it. It is mainly used for weather forecasting, natural disaster monitoring and global environmental change research. The design of the solar reflection band The onboard calibration accuracy is better than 5%, and it is used to monitor the relative attenuation trend of MERSI radiation response in the visible light shortwave infrared band. The onboard calibration of MERSI in the solar reflection band is mainly performed by the VOC visible infrared onboard calibrator and the SV cold sky observation. It consists of two parts and belongs to the integrating sphere method in the on-board calibration equipment.

A star- and moon-based approach. The change rate of solar radiation in the past 15 years does not exceed 0.2%, which can be regarded as a Lambertian light source with uniform and stable brightness. There is no atmosphere on the surface of the moon, and the moon is the brightest light source radiation except the sun when the sensor observes The moon's reflectivity changes less, and the stable reflection characteristics make the moon a reference radiation source for satellite sensor calibration.

MODIS [20], SeaWiFSl [21], Hyperionl [22], etc. have all carried out lunar observations. They compared the solar radiance data reflected from the observed lunar surface with the solar radiance data obtained through the diffuser to determine the solar diffuse On-orbit performance of the board. The CLARREO program in the United States has designed a lunar observation function to evaluate the stability of the visible short-wave infrared reference payload on-orbit calibration. The FY-3C medium-resolution spectral imager MERSI has added the function of observing the moon [23], and has carried out radiometric calibration in the visible and near-infrared bands, realizing the dynamic tracking and evaluation of the radiometric calibration coefficient of the MERSI solar reflection channel.

High-resolution commercial optical remote sensing satellites in Europe and the United States use the stable radiation characteristics of stars and the stable reflection characteristics of the moon to perform high-precision on-orbit calibration. In the north and south poles and the back-illuminated regions of the satellite's flight, each orbit has the opportunity to image and calibrate the stars of different magnitudes and the moon with different phase angles in the deep space. Using stellar point target calibration, it is necessary to select an appropriate magnitude. Since the point target imaging is greatly affected by discrete sampling, it is necessary to accurately estimate the sampling center. To use the moon for calibration, it is necessary to make a special radiation model for the moon. The WorldView-3 satellite, launched on August 13, 2014, has a full-color 0.31 m resolution, a visible-near-infrared multispectral resolution of 1.24 m, and a short-wave infrared multispectral resolution of 3.72 m. Using the satellite's own characteristics, the on-orbit absolute radiation calibration and relative radiation calibration are carried out with high precision and high frequency for the stars and the moon, and the accuracy of the absolute radiation calibration is better than 5% [11].

3.3 Based on the Site Calibration

The method based on on-board calibration equipment has the advantages of high calibration accuracy and is not affected by the surface and atmosphere. However, this method needs to carry on-board calibration equipment, which is difficult to achieve technically, and the cost of satellite development is high. The attenuation of the device itself will also reduce the accuracy of onboard calibration. The calibration method based on stars and moons has many limitations. First of all, it is necessary to select suitable stars and continuously observe, and build a special radiation model, and the point target imaging is greatly affected by the discrete sampling phase. Second, the satellite observation attitude requires more attention. The error in the short-wave infrared and thermal infrared bands is higher than that in the visible light band. Therefore, in the late 1970s and early 1980s, a group of scientists represented by Professor Slater of the United States proposed to use the large-scale, uniform and stable ground objects on the earth's surface to realize the on-orbit absolute radiation calibration of remote sensors [24] On-orbit field calibration is to carry out satellite-ground synchronization experiments at the ground radiation calibration field at the time of satellite transit, and use the surface and atmospheric parameters of the experimental site to realize the on-orbit radiation calibration of the sensor, which is the most widely used by remote sensing workers. Methods. There are three types of site calibration methods: reflectance-based method, irradiance-based method and radiance-based method.

The selection of the calibration site is based on the method focus of the calibration site. Since the last century, the United States has established the White Sands Calibration Test Site at the White Sands Missile Base WSMR (White Sands Missle Range) and the Edwards Air Force Base EAFB (Edwards Air Force Base). Sand Test Site) and Railroad Valley Playa Proving Ground. Subsequently, various countries have successively developed a number of radiometric calibration sites, including: the Newell test site in Canada, CNES (Centre National d'Etudes Spatiales) and INRA (Institut National de la Recherche

Agronomique) in France. The La Crau radiation correction field established near the city of Marseille in southeastern France, the radiation field established by the European Space Agency (ESA) in the Sahara Desert in Africa, and the Lake Frome radiation field established by Japan and Australia in northern Australia. The Dunhuang calibration field and the Qinghai Lake calibration field established in China have successfully achieved absolute radiation calibration of FY series satellites, HJ satellites, GF series satellites, HY series satellites and military satellites based on these two experimental sites.

Since 1987, researchers have carried out Landsat-5/TM, Landsat-7/ETM+, SPOT, MODIS, SeaWiFS, ALI, Hyperion, lkonos, ASTER, MISR and other sensors based on the White Sands calibration field in the United States. Field radiometric calibration, the on-orbit calibration coefficients of multiple sensors in different periods were obtained [25–28]. The La Crau test site based in French has completed the on-orbit calibration of sensors such as NOAA-14/AVHRR, Orbitview-2/SeaWIFS, SPOT-4/VGT, Landsat-5/TM and SPOT-2/HRV, and achieved comparative results. Good results [28, 29]. The Commonwealth Scientific and Industrial Research Organization (CSIRO) of Australia has achieved on-orbit calibration of EO-1/ALI and EO-1/Hyperion sensors based on calibration fields such as Tinga Tingana, Uardry and Lake Frome in Australia. Based on the standard results, the on-orbit radiation characteristics and application potential of the sensor were analyzed [30]. Based on the Railroad Valley Playa and Ivanpah Playa in the United States and the Tsukuba calibration field in Japan, the on-orbit field calibration of sensors such as Terra/ASTER, ADEOS/AVNIR and ADEOS/OCTS [31–33].

Every summer, the China Resources Satellite Application Center will test the four CCD sensors of HJ-1A/1B, the MUX sensor of ZY-3 01/02, the PMS sensor of ZY-3 02C, and the two PMS sensors of GF-1 at the Dunhuang calibration field every summer. Sensors, four WFV sensors of GF-1, two PMS sensors of GF-2, PAN and WFI sensors of CBERS 04, and PMS sensors of GF-4 are calibrated on-orbit, and the radiation calibration is collected through satellite-ground synchronization measurement. All the data required, and the calibration results will be published on its official website once a year for researchers to download and use.

The reflectance-based method is to measure the reflectivity factor of the ground target and atmospheric optical parameters (such as the optical thickness of the atmosphere, the water vapor content of the atmospheric column, etc.) synchronously when the satellite is over the top, and then use the atmospheric radiative transfer model to calculate the radiance value at the entrance pupil of the remote sensor [12]**, with high accuracy.** The correspondence between the radiance L at the entrance pupil and the apparent reflectance ρ at the top of the atmosphere is achieved in Eq. 1:

$$\rho = \frac{L \cdot d_{ES}^2 \cdot \pi}{E_{sun} \cdot \cos\theta_S} \tag{1}$$

where L is the apparent radiance at the top of the atmosphere, d_{ES} is the Sun-Earth distance expressed in 1AU at the time of imaging, E_{sun} is the average solar spectral radiance at a distance of 1AU outside the atmosphere, θ_S is the solar zenith angle (90°-Sun height angle).

The Mapping Satellite-1 sensor satellite uses the reflectivity-based method for on-orbit radiometric calibration, and the accuracy is better than 5% when compared with the measured reflectivity of the grassland [34].

The irradiance-based method, also known as the improved reflectance method, uses the downward diffusion and total radiance measured on the ground to determine the apparent reflectance at the height of the satellite remote sensor, and then determine the radiance at the entrance pupil of the remote sensor. This method uses an analytical approximation to calculate the reflectivity, which can greatly reduce computational time and computational complexity. The apparent reflectance can be expressed in Eq. 2 as [14]:

$$\rho^*(\theta_V, \theta_S, \varphi_V, \varphi_S) = \frac{\pi L_\lambda(\theta_V, \theta_S, \varphi_V - \varphi_S)}{E_{o\lambda}} \tag{2}$$

In the formula, $L_\lambda(\theta_V, \theta_S, \varphi_V - \varphi_S)$ is the radiance from the space measured by the satellite sensor, $E_{o\lambda}$ is the solar irradiance outside the atmosphere, $\theta_V, \varphi_V, \theta_S, \varphi_S$ represent the sensor observation and the day of the sun, respectively. Vertex and Azimuth.

The FY-1C meteorological satellite uses the irradiance-based method and uses the Dunhuang radiation correction field to perform absolute radiometric calibration on the six visible and near-infrared channels [14].

The radiance-based method uses a radiometer that has undergone strict spectrum and radiation calibration, and realizes a synchronous measurement similar to the observation geometry of a satellite remote sensor through an aviation platform. The radiance measured by the airborne radiometer is used as a known quantity to calibrate the remote sensor in flight. Finally, the error of the radiation correction coefficient is mainly based on the calibration error of the radiometer. It is only necessary to correct the atmosphere above the flight altitude, which avoids the correction error of the bottom atmosphere and is conducive to improving the accuracy. In Eq. 3, the correspondence between the image DN value and the apparent radiance L at the top of the atmosphere at the entrance pupil is achieved:

$$L = Gain * DN * \left(\frac{Abs\_factor}{\Delta\lambda}\right) + offset \tag{3}$$

In the formula, L is the apparent radiance at the top of the atmosphere, DN is the gray value of the image, Gain is the absolute scaling factor gain, Offset is the offset, and Abs_factor is the absolute scaling factor, which is related to the spectral response function of the remote sensor, imaging $\Delta\lambda$ is the effective bandwidth.

Intercalibration uses a sensor with complete calibration equipment as a reference, obtains the image pair imaged by the reference sensor and the sensor to be calibrated in the same area at the same time, performs spectral matching and other processing, and obtains the radiometric calibration coefficient of the sensor to be calibrated [9]**], the accuracy of which depends on the working quality of the reference satellite** [35].

The main step is to connect two satellite sensors that observe the same target at the same time and at the same angle, and they can be regarded as the same. The sensor to be calibrated can be calculated from the reflectivity of the reference satellite.

$$\rho_S = \frac{\pi \cdot L_S \cdot d^2}{E_S \cdot \cos\theta_S} \tag{4}$$

Among them, ρ is the apparent reflectivity of the sensor, L is the apparent radiance, d is the sun-earth distance factor, θ is the solar zenith angle, and E is the solar irradiance at the top of the atmosphere.

Chander took ETM+ as the reference sensor and the stable desert as the calibration field, realized the cross-radiation calibration of the TM sensor, and obtained the calibration attenuation relationship of the TM sensor through calculation. The scaling coefficients were revised to improve the scaling accuracy of the TM data [36]. Feng et al. chose the Dunhuang calibration field, and used Landsat-8/OLI as the reference sensor to perform cross-radiometric calibration on the four WFV sensors of GF-1; selected the BRDF product of MODIS to invert the reflectivity of the surface, and selected the gas of MODIS. The inversion of TOA reflectance of sol products has been verified, and the accuracy of cross-radiation calibration is controlled within 8% [37]. The cross-calibration method has the advantages of low calibration cost, high frequency, and can realize historical data calibration. However, the difficulty of cross-calibration is that the number of valid image pairs that can be obtained every year is very small, and it is difficult to achieve high-frequency calibration. Moreover, the accuracy of cross-calibration mainly depends on the accuracy of the reference source. In order to achieve high absolute radiation calibration accuracy, it is necessary to plan to develop very high-precision calibration satellites. The calibration is passed on to other satellites. This method is less economical.

4 Summary and Outlook

Due to the high-voltage power transmission process of the power grid, the transmission lines inevitably pass through uninhabited areas, especially in forest-rich areas, where wildfire disasters are more likely to occur, resulting in the loss of rights and interests of power grid operating companies and forest ecosystems. Based on the needs of power grid wildfire monitoring, this paper summarizes the status of satellite remote sensing methods for detecting wildfires in forests, and makes a detailed summary of the pre-orbit radiation calibration work of satellite sensors to monitor wildfires. The existing mainstream radiation calibration methods are mainly divided into The on-satellite calibration equipment method is based on the star and moon method, based on the calibration field method (which is divided into the reflectance method, the irradiance basis method and the radiance basis method based on the calibration field method), and the cross calibration method. At present, as the remote sensing sensors carried by emerging satellites have wider width, higher spatial resolution, and more sensor spectrums, their applications in fire detection and other fields are becoming more and more in-depth, and with the improvement of remote sensing image quality, popular machines Learning and deep learning algorithms can be applied to remote sensing images to further improve the accuracy of land object classification, disaster monitoring and other applications. The basis of all this is to calibrate the radiance at the entrance pupil of the satellite. Moreover, with the enhanced flexibility of the remote sensing satellite carrying platform, the joint calibration of multi-method and multi-source data can also be realized in the future.

References

1. Liu, M., et al.: Research on the risk assessment model and assessment method of transmission line mountain fire fault. Power Syst. Prot. Control **44**(06), 82–89 (2016)
2. Shen, X., Du, Y., Wang, R., Zhao, K., Qin, C.: Inclination measurement of transmission line towers based on ground-based lidar. J. Electron. Measur. Instrum. **31**(04), 516–521 (2017). https://doi.org/10.13382/j.jemi.2017.04.004
3. Zhang, Z., Zhang, C.: Transmission line wildfire monitoring scheme based on infrared detectors. Jiangsu Electr. Eng. **35**(03), 57–59+63 (2016). https://doi.org/10.19464/j.cnki.cn32-1541/tm.2016.03.015
4. Sun, M., Wang, Q., Song, Y., Chen, Y.: Satellite mountain fire monitoring and positioning of transmission lines based on image recognition technology. Autom. Technol. Appl. **38**(01), 65–69 (2019)
5. Cao, C.: Application of space remote sensing in power grid line safety inspection. Satellite Appl. (10), 22–25 (2021)
6. Man, Y., Chen, S.: Research progress on absolute radiation calibration of optical remote sensing satellites in orbit [J/OL]. China Space Science and Technology: 1–10 (2022). http://kns.cnki.net/kcms/detail/11.1859.V.20220513.2127.008.html
7. Tanaka, K., Okamura, Y., Mokuno, M., et al.: First year on-orbit calibration activities of SGLI on GCOM-C satellite. In: Earth Observing Missions and Sensors: Development, Implementation, and Characterization V, vol. 10781, pp. 101–110. SPIE (2018)
8. Palmer, J.M.: Calibration of satellite sensors in the thermal infrared. In: Infrared Technology XVIII, vol. 1762, pp. 108–117. SPIE (1993)
9. Wang, K.: Research on Jilin-1 Spectral Star Cross Calibration Method Based on Fengyun-3 Satellite. Jilin University (2022). https://doi.org/10.27162/d.cnki.gjlin.2022.000772
10. Xiong, X., Angal, A., Barnes, W.L., et al.: Updates of moderate resolution imaging spectroradiometer on-orbit calibration uncertainty assessments. J. Appl. Remote Sens. **12**(3), 034001 (2018)
11. Kuester, M., Ochoa, T.: Improvements in calibration, and validation of the absolute radiometric response of MAXAR earth-observing sensors. In: Joint Agency Commercial Imagery Evaluation (JACIE) Workshop, Reston, VA, USA (2019)
12. Dong, Y., Lv, J., Song, Q., et al.: Introduction to the principle and process of reflectivity-based radiation calibration. Sci. Technol. Innov. Appl. (24), 71–72 (2016)
13. Cui, Y.: Research on Spectral Imager Calibration Technology. Graduate School of Chinese Academy of Sciences (Xi'an Institute of Optics and Fine Mechanics) (2009)
14. Hu, X., Zhang, Y., Qiu, K.: Absolute radiometric calibration of visible and near-infrared channels of FY-1C meteorological satellite using irradiance-based method. J. Remote Sens. (06), 458–464 (2003)
15. Gao, H., Gu, X., Yu, T., Li, X., Gong, H., Li, J.: Research progress on visible and near-infrared channel radiation calibration of spaceborne optical remote sensors. Remote Sens. Inf. (04), 117–128 (2010)
16. Hu, Y.: Research on key technologies for quantitative measurement of wide-format high-resolution thermal imaging cameras. University of Chinese Academy of Sciences (Shanghai Institute of Technical Physics, Chinese Academy of Sciences) (2021). https://doi.org/10.27581/d.cnki.gksjw.2021.000030

17. Fox, N., Green, P.: Traceable radiometry underpinning terrestrial-and helio-studies (TRUTHS): an element of a space-based climate and calibration observatory. Remote Sens. **12**(15), 2400 (2020)
18. Martimort, P., Fernandez, V., Kirschner, V., et al.: Sentinel-2 MultiSpectral imager (MSI) and calibration/validation. In: 2012 IEEE International Geoscience and Remote Sensing Symposium, pp. 6999–7002. IEEE (2012)
19. Revel, C., Dick, A., Lonjou, V., et al.: Results from the Radiometric Absolute Calibration of Sentinen-2A and Sentinel-2B (2017)
20. Xiong, X., Sun, J.Q., Chiang, K., et al.: MODIS on-orbit characterization using the Moon. In: Sensors, Systems, and Next-Generation Satellites VI, vol. 4881, pp. 299–307. SPIE (2003)
21. Werij, H.G.C., Kruizinga, B., Olij, C., et al.: Calibration aspects of remote sensing spaceborne spectrometers. In: Earth Observing System, vol. 2820, pp. 126–137. SPIE (1996)
22. Barry, P., Segal, C., Pearlman, J., et al.: Hyperion data collection: performance assessment and science application. In: Proceedings of the IEEE Aerospace Conference, vol. 3, p. 3. IEEE (2002)
23. Wu, R., Zhang, P., Yang, Z., Hu, X., Ding, L., Chen, L.: Calibration, tracking and monitoring of remote sensors based on lunar reflection. J. Remote Sens. **20**(02), 278–289 (2016)
24. Holm, R.G.: The Absolute Radiometric Calibration of Space-Based Sensors. The University of Arizona (1987)
25. Slater, P.N., Biggar, S.F., Holm, R.G., et al.: Reflectance-and radiance-based methods for the in-flight absolute calibration of multispectral sensors. Remote Sens. Environ. **22**(1), 11–37 (1987)
26. Biggar, S.F., Slater, P.N., Gellman, D.I.: Uncertainties in the in-flight calibration of sensors with reference to measured ground sites in the 0.4–1.1 μm range. Remote Sens. Environ. **48**(2), 245–252 (1994)
27. Biggar, S.F., Dinguirard, M.C., Gellman, D.I., et al.: Radiometric calibration of SPOT 2 HRV: a comparison of three methods. In: Calibration of Passive Remote Observing Optical and Microwave Instrumentation, vol. 1493, pp. 155–162. SPIE (1991)
28. Thome, K.J., Arai, K., Tsuchida, S., et al.: Vicarious calibration of ASTER via the reflectance-based approach. IEEE Trans. Geosci. Remote Sens. **46**(10), 3285–3295 (2008)
29. Teillet, P.M., Fedosejevs, G., Gauthier, R.P., et al.: Radiometric calibration of multiple Earth observation sensors using airborne hyperspectral data at the Newell County rangeland test site. In: Earth Observing Systems IV, vol. 3750, pp. 470-481. SPIE (1999)
30. Barry, P., Jarecke, P.J., Pearlman, J., et al.: Radiometric calibration validation of the Hyperion instrument using ground truth at a site in Lake Frome, Australia. In: Imaging Spectrometry VII, vol. 4480, pp. 242–246. SPIE (2002)
31. Arai, K.: Atmospheric correction and vicarious calibration of ADEOS/AVNIR and OCTS. Adv. Space Res. **25**(5), 1051–1054 (2000)
32. Arai, K.: Early results from the vicarious calibration of Terra/ASTER/SWIR. Adv. Space Res. **28**(1), 77–82 (2001)
33. Arai, K.: Vicarious calibration of the solar reflection channels of radiometers onboard satellites through the field campaigns with measurements of refractive index and size distribution of aerosols. Adv. Space Res. **39**(1), 13–19 (2007)
34. Huang, H., Yi, W., Qiao, Y., Du, L.: On-orbit radiometric calibration method of "Tianhui-1" satellite. J. Remote Sens. **16**(S1), 22–27 (2012)
35. Yang, A.: Research on the VNIR band cross-radiometric calibration method and system of domestic optical satellite remote sensing data. University of Chinese Academy of Sciences (Institute of Remote Sensing and Digital Earth, Chinese Academy of Sciences) (2017)
36. Chander, G., Markham, B.L., Barsi, J.A.: Revised Landsat-5 thematic mapper radiometric calibration. IEEE Geosci. Remote Sens. Lett. **4**(3), 490–494 (2007)

37. Feng, L., Li, J., Gong, W., et al.: Radiometric cross-calibration of Gaofen-1 WFV cameras using Landsat-8 OLI images: a solution for large view angle associated problems. Remote Sens. Environ. **174**, 56–68 (2016)
38. Xu, Y.: Analysis of the application status and development trend of photogrammetry and remote sensing technology. Sci. Technol. Inf. **15**(14), 49–50 (2017)
39. Fan, G., et al.: Research and application of satellite remote sensing monitoring of fire around transmission lines. Mineral Explor. **12**(08), 1844–1851 (2021)
40. Zhang, B.: Current situation and future prospects of contemporary remote sensing technology development. Proc. Chin. Acad. Sci. **32**(07), 774–784 (2017). https://doi.org/10.16418/j.issn.1000-3045.2017.07.012
41. Lin, Y., et al.: A review of forest fire monitoring technology along transmission lines. Forestry Environ. Sci. **35**(05), 122–126 (2019)
42. Zhang, X.: Detection of land cover changes in power transmission corridors and assessment of wildfire susceptibility based on satellite remote sensing. Wuhan University (2017)
43. Pearlman, J.S., Barry, P.S., Segal, C.C., et al.: Hyperion, a space-based imaging spectrometer. IEEE Trans. Geosci. Remote Sens. **41**(6), 1160–1173 (2003)
44. Zhou, G., He, J., Zhao, H., et al.: Cross-radiometric calibration of spaceborne imaging spectrometer based on precise spectral response matching. Spectrosc. Spectral Anal. **32**(12), 3416–3421 (2012)
45. Goetz, A.F.H., Vane, G., Solomon, J.E., et al.: Imaging spectrometry for earth remote sensing. Science **228**(4704), 1147–1153 (1985)
46. Hochberg, E.J., Roberts, D.A., Dennison, P.E., et al.: Special issue on the Hyperspectral Infrared Imager (HyspIRI): emerging science in terrestrial and aquatic ecology, radiation balance and hazards. Remote Sens. Environ. **167**, 1–5 (2015)
47. Tian, C.: Research and Analysis of Gaofen-4 Cross-radiation Calibration Technology. Nanjing University of Information Technology (2020)
48. Chen, H., Li, S., Si, X., et al.: On-orbit absolute radiometric calibration of multispectral cameras based on gray-scale targets. J. Remote Sens. (S1), 28–34 (2012)
49. Helder, D., Thome, K.J., Mishra, N., et al.: Absolute radiometric calibration of Landsat using a pseudo invariant calibration site. IEEE Trans. Geosci. Remote Sens. **51**(3), 1360–1369 (2013)
50. Angal, A., Xiong, X., Wu, A., et al.: Multitemporal cross-calibration of the Terra MODIS and Landsat 7 ETM+ reflective solar bands. IEEE Trans. Geosci. Remote Sens. **51**(4), 1870–1882 (2013)
51. Shrestha, M., Hasan, M.N., Leigh, L., et al.: Extended pseudo invariant calibration sites (EPICS) for the cross-calibration of optical satellite sensors. Remote Sens. **11**(14), 1676 (2019)
52. Liu, Q., Yu, T., Gao, H.: Radiometric cross-calibration of GF-1 PMS sensor with a new BRDF model. Remote Sens. **11**(6), 707 (2019)
53. Zhang, Y.: Research on cross-calibration of multispectral cameras of ZY-3 satellite. Chang'an University (2014)
54. Li, J., Wang, R., Zhu, L., et al.: On-orbit geometric calibration of "Tianhui-1" satellite mapping camera. J. Remote Sens. (S1), 35–39 (2012)
55. Wang, M., Tian, Y., Cheng, Y.: Current status and prospect of on-orbit geometric calibration of high-resolution optical remote sensing satellites. J. Wuhan Univ. Inf. Sci. Ed. **42**(11), 1580–1588 (2017)

Design and Research of Segmented Ice Melting System for 10 kV Distribution Network

Xiang Cai(✉), Qingjun Huang, Yuan Zhu, Xiudong Zhou, Shiyi Sun, and Zehong Chen

State Key Laboratory of Disaster Prevention and Reduction for Power Grid Transmission and Distribution Equipment, State Grid Hunan Electric Company Limited Disaster Prevention and Reduction Center, Changsha 410129, China
941668991@qq.com

Abstract. The ice disaster which lasted for dozens of days in 2008 caused serious damage to China's power grid, and the existing ice melting system is difficult to meet all the ice melting needs. In order to solve the above problems, a new segmented AC ice melting system is developed in this paper. Firstly, the structure of segmented AC ice melting system is proposed, which can directly extract electricity from 10 kV lines to realize ice melting at the end of the line or multi-branch lines. Then, the principle of segmented ice melting system is analyzed, and the ice melting voltage, current and system capacity are defined. After that, the detailed electrical and geometric parameters of each part of the system are designed. Finally, the detailed melting scheme of the segmented melting system is developed. This study is of great significance to solve the icing problem at the end of the line and improve the economy and flexibility of ice melting.

Keywords: Ac ice melting system · Sectional type · Ice melting scheme

1 Introduction

China has a vast territory, which is located in the middle latitudes, and the climate is humid, which leads to the icing of transmission lines in winter. According to statistics, in the severe ice and snow disasters that occurred in 2008, the icing period of the lines lasted for dozens of days, resulting in more than 30,000 power outages across the country, and power outages occurred in more than 100 cities and counties, resulting in serious economic losses and seriously affecting the quality of life of the people [1–3]. Therefore, how to solve the problem of line icing, improve the reliability of power supply and reduce the occurrence of tower breakage accidents is a key research direction at present [4–6].

Aiming at the problem of transmission line icing, scholars at home and abroad mainly carry out research in the fields of mechanical deicing, thermal deicing and so on. Due to the shortcomings of mechanical deicing, such as low melting efficiency, easy to damage wires and so on, there are many researches at present, and the more widely used deicing method is thermal deicing. The ways of thermal deicing include using laser irradiation to

H. Yang et al. (Eds.): SmartGIFT 2022, LNICST 483, pp. 153–162, 2023.
https://doi.org/10.1007/978-3-031-31733-0_14

flow the wire to produce Joule heat and so on. On the one hand, laser irradiation requires large laser power, high-power laser device is difficult to develop, and low laser power will lead to low ice melting efficiency [7]. Therefore, the research of scholars at home and abroad mainly focuses on putting a large current into the transmission line, making the conductor produce joule heat, so as to realize the line deicing and deicing.

In the aspect of Joule thermal deicing, scholars mainly studied the fixed melting system and mobile melting system according to the arrangement and structure of the system. The fixed ice melting system is studied in reference [8–10], the composition of the system is studied and related tests are carried out in paper [8], and the ice melting experiments are carried out in paper [9, 10] based on the fixed ice melting system. However, the fixed ice melting system can only be built inside the substation and can only meet the ice melting needs of a certain substation. In order to solve the problem of multi-point icing, a large number of systems need to be arranged, and the economy is difficult to meet the requirements. In addition, part of the icing section is located at the end of the line, and the fixed ice melting system can not meet the ice melting demand. Literature [11–13] has carried out research on mobile ice melting system, which is deployed on large vehicles to solve the problem of ice melting in multi-point icing areas. However, the mobile ice melting system needs to be equipped with a special generator set to provide the power needed for ice melting, and the ice melting power supply occupies a large amount of volume of the whole system. According to the comprehensive research of scholars, there is still a lack of an economical ice-melting system and scheme that can meet the needs of multi-point ice melting.

In this paper, a segmented ice melting system is designed and studied, which takes electricity directly from the 10 kV distribution network and installs the system near the line that needs ice melting. No need to configure the power car, equipped with multiple groups of ice-melting short switch can realize the ice-melting of multiple lines. It not only solves the needs of multi-point ice melting and ice melting at the end of the line, but also improves the economy of ice melting and saves social resources.

2 Structure of Segmented Ice Melting System

The structure of the segmented ice melting system is shown in Fig. 1, which can be seen in Fig. 1. The segmented ice melting system consists of six parts, namely, multi-position ice melting transformer, measurement and protection unit, column switch, input isolation knife gate, output isolation knife gate and container shell.

10 kV transmission line, through the column switch, through the input isolation switch, connected with the multi-gear ice-melting transformer. The multi-gear ice-melting transformer is connected to the transmission line through the output switch. At this time, the end of the transmission line is short-connected to form an ice-melting current loop, and the current flows through the wire to produce joule heat to realize the ice melting of the transmission line. In this process, the measurement and protection unit monitors the voltage at both ends of the side of the multi-position ice-melting transformer and the current flowing through the side of the transformer in real time, and trips when overvoltage and overcurrent are detected to protect the multi-position ice-melting transformer.

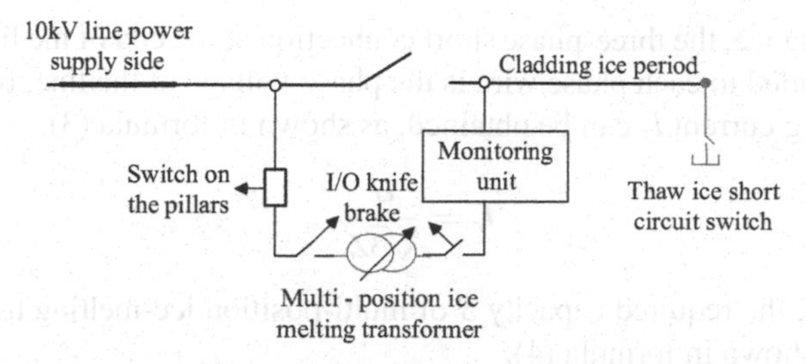

Fig. 1. Structure diagram of segmented ice melting system

3 Principle of Segmented Ice Melting System

The single-line equivalent circuit diagram of the segmented ice melting system is shown in Fig. 2. Figure 2 is a single line diagram, and the actual ice melting adopts three-phase AC melting. In Fig. 2, U_0 represents the primary input line voltage of the ice-melting transformer, U represents the secondary output line voltage, R represents the line resistance and X represents the line reactance.

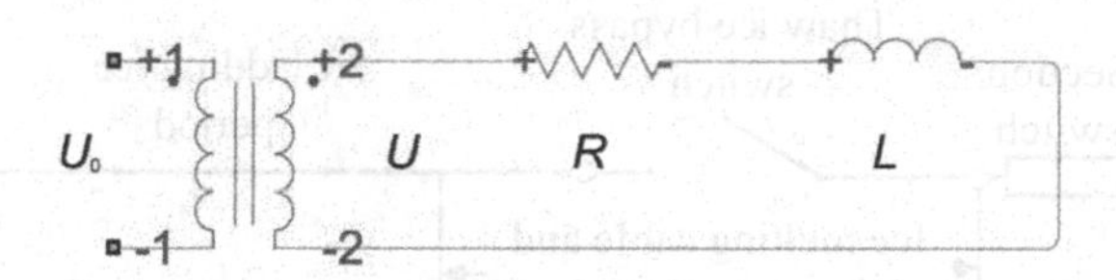

Fig. 2. Equivalent circuit diagram of segmented ice melting single wire

The multi-position ice-melting transformer takes electricity directly from the line, that is, the input voltage of the ice-melting transformer is the line voltage U_0 of the transmission line. Different transmission line conductors can withstand different ice-melting currents. Taking LGJ-70 as an example, the minimum ice-melting current is 290 A and the maximum ice-melting current is 420 A. At the same time, the unit resistance Z_d of the wire can be known from the wire type, as shown in formula (1).

$$Z_d = R + jX \tag{1}$$

In formula (1), R represents the resistance per unit length of the wire, and X represents the reactance per unit length of the wire. According to the actual icing area, we can know the actual melting line length, recorded as L. The single-phase resistance Z of the ice-melting circuit can be obtained, as shown in formula (2).

$$Z = L \cdot Z_d \tag{2}$$

According to formula (2) and the range of deicing current of the wire, the actual deicing voltage U can be selected.

When melting ice, the three-phase short connection at the end of the line is required, so the voltage added to each phase wire is the phase voltage of the line, from which the actual ice melting current I_r can be obtained, as shown in formula (3).

$$I_r = \frac{U}{\sqrt{3}Z} \tag{3}$$

Furthermore, the required capacity S of multi-position ice-melting transformer can be obtained, as shown in formula (4).

$$S = \sqrt{3}U \cdot I_r \tag{4}$$

4 Composition and Parameters of Segmented Ice Melting System

The detailed schematic diagram of the segment melting system is shown in Fig. 3. It can be seen from Fig. 3 that the structure of the segmented melting system is complex. The parameters of each component of the system are described below.

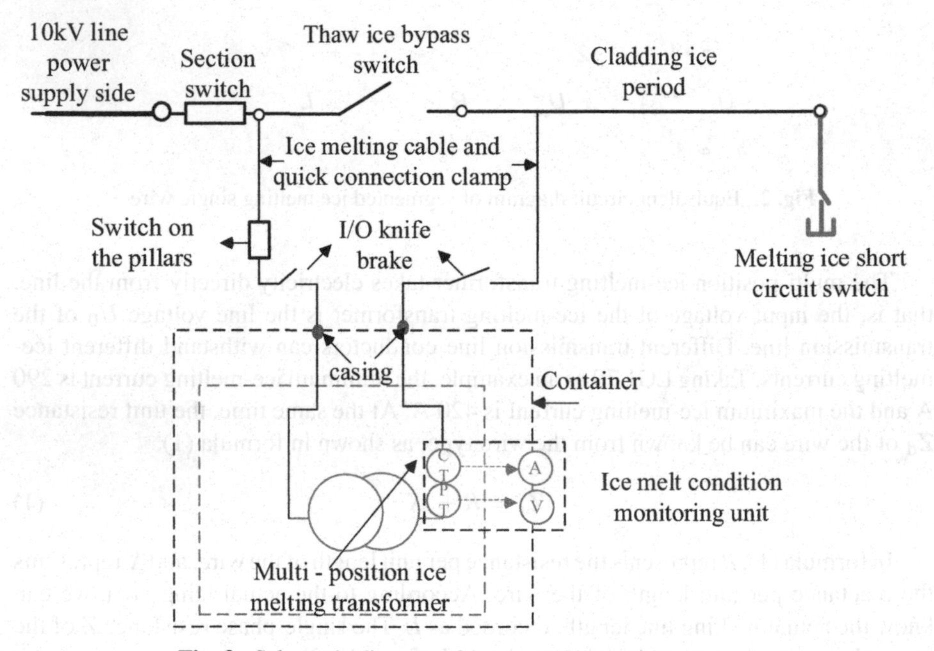

Fig. 3. Schematic diagram of segmented ice melting system

4.1 Parameter Design of Multi-position Transformer

Gear ice-melting transformer is the most important component in the segmented ice-melting system. The transformer gear is the most important parameter of the transformer, and the transformer gear takes into account the ice melting needs of each wire type. Therefore, it is necessary to calculate the minimum ice melting current and maximum ice melting current of each type of wire.

(1) **Analysis of minimum Ice melting current of conductor**

The calculation formula of the minimum melting current of wire is shown in formula (5).

$$I_{\min} = \sqrt{\frac{\Delta t}{R_0(R_{T0} + R_{T1})}} \tag{5}$$

In formula (5), $I_{\min}$ represents the minimum ice melting current (A); R_0 represents the resistance per unit length of the wire at 0 °C (Ω / m); Δt represents the difference between the conductor temperature and the external temperature (°C), R_{T0} represents the equivalent ice conduction thermal resistance (°C·cm/W), and R_{T1} represents the equivalent thermal resistance of convection and radiation. The calculation formulas of R_{T0} and R_{T1} are shown in formula (6) and formula (7), respectively.

$$R_{T0} = \frac{\lg D/d}{273\delta} \tag{6}$$

$$\begin{cases} R_{T1} = \frac{1}{0.09D+0.22+0.73(VD)^{2/3}}(glaze) \\ R_{T1} = \frac{1}{0.04D+0.73(VD)^{3/4}}(rime) \end{cases} \tag{7}$$

In formula (6), D represents the outer diameter of the iced wire (cm), d represents the wire diameter (cm), δ represents the thermal conductivity (W/cm °C), and in formula (7), V represents the external wind speed (m). With the simultaneous formula (5)–(7), the minimum ice melting current can be obtained when the surface of the wire is 0 °C .

(2) **Analysis of maximum Ice melting current of conductor**

According to the national standard GB 50545-2010, the temperature rise of aluminum-clad steel strands should be in the range of +80 °C and 100 °C when the maximum carrying capacity is reached. In this paper, the intermediate value, that is, the temperature rise of the wire is 90 °C, is taken to calculate the maximum ice-melting current of the wire. In the simultaneous formula (5)–(7), the resistance in formula (5) is modified to the resistance of the wire at 90 °C, and the maximum ice melting current of the wire can be obtained by raising the temperature of the wire to 90 °C.

Based on the above results, the minimum and maximum ice melting current of each type of wire with ice thickness of 10 mm are calculated, as shown in Table 1.

Table 1. Minimum and maximum ice melting currents for different conductors

Wire model	Minimum ice melting current (A)	Maximum ice melting current (A)
LGJ-35	200	300
LGJ-50	230	350
LGJ-70	290	420
LGJ-95	360	520
LGJ-120	420	600
LGJ-150	480	600

Transformer capacity is designed as 2.1 MVA, rated input 10 kV. During the actual ice melting, the intermediate value of the minimum ice melting current and the maximum ice melting current of each wire is generally taken. According to Table 1, the output voltage of the transformer is designed as 2.4, 2.0, 1.6, 1.2, 1.0, 0.8 kV, with a rated current of 500 A, which can meet the ice-melting needs of distribution lines.

The scattered mode of the transformer is air-cooled, the transformer is equipped with a CT and a PT measurement, and corresponding to a group of passive voltmeters and ammeters to display the ice-melting output voltage and current in real time. The detailed design dimensions of the multi-position transformer are shown in Fig. 4. Structure size of transformer in Fig. 4: 2.0*1.3*2.2 m, weight 4.0 t.

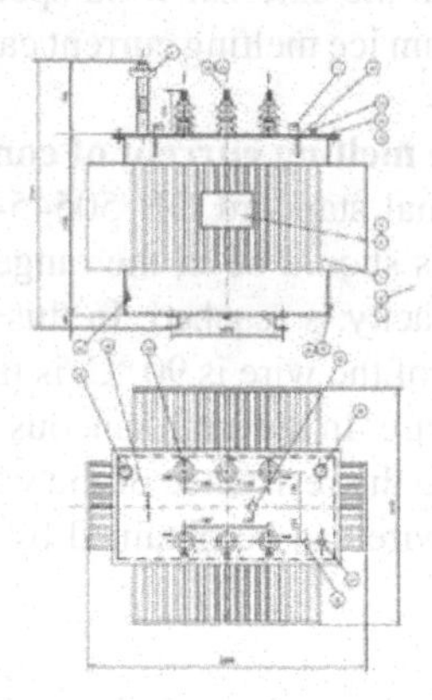

Fig. 4. Dimension design diagram of multi-position transformer

4.2 Parameter Design of Isolation Knife Gate

(1) the segmented ice melting system is equipped with a set of ice melting input isolation knife gate, a set of output knife gate, a set of bypass knife gate, a set of post switch (including secondary and external tripping function), 2 sets of ice melting short switch, a total of 5 knife gates, a set of on-column switches.
(2) switch rated voltage 10 kV, rated current 630 A.

4.3 Parameter Design of Ice-Melting Cable

(1) the segmented ice-melting system is equipped with a set of three-phase input cables and a set of three-phase ice-melting output cables.
(2) input the rated parameters of ice melting cable: input 10 kV, 200 A, single core, 50 m per phase of three phases.
(3) rated parameters of output ice-melting cable: input 6 kV, 600 A, single core, 50 m per phase

4.4 Parameter Design of Ice-Melting Voltage and Current Measurement Protection Unit

The ice-melting voltage and current measurement protection unit mainly detects the ice-melting voltage and ice-melting current, and automatically records the relevant data curve. The fault signals such as overvoltage and overcurrent are integrated and sent to the post switch for protection as a tripping signal. At the same time, the ice melting state can be uploaded to the remote master station, which is convenient for other off-site personnel to check the ice melting status in real time through communication software.

All the above devices are integrated into the container to reduce the damage caused by the external environment to the ice-melting equipment, and the arrangement of the ice-melting parts in the centralized box is shown in Fig. 5.

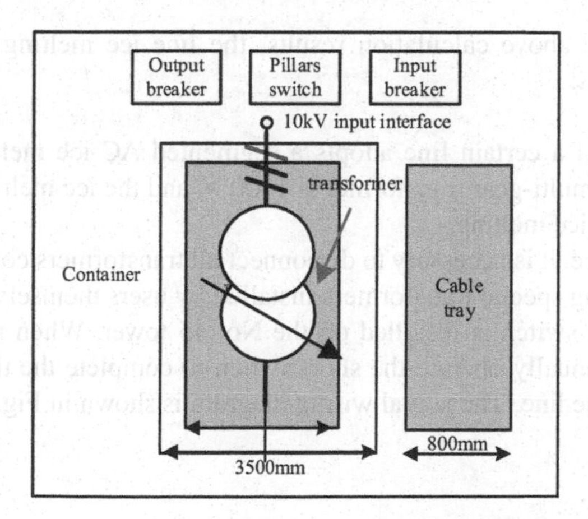

Fig. 5. Layout of ice-melting components

5 Ice Melting Scheme of Segmented Ice Melting System

Taking the 10 kV transmission line in a certain area as an example, after on-site investigation, the wire parameters of the transmission line are shown in Table 2.

Table 2. Conductor parameters of transmission lines

Wire model	Ice line length (km)	Wire resistance per unit length (Ω/km)	Unit length wire reactance (Ω/km)	Ice melting access point	Ice melting short contact
LGJ-70	4.7	0.408	0.569	No. 1 tower	No. 45 tower

According to the parameters in Table 1, the total impedance of ice melting line is calculated by simultaneous formula (1) and formula (2).

$$Z = 4.7 \times (0.408 + 0.569j) = 2.676\Omega \tag{8}$$

The transformer gear is 1600 V, the formula (8) is substituted for (3), and the ice melting current is calculated to be

$$I_r = \frac{1600}{\sqrt{3} \times 2.676} = 345\,\text{A} \tag{9}$$

By substituting formula (9) for (4), the capacity of multi-position ice-melting transformer is obtained.

$$S = \sqrt{3} \times 1600 \times 345 = 957\,\text{kVA} \tag{10}$$

According to the above calculation results, the line ice melting scheme can be established as follows:

(1) A branch line of a certain line adopts a segmented AC ice melting system, the voltage gear of multi-gear transformer is 1600 V, and the ice melting mode adopts three-phase AC ice melting.
(2) When melting ice, it is necessary to disconnect all transformers connected to tower 1 × 45, including special transformers installed by users themselves.
(3) The ice-melting switch is installed on the No. 45 tower. When melting ice, it is necessary to manually operate the short switch to complete the three-phase short connection of the line. The actual wiring diagram is shown in Fig. 6.

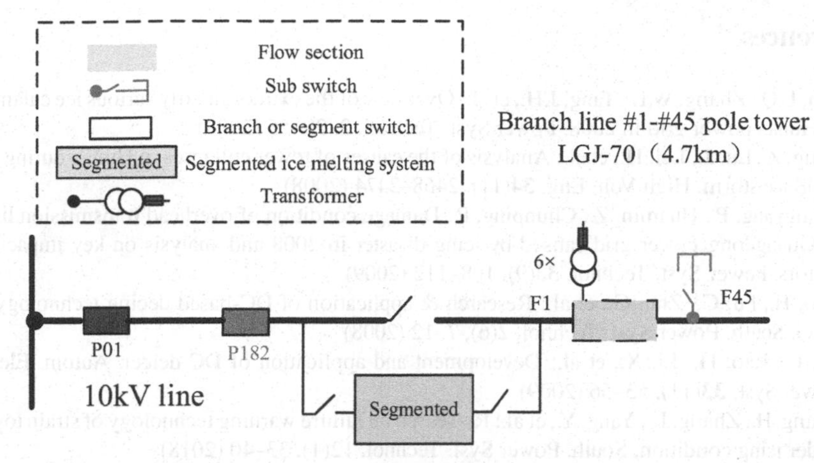

Fig. 6. Actual ice melting wiring diagram of the line

(4) blackout range: all stations connected to tower 1: 45.
(5) during the ice melting period, the temperature rise of the bare wire was measured at Tower 1 and Tower 45 respectively to ensure that the temperature rise was less than 90 °C.
(6) after melting ice, close the transformers in all the stations connected to the line, and finally restore the power supply to the line.

6 Conclusion

A new type of AC ice melting system is studied in this paper. For the segmented ice melting system, the structure, ice melting principle, equipment, parameters and ice melting scheme of the ice melting system are studied. The main conclusions are as follows:

(1) the segmented AC ice melting system takes electricity directly from the line and is installed near the icing area, and the multi-branch ice melting of the transmission line can be realized directly by regulating the voltage of the multi-gear transformer. The utility model has the advantages of convenience, rapidity and economy.
(2) the segmented AC ice melting system is mainly composed of multi-gear transformer, isolation switch, ice melting cable, measurement and protection unit and container. The electrical and geometric parameters of each component are studied in detail.
(3) the ice melting principle of segmented AC ice melting system is studied, and the ice melting current, ice melting voltage and system capacity are determined. And the detailed implementation plan of ice melting is worked out in turn.

Acknowledgement. This research was supported by the Science and Technology project of State Grid Hunan Electric Power Co., LTD. "Study on efficient ice melting technology for wind power lines" (5216AF210005).

References

1. Pan, L.Q., Zhang, W.L., Tang, J.H., et al.: Overview of the extraordinarily serious ice calamity to Hunan power grid in 2008. Power Syst. Technol. **2**, 20–25 (2008)
2. Jiang, Z., Lu, J., Lei, H., et al.: Analysis of the causes of tower collapses in Hunan during the 2008 ice storm. High Volt. Eng. **34**(11), 2468–2474 (2008)
3. Xiangyang, P., Huamin, Z., Chunping, P.: Damage condition of overhead transmission lines in Guangdong power grid caused by icing disaster in 2008 and analysis on key impacting factors. Power Syst. Technol. **33**(9), 108–112 (2009)
4. Rao, H., Fu, C., Zhu, G., et al.: Research & application of DC-based decing technology in CSG. South. Power Syst. Technol. **2**(6), 7–12 (2008)
5. Fu, C., Rao, H., Li, X., et al.: Development and application of DC deicer. Autom. Electr. Power Syst. **33**(11), 53–56 (2009)
6. Zhang, H., Zhang, L., Yang, Y., et al.: Re-search on failure warning technology of strain tower under icing condition. South. Power Syst. Technol. 12(1), 33–40 (2018)
7. Qi, L.: Laser Deicing Theoritical and Experimental Research for Transmission Lines. Wuhan, Huazhong University of Science & Technology (2012)
8. Zhang, J., Ke, Z., Ma, D., et al.: Design and Simulation of Large-capacity DC Ice-melting Systems
9. Yang, Y., Li, C., Wang, K., et al.: Study on configuration of valve side voltage transformer in DC de-icing device. Power Capacit. React. Power Compens. **40**(6), 49–53 (2019)
10. Yao, Z., Liu, T., Zhang, A.L., et al.: Research & application on DC de-icing technology. Power Syst. Prot. Control **38**(21), 57–62 (2010)
11. Liu, D., He, Z., Fan, R., et al.: Research on relocatable DC ice-melting equipment based on switchable device. Power Syst. Technol. **36**(3), 228–233 (2012)
12. Cui, J., Xu, J., Jiang, W., et al.: Design of DC deicing power supply for lightning protection and anti-icing disaster ground wire system of 220 kV overhead line. **57**(12), 209–217+224 (2021)
13. Rao, C., Bi, R., Liang, Y. et al.: Development on MMC-based mobile DC De-icing device with STATCOM function. **42**(2), 29–35 (2021)

Effect of SnO_2 Doping on the Performance of High Voltage ZnO Varistors

Bowen Wang[1], Zhiyao Fu[1(✉)], and Anting Kong[2]

[1] State Key Laboratory of Disaster Prevention and Reduction for Power Grid Transmission and Distribution Equipment, State Grid Hunan Electric Power Company Disaster Prevention and Reduction Center, Changsha 410100, China
jxfzy0602@163.com

[2] College of Sciences, Shanghai University, Shanghai 200444, China

Abstract. The effect of the SnO_2 doping on the structure and the electrical performance of ZnO varistors with high voltage was systematically studied. When the doping amount of SnO_2 was small, the main effect was to promote the growth of grains. As the doping amount increased, SnO_2 led to the formation of the Zn_2SnO_4 spinel, inhibiting the growth of ZnO grains. The donor concentration, the boundary barrier and the surface state density decreased first and then increased, respectively. By proper SnO_2 doping, the key performance parameters of the high voltage varistors were improved, where the breakdown voltage gradient was increased from 193.0 to 208.5 $V \cdot mm^{-1}$, the voltage ratio was reduced from 1.74 to 1.73, and the 2 ms square waveform impulse energy withstanding capacity was increased from 200 to 250 A.

Keywords: SnO_2 Doping · ZnO Varistors · Energy withstanding Capacity · Doping Amount

1 Introduction

Zinc oxide varistor is a kind of semiconductor ceramic element made of ZnO as the main material and various additives [1–7]. ZnO varistors have been used for the pro-tection of power transmission and distribution because of their excellent voltage de-pendent property, fast response time and strong energy withstanding capacity [8–12].

Doping can improve the nonlinear voltammetry characteristics of ZnO varistors, increase or decrease grain resistance, promote or inhibit the growth of grains, thus affecting the properties of ZnO varistors [13–17]. Therefore, doping is an important way to improve the performance of ZnO varistors. As a flux, SnO_2 doping can reduce the phase transition temperature of Bi_2O_3 in the sintering process, so as to reduce the potential gradient of the varistors, which is mostly used in low gradient varistors or high energy varistors. Zou Qingwen [18] doped SnO_2 into ZnO varistors and found that the total amount of additives in the new formulation system was significantly decreased, and the protection ability was stronger. Zhijun Xu et. al. [19] investigated the effects of SnO_2

H. Yang et al. (Eds.): SmartGIFT 2022, LNICST 483, pp. 163–172, 2023.
https://doi.org/10.1007/978-3-031-31733-0_15

on the ZnO varistor ceramics. They found that a small amount of SnO_2 caused a high nonlinear coefficient, lower leakage current, as well as noticeably higher breakdown voltage gradient. There have been several reports on the effect of SnO_2 doping on low voltage ZnO varistors, but there are few reports on the influence of SnO_2 doping on the performance, especially on the large energy withstanding capacity of the varistors with high voltage used in power transmission and distribution systems.

Herein, the effect of SnO_2 doping on the properties of the high voltage ZnO varistors was studied in detail. The influence of the doped SnO_2 on the donor concentration, surface density of states, and grain boundary barrier of ZnO varistors was estimated. With appropriate doping amount, the potential gradient, residual voltage ratio and large energy withstanding capacity of the ZnO varistors were enhanced compared to those of the varistors without SnO_2 doping.

2 Experimental Procedure

The ZnO varistor is composed of ZnO (95 mol%) as main material and the other oxides (5 mol%) including Cr_2O_3, Bi_2O_3, Co_2O_3, $MnCO_3$, Sb_2O_3, NiO and SnO_2 (x mol%, x = 0, 0.1, 0.2, 0.3, 0.4, and 0.5) as additives. The samples were named as D0, D1 - 5 according to the content of SnO_2. The ZnO powder and the additive powder were ball milled for 24 h. Centrifugal spray dryer (LZG-5, Wuxi Fenghua Drying Equipment Co., LTD, China) was used for spray granulation of the total slurry. A powder hydraulic press (Y79-25, Shanghai Huci Electric Appliance Development Co., LTD, China) was used for pressing. The green discs were heated to 500 °C to remove organics, then were sintered at 1200 °C to obtain the varistors. Both sides of the sintered samples were coated with Al electrodes.

The crystal phase of the samples was analyzed by an X-ray diffractometer. The morphology of the samples was characterized by a scanning electron microscope. Breakdown voltage U_{1mA}, leakage current I_L, nonlinear coefficient α, and E-J characteristic curve of the samples were measured by a DC varistor parameter tester. The C-V characteristic parameters were tested by a precision impedance analyzer. The donor concentration N_d, the height of the Schottky barrier φ and the surface density N_s were calculated from the C-V plots according to the equation $(\frac{1}{C_b} - \frac{1}{2C_0})^2 = \frac{2(\varphi - V_b)}{q\varepsilon_0\varepsilon_r N_d}$, where C_b is the grain boundary capacitance per unit area, C_0 is the C_b value when the applied bias is 0, and V_b is the bias of the individual grain boundary, φ is the barrier height, q is the charge of an electron, ε_0 and ε_r are the vacuum permittivity and the ZnO relative permittivity, respectively [20, 21]. The aging performance of the varistors was tested by a varistor accelerated aging tester under an AC voltage of $85\%U_{1\,mA}/\sqrt{2}$ at 135 °C for 96 h. The aging performance was evaluated using the aging coefficient K_{ct} ($K_{ct} = P_{96}/P_1$). P_{96} is the power consumption after 96 h, P_1 is the power consumption after 1 h. A K_{ct} value less than 1 indicates a good aging performance.

3 Results and Discussion

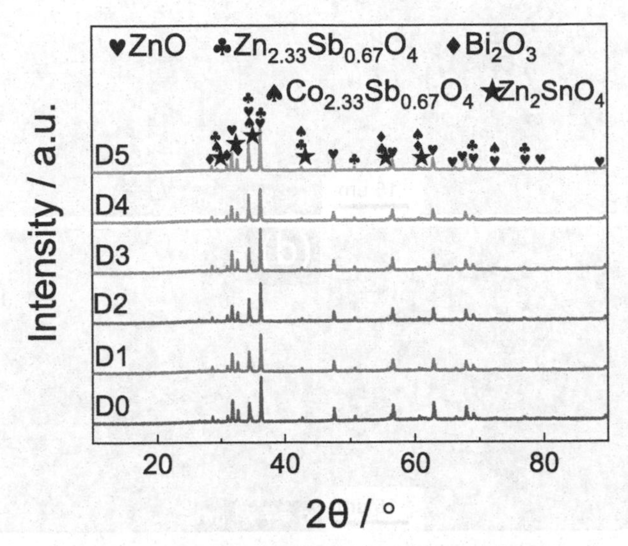

Fig. 1. XRD patterns of ZnO varistors of D0 - D5.

Figure 1 displays the XRD patterns of the ZnO varistors with different SnO_2 doping content. The main structure is composed of hexagonal crystalline ZnO phase, bismuth-rich phase δ-Bi_2O_3 and spinel phases $Zn_{2.33}Sb_{0.67}O_4$ and Zn_2SnO_4. The diffraction patterns of all samples are similar, indicating that SnO_2 does not have a visible effect on the crystal phase of ZnO varistors, which may be because the content of SnO_2 is small.

Figure 2 shows the SEM images of the ZnO varistors with different contents of SnO_2. The average grain size of the sample without SnO_2 was 8.16 μm. With the increase of SnO_2, the grain size increases to 8.98 μm, and then decreases to 7.24 μm. When the doping amount of SnO_2 is small, the main effect is to reduce the phase transition temperature of Bi_2O_3, make the liquid phase form at lower temperature, promoting the grain growth [18]. The grain size distribution of samples D1 - D5 gradually changed from uneven to uniform, and the average grain size gradually decreased, because as the SnO_2 content increased, the inhibiting effect of the spinel on the grain growth was enhanced.

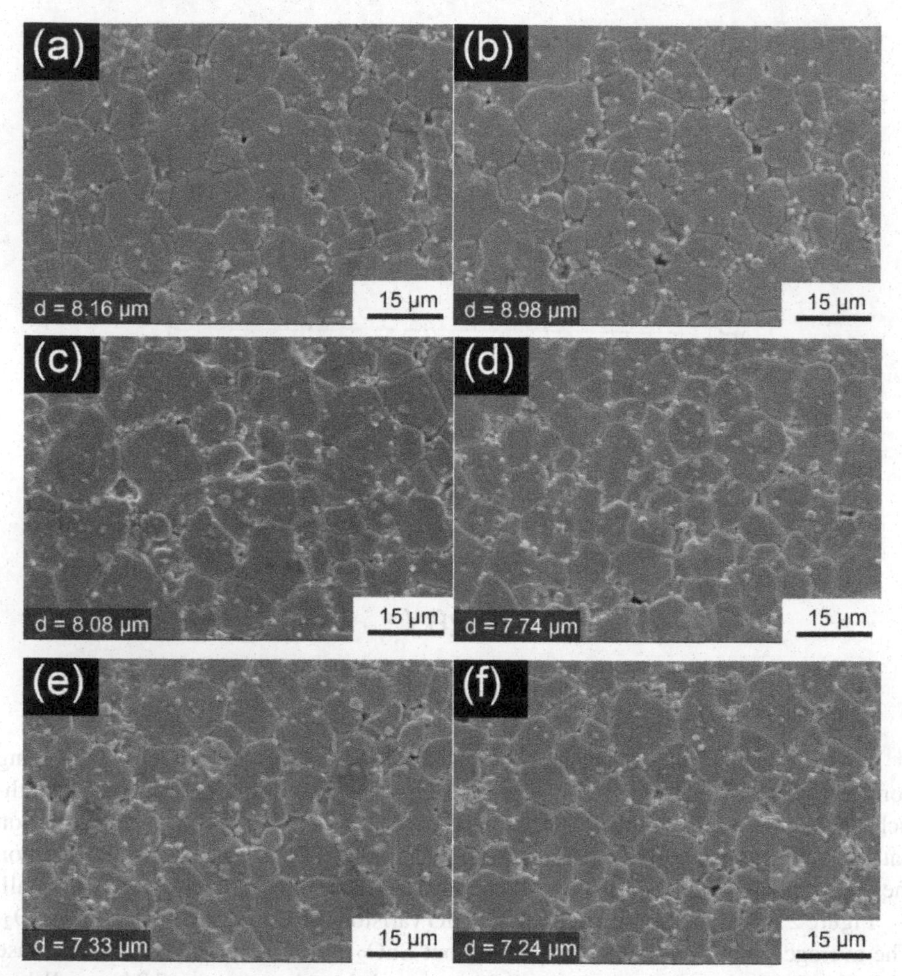

Fig. 2. SEM images of the ZnO varistors of (a) D0, (b) D1, (c) D2, (d) D3, (e) D4, and (f) D5.

Figure 3 (a) shows the potential gradient curves of the ZnO varistors with different amounts of SnO_2 doping. As the SnO_2 amount increases, the potential gradient decreased first from 193.0 to 190.5 $V{\cdot}mm^{-1}$, then increased to 218.9 $V{\cdot}mm^{-1}$. The decrease of the potential gradient is due to the appearance of some voids in the grain and the increase of the grain size. As SnO_2 increases gradually, the grain size decreases and the distribution is uniform, so the potential gradient for D2 - D5 is increasing.

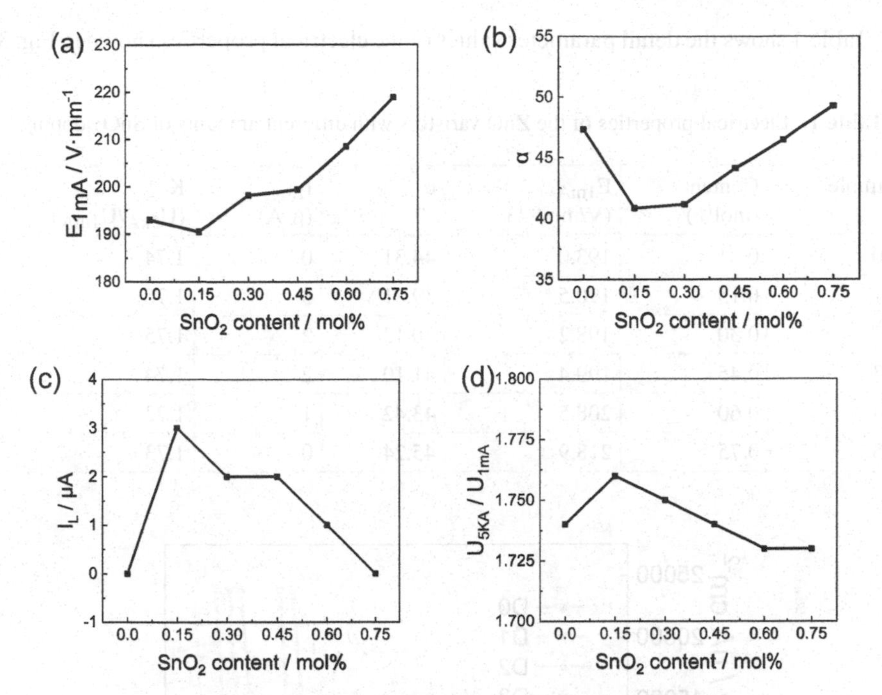

Fig. 3. Properties of ZnO varistors including breakdown voltage gradient (a), nonlinear coefficient (b), leakage current (c) and residual voltage ratio (d) as functions of the SnO_2 content.

Figure 3 (b) displays the variation curve of the nonlinear coefficient of the varistors with different SnO_2 doping contents. With the increasing of the SnO_2 content, the non-linearity decreases first and then increases. The nonlinear decrease of D1 is due to the lack of spinel particles and uneven distribution. With the increase of the SnO_2 content, the Zn_2SnO_4 spinel was formed on the grain boundary. Spinel particles hindered ion migration and increased the barrier height of the grain boundary.

Figure 3 (c) shows the leakage current curve of the ZnO varistors with different SnO_2 doping contents. With the increase of the SnO_2 content, the leakage current firstly increased and then decreased. According to the formula $J = J_0 exp\left(-v\varphi_B^{\frac{3}{2}}/E\right)$, where J is the current density, J_0 is the current density when the bias is 0, J is inversely proportional to φ, that is, inversely proportional to the nonlinearity [22].

Figure 3 (d) displays the variation of the residual voltage ratio of the ZnO varistors as a function of the SnO_2 doping amount. As the SnO_2 doping amount increases, the residual voltage ratio increased first and then decreased, because E_{5kA} is inversely proportional to E_{1mA}, according to the formula $K = E_{5kA}/E_{1mA}$.

Table 1 shows the detail parameter values of the electrical properties shown in Fig. 3.

Table 1. Electrical properties of the ZnO varistors with different amounts of SnO_2 doping.

Sample	Content (mol%)	E_{1mA} (V/mm^{-1})	α	I_L (μ A)	K (U_{5kA}/U_{1mA})
D0	0	193.0	44.31	0	1.74
D1	0.15	190.5	39.81	3	1.76
D2	0.30	198.2	40.12	2	1.75
D3	0.45	199.4	41.10	2	1.74
D4	0.60	208.5	43.42	1	1.73
D5	0.75	218.9	45.24	0	1.73

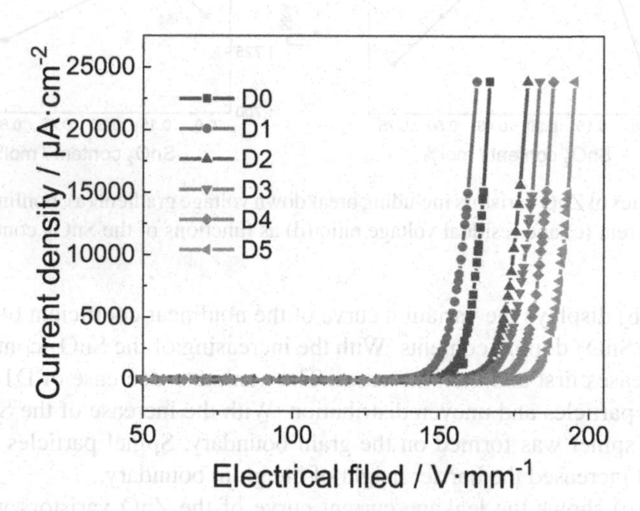

Fig. 4. Electrical field - current density curves of the ZnO varistors with different amounts of SnO_2 doping.

Figure 4 shows the E-J curves of ZnO varistors with different SnO_2 doping contents. The characteristic parameters extracted from the E-J curves are in agreement with those measured by the varistor parameter tester displayed in Table 1, which confirms the validity of the data.

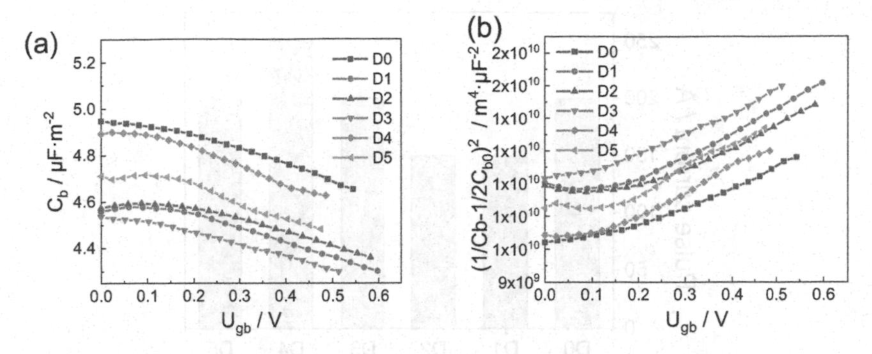

Fig. 5. C-V curves of ZnO varistors with different amounts of SnO_2 doping.

Table 2. Schottky barrier parameters of the ZnO varistors doped with different amounts of SnO_2 doping.

Sample	φ (eV)	$N_d(10^{18}\ m^{-3})$	$N_s(10^{23}\ m^{-2})$
D0	1.61	2.23	5.73
D1	1.33	1.81	4.72
D2	1.35	1.89	4.87
D3	1.33	1.85	5.16
D4	1.65	2.32	6.61
D5	1.77	2.32	7.09

Figure 5 and Table 2 show the C-V curves of the ZnO varistors and the Schottky barrier characteristic parameters calculated from the curves, respectively. As the SnO_2 content increases, the donor concentration N_d and the surface state density N_s decrease first and then increase, while the grain boundary barrier φ firstly decreases and then increases. The decrease of the donor concentration might because SnO_2 promoted the formation of more liquid phase during sintering, allowing more additives to be incorporated into the Bi-rich phase instead of permeating to ZnO. The increase of N_d and N_s is because Sn^{4+} enters the ZnO lattice and becomes donor doping, increasing the donor concentration. Meanwhile, the oxygen produced by the decomposition of SnO_2 at high temperature increases the partial pressure of oxygen at the grain boundaries, resulting in more surface state density, according to the equation $SnO_2 \leftrightarrow 2Sn_{Zn}^{\cdot\cdot} + 2e' + O_2$.

Figure 6 shows the 2 ms square-waveform energy withstanding capacity of the ZnO varistors with different amounts of SnO_2 doping. As the SnO_2 content increases, the maximum energy withstanding capacity first decreases, then increases to 250 A at sample D4, and then decreases to 200 A at D5. The weakening of the energy withstanding capacity from sample D0 to D1 is due to the uneven grain distribution and more cavities in the ceramic. The improvement of the energy withstanding capacity from D1 to D4 is due to the more uniform grain distribution. The decrease of the energy withstanding capacity from D4 to D5 may be due to the fact that the donor doping has been saturated,

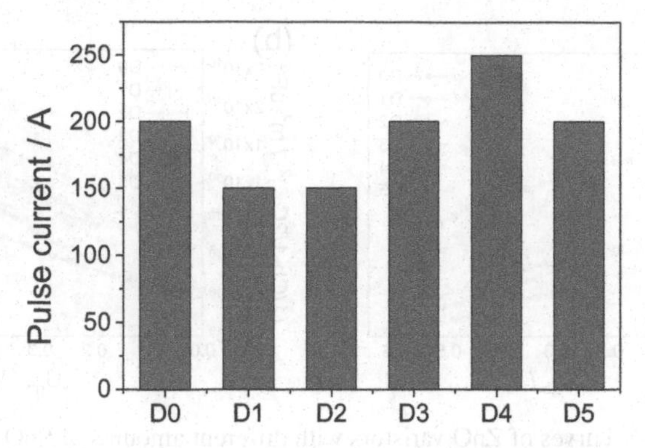

Fig. 6. 2 ms energy withstanding capacity of the ZnO varistors with different amounts of SnO_2 doping.

and the grain resistance cannot further decrease, while the number of grain boundaries further increases, which further aggravates the internal stress.

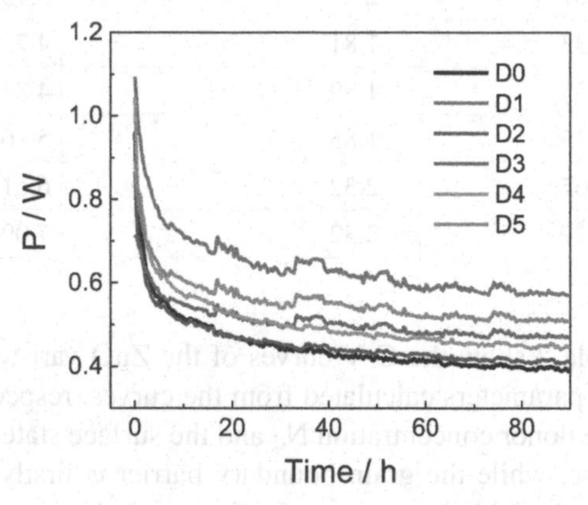

Fig. 7. Accelerated aging performance of the ZnO varistors with different amounts of SnO_2 doping.

In order to verify whether the ZnO varistors can run stably in the circuit, we tested the accelerated aging performance of the samples for 96 h. The accelerated aging curves are shown in Fig. 7, and the performance parameters are displayed in Table 3. The power consumption of D0 - D5 decreases first and then stabilizes as time goes on, and the K_{ct} of all the varistors is less than 1, indicating that all samples can run stably in the circuit. The power consumption is the product of the loading voltage and current of the sample, so the power consumption during aging is roughly proportional to the breakdown voltage gradient and the leakage current [4, 23]. D0 has the second smallest breakdown voltage gradient and the smallest leakage current, thus its aging power consumption is the least. D1 has the smallest breakdown voltage gradient, however, its leakage current is the largest, so its aging power consumption is the largest.

Table 3. Accelerated aging parameters of the ZnO varistors with different amounts of SnO_2 doping.

No	P_{1h} (W)	P_{96h} (W)	K_{ct}
D0	0.77	0.39	0.50
D1	0.97	0.58	0.60
D2	0.73	0.41	0.56
D3	0.69	0.48	0.70
D4	0.85	0.45	0.53
D5	0.77	0.50	0.65

4 Conclusions

This work systematically explored the influence of SnO_2 on the microstructure and the performance of the ZnO varistors. When the doping amount of SnO_2 was small, the main effect was to reduce the phase transition temperature of Bi_2O_3 and promote the ZnO grain growth. As the doping amount increased, SnO_2 led to the formation of the Zn_2SnO_4 spinel, inhibited the ZnO grain growth, promoted the uniform distribution of grains, and improved the uniformity of the structure of the ZnO varistors. During sintering process, Sn^{4+} entered the ZnO lattice, increasing the donor concentration. The oxygen produced by the decomposition of SnO_2 increased the partial pressure of oxygen at the grain boundaries, resulting in more surface state density. Sample D4 has the best comprehensive performance with the potential gradient of $208.5\ V \cdot mm^{-1}$, the nonlinear coefficient of 43.42, the leakage current density of 1 μA, the 5 kA voltage ratio of 1.73, the energy withstanding capacity of 250 A suffering from 18 shocks of 2 ms square waveform pulse impacts, and the ageing coefficient K_{ct} of 0.53.

Acknowledgements. We acknowledge the fund support of Science and Technology Project of State Grid Hunan Electric Power Company (grant 5216AF210004).

References

1. Wang, M., et al.: High improvement of degradation behavior of ZnO varistors under high current surges by appropriate S_b2O_3 doping. J. Eur. Ceram. Soc. **41**(1), 436–442 (2021)
2. Ruan, X., et al.: Effects of dispersant content and pH on dispersion of suspension, microstructures and electrical properties of ZnO varistors. Ceram. Int. **46**(9), 14134–14142 (2020)
3. Liu, W., Zhang, L., Kong, F., Wu, K., Li, S., Li, J.: Enhanced voltage gradient and energy absorption capability in ZnO varistor ceramics by using nano-sized ZnO powders. J. Alloys Compd. **828**, 154252 (2020)
4. Meng, P., Zhao, X., Fu, Z., Wu, J., Hu, J., He, J.: Novel zinc-oxide varistor with superior performance in voltage gradient and aging stability for surge arrester. J. Alloys Compd. **789**, 948–952 (2019)

5. Roy, S., Das, D., Roy, T.K.: Nonlinear electrical properties of ZnO-V_2O_5 based rare earth (Er2O3) added varistors. J. Electron. Mater. **48**(9), 5650–5661 (2019)
6. Zhao, M., Li, X., Li, T.Y., Shi, Y., Li, B.W.: Effect of Y_2O_3, Nd_2O_3 or Sm_2O_3 on the microstructure and electrical properties of ZnVMnNbO varistor ceramics. J. Mater. Sci. Mater. Electron. **30**(1), 450–456 (2019)
7. Roy, S., Roy, T.K., Das, D.: Grain growth kinetics of Er2O3 doped ZnO-V_2O_5 based varistor ceramics. Ceram. Int. **45**(18), 24835–24850 (2019)
8. Zhao, M., Wang, Y.-H., Sun, T.-T., Song, H.-H.: Effect of bismuth and vanadium as the varistor forming element in ZnO-based ceramics. J. Mater. Sci. Mater. Electron. **31**(11), 8206–8211 (2020)
9. Gunnewiek, R.F.K., Perdomo, C.P.F., Cancellieri, I.C., Cardoso, A.L.F., Kiminami, R.H.G.A.: Microwave sintering of a nanostructured low-level additive ZnO-based varistor. Ceram. Int. **46**(10), 15044–15053 (2020)
10. Roy, S., Das, D., Roy, T.K.: Influence of sintering temperature on microstructure and electrical properties of Er_2O_3 added ZnO-V_2O_5-MnO_2-Nb_2O_5 varistor ceramics. J. Alloys Compd. **749**, 687–696 (2018)
11. Meng, P., et al.: Stable electrical properties of ZnO varistor ceramics with multiple additives against the AC accelerated aging process. Ceram. Int. **45**(8), 11105–11108 (2019)
12. Zhao, H., Hu, J., Chen, S., Xie, Q., He, J.: Improving age stability and energy absorption capabilities of ZnO varistors ceramics. Ceram. Int. **42**(15), 17880–17883 (2016)
13. Ruan, X., et al.: Effects of SiO_2/Cr_2O_3 ratios on microstructures and electrical properties of high voltage gradient ZnO varistors. J. Mater. Sci. Mater. Electron. **30**(13), 12113–12121 (2019)
14. Cheng, L.-H., et al.: Electrical properties of Al_2O_3-doped ZnO varistors prepared by sol–gel process for device miniaturization. Ceram. Int. **38**, S457–S461 (2012)
15. Zhu, J., Qi, G., Yang, H., Wang, F.: Microstructure and electrical properties of Pr 6 O 11 doped ZnO-Bi_2O_3-based varistors. J. Mater. Sci. Mater. Electron. **22**(1), 96–100 (2011)
16. He, J., Hu, J., Lin, Y.: ZnO varistors with high voltage gradient and low leakage current by doping rare-earth oxide. Sci. China Ser. E Technol. Sci. **51**(6), 693–701 (2008)
17. Canikoğlu, N., Toplan, N., Yıldız, K., Toplan, H.Ö.: Densification and grain growth of SiO_2-doped ZnO. Ceram. Int. **32**(2), 127–132 (2006)
18. Qingwen, Z.: Study on the amelioration of the formula of ZnO varistor, Xidian University (2012)
19. Shuai, M., Xu, Z., Chu, R., Hao, J., Li, G.: Influence of SnO_2 on ZnO–Bi_2O_3–Co_2O_3 based varistor ceramics. Ceram. Int. **41**(9), 12490–12494 (2015)
20. He, J., Long, W., Hu, J., Liu, J.: Nickel oxide doping effects on electrical characteristics and microstructural phases of ZnO varistors with low residual voltage ratio. J. Ceram. Soc. Jpn. **119**(1385), 43–47 (2011)
21. Wang, X., Ren, X., Li, Z., You, W., Shi, L.: A unique tuning effect of Mg on grain boundaries and grains of ZnO varistor ceramics. J. Eur. Ceram. Soc. **41**(4) (2020)
22. Zhao, H., Hu, J., Chen, S., Xie, Q., He, J.: Tailoring the high-impulse current discharge capability of ZnO varistor ceramics by doping with Ga_2O_3. Ceram. Int. **42**(4), 5582–5586 (2016)
23. Meng, P., et al.: Stable electrical properties of ZnO varistor ceramics with multiple additives against the AC accelerated aging process. Ceram. Int. (2019)

Simulation Generation Algorithm for Foggy Images in Natural Scenes

Jianping Liu(✉), Qing Ye, Shizhuo Qiu, and Yuze Liu

School of Electrical and Information Engineering, Changsha University of Science and Technology, Changsha 410114, Hunan, China
799372927@qq.com

Abstract. The foggy environment seriously affects the automatic inspection or cruise monitoring of outdoor equipment in the power system. Aiming at the lack of fog image data sets, a fog simulation image generation algorithm based on depth estimation was proposed. First of all, by unsupervised depth estimation model building the depth map of an outdoor clear picture. Then using feature fusion to refine the depth chart details. By setting the atmospheric extinction coefficient for transmittance figure. Dark channel method is used to estimate the atmospheric light value of the image. Finally, the fog simulation images are obtained based on the atmospheric scattering model. The experimental results show that the method improves the depth map effectively, and the generated fog simulation image is reliable. The average error rate of fog simulation is 6.2%, which solves the problem of excessive uneven fog edge, and the fog simulation image effect is very good in low visibility. Generating fog images with different visibility labels can solve the problem of lack of fog datasets.

Keywords: Fog Simulation · Depth Estimation · Automatic Inspection

1 Introduction

Under fog weather conditions, the scattering and absorption of light caused by a large number of tiny water droplets suspended in the atmosphere greatly reduce the visibility, resulting in lower image quality and affecting the accuracy of computer vision, such as automatic driving, object detection, robot inspection of power system equipment, etc. Therefore dehazing and sharpening of video images has become a key research content in computer vision. A large number of machine learning and deep learning dehazing algorithms need to be trained on foggy images. Due to the randomness of fog, it is difficult to collect image data sets under real fog scenes, and the number of existing natural foggy image datasets is difficult to meet the needs of research and training.

Based on Koschmieder's law [1], the influence of atmospheric medium on image information in foggy outdoor environment depends on the distance between scene information and image acquisition equipment, that is, scene depth. The authenticity of fog simulation image depends on the authenticity of the generated scene depth. Researchers

H. Yang et al. (Eds.): SmartGIFT 2022, LNICST 483, pp. 173–185, 2023.
https://doi.org/10.1007/978-3-031-31733-0_16

have used a variety of methods to obtain scene depth, including direct measurements using LiDar equipment and methods based on two images and videos. Methods in computer vision include binocular disparity depth estimation, optical flow method, monocular depth estimation, etc. In the aspect of scene depth estimation, monocular depth estimation based on unsupervised learning has become a hot research topic in this field because it does not rely on depth truth value during network training. Gary [2] proposed the use of stereo images to realize unsupervised monocular depth estimation without depth label, and its working principle is similar to autoencoder. Based on the above work, Godard [3] uses the consistency of left and right views to realize unsupervised depth prediction, further adding details and improving resolution. However, the above methods have limited ability to predict depth, and the prediction effect is not good for the scene with rich details. Chen [5] created a new dataset 'Depth in the Wild', which contained the relative Depth relationship between any image and random points in the image, and proposed an algorithm to estimate Depth by using the relative Depth relationship. The algorithm can restore the details of the image well, but the prediction depth needs to be improved.

In summary, the existing fog simulation methods are mainly based on the real information or binocular disparity data to obtain the depth map, but from the reality, it is difficult to obtain the real depth information and binocular image. Therefore, this paper conducts monocular depth estimation based on unsupervised learning of real scenes, uses feature fusion to refine the depth map details, and combines atmospheric scattering model to generate high-quality fog simulation images.

2 Atmospheric Scattering Model

Under fog conditions, there are a large number of suspended particles in the atmosphere to absorb and scatter light [6], which makes the imaging results of the detection system degrade. There are two main reasons: first, the reflected light of the target is absorbed and scattered by the suspended particles, resulting in the attenuation of brightness and contrast; Second, ambient light such as atmospheric light forms background light due to the scattering effect of medium, and is stronger than the target reflected light, which often makes the image blurred. Therefore, the light source of foggy image imaging is mainly the light that the target reflected light attenuates to the imaging system and the atmospheric light that the light source is scattered by particles. Based on this principle, the atmospheric scattering model widely used today is simplified, and its mathematical model expression is as follows.

$$I(x) = J(x)t(x) + A(1 - t(x)) \tag{1}$$

$$t(x) = e^{-\beta d(x)} \tag{2}$$

where I(x) is the foggy image; J(x) is the clear image; A is the atmospheric light value at infinity; t(x) is the atmospheric transmittance map, formula (2) is the expression of the transmission map, where β is the atmospheric scattering coefficient, d(x) is the distance between the target and the camera, also known as scene depth, and the depth map is represented by thermal image quantification.

Based on the above atmospheric scattering model and its principle, the fog-free clear images in natural environment are simulated as foggy images. Under the premise that the atmospheric scattering coefficient is determined by the visibility, the estimation of depth map, transmittance map and atmospheric light value becomes the main content of the study.

3 Parameters Estimation

3.1 Estimation of Atmospheric Light Values

Since the clear original image does not have the influence of large pixel points caused by fog [7–9], its atmospheric light value can be directly estimated by using the pixel point of the brightest region in the image, which is generally the value of the sky region or infinity. However, the single brightest pixel in the image tends to appear on small white objects, such as vehicles and white floor tiles, and the atmospheric light value determines whether the fog color is normal after fog simulation. Therefore, the dark channel [11] method is used to estimate the atmospheric light value.

In the clear image without sky area, the dark channel approaches 0, while in the original image with sky area, the pixels close to the sky area do not approach 0. Therefore, the dark channel can be used to screen the sky area, and the three-channel pixels in this area are averaged, so as to obtain the estimated value of atmospheric light. If there is no sky area, the first 0.1% pixel in the dark channel corresponding to the brightest pixel in the original image is used as the estimate value of atmospheric light.

3.2 Depth Map Estimation

The self-supervised monocular depth estimation method is trained with video sequences or continuous images, which can input any monocular image and output a reliable depth map. In this paper, the *manydepth* [12] model is used to obtain image depth. Using the cost-volume [14] method in multi-view depth estimation [13], the model replaces the original binocular image with a pair of front and rear frame images, overcoming the scale ambiguity problem in depth estimation. The model is composed of pose estimation network, cost-volume construction and depth estimation network. The block diagram is shown in Fig. 1.

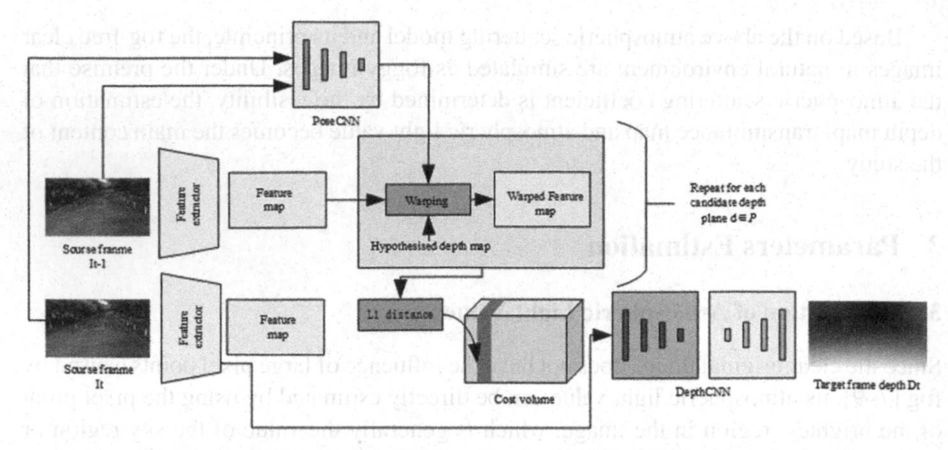

Fig. 1. Self-supervised monocular depth estimation framework

Pose Estimation Network

Here, two adjacent frames of images are used to estimate the pose of the camera $T_{t \to t+n}$ $(n = -1)$, and the pose network is trained with the images of past adjacent frames. Then the pose is described as (3).

$$T_{t \to t+n} = \theta_{pose}(I_t, I_{t+n}) \tag{3}$$

Building a Cost-Volume

Cost-Volume is described as the difference in pixels of adjacent frames at different depths, but it is not the difference in images but the difference in features. According to the maximum depth d_{max} and minimum depth d_{min}, several planes P are divided in the vertical direction of the I_t optical axis. Then, $F_{t+n \to t,d}$, $d \in P$ is obtained by using the camera pose information and the internal reference matrix to transform the features of the source image. The cost-volume is obtained by making the absolute value of the difference between the source image features and the target image features. Finally, it is combined with the features of the target image to get the depth estimation map through the decoder.

Depth Estimation Network

The *manydepth* model is trained using multiple image sequences, so the depth estimation part is described as follows.

$$D_t = \theta_{depth}(I_t, I_{t-1}, \ldots, I_{t-n}) \tag{4}$$

Formula (4) shows that the model uses the image data of past frames as input to train and predict depth $(n = -1)$. The estimation of camera pose $T_{t \to t+n}$ using the current estimated depth D_t and pose estimation network θ_{pose} is used to reconstruct the scene, but only using pixels from adjacent frames $(n = -1)$, which is described as follows.

$$I_{t+n \to t} = I_{t+n} \langle pr(D_t, T_{t \to t+n}, K) \rangle \tag{5}$$

where <> represents the sampling operator and pr represents the 2D coordinates of the depth returned when *pr* reprojected into the camera of I_{t+n}. For each pixel, the loss of the best-matched source image is optimized by selecting the smallest pixel on the reconstruction loss *pe*, which can be expressed as follows.

$$L_p = \min_n pe(I_t, I_{t+n \to t}) \tag{6}$$

Refinement of the Depth Map

It is found that the resolution of the input image has the following two effects on the quality of the depth map. When the low resolution image is input, the generated depth map has good depth consistency, but the image detail performance is poor. When a high-resolution image is input, the predicted depth map has good image details but poor depth consistency performance. The results are shown in Fig. 2 and Fig. 3.

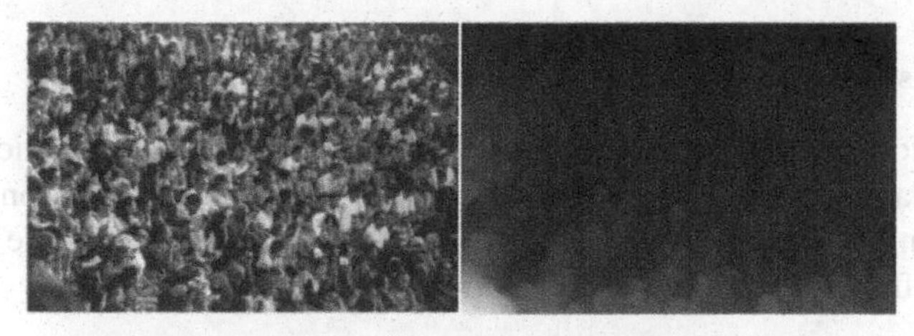

Fig. 2. High resolution image and its depth map

Fig. 3. Low image and its depth map

Figure 2 and Fig. 3 show that the characteristics of the monocular depth estimation network vary with the resolution of the input image, and the main reason is that the network receptive field is limited, and the size of the receptive field mainly relies on the network structure and the resolution of the training datasets, depth estimation depends on the image context clues, when image clues in farther than receptive field, the network cannot accept enough information.

To solve the above problem, we generate multiple depth maps for the individual images to be merged to achieve results with high frequency details with a consistent overall structure. The Pixel2pixel [16] structure with 10-layer U-net [15] is used as the generator of the merge network, which accepts two depth maps with different resolutions. After the two depth maps are resized, different sampling patches are selected according

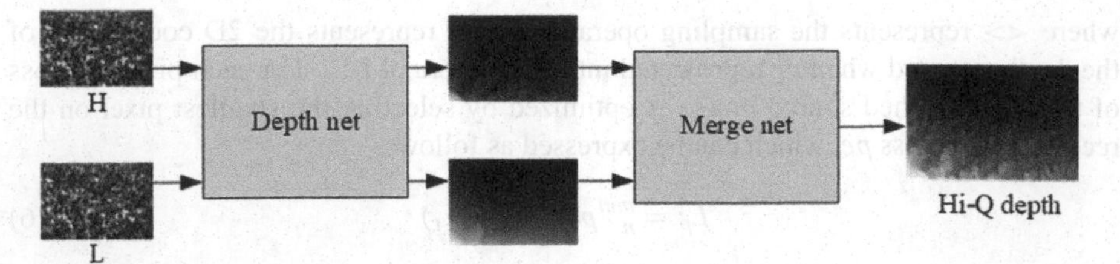

Fig. 4. Multi-scale fusion

to the set gradient, and then multi-scale fusion is performed through the Pixel2Pixel generator. Specific steps are shown in Fig. 4.

Figure 4 shows that by adding the Merge network, the depth image has the accurate and consistent scene structure of the boundary, which lays a foundation for the subsequent calculation of the transmittance map of fog images.

3.3 Transmission Map Estimation

According to formula (2), it can be concluded that the atmospheric extinction coefficient β is an important parameter to generate the transmittance map in addition to the depth map. According to *Koschmieder's* law, visibility is closely related to the atmospheric extinction coefficient, and the specific relationship is as follow.

$$V = -\frac{ln\sigma}{\beta} \tag{7}$$

where V is visible distance, namely visibility; β is the same as formula (2), is the atmospheric extinction coefficient, σ is the visual contrast threshold, generally 0.02 or 0.05, this paper takes 0.05; Based on this law, the corresponding β value can be generated according to the required visibility value, so that the estimated depth map can be used to calculate the pixels in the image one by one, and the corresponding transmittance map can be estimated.

Thus, the depth map, transmittance map and atmospheric light value needed for fog simulation are estimated. Foggy images with different visibility can be simulated according to the principle shown in formula (1): First use natural environment without clear mist image depth map estimation and atmospheric optical value estimation, then selected need visibility of atmospheric extinction coefficient is calculated, thus to estimate transmittance using atmospheric scattering model finally from the clear picture to the fog simulation, get visibility standard and the actual situation of image contrast. The process is shown in Fig. 5.

4 Results and Discussion

4.1 Improved Depth Map Image Contrast

The outdoor natural environment images captured by the camera were used for the experiment with a resolution of 1920 × 1080. Fog simulation was carried out before

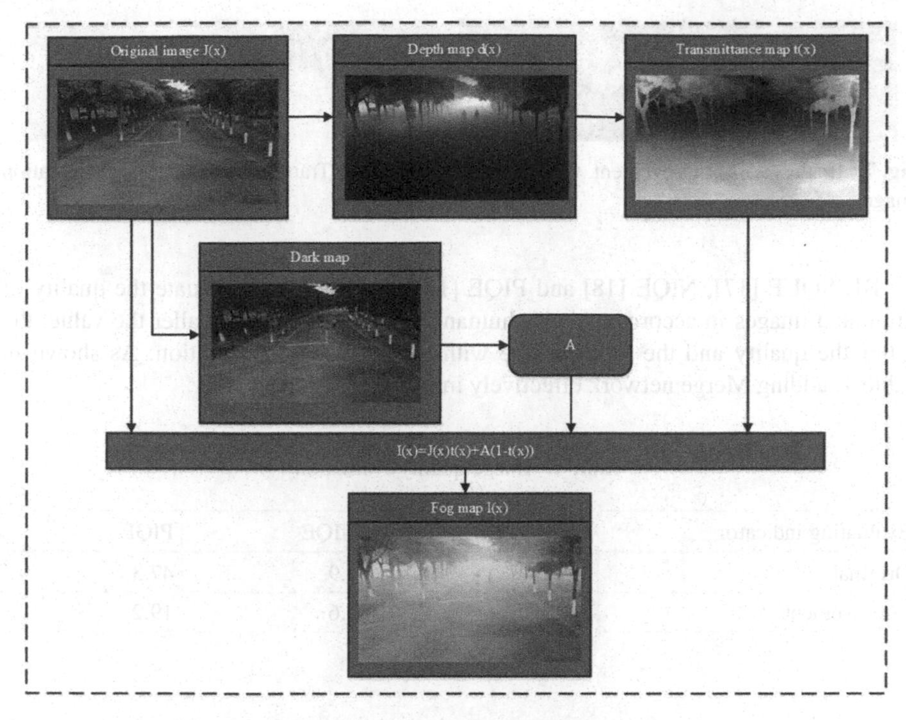

Fig. 5. Fog diagram simulation process

and after the improvement. As can be seen from Fig. 6, the perspective of the depth map and transmittance map without improvement is too smooth, the details of the image information are lacking, and the furthest depth of the depth map is not consistent with the actual situation, resulting in too uniform fog in the perspective of the fog map. There is no transition between the fog area and the non-fog area, which is inconsistent with the real foggy image. Multi-scale feature fusion is used to improve the depth map. First, the original image is clipped by line, and the original image and the clipped image with two different resolutions are respectively input into the depth estimation model, and the obtained results are merged to obtain the improved depth map. It can be seen from Fig. 7 that the details of the depth map and transmittance map are obvious, which are more real than Fig. 6. The simulated fog map also has obvious depth information, and there is a good transition between the fog area and the non-fog area, which is in line with the actual situation.

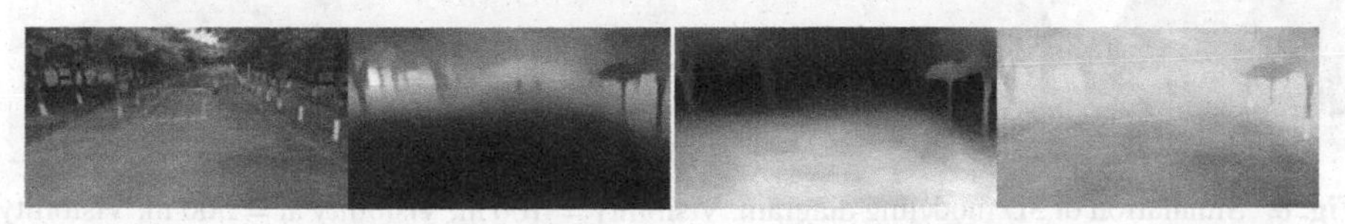

Fig. 6. Images without improvement. Clear image; Depth map; Transmission map; Fog simulation image

Fig. 7. Images with improvement. Clear image; Depth map; Transmission map; Fog simulation image

BRISQUE [17], NIQE [18] and PIQE [19] are selected to evaluate the quality of simulated images in accordance with human visual effects. The smaller the value, the better the quality and the more in line with human visual observation. As shown in Table 1, adding Merge network effectively improves fog map quality.

Table 1. Image quality evaluation

Evaluating indicator	BRISQUE	NIQE	PIQE
Original	27.7	2.9	47.3
Improvement	24.3	1.6	19.2

4.2 Foggy Images Under Different Scenes

In meteorology, the intensity of fog is described by visibility, which is the maximum distance the human eye can identify an object from a background, usually the sky near the horizon. In the following, fog ($V = 100$ m), medium fog ($V = 500$ m) and mist ($V = 800$ m) were simulated through images of three different scenes in 3D composite image, cruise map of power equipment and urban road map in Cityscape datasets, as shown in Fig. 8, Fig. 9 and Fig. 10 (Table 2).

Table 2. The relationship of visibility and fog concentration

Category	Dense fog	Big fog	Moderate fog	Mist
Visibility(km)	<0.2	0.2~0.5	0.5~1.0	1.0~5.0

Fig. 8. Simulation of 3D modeling diagram. Visibility = 100 m; Visibility at = 500 m; Visibility = 800 m

Fig. 9. Simulation of urban road map. Visibility = 100 m; Visibility = 500 m; Visibility = 800 m

Fig. 10. Simulation of cruise map. Visibility = 100 m; Visibility = 500 m; Visibility = 800 m

4.3 Quality Evaluation of Foggy Simulated Images

In order to verify the validity of the simulated foggy images, the simulated foggy images were compared with the real foggy images. Figure 12 shows the real fog images when the visibility is 100 m, 300 m, 500 m and 800 m. Figure 13 shows the images with visibility of 100 m, 300 m, 500 m and 800 m in fog simulation of the same scene without fog. Figure 11 is a clear image, which is used to simulate the above real foggy images. From the subjective evaluation of human vision, the fog degree of images is similar, the image features are calculated and evaluated, and the image quality is compared using the evaluation index of image sharpness without reference.

Fig. 11. A clear image of the same scene.

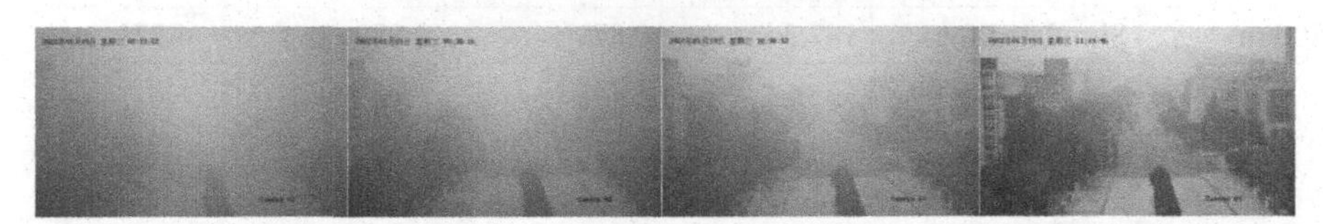

Fig. 12. Real fog. Visibility = 100 m; Visibility = 300 m; Visibility = 500 m; Visibility = 800 m.

Laplacian [20] gradient function, SMD function, SMD2 function [21] and information entropy [22] function, which are commonly used to evaluate image sharpness without reference, are used for quantitative evaluation. Laplacian gradient function adopts

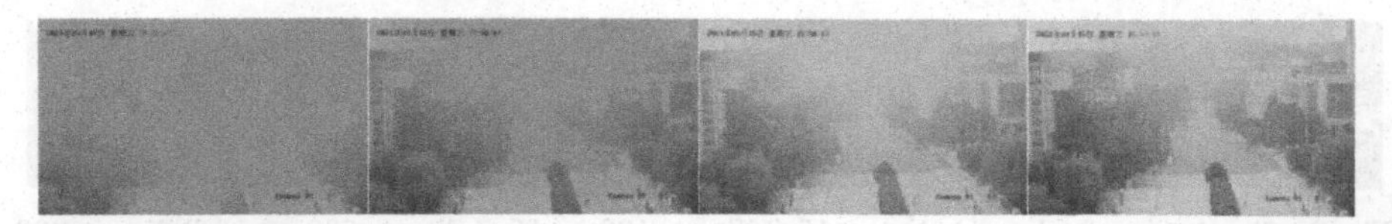

Fig. 13. Simulated fog image. Visibility = 100 m; Visibility = 300 m; Visibility = 500 m; Visibility = 800 m.

Laplacian operator to extract horizontal and vertical gradient values respectively for convolution operation. The higher the gradient value, the clearer the image is. The SMD function is also used to accumulate the sum of the absolute values of the difference between the gray values of adjacent pixels in two directions as the function value. The higher the value, the clearer the image will be. The SMD2 function multiplicate the two gray differences in each pixel neighborhood and then accumulates pixel by pixel, which improves the former shortcoming. The operation of multiplication and division is used to expand useful information. The larger the value, the clearer the image will be. The information Entropy function measures the richness of image information. The larger the value of the function, the richer the information and the more detailed features. Although the above indicators have certain limitations, generally speaking, the closer the value between the foggy image and the simulated image, the more realistic the simulated image is (Table 3).

Table 3. Comparison of evaluation indicators

Visibility	Category	Laplacian	SMD(107)	SMD2(107)	Entropy
100 m	Real fog	80.5	0.335	0.966	3.968
100 m	Simulated fog	79.3	0.331	0.953	3.637
300 m	Real fog	140.3	0.732	1.334	4.212
300 m	Simulated fog	139.1	0.712	1.322	4.207
500 m	Real fog	160.7	0.882	1.912	4.334
500 m	Simulated fog	159.1	0.812	2.121	4.451
800 m	Real fog	189.6	0.901	2.874	4.673
800 m	Simulated fog	187.3	0.873	2.889	4.771

4.4 Generation of Foggy Datasets

Using the above fog image generation algorithm, 765 urban road images are selected from Cityscape datasets to generate a total of 7650 fog data sets with visibility labels of 50 m, 100 m, 200 m, 300 m, 400 m, 500 m, 600 m, 700 m, 800 m and 900 m. The data sets are real and reliable. It can be used in many machine vision fields such as image recognition and object detection. Part of the datasets are shown in Fig. 14.

Fig. 14. Datasets of simulated foggy image. Visibility = 50 m; Visibility = 200 m; Visibility = 400 m

5 Conclusions

Aiming at the urgent needs of fog simulation technology, this paper proposes a fog simulation method based on improved self-supervised monocular depth estimation. Based on the atmospheric scattering model, detailed depth images were generated by multi-scale feature fusion and improved *manydepth* model. Then, the transmittance map was obtained by given visibility, and the dark channel map was used to estimate the atmospheric light value by distinguishing the sky region, so as to generate simulated fog datasets with different visibility. Through the comparison of 15 groups of experimental data, the fog simulation image conforms to human visual effect. This method is suitable for outdoor images with a small proportion of sky background, and its average fog simulation error rate is 6.2%, which indicates that the fog simulation method proposed in this paper is reliable and can solve the problems of lack of data sets and missing visibility data in fog days. It can be widely used in fog image recognition, visibility detection and fog target detection and other fields.

Acknowledgements. We acknowledge the support of Changsha University of Science and Technology Graduate Research Innovation Program (Grant No. 1208035).

References

1. Horvath, H.: On the applicability of the Koschmieder visibility formula. Atmos. Environ. 5(3), 177–184 (1967)
2. Garg, R., Bg, V.K., Carneiro, G., et al.: Unsupervised CNN for single view depth estimation: geometry to the rescue. In: Leibe, B., Matas, J., Sebe, N., Welling, M. (eds.) Computer Vision – ECCV 2016. ECCV 2016. LNCS, vol. 9912, pp. 740–756. Springer, Cham (2016). https://doi.org/10.1007/978-3-319-46484-8_45
3. Godard, C., Mac Aodha, O., Brostow, G.J.: Unsupervised monocular depth estimation with left-right consistency. In: Proceedings of the IEEE Conference on Computer Vision and Pattern Recognition, pp. 270–279 (2017)

4. Mansour, M., Davidson, P., Stepanov, O., et al.: Relative importance of binocular disparity and motion parallax for depth estimation: a computer vision approach. Remote Sens. **11**(17), 1990 (2019)
5. Chen, W., Fu, Z., Yang, D., et al.: Single-image depth perception in the wild. Adv. Neural Inf. Process. Syst. **29** (2016)
6. Nayar, S.K., Narasimhan, S.G.: Vision in bad weather. In: Proceedings of the Seventh IEEE International Conference on Computer Vision, pp. 820–827 (1999)
7. Song, H.S., Liu, Y.P., Zheng, H.L., et al.: Road visibility detection based on priori theory of dark and bright primary colors. Laser Optoelectron. Progress **58**(6), 94–100 (2021)
8. Wang, J., Liu, Y.Y., Zhang, X.W., et al.: Summary of atmospheric light value estimation methods in haze images. Laser J. **42**(9), 6–10 (2021)
9. Yang, Y., Lu, X.X.: An image dehazing method combing adaptive brightness transformation inequality to estimate transmittance. J. XI'AN JIAOTONG Univ. **55**(6), 69–76 (2021)
10. Yu, M.J., Zhang, H.F.: Single-image dehazing based on dark channel and incident light assumption. J. Image Graph. **19**(12), 1812–1819 (2014)
11. He, K., Jian, S., Tang, X., et al.: Single image haze removal using dark channel prior. IEEE Trans. Pattern Anal. Mach. Intell. **33**(12), 2341–2353 (2011)
12. Watson, J., Mac Aodha, O., Prisacariu, V., et al.: The temporal opportunist: self-supervised multi-frame monocular depth. In: Proceedings of the IEEE/CVF Conference on Computer Vision and Pattern Recognition, pp. 1164–1174 (2021)
13. Long, X., Liu, L., Li, W., et al.: Multi-view depth estimation using epipolar spatio-temporal networks. In: Proceedings of the IEEE/CVF Conference on Computer Vision and Pattern Recognition, pp. 8258–8267 (2021)
14. Choi, S., Park, J., Yu, W.: Resolving scale ambiguity for monocular visual odometry. In: 2013 10th International Conference on Ubiquitous Robots and Ambient Intelligence (URAI), pp. 604–608. IEEE (2013)
15. Ronneberger, O., Fischer, P., Brox, T.: U-Net: convolutional networks for biomedical image segmentation. In: IEICE Transactions on Fundamentals of Electronics, Communications and Computer Sciences (2015). abs/1505.04597
16. Mishra, P., Herrmann, I.: GAN meets chemometrics: segmenting spectral images with pixel2pixel image translation with conditional generative adversarial networks. Chemom. Intell. Lab. Syst. **215**, 104362 (2021)
17. Mittal, A., Moorthy, A.K., Bovik, A.C.: No-reference image quality assessment in the spatial domain. IEEE Trans. Image Process. Publ. IEEE Signal Process. Soc. **21**(12), 4695 (2012)
18. Mittal, A., Soundararajan, R., Bovik, A.C.: Making a completely blind image quality analyzer. IEEE Signal Process. Lett. **20**(3), 209–212 (2013)
19. Venkatanath, N., Praneeth, D., Chandrasekhar, B., et al.: Blind image quality evaluation using perception based features. In: Proceeding of the 21st National Conference on Communications, pp. 1–6, Washington, USA. IEEE (2015)
20. Yao, Y., Abidi, B., Doggaz, N., et al.: Evaluation of sharpness measures and search algorithms for the auto focusing of high-magnification images. Phys. A Stat. Mech. Appl. **6246**, 62460G-62460G-12 (2006)
21. Li, Y.F., Chen, N.N., Zhang, J.C.: Fast and high sensitivity focusing evaluation function. Appl. Res. Comput. **27**(4), 1534–1536 (2010)
22. Sen, A.: Quantum entropy function from AdS 2/CFT 1 correspondence. Int. J. Mod. Phys. A **24**(23), 4225–4244 (2009)
23. Song, S., Chandraker, M.: Robust scale estimation in real-time monocular SFM for autonomous driving. In: Proceedings of the IEEE Conference on Computer Vision and Pattern Recognition, pp. 1566–1573 (2014)
24. Yuan, W., Gu, X., Dai, Z., et al. New crfs: Neural window fully-connected crfs for monocular depth estimation. arXiv preprint arXiv:2203.01502 (2022)

25. Mahmud, R., Buyya, R.: Modelling and simulation of fog and edge computing environments using iFogSim toolkit. Fog edge Comput. Princ. Paradig. 1–35 (2019)
26. Wang, Y.K., Fan, C.T.: Single image defogging by multiscale depth fusion. IEEE Trans. Image Process. **23**(11), 4826–4837 (2014)
27. Graffieti, G., Maltoni, D.: Artifact-free single image defogging. Atmosphere **12**(5), 577 (2021)

Improved YOLOX Transmission Line Insulator Identification

Zhongqi Zhao[1](✉), Qing He[2], Sixuan Dai[2], and Qiongshuang Tang[2]

[1] Haibei Power Supply Company, State Grid Qinghai Power Company, Haiyan 812200, China
254739027@qq.com

[2] School of Electrical and Information Engineering, Changsha University of Science and Technology, Changsha 410114, China

Abstract. Aiming at the problem of low recognition accuracy of insulators in power system transmission lines and the recognition results contain many backgrounds, this paper proposes a high-performance detection model by combining the improved YOLOX target detection algorithm with the rotating frame detection algorithm. Firstly, the backbone network of YOLOX is replaced with ConvNext with a larger receptive field to improve the feature learning ability of the model for insulators. Secondly, the fusion between the output features of the feature pyramid pooling module is enhanced using the channel disorder operation. Finally, the angle classification of the detection frame is added to the network to realize the rotation frame detection and reduce the background interference in the recognition result. The model is trained and tested with manually marked aerial photography data. The test results show that the method has high accuracy in insulator identification and meets the high-performance detection requirements.

Keywords: Insulator identification · Target detection · Rotating box detection · Feature pyramid pooling

1 First Section

1.1 A Subsection Sample

In the power system, the safety of transmission lines is the primary factor for the failure-free operation of the power grid, so the grid needs to be inspected regularly. The traditional inspection mode requires employees to go to the site for inspection, which needs a lot of human and material resources and is inefficient.

Because of the rapid development of unmanned aerial vehicle (UVA) technology, using UVA instead of manual operation can simplify the work pattern and reduce the risk of aerial operation [1]. In order to accelerate the transformation of traditional inspection work mode to automatic operation mode, the power grid company has adopted a combination of helicopter and laser point cloud scanning to achieve full coverage of transmission line images. At present, the "machine patrol as the main, human patrol as a supplement" of "machine patrol + human patrol" operation and maintenance mode

H. Yang et al. (Eds.): SmartGIFT 2022, LNICST 483, pp. 186–199, 2023.
https://doi.org/10.1007/978-3-031-31733-0_17

has basically formed, transmission line operation and maintenance level continues to improve [2]. In order to be safe and stable, power transmission conductors are generally erected at high altitudes through poles and towers. The function of insulators is to ensure that the conductor is insulated from the tower and the earth, with the characteristics of high voltage resistance and mechanical stress resistance. However, the complex outdoor environment causes insulators to be damaged, partially dislodged, dirty, etc., which can easily lead to power line operation failure, it is necessary to replace the detected damaged insulator [3], and insulator detection provides significant data support for it.

In the traditional insulator identification algorithm, researchers use the edge features, histogram features, and color features of insulators as the basis for the identification of insulators. Reference [4] uses Euclidean distance to match insulator features extracted by Canny edge detection to intelligently identify insulators. Reference [5] uses the Dirichlet distribution combined with relative entropy to obtain the semantic relevance of features and improve the recognition accuracy. Traditional algorithms rely on human a priori knowledge, which requires manual design of classification features and increases the complexity of the algorithm.

The development of Graphics Processing Unit (GPU) technology has facilitated the widespread application of deep learning technology. In the insulator identification task, the deep learning model is constructed so that the model can learn the contextual semantic information of insulators autonomously and complete the automatic insulator identification work, which simplifies the complexity of the identification process and improves the work efficiency. The target detection algorithm can complete the insulator recognition and get the insulator location information through logistic regression. It can be mainly divided into two categories, single-stage detection algorithms including SSD [6], YOLO [7], RetinaNet [8], etc., and two-stage detection algorithms including R-CNN [9], Fast R-CNN [10], Faster R-CNN [11], etc.

Reference [12] applied the Faster R-CNN detection algorithm to the insulator identification task of transmission lines, completed the identification of different types of insulators, and proved the effectiveness of the algorithm. Based on Faster RCNN, the reference [13] uses an attention mechanism to improve each feature extraction module, forcing the network to learn channel feature correlation, suppressing background interference, and improving model accuracy. Reference [14] uses the YOLOV2 detection algorithm to identify insulators and combines fault diagnosis technology to complete insulator defect discrimination. Reference [15] uses multi-feature fusion technology to enhance the detailed information of small objects and then combines spatial attention mechanisms to optimize model performance. To address the problem of little semantic information, reference [16] uses multi-scale feature fusion to enhance the semantic features of targets and optimize the scale scaling module. The model is made more suitable for insulator identification with a large-scale span. To achieve real-time detection requirements, reference [17, 18] replaces the traditional convolution operation with depth-separable convolution. It can reduce the computational complexity of the model and improve the efficiency of the algorithm under the premise of ensuring accuracy.

Deep learning techniques have significantly improved the automation of transmission line inspection, and the accuracy of the current single-stage algorithm in the target detection network is improved to a high level of accuracy. Based on this, this paper proposes an insulator identification model with an improved YOLOX algorithm to improve the detection accuracy of insulator identification.

2 Detection Network

2.1 YOLO Network

In 2015, Redmon et al. proposed the yolov1 detection algorithm, which is a single-stage target detection algorithm and an anchors-free target detection algorithm.

Subsequent authors proposed V2 and V3 versions, in which V2 introduced the idea of anchors and proposed to use of a stronger feature extraction network, V3 version proposed a stronger backbone feature extraction network DarkNet53 and introduced the idea of FPN to detect multi-scale targets, among which the V3 algorithm is one of the most widely used algorithms. Later, some scholars proposed V4 and V5 versions based on the V3 version, which improved the speed and accuracy of the model. The V4 and V5 models have similar structures, but the V5 version is very friendly to engineering deployment. In July 2021, Megvii Technology released the YOLOX target detection algorithm.

2.2 YOLO Network

YOLOX is an anchors-free algorithm, YOLOV4 and YOLOV5 use the idea of hyperparameter evolution to update their hyperparameters during training, which will lead the algorithm to over-optimization on anchors, so the authors do not improve on V4 and V5 structure, but on the model of YOLOV3-SPP. The model structure of YOLOX is shown in Fig. 1. Conv in the figure represents convolution, BN represents batch normalization, and Sibu represents activation function.

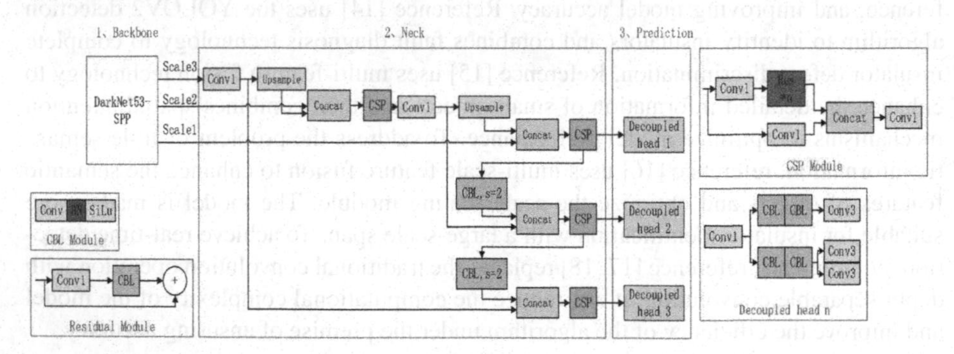

Fig. 1. YOLOX structure diagram.

In the backbone network, the feature extraction module is consistent with that in the YOLOV3-SPP algorithm, and both use DarkNet53 to extract higher-order semantic features and the SPP module to extract multi-scale features. The feature fusion module introduces the PAN structure based on the FPN structure. The shallow feature map contains more local detail information, and the local detail information is beneficial to the regression task, and the deep feature map contains more higher-order semantic features, and the higher-order semantic information is beneficial to the classification task.

The fusion of shallow and deep features can obtain a feature mapping of the two attributes, thus improving the detection performance of the model. In the prediction module, a Decoupled Head (DH) strategy is used to decouple the prediction branches, where the output branches of classification and regression share a single convolutional layer in YOLOV3. Since the classification branch requires more higher-order semantic information and the regression branch requires more local detail information. On this basis, the output of the classification branch is separated from the branch of the regression output and use two-way convolution to perform the regression task and the regression task separately. The addition of DH improves the detection accuracy of the model and speeds up the convergence of the network.

2.3 Optimization Strategy

It is well known that the detection algorithm based on anchors based has the problems of difficult adjustment of hyperparameters and poor versatility. To obtain better detection performance, the V3 algorithm sets three a priori boxes of different sizes to improve the detection accuracy of the model, but it reduces the detection speed of the model to a certain extent.

A large number of anchors free algorithms have emerged in recent years, which eliminate a large number of tuning links, reduce the complexity of the algorithm, and are no longer limited by the setting of anchors for extreme size targets, which can improve the detection performance of the model. The YOLOV3 algorithm is combined with the detectors of anchors free to extract the target detection algorithm of anchors free. The detection algorithm based on anchors free changes the original prediction of 3 different sizes of boxes in one location into 1 box, which reduces the computation of the model in the detection head link and improves the detection speed of the model. The performance of the target detection algorithm depends to some extent on the label assignment of positive and negative samples. The assignment of positive and negative samples is according to the Intersection over Union (IoU) ratio of the ground truth and the prior frame. However, the assignment of positive and negative samples is different in different situations (obscured), and at this point, the label assignment is regarded as an optimal transmission problem, and the simOTA label assignment method is proposed. The detection accuracy of the model is improved by proposing a cost matrix to select the a priori frame corresponding to the position with the smallest cost as the positive sample to match the ground truth.

3 Model Improvement

3.1 ConvNext

Reference [19] proposes a neural network model with a larger sensory field with a Base Unit (BU) as shown in the a-plot in Fig. 2b. Firstly, the input is goes through a deep separable convolution of size 7 × 7 for feature extraction, and the larger the convolution kernel, the wider the feature area learned. Then the features are up-dimensioned and down-dimensioned using two 1 × 1 ordinary convolutional operations to obtain more abstract semantic information, and finally the features are summed and fused with those of the residual mapping branch. The downsampling operation can reduce the input feature resolution and the computational complexity of the model. This paper shows the Down Sample Uint (DSU) in Fig. 2b, a 3 × 3 depth-separable convolution is added to the residual mapping, while the step size of the 7 × 7 depth-separable convolution is 2, which is applied to double the feature resolution and double the number of channels.

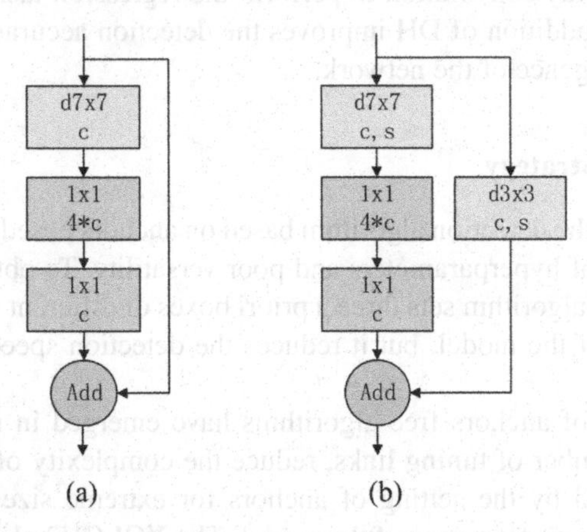

Fig. 2. ConvNext module. (a) Base Unit (BU); (b) Down Sample Uint (DSU).

3.2 Spatial Pyramid Pooling Module

In this paper, SPP [20] has been modified adaptively, and its structure is shown in Fig. 3. Firstly, four sets of feature compression vectors are obtained by using four sets of maximum pooling operations with different sizes for the input features. To reduce the number of parameters of the module and to ensure that the feature dimension of each group of features is consistent with the input when stitching, so compress its channel dimension by a factor of 4 using 1 × 1 convolution operation. Then the feature resolution is restored using upsampling, and the four groups of features are combined in the channel dimension, and the combined results are summed and fused with the original input features. Finally, to increase the transferability of information between features, a Channel Shuffle operation is used to reorder the final results in the channel dimension.

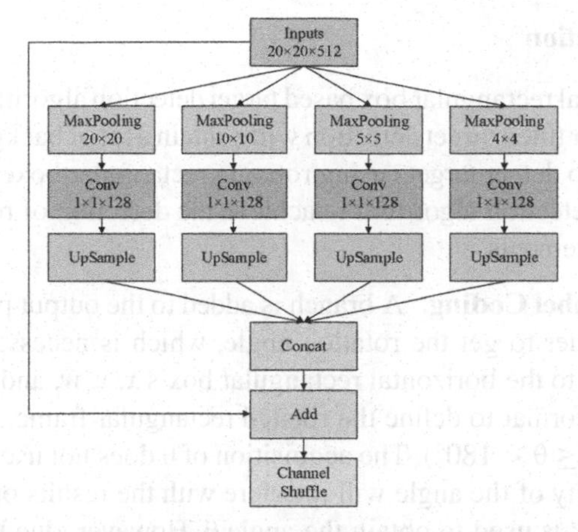

Fig. 3. ConvNext module. (a) Base Unit (BU); (b) Down Sample Uint (DSU).

Table 1. Backbone network

name	size	layer
Inputs	640 × 640 × 3	-
Conv1	320 × 320 × 32	BU × 1 DSU × 1
Conv2_x	160 × 160 × 64	BU × 2 DSU × 1
Conv3_x	80 × 80 × 128	BU × 5 DSU × 1
Conv4_x	40 × 40 × 256	BU × 2 DSU × 1
Conv5_x	20 × 20 × 512	BU × 1 DSU × 1
	20 × 20 × 512	SPP × 1

3.3 Backbone

To improve the model feature learning capability, the original backbone network in YOLOX is replaced using the network structure in Table 1. The network input size is 640 × 640 × 3. In the first level of features, 1 BU module and 1 DSU module are used to learn shallow features, and change the resolution of the features to half and double the number of channel dimensions. Similarly, in the second level of features, 2 BU modules and 1 DSU module are used to learn the features. In the third level features, 5 BU modules and 1 DSU module are used to learn the features, in the fourth level feature, 2 BU modules and 1 DSU module learning features are used, and in the fifth level, 1 BU module and 1 DSU module are used to learn the features. Finally, the improved SPP module is used to acquire multi-scale features.

3.4 Rotation Detection

YOLOX is a horizontal rectangular box based target detection algorithm, using a horizontal rectangular box for tilted target detection will contain a lot of background information. The best practice is to detect targets using rotating rectangular boxes, so this paper uses the YOLOX target detection algorithm to achieve the detection of rotating targets, with the following improvements.

Circular Smooth Label Coding. A branch is added to the output port of the network's detection head in order to get the rotation angle, which is necessary for rotating box detection in addition to the horizontal rectangular box's *x*, *y*, *w*, and h dimensions. This paper uses longside format to define the rotated rectangular frame, which is the format of *x*, *y*, *w*, *h*, and θ ($0 \leq \theta < 180°$). The acquisition of θ does not use the regression task, because the periodicity of the angle will interfere with the results of the regression, but the classification task is used to obtain the angle θ. However, due to the periodicity of the angle, a simple one-hot encoding cannot be used. Instead, the encoding method of the Circular Smooth Label (*CSL*) proposed in reference [21] is used to classify the angle of the box. Its expression The formula is shown in formula 1:

$$CSL(x) = \begin{cases} g(x), \ \theta - r < x < \theta + r \\ 0, \ else \end{cases} \tag{1}$$

where θ denotes the current rotation angle of the real frame, r denotes the window radius, whose default value is 6, and *g(x)* denotes the window function.

The window function expression is shown in formula 2, and its related expressions in formula 3 and 4 are respectively shown. The window function meets periodicity and symmetry.

$$g(x) = e^{-\frac{(x-\mu)^2}{2\delta^2}} \tag{2}$$

$$g(x) = g(x + KT), \ K \in N, T = 180/\omega \tag{3}$$

$$0 \leq g(\theta + \varepsilon) = g(\theta - \varepsilon) \leq 1, \ |\varepsilon| < r \tag{4}$$

where the mean $\mu = 0$, the variance $\delta = 0$, and N is the set of natural numbers.

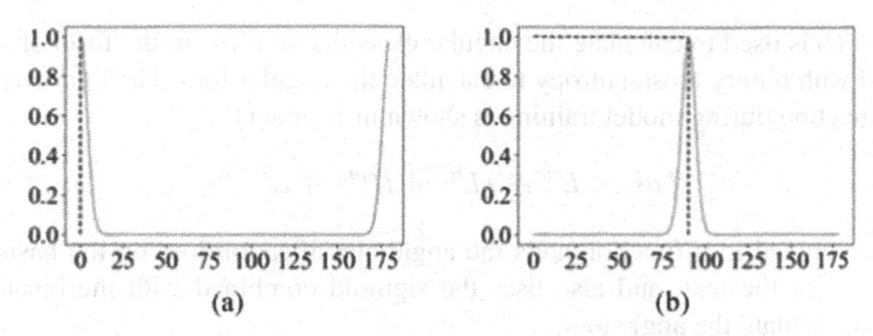

Fig. 4. *CSL* encoded label score map. (a) θ = 0°; (b) θ = 90°.

When the true θ value is 0° or 90°, the corresponding *CSL* coded label scores are shown in the left and right plots in Fig. 4, respectively, where the horizontal axis indicates the angle value and the vertical axis indicates the coded label score.

Loss Function Optimization. There are two places in YOLOX where the loss function needs to be calculated, the first time the loss is found for constructing the cost matrix for label assignment with the loss function shown in in formula 5, and this time the loss is calculated simply for screening positive and negative samples.

$$
\begin{aligned}
Cost &= L^{cls} + \lambda L^{reg} + L_1 \\
L_1 &= \begin{cases} -1000, \ if \ in \, center \, or \, r \leq 2.5 \\ 0, \text{ else} \end{cases}
\end{aligned}
\tag{5}
$$

where the classification loss (L^{cls}) uses a binary cross-entropy loss function, the regression loss (L^{reg}) uses an iou loss function, λ is used to control the ratio of the two loss weights, and λ defaults to 3. The L_I in formula is equivalent to adding more prior information to the equivalent, increasing the degree of matching of the high-quality prior (the center of the grid is within the range of the true box or 2.5 grid).

A second calculation of the loss is used to optimize the model with the loss function shown in formula 6.

$$
Loss = L^{cls} + \lambda L^{reg} + L^{conf} \tag{6}
$$

The equation contains classification loss, confidence loss and regression loss, where the binary cross-entropy loss function is used for classification loss, and confidence loss, and λ is used to control the regression loss weight ratio, which is 5 by default. This paper also uses the approach proposed in reference [22] to swap the true labels of confidence with the true labels of classification, which is used to solve the inconsistency between the training session and the testing session of the network due to the absence of supervised signals in the confidence output of some boxes during training. Since the output branch of the improved algorithm has an additional branch for rotation angle classification, the loss function in YOLOX needs to be improved. The improved cost function at label assignment is given in formula 7.

$$
Cost = L^{cls} + \lambda L^{reg} + L_1 + L^{\theta-cls} \tag{7}
$$

where (θ-*cls*) is used to calculate the angular classification loss in the form of sigmoid combined with binary cross-entropy to calculate the angular loss. The improvement of the loss function during model training is shown in formula 8.

$$Loss = L^{cls} + \lambda L^{reg} + L^{conf} + L^{\theta-cls} \tag{8}$$

The optimized loss function adds the angle classification loss on the basis of the original loss in the text, and also uses the sigmoid combined with the binary cross entropy to calculate the angle loss.

4 Experimental Results and Analysis

4.1 Data Set Introduction and Data Enhancement

The experimental data are obtained from aerial image maps, of which 1500 are in the training set and 300 are in the test set. The insulators in the image maps are labeled using the Labelme tool, which is divided into two modes: rectangular box labeling and rotating rectangular box labeling, and the results are shown in Fig. 5. Where a is the rectangular box labeling result, which contains more background, and b is the rotating box labeling result.

Fig. 5. Annotation mode. (a) Rectangular box labeling; (b) Rotated box annotation.

In view of the difficulty of image data acquisition, tedious and time-consuming labeling, and considering that the neural network model requires more data for fitting in the process of learning target features, the training set is subjected to data enhancement processing. Insulators have directional feature invariance in spatial location, scale variability in shape, and obscured phenomenon in shooting angle. Therefore, this paper uses the data enhancement methods of mirror image enhancement, multi-scale scaling, and random erasure to expand the training data to 3,000 sheets.

4.2 Experimental Environment

The code used for the experiments in this paper runs on a deep learning server configured with an RTX3090 graphics card, 24G of current memory, and 32G of running memory. A neural network model is built using the Tensorflow 2.0.0 deep learning framework.

4.3 Learning Rate Setting

The number of iterations for each model is set to 100, and the Adam optimizer is selected. In the process of searching for the global optimal solution of the model, using a larger learning rate at the early stage of training can avoid the model from falling into the local optimal solution, and at the same time, it should ensure that the learning rate decays at a smaller rate. And in the middle of training, the parameters of each model are more stable, so the learning rate decay should be accelerated. In the late training period, the learning rate should be slowed down in order to prevent the model parameters from oscillating and becoming unstable due to too large a change in the learning rate. Therefore, this paper uses the "cosine annealing" learning rate decay strategy as shown in Fig. 6, and the learning rate decrease helps the model converge.

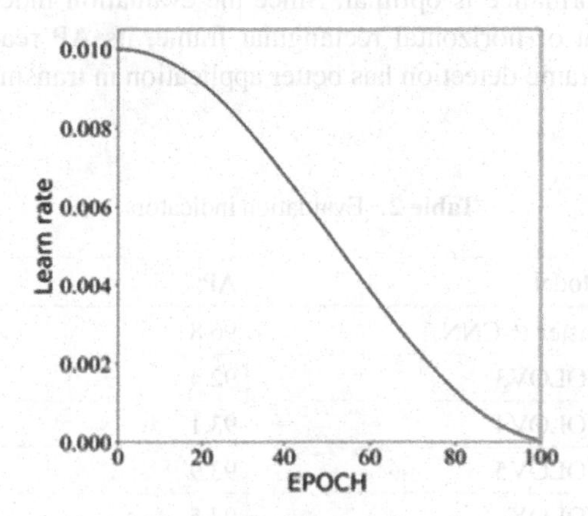

Fig. 6. Cosine annealing.

4.4 Experimental Results

In order to better evaluate the model performance, Precision (P), Recall (R), and Average Precision (AP) evaluation metrics are selected for analysis in this paper. First, TP is defined to denote the number of detected frames with IoU greater than a specified threshold, FP denotes the number of detected frames with IoU less than a specified threshold, and FN denotes the number of undetected true frames. The meaning of each indicator representation is shown below.

Precision (P). The precision represents the probability of the true being an insulator in the sample predicted to be an insulator. The expression is calculated as follows.

$$P = \frac{TP}{TP + FP} \tag{9}$$

Recall (R). The recall represents the probability of predicting a positive sample among the samples that are truly insulators. The expression is as follows.

$$R = \frac{TP}{TP + FN} \tag{10}$$

Average Precision (AP). The average precision is defined as plotting a curve on two-dimensional coordinates using a combination of different P-point coordinates and R-point coordinates, and the area of the curve is the AP of a single category.

4.5 Qualitative and Quantitative Analysis

Comparison of Each Index. The results of model evaluation index comparison are shown in Table 2. In this paper, the improved algorithm is compared with the current mainstream detection algorithm, and the two-stage algorithm Faster RCNN has higher accuracy than YOLOV3-YOLOV5, but the YOLOX algorithm performs better, in which the AP of the improved model reaches 98.7%, which is 1.2% higher than the YOLOX model, and the performance is optimal. Since the evaluation index of rotating frame is different from that of horizontal rectangular frame, its AP reaches 90.8%, which proves that rotating frame detection has better application in transmission line insulator detection.

Table 2. Evaluation indicators

Model	AP%
Faster R-CNN	96.8
YOLOV3	92.4
YOLOV4	93.1
YOLOV5	93.9
YOLOX	97.5
Ours	98.7
R-YOLOX	90.8

Horizontal Frame Detection Results. The effect of the improved model in the horizontal frame detection is shown in Fig. 7, which shows that the insulator as a whole can be well detected. The improved SPP module enables the model to have better characterization capability in terms of multi-scale features, and the smaller insulators in the figure can be well identified. In addition, this paper uses the on-the-fly data erasure enhancement method to effectively alleviate the difficult identification problem caused by the obscured insulators. However, it can be seen from the results that the rectangular box where the insulators are detected contains a large background, which can easily bring interference to the insulator fault detection.

Detection Results of Rotating Frame. In order to reduce the interference of complex background in the recognition results, this paper uses the idea of rotating frame target detection to get the position information of the rotating frame by regressing the position coordinates as well as the angle classification, and its detection results are shown in Fig. 8.

Fig. 7. Horizontal box detection results.

Fig. 8. Detection results of rotating frame

The rotating frame is the main body of the insulator, and there is less background in the frame, which largely reduces the false detection caused by background interference.

4.6 Ablation Experiments

In order to test the insulator recognition effect of the improved network, ablation experiments are set up in this paper, as shown in Table 3, to verify the detection effect of the proposed model by adding improvement steps step by step. The original YOLOX algorithm can achieve 97.5% AP, which is improved by 0.8% points by using ConvNext to improve the backbone feature extraction network and improve the model feature learning capability. Enhancing the output feature fusion by adding channel disorder operation in the SPP module, which achieves 98.7% AP. Finally, using the rotated rectangular frame for target detection, the obtained R-YOLOX model performance can also reach 90.8% with excellent performance.

Table 3. Evaluation indicators

Model	AP%
Original YOLOX	97.5
Improved YOLOX (ConvNext)	98.3
Improved YOLOX (ConvNext + Channel Shuffle)	98.7
R-YOLOX	90.8

5 Conclusion

In this paper, based on the YOLOX detection algorithm, the DarkNet53 is replaced by a backbone network with a larger feeling field, which can make the model learn larger local features, while the use of depth-separable convolution in the backbone network ensures the high-speed of the model. The features output from the spatial pyramid pooling module are independent in the channel dimension, and this paper uses the channel disorder operation to increase the information interactivity between its features and enhance the feature fusion capability. And the idea of rotating frame detection is added to reduce the interference of background in the recognition results and provide good data support for insulator fault recognition, and the final model is optimal in terms of accuracy.

References

1. Chen, F.X., Yang, L., Xie, C., et al.: Unmanned aerial vehicle transmission line patrol technology and its application. Technol. Innov. Appl. **11**(25), 174–176 (2021)
2. Wang, L.F.: Research and Application of UAV in Transmission Line Patrol. Doctor, North China Electric Power University (2018)
3. Liu, Z., Zhang, L.M., Geng, M.X., et al.: Target detection method for high voltage cable based on improved faster R-CNN. J. Intell. Syst. **14**(04), 627–634 (2019)
4. Yao, X.T., Liu, L., Li, Z.Y.: Catenary insulator recognition method based on canny edge feature points. Electr. Porcelain Arrester **01**, 142–148 (2020)
5. Wu, W.H., Sun, L., Wang, G.Z., et al.: Recognition and classification based on synonyms for the allocation of railway catenary insulator. Electr. Porcelain Arrester **01**, 156–160 (2020)
6. Liu, W., Anguelov, D., Erhan, D., Szegedy, C., Reed, S., Fu, C.-Y., Berg, A.C.: SSD: single shot multibox detector. In: Leibe, B., Matas, J., Sebe, N., Welling, M. (eds.) ECCV 2016. LNCS, vol. 9905, pp. 21–37. Springer, Cham (2016). https://doi.org/10.1007/978-3-319-46448-0_2
7. Redmon, J., Farhadi, A.: Yolov3: an incremental improvement, arXiv preprint https://doi.org/10.48550/arXiv.1804.02767
8. Lin T, Y., Goyal, P., Girshick, R., et al.: Focal loss for dense object detection. In: Proceedings of the IEEE International Conference on Computer Vision, 2017, pp. 2980–2988. IEEE (2017)
9. Girshick, R., Donahue, J., Darrell, T., et al.: Rich feature hierarchies for accurate object detection and semantic segmentation. In: Proceedings of the IEEE Conference on Computer Vision and Pattern Recognition, 2014, pp. 580–587.IEEE (2014)
10. Girshick, R.: Fast R-CNN. In: Proceedings of the IEEE International Conference on Computer Vision, pp. 1440–1448, IEEE (2015)

11. Ren, S., He, K., Girshick, R., et al.: Faster R-CNN: towards real-time object detection with region proposal networks. In: Advances in Neural Information Processing Systems, vol. 28 (2015)
12. Cheng, H.Y., Zhai, Y.J., Chen, R.: Based on Faster R-CNN insulator in aerial image recognition. J. Mod. Electron. Technol. **42**(02), 98–102 (2019)
13. Zhao, W.Q., Cheng, X.F., et al.: Attention mechanism and Faster RCNN for insulator recognition. J. Intell. Syst. **15**(01), 92–98 (2020)
14. Lai, Q.P., Yang, J., Tan, B.T., et al.: Insulator automatic identification and defect diagnosis model based on YOLOv2 network. China Power **52**(07), 31–39 (2019)
15. Wang, T.: Research on Recognition and Location of Insulators in Aerial Images Based on SSD. Master, School of Control and Computer Engineering (2021)
16. Zhao, W.Q., Zhang, H.M., Xu, M.F.: Insulator recognition based on an improved scale-transferrable network. J. Image Graph. **26**(11), 2561–2570 (2021)
17. Hong, G.: Research on identification and positioning of insulators based on lightweight algorithm UAV images. Inner Mongolia Sci. Technol. Econ. **21**, 83–85 (2019)
18. Tang, L., Wang, S.Q., Jin, H.B., et al.: Intelligent Electric Power,50(02), 69–74 (2022)
19. Liu, Z., Mao, H., Wu, C.Y., et al.: A ConvNet for the 2020s, arXiv preprint https://arxiv.org/abs/2201.03545
20. He, K., Zhang, X., Ren, S., et al.: Spatial pyramid pooling in deep convolutional networks for visual recognition. IEEE Trans. Pattern Anal. Mach. Intell. **37**(9), 1904–1916 (2015)
21. Yang, X., Yan, J.: Arbitrary-oriented object detection with circular smooth label. In: Vedaldi, A., Bischof, H., Brox, T., Frahm, J.-M. (eds.) ECCV 2020. LNCS, vol. 12353, pp. 677–694. Springer, Cham (2020). https://doi.org/10.1007/978-3-030-58598-3_40
22. Li, X., Wang, W., Wu, L., et al.: Generalized focal loss: learning qualified and distributed bounding boxes for dense object detection. In: Advances in Neural Information Processing Systems, vol. 33, pp. 21002–21012 (2020)

Industry 4.0 Applications

Electricity Anomaly Detection Research of Flue-Cured Tobacco Users Considering the Characteristics of Industry Electricity Consumption Behavior

Xu Zhengyi[1(✉)], Yang Jianping[1], and Liang Yunhua[2]

[1] Safety Supervision Center of State Grid, Hunan Electric Power Co., Ltd., Changsha 410004, China
1182667599@qq.com

[2] State Grid Hunan Electric Power Company Extra High Voltage Substation Company, Changsha 410004, China

Abstract. Power theft inspection is an effective means to improve the operating income of power supply enterprises. However, in practice, there has been a problem that the accuracy rate of power theft detection is not high. Cluster analysis of power consumption behaviors by subdividing power users by industry will not only make it possible to extract characteristic index items that accurately describe user behaviors in combination with industry power consumption behavior characteristics, but also reduce user classification dimensions and false positives for power theft detection. Rate is the development direction of promoting the practical application of data-driven power theft detection. This article takes flue-cured tobacco users as the object. Firstly, it analyzes the industry electricity consumption patterns of flue-cured tobacco users, and then based on the statistical analysis of industry characteristics, establishes power consumption index characteristic items that accurately describe the industry characteristics of flue-cured tobacco users. The propagation clustering algorithm performs cluster analysis of users in flue-cured tobacco industry. Numerical simulation results show that the proposed method can not only accurately identify misclassified non-flue-cured tobacco users such as public properties in rural areas, reduce the scope of power theft detection, but also effectively detect specific types of flue-cured tobacco specific power stealing behavior.

Keywords: Industry Electricity Characteristics · Electricity Theft Detection · Tobacco Load · AP Clustering

1 Introduction

At present, The State Grid Corporation of China have achieved complete collection of electricity consumption information, and can basically grasp the user's electricity consumption data and customer information timely and accurately [1]. On this basis,

H. Yang et al. (Eds.): SmartGIFT 2022, LNICST 483, pp. 203–217, 2023.
https://doi.org/10.1007/978-3-031-31733-0_18

the production technicians summarized the indicators of exact physical meaning such as zero-sequence current, power reversal and voltage loss of electric meters for low-voltage users based on their experience, which can accurately identify abnormal electricity consumption behaviors. However, this type of method is mainly applicable to specific stealing methods, and the coverage of stealing methods is limited. Electric power scientists and technicians have carried out a large number of data-driven electricity anomaly detection research mainly from two aspects: unsupervised cluster analysis and supervised classification analysis, focusing on massive electricity metering data. Among them, unsupervised anomaly recognition is generally based on user data to calculate characteristic index items and then perform cluster analysis, identify abnormal users according to category [2]. Supervised electricity theft detection takes known electricity thieves as negative samples, summarizes the regular characteristics of the negative samples on the feature index items, and then evaluates the degree of difference between the detected users and the negative samples, thereby identifying abnormal users.

The core of the data-driven electricity theft detection method lies in two aspects: the selection of characteristic index items and the algorithm design. Electricity thieves usually have performance in specific aspects of metering data and user information. Commonly used characteristic index items in electricity anomaly detection mainly include the following categories:

(1) User payment records and credit information: users with bad credit have a significantly higher probability of abnormal electricity usage than general users. Credit evaluations such as the payment records of marketing systems and the on-site inspections times are commonly used characteristic index items [3–5].
(2) Consumer electricity consumption, volatility and fluctuation range: Electricity theft is often manifested as a trend of decline in electricity consumption. Most documents regard the load curve and fluctuation interval composed of daily or monthly electricity and their volatility as characteristic index items, and according to the abnormal changes in power consumption, the theft is identified [6–8].
(3) Reporting capacity utilization and power factor: In addition to abnormal power consumption, users may also leave traces in other aspects. For example, industrial and commercial users need to pay capacity electricity charges based on reported capacity, so there may be a certain proportional relationship between actual load and reported capacity [9]. In addition, power theft mainly focuses on reducing the power metering, and sudden abnormalities in the power factor may occur. Such indirect factors can also be used as characteristic index items.

On the basis of the aforementioned characteristic index items, researchers have explored the use of various algorithms to accurately identify abnormal electricity consumption. After completing the cluster analysis, outlier detection is required to identify outliers from the clustering results. The local outlier factor proposed in [10] can characterize the isolation degree of a sample by comparing the local density of an object and its neighbors in the data set, and can be used to detect outliers. [11] proposed an outlier identification method based on gridding local outlier factors, which significantly simplified the complexity of outlier analysis in low-density areas and improved the algorithm efficiency. Since there may be a strong correlation between the feature index items, this paper also uses principal component analysis to reduce the dimension of the feature index items to improve the accuracy of the algorithm. Literature [7] uses Gaussian kernel function to improve the local outlier factor algorithm for user clustering on the basis of feature index dimensionality reduction, which better solves the problem of threshold setting for outlier judgment. In Irish commercial and residential user data. The test samples constructed above have a higher recognition accuracy. Literature [12] extended the horizontal load clustering between users to the vertical clustering of the users themselves, using the bulldozer algorithm for horizontal and vertical clustering, and using the user's electricity consumption behavior pattern. Aiming at the problem of high false alarm rate due to insufficient negative samples for electricity theft detection methods, literature [13] combined the ROC curve to optimize the classification threshold, and used the real-valued deep confidence network to detect the abnormal electricity consumption data for daily electricity data.

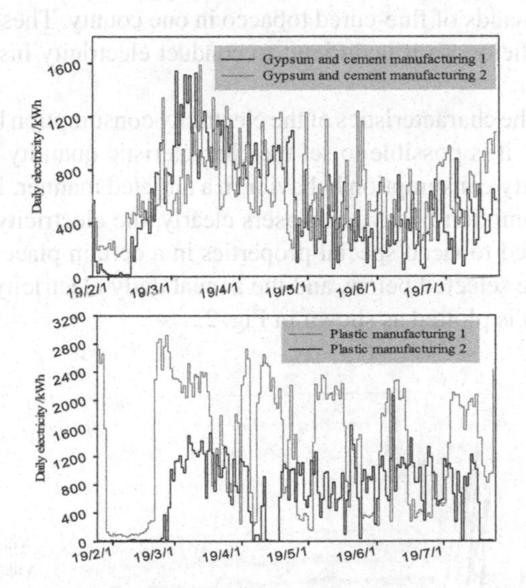

Fig. 1. Village tobacco roasting electricity consumption standardization curve.

It should be pointed out that the existing researches mostly design characteristic index items around abnormal changes in power consumption, which are prone to false alarms themselves for the following reasons. Existing power theft algorithms implicitly require users to have a basically stable power consumption, but from the Fig. 1, we can see that the power demand of a considerable number of users depends on the order demand, and large or trending fluctuations in power are normal. Industrial users with relatively stable electricity demand may have abnormal low electricity under external interference such as environmental protection inspection and safety inspection.

The aforementioned characteristic index items are distilled out of the industry background. Although this can better take into account the universality of users in different industries, the index items designed around power changes have the defects of insufficient reliability and sensitivity, which may easily lead to false alarms, and the defects of this index item itself are difficult to solve from the algorithm design level. To the best knowledge of the authors, it is possible to extract industrial characteristic index items and detect abnormal electricity consumption by taking advantage of the similar characteristics of users in the same industry in terms of composition, consumption behavior and production scheduling mode of electric equipment.

2 Industry Characteristics Analysis of Flue-Cured Tobacco Users

Electric flue-cured tobacco is a typical case of promoting electric energy substitution strategy in rural areas recent years [13]. As electric roasting can automatically control the temperature of the roasting barn with high precision, it can not only reduce labor and fuel costs significantly, but also improve the quality of tobacco leaves. At present, electric flue-cured tobacco has been widely promoted and applied. In some tobacco producing areas, there are thousands of flue-cured tobacco in one county. These special properties are scattered in the fields, so it is difficult to conduct electricity inspection in a timely and effective manner.

Combined with the characteristics of the electricity consumption behavior of the flue-cured tobacco users, it is possible to set the characteristic quantity that can accurately describe the electricity consumption behavior in a targeted manner. In order to manifest the electricity consumption behavior of users clearly, the electricity consumption data of 4 typical flue-cured tobacco special properties in a certain place from June 1, 2016 to April 30, 2017 are selected below, and the annual daily electricity consumption data after standardization is plotted as shown in Fig. 2.

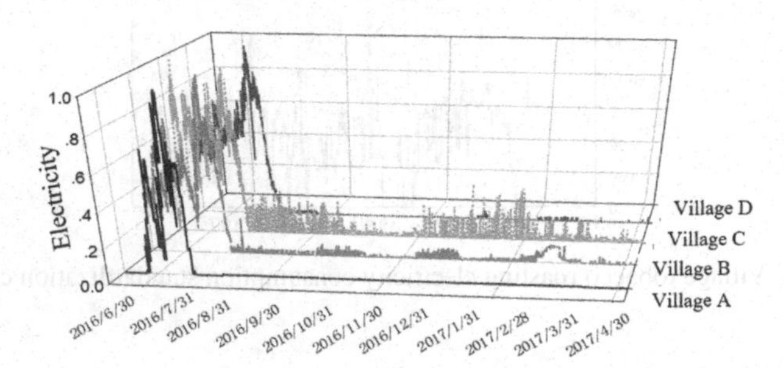

Fig. 2. Standardization daily electricity consumption in a year.

The characteristics of daily electricity consumption are analyzed as follows:

(1) The capacity of the flue-cured tobacco special properties is generally between 90~150 kW, and several barns are connected underneath, and each barn has a single-phase load, and the electric heating power is about 3~5 kW. Each barn can operate independently and does not have the characteristics of three-phase load balance. Therefore, it is not appropriate to use three-phase balance as a characteristic index to describe the electricity consumption behavior of flue-cured tobacco users.

(2) The flue-cured tobacco special properties mainly supplies the flue-cured tobacco load. The electricity consumption in the mature season of tobacco leaves in June and July reaches its peak, which is significantly higher than other periods. During the flue-cured tobacco season, the daily electricity consumption has obvious daily changes. From the Fig. 2 we can see that, taking the average daily power consumption of 4 special properties in June and July as the reference value, the calculated maximum daily power difference before and after the flue-cured tobacco season can reach 1.40, 0.36, 0.76, and 0.29, respectively. Because the flue-cured tobacco special properties load has obvious inter-day volatility during the flue-cured tobacco season, it is difficult to identify the abnormal electricity consumption based on the electricity abnormality.
(3) Other periods outside the flue-cured tobacco season are obviously light-loaded, with low electricity consumption and a stable trend, showing a continuous low electricity consumption state.

From the daily electricity data of the flue-cured tobacco special properties, it is difficult to identify abnormal electricity consumption based on the three-phase symmetry of the load or the inter-day electricity changes. It is necessary to combine the flue-cured tobacco technological process to extract characteristic index items from other time scales. The electricity consumption curve of the flue-cured tobacco special properties during one week of the flue-cured tobacco season is drawn as shown in Fig. 3. For the convenience of comparison, the weekly electricity curve of the commuter change in the local rural area is also drawn.

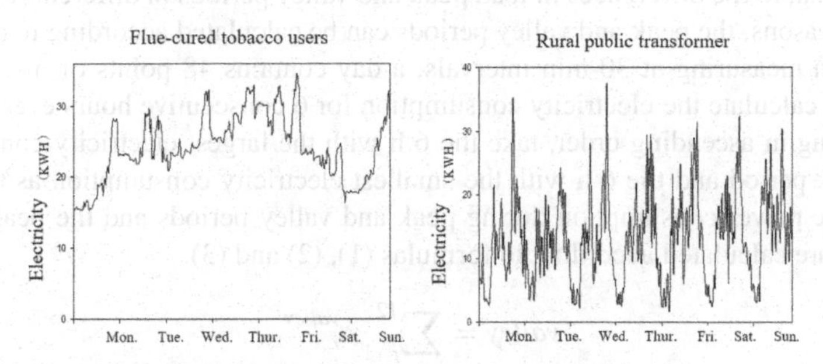

Fig. 3. Weekly power consumption of different types of users

It can be seen from the figure that the daily load curve of the public properties in rural areas has clear peaks and valleys according to the time changes of daily life. The electricity consumption at night is significantly lower than that during the day, which has outstanding daily cycle characteristics. The load of the common transformers in the station area fluctuates obviously on an hourly scale, and appears as a large number of burrs on the weekly electricity curve.

Although the daily power of flue-cured tobacco has obvious fluctuations, the load of flue-cured tobacco has strong continuity on an hourly scale. According to the technical requirements of tobacco leaf roasting, it takes about 7 days to roast tobacco leaves, during which interruption of roasting will cause the tobacco leaves to re-moisture and economic loss. In order to keep the curing barn continuously dry and constant temperature, the flue-cured tobacco load remains basically stable. Only when the barn completes the roasting and moves out the cured tobacco leaves and moves into the to-be-cured tobacco leaves, there will be obvious load fluctuations. Therefore, the flue-cured tobacco users have relatively stable load on the hourly scale of the flue-cured tobacco season, and there will be no burr-like fluctuations and no load interruptions. Taking the two users in Fig. 4 as an example, taking a week's average daily power as a reference value, the flue-cured tobacco users' cumulative power fluctuation rate per week is 0.8202, while the Taiwan communal variable fluctuation rate can reach 7.2089, which is significantly higher than the former. Therefore, the cumulative fluctuation rate can better characterize the strong continuity of flue-cured tobacco load.

The load of flue-cured tobacco is limited by the technological process, with strong continuity, no daily periodicity, and the peak-valley difference between day and night is significantly smaller than that of ordinary production and living users.

3 First Section Construction of Industry Characteristic Index Items

3.1 Valley Peak Load Ratio

Please note that the first paragraph of a section or subsection is not indented. The first paragraphs that follows a table, figure, equation etc. does not have an indent, either. In order to adapt to the differences in load peak and valley periods in different regions and different seasons, the peak and valley periods can be calculated according to daily load data. When measuring at 30-min intervals, a day contains 48 points of measurement data. First, calculate the electricity consumption for 6 consecutive hours every 30 min. After sorting in ascending order, take the 6 h with the largest electricity consumption as the peak period and the 6 h with the smallest electricity consumption as the valley period. The power consumption during peak and valley periods and the peak-to-peak load ratio are calculated according to formulas (1), (2) and (3).

$$valley = \sum_{i=1}^{12} a_i^{valley} \tag{1}$$

$$peak = \sum_{i=1}^{12} a_i^{peak} \tag{2}$$

$$ratio = valley / peak \tag{3}$$

The peak load ratio of flue-cured tobacco season can describe the behavior characteristics of flue-cured tobacco users effectively. The trough-peak load ratios of the four typical flue-cured tobacco users in Fig. 2 during the flue-cured tobacco season are calculated daily, and their box-line diagrams are drawn as shown in Fig. 4.

It can be seen from Fig. 4 that the median peak-to-peak load ratios of the four typical flue-cured tobacco users are all between 0.8 and 1, and the range between the upper and lower quartiles is small, indicating that the peak-to-valley load difference during the maturity period of tobacco leaves is relatively small. There are obvious differences among users in common residential areas, and the low-peak load ratio can effectively identify the characteristics of flue-cured tobacco load behavior.

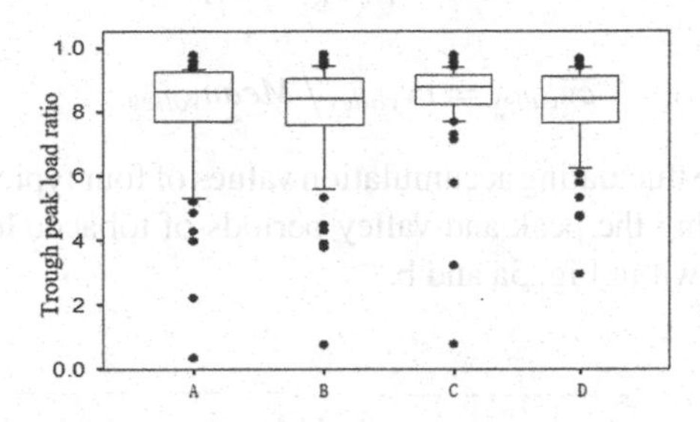

Fig. 4. Box line chart of electricity consumption ratio during peak and valley time span.

3.2 The Cumulative Volatility of Peaks and Valleys

Except for the trough-to-peak load ratio, the flue-cured tobacco load is relatively stable with a small cumulative change rate on an hourly scale, and can also be used to characterize the industry. Flue-cured tobacco users have a very low cumulative power fluctuation rate during the peak and low load periods, while other users may only show a lower cumulative power fluctuation rate during the night low-load period. To facilitate the multi-dimensional characterization of user behavior, the load can also be reduced. The cumulative volatility of power during peak and trough periods is collectively used as a feature item.

After calculating and determining the peak-valley period of each day according to the method described in the previous section, for 30-min interval measurement data, the cumulative value of peak and valley period fluctuations can be calculated according to formula (4) and formula (5).

$$cv_{peak} = \sum_{i=1}^{12} b_{i-1,i}^{peak} \tag{4}$$

Among them, $b_{i-1,i}^{peak} = |a_i - a_{i-1}|$

$$cv_{valley} = \sum_{i=1}^{12} b_{i-1,i}^{cvlley} \tag{5}$$

Among them, $b_{i-1,i}^{valley} = |a_i - a_{i-1}|$

In order to facilitate the comparison among users of different power consumption levels, after calculating the peak and valley load averages in formulas (6) and (7), according to formulas (8) and (9), the unified dimension of the peak and valley period fluctuation cumulative value is obtained after the value.

$$Mean_{peak} = \sum_{i=1}^{12} a_i / 12 \tag{6}$$

$$Mean_{valley} = \sum_{i=1}^{12} a_i / 12 \tag{7}$$

$$\overline{cv}_{peak} = cv_{peak} / Mean_{peak} \tag{8}$$

$$\overline{cv}_{valley} = cv_{valley} / Mean_{valley} \tag{9}$$

After analyzing the fluctuating accumulation values of four typical flue-cured tobacco special properties during the peak and valley periods of tobacco leaf maturity, the box plots are drawn as shown in Fig. 5a and b.

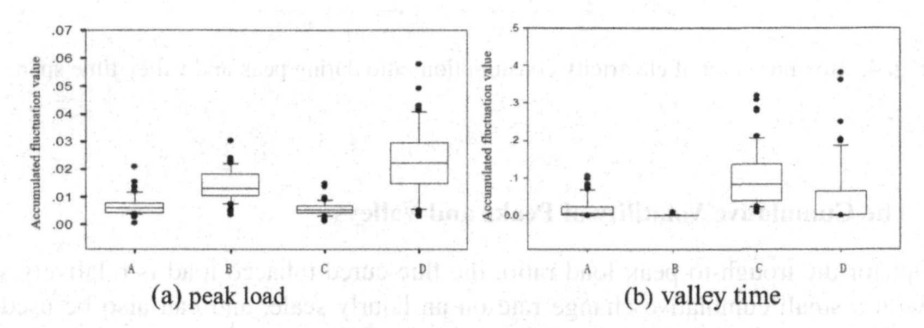

(a) peak load (b) valley time

Fig. 5. Accumulated variation of load curve.

The median cumulative volatility of the four typical users during the peak load period of the flue-cured tobacco season is between 0–0.02. The range between the upper and lower extensions of the boxes in Village B and Village D is slightly larger than that in Village A and Village C, and is stable within 0.03. There are outliers outside the tentacles of the box plot, but all samples including outliers are concentrated within 0.07. The median of the cumulative power volatility during the valley period is distributed between 0–0.1. All data points including anomalies are distributed within 0.4, and the overall distribution is relatively scattered.

4 Load Clustering Based on Nearest Neighbor Propagation Algorithm

4.1 A Subsection Sample Nearest Neighbor Propagation Algorithm

The nearest neighbor propagation algorithm is a clustering algorithm based on the transmission of nearest neighbor information. It has no need to specify the number of clusters, no need to select initial values. The cluster center point is the prominent advantage of the sample points that exist in the data set and the square and small errors of the clustering results, which are widely used in image, text and signal processing fields [14, 15].

The nearest neighbor propagation algorithm is based on the similarity matrix of the data set. At the initial stage, all samples are regarded as potential clustering center points, and the attraction is recursively transmitted along the node line until the optimal cluster representative point set is found, so that the sum of similarities between all data points and corresponding cluster representative points is the largest. Among them, attractiveness is the degree to which data points are selected as cluster representative points of other data. The following describes the specific process of the nearest neighbor propagation algorithm in conjunction with Fig. 6.

a) The goal of clustering is to minimize the distance between the data points and the class representative points. Euclidean distance is selected as the similarity measure between data points. The similarity between any two points x_i and x_k is:

$$s(i,k) = -d_{i,k} = -\|x_i - x_k\| \tag{10}$$

b) Initialize the attraction matrix R and the attribution matrix A, use the attraction matrix R and the attribution matrix A to represent the two types of information between the data points, $r(i,k)$ represents the attraction from the point x_i to the candidate representative point x_k, and indicates the degree to which x_k is suitable as the class representative point of x_i; $a(i,k)$ is the degree of belonging from the point x_k to x_i, which indicates the suitability of x_i to select x_k as the class representative point.
c) Calculate $r(i,j)$and $a(i,j)$

$$r(i,k) = \begin{cases} s(i,k) - \max\limits_{j \neq k}\{a(i,j) + s(i,j)\}, i \neq k \\ s(i,k) - \max\limits_{j \neq k}\{s(i,j)\}, i = k \end{cases} \tag{11}$$

$$a(i,k) = \begin{cases} \min\left\{0, r(k,k) + \sum_{j \neq k} \max\{r(j,k), 0\}\right\}, i \neq k \\ \sum_{j \neq k} \max\{r(j,k), 0\}, i = k \end{cases} \tag{12}$$

d) Iteratively update $r(i, j)$ and $a(i, j)$ to introduce the attenuation coefficient λ; the updated value is (1−λ) times the calculated value in this round plus λ times the previous round value.

$$r_{t+1}(i,k) = \lambda * r_t(i,k) + (1-\lambda) * r_t(i,k) \tag{13}$$

$$a_{t+1}(i,k) = \lambda * a_t(i,k) + (1-\lambda) * a_t(i,k) \tag{14}$$

e) Sum the attribution and attractiveness of each data point to determine the cluster center. Among them, for data point i, when $a(i,k) + r(i,k)$ achieves the maximum value, if $i = k$, the data point i is determined to be the cluster center, if $i \neq k$, the data point is determined k is the cluster center.

$$k = \arg\max\{a(i,k) + r(i,k)\} \tag{15}$$

f) When the number of iterations of the cluster center is equal to the preset maximum number of iterations of the cluster center, clustering ends when the cluster center still does not change or the number of iterations equals the preset maximum number of iterations.

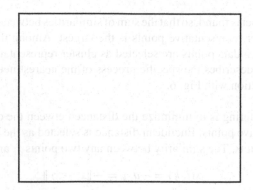

Fig. 6. Iterative diagram of AP clustering algorithm

4.2 Load Clustering Based on Nearest Neighbor Propagation Algorithm

The nearest neighbor propagation algorithm is used for cluster analysis of flue-cured tobacco users. First, obtain the electricity consumption data of each user in the same time period at equal intervals, and calculate the peak-to-peak electricity consumption ratio, the cumulative fluctuation rate of the peak-hour electricity consumption, and the cumulative fluctuation rate of the valley-hour electricity consumption. If the acquired electricity consumption data contains s days, each user will correspond to a $1 \times (3\ s)$ vector.

The similarity matrix is the initialization matrix of the algorithm. There is an $n \times n$ similarity matrix for n users, and each value represents the similarity between two users. The diagonal element is recorded as preference, which is the similarity between the user and itself. The calculation result is 0 according to the Euclidean distance formula, so the preference value is the median of all similarity elements. The larger the value, the clustering that can be obtained the greater the number.

When updating attractiveness and attribution, attractiveness means that user k is more suitable as the clustering center of i than other users. For other users k', $s(i, k')$ represents the similarity between users i and k'. Redefine the index $a(i, k')$ to indicate the degree of recognition of user i to k' as its cluster center. By calculating the value of $s(i, k') + a(i, k')$, k' can be obtained as the suitability of the cluster center of i; among all other users k', find $\max\left\{a(i, k^{'}) + s(i, k^{'})\right\}$, and finally calculate $s(i, k) - \max\left\{a(i, k^{'}) + s(i, k^{'})\right\}$ get user k's attractiveness to i, where $k \neq k^{'}$; For attribution, first calculate user k's attractiveness to other users $r(i', k)$, and then the cumulative summation represents the attractiveness of user k to other users $\sum_{i^{'} \neq k} \max\left\{r(i^{'}, k), 0\right\}$, plus $r(k, k)$, this value reflects how much user k should not be divided into other cluster centers, and $\min\left\{0, r(k, k) + \sum_{i^{'} \neq k} \max\left\{r(i^{'}, k), 0\right\}\right\}$ can be get.

Finally, sum the user attraction and attribution to find the cluster center that maximizes $a(i, k) + r(i, k)$. If $i = k$, then the cluster center is i itself, if $i \neq ki \neq k$, the cluster center is k.

In order to evaluate the results of the clustering algorithm, the Purity index is used as the evaluation standard, which is defined as the proportion of the correct clustered data to the total data.

$$Purity(W, X) = 1 \Big/ N \sum_j \max |\omega_k \cap x_j| \tag{16}$$

Among them, $W = \{w_1, w_2, \cdots, w_k\}$ is the set of clusters, w_k represents the k-th cluster set, $X = \{x_1, x_2, \cdots, x_n\}$ is the data set, and x_j represents the j-th data, N represents the total number of data. The value of this index is between 0–1. When it is 0, the clustering result is completely wrong, and when it is 1, the clustering result is completely correct. The Purity index can directly reflect the performance of the clustering algorithm, and the accuracy of the constructed feature index can be judged according to the evaluation index to describe the electricity consumption behavior of flue-cured tobacco users.

5 Numerical Simulation

From the electricity consumption information collection system, 200 users whose industry attribute is the tobacco industry are selected to conduct electricity abnormality detection. In the actual system, there may be errors in industry attributes caused by registration errors and user business changes. In order to simultaneously test the clustering algorithm's ability to detect users with incorrect industry attributes, it also involved 20 rural public changes. In order to fully characterize the characteristics and trends of the electricity consumption of flue-cured tobacco users in the mature season of tobacco leaves, the electricity consumption data is selected from the 30-min interval data of the 2016 flue-cured tobacco season (from June 1 to July 30).

The parameters of the nearest neighbor propagation clustering algorithm are set as follows: the attenuation coefficient λ is 0.5, the maximum number of iterations is 500 times, the maximum number of iterations that the cluster center does not change is 50 times, and the reference degree is set to all values in the similarity matrix The median. In addition, K-means, FCM fuzzy C-means clustering algorithm, and DBSCAN are also used to cluster the data set. Because users may be special properties in normal flue-cured tobacco and abnormal flue-cured tobacco, and public changes in rural life, the number of clusters is set to 3 in the K-means and FCM algorithms. Each clustering algorithm uses Purity index to evaluate the performance of the algorithm, and the evaluation index can be shown in Table 1.

The nearest neighbor propagation clustering algorithm divides the test user data into 5 categories. Except for flue-cured tobacco users and rural living areas, it is found that 4 of the 20 rural areas that are mixed are actually brick factory users and are individually identified as one. In addition, the two flue-cured tobacco special properties are separately identified as two categories; the number of clusters is more than the expected 3 categories. The Purity index of cluster recognition is 0.9818, which has the highest correct rate among the four clustering algorithms. Among them, 4 flue-cured tobacco users are classified as rural living areas. In-depth understanding shows that the local capacity is insufficient due to the lack of distribution and the residents' load is connected to the flue-cured tobacco transformation, which leads to clustering errors. It needs to be pointed out that the neighbor propagation algorithm parameters setting is simple, and the clustering effect is stable under different parameter settings.

The nearest neighbor propagation algorithm can not only accurately cluster and distinguish normal/abnormal flue-cured tobacco users based on user characteristic indicators, but also identify non-cured tobacco users with other industry attributes mixed with test data.

The parameter setting has a significant impact on the clustering effect of the DBSCAN algorithm. After a large number of parameter setting tests, users can also be divided into 5 categories under optimal conditions, and the Purity index can reach up to 0.9545.

K-means and FCM clustering algorithms are clustered according to the preset number of clusters of 3 types, and the clustering effect is obviously inferior to DBSCAN and neighbor propagation clustering algorithms.

Table 1. Results of clustering algorithm evaluation indicators.

Algorithm	Number of clusters	Purity Metrics
K-means	3	0.7955
FCM	3	0.8455
DBSCAN	5	0.9545
AP	5	0.9818

Table 2. Cluster contain users and division accuracy.

	User	Accuracy
Cluster 1	Flue-cured Tobacco Specialized User (194 households)	100%
Cluster 2	Rural public change (16 households), Flue-cured Tobacco Specialized User (4 households)	80%
Cluster 3	Brick factory (4 households)	100%
Cluster 4	Abnormal Flue-cured Tobacco Special Change User A (1 household)	100%
Cluster 5	Abnormal Flue-cured Tobacco Special Change User B (1 household)	100%

According to the classification of neighbor propagation clustering, the 4 flue-cured tobacco special properties were mistakenly classified as the rural public properties. The specific conditions are listed in Table 2. In order to compare the characteristic indicators of different clusters, the 60-day average values of the peak cumulative volatility, trough cumulative volatility and trough peak load ratio of various cluster centers are listed in Table 3, and each cluster center is listed on June 1st. The electricity consumption curve up to July 30 is drawn as shown in Fig. 7. Each sub-graph corresponds to the set of flue-cured tobacco users, the set of communal transformers in rural areas, the set of brick factory users, the abnormal flue-cured tobacco user A, and the abnormal flue-cured tobacco user B. It can be seen from the chart that:

(1) The characteristic items of various cluster centers are significantly different. Cluster center 1 is a flue-cured tobacco user with strong load continuity and low cumulative volatility, and the cumulative volatility is significantly lower than other cluster centers; center 2 is a rural station with obvious daily cycles. Center 3 is a brick factory user with strong cumulative volatility, and the cumulative volatility is significantly higher than that of all other cluster centers; center 4 and 5 have obvious index differences, and they are two abnormal flue-cured tobacco users. From the curve characteristics and index items, the clustering results are reasonable.
(2) Cluster 4 and cluster 5 are applied to the load of abnormal flue-cured tobacco users A and B. Among them, abnormal user A only has normal power consumption during the first few days of the flue-cured tobacco season in June, and abnormal user B has continuous electricity consumption for 5 days separated in mid-June, which violates the rules of continuity requirements for flue-cured tobacco, which is significantly different from typical flue-cured tobacco users, and can be judged as abnormal electricity consumption.

Table 3. 30-day mean of cluster center features.

	Peak cumulative volatility	Trough cumulative volatility	Trough peak load ratio
Cluster 1	0.922	0.827	0.696
Cluster 2	5.185	5.975	0.610
Cluster 3	13.006	14.014	0.434
Cluster 4	6.142	0.517	0.001
Cluster 5	4.767	3.761	0.334

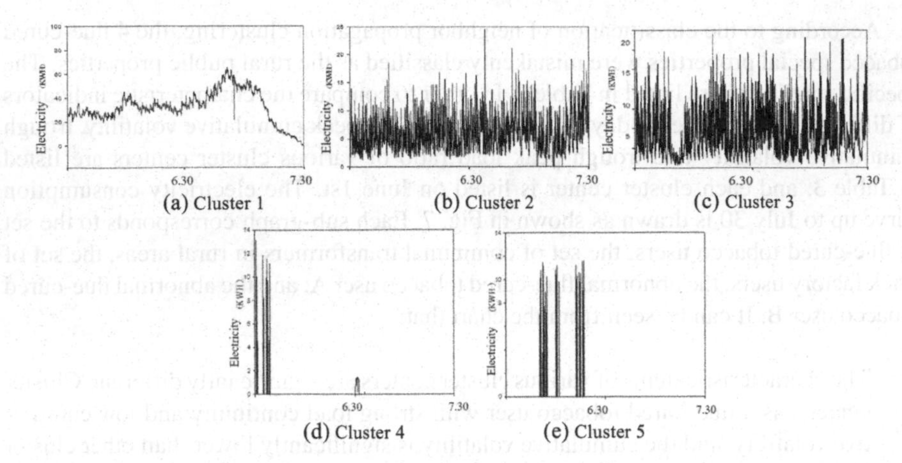

Fig. 7. Load profile of Clustering center

6 Conclusion

In this paper, users in the same industry have similar characteristics of electricity consumption behavior, and propose an abnormal electricity detection method considering the electricity consumption characteristics of users in the industry. Combined with users of flue-cured tobacco, explore the extraction of characteristic index items by sub-sector and detect abnormal electricity consumption. The characteristic index items that can accurately describe the electricity consumption characteristics of flue-cured tobacco users are adopted. The nearest neighbor propagation algorithm is used to perform cluster analysis on the actual flue-cured tobacco special change and the rural public transformer according to the extracted characteristic index items. The analysis results show that the proposed method not only accurately identifies the flue-cured tobacco special change users with abnormal electricity consumption, but also can effectively distinguish them. Specialized users of non-flue-cured tobacco mixed in due to wrong industry attributes.

References

1. Hao, R., Ai, Q., Xiao, F.: Architecture based on multivariate big data platform for analyzing electricity consumption behavior. Electr. Power Autom. Equip. **37**(8), 20–27 (2017)
2. Cheng, C., Zhang, H., Jing, Z., et al.: Study on the anti-electricity stealing based on outlier algorithm and the electricity information acquisition system. Power Syst. Protect. Control **43**(17), 69–74 (2015)
3. Su, S., Li, K., Yan, Y., et al.: The resident load consumption pattern classification model based on density spatial clustering and gravitational search algorithms. Electr. Power Autom. Equip. **38**(1), 129–136 (2018)
4. Nagi, J., Yap, K.S., Tiong, S.K., et al.: Nontechnical loss detection for metered customers in power utility using support vector machines. IEEE Trans. Power Deliv. **25**(2), 1162–1171 (2010)
5. Chen, Q., Zheng, K., Kang, C., et al.: Detection method of abnormal electricity consumption: review and Prospect. Autom. Electr. Power Syst. **42**(17), 189–198 (2018)

6. Sun, Y., Li, S., Cui, C., et al.: Detection method of power data outliers based on Gaussian kernel function. Grid Technol. **42**(5), 1595–1604 (2018)
7. Marcelo, Z., Edgard, J., Marcelo, P., et al.: A tunable fraud detection system for advanced metering infrastructure using short lived-patterns. IEEE Trans. Smart Grid **10**(1), 830 (2019)
8. Monedero, I., Biscarri, F., León, C., et al.: Detection of frauds and other non-technical losses in a power utility using Pearson Coefficient, Bayesian networks and decision trees. J. Electr. Power Energy Syst. **34**, 90–98 (2012)
9. Breuning, M.M., Kriegel, H.P., Ng, R.T., et al.: LOF: identifying density-based local outliers. ACM Sigmod Int. Conf. Manage. Data **9**(2), 93–104 (2000)
10. Zhuang, C., Zhang, B., Hu, J., et al.: Anomaly detection for power consumption patterns based on unsupervised learning. Proc. CSEE **36**(2), 379–387 (2016)
11. Feng, Z., Tang, W., Wu, Q., et al.: Users' consumption behavior clustering method considering longitudinal randomness of load. Power Autom. Equip. **38**(9), 39–44 (2018)
12. Zhang, C., Xiao, X., Zheng, Z.: Electricity theft detection for customers in power utility based on real-valued deep belief network. Power Syst. Technol. **43**(3), 1083–1091 (2019)
13. Peng, X., Lai, J., Chen, Y.: Application of clustering analysis in typical power consumption profile analysis. Power Syst. Protect. Control **42**(19), 68–73 (2014)
14. Li, L., Liu, T.: PV power forecasting based on AP-ESN. Electr. Power Autom. Equip. **36**(7), 41–46 (2016)
15. Hang, W., Jiang, Y., Liu, J., et al.: Transfer affinity propagation clustering algorithm. J. Softw. **27**(11), 2796–2813 (2016)

Direct Power Supply Identification Method of PV Power Based on Affinity Propagation Clustering

Hanjun Deng[1,2], Xing He[1,2](✉), Rui Huang[1,2], Yuping Su[1,2], Suihan Zhang[1,2], and Wenwei Zeng[1,2]

[1] State Grid Hunan Electric Power Company Limited, Changsha 410000, Hu'nan, China
2065057002@qq.com

[2] Hunan Province Key Laboratory of Intelligent Electrical Measurement and Application Technology, Changsha 410000, Hunan, China

Abstract. At present, the marketization of distributed photovoltaic power generation faces problems such as the trading model is still immature and the trading mechanism is complicated, which makes the management of distributed energy trading very difficult. In this paper, a direct power supply identification method based on affinity propagation (AP) clustering is proposed. First, the historical PV output data of the station or neighboring stations are used to obtain the output data of the "same type" PV arrays for reference. Then, the AP clustering algorithm is used to cluster the power generation data in the same temperature segment, and the PV power sources suspected of direct power supply are identified according to the corresponding relationship between the clustering results and the electricity sales state. Finally, the proposed method is verified by the actual operation data in a certain area. The simulation results verify the effectiveness of the proposed method for the identification of direct PV power supply, and provide a reference for the subsequent on-site inspection of power grid companies.

Keywords: Photovoltaic Power · Direct Power Supply Identification · Affinity Propagation Clustering · Correlation Coefficient

1 Introduction

The direct power supply (DPS) is conducive to the local consumption of distributed photovoltaic (PV) [1–3]. It is also conducive to the implementation of "double carbon" and energy conservation and emission reduction policies. The Notice on the Pilot of Distributed Generation Market Trading (2017) No. 1901 also explicitly supports the relevant mode of electricity trading between distributed generation project units and

Fund project: This work was supported in part by the State Grid Hunan Electric Power Co., Ltd. 2022 "New Research Control Model" Pilot Project (5216AG220007); in part by the Changsha Science and Technology Project of Hunan Province under Grant (kq2202213).

H. Yang et al. (Eds.): SmartGIFT 2022, LNICST 483, pp. 218–228, 2023.
https://doi.org/10.1007/978-3-031-31733-0_19

nearby power users within the distribution network. According to a series of policies, it is obvious that the state encourages distributed PV projects to participate in DPS. However, due to the volatility and randomness of distributed PV output, it usually cannot fully meet the electricity demand of DPS users. It still needs the power system to provide full capacity investment, but it does not bear the corresponding transmission and distribution price. This means that customers who do not participate in the DPS will share more of the transmission and distribution costs. In addition, the DPS site is prone to the occurrence of electricity theft [4–6]. The mode of DPS also has some influence on power quality management [7–9]. In order to standardize the trading behavior of distributed PV power market, it is necessary to provide a DPS identification method of distributed PV power as an auxiliary means for the implementation of new energy policy.

The classification and abnormal identification of load data have been studied in the literature, but the abnormal identification of PV power generation data is less studied. In [10], a detection method with low false alarm rate based on identification of production and operation status is proposed. The false alarm rate of abnormal load identification is reduced by studying the corresponding relationship between various production and operation states of load and three-phase power. In [11], a power data anomaly detection method based on Holt-winters model and DBSCAN clustering is proposed. It can improve the accuracy of detection by clustering the residual term obtained by subtracting the predicted value and the real value.

Unlike load power consumption, the DPS of PV behavior is more difficult to identify and classify due to the randomness and uncertainty of PV. The existing research method is to predict the PV output and identify whether there is any abnormality by comparing the predicted data with the actual measured data. In [12], a comparison method for PV day-ahead prediction models based on deep learning neural networks is proposed. The method shows that the hybrid prediction model based on convolutional neural network and long short-term memory network has the best effect. In [13], a PV prediction method based on deep convolutional neural network and meta-learning is proposed, which achieves high accuracy and reliability of day-ahead prediction. In [14], a graphical modeling method for PV prediction based on multiple meteorological factors is proposed, which improves the accuracy of PV day-ahead forecasting. However, there are many factors affecting the prediction of PV, including climate, temperature, weather and geographical environment. The existing methods cannot comprehensively consider all the influencing factors.

There are many factors that affect the output of the PV array, such as climate, temperature, weather, solar radiation, and shade. In [15], a prediction method based on regional similarity is proposed, but the factors such as shading, dust and attenuation during the use of PV arrays are not considered. In this paper, a DPS identification method of PV output in the same area based on AP clustering is proposed. Firstly, through the basic data such as the model and installation date of PV arrays in the same area, the PV arrays of the same type and area are found. Through the correlation analysis of historical output data, the clustered PV power supply set is found. Then, the AP clustering algorithm is used to cluster the power generation data in the same temperature segment to find out the corresponding relationship between the clustering results and the state of PV power supply, so as to identify the PV power supply suspected of DPS. Finally, 10 distributed

PV power sources in a region are taken as an example to verify the effectiveness of the proposed method.

2 Output Correlation Analysis of Photovoltaic Power Supply

Since the capacity of each PV power supply is different, the power generation and grid-connected power P used in the calculation of this paper are calculated by taking the power value corresponding to the 100 kW capacity PV power supply.

$$P = \frac{P_{act}}{P_e} \times 100 \tag{1}$$

where P_{act} represents the actual value of power. P_e represents the rated power of the corresponding PV power supply.

The climatic conditions, solar radiation amount and other conditions of PV power in the same area are similar, but the shading, dust, attenuation and other factors in the process of use are different. Through the basic data such as the model and installation date of PV arrays in the same area, the interference of these factors can be eliminated by finding out the PV arrays in the same type and area as a reference. However, due to the different factors such as solar cell module tilt Angle, energy conversion efficiency and maximum power point tracking (MPPT), the output data of these PV power sources do not necessarily have sufficient similarity.

As an evaluation index to measure the degree of linear correlation between two variables, the correlation coefficient can be used to measure the output similarity between PV power sources. In this paper, Pearson Correlation Coefficient (PCC) is used to measure and screen out the PV power sources suitable for analysis together. Assuming that the corresponding variables of PV power supply a and b are P_a and P_b. The generation data of PV power supply is selected as a variable at an interval of 15min, and the correlation coefficient of PV power supply a and b is:

$$r\left(P^a, P^b\right) = \frac{\frac{1}{n}\sum_{i=1}^{n}\left(P_i^a - \overline{P}^a\right)\left(P_i^b - \overline{P}^b\right)}{\sqrt{\sum_{i=1}^{n}\left(P_i^a - \overline{P}^a\right)^2}\sqrt{\sum_{i=1}^{n}\left(P_i^b - \overline{P}^b\right)^2}} \tag{2}$$

where n represents the number of time intervals in a day. ${P_i}^a$ and ${P_i}^b$ represent the output of PV power supply a and b at the i-th moment, respectively. $\overline{P}^a$ and $\overline{P}^b$ represent the average output of PV power supply in a day, respectively. The range of PCC is [0, 1]. PCC > 0 represents positive correlation between variables, and larger PCC represents the stronger correlation.

Assuming that the total number of PV power sources is N_a in a region. The correlation coefficient of each power source can be calculated to form the correlation coefficient matrix of the region.

$$R = \left[r\left(P^a, P^b\right)\right]_{N_a \times N_a} \tag{3}$$

In order to improve the differentiation, the data of each PV power source in the same area for one day and one hour are counted separately as variables to calculate the correlation coefficient matrix. According to the correlation coefficient less than 0.5 in the correlation coefficient matrix, the PV power sources with low correlation are screened out. Thus, the PV power population calculated together is obtained.

3 The Identification of PV Power Sales Status

For the PV power supply with strong correlation in the same station area, the power generation data at the same temperature is selected as the research sample with the resolution of 15 min. Assume that there is no DPS for PV power supply in a certain station, so the grid-connected power is the generation power. The three-phase grid-connected power curves of two typical days at 25–35 °C are shown in Fig. 1 and Fig. 2, respectively. The PV power supply had stable weather on the first day. The power fluctuation is small, and the curve presented a single peak shape. The next day is rainy and there was a temporary shortage of power generation. The curve shows a double peak shape in Fig. 2.

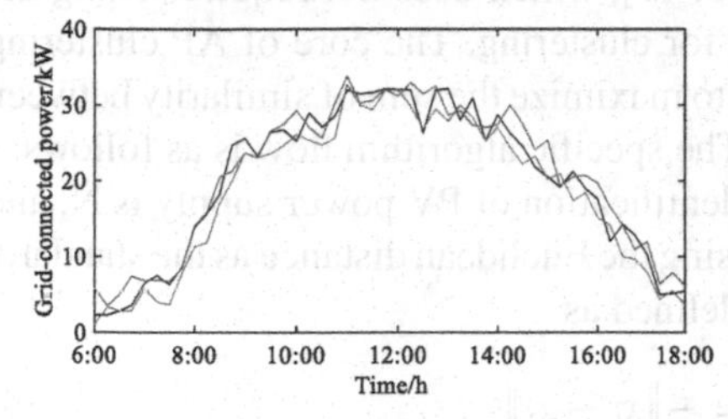

Fig. 1. The grid-connected power on the first day

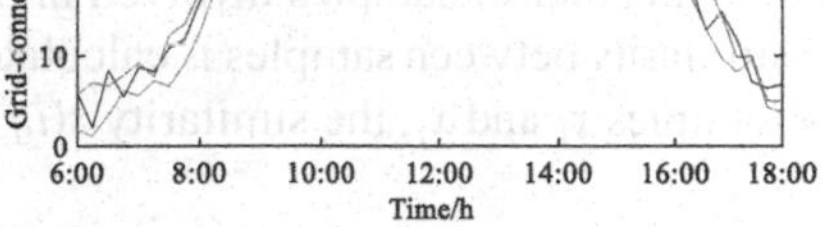

Fig. 2. The grid-connected power on the second day

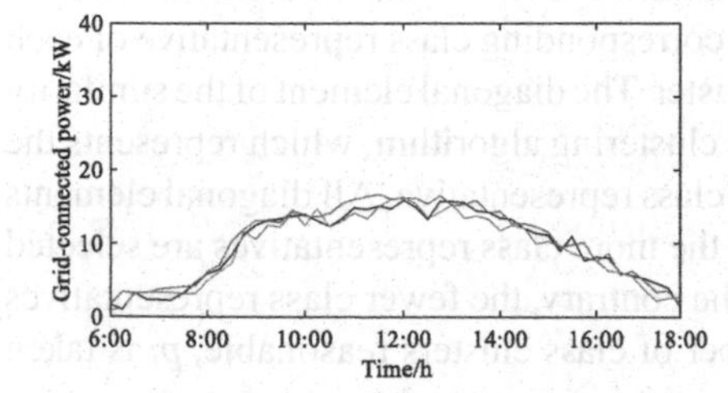

Fig. 3. The grid-connected power under "factory power sale"

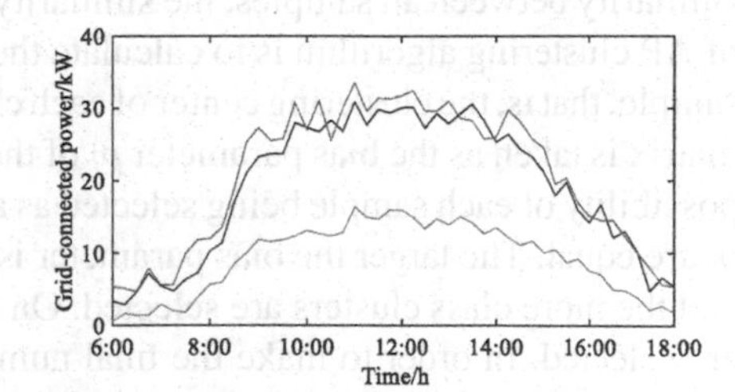

Fig. 4. The grid-connected power under "residential customers power sale"

DPS from PV power sources is mainly divided into two types of power sales to residential customers and power sales to factories. The power consumption of the factory is mainly high-power three-phase equipment, and the three-phase power is basically balanced. The power consumption is large, which is easy to cause the continuous large power shortage of PV power supply. It is shown in Fig. 3. The residential power consumption is mainly single-phase equipment with small power, which is easy to cause three-phase power imbalance of PV power supply. It is shown in Fig. 4.

According to Figs. 1, 2, 3 and 4: Under the same temperature conditions, the maximum daily power generated by PV power will not be significantly different. The power of the three phases is basically balanced. No matter what form of direct power supply will have a certain impact on the grid-connected power. In the case of "factory power sale", the three-phase grid-connected power of PV power supply will be significantly reduced. In the case of "residential customers power sale", the grid-connected power of PV power will appear three-phase imbalance. These differences can be used as the basis for the identification of direct power supply of PV power.

4 Direct Supply Power of PV Identification Based on AP Clustering Algorithm

The daily grid-connection curves of PV power sources with high correlation in the same station area under the same temperature are taken as samples, and the corresponding clustering algorithm is designed to identify whether there is DPS. Due to the random and changeable weather conditions, the number of clusters is difficult to determine. In this paper, the AP clustering algorithm [16, 17], which does not require setting the number of class families in advance, is used for clustering. The core of AP clustering algorithm is to find the set of optimal samples to maximize the sum of similarity between all samples and the nearest optimal sample. The specific algorithm flow is as follows:

The number of samples involved in the identification of PV power supply is N, and the similarity between samples is calculated using the Euclidean distance as the standard. For samples x_i and x_j, the similarity $s(i,j)$ is defined as

$$s(i,j) = -d_{i,j} = -\|x_i - x_j\| \tag{4}$$

where $d_{i,j}$ denotes the Euclidean distance between samples x_i and x_j. By calculating the similarity between all samples, the similarity matrix $S \in R^{N \times N}$ can be formed. The goal of AP clustering algorithm is to calculate the corresponding class representative of each sample, that is, the clustering center of each cluster. The diagonal element of the similarity matrix is taken as the bias parameter p_i of the clustering algorithm, which represents the possibility of each sample being selected as a class representative. All diagonal elements p_i are equal. The larger the bias parameter is, the more class representatives are selected and the more class clusters are selected. On the contrary, the fewer class representatives are selected. In order to make the final number of class clusters reasonable, p_i is taken as the median of all elements in the similarity matrix.

The class representation is calculated by the attractiveness index and the attribution index. The attractiveness index $b(i,j)$ represents x_j as the class representative fit of x_i and is a parameter of x_i pointing to x_j. All the attractiveness indices form the attractiveness matrix $B \in R^{N \times N}$. The attribution index $a(i,j)$ represents the probability that x_i chooses x_j as a class representative and is a parameter of x_j pointing to x_i. All the attribution indices form the attribution matrix $A \in R^{N \times N}$. The initial values of the attractiveness matrix B and the attribution matrix A are taken as zero matrices.

$$b_0(i,j) = 0 \tag{5}$$

$$a_0(i,j) = 0 \tag{6}$$

The latter one attractiveness matrix element $b_1(i,j)$ and the attribution matrix element $a_1(i,j)$ are calculated as follows.

$$b_1(i,j) = \begin{cases} s(i,j) - \max\limits_{k \neq j}\{a_0(i,k) + s(i,k)\}, & i \neq j \\ s(i,j) - \max\limits_{k \neq j}\{s(i,k)\}, & i = j \end{cases} \tag{7}$$

$$a_1(i,j) = \begin{cases} \min\left\{0, b_0(j,j) + \sum_{k \neq j} \max\{b(k,j), 0\}\right\}, & i \neq j \\ \sum_{k \neq j} \max\{b(k,j), 0\}, & i = j \end{cases} \tag{8}$$

The number of iterations is denoted by t. The attractiveness matrix element $b_{t+1}(i,j)$ and the attribution matrix element $a_{t+1}(i,j)$ are calculated by iterating the following equation.

$$b_{t+1}(i,j) = \lambda \times b_{t-1}(i,j) + (1-\lambda) \times b_t(i,j) \tag{9}$$

$$a_{t+1}(i,j) = \lambda \times a_{t-1}(i,j) + (1-\lambda) \times a_t(i,j) \tag{10}$$

where λ represents the attenuation coefficient of the AP clustering algorithm, also known as the damping factor, which mainly affects the iterative convergence speed.

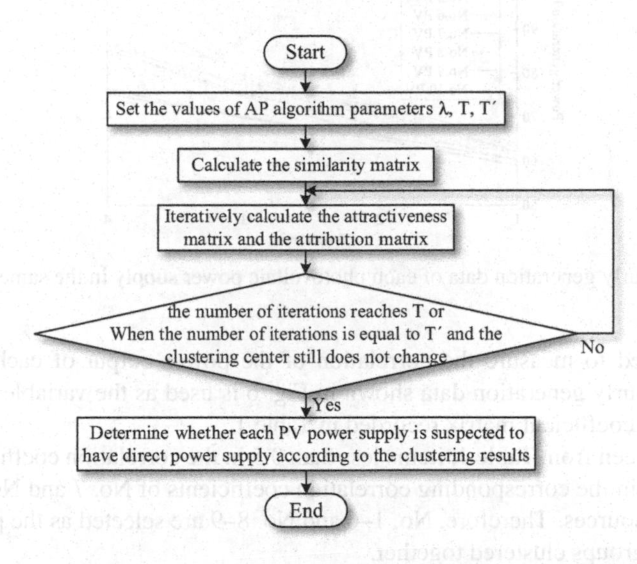

Fig. 5. Flowchart of direct power supply identification for PV power based on AP clustering algorithm

The sum of the attractiveness matrix elements $b_t(i,j)$ and the attribution matrix elements $a_t(i,j)$ obtained at each iteration step is calculated, and the sample x_j corresponding to the largest sum is the class representative of sample x_i.

$$sum = b_t(i,j) + a_t(i,j) \tag{11}$$

Find all the class representatives of each iteration and determine the cluster center. The iteration process ends when the number of iterations reaches T or when the number of iterations is equal to T′ and the clustering center still does not change. According to the final clustering results, the direct power supply corresponding to each sample can be identified. The whole AP clustering process can be expressed as Fig. 5.

5 Case Study

5.1 Output Correlation Analysis

The case study was conducted with 10 PV power sources of the same type in a certain station. These PV arrays are similar in terms of shading, dust, and attenuation during use. The hourly generation data of each photovoltaic power supply in the same time period is shown in Fig. 6.

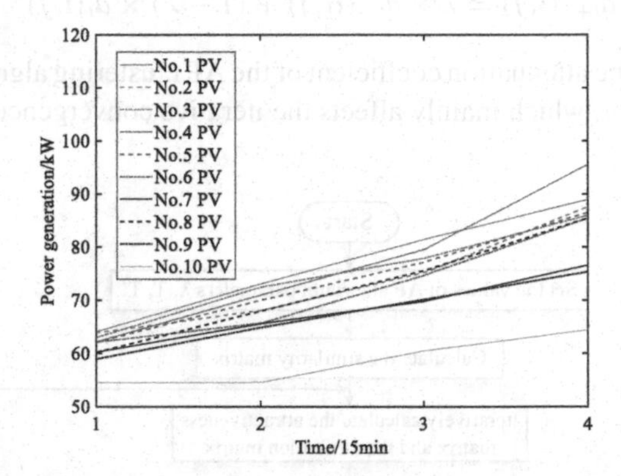

Fig. 6. The hourly generation data of each photovoltaic power supply in the same time period

PCC is used to measure the correlation of the power output of each PV power source. The hourly generation data shown in Fig. 6 is used as the variable to calculate the correlation coefficient matrix recorded in Table 1.

As can be seen from Table 1, items less than 0.5 in the correlation coefficient matrix mainly appear in the corresponding correlation coefficients of No. 7 and No. 10 photovoltaic power sources. Therefore, No. 1–6 and No. 8–9 are selected as the photovoltaic power supply groups clustered together.

5.2 The Direct Power Supply Identification of Photovoltaic Power Supply

All daily three-phase power generated by PV power sources 1–6 and 8–9 at 25–35 °C in the past year are selected as samples for analysis. The total number of samples is 163.

Table 1. The correlation coefficient matrix of each photovoltaic power source.

PV	1	2	3	4	5	6	7	8	9	10
1	1	0.9812	0.9693	0.9672	0.9125	0.9813	0.5795	0.9524	0.7324	0.2538
2	0.9812	1	0.9005	0.9854	0.9558	0.9955	0.4757	0.9132	0.8364	0.2826
3	0.9693	0.9005	1	0.9104	0.9846	0.9871	0.5566	0.9980	0.7912	0.3178
4	0.9672	0.9854	0.9104	1	0.9864	0.8842	0.5815	0.8983	0.7725	0.2805
5	0.9125	0.9558	0.9846	0.9864	1	0.9440	0.5505	0.9936	0.7810	0.4014
6	0.9813	0.9955	0.9871	0.8842	0.9440	1	0.5397	0.9752	0.7847	0.1926
7	0.5795	0.4757	0.5566	0.5815	0.5505	0.5397	1	0.5560	0.6737	0.6138
8	0.9524	0.9132	0.9980	0.8983	0.9936	0.9752	0.5560	1	0.7906	0.3334
9	0.7324	0.8364	0.7912	0.7725	0.7810	0.7847	0.6737	0.7906	1	0.6706
10	0.2538	0.2826	0.3178	0.2805	0.4014	0.1926	0.6138	0.3334	0.6706	1

The AP clustering algorithm is used to cluster these samples. The damping factor λ is 0.5. The bias parameter *p* is taken as the median of all terms of the similarity matrix *S* ranked from largest to smallest. The maximum number of iterations T is 400. The maximum number of iterations T′ is 40 if the clustering center does not change. The three-phase grid-connected power curves corresponding to each cluster center are shown in Figs. 7, 8, 9, 10, 11 and 12.

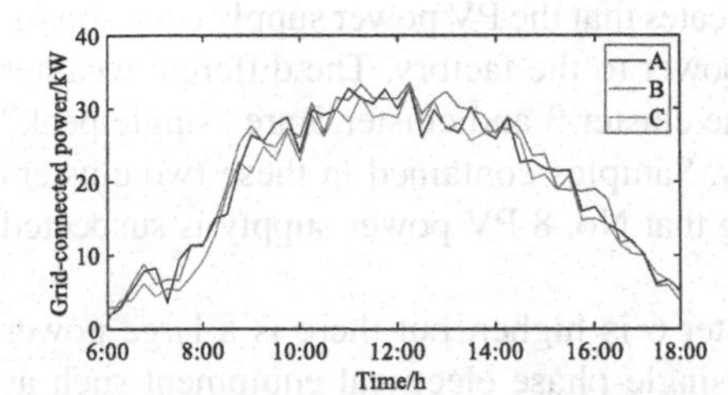

Fig. 7. The grid-connected power of class cluster center 1.

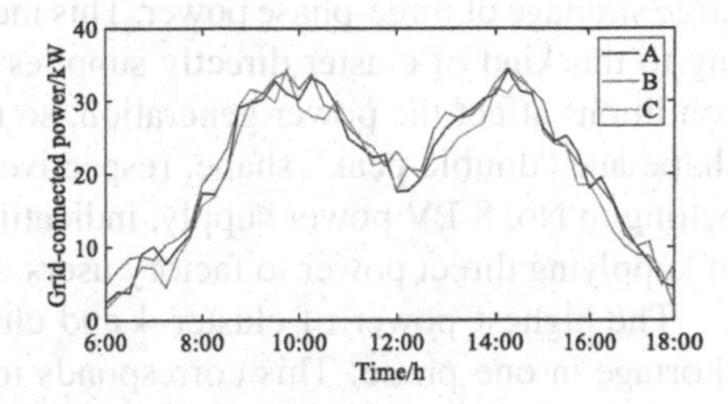

Fig. 8. The grid-connected power of class cluster center 2.

Cluster 1 represents the three-phase grid-connected power without direct power supply. The power generation is high, and the power of the three phases is basically balanced. The weather conditions corresponding to this kind of cluster are good, and the power generation first rises and then declines with the advance of time, presenting a "single peak" shape.

Cluster 2 shows a "double peak" shape, which corresponds to the brief rainy days during the day. The power generation power showed a temporary drop during the day and then rebounded to a higher state. The highest grid-connected power of photovoltaic power is close to the cluster 1, and the three-phase power is basically balanced. This type of cluster also corresponds to the case of no DPS.

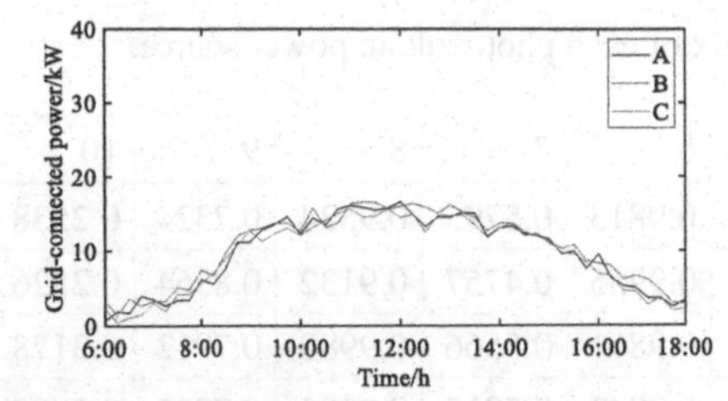

Fig. 9. The grid-connected power of class cluster center 3.

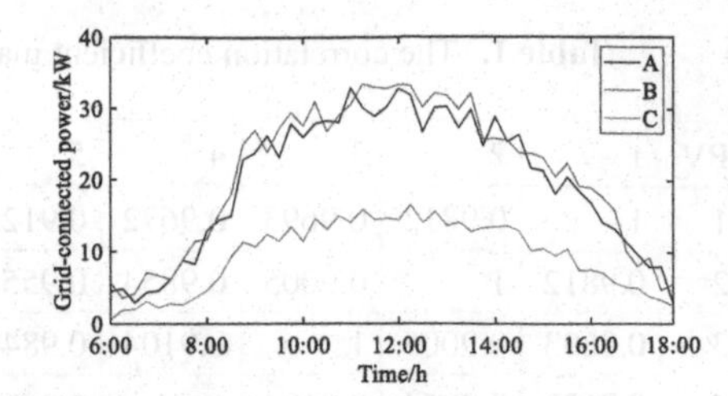

Fig. 10. The grid-connected power of class cluster center 4.

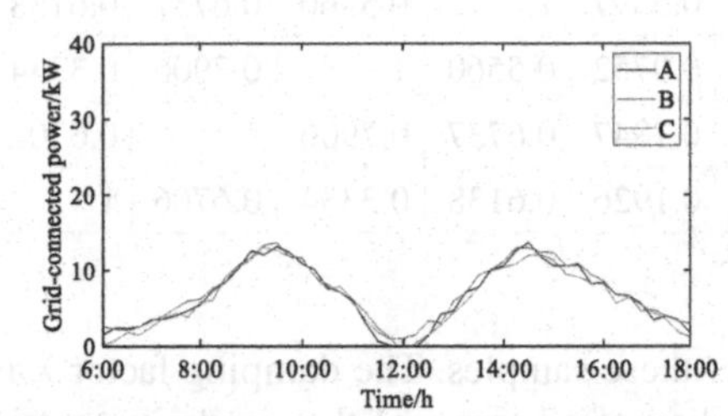

Fig. 11. The grid-connected power of class cluster center 5.

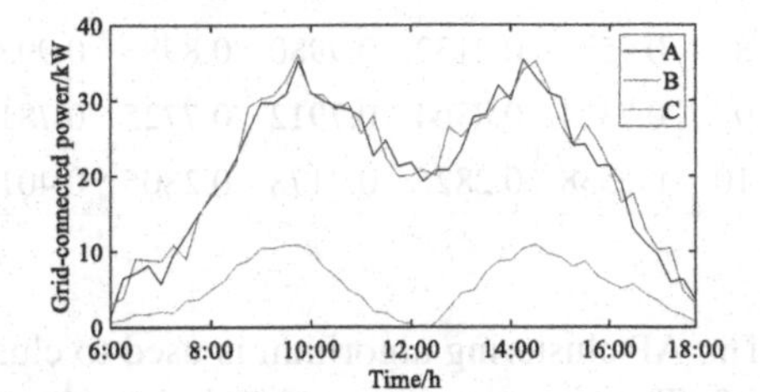

Fig. 12. The grid-connected power of class cluster center 6.

The three-phase power of cluster 3 and cluster 5 is basically balanced, but there is a large shortage of three-phase power. This indicates that the PV power supply corresponding to this kind of cluster directly supplies power to the factory. The different weather conditions affect the power generation, so the cluster 3 and cluster 5 are "single peak" shape and "double peak" shape, respectively. Samples contained in these two clusters belong to No. 8 PV power supply, indicating that No. 8 PV power supply is suspected of supplying direct power to factory users.

The highest power of cluster 4 and cluster 6 is higher, but there is a large power shortage in one phase. This corresponds to single-phase electrical equipment such as household appliances. The PV power supply corresponding to this kind of cluster directly supplies power to residential users. The different curve shapes of cluster 4 and cluster 6 are also caused by different weather states. The samples contained in these two clusters belong to No. 9 PV power supply, indicating that No. 9 PV power supply is suspected of supplying direct power to residential users.

In summary, the suspicion of DPS of No. 8 and No. 9 PV power supply is identified by AP clustering algorithm.

6 Conclusion

The identification method of DPS based on AP clustering algorithm proposed in this paper can effectively identify the DPS of PV power. The differences in climate, light intensity and other factors can be reduced by selecting the PV power source in the same station for analysis. Choosing the same type of PV power supply can reduce the shading, dust, attenuation and other factors. The output correlation of each PV power supply can be measured by the correlation coefficient, and the PV power supply with low correlation can be screened out. The AP clustering algorithm is used to divide the three-phase grid-connected power curves of each PV power supply at the same temperature into different clusters. The characteristics of the grid-connected power of each type of cluster can be used to know whether the corresponding sample is suspected of having direct power supply. Further, it can judge which type of DPS exists and provide reference for the on-site inspection of the power supply company.

References

1. Singh, A.K., Parida, S.K.: A review on distributed generation allocation and planning in deregulated electricity market. Renew. Sustain. Energy Rev. **82**, 4132–4141 (2018)
2. Nguyen, S., Peng, W., Sokolowski, P., et al.: Optimizing rooftop photovoltaic distributed generation with battery storage for peer-to-peer energy trading. Appl. Energy **228**, 2567–2580 (2018)
3. Georgilakis, P.S., Hatziargyriou, N.D.: Optimal distributed generation placement in power distribution networks: models, methods, and future research. IEEE Trans. Power Syst. **28**(3), 3420–3428 (2013)
4. Jokar, P., Arianpoo, N., Leung, V.C.M.: Electricity theft detection in AMI using customers' consumption patterns. IEEE Trans. Smart Grid **7**(1), 216–226 (2015)
5. Shaaban, M., Tariq, U., Ismail, M., et al.: Data-driven detection of electricity theft cyberattacks in PV generation. IEEE Syst. J. (2021)
6. Ismail, M., Shaaban, M.F., Naidu, M., et al.: Deep learning detection of electricity theft cyber-attacks in renewable distributed generation. IEEE Trans. Smart Grid **11**(4), 3428–3437 (2020)
7. Campanhol, L.B.G., Da Silva, S.A.O., De Oliveira, A.A., et al.: Power flow and stability analyses of a multifunctional distributed generation system integrating a photovoltaic system with unified power quality conditioner. IEEE Trans. Power Electron. **34**(7), 6241–6256 (2018)
8. Miller, W., Liu, A., Amin, Z., et al.: Power quality and rooftop-photovoltaic households: an examination of measured data at point of customer connection. Sustainability **10**(4), 1224 (2018)
9. Kharrazi, A., Sreeram, V., Mishra, Y.: Assessment techniques of the impact of grid-tied rooftop photovoltaic generation on the power quality of low voltage distribution network-a review. Renew. Sustain. Energy Rev. **120**, 109643 (2020)
10. Du, Z., Su, S., Liu, Z., et al.: Second inspection method for electricity theft detection with low false alarm rate based on identification of production and operation status. Autom. Electr. Power Syst. **45**(02), 97–104 (2021)
11. Xiao, Y., Zheng, K., Yu, Z., et al.: Power data anomaly detection based on holt-winters model and DBSCAN clustering. Power Syst. Technol. **44**(03), 0320 (2020)
12. Wang, K., Qi, X., Liu, H.: A comparison of day-ahead photovoltaic power forecasting models based on deep learning neural network. Appl. Energy **251**, 113315 (2019)
13. Zang, H., Cheng, L., Ding, T., et al.: Day-ahead photovoltaic power forecasting approach based on deep convolutional neural networks and meta learning. Int. J. Electr. Power Energy Syst. **118**, 105790 (2020)
14. Cheng, L., Zang, H., Ding, T., et al.: Multi-meteorological-factor-based graph modeling for photovoltaic power forecasting. IEEE Trans. Sustain. Energy **12**(3), 1593–1603 (2021)

15. Lu, S., Peng, S., Yang, Y., et al.: Identification method of abnormal photovoltaic users based on mean impact value and heuristic forward searching. Electr. Power Autom. Equip. **42**(02), 106–111 (2022)
16. Frey, B.J., Dueck, D.: Clustering by passing messages between data points. Science **315**(5814), 972–976 (2007)
17. Wang, K., Zhang, J., Li, D., et al.: Adaptive affinity propagation clustering. arXiv preprint arXiv:0805.1096 (2008)

An Optimized Depth Complementation of Transparent Objects Based Robotic Arm Grasping System

Zhaojian Gu[1,2], Hongbo Chen[3], Ping Zhu[3], Mingyu Gao[1,2](✉), and Yan Huang[4]

[1] School of Electronics and Information, Hangzhou Dianzi University, Hangzhou 310018, China
mackgao@hdu.edu.cn
[2] Zhejiang Provincial Key Lab of Equipment Electronics, Hangzhou 310018, China
[3] Zhejiang Fangyuan Test Group Co., Ltd., Hangzhou 311222, China
[4] China Southern Power Grid Energy Development Research Institute Co., Ltd., Guangzhou 310027, China

Abstract. In this paper, we propose a method to implement a robotic arm for grasping transparent objects and apply it to the grasping of transparent test tubes. Test tubes are one of the frequently used experimental equipment in the chemical industry, and many steps in the experimental process require the use of test tubes to hold reagents. However, as a transparent object, the test tube has unique visual characteristics, which makes it difficult for general-purpose RGB-D cameras to capture its complete depth information. To solve this problem and improve the grasping quality, we propose a robotic arm grasping system using depth completion combined with point clouds. Specifically, we propose a depth learning method to complement the original depth image of transparent objects. In addition, the coordinate transformation relationship between the camera and the robotic arm is obtained by a hand-eye calibration system, while the grasping is performed based on a point cloud map generated from the complementary depth image. Experiments show that our method can significantly improve the depth complementary performance of the transparent object images and achieve accurate grasping by the robotic arm.

Keywords: Transparent Objects Detection · Depth Completion · Robot Grasping

1 Introduction

In order for a robot to accurately perform its tasks, traditional robot programming requires strict designation of start and stop positions, which makes the robot extremely demanding for the working environment. With the rapid development of computer vision, robots are no longer limited to fixed and repetitive tasks, but can achieve automatic identification and grasping of different target objects by processing the images acquired by cameras [1, 2].

Although there are many methods to achieve object recognition [3–6], the unique visual characteristics such as reflectivity and refraction of transparent objects [7] lead

H. Yang et al. (Eds.): SmartGIFT 2022, LNICST 483, pp. 229–240, 2023.
https://doi.org/10.1007/978-3-031-31733-0_20

to the fact that most algorithms are still ineffective in recognizing transparent objects. Recent work based on deep learning has achieved good results in depth completion [8, 9], by introducing features such as surface normal and occlusion boundaries to complete the original depth [10]. However, most of the depth-completion methods ignore transparent objects and predict their true depth only from the approximation of the surface or distortion behind the transparent region, which cannot recognize the transparent object, and the lack of depth information can cause serious errors in the robot grasping system [11]. Sajjan et al. [7] optimize the initial depth estimation for the transparent object surface by introducing a mask of the transparent object, and use parallel jaws to achieve 72% grasping success rate. However, this cannot satisfy the accuracy and stability required for industrial application scenarios.

In this paper, we improve the depth complementation model for transparent objects to generate a more complete depth map, and combine the point cloud data generated from the complete depth map to obtain the position of the transparent objects in the world coordinate system [12, 13], and apply it to the robotic arm grasping system.

The main contributions of this paper are as follows:

(1) The clear grasp algorithm is improved to optimize the depth map of transparent objects to obtain the complete point cloud data, and applied to the robotic arm operating system.
(2) By processing the test tube point cloud data and combining the cubic non-uniform B-sample interpolation, the path of the robotic arm in Cartesian space is planned to achieve stable grasping of the transparent test tube. Our grasping system can achieve nearly 93% grasping success rate for transparent test tubes.

2 Related Work

2.1 Detecting Transparent Objects

The recognition of transparent objects has been a challenge in computer vision and physical fields, and traditional detection methods rely on the unique optical properties possessed by transparent objects, such as the use of charge-coupled devices [14], ground-separated stereo techniques [15], and visual shell refinement [16]. Recent methods are to predict the boundary range of transparent objects by deep learning models for their accurate localization, such as SSD models [17] and RCNN models [18]. Agastya et al. [19] proposed a transparent object segmentation method combining multimodal images and deep learning by using polarization cameras to capture multimodal maps. Sajjan et al. [7] proposed a 3D shape of transparent objects estimation method by predicting surface normal, masks and occlusion boundaries, using Cholesky optimization to estimate the 3D geometry of transparent objects in a single RGB-D image. However, the depth maps produced by these methods may not meet the stable grasping requirements of a real robot arm operating system for transparent objects. Tang et al. [20] proposed to use Generative Adversarial Networks to complement the depth maps of transparent objects, however, it requires retraining all surface normal, occlusion boundaries, and masks, which is time-consuming.

2.2 Depth Completion

With the development of depth sensing technology, commercial RGB-D cameras can achieve accurate estimation of depth, but when the surface of the object is too smooth and influenced by light, the camera obtains a depth map with a part of the data missing. Depth complementation aims to predict the missing depth data to generate a complete depth image. Zhang et al. [10] obtained geometric information of the target by predicting surface normal and occluded boundaries of RGB images, which is still insufficient for predicting depth images of transparent objects. Sajjan et al. [7] removed all depth pixels from the surface of transparent objects in the original depth map and used a linear system based on geometric constraints for depth prediction, which still had a portion of depth missing in the original depth map except for transparent objects due to the illumination environment, which was not conducive to depth reconstruction. We further processed the original depth map with a fast depth complement module (FDC) [21] to improve the accuracy of the depth complement of transparent objects.

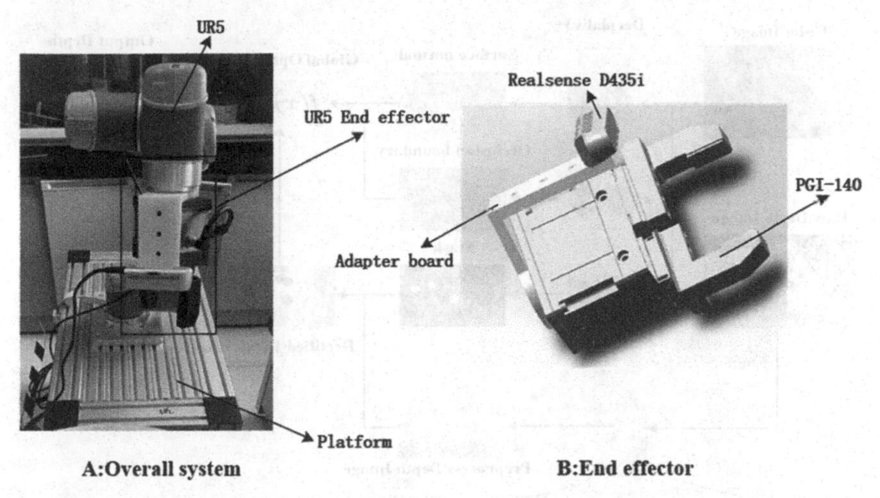

Fig. 1. Part A is the overall hardware of the robot system and part B is the end effector model of robot.

2.3 Robot Grasping

Point clouds have been applied in several ways for motion trajectory planning. Krusi et al. [22] achieved autonomous navigation in complex 3D terrain by means of unordered point cloud maps. Kuntz et al. [23], used point clouds to represent anatomical structures inside the patient's body, enabling the robot to automatically reach the surgical target inside the body while avoiding obstacles. We propose the use of point clouds to locate specific location information of transparent test tubes, and the grasping system mainly considers the trajectory based on the motion of the end gripper jaws, including the inverse kinematic solution of the robot arm based on Jacobi matrix, and a Fourier series based approximation of the robot's kinematic.

The waypoints of the grasping system are generated by the sampling-based Rapid Exploration Random Tree (RRT) algorithm [24], while the smooth trajectory is optimized by the cubic non-uniform B spline interpolation and TOPP algorithms [25]. Our system is shown in Fig. 1.A. The end-effector used by the robot arm to implement the grasping is a PGI motorized gripper, whose model is shown in Fig. 1.B.

3 Method

3.1 Depth Refinement Model

As shown in Fig. 2, given a single RGB-D image of a transparent object, surface normal, occlusion boundaries, and masks of transparent objects are first obtained from the color image. Then, the original depth image is quickly depth-complemented by a classical image processing algorithm, and the processed multiple features are used as input for global optimization to further refine the globally optimized output depth estimate.

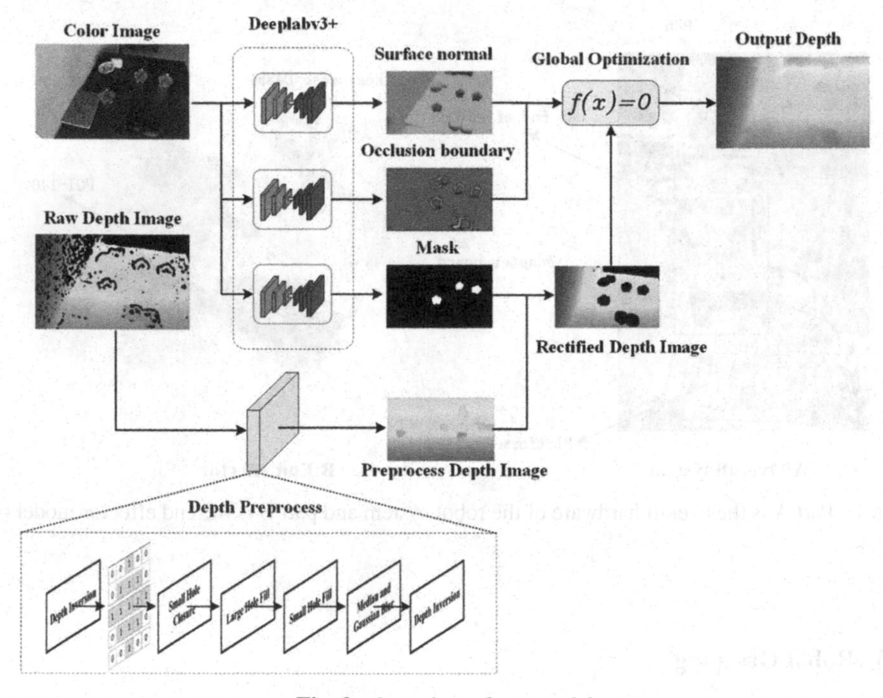

Fig. 2. Overview of our model.

Data Preprocessing. Depth complementation of transparent objects requires the use of surface normal and occlusion boundaries to provide geometric information about the object. Where the ground truth of the surface normal of a transparent object is estimated by obtaining point cloud data of an opaque object that has exactly the same shape as the transparent object and is located at the same position, while the ground truth of the occlusion boundary is predicted by the depth and mask of the same opaque object.

Initial Depth Complement. For the visual properties of transparent objects, Sajjan et al. [7] modified the original depth map by removing the masks of transparent objects. Considering the efficiency and accuracy, we first perform a fast preprocessing of the original depth map by using the classical image processing method [21] to repair the missing depth in it due to factors such as lighting environment except for transparent objects.

The process of the original depth map processing can be described as finding a function f' to approximate the true function:

$$f(I, D_{raw}) = D_{dense} \tag{1}$$

where $I \in R^{M \times N}$ is the original color image, $D_{raw} \in R^{M \times N}$ is the original depth map, and $D_{dense} \in R^{M \times N}$ is the processed depth map, which is the same size as I and D_{raw}. The process can be formulated as:

$$\min\left|\left|f'(I, D_{raw}) - f(I, D_{raw})\right|\right|_F^2 = 0 \tag{2}$$

The function f' can be implemented by the image processing operation as shown in Fig. 3.

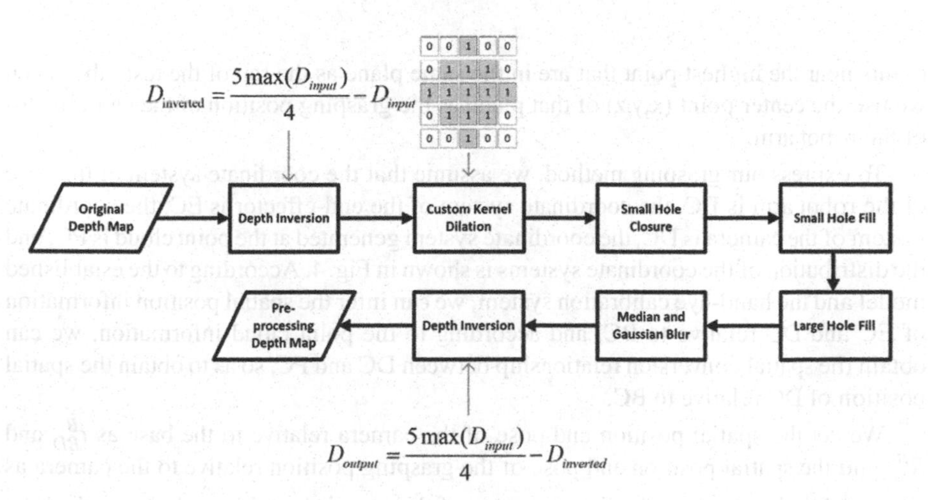

Fig. 3. Preprocess of depth map.

where $D_{intered}$ denotes the inverted depth map, and $\max(D_{input})$ denotes taking the maximum value of the depth of the input depth map. Considering the application scenario, we removed the module that extends to the top of the frame, making it more focused on the immediate target.

Point Cloud for Grasping. We use transparent test tubes as the experimental object and first obtain the position of the transparent test tube in space from the complete depth map and generate a point cloud map. Since the test tube is placed on the test tube holder, we traverse all the point cloud data to find the highest point and use to search all the

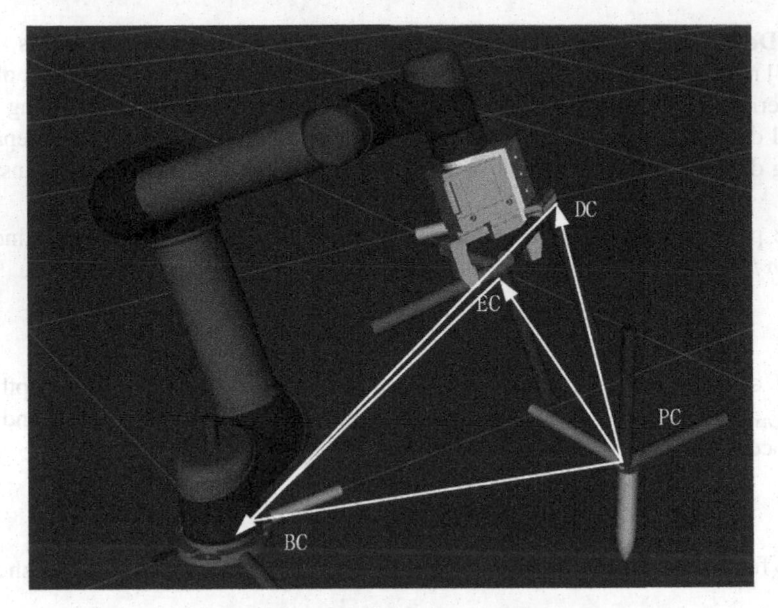

Fig. 4. Robot coordinate system.

points near the highest point that are in the same plane as the top of the test tube. Then we use the center point (x,y,z) of that plane as the grasping position of the end-effector of the robot arm.

To express our grasping method, we assume that the coordinate system of the base of the robot arm is BC, the coordinate system of the end-effector is EC, the coordinate system of the camera is DC, the coordinate system generated at the point cloud is PC, and the distribution of the coordinate systems is shown in Fig. 4. According to the established model and the hand-eye calibration system, we can infer the spatial position information of EC and DC relative to BC, and according to the point cloud information, we can obtain the spatial conversion relationship between DC and PC, so as to obtain the spatial position of DC relative to BC.

We set the spatial position and pose of the camera relative to the base as $t_{BD}^{\vec{B}}$ and R_D^B, and the spatial position and pose of the grasping position relative to the camera as $t_{DP}^{\vec{D}}$ and R_P^D, then the transformation matrix of the grasping position relative to the base coordinate system of the robot arm is as follows:

$$\begin{cases} {}^BT_P = {}^BT_E{}^ET_D{}^DT_P \\ {}^DT_P = \begin{bmatrix} R_P^D & t_{DP}^{\vec{D}} \\ 0 & 1 \end{bmatrix} \\ {}^BT_E{}^ET_D = \begin{bmatrix} R_D^B & t_{BD}^{\vec{B}} \\ 0 & 1 \end{bmatrix} \end{cases} \tag{3}$$

4 Experiments

4.1 Experimental Environment and Dataset

The hardware and software environments for the experiments are as follows: a server with Ubuntu 20.04, GTX3070 GPU, deep learning framework Pytorch1.11.0, Python 3.8.

We use Clear Grasp's dataset for evaluation, which contains more than 50,000 synthetic RGB-D images, as well as 286 real-world images of transparent objects. Opaque objects are used to overlay transparent objects to obtain realistic depth information. The ground truth of occlusion boundaries is generated from the depth maps of opaque objects as well as masks, and point cloud data are generated from the depth maps to obtain the ground truth of surface normal for training. We use 5 known real-world objects in Clear Grasp's dataset as testing set.

4.2 Performance Metrics

For depth-completion, we use the same metric as in the previous work: the RMSE, REL, MAE and the percentage of pixels of the ground truth where the predicted depth falls within the threshold percentage error called δ [26, 27]:

$$\delta = |\text{predicted} - \text{true}|/\text{true} \tag{4}$$

where δ is 1.05, 1.10 or 1.25.

For grasp detection, we use multiple depth completion methods for grasping, and each method is repeated 100 times, and we calculate the grasping success rate:

$$rate = \frac{successful\ picks}{picking\ attempts} \tag{5}$$

as the evaluation metric.

4.3 Comparison with Other Depth Completion Algorithm

We compare the performance of Fast Depth Completion (FDC) [21], Deep Depth Completion (DDC) [10], Clear Grasp [7] and our method, and the performance of depth completion is shown in Table 1.

We can observe that the poor performance of the model using the traditional depth-completion algorithm alone, which reasons may be that it does not consider the unique visual properties possessed by transparent objects, ignoring its local details and contour boundaries. Compared to the aforementioned methods, Clear Grasp obtains a larger performance improvement due to the geometric information obtained from the RGB image prediction and the correction of the input depth map. The best performance of our proposed method is obtained due to the further processing of depth information, which eliminates a large amount of uncertain depth information in the input depth map and achieves a more accurate optimization.

The results of depth complementation are shown in Fig. 5, and it can be observed that our method obtains relatively complete depth information. As shown in the figure, the shapes and contours of transparent objects in the circles can be well.

Table 1. Depth completion results of the approaches.

	Error Metrics			Accuracy Metrics		
Model	RMSE ↓ (m)	REL ↓ (m)	MAE ↓ (m)	$\delta_{1.05}$ ↑ (%)	$\delta_{1.10}$ ↑ (%)	$\delta_{1.25}$ ↑ (%)
FDC	0.127	0.142	0.078	48.04	66.63	88.24
DDC	0.054	0.081	0.045	44.53	69.71	95.77
Clear Grasp	0.039	0.051	0.029	72.86	86.99	95.63
Ours	0.035	0.046	0.026	75.81	89.04	96.19

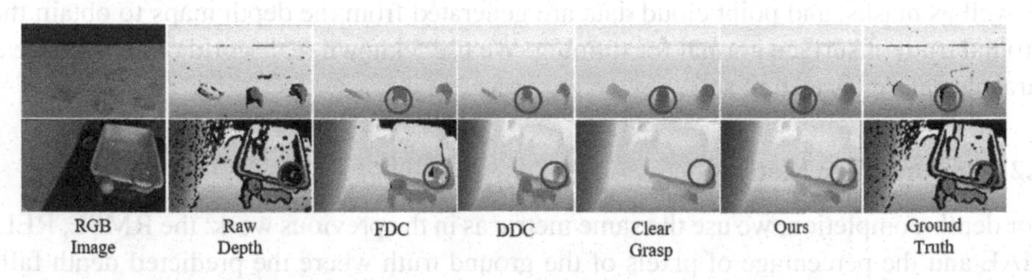

Fig. 5. Comparison of depth completion effects of multiple approaches.

4.4 Ablation Study

The preprocessing module of the depth image uses depth inversion, hole closure and fill methods to complement the depth information. We compare the effects of using different hole methods and eliminating depth inversion in the preprocessing module, and we denote the method without the depth inversion module as Ours-I, the method without small hole closure as Ours-Shc, the method without small hole fill as Ours-Shf and the method without large hole fill as Ours-Lhf. Table 2 summarizes the preprocessing performance of various variants of the module.

Table 2. Ablation results of the preprocessing module.

	Error Metrics			Accuracy Metrics		
Model	RMSE ↓ (m)	REL ↓ (m)	MAE ↓ (m)	$\delta_{1.05}$ ↑ (%)	$\delta_{1.10}$ ↑ (%)	$\delta_{1.25}$ ↑ (%)
Ours-I	0.064	0.085	0.048	49.87	74.85	92.66
Ours-Shc	0.035	0.046	0.026	75.73	88.98	96.18
Ours-Shf	0.036	0.047	0.027	75.55	88.72	95.85
Ours-Lhf	0.037	0.048	0.027	74.92	88.4	95.53
Ours	0.035	0.046	0.026	75.81	89.04	96.19

The depth map after the variant complementation by our method is shown in Fig. 6, it can be observed that the model after depth inversion obtains a clearer outline of transparent objects, while hole closure and hole fill also play a certain role.

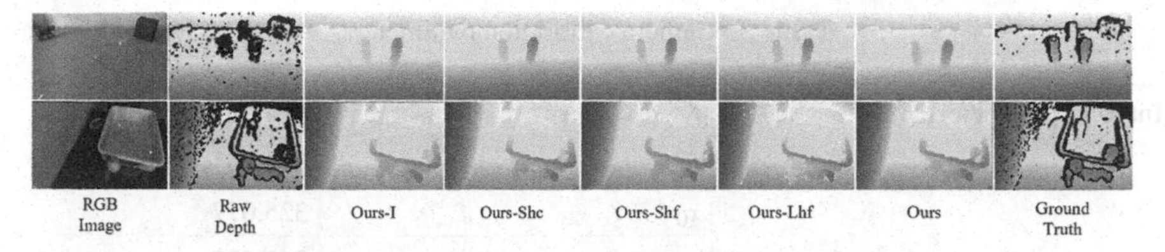

Fig. 6. Comparison to the variants of our method.

Fig. 7. Part A is camera internal parameters calibration and part B is Camera external parameters calibration.

4.5 Eye-to-Hand Calibration System

In order for the robotic arm to obtain the position of the object in the image in space, the camera needs to be calibrated. This includes the calibration of the internal parameters of the camera and the calibration of the external parameters. The internal calibration is used to correct the distortion of the image due to the distortion of the camera lens, and the external calibration is used to reconstruct the 3D scene. We use Zhang Zhengyou calibration method [28] for internal calibration, as shown in Fig. 7.A. Using a 9x7 checkerboard calibration plate of size 20 mm to calculate the internal parameters and aberration coefficients of the camera by shooting from multiple angles.

For external calibration, we use the eye-in-hand calibration method, as shown in Fig. 7.B. We move the robot arm to different positions while keeping the calibration plate within the field of view of the camera, and obtaining the motion samples of multiple points for the calculation of parameters. The specific parameters of the camera are shown in the Table 3.

4.6 Accuracy of Grasp System

We use the acquired complete depth map as input to the robot grasping system to observe the effect of depth complementation on the grasping performance of transparent objects. In this experiment, we place transparent test tubes on an experiment-specific test tube rack, capture RGB-D images by a Realsense D435i camera, and control the robotic

Table 3. Camera calibration parameters.

Internal parameters	f_x	614.367
	f_y	614.705
	x_0	325.077
	y_0	240.572
T	Position x	0.409
	Position y	0.466
	Position z	0.516
R	Orientation x	0.840
	Orientation y	−0.520
	Orientation z	0.043
	Orientation w	−0.149

arm to achieve the grasping of transparent test tubes by point cloud information. The point cloud maps obtained before and after depth complementation using our method are shown in Fig. 8, and the snapshots of the UR5 grasping transparent test tubes are shown in Fig. 9. We tested different methods to grasp the test tube 100 times, and if the error between the robot's end-effector coordinate system position and the predicted test tube coordinate position is less than 0.1 cm, the grasping is successful, and the success rate is shown in the Table 4. It can be observed that our method has the best grasping performance.

Fig. 8. Part A is the raw point cloud map and part B is the processed point cloud map

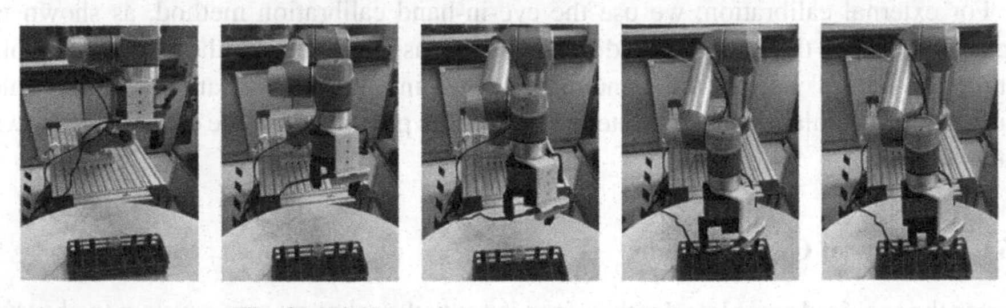

Fig. 9. UR5 grasping transparent test tube process

Table 4. Performance of grasping test tube

Method	Success rate (%)
Raw Depth	4
FDC	53
DDC	67
Clear Grasp	87
Ours	93

5 Conclusion

In this paper, we obtain more complete depth information of the transparent object by preprocessing the original depth map using the fast depth complement method, and obtain the point cloud data of the transparent object by the complete depth information to obtain its position information in the real world and control the robotic arm for grasping. The results show that the system can achieve stable grasping of transparent objects. This study is beneficial to advance the intelligence of chemical laboratory and reduce the labor cost. In future work, we will try to use the dual-arm robot to perform the tasks in chemistry experiments for test tube manipulation and to improve the robustness of the predictive occlusion boundary algorithm in complex laboratory environments.

References

1. Lu, C.: Kalman tracking algorithm of ping-pong robot based on fuzzy real-time image. J. Intell. Fuzzy Syst. **38**(4), 3585–3594 (2020)
2. Zhang, Y., Cheng, W.: Vision-based robot sorting system. In: Materials Science and Engineering, vol. 592, p. 1. IOP Publishing (2019)
3. Tanwani, A.K., Mor, N., Kubiatowicz, J.: A fog robotics approach to deep robot learning: application to object recognition and grasp planning in surface decluttering. In: International Conference on Robotics and Automation (ICRA), pp. 4559–4566. IEEE (2019)
4. Hossain, D., Capi, G., Jindai, M.: Optimizing deep learning parameters using genetic algorithm for object recognition and robot grasping. J. Electron. Sci. Technol. **16**(1), 11–15 (2018)
5. Cartucho, J., Ventura, R., Veloso, M.: Robust object recognition through symbiotic deep learning in mobile robots. In: International Conference on Intelligent Robots and Systems (IROS), pp. 2336–2341. IEEE (2018)
6. Dong, Z., Ji, X., Zhou, G.: Multimodal neuromorphic sensory-processing system with memristor circuits for smart home applications. IEEE Trans. Ind. Appl. (2022)
7. Sajjan, S., Moore, M., Pan, M.: Clear grasp: 3D shape estimation of transparent objects for manipulation. In: International Conference on Robotics and Automation (ICRA), pp. 3634–3642. IEEE (2020)
8. Sperling, L., Lämmer, S., Leipzig, S.: Uncertainty-aware evaluation of machine learning performance in binary classification tasks. J. WSCG **30**(1), 63–71 (2022)
9. Lu, K., Barnes, N., Anwar, S.: From depth what can you see? Depth completion via auxiliary image reconstruction. In: Proceedings of the IEEE/CVF Conference on Computer Vision and Pattern Recognition, pp. 11306–11315. IEEE (2020)

10. Zhang, Y., Funkhouser, T.: Deep depth completion of a single RGB-D image. In: Proceedings of the IEEE Conference on Computer Vision and Pattern Recognition, pp. 175–185. IEEE (2018)
11. Ji, X., Dong, Z., Lai, C.S.: A brain-inspired in-memory computing system for neuronal communication via memristive circuits. IEEE Commun. Mag. **60**(1), 100–106 (2022)
12. Ten Pas, A., Platt, R.: Using geometry to detect grasp poses in 3D point clouds. Rob. Res. **2**, 307–324 (2018)
13. Mahler, J., Liang, J., Niyaz, S.: Dex-Net 2.0: deep learning to plan robust grasps with synthetic point clouds and analytic grasp metrics. Robot.: Sci. Syst. (2017)
14. Jamaludin, J., Rahim, R.A., Rahiman, M.H.F.: Optical tomography system using charge-coupled device for transparent object detection. Int. J. Integr. Eng. **10**(4) (2018)
15. Phillips, C.J., Derpanis, K.G., Daniilidis, K.: A novel stereoscopic cue for figure-ground segregation of semi-transparent objects. In: International Conference on Computer Vision Workshops (ICCV Workshops), pp. 1100–1107. IEEE (2011)
16. Zuo, X., Du, C., Wang, S.: Interactive visual hull refinement for specular and transparent object surface reconstruction. In: Proceedings of the IEEE International Conference on Computer Vision, pp. 2237–2245. IEEE (2015)
17. Khaing, M.P., Masayuki, M.: Transparent object detection using convolutional neural network. In: Zin, T.T., Lin, J.-W. (eds.) ICBDL 2018. AISC, vol. 744, pp. 86–93. Springer, Singapore (2019). https://doi.org/10.1007/978-981-13-0869-7_10
18. Lai, P.J., Fuh, C.S.: Transparent object detection using regions with convolutional neural network. In: IPPR Conference on Computer Vision, Graphics, and Image Processing, p. 2 (2015)
19. Kalra, A., Taamazyan, V., Rao, S.K.: Deep polarization cues for transparent object segmentation. In: Proceedings of the IEEE/CVF Conference on Computer Vision and Pattern Recognition, pp. 8602–8611 (2020)
20. Tang, Y., Chen, J., Yang, Z.: DepthGrasp: depth completion of transparent objects using self-attentive adversarial network with spectral residual for grasping. In: 2021 IEEE/RSJ International Conference on Intelligent Robots and Systems (IROS), pp. 5710–5716. IEEE (2021)
21. Ku, J., Harakeh, A., Waslander, S.L.: In defense of classical image processing: fast depth completion on the CPU. In: 2018 15th Conference on Computer and Robot Vision (CRV), pp. 16–22. IEEE (2018)
22. Krüsi, P., Furgale, P., Bosse, M.: Driving on point clouds: motion planning, trajectory optimization, and terrain assessment in generic nonplanar environments. J. Field Robot. **34**(5), 940–984 (2017)
23. Kuntz, A., Fu, M., Alterovitz, R.: Planning high-quality motions for concentric tube robots in point clouds via parallel sampling and optimization. In: 2019 IEEE/RSJ International Conference on Intelligent Robots and Systems (IROS), pp. 2205–2212. IEEE (2019)
24. Véras, L.G.D.O., Medeiros, F.L.L., Guimarães, L.N.F.: Systematic literature review of sampling process in rapidly-exploring random trees. IEEE Access **7**, 50933–50953 (2019)
25. Pham, Q.C.: A general, fast, and robust implementation of the time-optimal path parameterization algorithm. IEEE Trans. Robot. **30**(6), 1533–1540 (2014)
26. Huang, Y.K., Wu, T.H., Liu, Y.C.: Indoor depth completion with boundary consistency and self-attention. In: Proceedings of the IEEE/CVF International Conference on Computer Vision Workshops. IEEE (2019)
27. Dong, Z., Qi, D., He, Y.: Easily cascaded memristor-CMOS hybrid circuit for high-efficiency Boolean logic implementation. Int. J. Bifurc. Chaos **28**(12), 1850149 (2018)
28. Zhang, Z.: A flexible new technique for camera calibration. IEEE Trans. Pattern Anal. Mach. Intell. **22**(11), 1330–1334 (2000)

Development of a Fast DC Switch Based on Electromagnetic Repulsion Mechanism

Sheng-qin Xu(✉), Li-xue Chen, and Zhao Yuan

Huazhong University of Science and Technology, Wuhan, China
xvshengqin@hust.edu.cn

Abstract. This paper introduces the overall structure design of a high-speed, medium-voltage compact fast DC switchgear. This device is driven by an electromagnetic repulsion disc, and uses a bistable spring as a holding device to maintain the opening and closing state. We calculated the steady-state heating of the switch under rated current for a long time, the results show that the steady-state heat generation of the through-flow part can meets the requirements of relevant standards. Then we calculated the breaking field strength of the isolation fracture, the breaking capacity of the switch at the rated distance meets the requirements of the rated voltage. The electromagnetic repulsion force on the repulsive disk and the stress distribution of the kinematic structure show that, the operating mechanism of the device can meet the requirements of opening distance greater than 5 mm within 1 ms. The closing time of this switch is less than 5 ms, the material and mechanical properties can meet the requirements. The above analysis shows that this device can meet the needs of medium-voltage DC systems for compact and fast DC switches.

Keywords: Fast transfer switch · Electromagnetic repulsion mechanism · DC switch

1 Introduction

With the development of science and technology in various countries, DC power systems have been applied in various fields, such as DC power transmission and distribution, and ship power [1, 2]. With the further increase in the power demand in the ship system, the medium voltage DC integrated power system has become the focus of current research. The structure of the medium-voltage DC system needs to have the ability to quickly disconnect and clear the fault, and at the same time, it can quickly isolate the faulty part of the system to ensure the stable operation of the rest of the system. Due to the short power lines, low equivalent impedance value and small time constant of the ship power system, when a short circuit fault occurs in the system, the current in the line will increase rapidly, so a DC circuit breaker that can quickly act to cut off the fault current is required. Device. At present, there are two main types of DC circuit breakers: hybrid DC circuit breakers and mechanical DC circuit breakers. In these two types of DC circuit

H. Yang et al. (Eds.): SmartGIFT 2022, LNICST 483, pp. 241–253, 2023.
https://doi.org/10.1007/978-3-031-31733-0_21

breakers [3, 4], the fast mechanical switch is an important component, and its action speed is related to the breaking speed of the DC circuit breaker, so it is required to have fast action capability. The fast DC switch can also be used as the isolation switch of the DC system to quickly cut off the faulty part of the system to ensure the stable operation of the rest of the system.

This paper introduces the overall structural design of a compact ultra-fast medium-voltage DC switchgear. To meet the needs of fast action. This DC switch device is based on the principle of electromagnetic repulsion disc, uses electromagnetic repulsion to quickly start the moving contacts, reaches the rated opening distance within 1ms, and then maintains a sufficient separation distance between the moving and static contacts through the holding device to withstand the system voltage. In order to consider environmental protection requirements, nitrogen gas with several times atmospheric pressure is used as insulating medium inside the switch. The performance of the device is verified by the multi-physics finite element simulation software COMSOL to meet the design requirements.

2 Overall Structure of the Equipment

The 3D model of the switch (without the casing) is shown in Fig. 1. This is a DC switchgear with a rated voltage of 6 kV and a rated current of 2 kA. It consists of an internal flow part, an opening and closing operating mechanism and an external supporting structure. The overall height of the device is about 35 cm, and the outer radius is about 13 cm. The design of the through-flow part and the opening and closing operating mechanism will be verified in the following chapters.

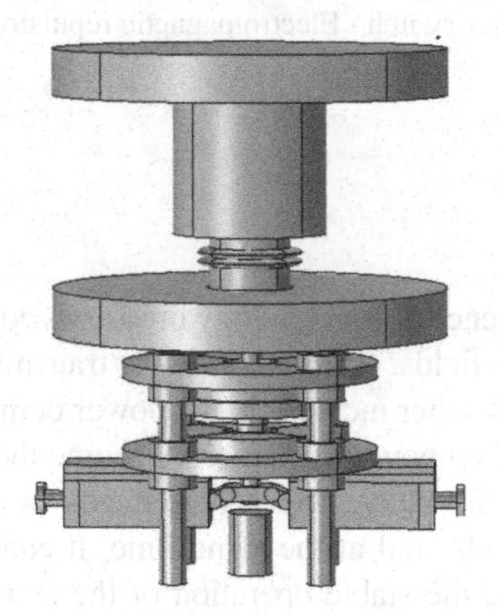

Fig. 1. 3D model of the quick switch.

3 Current-Carrying Part Design

Since the DC switch adopts a fully enclosed structure, that is, all moving parts are located inside the casing. In order to meet the electrical connection requirements, the strap contact finger structure is used as the electrical connection component between the movable contact and the external outgoing terminal. To sum up, the overall flow-through part includes four parts: the moving contact connected with the operating mechanism, the static contact and its external connection part, the transitional outgoing terminal connected with the outgoing terminal, the connecting moving contact and transitional outgoing wire The sliding finger structure of the terminal.

Since the sliding contact finger structure is sleeved on the periphery of the moving contact, there are certain requirements on the perimeter of the cross-sectional area of the moving contact. The radius of the moving contact of the designed plate electrode is 2.7 cm, the length is 5.3 cm, and the radius of the static contact is the same as that of the moving contact. The contact material is chrome bronze, the minimum flow area is 2290 mm^2, and the flow capacity can reach 4 kA, which meets the rated current requirements.

The 2D model of the current-carrying part is shown in Fig. 2. The middle diameter of the static contact holding spring is 47 mm, the wire diameter is 7.5 mm, the material is high-conductivity beryllium bronze C17500, the effective number of turns is 3, and the spring stiffness coefficient is about 1524 N/mm, the design closing retention force is 1500 N.

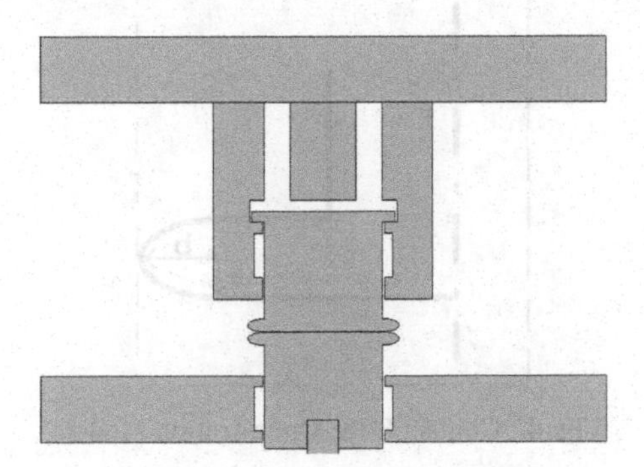

Fig. 2. 2D model of the current-carrying part.

According to relevant standards, the temperature rise of the electrical switch contact part at an ambient temperature of 40°C should not exceed 35 K, that is, the long-term operating temperature at an ambient temperature of 40°C should not exceed 75°C. The steady-state thermal calculation result of adding the rated current to the current-carrying part is shown in Fig. 3. When the external ambient temperature is 40°C, the maximum internal temperature rise is 30 K, which meets the standard requirements.

When the distance between the moving and static contacts is short, the electric field distribution between the contacts is relatively uniform. However, in order to improve the insulation breakdown level at the contact edge, the shape at the contact edge needs to be optimized.

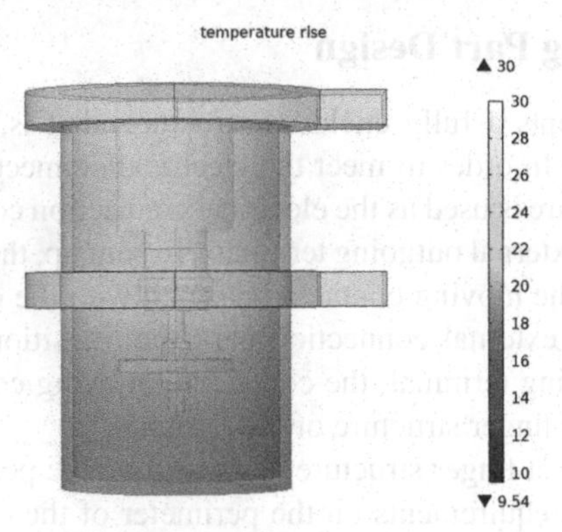

Fig. 3. Current-carrying part temperature rise distribution.

Using the scheme shown in Fig. 4 to carry out the optimization design, the electric field optimization results are shown in Fig. 5, *a* is 3 mm, the ratio of the long and short axes is 2.6, the field strength distribution between the poles is relatively uniform, and the maximum field strength is 1.24 kV/mm. When the pressure is 1.6 times the atmospheric pressure, the 5 mm withstand voltage level of nitrogen is already 20 kV which meets the withstand voltage requirement.

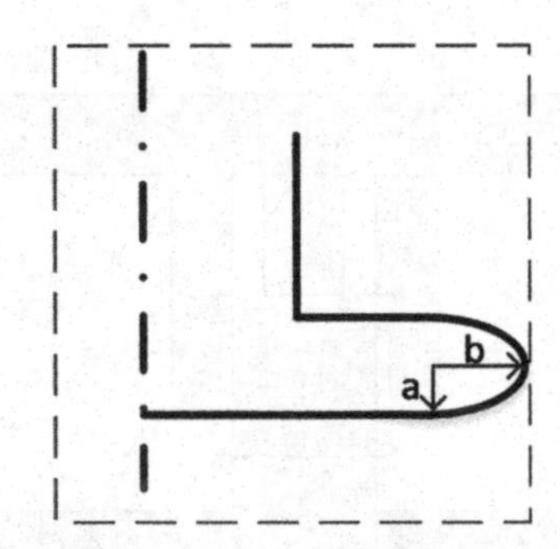

Fig. 4. Contact Edge Optimization Model.

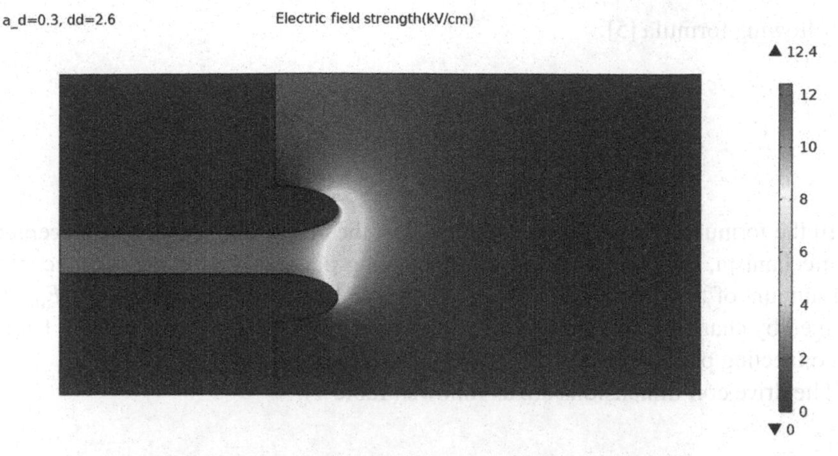

Fig. 5. Optimized electric field intensity distribution.

4 Operating Mechanism Design

4.1 Simulation Model Establishment

The isolation switch action mechanism based on the coil-disc electromagnetic repulsion mechanism mainly includes three parts: a driving device, a holding device and a buffer device. The principle of the driving device is as follows: the pre-charged capacitor C is discharged to the closing or opening coil to generate a pulse current, and the repulsive disc is subjected to electromagnetic thrust due to the induced eddy current, thereby driving the connecting rod to move to realize the closing or opening of the switch.

Based on the composition and driving principle of the electromagnetic repulsion mechanism, the force characteristics of the mechanism are further discussed. The electromagnetic repulsion borne by the repulsion disc is the driving force for the action of the mechanism, and the electromagnetic repulsion can be expressed as:

$$F = \frac{\mathrm{d}W}{\mathrm{d}z} = \frac{i_1 i_2 \mathrm{d}M}{\mathrm{d}z} \quad (1)$$

It can be seen from the above formula that the electromagnetic repulsion force F is related to the current i_1 in the excitation coil, the eddy current i_2 in the repulsion disk, and the derivative of the mutual M inductance to the displacement z, and it is difficult to directly obtain the analytical results. In the finite element analysis, the Lorentz force on the repulsive disk can be obtained by field calculation.

In addition to the electromagnetic driving force, the mechanism is also affected by other reaction forces during the operation, including: the opening and closing holding force provided by the holding device, the buffer force, the friction force, the gravity, etc.

The bistable spring retaining device has the advantages of convenient output adjustment, simple structure and compact installation space, and is currently widely used in electromagnetic repulsion mechanisms. Its output characteristics can be described by the following formula [5]:

$$F_h = 2k\frac{\left(x_0 - l_0 + \sqrt{l_0^2 - (z - z_0)^2}\right)(z - z_0)}{\sqrt{l_0^2 - (z - z_0)^2}} \tag{2}$$

In the formula, k is the elastic coefficient of the coil spring, z is the displacement of the mechanism, l_0 is the length of the connecting plate, and x_0 is the spring compression amount of the holding device when z is equal to z_0. The holding force F_h can be changed by changing the spring rate, the amount of pre-compression and the length of the connecting plate.

The drive coil dimensions are as follows (Table 1):

Table 1. Drive coil dimensions.

part	outer diameter	inside diameter	number of turns	single turn width	single turn height
value	100 mm	40mm	20	1 mm	7 mm

The size parameters of the repulsion disc are as follows (Table 2):

Table 2. Repulsion disc size.

part	outer diameter	width	Circumference width	Circumference height	Bevel chamfer radius
value	10 cm	1 cm	5 mm	1 cm	1 cm

The cross-sectional model of the repulsive disc and coil is shown below (Fig. 6):

The height of the repulsion disc fixing nut is 5mm, and the radius of the pull rod is 7mm. The material of the repulsion disc is 7075 aluminum alloy, and the material of the tie rod and nut is TC4 titanium alloy. Its material parameters are shown in Table 3:

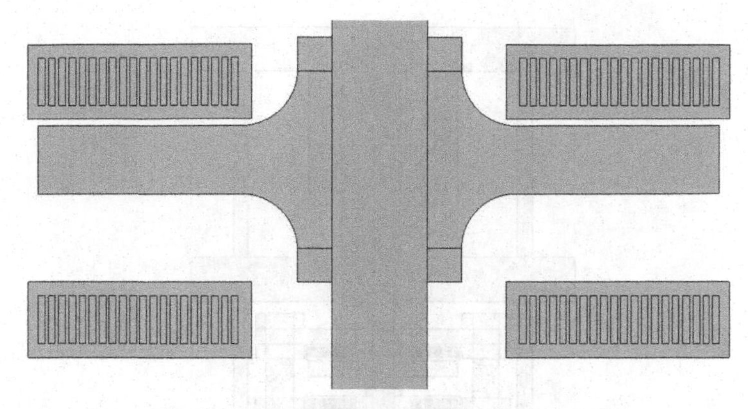

Fig. 6. Repulsion disk and coil section model.

Table 3. Kinematic structure material parameters.

Material	part	tensile strength/MPa	Yield Strength/MPa	Elastic Modulus	Poisson's ratio
7075-T651	repulsion disc	560	540	7.0e10	0.33
TC4	drive rod、connector	895	860	1.1e11	0.34

The bistable spring retaining device is designed as follows:

The middle diameter of the spring is 20 mm, the wire diameter is 5 mm, the effective number of turns is 7, the axial intercept is 10 mm, the material is SWPB, the stiffness coefficient is about 150 N/mm, and the pre-compression is 10 mm, which can be adjusted by the rear screw. The central opening of the connecting plate on the upper part of the device is a part of the tie rod positioning device.

Figure 8 shows the overall structure of the plate electrode isolation switch after installing the motion mechanism fixing frame and the bistable spring holding device. The mass of the moving part of the switch is about 1.34 kg (Fig. 7).

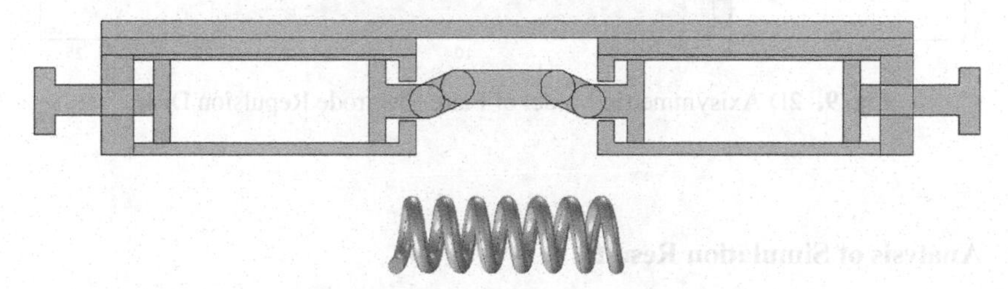

Fig. 7. Bistable spring structure diagram.

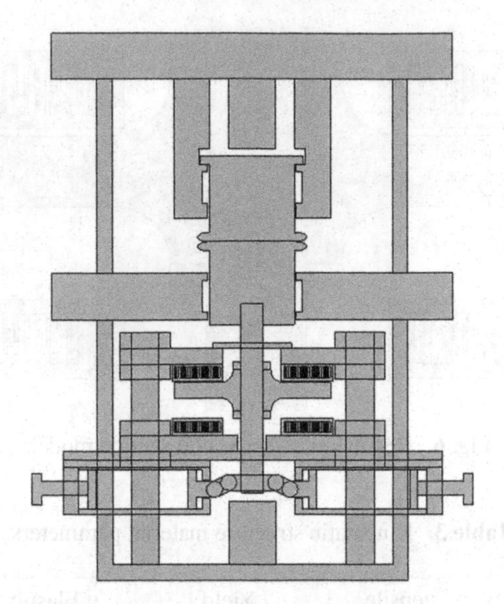

Fig. 8. DC Switch Section Model.

The designed opening capacitor capacity is 1200 μF, the charging voltage is 1.2 kV, and the simplified opening model is established as shown in Fig. 9:

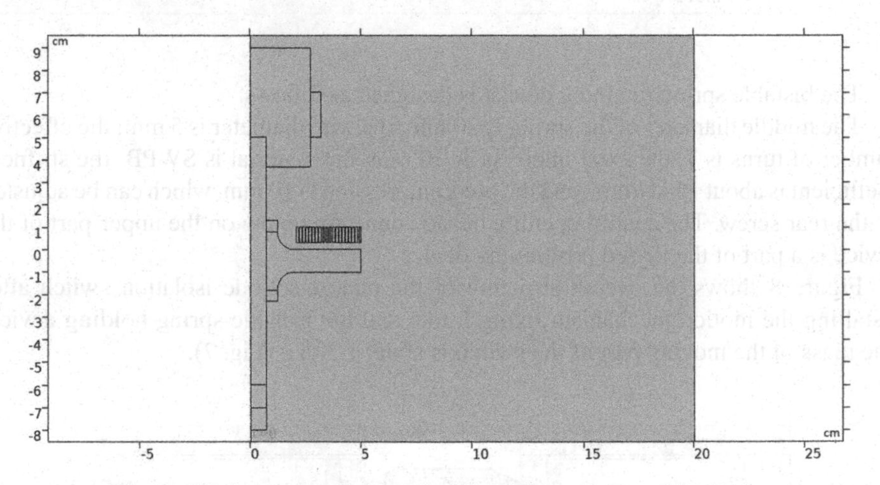

Fig. 9. 2D Axisymmetric Model of Plate Electrode Repulsion Disk.

4.2 Analysis of Simulation Results

The results obtained from the flexible body transient simulation are shown in the figure below:

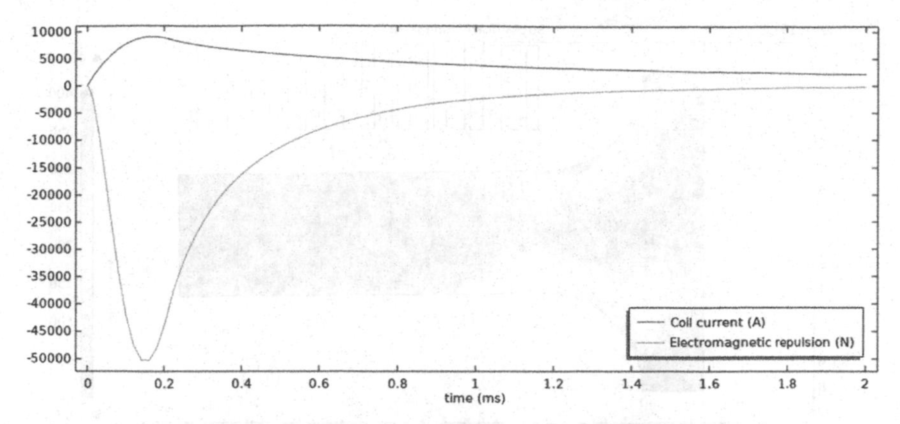

Fig. 10. Coil Current and Electromagnetic Repulsion.

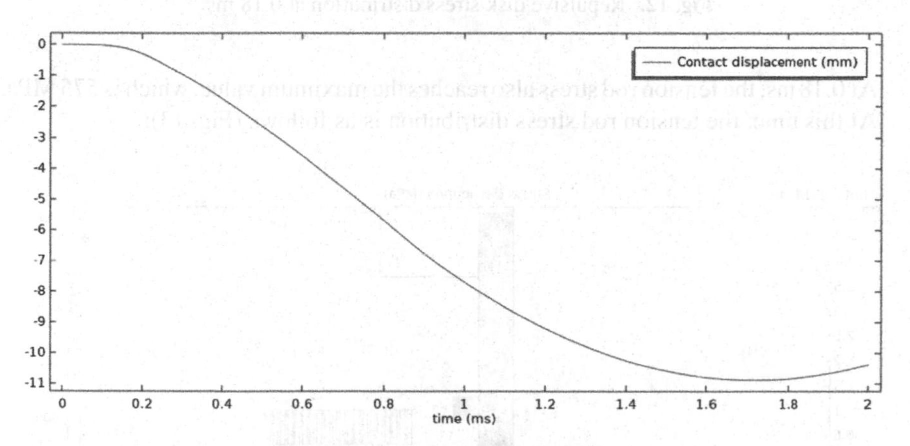

Fig. 11. Displacement vs Time Plot.

It can be seen from Fig. 10 that the peak value of the electromagnetic repulsion is about 50 kN, compared with which the frictional resistance and gravity are negligible. It can be seen from Fig. 11 that the moving contact reaches the rated opening distance of 5mm at 0.8 ms, reaches the opening position at 1.7 ms, and the opening distance is 10 mm.

The maximum stress on the repulsion disc during the movement is 404 MPa, which is reached at 0.18 ms. At this time, the stress distribution of the repulsion disc is as follows (Fig. 12):

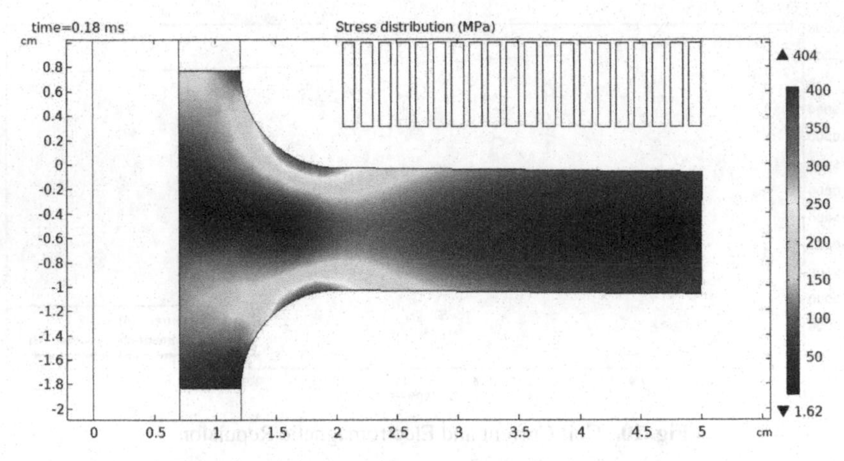

Fig. 12. Repulsive disk stress distribution at 0.18 ms.

At 0.18 ms, the tension rod stress also reaches the maximum value, which is 575 MPa. At this time, the tension rod stress distribution is as follows (Fig. 13):

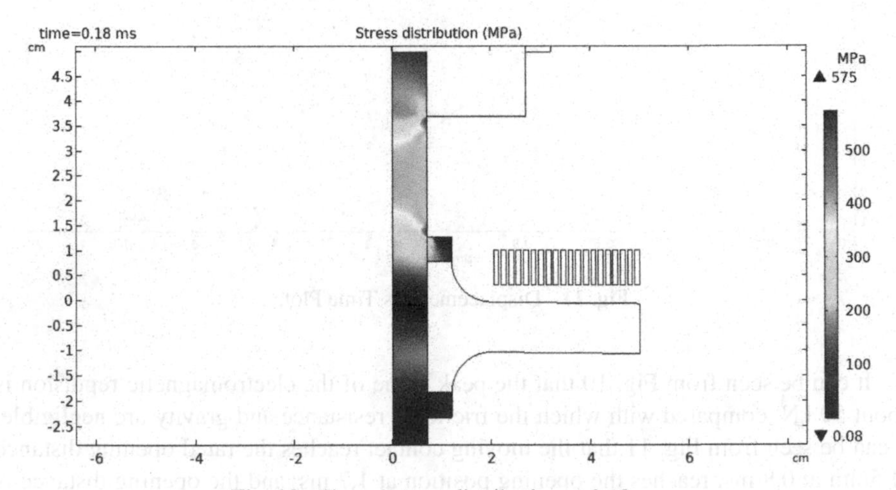

Fig. 13. Tie rod stress distribution at 0.18 ms.

The maximum stress during the entire movement is as follows (Fig. 14):

From the mechanical properties of the material, it can be known that the disk and the tie rod can meet the requirements in the whole process.

Set the closing capacitor capacity to 1100 μF and the charging voltage to 1.2 kV. The flexible body simulation results are shown in the following figure:

It can be seen from Fig. 15 that the peak value of the electromagnetic repulsion is about 36 kN when the gate is opened. It can be seen from Fig. 16 that the moving contact can reach the closing position within 5 ms.

The maximum stress during the entire movement is as follows (Fig. 17):

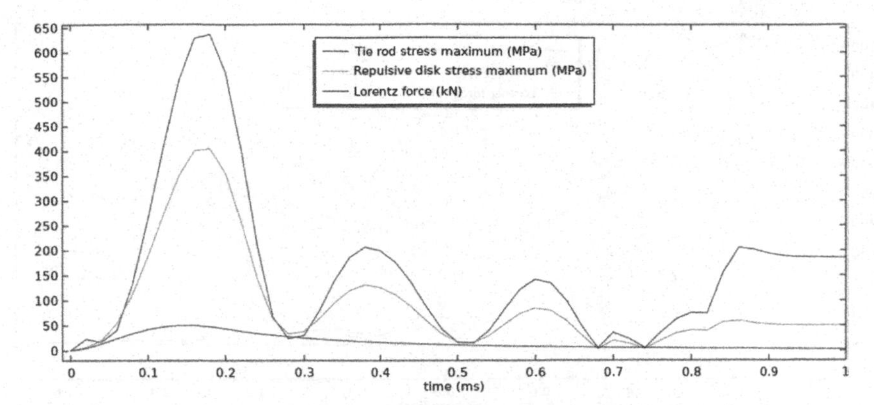

Fig. 14. Electromagnetic force and component stress curve.

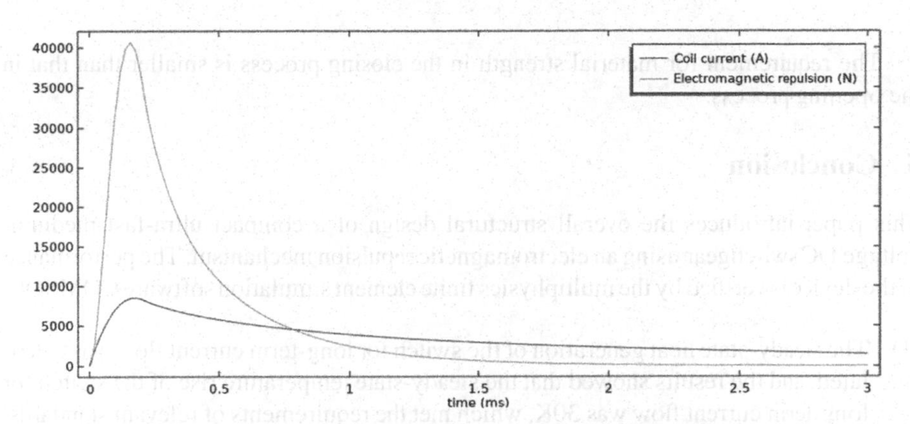

Fig. 15. Coil Current and Electromagnetic Repulsion (closing).

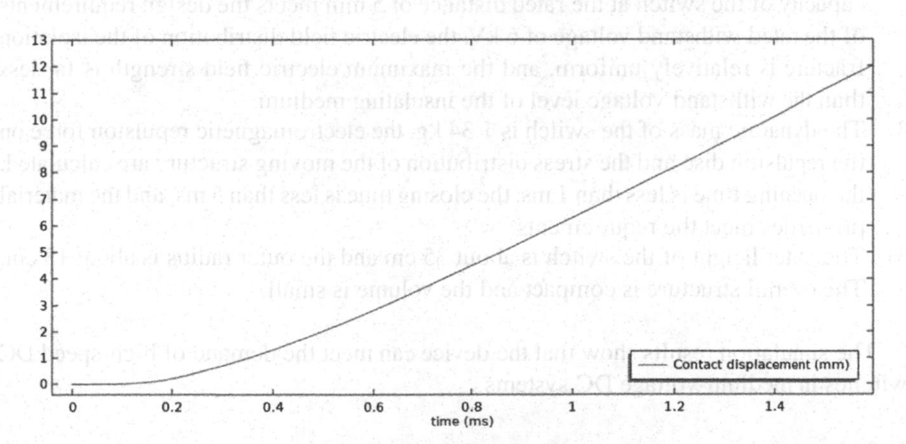

Fig. 16. Displacement vs Time Plot (closing).

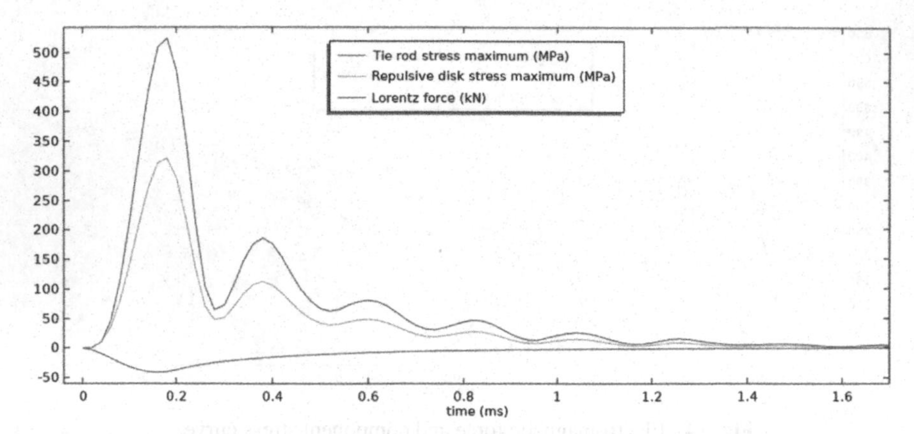

Fig. 17. Electromagnetic force and component stress curve (closing).

The requirement for material strength in the closing process is smaller than that in the opening process.

5 Conclusion

This paper introduces the overall structural design of a compact ultra-fast medium-voltage DC switchgear using an electromagnetic repulsion mechanism. The performance of the device is verified by the multiphysics finite element simulation software COMSOL:

(1) The steady-state heat generation of the switch for long-term current flow was calculated, and the results showed that the steady-state temperature rise of the switch for long-term current flow was 30K, which met the requirements of relevant standards.
(2) Calculated the electric field intensity distribution, and verified that the rated breaking capacity of the switch at the rated distance of 5 mm meets the design requirements of the rated withstand voltage of 6 kV, the electric field distribution of the isolation fracture is relatively uniform, and the maximum electric field strength is far less than the withstand voltage level of the insulating medium.
(3) The dynamic mass of the switch is 1.34 kg, the electromagnetic repulsion force on the repulsion disc and the stress distribution of the moving structure are calculated, the opening time is less than 1 ms, the closing time is less than 5 ms, and the material properties meet the requirements.
(4) The outer height of the switch is about 35 cm and the outer radius is about 13 cm. The overall structure is compact and the volume is small.

The simulation results show that the device can meet the demand of high-speed DC switches in medium-voltage DC systems.

References

1. Zhang, Y.N., Tang, J.H.: The busbar architecture choice of integrated power system for US and UK future surface ship. Ship Sci. Technol. 34(5), 136–139 (2012)

2. Fu, L.J., Liu, L.F., Wang, G.: The research progress of the medium voltage DC integrated power system in China. Chinese J. Ship Res. **11**(1), 72–79 (2016)
3. He, J.J., Yuan, Z., Zhao, W.T.: Review of DC circuit breaker technology development. Southern Power Syst. Technol. **9**(02), 9–15 (2015)
4. Liu, L.H., Ye, Z.H., Fu, L.J.: Research & development status and prospects of fast DC circuit breakers. Proc. CSEE **37**(04), 966–978(2017)
5. Wen, W., Huang, Y.: Research on operating mechanism for ultra-fast 40.5-kV vacuum switches. Power Delivery, IEEE Trans. **30**(6), 2553–2560(2015)

Flexible Planning and Regulation Techniques in Smart Grids

Research on Low Carbon Development Planning of Public Transportation Energy Based on System Dynamics

Yawen Zeng, Jianyu Hu, Jing Li, and Keqi Huang(✉)

China Energy Engineering Group Hunan Electric Power Design Institute Co., Ltd., Changsha, China

452681077@qq.com

Abstract. Due to current energy shortage and climate change in China, it is necessary to predict the energy demand and carbon emission of urban passenger transport in the future. Firstly, the urban passenger transport is divided into three parts: bus, taxi and car, and the demand of future urban passenger transport is forecasted by using the national energy technology model. Modeling the urban passenger transport network from a System dynamics perspective. In the transport part, the number of vehicles, the proportion of fuel types and the energy consumption per 100 km are considered, and the energy consumption of transport travel is calculated by using the transport energy consumption equation. Using 2021 as the base year, four scenarios were set to assess the energy saving and emission reduction potential under different policy needs, including keeping the baseline scenario of urban development inertia, considering the speed limit of urban vehicles and further optimizing the speed control scenario of public transport system, and considering the promotion of shared mode of travel shared scenarios, and according to the national renewable energy automobile industry development planning overall goal of electric vehicle scenario. This paper analyzes travel demand, energy consumption demand and carbon emission intensity under different scenarios, and puts forward policy suggestions on public transportation energy saving and emission reduction planning.

Keywords: public transportation development planning · low carbon energy · energy saving and emission reduction · system dynamics

1 Introduction

Transportation is an important department carrying out human social and economic activities. With the advancement of urbanization and the increasing demand for transportation in China, the energy consumption and carbon emissions of Transportation show a growing trend. In terms of global greenhouse gas emissions, the transportation industry has surpassed industry and construction, becoming the second largest emission

H. Yang et al. (Eds.): SmartGIFT 2022, LNICST 483, pp. 257–271, 2023.
https://doi.org/10.1007/978-3-031-31733-0_22

sector in the world [1]. As an important part of transportation, urban passenger transport should contribute to energy conservation and emission reduction. So there are two problems:

First, how to evaluate the energy consumption and carbon emission level of urban passenger transport, and provide methods and basis for the government to formulate energy conservation and emission reduction targets for urban passenger transport? Second, how to reduce the energy consumption and carbon emission level of urban passenger transport through policy means while trying to meet the travel needs of residents?

Chinese urban passenger transport energy consumption and carbon dioxide emissions may show a sustained and rapid growth trend in the coming period, mainly considering:

(1) The fuel structure of urban traffic vehicles is single, and most of them use petroleum products such as gasoline and diesel. The excessive use of fossil fuels will lead to the continuous increase of greenhouse gases and pollutants; (2) The further improvement of urbanization rate and the rise of residents' income not only bring about the increase of travel demand, but also cause the rapid growth of car ownership [2]; (3) The travel sharing rate of public transport has not reached the international advanced level. Only a few cities have a public transport travel sharing rate of 50% [3], most of which are below 40%, and some big cities are even less than 10%, which still has great room for improvement.

Therefore, it is of great significance to scientifically predict the energy consumption and emissions of urban passenger transport in the future and take active measures to intervene its rapid growth.

However, due to the diversification of urban passenger transport residents' travel modes and types of motor vehicles, how to change urban residents' travel modes, how to choose travel modes, and how to develop vehicle technology in the future under the situation of social and economic transformation, these uncertain factors lead to the prediction of urban passenger transport energy demand and carbon emissions is very complex and full with great uncertainty.

Existing relevant studies have analyzed and predicted energy consumption and carbon emissions in many fields in terms of model tools and prediction means. As a key industry of energy consumption, transportation industry has always been the research object of scholars. Internationally, the prediction methods of transportation energy consumption and carbon emissions mainly use bottom-up micro prediction models, supplemented by some top-down macro prediction models. As the main tool for predicting transportation energy consumption and carbon emissions, micro prediction models include long-term energy alternative planning system (LEAP) model, terminal energy consumption model, Primes-Tremove and so on.

Domestic researchers often use some more direct prediction methods. Including exponential decomposition method [4, 5], the elastic coefficient method [6], regression model [7, 8], time series prediction model [9], and combined prediction model [10], etc. These methods are mainly used to predict various passenger and freight traffic volume or passenger and freight turnover, combined with energy intensity, and then predict energy consumption and carbon emissions.

However, both macro and micro energy consumption prediction models have shortcomings: macro models are usually difficult to describe the role of technological progress, which affects the prediction results; However, micro models are weak in analyzing the impact of economy, and often overestimate the impact of economy on the model [11]. The system dynamics method can partially solve this contradiction by examining the research object from the perspective of system.

The urban passenger transport is divided into three parts: bus, taxi and car. The urban passenger transport level is counted from the perspective of the sharing rate of urban passenger transport modes and the average travel intensity, and the national energy technology model is used to predict the passenger transport demand of urban transport in the future. The urban passenger transport network is modeled from the perspective of system dynamics, which organically links transportation with social, economic and environmental modules. In the transportation part, the number of vehicles, the proportion of fuel types and energy consumption per 100 km are considered, and the energy consumption of transportation travel is calculated by using the transportation energy consumption equation. Based on the predicted passenger transport demand, the regional urban transport energy consumption and carbon emissions can be divided and calculated from a systematic perspective.

Taking a city as a case study, this paper provides a method for evaluating and predicting urban passenger transport energy consumption and carbon emissions through the verification, calculation and analysis of the model. Taking 2021 as the base year, four scenarios are set to evaluate the potential of energy conservation and emission reduction under different policy needs, including the benchmark scenario of maintaining the inertia of urban development, the speed control scenario of considering the city's speed limit for cars and further optimizing the public transport system, the shared travel scenario considering the promotion of shared travel mode, and the electric vehicle scenario according to the overall goal of the national renewable energy vehicle industry development plan. By comparing and analyzing the travel demand, energy consumption demand and carbon emission intensity under different scenarios, the results show that the speed control, shared travel and electric vehicle policies have changed the travel mode and energy technology structure to a certain extent, especially the fossil fuel consumption in the electric vehicle scenario will be largely replaced by power consumption.

At the same time, it can evaluate the energy conservation and emission reduction potential of the city in urban passenger transport, and put forward relevant suggestions and development plans for the government in the field of energy conservation and emission reduction in urban passenger transport.

2 Prediction Model of Urban Passenger Transport Demand

2.1 National Energy Technology Model

The optimization principle of the national energy technology (Net Transport) model is to minimize the total cost of vehicle technology that meets the service demand in the planning year. The total cost is decomposed into the annual initial acquisition cost of new technology, the operation and maintenance cost and fuel cost of all equipment in the planning year. In addition, energy tax and emission tax can be increased according to the setting of scenarios.

$$\min TC_t = \sum_j \left(\sum_l (AIC_{t,j,l} + OM_{t,j,l} + FC_{t,j,l})\right) + \sum_e K_e Q_{t,e} + \sum_m K_m Q_{t,m} \quad (1)$$

where, t represents the planning year; l represents the means of transportation, including bus and trolley bus, rail transit, taxi, car and electric bicycle; l represents the vehicle technology category, distinguishing fuel types and energy efficiency levels; e indicates the type of energy, including gasoline, diesel, natural gas, liquefied petroleum gas, bio-gasoline, electricity, etc. m indicates the type of gas produced by the fuel consumed by the vehicle, such as CO_2; TC_t represents the total cost of the planning year; $AIC_{t,j,l}$ represents the annual initial acquisition cost of vehicle technology l of mode j; $OM_{t,j,l}$ represents the annual operation and maintenance cost of transportation mode j vehicle technology l; $FC_{t,j,l}$ represents the annual fuel cost of transportation mode j vehicle technology l; K_e represents the energy tax levied on behalf of energy consumption units; $Q_{t,e}$ represents energy consumption of e; K_m represents emission tax levied on behalf of emission unit gas m; $Q_{t,m}$ represents gas emissions of m.

The initial investment cost of the new transportation mode j vehicle technology l in the t year is converted by the total initial investment cost $IC_{t,j,l}$ at the depreciation rate $\alpha_{j,l}$, as shown in formula (2):

$$AIC_{t,j,l} = IC_{t,j,l} \frac{\alpha_{j,l}(1+\alpha_{j,l})^{T_{j,l}}}{(1+\alpha_{j,l})^{T_{j,l}} - 1} \quad (2)$$

where, $IC_{t,j,l}$ represents the total cost of initial acquisition of vehicle technology l of transportation mode j; $\alpha_{j,l}$ represents the depreciation rate of vehicle technology l of transportation mode j; $T_{j,l}$ represents the service life of vehicle technology l of transportation mode j. Formula (2) apportions the initial total purchase cost of vehicles to each year within the service life, so as to obtain the annualized investment cost.

The fuel cost $FC_{t,j,l}$ of transportation mode j vehicle technology l year is calculated by formula (3), which is related to the total annual energy consumption and energy price of vehicles:

$$FC_{t,j,l} = \sum_e Q_{t,j,l,e} O_{t,j,l} Price_{t,e} \quad (3)$$

where, $Q_{t,j,l,e}$ represents the consumption of t transportation mode j vehicle technology l energy e in the planning year; $O_{t,j,l}$ represents the operation quantity of transportation mode j vehicle technology l in the planning year t; The product of the operating quantity and the annual transportation capacity of the unit vehicle technology of mode j represents the service volume provided by mode j vehicle technology l in the planning year, which is optimized by the model based on the principle of cost minimization. In addition, the number of operations should not exceed the number of vehicles owned by transportation mode j and vehicle technology l in the planning year. $Price_{t,e}$ represents the unit price of energy e in the planning year t.

The energy consumption $Q_{t,j,l,e}$ of mode j vehicle technology l in the planning year is calculated from the driving mileage of mode j vehicle technology l and the unit energy consumption of the vehicle. The gas emission $Q_{t,j,l,m}$ is related to energy consumption and gas emission factor, as shown in formula (4) and formula (5):

$$Q_{t,j,l,e} = X_{t,j,l}E_{t,j,l,e} \tag{4}$$

$$Q_{t,j,l,m} = Q_{t,j,l,e}f_{t,e} \tag{5}$$

where, $X_{t,j,l}$ represents the annual driving mileage of vehicle technology l of mode j; $E_{t,j,l,e}$ represents the energy consumption per unit mileage of transportation mode j vehicle technology l; $f_{t,e}$ represents the emission factor of energy e with respect to gas m.

The energy consumption $Q_{t,e}$ (Gas m emission) of the transportation department in the planning year is multiplied by the annual single vehicle energy consumption (Annual single vehicle emission) of the transportation mode j vehicle technology l by the operation quantity $Q_{t,j,l}$ in the planning year, as shown in formulas (6) and (7):

$$Q_{t,e} = \sum_{j}\sum_{l} Q_{t,j,l,e}O_{t,j,l} \tag{6}$$

$$Q_{t,m} = \sum_{j}\sum_{l} Q_{t,j,l,m}O_{t,j,l} \tag{7}$$

2.2 Prediction Model of Urban Passenger Transport Demand

This paper establishes a prediction model of urban passenger transport demand based on the classification of cities from the size of population development. The model considers the number of future urban residents in cities with different population sizes, residents' travel intensity, the sharing rate of each travel mode and the travel distance of each travel mode. Using this model, we can get the passenger turnover of various travel modes in cities with different population sizes in the future.

The passenger transport turnover Dfj of mode j in the future is calculated by the urban passenger transport demand generation model, as shown in formula (8):

$$D_j^f = \sum_{i} P_iI_iS_{j,i}DIS_{j,i}365 \tag{8}$$

where, i represents the city level classified by population size; P_i represents the total population of grade i cities; I_i represents the number of trips per capita of grade i urban residents (times/person/day); $S_{j,i}$ represents the travel sharing rate of public transportation modes j of grade i; $DIS_{j,t}$ represents the average travel distance (km/time/person) of grade i public transportation mode j (Fig. 1).

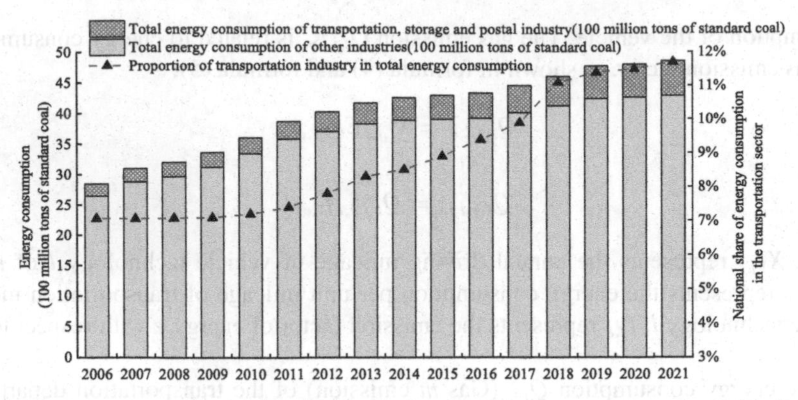

Fig. 1. Energy consumption and national ratio in transportation, storage and postal industries.

3 Construction of Urban Passenger Transport Network Module Based on System Dynamics

On the basis of system dynamics, the urban passenger transport is modeled, which is divided into three modules: bus, taxi and car. At the same time, the data statistics are carried out from the number of vehicles, the proportion of fuel types and the energy consumption of 100 km, and the energy consumption of transportation travel is calculated by using the transportation energy consumption equation (Fig. 2).

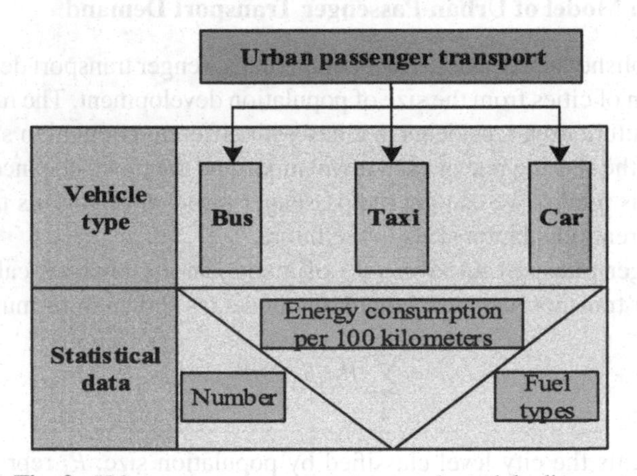

Fig. 2. Urban passenger transport network module diagram.

3.1 Data Related to the Number of Vehicles and the Proportion of Fuel Types

Take a city as a reference, and make statistics on the proportion of transportation vehicles and fuel types in the city from 2010 to 2021 (see in Tables 1, 2, 3 and 4).

Table 1. Number of Transportation Vehicles in the City from 2010 to 2021.

Date	Bus	Taxi	Car
2010	832	2241	130691
2011	891	2333	171145
2012	1018	2344	211600
2013	1124	2344	259681
2014	1119	2401	307267
2015	1294	2595	500197
2016	1837	3052	751307
2017	2488	3607	1102630
2018	3241	4783	1403319
2019	4609	5791	1702806
2020	5573	6700	2100074
2021	6730	7880	2551054

Table 2. Proportion of Bus Fuel Types in the City from 2010 to 2021.

Time	LNG	Gasoline	Electric	Petrol/electric hybrids
2010	0	100%	0	0
2011	0	100%	0	0
2012	3.9%	96.1%	0	0
2013	21.2%	78.8%	0	0
2014	21.4%	78.6%	0	0
2015	23.7%	76.3%	0	0
2016	26.9%	56.5%	3.8%	12.8%
2017	30.1%	46.1%	7.9%	15.9%
2018	32%	39.2%	12.4%	16.4%
2019	29.8%	28.5%	19.2%	22.5%
2020	20.8%	23.4%	25.1%	30.7%
2021	13.3%	20.9%	30.7%	35.1%

3.2 Energy Consumption Per 100 km of Urban Vehicles

The parameter setting of the base period of 100 km energy consumption of urban vehicles in the city follows the following principles: assign values according to the order of the city's survey data > literature data > locomotive test data provided by the network.

Table 3. Proportion of Taxi Fuel Types in the City from 2010 to 2021.

Time	LNG	Gasoline	Electric	Petrol/electric hybrids
2010	0	100%	0	0
2011	0	100%	0	0
2012	56.1%	43.9%	0	0
2013	56.1%	43.9%	0	0
2014	61.7%	38.3%	0	0
2015	61.7%	38.3%	0	0
2016	61.7%	38.3%	0	0
2017	59.9%	40.1%	0	0
2018	56.3%	43.7%	0	0
2019	50.5%	37.5%	0	12%
2020	37.8%	36.8%	5%	20.4%
2021	28.7%	30.9%	15.1%	25.3%

Table 4. Proportion of Car Fuel Types in the City from 2010 to 2021.

Time	Gasoline	Electric	Petrol/electric hybrids
2010	100%	0	0
2011	100%	0	0
2012	100%	0	0
2013	100%	0	0
2014	100%	0	0
2015	100%	0	0
2016	90%	0	10%
2017	85.5%	0	14.5%
2018	75.6%	5.3%	19.1%
2019	62%	13.6%	24.4%
2020	50.9%	20.9%	28.2%
2021	41.4%	25.7%	32.9%

For the situation that there are many values in the literature, this paper will refer to the authority of published journals and try to use “intermediate data” for quotation.

Since most documents do not indicate the specific year corresponding to the value in the assignment of 100 km energy consumption, this paper adopts a fuzzy treatment for this part of the data, in principle, the same data is used in 2021 and 2015, and slightly adjusted according to other data sources. As shown in the Table 5 for the parameter settings.

Table 5. Energy Consumption Per 100 km of Various Transportation Vehicles in the City in 2021.

Vehicle	Gas (m3)	Diesel (Gasoline) oil (L)	Electric (kWh)	Petrol/electric hybrids	
				gasoline	electric
Bus	29.62	38.88	87.6	29.03	3.78
Taxi	9.45	10.15	16.71	2.53	8.4
Car	9.28	8.16	18.01	2.32	7.78

3.3 Public Transportation Passenger Transport Level

The data of public transport share rate and average daily mileage of buses are estimated according to the mileage in the Yearbook, passenger volume and number of residents' trips; The average passenger capacity of taxis is set according to the literature value. Transfer times, annual mileage of cars and annual mileage of taxis are considered through the survey data (Table 6).

Table 6. The Level of Public transportation and Passenger Transport in the City in 2021.

Taxi sharing rate	Bus sharing rate	Number of trips per capita	Annual mileage of taxi (km)	Transfer times	Annual mileage of car (km)	Average passenger capacity of taxi (person)	Average daily mileage of buses (km)
4.92%	7.74%	2.75	12198	1.24	8313	1.38	132

3.4 Prediction and Calculation Method of Energy Consumption and Carbon Emission

Combined with the prediction of passenger transport demand in Sect. 2, this section divides the transportation energy consumption into three modules from the perspective of system dynamics and calculates the consumption and carbon emissions of each module based on the prediction of passenger transport demand, so as to obtain the predicted energy consumption and carbon emissions.

This paper uses the transportation energy consumption equation to calculate the energy consumption of transportation travel. The energy consumption of different travel modes and types of transportation energy technology can be expressed as a nonlinear equation of travel time, and the travel time of each means of transportation is calculated according to the driving speed of the relevant means of transportation. The energy consumption per unit distance of traveler's choice of travel mode *m* and technology *t* is as follows (9):

$$E_{i,m,t} = \frac{e_{i,m,t}(e_1 + e_2(\frac{1}{t_{i,m,t}}) + e_3 t_{i,m,t})}{f_{i,m}} \tag{9}$$

where, $e_{i,m,t}$ represents the exogenous parameters that calibrate the energy consumption of different vehicles and technology types; e_1, e_2, e_3 represent the given parameters used to evaluate traffic energy consumption; $t_{i,m,t}$ represents travel time; $f_{i,m}$ represents the load factor of the vehicle.

Taking 2021 as an example, using the above calculation method, we can get the passenger transport energy consumption and composition and total carbon emission composition of the city in 2021 (Fig. 3).

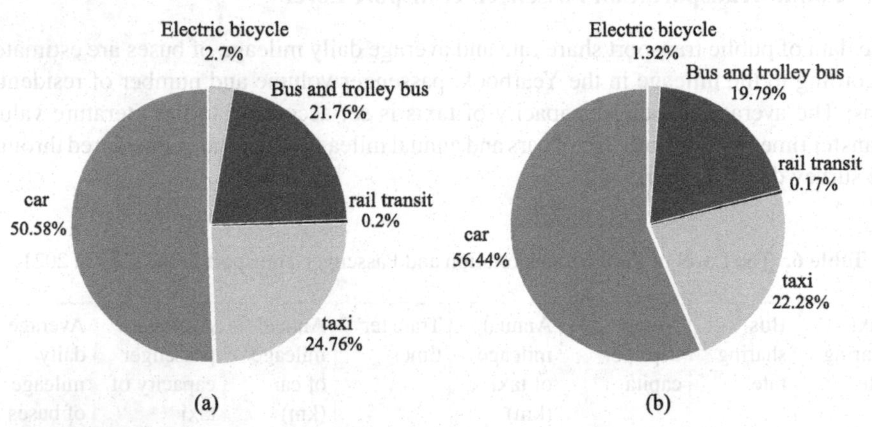

Fig. 3. Urban passenger traffic energy consumption composition (a) and carbon emission composition (b).

4 Case Study

4.1 Scene Settings

This paper sets 2021 as the base year. Four different scenarios are set to evaluate the energy conservation and emission reduction potential of public transportation energy in a city under different policy needs.

Scenario 1: the benchmark scenario of maintaining the inertia of urban development.
Scenario 2: consider the speed control scenario in which the city adopts a speed limit for cars and further optimizes the public transport system.

Scenario 3: shared travel scenario considering the promotion of shared travel mode. Scenario 4: electric vehicle scenario according to the overall goal of the national renewable energy vehicle industry development plan.

4.2 Analysis of Simulation Results

The travel demand of the city from 2010 to 2060 is shown in Fig. 4. In the benchmark scenario, due to economic development, urbanization and population changes, the total demand for travel increased from 3.1 billion person kilometers in 2010 to 5.8 billion person kilometers in 2060. In the benchmark scenario without any exogenous policies, car travel accounted for the largest proportion. Travel demand is driven by population growth, economic development, land use, travel mode, technological progress and other factors. Since the travel mode and transportation technology in the benchmark scenario do not change significantly without exogenous policy impact, the change of traffic demand is mainly affected by the future population and economic growth path.

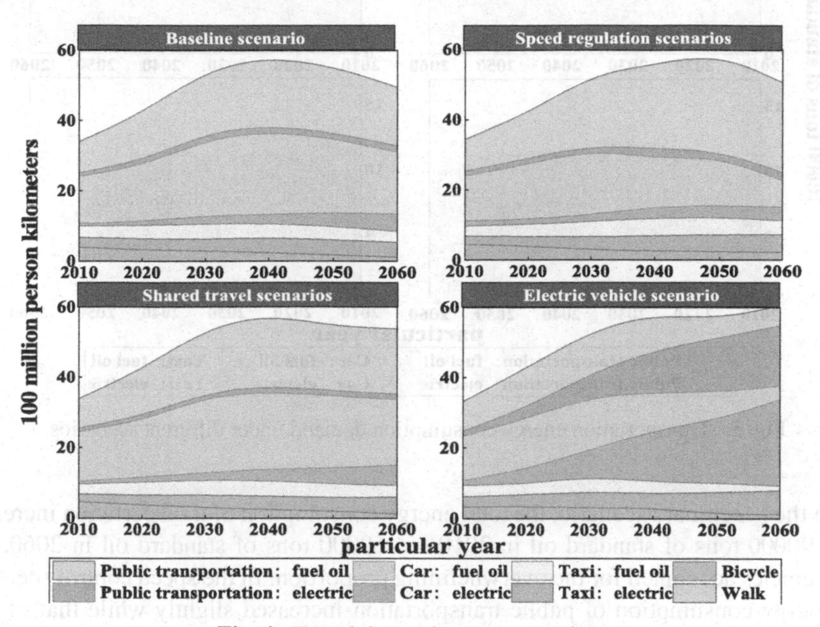

Fig. 4. Travel demand across scenarios.

According to the predicted value in SSPS, the future population change of the city will show a trend of first rising and then falling. Therefore, the traffic demand also shows a similar change path. In terms of energy technology types, due to the decline in battery costs and vehicle costs brought about by technological development and the comparative advantage of energy prices, the proportion of electric vehicles in car travel demand rose to 18% by 2060. The speed control scenario significantly changed the structure of travel mode. The travel demand of public transport increased from 2.1 billion person kilometers in the benchmark scenario to 2.9 billion person kilometers in 2060, while the travel demand of cars decreased from 2.5 billion person kilometers in the benchmark scenario to 1.6 billion person kilometers. The number of car trips in the shared travel scenario increased slightly, because the promotion of shared travel mode has reduced the transportation cost of car travel to a certain extent. There are significant changes in the structure of transportation energy technology in the electric vehicle scenario, and the electric vehicle technology has increased significantly in the three motorized travel modes.

Traffic energy consumption and structure also show significant differences in different scenarios (Fig. 5).

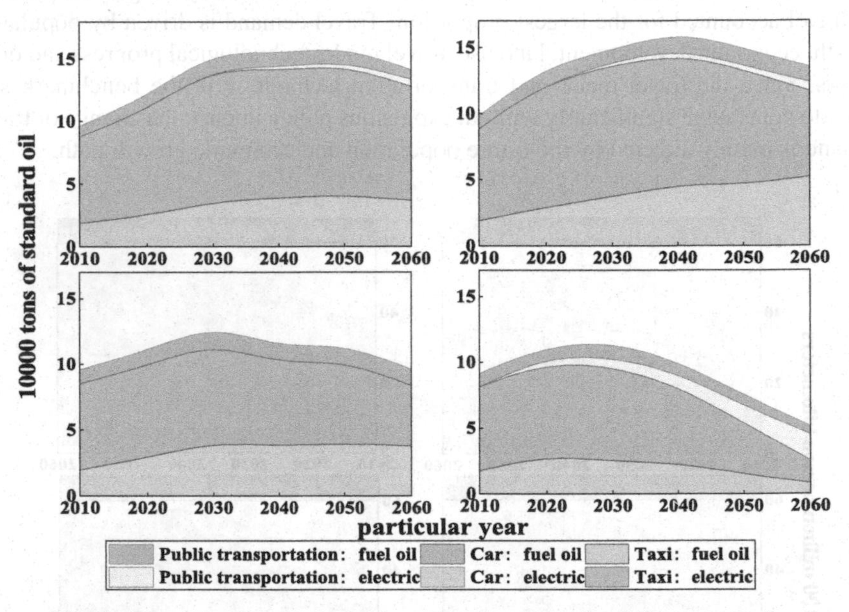

Fig. 5. Transportation energy consumption demand under different scenarios.

In the benchmark scenario, the total energy consumption of transportation increased from 90000 tons of standard oil in 2010 to 160000 tons of standard oil in 2060, and fuel vehicles accounted for the overwhelming proportion. In the speed control scenario, the energy consumption of public transportation increased slightly while that of cars decreased slightly, because speed control made more people use public transportation to replace cars. Shared travel reduces energy consumption by reducing the energy intensity of per capita travel. In 2050, the energy consumption of cars will drop from 110000 tons of standard oil in the benchmark scenario to 60000 tons of standard oil. Due to the technological progress brought about by the electric vehicle scenario, the energy consumption structure has changed greatly, and the power demand in the electric vehicle scenario has gradually increased instead of the use of fossil fuels.

The transportation energy demand in the four scenarios shows the characteristics of rising at first and then falling, which is consistent with the changing trend of transportation travel demand, and it is mainly affected by the future population growth path of the city. The implementation of speed control, shared travel and electric vehicle policies will accelerate the transportation energy demand to enter the declining stage faster.

The medium and long-term traffic emission path of the city is shown in the Fig. 6.

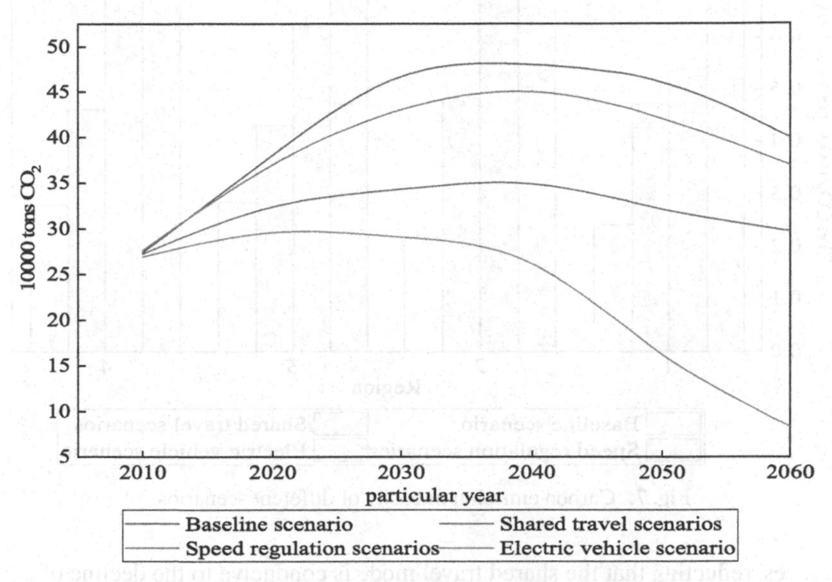

Fig. 6. Carbon emission pathways of different scenarios.

In the benchmark scenario, the total carbon emissions increased from 250000 tons in 2010 to 420000 tons in 2050. The speed control scenario can reduce carbon emissions to a certain extent, from 420000 tons in the benchmark scenario to 390000 tons in 2050. In the shared travel scenario, the change path of carbon emissions is more moderate. Due to the promotion of shared travel mode, carbon emissions increased slowly from 2010 to 2030, and decreased from 2030 to 2060. The electric vehicle scenario shows the most significant carbon emission reduction potential, which will be reduced to 160000 tons in 2050, even lower than the emission value in the benchmark year of 2010. It can be seen that the electric vehicle policy can decouple carbon emissions from the growth of travel demand. At the same time, to reflect the spatial differences in the development of transportation energy, four regions with different development conditions in the city are taken as examples.

It can be seen from the Fig. 7 reflects that the carbon emission intensity of four regions under different scenarios in 2060, which is used to measure the carbon emission per unit of travel demand. The carbon emission intensity of different scenarios shows the same change law as the carbon emission path in the four zones.

However, under the same scenario, carbon emission intensity shows certain spatial differences in different regions. In the benchmark scenario, speed control scenario and electric vehicle scenario, the carbon emission intensity in the central urban area is lower than that in other areas. However, the shared travel scenario shows the opposite spatial

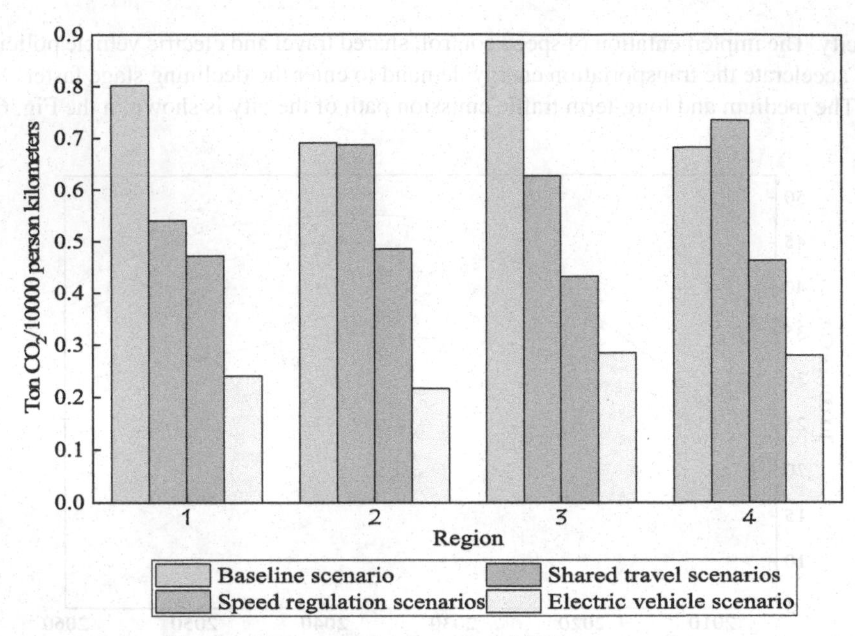

Fig. 7. Carbon emission intensity of different scenarios.

differences, reflecting that the shared travel mode is conducive to the decline of carbon emission intensity in the suburbs.

5 Conclusion

From the perspective of system dynamics, this paper constructs a system dynamics model for predicting energy consumption and carbon emissions of urban passenger transport based on the pre-measurement of urban passenger transport demand. Taking a city as an example, the energy consumption and carbon emission of public transportation in this city are predicted and analyzed. The simulation results show that there is a strong correlation between energy consumption and carbon emissions of urban passenger transport, indicating that the efficiency of urban passenger transport in energy conservation and carbon emission reduction is consistent.

The low carbon transport planning policy has a significant effect on energy conservation and emission reduction of urban passenger transport. Under the low-carbon scenario, the passenger transport in the city will generate 123300 tons of standard coal energy savings and 205700 tons of CO_2 emission reductions. Cars are the primary contributors to the energy consumption and carbon emission reduction of urban passenger transport, followed by taxi, and third is bus. As a priority travel mode recommended by the state, they will maintain a high share of public transport in the next few years.

References

1. Barczak, R.F., Duarte, F.S.: Environmental impacts of urban mobility: five categories of mitigating measures. Revista Brasileira de Gestão Urbana **4**(1), 13–32 (2012)

2. Wang, H.P.F., Zhang, X.Y.S.: Spatial heterogeneity of factors influencing transportation CO_2 emissions in Chinese cities: based on geographically weighted regression model. Air Qual. Atmos. Health **13**(8), 977–989 (2020)
3. Hao, J.J.F., Liu, X.Q.S., Shen, X.J.T., et al.: Bilevel programming model of urban public transport network under fairness constraints. Discrete Dyn. Nat. Soc. (2019)
4. Mourrain, B.F.: Polynomial exponential decomposition from moments. Found. Comut. Math. **18**(6), 1435–1492 (2018)
5. Yanev, G.P.F., Chakraborty, S.S.: A characterization of exponential distribution and the Sukhatme-Renyi decomposition of exponential maxima. Stat. Probab. Lett. **110**, 94–102 (2016)
6. Yasuhiro, S.F., Azusa, T.S., Hideki, N.T.: International analysis on social and personal determinants of traffic violations and accidents employing logistic regression with elastic net regularization. IATSS Res. **46**(1), 36–45 (2022)
7. Daniel, V.F., Roger, G.S., Marta, S.T., et al.: Automatic modeling of socioeconomic drivers of energy consumption and pollution using Bayesian symbolic regression. Sustain. Prod. Consum. **30**, 596–607 (2022)
8. Zhang, M.M.F., Zhang, S.C.S., Lee, C.C.T., et al.: Effects of trade openness on renewable energy consumption in OECD countries: new insights from panel smooth transition regression modelling. Energy Econ. **104**, 105–649 (2021)
9. Mohammed, A.J.F., Aurora, G.V.S., Antonio, F.S.T., et al.: A hybrid neuro-fuzzy inference system-based algorithm for time series forecasting applied to energy consumption prediction. Appl. Energy **268**(15), 114–977 (2020)
10. Roberto, Á.F.F., Sergio, C.C.S., Francesc, C.L.T.: A probabilistic approach for determining the influence of urban traffic management policies on energy consumption and greenhouse gas emissions from a battery electric vehicle. J. Clean. Prod. **236**, 117–604 (2019)
11. Bahareh, O.F., Ali, M.S., Shahabaldin, R.T., et al.: Asymmetric impacts of economic uncertainties and energy consumption on the ecological footprint: implications apropos structural transformation in South Korea. Fuel **322**, 124–180 (2019)

Two-Stage Dynamic Voltage/Var Control in Distribution Network Considering Uncertain Distributed Generations

Feng Qiao[1(✉)], Xinxin Lv[1], and Jingjie Huang[2]

[1] Zhejiang Sci-Tech University, Hangzhou 0571, Zhejiang, China
feng.qiao@zstu.edu.cn

[2] Changsha University of Science and Technology, Changsha 0731, Hunan, China

Abstract. After integrating distributed generators (DGs), the voltage/var control in distribution networks requires addressing multiple objectives, including power loss reduction, lifetime saving of mechanical switching voltage control devices and uncertain power output of DGs. Therefore, this paper proposes a two-stage voltage/var control method for distribution networks with uncertain power generation from DGs. A dynamic voltage/var optimisation model is formulated in the primary optimisation stage. It dispatches all the voltage/var controllers to minimise the action times of mechanical switching devices and the total active power loss over the day. The second stage consists of a stochastical optimisation model in which probabilistic scenarios replace the deterministic parameters of DGs and loads. The Monte Carlo approach and K-mean clustering technic are utilised to generate the scenarios to be used in the second stage. The DGs' setpoints are recursively calculated to address the uncertainties. The proposed method is tested on a modified IEEE 33-node distribution network. The effectiveness of the method is demonstrated through the simulation results.

Keywords: voltage/var control · dynamic optimisation · stochastical modelling

1 Introduction

The distribution network is being evolved from a traditionally radial system to a multiterminal grid with high penetration of distributed generators (DGs). This evolved system imposes a challenge in achieving voltage control objectives. With the increasing integration of DGs, reversed power flow makes traditional voltage/var control (VVC) schemes invalid because the downstream power injections are unpredictable to traditional voltage control devices. The supply reliability and system stability can severely deteriorate if the voltage deviates from

This work was supported by Science Foundation of Zhejiang Sci-Tech University (ZSTU) under Grant No. 21022096-Ys.

H. Yang et al. (Eds.): SmartGIFT 2022, LNICST 483, pp. 272–283, 2023.
https://doi.org/10.1007/978-3-031-31733-0_23

the safety limit. Thus, extensive research has been proposed to achieve reduced active power loss and optimised node voltage quality by considering DGs' participation [1,2].

A distributed coordinated voltage control scheme was proposed in [3]. The gradient projection method and model predictive control were utilised to formulate the controllers for on-load tap changers (OLTCs), static synchronous compensators and DGs in the system. The voltage violation caused by distributed photovoltaic (PV) generation was addressed in [4]. A two-stage coordinated control was utilised to achieve the VVC objectives by considering multiple operation modes of PV inverters. The local voltage control method proposed in [5] aimed at mitigating the overvoltage caused by DGs. It utilised enhanced power factor voltage control methods that adjust active and reactive power with PI controllers to regulate the voltage. The voltage control scheme in [6] have considered different control time scales of traditional switching equipment and distributed power supply when establishing the voltage/var optimisation model. It achieved voltage control objectives through coordinated control under multiple time scales. The dynamic VVC optimisation model in [7] limited the total action numbers of switching voltage regulating equipment which effectively reduces the operating loss of mechanical controllers. Furthermore, the dynamic optimisation was also established in [8]. The second-order cone relaxation technic was utilised to reduce the complexity of solving the dynamic optimisation model. In [9], the power electronic soft switch was considered. The system voltage was further optimised by utilising the characteristics of the soft switch that can quickly control the active and reactive power flow. In [10], the dynamic voltage control was established. The fast control characteristics of power electronic devices were utilised to improve the dynamic voltage quality in the time segment after adjustment of the traditional reactive power compensation devices. A combined centralised and decentralised voltage control scheme was proposed in [11]. It combined the local control of DGs with a centralised optimisation model to achieve system-level dynamic voltage/var coordination. Literature [12] proposed a data-driven coordinated voltage control scheme. Based on real-time measurements, it realised a coordinated and optimised control for multiple voltage regulating devices under different time scales. In [13], a two-layer VVC model was proposed that integrates the optimal operation model of the microgrid into the distribution network voltage control. The model was established based on Stackelberg game theory and described the game relationship between microgrid and distribution network. A quantification method of voltage control contribution for the grid-tied microgrids was proposed in [14] where the fair resource allocation theory was utilised. A multi-objective VVC model was established to maximises the voltage control contribution of grid-connected microgrids in the distribution network.

The above-reviewed VVC schemes improve the system voltage quality for the distribution network with DGs. Most of these schemes prioritised the objective of active power loss reduction. However, only a few of them address the wear and tear of mechanical voltage controllers such as OLTC and shunt capacitors (SCs).

Furthermore, the impact of DGs' uncertain generations on the voltage control objectives is inadequately discussed. Since the fluctuated power generations of DGs could lead to decreased life duration of mechanical devices and node voltage violation, it is required to simultaneously consider various factors, including the active power loss, the lifetime of OLTC and SCs and uncertain generation of DGs. Therefore, this paper proposes a two-stage voltage/var control model that addresses multiple factors. The primary optimisation stage calculates the setpoints of OLTC, SCs and DGs. These devices are coordinately controlled in the first stage optimisation to minimise the action times of OLTC and SCs and active power loss in the system. The secondary optimisation stage address the uncertainty of DGs' active power forecasts. The setpoints of OLTC and SCs determined in the first stage are treated as input, while the DGs' reactive power can be recursively adjusted. The Monte Carlo sampling approach and K-means technic are utilised to generate the scenarios for secondary stage optimisation.

The rest of the paper is organised as follows: Sect. 2 formulates the coordinated voltage/var dispatch model and presents the two-stage voltage optimisation strategy. Section 3 introduces the simulation system and presents the results and discussions. Section 4 concludes the paper.

2 Two-Stage Voltage/Var Optimisation Strategy

The proposed VVC method aims to address cost reduction and parameter uncertainty simultaneously. Thus, a new two-stage voltage optimisation strategy is utilised in this paper. In the primary stage, all the DGs' forecasted generations and loads are assumed as deterministic parameters. VVC controllers such as OLTC, SCs and DGs are coordinately controlled to achieve the optimisation objectives. In the secondary stage, a stochastic dispatch model is formulated by introducing probabilistic scenarios. The OLTC and SCs remain in the first-stage positions while the setpoints of DGs are recursively calculated to address the newly introduced uncertainties.

2.1 Primary Stage Optimisation

In the primary stage, a VVC optimisation model is formulated based on the DistPF [15]. The objective function (1) consists of three terms. The first term minimises the aggregated active power loss along the distribution lines. The second and third terms minimise the action times of OLTC and SCs over the whole period. Three weights α_1, α_2 and α_3 scale the objectives. In this paper, α_1 takes the largest value among the three weights because the power loss reduction is considered the primary objective. The weight α_2 takes a large value while the weight α_3 is the smallest because the operation cost of OLTC is usually higher than SCs. The control variable set u consists of OLTC's setpoint tap, SC's setpoint k and DG's reactive power Q^{DG}. The set s includes all the state variables such as bus voltage and power flow in the system. It is worth noting that using the second and third objectives constitutes a dynamic optimisation model, which increases the computation complexity. Still, it is economically necessary as the minimised action times of OLTC and SCs will significantly contribute to their life duration.

$$\min f(u,x) = \alpha_1 P_{loss} + \alpha_2 C_{OLTC} + \alpha_3 C_{SC}$$
$$P_{Loss} = \sum_{h=1}^{H}\sum_{i=1}^{L} R_i \frac{P_i^2(h)+Q_i^2(h)}{V_S^2}$$
$$C_{OLTC} = \sum_{h=1}^{H-1}\sum_{i=1}^{O} |tap_i(h+1) - tap_i(h)| \tag{1}$$
$$C_{SC} = \sum_{h=1}^{H-1}\sum_{i=1}^{J} |k_i(h+1) - k_i(h)|$$

The objective function is applied by following certain constraints, which are categorised into (2) and (3). The set (2) includes all the equality constraints representing each distribution bus's voltage and power balance.

$$\begin{cases} V_{i+1}(h) = V_i(h) - \dfrac{P_i(h)R_i + Q_i(h)X_i}{V_S} \\ V_1(h) = V_N + tap(h)\Delta V_{tap} \\ P_{i+1}(h) = P_i(h) - P_{i+1}^{Load}(h) + P_{i+1}^{DG}(h) \\ Q_{i+1}(h) = Q_i(h) - Q_{i+1}^{Load}(h) + Q_{i+1}^{DG}(h) + k_i(h)\Delta Q_i \end{cases} \tag{2}$$

The set (3) consists of the constraints for bus voltage, the adjustment range of OLTC and SCs and the control capacity of DGs. Note that the DGs' reactive power can be regulated in four-quadrant as they interface to the system via converters. Table 1 defines the variables in the formulated model.

$$\begin{cases} V^{min} \le V_i(h) \le V^{max} \\ 0 \le k_i(h) \le k_i^{max} \\ tap^{min} \le tap(h) \le tap^{max} \\ |Q_i^{DG}(h)| \le \sqrt{(S_i^{DG})^2 - (P_i^{DG}(h))^2} \end{cases} \tag{3}$$

In this stage, the forecasted loads and active power from DGs are assumed as accurate. Therefore, there are no uncertain variables in the optimisation model. The control variables in this stage include the action sequences of OLTC and SCs and the reactive power of DGs.

2.2 Secondary Stage Optimisation with Stochastical Modelling

In the secondary stage, uncertain parameters are introduced to formulate a stochastical optimisation model. The forecasted parameters for DGs and loads are replaced by their probabilistic scenarios. Considering that the reduced wear and tear of OLTC and SCs are expected to save their lifetime, their setpoints

Table 1. Nomenclature for variables in the dispatch model.

Name	Definition
h	Time interval
H, L	Time horizon and distribution line set
O, J	Device set of OLTCs and SCs
V_i	The voltage of bus i
P_i,Q_i	Active and reactive power flow
R_i,X_i	Resistance and reactance
V_S	Nominal voltage
tap	Tap position of OLTC
ΔV_{tap}	Tap step of OLTC
k_i	Position of the shunt capacitor i
ΔQ_i	Step size of shunt capacitor i
P_i^*,Q_i^*	Active and reactive power of component *
S_i^*	Capacity of DG i
$(\star)^{min}$	Minimal value of variable *
$(\star)^{max}$	Maximal value of variable *

calculated in the primary stage are treated as input in the secondary stage optimisation. However, the setpoints of DGs are recursively calculated as frequent adjustment of electronically interfaced DGs is more economical to address the newly introduced uncertainties. Therefore, the optimisation objective in this stage is formulated in (4). The control variable set $u^{'}$ includes all the DGs' setpoints, and s is the scenario index.

$$\min\ f(u^{'}, x, s) = \sum_{h=1}^{H}\sum_{i=1}^{L} R_i \frac{P_i^2(h,s) + Q_i^2(h,s)}{V_S^2} \tag{4}$$

The probabilistic scenarios of loads and DGs are generated by (5). The terms $\widehat{P}_i^{Load}(h,s)$, $\widehat{Q}_i^{Load}(h,s)$ and $\widehat{P}_i^{RG}(h,s)$ are utilised to model the possible deviation of parameters. The Monte-Carlo sampling method is utilised to generate the probabilistic deviation terms. The probability for each of them follows a normal distribution. The original deterministic parameters are chosen as the mean values, and the standard deviations for loads and DGs are 3% and 5%, respectively. Therefore, for each scenario s, the parameters $P_i^{Load}(h,s)$, $P_i^{Load}(h,s)$ and $P_i^{Load}(h,s)$ will deviate from their deterministic values according to the probabilistic deviations.

$$\begin{cases} P_i^{Load}(h,s) = P_i^{Load}(h) + \widehat{P}_i^{Load}(h,s) \\ Q_i^{Load}(h,s) = Q_i^{Load}(h) + \widehat{Q}_i^{Load}(h,s) \\ P_i^{RG}(h,s) = P_i^{RG}(h) + \widehat{P}_i^{RG}(h,s) \end{cases} \tag{5}$$

A large number of scenarios will be produced after Monte-Carlo sampling. To select representative scenarios, the K-means clustering approach is utilised. It is an iterative data-partitioning algorithm that assigns N parameters to exactly one of K clusters defined by centroids, where K is chosen before starting the algorithm. Initially, the approach chooses k centroids by K-means++ algorithm [16]. Then the following steps repeat until cluster assignments do not change: First, assign each parameter to the cluster with the closest centroid using the squared Euclidean distance between parameters to each cluster centroid, or individually assign each parameter to a different centroid if doing so decreases the sum-of-squares point-to-cluster-centroid distances; Then, update K centroids by calculating the average of the parameters in each cluster.

Alternatively, the K-means clustering can be represented by objective function (6) and (7) [17]. It applies (6) to minimise the closeness to cluster centroids while utilises (6) to seek the minimised sum-of-squares point-to-cluster-centroid distances. ξ is the parameter that needs to be clustered, and pi_x is the uniform weight of the parameter. k is the cluster index and m_k represents the centroid in cluster C_k. $dist(*)$ is represented as the squared Euclidean distance. n_k represents the number of feature sets n_k.

$$\min \sum_{k\in K} \sum_{\xi\in C_k} \pi_\xi dist(\xi, m_k) \tag{6}$$

$$\min \sum_{k\in K} \frac{1}{2n_k} \sum_{\xi_i,\xi_j\in C_k} ||\xi_i - \xi_j||^2 \tag{7}$$

3 Numerial Simulation

3.1 Simulation System

The proposed VVC was tested on a modified IEEE 33-bus distribution network as shown in Fig. 1. The raw data of the system is obtained from [15]. The modifications include an OLTC, three SCs and four DGs. The DGs on bus 14 and 30 are small wind turbine generators, while the DGs on bus 25 and 8 are photovoltaic generators. Their maximum generations are 2 MVA, 3 MVA, 1.5 MVA and 1MVA, respectively. The OLTC has 20 steps and 0.05 pu step size. The SC at bus 2 has 5 steps, while both the SCs at bus 25 and 30 have 3 steps. The step size of all the SCs is 0.1 MVAr. Moreover, the original loads are timed by 4 to accommodate the augmented power generation. The timed loads and the maximum generations of DGs are treated as base data. The base data is multiplied by the coefficients obtained from [13] to produce the DGs' generations and loads over the next 24 h. Figure 2 shows the produced DGs' generations.

3.2 Results and Discussions

Primary Voltage Optimisation Results: The total active power loss is 18.52 MW and the average node voltage deviation is 2.06 pu in the original system.

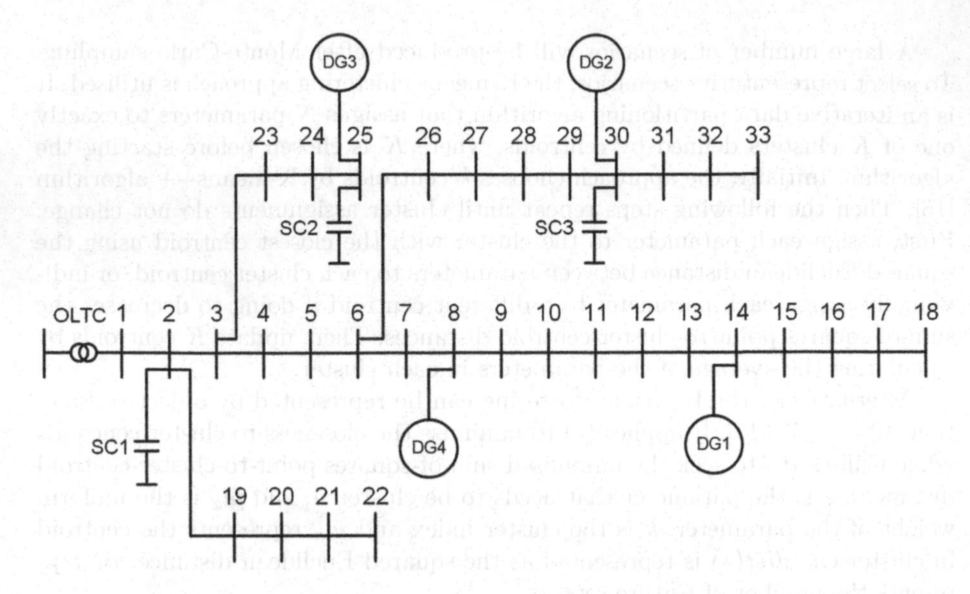

Fig. 1. Modified IEEE 33-bus distribution network.

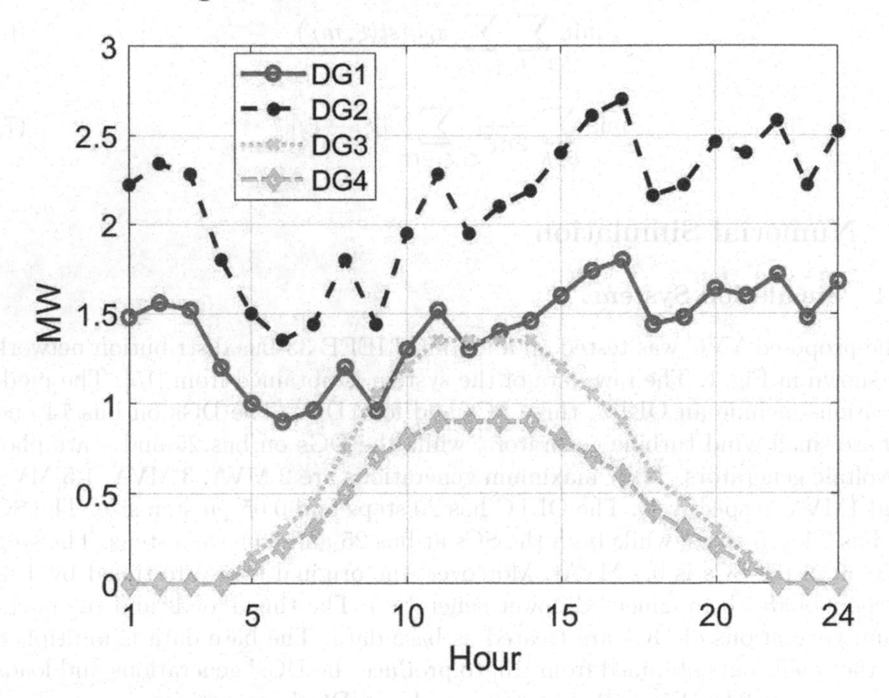

Fig. 2. Day-ahead DGs' generations for numerical simulation.

After applying the primary stage optimisation, the power loss reduces to 3.85 MW and the average voltage deviation decreases to 0.551 pu. The enhanced VVC performance is due to the fact that all the devices are coordinately dispatched in the proposed model. Figure 3 shows the coordinated pattern in the setpoints of OLTC, SCs and DGs. The OLTC only adjusts two times, and three SCs remain at the original position throughout the day. However, all the DGs actively change their reactive power in responding to the load variations. Figure 4 shows the bus voltages over 24 h. It can be seen that the voltage of each bus secures in the safety range from 0.95 pu to 1.05 pu.

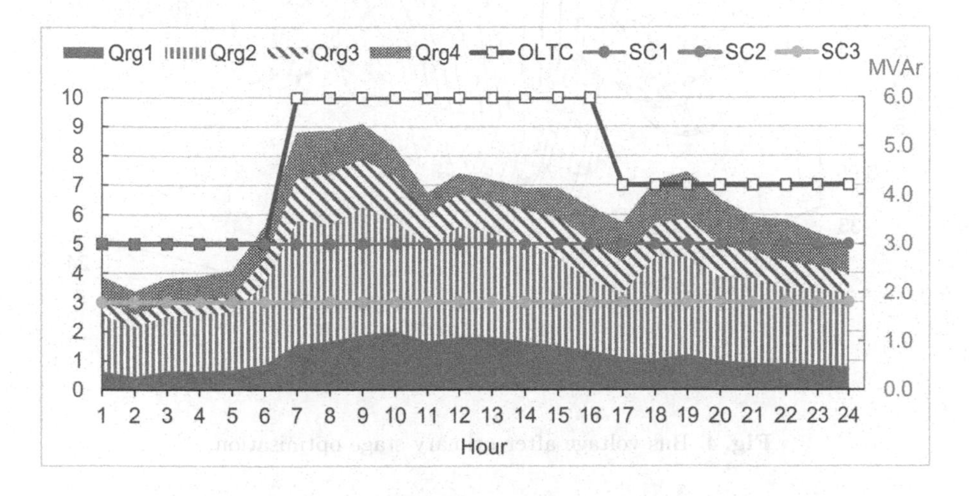

Fig. 3. Setpoints of OLTC, SCs and DGs in the primary stage.

Scenarios Production and Reduction: In the secondary optimisation stage, probabilistic scenarios are produced to replace the deterministic data of loads and DGs. By using the Monte-Carlo sampling method, 3000 scenarios are constructed, and their probability follows the normal distribution as stated in Sect. 2.2. Then, five representative clusters are calculated by the K-means clustering approach. Finally, the five cluster centroids are selected as the representative scenarios. The probability of each scenario depends on the number of points in the corresponding cluster.

To illustrate the clustering approach, the clustered data of DG1 is selected to be shown here. Figure 5(a) shows the five clusters and centroids for DG1's generation at hour 1. Figure 5(b) shows the generation of DG1 in five scenarios. The probabilities of DG1s' active power generation at the first hour in the five representative scenarios are listed in Table 2. Due to the page limit, the probabilities of other DGs and loads are not shown here. The secondary optimisation model is solved for all the scenarios. The expected value of parameters and objective function are obtained by Eq. (8) and (9). $X_i(s)$ represent the i_{th} parameter in scenario s, such as $P_i^{DG}(s)$ and $P_i^{Load}(s)$. S is the scenario set, and I is the parameter set.

$$X_e = \sum_{s=1}^{S} Prob_i(s) \times X_i(s) \tag{8}$$

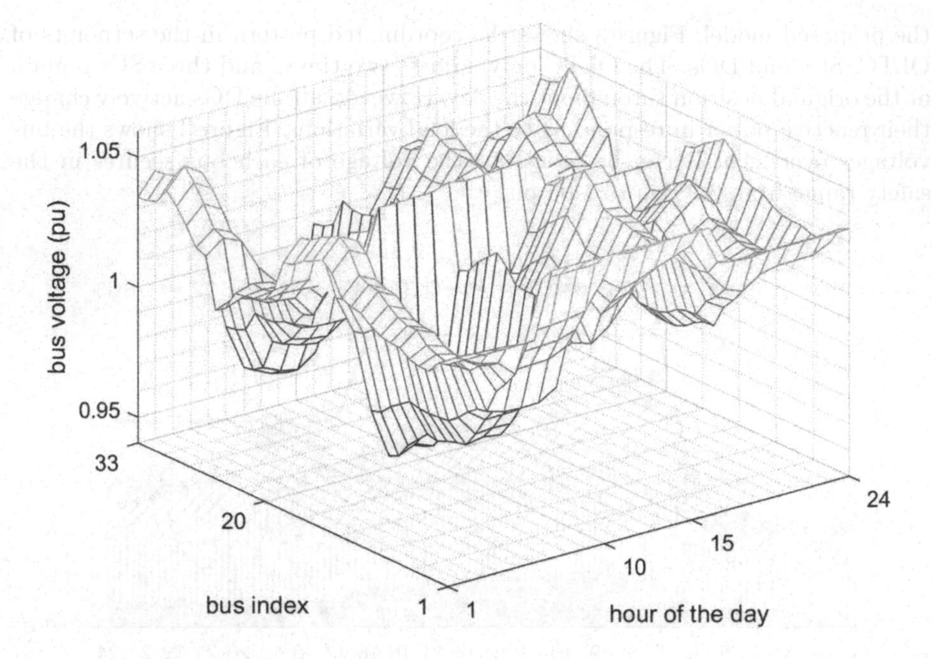

Fig. 4. Bus voltage after primary stage optmisation.

$$f_e^{'} = \sum_{s=1}^{S} Prob(s) \times f^{'}(s) = \sum_{s=1}^{S} [\prod_{i=1}^{I} Prob_i(s)] \times f^{'}(s) \quad (9)$$

Table 2. Probablity for DG1's generation at hour 1 in scenarios.

Index of scenari	DG1's generation (MW)	Probability
1	1.609	24%
2	1.424	18%
3	1.481	17%
4	1.350	21%
5	1.538	19%

Secondary Voltage Optimisation Results: In the secondary stage, all the representative scenarios are solved. The expected results are calculated by (8) and (9). Compared to the results of the primary stage, the power loss slightly increases to 4.07 MW while the voltage deviation decreases to 0.549 pu. The deterministic and expected values for DGs' reactive power are compared in Fig. 6.

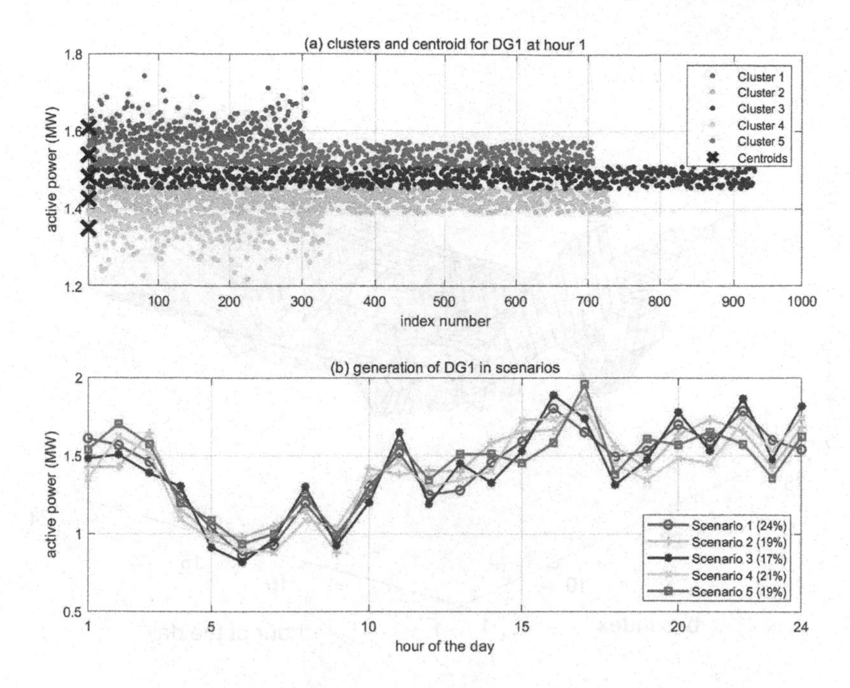

Fig. 5. DG1's parameters in scenarios.

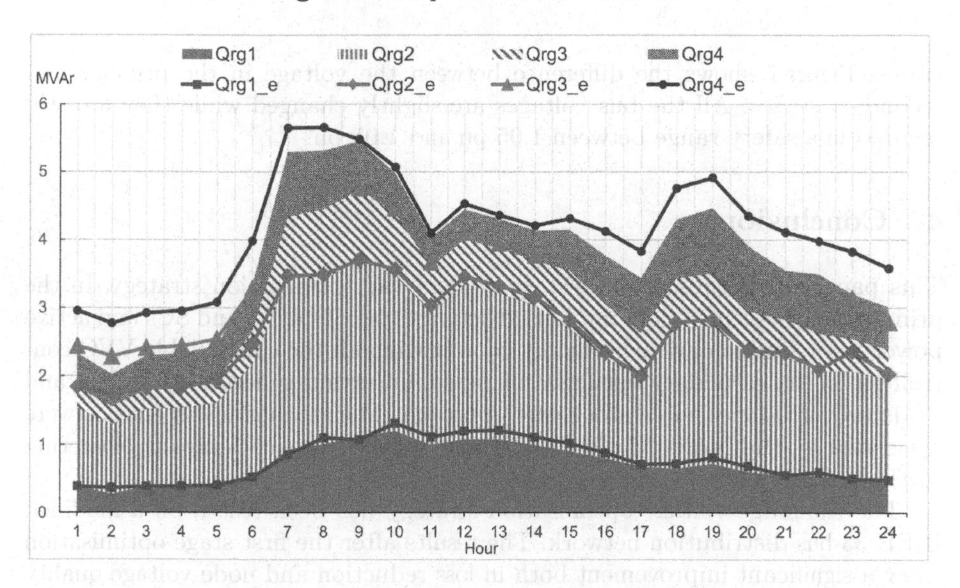

Fig. 6. Comparative results of reactive power of DGs.

The difference between deterministic and expected values indicates that the optimisation results are sensitive to the uncertainties constructed in Subsect. 3.2. Due to the change of DGs' setpoints, the voltage for each node correspondently

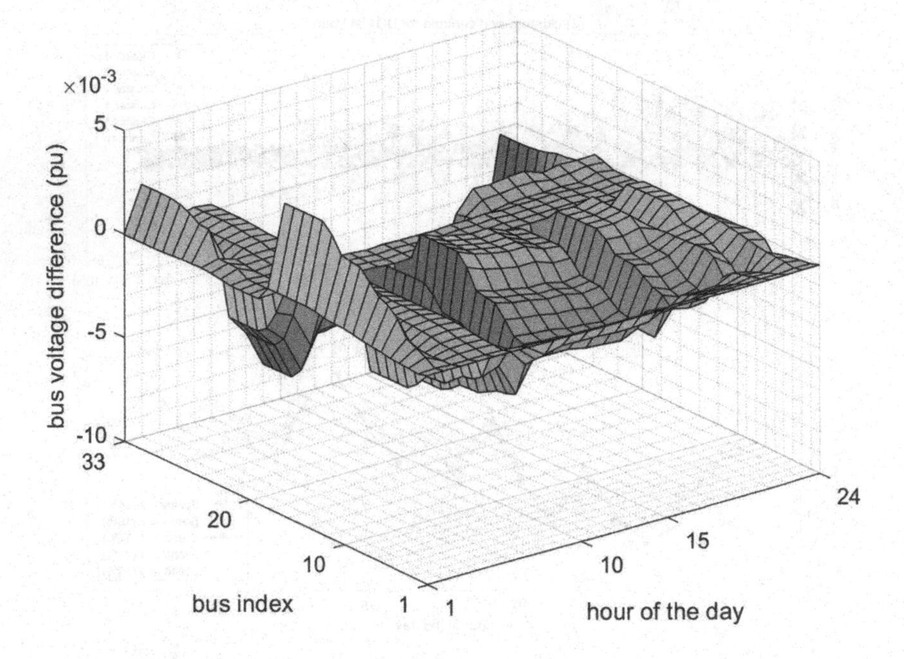

Fig. 7. Bus voltage difference between primary and secondary stage.

varies. Figure 7 shows the difference between the voltage in the primary and secondary stages. All the bus voltages are slightly changed while they are still secured in a safety range between 1.05 pu and 1.05 pu.

4 Conclusion

This paper has proposed a two-stage voltage/var optimisation strategy. In the primary stage optimisation, minimised action times of OLTC and SCs and active power loss reduction are achieved by coordinating all the controllable VVC controllers. In the secondary optimisation stage, uncertain generations of DGs and loads are introduced via a stochastic approach. The stochastical scenarios were generated by the Monte-Carlo technic and reduced by the k-means clustering method.

The two-stage voltage optimisation strategy has been tested on a modified IEEE 33-bus distribution network. The results after the first stage optimisation show a significant improvement both in loss reduction and node voltage quality in comparison with the original system. The second stage optimisation was performed by applying probabilistic scenarios. The setpoints of DGs' reactive power are adjusted in response to the uncertainties, and the expected values of active power loss and node voltage deviation vary. The results demonstrate that the optimisation results are sensitive to uncertainties. To further improve the voltage control performance under uncertain distributed generations, the impact of uncertain parameters on the optimisation results should be studied in detail in future works.

References

1. Murray, W., Adonis, M., Raji, A.: Voltage control in future electrical distribution networks. Renew. Sustain. Energy Rev. **146**, 111100 (2021)
2. Yuanyuan, C., et al.: Network partition and voltage coordination control for distribution networks with high penetration of distributed PV units. IEEE Trans. Power Syst. **33**(3), 3396–3407 (2018)
3. Wenshu, J., et al.: Distributed coordinated voltage control for distribution networks with DG and OLTC based on MPC and gradient projection. IEEE Trans. Power Syst. **37**(1), 680–690 (2021)
4. Shiwei, L., et al.: Two-stage voltage control strategy in distribution networks with coordinated multimode operation of PV inverters. IET Renew. Power Gener. **17**(1), 66–82 (2023)
5. Lundberg, M., Samuelsson, O., Hillberg, E.: Local voltage control in distribution networks using PI control of active and reactive power. Electr. Power Syst. Res. **212**, 108475 (2022)
6. Yan, X., et al.: Multi-timescale coordinated voltage/var control of high renewable-penetrated distribution systems. IEEE Trans. Power Syst. **32**(6), 4398–4408 (2017)
7. Chen, L., Deng, Z., Xu, X.: Two-stage dynamic reactive power dispatch strategy in distribution network considering the reactive power regulation of distributed generations. IEEE Trans. Power Syst. **32**(2), 1021–1032 (2018)
8. Lai, X., Ma, X., Bai, Y.: Dynamic reactive power optimization method based on mixed integer second-order cone programming. Autom. Electr. Power Syst. **41**(17), 37–42 (2017)
9. Peng, L., et al.: Coordinated control method of voltage and reactive power for active distribution networks based on soft open point. IEEE Trans. Sustain. Energy **8**(4), 1430–1442 (2017)
10. Muhammad, A., et al.: Coordinated voltage control strategy for voltage regulators and voltage source converters integrated distribution system. IEEE Trans. Ind. Appl. **55**(4), 4235–4246 (2019)
11. Bidgoli, H.S., Van Cutsem, T.: Combined local and centralized voltage control in active distribution networks. IEEE Trans. Power Syst. **33**(2), 1374–1384 (2017)
12. Jabr, R.A., Džafić, I.: Sensitivity-based discrete coordinate-descent for volt/var control in distribution networks. IEEE Trans. Power Syst. **31**(6), 4670–4678 (2016)
13. Qiao, F., Ma, J.: Coordinated voltage/var control in a hybrid AC/DC distribution network. IET Gener. Transm. Distrib. **14**(11), 2129–2137 (2020)
14. Qiao, F., Ma, J.: Voltage/var control for hybrid distribution networks using decomposition-based multiobjective evolutionary algorithm. IEEE Access **8**, 12015–12025 (2020)
15. Baran, M.E., Wu, F.F.: Network reconfiguration in distribution systems for loss reduction and load balancing. IEEE Trans. Power Deliv. **42**, 1401–1407 (1989)
16. Sergei Vassilvitskii., and Arthur, David.: k-means++: The advantages of careful seeding. In Proceedings of the eighteenth annual ACM-SIAM symposium on Discrete algorithms, pp. 1027–1035 (2006)
17. Wu, J.: Advances in K-Means Clustering: A Data Mining Thinking, 1st edn. Springer, Heidelberg (2012). https://doi.org/10.1007/978-3-642-29807-3

Energy Management for SOFC Hybrid DC Microgrids When External Power Goes Up

Lin Zhang[1], Quanmin Niu[1], Yu Deng[1], Feng Wang[1], Chao Xie[1], Jinjing Wang[1], Jian Zhang[2], and Hongtu Xie[2](✉)

[1] Department of Early Warning Technology, Air Force Early Warning Academy, Wuhan 430019, China

[2] School of Electronics and Communication Engineering, Shenzhen Campus of Sun Yat-sen University, Shenzhen 518107, China
xiehongtu@mail.sysu.edu.cn

Abstract. In the solid oxide fuel cell (SOFC) hybrid direct-current (DC) microgrids, the energy management for the high efficiency, fast power transients and thermal safety are the main difficult task for considering. In this article, the composition of the SOFC hybrid DC microgrids including the SOFC, lithium battery and supercapacitor is established, and then its stable operating requirement is discussed. Moreover, the control and optimization strategies, including the energy management techniques are designed for the SOFC, battery and supercapacitor to remedy the defects of the slow SOFC power transients. Among the energy management techniques, the control scheme based on the SOFC system optimal operating points (OOPs) is established to realize highest efficiency and static thermo-safety. Moreover, the voltage and current control strategy based on the proportional plus integral (PI) controller is set up to maintain load terminal voltage to 220 V. In the end, the experimental results are shown to verify the effectiveness of the proposed control strategies. In addition, the SOFC/battery/supercapacitor-based DC microgrids shows the comparative advantage in the fast load tracing.

Keywords: Solid oxide fuel cell · Energy management techniques · Direct-current microgrids · High efficiency · Fast power transients · Thermal safety

This work is supported by the Guangdong Basic and Applied Basic Research Foundation (Grants No. 2021A1515010768 and No. 2023A1515011588), the Shenzhen Science and Technology Program (Grant No. 202206193000001, 20220815171723002), the National Natural Science Foundation of China (Grants No. 62203465, No. 62001523, No. 62201614 and No. 6210593), the Science and Technology on Near-Surface Detection Laboratory Pre-Research Foundation (Grant No. 6142414200607), the Science and Technology Talents Foundation of Air Force Early Warning Academy (Grant No. 2021KJY11), and the Fundamental Research Funds for the Central Universities, Sun Yat-sen University (Grant No. 23lgpy45.)

Lin Zhang and Hongtu Xie are the co-first authors, who share the first authorship and have contributed equally to this work.

H. Yang et al. (Eds.): SmartGIFT 2022, LNICST 483, pp. 284–294, 2023.
https://doi.org/10.1007/978-3-031-31733-0_24

1 Introduction

The microgrid is one of the fastest growing smart power systems, which plays an important role in the incremental electric power consumption [1–3]. Among the microgrids, the direct-current (DC) microgrids pay the more attention due to the advantages of the efficiency, reliability, high power quality, reduced power loss, improving transactive energy and the elimination of frequency and phase control [4, 5]. The distributed generations can be selected as the fuel cells (FCs), battery, supercapacitor, wind and solar photovoltaics (PV) [2, 3].

Among the several novel propositions, the SOFC are one of the most popular and efficient FCs-based DC microgrids. In especial, it can generate the electricity directly from the electrochemical reaction with the least spread of the pollution compared to the conventional energy production methods [6]. However, as the SOFC operates in the medium-high temperature, the poor thermal response must be given priority to consider. What's more, the lack of the external load following and system efficiency should also be addressed [7, 8]. To solve these issues and many others, our group and other teams have done a lot of works.

Currently and in the future, thermal safety control in the SOFC-based DC microgrids is critical. Our previous works have studied the operational safety by considering the temperature constraints in SOFC system. Some researches design the system controller to provide excess air to cool the SOFC stack [9–11], including a PI controller, a multivariable controller and so on. All the above controllers are suitable for SOFC system overheat control. Another point to consider is getting high efficiency output in FCs-based DC microgrids, our and other groups have many groundbreaking researches on it. Especially, the optimal operation points (OOPs) and the corresponding optimize external load power switch schemes have been discussed to obtain the maximum output efficiency [12–15]. Huang has studied the impact of the fuel utilization (FU) on the net efficiency of SOFC stand-alone system [12]. Zhu has proposed a novel combined cooling, heating and power (CCHP) system. The system has a high electrical efficiency of 52% and overall efficiency of 75%. Based on above, the parameter study and multiple objective optimization are conducted to get higher output efficiency [13]. Zhu also has optimized the system efficiency by controlling the SOFC fuel utilization through the parametric analysis [14]. Tan assesses the integrated energy efficiency ratio and CO_2 emission trend to obtain a much higher primary energy efficiency [15]. However, all the maximum efficiency obtained in the SOFC system at the intersection of the safety constraints. Few scholars research related the topics that ensure process safety and simultaneously optimizes the energy-efficiency.

The rapid load following is another key point in system control objective of SOFC-based DC microgrids. Plenty of the control schemes have been presented and investigated to maintain quick power following. Kandepu has developed a control architecture at the cost of the output efficiency for a SOFC-GT-based independent station [16]. Wang has proposed a novel operating method by combining the multi-controlled circuits with the protective circuits to achieve the rapid external load tracing and safety reliability and maintain-ability in SOFC system [17]. However, the quick-speed load following on the basis of optimal efficiency and thermal safety in static operating conditions should be focused on in this paper.

The main purpose of this article is to design the energy management scheme of the SOFC hybrid DC microgrids considering the system efficiency, fast power transients and thermal safety. This paper is organized as followings. Section 2 presents a SOFC hybrid DC microgrid architecture, containing stand-alone SOFC, lithium battery and supercapacitor, and then deals with its essential operational requirements. Section 3 presents the energy management and control strategies of the SOFC hybrid DC microgrids. The article finally gives the conclusion in Sect. 4.

2 SOFC Hybrid DC Microgrid System Architecture

The overall structure and distribution of the SOFC hybrid DC microgrids system is shown in Fig. 1. It mainly consists of the SOFC independent station, the lithium battery, the super capacitor, the DC/DC boost converters, the DC microgrids network and DC load. The battery and supercapacitor are preferred with the combinations because of the SOFC cannot reimburse for the fast load following [18, 19], and the required transient power is supplied to the DC bus by the battery and supercapacitor. The DC/DC boost converters are provided to maintain the quick-speed external load requirements and system reliability improving [20].

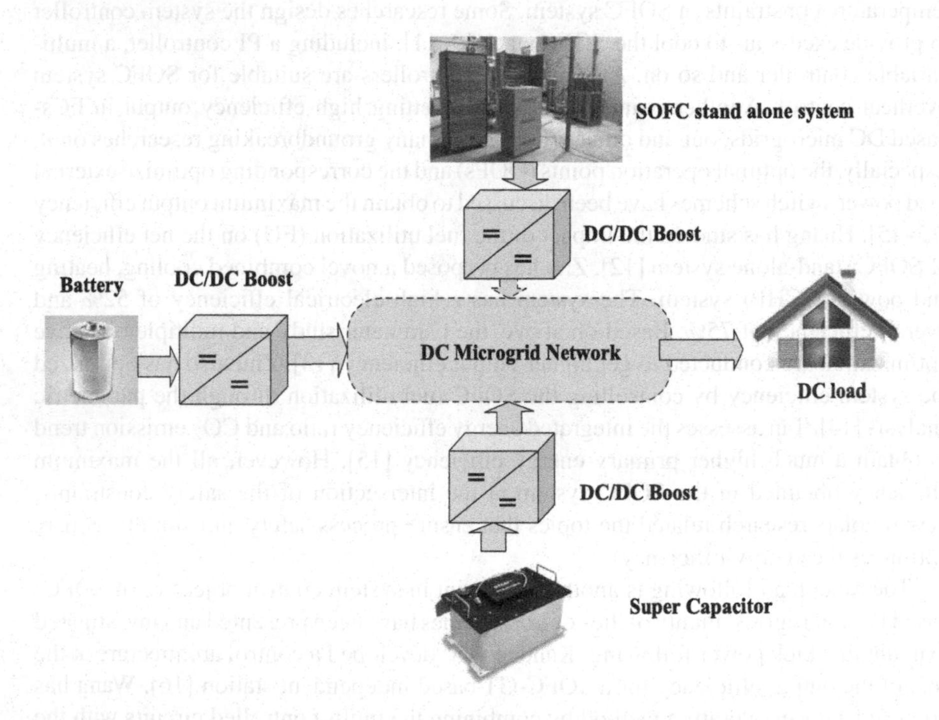

Fig. 1. Schematic diagram of the SOFC hybrid DC microgrids.

The systematic architecture of the SOFC is shown in Fig. 2. It mainly consists of two modules: the balance of plant (BOP) and SOFC stack. BOP plays an auxiliary role in SOFC system generation, it mainly consists the gas feed pipes and valves, the secondary heat exchangers, the tail gas recovery unit (burner). The stack operating power range is about 1 kW to 6 kW in different working conditions. The SOFC electrical output energy is provided by gas electrochemical reaction directly in stack. The main function of secondary heat exchangers is to reduce the stack cathode and anode inlet temperature difference. The heat source inlet heat exchangers are derived from burner. The main role of burner is to increase fuel utilization by making the exhaust gas burn completely. Meanwhile, an extra-second air bypass manifold is added to SOFC system to prevent excessive temperature in stack.

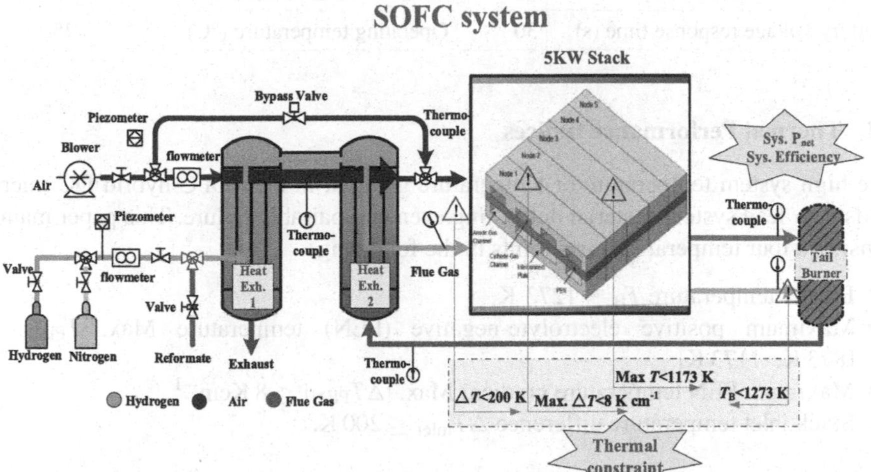

Fig. 2. Overall SOFC stand-alone system layout.

Our early works have studied the SOFC system structure, the simulation stratagem, the parameter and system-level optimization and the control strategies [21–24]. The battery of Li_ion is considered in our paper as it has been proving of the good energy density and electrical efficiency compared to other energy modes. Supercapacitor is known as the Electric Double Layer Capacitors (EDLCs), which can charge and discharge the more electrical energy because of its high capacitance. Their simulation process can be referred to [25].

Moreover, the interrelating parameter of Li_battery and supercapacitor models are listed in Table 1.

Table 1. Input parameters of the battery and supercapacitor models

Battery		Supercapacitor	
Nominal voltage (V)	28	Rated capacitance (F)	15.6
Rated capacity (Ah)	6.6	Equivalent series resistance DC (Ω)	2.1e−3
Maximum capacity (Ah)	40	Rated voltage (V)	16
Fully charged voltage (V)	32.42	Surge voltage (V)	18
Nominal discharge current (A)	17.4	Number of series capacitor	6
Internal resistance (Ω)	0.012	Number of parallel capacitor	1
Capacity (Ah)@Nominal voltage	36.17	Number of layer*	6
Initial state-of-charge (%)	90	Molecular radius (m)*	4e−10
Battery voltage response time (s)	30	Operating temperature (°C)	25

2.1 Thermal Performance Indices

The high system temperature or temperature gradient in the SOFC hybrid DC micro-grids may lead system material deforming even unrepairable failure. This paper mainly considers four temperature constraints in the following.

(1) Burner temperature $T_B \leq 1273$ K.
(2) Maximum positive electrolyte-negative (PEN) temperature Max. $T_{PEN} \in [873\,\text{K},\ 1173\,\text{K}]$.
(3) Maximum PEN temperature gradient Max. $|\Delta T_{PEN}| \leq 8\,\text{Kcm}^{-1}$.
(4) Stack inlet temperature difference $\Delta T_{inlet} \leq 200\,\text{K}$.

2.2 System Efficiency Indices

In addition to the thermal safety, the system efficiency indices mainly include the operating parameters. The combined operation parameters, including the system inlet air flow rate (F_{air}), fuel flow rate (F_{H2}), system current (I_S), and bypass valve opening ratio (*BP*), are selected as assemble regulating variables in our paper. The range of their values are in the following.

(1) Inlet air flow rate $F_{air} > 0$;
(2) Inlet fuel flow rate $F_{H2} > 0$;
(3) SOFC system current $I_S \in [10\,\text{A},\ 70\,\text{A}]$.
(4) Bypass valve opening ratio $BP \in [0,\ 0.3]$.

Based on these performance indices, and comprehensive considering system thermoelectric synergy, as well as thermal safety and high efficiency. The optimal operating points (OOPs) are manipulated to achieve all the above operating requirements above. The OOPs under different operating power have been processed in the static state by the traversal optimization strategy in our previous studies in [21–24], as shown in Table 2.

Table 2. OOPs of the SOFC stand-alone system

P_{net} (W)	I_s(A)	F_{air} (mol/s)	F_{H2}(mol/s)	*BP* (%)
1000	10	0.09920	0.00772	0.2
2000	20	0.19841	0.01543	0.1
3000	32	0.34390	0.02469	0
4000	44	0.43649	0.03419	0
5000	52	0.57538	0.04774	0

3 Energy Management and Control Strategies

The response time of the SOFC-based DC/DC microgrid output power is within tens of second, which is insatiable for the rapid external load following. Especially in the scenarios of external load power rising. In this section, the SOFC hybrid DC microgrids are analyzed to highlight the load power rising transients.

The control and energy management strategies for the SOFC hybrid DC microgrid is shown in Fig. 3(a), for the purpose of the fast load following, thermal management and high efficiency. The DC demanded voltage is controlled by the voltage and current regulator (Fig. 3(b)) though their associated boost converters. The DC/DC converter can allow the voltage conversion as well as the full control of the fuel cell current and DC bus voltage. The average value of the DC/DC converter models can be referred to [26] for this study. The optimal regulator mainly control the load demanded power by referring to the OOPs. What's more, as three sources of the energy is introduced here, the energy management strategies (Fig. 3(c)) should be analyzed to highlight the fast load following.

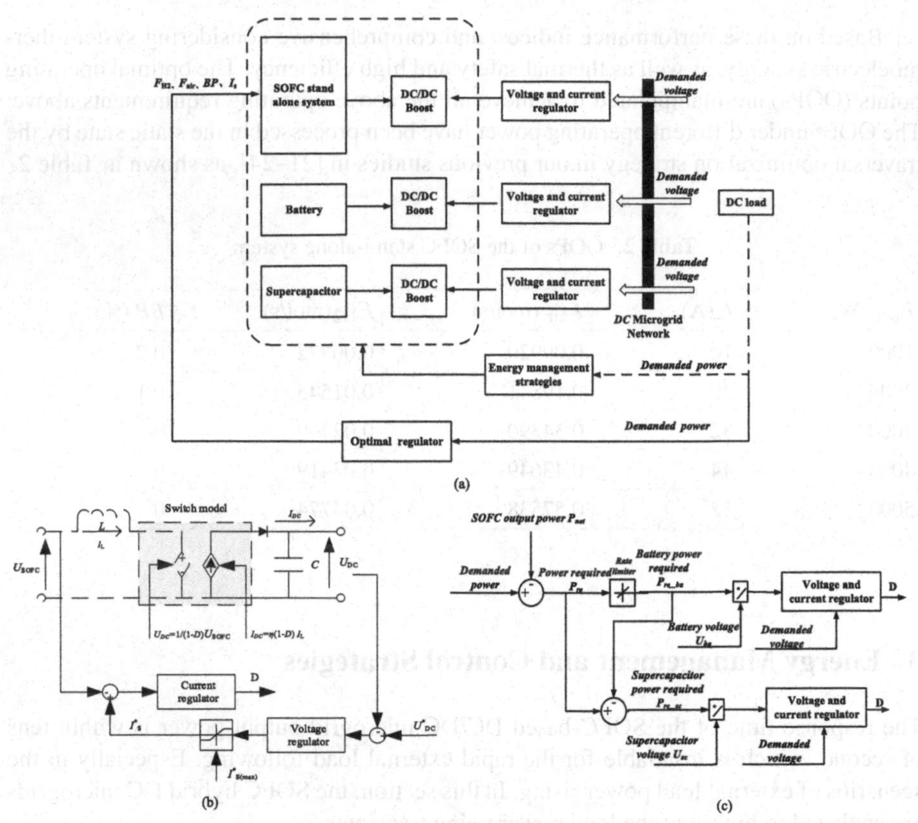

Fig. 3. Control and energy management strategies. (a) The overall control layout; (b) Boost type DC/DC converter model; (c) Energy management strategies.

As shown in Fig. 3(c), the system energy management strategies are designed based on SOFC system net output power (P_{net}) and the load demanded power. Their difference is the power required during the external load power step up. The battery and supercapacitor mainly provide the required energy. The required battery power is adopted by the power slope limitation, then the residual required power can be provided by the supercapacitor. Then, their input current of the DC/DC boost converter can be obtained from their required energy and voltage.

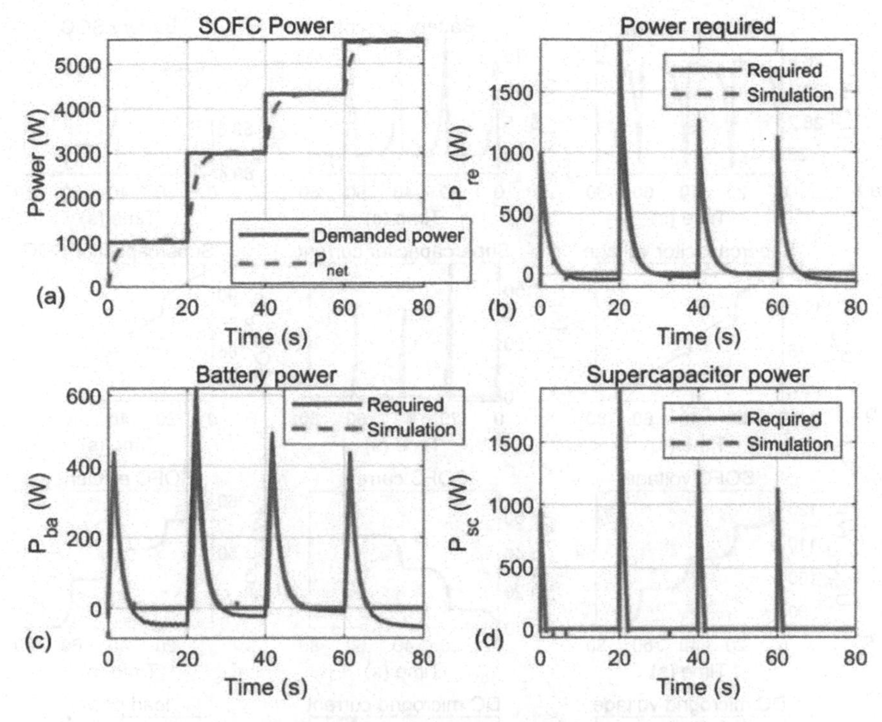

Fig. 4. Power results for the energy management strategies.

The power results of the above introduced control scheme is demonstrated as Fig. 4. The simulation results show the favorable power provided to the DC microgrid to remedy the defects of the slow SOFC power transients (Fig. 4(a)), and they all show the high accuracy according to the calculated required power (Fig. 4(b)–Fig. 4(d)).

Performance of the related electrical results in the SOFC hybrid DC microgrids is observed in Fig. 5. The electrical output characteristics (i.e. the voltage, current, SOC and system efficiency) of the supercapacitor and SOFC independent power generation system all changes with the external load demand (Fig. 5(a)–Fig. 5(c)). Especially, the SOFC system is operated near highest efficiency by the introduced optimal control method based on OOPs. Figure 5(d) shows the DC microgrid voltage is well controlled to 220 V. Moreover, the response time of the load power in the SOFC hybrid DC microgrid is within seconds, which shows the superiority in comparison with the SOFC-based DC microgrid.

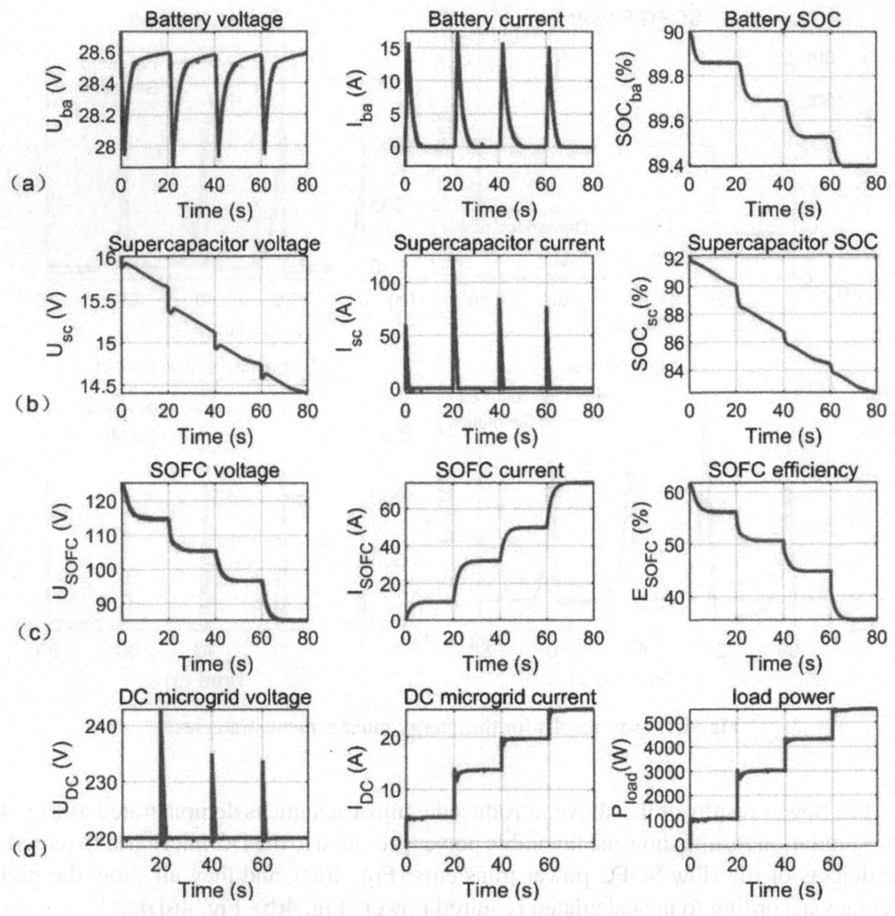

Fig. 5. Related electrical results in the SOFC hybrid DC microgrids. (a) Battery; (b) Supercapacitor; (c) SOFC; (d) DC microgrid load.

4 Conclusion

This paper presented the energy management strategies for the SOFC hybrid DC microgrids from the perspective of the high output efficiency, thermal safety and rapid load tracing response. The architecture of the SOFC hybrid DC microgrids including the SOFC, lithium battery and supercapacitor is first introduced. Then, the system essential operational requirements, including the thermal performance indices, system efficiency indices and the OOPs are introduced and discussed. Considering the high system efficiency, static thermal safety constraints and rapid external load following, the control and energy management strategies to highlight the fast load following for the SOFC hybrid DC microgrid is introduced. As expected, the favorable power response time is achieved with in seconds, as the battery and supercapacitor can remedy the defects of the slow SOFC power transients. To conclude, the SOFC hybrid DC microgrid has a great superiority in the fast load tracing, especially when the external power step up. An alternative is to design the multi-objective optimization energy management strategies to optimize all the performance criteria in the SOFC hybrid DC microgrid, which is the next topic in our further studies.

References

1. Xu, L., Ibragimova, A., Shilova, K.: Analysis of international practice in the use of renewable energy sources (RES). In: IOP Conference Series: Earth and Environmental Science, pp. 0121880–1–0121880–6. IOP Publishing Ltd., Moscow (2022)
2. Deng, Y., Zhang, Y., Luo, F., Mu, Y.: Operational planning of centralized charging stations utilizing second-life battery energy storage systems. IEEE Trans. Sustain. Energy **12**(1), 387–399 (2021)
3. Zhang, Y., Xu, Y., Yang, H., Dong, Z., Zhang, R.: Optimal whole-life-cycle planning of battery energy storage for multi-functional services in power systems. IEEE Trans. Sustain. Energy **11**(4), 2077–2086 (2020)
4. Eid, A.: Utility integration of PV-wind-fuel cell hybrid distributed generation systems under variable load demands. Int. J. Electr. Power Energy Syst. **62**(11), 689–699 (2014)
5. Srinivasan, M., Kwasinski, A.: Control analysis of parallel DC-DC converters in a DC microgrid with constant power loads. Int. J. Electr. Power Energy Syst. **122**(4), 1–9 (2020)
6. Wang, Y., Li, S., Sun, H., Huang, C.: The utilization of adaptive African vulture optimizer for optimal parameter identification of SOFC. Energy Rep. **8**, 551–560 (2022)
7. Mumtaz, S., Khan, L., Ahmed, S., Badar, R.: Indirect adaptive soft computing based wavlet-embedded control paradigms for WT/PV/SOFC in a grid/charging station conneced hybrid power system. PLoS ONE **13**(4), 1–17 (2018)
8. Pranita, R., Sanjoy, K., Sujit, K.: Renewable energy generation system connected to micro grid and analysis of energy management: a critical review. Int. J. Power Electron. Drive Syst. **13**(1), 470–479 (2022)
9. Sorrentino, M., Pianese, C., Guezennec, Y.: A hierarchical modeling approach to the simulation and control of planar solid oxide fuel cells. J. Power Sources **180**(1), 380–392 (2008)
10. Huo, H., Wu, Y., Liu, Y., Gan, S., Kuang, X.: Control-oriented nonlinear modeling and temperature control for solid oxide fuel cell. J. Fuel Cell Sci. Technol. **7**(4), 0410051–0410059 (2010)
11. Hajimolana, S., Tonekabonimoghadam, S., Hussain, M., Chakrabarti, M., Jayakumar, N., Hashim, M.: Thermal stress management of a solid oxide fuel cell using neural network predictive control. Energy **62**(1), 320–329 (2013)
12. Huang, S., Yang, C., Chen, H., Zhou, N., Tucker, D.: Coupling impacts of SOFC operating temperature and fuel utilization on system net efficiency in natural gas hybrid SOFC/GT system. Case Stud. Therm. Eng. **31**(101868), 1–12 (2022)
13. Zhu, P., et al.: Achieving high-efficiency conversion and poly-generation of cooling, heating, and power based on biomass-fueled SOFC hybrid system: performance assessment and multi-objective optimization. Energy Convers. Manag. **240**(114245), 1–18 (2021)
14. Zhu, P., et al.: High-efficiency conversion of natural gas fuel to power by an integrated system of SOFC, HCCI engine, and waste heat recovery: Thermodynamic and thermo-economic analyses. Fuel **275**(117883), 1–13 (2020)
15. Tan, L., Dong, X., Gong, Z., Wang, M.: Analysis on energy efficiency and CO_2 emission reduction of an SOFC-based energy system served public buildings with large interior zones. Energy **165**(B), 1106–1118 (2018)

16. Kandepu, R., Imsland, L., Foss, B., Stiller, C., Thorud, B., Bolland, O.: Modeling and control of a SOFC-GT-based autonomous power system. Energy **32**(4), 406–417 (2007)
17. Wang, X., Lv, X., Mi, X., Spataru, C., Weng, Y.: Coordinated control approach for load following operation of SOFC-GT hybrid system. Energy **248**(123548), 1–15 (2022)
18. Armghan, H., Yang, M., Wang, M., Ali, N., Armghan, A.: Nonlinear integral backstepping based control of a DC microgrid with renewable generation and energy storage systems. Int. J. Electr. Power Energy Syst. **117**, 105613 (2020)
19. Ahmed, O.A., Bleijs, J.A.M.: Power flow control methods for an ultra capacitor bidirectional converter in DC microgrids–a comparative study. Renew. Sustain. Energy Rev. **26**, 727–738 (2013)
20. Liu, Z., Zhao, J., Zou, Z.: Impedance modeling, dynamic analysis and damping enhancement for DC microgrid with multiple types of loads. Int. J. Electr. Power Energy Syst. **122**(106183), 1–12 (2020)
21. Zhang, L., Li, X., Jiang, J., Li, S., Yang, J., Li, J.: Dynamic modeling and analysis of a 5-kW solid oxide fuel cell system from the perspectives of cooperative control of thermal safety and high efficiency. Int. J. Hydrogen Energy **40**, 456–476 (2015)
22. Zhang, L., Jiang, J., Cheng, H., Deng, Z., Li, X.: Control strategy for power management, efficiency-optimization and operating-safety of a 5-kW solid oxide fuel cell system. Electrochim. Acta **177**(20), 237–249 (2015)
23. Zhang, L., et al.: An optimization and fast load-oriented control for current-based solid oxide fuel cell system. J. Solid State Electrochem. **22**(9), 2863–2877 (2018). https://doi.org/10.1007/s10008-018-3996-x
24. Zhang, L., Shi, S., Jiang, J., Li, X.: Current-based MPC for operating-safety analysis of a reduced-order solid oxide fuel cell system. Ionics **25**(4), 1759–1772 (2018). https://doi.org/10.1007/s11581-018-2654-8
25. Tremblay, O., Dessaint, L.-A., Dekkiche, A.-I.: A generic battery model for the dynamic simulation of hybrid electric vehicles. In: IEEE Vehicle Power and Propulsion Conference, Arlington, TX, USA, pp. 284–289. IEEE (2007)
26. Zakzouk, N.E., Khamis, A.K., Abdelsalam, A.K., Williams, B.W.: Continuous-input continuous-output current buck-boost DC/DC converters for renewable energy applications: modelling and performance assessment. Energies **12**(11), 1–27 (2019)

Design and Implementation of Tracking Smart Car with Wireless Communication Functions

Jian Zhang[1,2], Yufan Liu[2], Ao Li[2], Jinshan Zeng[2], and Hongtu Xie[1](✉)

[1] School of Electronic and Communication Engineering, Shenzhen Campus of Sun Yat-sen University, Shenzhen, China
zhangj765@mail2.sysu.edu.cn, xiehongtu@mail.sysu.edu.cn

[2] School of Information Engineering, NanChang Hangkong University, Nanchang, China

Abstract. In order to realize the rapid and stable automatic tracking of the smart car, this paper designs and implements a tracking smart car with wireless communication function in the background of the National College Students Smart Car Competition of China. The system of the smart car includes hardware design, signal processing, and software algorithms. The hardware design mainly includes track information acquisition sensors, auxiliary control modules and communication modules. The software algorithms mainly includes the filtering and difference-ratio-sum algorithm, incremental Proportion Integration Differentiation (PID) and communication control algorithm. Firstly, the electromagnetic signal in the track is acquired by the inductance-capacitor pairs, and the deviation between the actual position of the smart car and the position of the electromagnetic wire laid in the central track is calculated. Then, the incremental PID control algorithm is used to calculate the pulse width modulation (PWM) signal according to the deviation, and the PWM signal is acted on the motor to drive the smart car to always drive along the central track, so as to achieve the purpose of automatic track guidance. The wireless communication module is used to achieve the communication between the two smart cars. Finally, a large number of hardware and software tests are carried out using the upper computer debugging tools. Experiments demonstrate that the smart car of this design can complete the communication task of two cars, can accurately achieve automatic tracking, and obtain higher speed performance.

This work was co-supported by the Guangdong Basic and Applied Basic Research Foundation under Grants 2021A1515010768 and 2023A1515011588, by the Shenzhen Science and Technology Program under Grant 202206193000001, 20220815171723002, by the National Natural Science Foundation of China under Grants 62203465, 62001523, 62201614 and 6210593, by the Science and Technology on Near-Surface Detection Laboratory Pre-Research Foundation under Grant 6142414200607, and by the Fundamental Research Funds for the Central Universities, Sun Yat-sen University under Grant 23lgpy45.

H. Yang et al. (Eds.): SmartGIFT 2022, LNICST 483, pp. 295–306, 2023.
https://doi.org/10.1007/978-3-031-31733-0_25

Keywords: Electromagnetic induction tracking smart car · Inductance-capacitor pairs · Proportion Integration Differentiation control · Difference-ratio-sum algorithm · Wireless communication between two cars

1 Introduction

With the improvement of the level of scientific and technological innovation, various technologies are developing in the direction of intelligence. As a key part of intelligent transportation, intelligent vehicle is a typical high-tech complex that integrates environmental perception, decision-making, interconnection communication, which concentrates on the modern sensing, information fusion, communications, artificial intelligence and automatic control [1]. The modern self-driving vehicle is an intelligent system that navigates autonomously along the main road, and the smart car system is a microcosm of the self-driving vehicles, there are many similarities between the two in terms of information acquisition, information processing and interconnection communication.

The National College Students Smart Car Competition of China is a creative science and technology competition with smart cars as the research object, an exploratory engineering practice activity for college students, and one of the science and technology competitions advocated by the Ministry of Education [2]. In order to solve the problem of slow speed and insufficient effect control strategies of the smart car, and the instability between smart car communications, this paper proposes the hardware design and software algorithms to realize a tracking smart car with wireless communication function [3], based on the author's entry that won the first prize of the national finals of the dual-cars relay group in the 16th National College Students Smart Car Competition of China.

2 System Hardware Design

The physical image of the smart car in this design is shown in Fig. 1, whose length, width and height is 30 cm, 25 cm and 20 cm, respectively. The hardware design mainly includes the microcontroller, inductance-capacitor sensor pairs, HC-05 Bluetooth module, NRF24L01 wireless communication module, HC-SR04 ultrasonic ranging module, photoelectric speed measurement coded sensor and motor drive module, which are selected for different tasks. The main information perception sensor is five inductance-capacitor pairs. The HC-05 Bluetooth module and NRF24L01 module are used for wireless debugging and communication.

2.1 Microcontroller

This design use the 32-bit microcontroller MM32F3277G9P produced by MindMotion as the core controller, with a operating frequency of 120 MHz and a supply voltage of 3.3 V. There are many peripheral interfaces in the MM32 microcontroller, such as the pulse width modulation (PWM), analog signal to digital signal interface, and the Universal Synchronous Asynchronous Receiver Transmitter (USART), which is used for communication. So the MM32 microcontroller

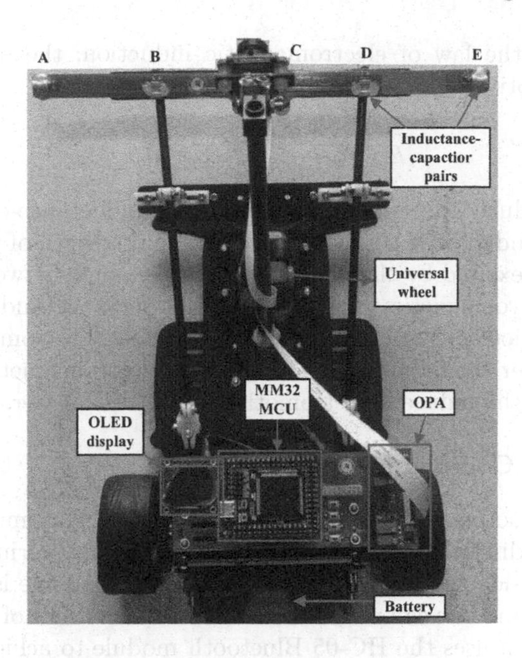

Fig. 1. Physical image of the smart car.

is sufficient to meet the needs of the competition. In addition, the MM32 microcontroller supports hardware division and hardware square operations, which can process the communication data more quickly.

2.2 Inductance-Capacitor Sensor Pairs

The race track is a closed curve, the center of the track is laid with electromagnetic guide line, that is a diameter within 0.1 to 1.0 mm enameled wire, which has the amplitude of 100 mA and frequency of 20 kHz alternating current. As uniformly changing electric field produces a constant magnetic field, the inductance is used to collected the information of the magnetic field, which reflects the relative position of the smart car and the center guide line. According to the formula for calculating the resonant frequency of a resonant circuit

$$f = \frac{1}{2\pi\sqrt{LC}} \tag{1}$$

So the 10 mH inductance and 6.8 nF capacitor pairs are used to collect the electromagnetic induction signal of the track. Five inductance-capacitor pairs A, B, C, D and E are used as sensors to detect the position of the smart car relative to the guide line, which is laid in the center of the track. The leftmost A and rightmost E inductance-capacitor pairs are used for normal tracking, the 45° oblique B and D are used to detect the cross road, and the intermediate C is used to assist in detecting roundbaout, as illustrated in Fig. 1.

According to the law of electromagnetic induction, the magnitude of the induced electromotive force in the circuit

$$E = n\frac{\Delta\Phi}{\Delta t} = nBLv\sin\theta \tag{2}$$

where E is the induced electromotive force by the inductance-capacitor pairs; n is the number of inductance coil windings; B is the strength of the induced electromagnetic field excited by the guide line; θ is the angle between the inductive coil and the electromagnetic wire. When the inductance and electromagnetic wires are perpendicular, θ is close to 90°, the induced electromotive force is the greatest. The closer the inductance coil is to the electromagnetic guide line, the B is greater, and the induced electromotive force E is greater.

2.3 Bluetooth Communication Module

The HC-05 Bluetooth module is a master-slave serial port module, which can be used for short-distance wireless communication. After pairing, the communication protocol inside the module is ignored, and the module is used as a serial port directly. The module can meet the communication needs of smart car within 10 m, so this design uses the HC-05 Bluetooth module to achieve the dual-cars communication [4]. In addition, the Bluetooth module can be connected using the Bluetooth of the mobile phone, so the mobile phone and the smart car can send data to each other, making the debugging of the smart car more convenient. The physical image of the HC-05 Bluetooth module is shown in Fig. 2.

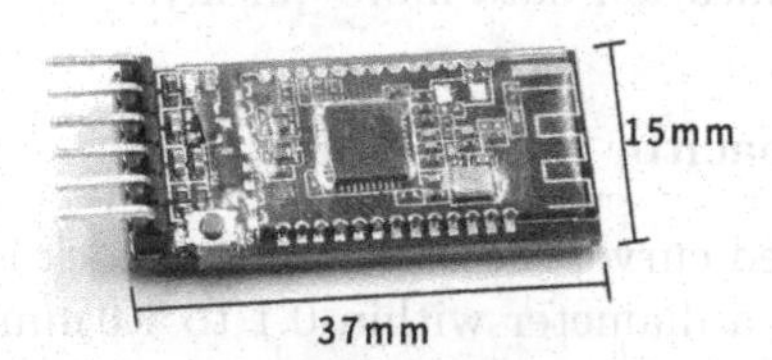

Fig. 2. Physical image of the HC-05 Bluetooth module.

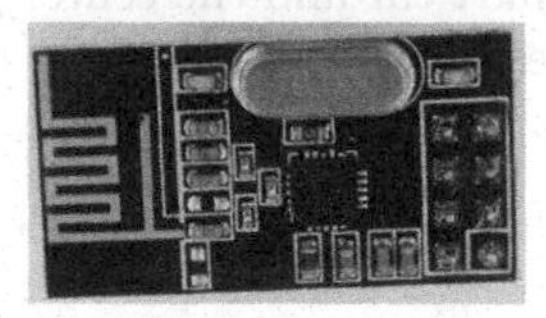

Fig. 3. Physical image of the NRF24L01 Module.

2.4 NRF24L01 Wireless Communication Module

Since the 16th dual-cars relay group requires the two smart cars to handover a ball and realize the accurate control of handover, this design uses the NRF24L01 wireless data transmission module for dual-cars communication [5].

The NRF24L01 module works in the 2.4 to 2.518 GHz frequency band, half-duplex, transceiver integration, using serial port for data transceiver, reducing the threshold of wireless applications. The NRF24L01 module transmits and receives 10 bytes of data with a test distance of about 70 m. And the module has the characteristics of automatic frequency hopping function, strong anti-interference ability, high transmission rate and small delay.

2.5 Ultrasonic Ranging Module

In order to realize the real-time, contactless distance measurement, this design uses the HC-SR04 ultrasonic ranging module to measure the distance between two smart cars. Ultrasonic ranging is calculated by means of the calculation of ultrasonic pulse echo crossing time, and then calculate the relative distance between the module and the measured target. The module can measure the distance within 0.04 to 4 m, and has the characteristics of accurate measurement, stability and high speed. The physical image of the ultrasonic module is illustrated in Fig. 4.

Fig. 4. Physical image of the HC-SR04 ultrasonic module.

Fig. 5. Physical image of the speed measurement sensor.

2.6 Speed Measurement Sensor

In order to ensure the closed-loop control of speed and improve the stability of the control, this design uses the photoelectric speed measurement coded sensor to measure the real-time speed of the smart car. The photoelectric speed measurement coded sensor can measure the speed of each moment of the car, and by integraling the time, can obtain the distance driven. The physical image of the sensor is illustrated in Fig. 5.

2.7 Motor Drive Module

The motor drive circuit of this design uses the HIP4082 chip to form an H-bridge drive circuit, and two motors require two H-bridge drive circuits. This design uses the hardware PWM technology, the frequency of the PWM signal is 17 kHz, by changing the duty cycle of the PWM signal, changing the open-time of the CMOS tube, so as to change the voltage at both ends of the motor to control the speed of the motor. If the left wheel rotates faster than the right wheel, then the car turns right, so as to change the direction of the car by changing the duty cycle of the PWM signal. The circuit diagram of the motor drive module is illustrated in Fig. 6, where the "M3" and "M4" are connected to the motor.

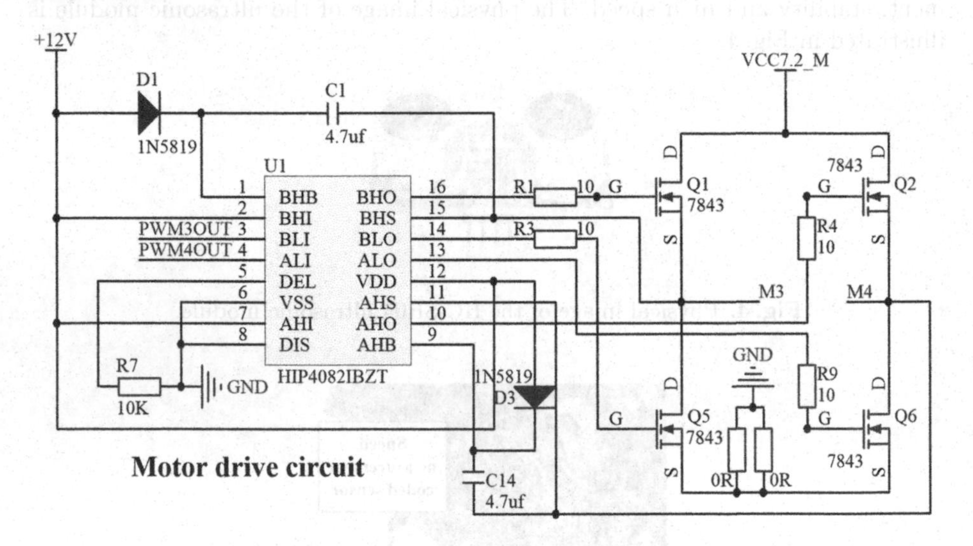

Fig. 6. Circuit diagram of the motor drive module.

3 Software Design

3.1 Electromagnetic Induction Signal Acquisition and Filtering

The process of software design is illustrated in Fig. 7. Firstly, the inductance-capacitor pairs, that is, the LC oscillation circuits installed in the smart car acquire the magnetic field information of the track. The acquired signal is an AC signal, which reflects the location of the smart car. The AC signal is input into the linear amplification circuit, and outputs a sine wave with larger amplitude, which is rectifying and filtering to a DC signal. Then the DC signal is sent into the 12-bit ADC interface of the microcontroller for ADC conversion.

Secondly, the converted digital signal is filtered to get the data of the information of the track. Then the data is normalized, the relevant information of the track is analyzed, which is used to classify the different track elements. And the difference-ratio-sum algorithm is used to calculated the deviation between the position of the smart car and the center guilde line of the track. Thirdly, the PID control algorithm is used to calculate the PWM signal corresponding to the deviation. Finally the PWM signal is acted through the drive circuit to the drive motor, which is used to control the smart car to go straight or turn. This design uses the wireless communication module to observe the intermediate variables of the real-time operation of the smart car.

Due to the presence of noise and interference in the system, it is important to perform the filtering algorithm. A weighted recursive average filtering method is used in this design. First take N sample values continuously as a queue, the length of the queue is fixed to N. Each time the new sampled data is input to the end of the queue, and the data of the team leader is removed. The weight of the team from tail to the head is decreased sequentially, then an average value is taken. The filtering algorithm is suitable for systems with the small sampling period, and changing the weights can change the sensitivity of the system. Besides, the median filtering algorithm is then used, and finally the Kalman filter is used for filtering. Filters can make the data smoother and reduce unnecessary jitter caused by sudden changes in the data.

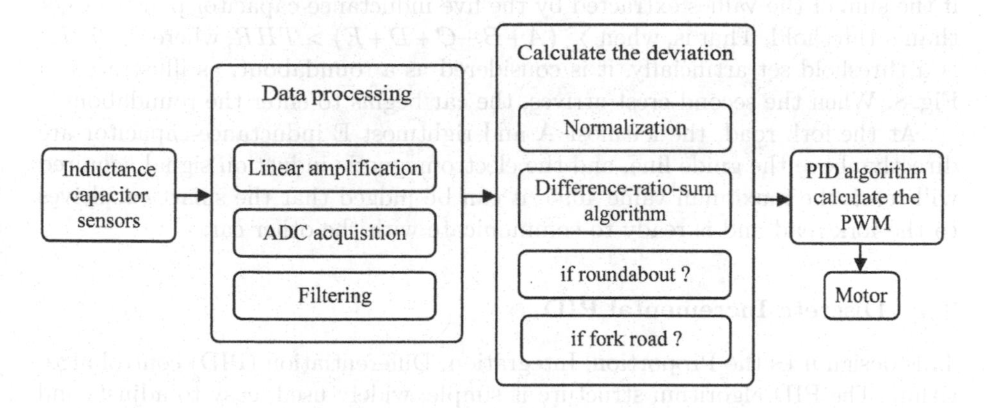

Fig. 7. The process of software design.

3.2 Normalization and Difference-Ratio-Sum Algorithm

Different tracks have different electromagnetic fields, the signal acquired by the inductance-capacitor pair sensor will also difference. In order to make the smart car adapt to different tracks, a normalization algorithm needs to be used. Firstly, acquire the maximum value of the inductance-capacitor pairs detected, the other values ratio to the maximum value, denoted as new values. Then the new values is multiplied by 4095, robustness of the algorithm will be better in that way.

If the values of the two symmetrically installed inductance-capacitor are ValueA and ValueE, the deviation calculated by the difference-ratio-sum algorithm is (ValueA-ValueE)/(ValueA+ValueE). The value of the deviation ranges from −1 to 1, and when multiplied by 4095, the value ranges from −4095 to 4095. According to the value and the positive situation of the deviation, the distance between the smart car and the center of the track can be quantitatively calculated.

The value calculated by the difference-ratio-sum algorithm do not vary with the fluctuation of the signal source, and the data is easy to use. Experiments demonstrate that it is possible to achieve a better implementation relying on electromagnetic sensors for basic tracking. As it is shown in Fig. 8, the A, B, C, D and E curves is the filtered value of five inductance-capacitor pairs senors.

3.3 Track Element Identification

Since the strength of the magnetic field at the roundabout is superimposed in the form of the vector, the strength of the magnetic field will become larger, and the value collected by the inductance will also be larger. The numerical variation of the five inductance-capacitor makes it easier to identify the roundabout. So, if the sum of the values extracted by the five inductance-capacitor pair is larger than a threshold. That is, when $\sum(A+B+C+D+E) > THR$, where the THR is a threshold set artificially, it is considered as a roundabout, as illustrated in Fig. 8. When the second crest arrives, the car begins to enter the roundabout.

At the fork road, the leftmost A and rightmost E inductance-capacitor are directly above the guide line, and the electromagnetic induction signal acquired will reach the maximum value 4095, it can be judged that the smart car drives to the fork road and is ready to communicate with the other car.

3.4 Discrete Incremental PID

This design uses the Proportion, Integration, Differentiation (PID) control algorithm. The PID algorithm structure is simple, widely used, easy to adjust, and with good stability. Since the microcontroller can only process the discrete digital signals, this design uses the discrete incremental PID. Below are the formulas of the discrete incremental PID [6].

$$\Delta u(k) = K_p[e(k) - e(k-1)] + K_i e(k) + K_d[e(k) - 2e(k-1) + e(k-2)] \quad (3)$$

where the K_p, K_i, K_d is proportion, integration, and differentiation coefficient respectively; $\Delta u(k)$ is the variation of the output; $e(k)$ is the error value between the target and the actual value this time; $e(k-1)$ is the error value between the target and the actual value last time, and $e(k-2)$ is the error value between the target and the actual value next-to-last time.

The leftmost and rightmost value of inductance-capacitor pairs are denoted as ValueA and ValueE, if the ValueA is larger than the ValueE, it means the car biases to the right. Then the deviation calculated by the difference-ratio-sum algorithm is positive, the output of the incremental PID control algorithm is also positive. So the right wheel runs faster than the left wheel, so as to drive the smart car to turn left, and vice versa. The PID control algorithm drives the smart car to always drive in the middle of the track. The impact of incremental PID is small when an error occurs, and the determination of the control increment is only related to the most recent k sample value, so it is easier to obtain better control effects by weighting.

4 Application of Wireless Communication Module

4.1 Bluetooth Module Communicate with the Upper Computer

When the smart car is dynamically debugged driving on the track, the data of the program running status and intermediate variables of the car should be monitored in real time, so as to detect the operation status of the car in order to improve the program. This design uses the HC-05 Bluetooth wireless transparent communication module to send the running status of the car, the distance between two cars and other information to the oscilloscope of the upper computer to observe the operation status of the program. The format of the communication protocol is { [0x03] [0xfc] [data] [0xfc] [0x03] }, so that a waveform transmission is completed. The waves of five inductance-capactior pairs is illustrated in Fig. 8, when these values skyrocket, it means the car come to the roundabout, and the program sets up a flag bit, as the light green curve illustrates.

When adjusting the parameters, uses the oscilloscope of the upper computer, outputs the PID intermediate variable waveform, according to the change range of the variable waveform as prior knowledge. And estimate the order of the magnitude and approximate range of the main amount of K_p, use this value as the starting point to adjust the parameters, and then increase K_i or K_d according to the performance requirements, which greatly reduces the time of parameter adjustment.

4.2 Communication Between the Two Smart Cars

In each edition of the annual smart car competition, communication between two smart cars is required to complete a specific task autonomously. Passing a ball and crossing each other are the tasks of the 16th smart car dual-cars competition, in this process, it cannot be directly contacted, and a wireless communication

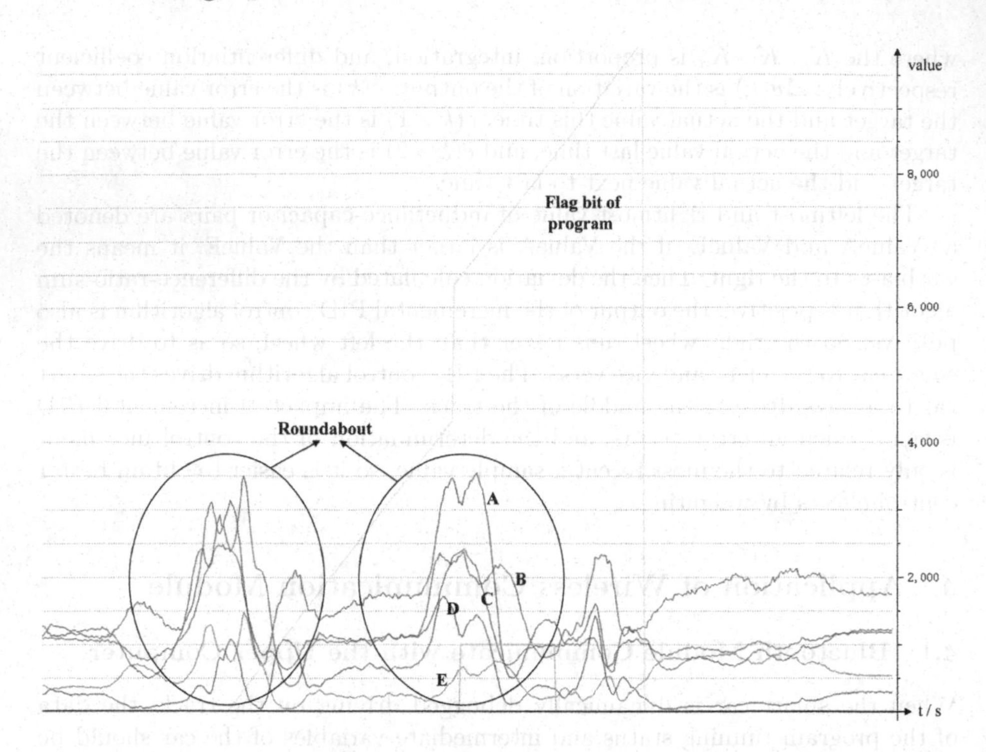

Fig. 8. Waves of virtual oscilloscope in the upper computer. Where the curves A, B, C, D, and E are the waves of five inductance-capacitor pairs, respectively. When two large crests are detected, it indicates that the car drives to the roundabout. The light green cure is the flag bit of the roundabout in the program. (Color figure online)

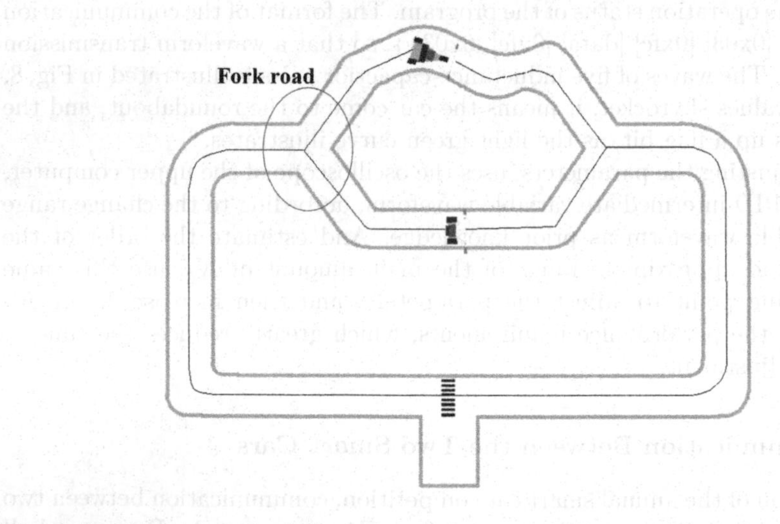

Fig. 9. Illustration of the fork road and the central black guideline. In the fork road, two cars handover a ball, and realize one car begins driving when the other car stops by wireless communciation.

module is required to complete the task of one car stopping and the other car starting to drive.

The receiving smart car is parked in the middle of the fork road, and the other ball delivery smart car takes the ping-pong ball from the starting line driving to the fork road, ready to pass the ball to the receiving car. When the ultrasonic sensor detects that the delivery car is within 40 cm away from the receiving car, the deceleration mark will be triggered, and the ball delivery car will slow down step by step, then the collision pass will be carried out.

The receiving car uses a infrared photoelectric switch module to detect whether the ball is successfully handed over. If the ball is successfully handed over, the receiving car immediately starts to drive forward, and the data [0x01] is sent every 10 ms through the NRF wireless communication module to the ball delivery car. If the rear ball delivery car receives the [0x01], the ball delivery car immediately stops to avoid the situation of crashing the receiving car out of the track, and sends seven answer data [0x02] continuously. As long as the receiving car receives a [0x02], the receiving car stop sending [0x01], and the communication ends.

When the receiving car runs around the track and drives to the fork road again, the data [0x60] is sent every 10 ms through the NRF wireless communication module to the ball delivery car. If the ball delivery car receives the data [0x60], the ball delivery car immediately begins to drive forward, and sends seven consecutive answer data [0x61] at the same time. Once the receiving car receives a [0x61], the receiving car stops sending [0x60], and the communication ends.

In the process of dual-cars communication, the data is repeated several times to prevent sensors and site interference and ensure the effectiveness of communication. After these multiple safeguard mechanisms, the success rate of the scheme used in this design to hand over the ball is more than 95.2%.

5 Conclusion

Taking the National College Students Smart Car Competition of China as the background, this paper designs a tracking smart car system with communication functions from the aspects of hardware design and software algorithms, and realizes a smart car with road information collection and analysis, automatic driving, and communication functions, which has good steady-state characteristics and fast dynamic response.

The actual test data is that the total length of the track is 68.6 m, and the two smart cars drive and relay for two laps, taking 57.1 s, and the average speed is about 2.4 m/s, which is faster than most smart cars in this competition. The test results demonstrate that the tracking algorithm, PID control algorithm and dual-cars communication scheme proposed in this design are stable and reliable, with low complexity, and can run on most 32-bit microcontrollers. This paper has a good reference for preparing for the National College Students Smart Car Competition, and has important theoretical significance and practical value in the field of automatic driving.

Acknowledgment. This work was co-supported by the Guangdong Basic and Applied Basic Research Foundation under Grants 2021A1515010768 and 2023A1515011588, by the Shenzhen Science and Technology Program under Grant 202206193000001, 20220815171723002, by the National Natural Science Foundation of China under Grants 62203465, 62001523, 62201614 and 6210593, by the Science and Technology on Near-Surface Detection Laboratory Pre-Research Foundation under Grant 6142414200607, and by the Fundamental Research Funds for the Central Universities, Sun Yat-sen University under Grant 23lgpy45.

References

1. Wu, Y., Li, S., Zhang, Q., et al.: Route planning and tracking control of an intelligent automatic unmanned transportation system based on dynamic nonlinear model predictive control. IEEE Trans. Intell. Transp. Syst. **23**(9), 16576–16589 (2022)
2. Zhuo, Q., Huang, K., Shao, B.: Learn to Design a Intelligent Vehicle: Challenge the Freescale Cup. Beihang University Press, Beijing (2007)
3. Zhu, J., Cao, H., Zhang, B., et al.: Multi-functional smart car based on wireless communication technology. In: 2020 IEEE International Conference on Mechatronics and Automation (ICMA), pp. 1275–1281. IEEE(2020)
4. Joshi, A., Gaonkar, P., Bapat, J.: A reliable and secure approach for efficient Car-to-Car communication in intelligent transportation systems. In: 2017 International Conference on Wireless Communications, Signal Processing and Networking (WiSPNET 2017), pp. 1617–1620, IEEE (2017)
5. Wang, C., Shen, Z., Tian, E., et al.: Multi-smart car control system design and research based on ZigBee. In: The 26th Chinese Control and Decision Conference (CCDC 2014), pp. 1490–1494. IEEE (2014)
6. Sudhapriya, K., Amudha, A., Divyapriya, S., et al.: Wireless vehicle control with speed adjustment. In: 2022 6th International Conference on Computing Methodologies and Communication (ICCMC 2022), pp. 583–588 (2022)

Optimal Wind Power Integration in Microgrid: A Dynamic Demand Response Game Approach

Fengchao Chen(✉), Xin Zhang, Zejian Qiu, and Junwei Zhao

Dongguan Power Supply Bureau, Guangdong Power Grid Corporation, Dongguan 523000, Guangdong, China
csgcfc@126.com

Abstract. The large-scale integration of renewables is very challenging due to their intermittency and fluctuations. With the growing interest in smart grids and smart metering systems, one promising option to tackle these challenges is to design demand-side management (DSM) algorithms. Such algorithms can shape the load to follow renewable energy generation, which is the focus of this paper. Based on field data, we model such intertemporal variations of the available wind power as a Markov chain. We formulate a dynamic potential game for efficient cost sharing among users to encourage user cooperation and participation in DSM programs to coordinate load with wind power generation. Further, we analyze the designed dynamic game over a long period and investigate the efficiency of the constructed game model at equilibrium. Then, we develop a *strategy proof* mechanism, which will reach a Nash equilibrium of the designed game. Simulation results show that, on average, the Nash equilibrium of the proposed game can reduce the generation cost by 25% compared to the case without demand side management. For the case of a windy day, the generation cost further reduces up to 91%.

Keywords: Smart Grid · Wind Power Integration · Demand Side Management · Markov Chain · Dynamic Game · Microgrid

1 Background

Renewable energy sources, particularly wind power, are becoming significant power generation technologies worldwide. However, wind power output's intermittency and inherent stochastic nature become the major bottleneck to reaching a considerable market penetration. One promising solution is to use fast-responding generators to compensate for the wind turbines' output fluctuations. Alternatively, we can implement advanced demand-side management (DSM) programs that adjust the controllable load to match the amount of available renewable power. We focus on the latter case. In an isolated microgrid, we want

This work was supported by the Science and Technology project of China Southern Power Grid Cooperation (No. GDKJXM20200475).

H. Yang et al. (Eds.): SmartGIFT 2022, LNICST 483, pp. 307–318, 2023.
https://doi.org/10.1007/978-3-031-31733-0_26

to study how to balance supply and demand efficiently [10] in the presence of wind power generation. An isolated microgrid comprises multiple local loads, local conventional generators, and local renewable generators. Therefore, understanding wind power integration in a microgrid can offer the first step toward large-scale penetration of renewable energy sources in a smart grid.

Integrating wind power into smart grid is already a well investigated topic. Cui *et al.* investigate forecast competition in energy imbalance market, taking the uncertainty of wind power into consideration in [4]. Furthermore, Cui *et al.* design the architecture of energy imbalance market with wind power in the form of blockchain in [3]. Gu *et al.* study deployment of power electronic devices into the distribution network, which can incentivize the distributed wind power integration in [9]. Wu *et al.* explore storage control with uncertainties of wind power generation in the framework of deep learning in [19]. Lu *et al.* conduct efficient economic dispatch via accurate wind power forecasting in the framework of end-to-end learning in [12]. Different from the previous work, our focus here is on applying game theory [8] to design a *decentralized* demand side management system, where users in a microgrid are independent decision makers and are interested in managing its own load to minimize its own energy expenses. A decentralized approach assures that users participate in the integration of renewable energy sources *voluntarily.*

Demand side management problem and demand response have also been explored by many researchers. Broadly speaking, demand side will adjust its load flexibly to obtain more benefits, such as [2,13]. Also, the vulnerability and robustness of demand side is also a significant problem, such as [5,6,11] and so on. Unlike the existing works, we address the demand side management design problem with focus on characterizing the interactions among users rather than generations. Furthermore, in this work, we apply dynamic game models which allows us to consider the decision dependencies over multiple periods of time. We feel that such consideration is critical for the integration of renewable energy resource, mainly due to the intermittency and inter-temporal variations such resource such as wind power.

2 System Model

A microgrid usually consists of local generators such as small-scale combined heat and power equipments, along with photovoltaic modules, small wind turbines, other renewable energy sources, heat and electricity storages, and controllable loads. Microgrids are expected to play a significant role in future electricity supply [10]. Our focus in this paper is on a simplified isolated microgrid, where a set of $\mathcal{N} = \{1, \ldots, N\}$ users. These users are supported by two kinds of generating resources. The first one is a conventional fast-responding generator, such as a gas turbines or a coal fired generator, whereas the other one is a wind turbine.

We design the demand side management problem for a period of time. And we divide the time period of interest into H time slots, *i.e.*, $\mathcal{H} = [1, \ldots, H]$. For example, we may choose $H = 24$ for daily planning. Other granularity, *e.g.*, 15 min time slots, may also be considered if needed.

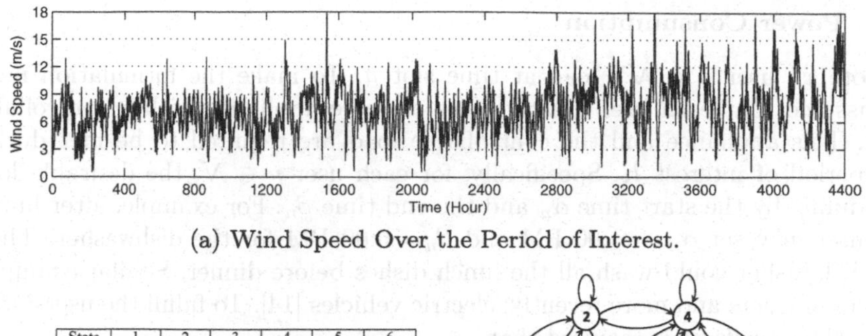

(a) Wind Speed Over the Period of Interest.

State	1	2	3	4	5	6
1	0.60	0.38	0.02	0.00	0.00	0.00
2	0.06	0.74	0.20	0.01	0.00	0.00
3	0.00	0.13	0.76	0.11	0.00	0.00
4	0.00	0.01	0.25	0.68	0.06	0.00
5	0.00	0.00	0.02	0.28	0.66	0.05
6	0.00	0.00	0.00	0.09	0.31	0.60

(b) Markov Transition Matrix. (c) Markov Chain State Model.

Fig. 1. The Markov chain model used in this study. The data are collected from [1].

2.1 Power Generation

The *total* generated power at each time slot $h \in \mathcal{H}$ includes the power generated by the conventional fast-responding fuel generator, denoted as v^h, and the power generated by the wind turbine, denoted as w^h. Note that the conventional power is used to supplement the gap between available wind power and users' total power demand.

We first characterize the wind power outputs. We assume the wind power outputs follow a stochastic process according to the wind speed. Specifically, we consider a simplified model where once the wind speed is given, the wind power output can be obtained according to the wind power versus wind speed curve. Figure 1(a) plots a sample measurement of the wind speed to highlight the volatility.

We employ the Markov chain to enable wind power output prediction. Based on field data, we identify six states. The first state is the case where the wind turbine output is between 0 and 30 kW. The other five states can be defined accordingly. We obtain the Markov chain transition probabilities as shown in Fig. 1(b) based on the collected data. We can observe that the transition probability matrix is, in fact, very sparse. That is, with a very high probability, the Markov chain will either stay at the current state or jump to an adjacent state, as illustrated in Fig. 1(c). The transition probability matrix enables the wind power output prediction at upcoming time slots. This is crucial for demand-side management as well as its associated decision-making. To the best of our knowledge, this is the first paper that integrates an explicit Markov chain model based on actual data for wind power in demand-side management.

2.2 Power Consumption

Denote x_n^h user $n \in \mathcal{N}$'s load at time slot h. To make the formulation neat, we assume that each user exactly owns a single appliance with a controllable load. This appliance and the controllable load are required to be met during the period of interest $\mathcal{H}$. Specifically, for each user $n \in \mathcal{N}$, the desirable load scheduling by the start time α_n and the end time β_n. For example, after lunch, the user may set α_n = 1:00 PM and β_n= 5:00 PM for the dishwasher. Thus, the dishwasher could wash all the lunch dishes before dinner. Similar examples include washers and more recently, electric vehicles [14]. To fulfill the users' load scheduling needs, it is required that

$$\sum\nolimits_{h=\alpha_n}^{\beta_n} x_n^h = E_n, \quad \forall n \in \mathcal{N}, \tag{1}$$

where E_n stands for the total energy consumption, which user n's appliance needs to consume for finishing the task. The energy profile x_n^h outside the time frame $[\alpha_n, \beta_n]$ should be zero. That is,

$$\begin{cases} x_n^h \geq 0, & \alpha_n \leq h \leq \beta_n, \\ x_n^h = 0, & \text{otherwise}, \end{cases} \quad \forall n \in \mathcal{N}. \tag{2}$$

Let $\boldsymbol{x}_n$ denote user n's energy consumption profile vector:

$$\boldsymbol{x}_n = [x_n^1, \cdots, x_n^H]. \tag{3}$$

User n's energy consumption feasible set can be characterized as follows:

$$\mathcal{X}_n = \left\{ \boldsymbol{x}_n \middle| \text{Constraints (1) and (2)} \right\}. \tag{4}$$

Finally, at each time slot h, the total load in the system summing over all users is denoted by

$$l^h = \sum\nolimits_{n \in \mathcal{N}} x_n^h. \tag{5}$$

2.3 Generation Cost

If the supply matches the demand in real-time, then clearly, it is not necessary to use the conventional backup generator. Otherwise, the microgrid operator must use the traditional generator to compensate for the supply-demand mismatch, which is primarily caused by the inaccurate forecast of renewable generation outputs. At each time slot h, the total conventional power needed can be calculated as follows $v^h = l^h - w^h$. Without loss of generality, we assume that the traditional generator available in the microgrid is a thermal generator. Thus, at each time slot h, we can model the power generation cost as a quadratic function [18]:

$$C(l^h - w^h) = k\,(l^h - w^h)^2 + s, \tag{6}$$

where the generation and maintenance cost of the wind power plant is assumed to be fixed and represented by the constant $s > 0$, as a *sunk cost*. That is, such a cost is independent of the exact value of wind power output [17]. Hence, as for demand side management, the model in (6) characterizes the total generation cost of the microgrid at time slot h to supply the total load l^h. From (6), we can observe that the microgrid operator will penalize any deviation (no matter whether the deviation is positive or negative) of load l^h from renewable energy supply w^h. For the case when $l^h < w^h$, the penalty comes from the fact that the *excessive* generated power challenges the power quality in the microgrid by deviating the voltage amplitude and frequency from their nominal values [16]. Therefore, the microgrid operator seeks to keep the total load at each time slot *as close as* possible to the total wind power outputs.

2.4 Centralized DSM Planning

Suppose we are allowed to adopt a centralized control. In that case, the microgrid coordinator can directly select $\boldsymbol{x} = (\boldsymbol{x}_n, \ \forall n \in \mathcal{N})$ and schedule the controllable load such that the load are kept as close as possible to the *expected* wind power outputs. Specifically, in a centralized design approach, we seek to solve the minimization problem as follows:

$$\begin{aligned} \mathbf{P1}: \ & \underset{\boldsymbol{x}_n, \ \forall n \in \mathcal{N}}{\textbf{minimize}} \ \mathbb{E}\left\{\sum\nolimits_{t=1}^{H}\left[k\left(l^t - w^t\right)^2 + s\right]\right\} \\ & \textbf{subject to} \ \ \boldsymbol{x}_n \in \mathcal{X}_n, \qquad \forall n \in \mathcal{N}. \end{aligned} \tag{7}$$

Note that problem **P1** is a static optimization problem. Next, we introduce its dynamic version where the centralized controller will decide each user's load profile time slot by time slot. For notational simplicity, we denote all the users' load profile from time slot l to time slot m as $\mathcal{U}_{t=l}^{m}$, that is

$$\mathcal{U}_{t=l}^{m} = \{x_n^t, \ \forall n \in \mathcal{N}\}_{t=l}^{m}. \tag{8}$$

Thus, mathematically, at time slot h, given all the users' load profile history, *i.e.*, $\mathcal{U}_{t=1}^{h-1}$ and the wind power history $\{w^t\}_{t=1}^{h-1}$, the controller tries to solve the following problem **P2**(h):

$$\begin{aligned} \mathbf{P1}(\mathrm{h}): \ & \underset{\mathcal{U}_{t=h}^{H}}{\textbf{minimize}} \ \mathbb{E}\left\{\sum\nolimits_{t=h}^{H}\left[k\left(l^h - w^h\right)^2 + s\right]\middle| w^{h-1}\right\} \\ & \textbf{subject to} \ \ \mathcal{U}_{t=h}^{H} \in \mathcal{X}^h, \end{aligned} \tag{9}$$

where $\mathcal{X}^h$ is the refined feasible solution set for $\mathcal{U}_{t=h}^{H}$. It can be obtained by the following two steps:

- For each $\mathcal{X}_n$, if $h \leq \alpha_n$, construct $\mathcal{X}_n^h = \mathcal{X}_n$. Otherwise, given user n's load profile history $\{x_n^t\}_{t=1}^{h-1} \in \mathcal{U}_{t=1}^{h-1}$, we could change constraint (1) to

$$\sum\nolimits_{t=h}^{\beta_n} x_n^t = E_n - \sum\nolimits_{t=\alpha_n}^{h-1} x_n^t. \tag{10}$$

Note in (10), $\{x_n^t\}_{t=\alpha_n}^{h-1}$ can be considered as the known constants. Hence, the only variables in (10) are the decision variables $\{x_n^t\}_{t=h}^{H} \in \mathcal{U}_{t=h}^{H}$. Together with constraint (2), we construct $\mathcal{X}_n^h$. That is

$$\mathcal{X}_n^h = \begin{cases} \mathcal{X}_n, & h \leq \alpha_n, \\ \{\{x_n^t\}_{t=h}^{H} | \text{Constraints (2) and (10)}\}, & \text{otherwise.} \end{cases} \tag{11}$$

- Construct

$$\mathcal{X}^h = \bigcup_{n \in \mathcal{N}} \mathcal{X}_n^h. \tag{12}$$

Both problem **P1** and problem **P2**(h) can be solved in a centralized fashion using various optimization methods [7]. However, in practice, users are independent decision makers and their behavior is not directly controlled by a centralized controller. Therefore, next, we propose an alternative approach that can lead to a distributed yet efficient solution to integrate renewable energy sources using dynamic game theory.

3 Cost-Sharing Game

In this section, we design a *decentralized* mechanism for efficient cost sharing. In the mechanism, we assume that each user, on his own, decides his energy consumption schedule at the beginning of each time slot. Specifically, each user decides to maximize its payoff based on the forecasts of wind power generation outputs based on the developed Markov chain. We want to emphasize that such decision-making is also coupled with other users' decisions. To share the total generation cost among all users in the microgrid, we define, at each time slot h, each user n's payoff function $f_n^h(\boldsymbol{x}_n, \boldsymbol{x}_{-n})$ as proportional to its total energy consumption over time interval $\mathcal{H}$:

$$f_n^h(x_n^h, x_{-n}^h) = \frac{-E_n}{\sum_{m \in \mathcal{N}} E_m} \mathbb{E}\left\{k(l^h - w^h)^2 + s\right\}, \tag{13}$$

where x_{-n}^h indicates the energy consumption scheduling profiles for all users *other than* user n at time slot h. We can see that each user's payoff function depends on not only the user's own load profile, but also other users' load profiles. This leads to a dynamic game model among users. In this paper, we consider a game with complete information, that is, at each time slot h, all the users have access to the wind power generation history, *i.e.*, $\{w^t\}_{t=1}^{h-1}$ and all the users' load profile history, *i.e.*, $\mathcal{U}_{t=1}^{h-1}$. Based on such information, the users can try to maximize their *expected* payoff during the rest of the game with the help of the Markov chain model. This yields our cost sharing game for microgrid (CSGM).

The solution concept for a dynamic game is the subgame perfect equilibrium.

3.1 Potential Game

For each subgame of *CSGM* at time slot $h \in \mathcal{H}$, we can verify that

$$\Phi(l^h, \ldots, l^H | w^{h-1}) = -\sum_{t=h}^{H} \mathbb{E}\left\{k\left(l^h - v^h\right)^2 + s | w^{t-1}\right\}$$

is in fact an ordinal potential function for *CSGM*. A game with an ordinal potential function is called an ordinal potential game (OPG). Thus, each subgame of *CSGM* at time slot $h \in \mathcal{H}$ is a finite-player OPG with several interesting properties that we will explain next.

3.2 Nash Equilibria Characterization of Subgames

For a finite-player OPG, a strategy profile is a Nash equilibrium *if and only if* it is a maximizer of the ordinal potential functions [15]. From this, together with (14), we can directly derive the following theorem.

Theorem 1. *At each time slot $h \in \mathcal{H}$, given the history profiles $\mathcal{U}_{t=1}^{h-1}$ and $\{w^t\}_{t=1}^{h-1}$, a strategy profile $\mathcal{U}_{t=h}^{H}$ is a Nash equilibrium of the subgame of* CSGM *at time slot h* if and only if *it is a maximizer to the optimization problem **P2**(h).*

However, since for a potential game, only the total load at each time slot h, *i.e.*, l^h matters, we reformulate the optimization problem $\mathbf{P2}$(h) with the constraints only depend on the total load $\{l^t\}_{t=h}^{H}$. By such replacement, we want to obtain a clearer insight of the game. First, at each time slot t, we define

$$\mathcal{N}_{\alpha}^{t} = \{\text{user } n | \alpha_n \leq t\}; \tag{14}$$

$$\mathcal{N}_{\beta}^{t} = \{\text{user } n | \beta_n \leq t\}. \tag{15}$$

Lemma 1. *At time slot $h \in \mathcal{H}$, given the history profiles $\mathcal{U}_{t=1}^{h}$, for any $\mathcal{U}_{t=h}^{H} \in \mathcal{X}^h$,* i.e., *any feasible solution for problem **P2**(h), there exists an $\boldsymbol{l}^h = (l^h, \ldots, l^H)$ that satisfies the following set of constraints:*

$$\sum_{n \in \mathcal{N}_{\beta}^{p}} E_n \leq \sum_{t=1}^{h} l^t + \sum_{t=h}^{p} l^t \leq \sum_{n \in \mathcal{N}_{\alpha}^{p}} E_n, \; h \leq p \leq H. \tag{16}$$

$$l^p \geq 0, \, h \leq p \leq H. \tag{17}$$

Note that, in Lemma 1, there could exist several different combinations of users' individual energy consumption schedules $\boldsymbol{x}$ that can lead to the same total load $\boldsymbol{l}$. We are now ready to characterize the subgame perfect equilibria (SPE) of *CSGM* in the following key theorem.

3.3 Subgame Perfect Equilibrium of CSGM

Theorem 2. *The total load profile* $\boldsymbol{l}^* = (l^{1*}, \ldots, l^{H*})$ *corresponding to any SPE* $\mathcal{U}^{*H}_{t=1}$ *of* CSGM*is the unique maximizer to the following sequence of optimization problem* ***P3(h)***:

$$\begin{aligned} \textbf{\textit{P3(h)}}: \ \underset{l^t,\ h \le t \le H}{\textbf{\textit{maximize}}} \quad & -\mathbb{E}\left\{\sum_{t=h}^{H}\left[k\left(l^t - w^t\right)^2 + s\right]\middle| w^{h-1}\right\} \\ \textbf{\textit{subject to}} \quad & \sum_{n \in \mathcal{N}_\beta^p} E_n \le \sum_{t=1}^{p} l^t \le \sum_{n \in \mathcal{N}_\alpha^p} E_n, h \le p \le H, \quad (18) \\ & l^p \ge 0,\ h \le p \le H. \quad (19) \end{aligned}$$

That is, each l^{h*} *in* $\boldsymbol{L}^*$ *is determined by the corresponding optimization problem* ***P3(h)***.

Note that problem **P3**(h) has to be solved time slot by time slot, since the wind power prediction will be updated at each time slot.

We conclude the section with the following remarks. First, we note that Theorems 2 provide an analytical approach to characterize the SPE of *CSGM*. Second, if *perfect predictions* are available on future wind power generation, then by solving problem **P1**, we can obtain the SPE for *CSGM* directly. However, since the wind power predictions are updated based on the new wind power measurements, *i.e.*, wind power generation history profile, as the game moves from one time slot to the next one, at each time slot $h \in \mathcal{H}$, the users may use and implement the SPE solution obtained by problem **P3**(h) only at the current time slot h. As time goes by, the SPE will be updated according to the new wind power measurements and predictions. Finally, we note that any $\boldsymbol{l}^*$ obtained from Theorems 2 characterizes the SPE in terms of the *total* load. However, there could exist several different combinations of users' *individual* energy consumption schedules $\boldsymbol{x}^*$ that can lead to the same aggregate load $\boldsymbol{l}^*$. Therefore, we also need to investigate individual load distributions at each equilibrium. This is what we will do next using mechanism design.

4 Mechanism Design

In this section, we design a mechanism to reach one SPE of *CSGM*. Our focus is to obtain the exact energy consumption schedule for each individual user. Note that, although *CSGM* may have multiple SPE, they are the same in terms of maximizing the potential function and hence minimizing the total generation cost in the system. Therefore, as long as all users choose their energy consumption schedules according to one of the SPE obtained in Sect. 3.2, optimal performance is guaranteed. However, the difficulty is to assure that users announce their local information truthfully. This can be tackled by developing mechanism design as we discuss next.

In order to reach the SPE of *CSGM* in a distributed fashion, it is required for each user $n \in \mathcal{N}$ to broadcast its own total energy consumption E_n, start time α_n and the end time β_n at the beginning such that all other users can also adjust their energy consumption schedules accordingly later on. Moreover, at each time slot h, the wind turbine needs to broadcast the upcoming expected wind power based on the new measure data w^{h-1}, *i.e.*, $\mathbb{E}\{w^h|w^{h-1}\}, \ldots, \mathbb{E}\{w^H|w^{h-1}\}$. The proposed DSM mechanism includes the following stages.

1. Each user n broadcasts E_n, α_n and β_n at time slot 1.
2. At each time slot h,
   - The wind turbine broadcasts the upcoming wind power to all the users.
   - Each user constructs $\mathcal{N}_h$ as the set of active users n whose $\alpha_n \leq h$ and $\beta_n \geq h$. That is,
   $$\mathcal{N}_h = \{\text{user } n | \alpha_n \leq h \leq \beta_n\}. \tag{20}$$
   - Each user computes the desirable total load at the Nash equilibrium, denoted by l_0^h, by solving **P3**(h).
   - Each user sorts the members in set $\mathcal{N}_h$ based on their end times β_n in an ascending order. Starting from the first with smallest finishing time, for the kth user in the sorted list, denoted by n_k, we also denote the available total energy consumption at the decision time slot is l_{k-1}^h. Then, set
   $$x_{n_k}^h = \max\left\{0, \min\left\{E_{n_k} - \sum_{t=1}^{h-1} x_{n_k}^t, l_{k-1}^h\right\}\right\}, \tag{21}$$
   - Update the available total energy consumption l_{k-1}^h to l_k^h according to the following equation:
   $$l_k^h = l_{k-1}^h - x_{n_k}^h. \tag{22}$$
   - Continue the process for the $k+1^{th}$ user in the sorted list until $l_k^h = 0$.
   - Each user n consumes x_n^h amount of power.

Note that, the second stage us implemented at each time slot h, *e.g.*, at every hour. At each time slot h, after the wind turbine broadcasts the upcoming wind power, each user computes its own load profile locally. They need keep a history of the previous computation results, *i.e.*, $\mathcal{U}_{t=1}^{h-1}$ to ensure the adequate information for the local computation in time slot h.

Next, we prove the optimality of this mechanism by showing that it achieves one SPE of *CSGM*. By Theorem 2, we can obtain the optimality of this mechanism in terms of minimizing the total energy cost in the system.

Theorem 3. *The designed mechanism will reach one SPE of* CSGM.

In our mechanism, we assume that based on the actual operating cost of the wind generator and conventional generator, the shared cost of each user will be collected at the end of the day. Then, we have the following theorem:

Theorem 4. *The designed mechanism is strategy proof.*

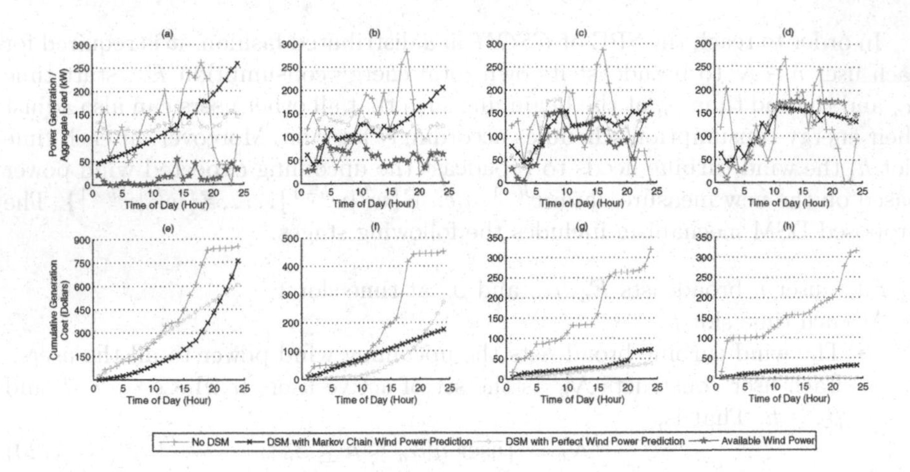

Fig. 2. Empirical results to highlight the performance of the proposed demand side management scheme. Subfigures (a)–(d) examine the performance under four weather conditions: (a) light/gentle breeze, (b) moderate/fresh breeze, (c) strong wind, and (d) (moderate) gale. Subfigures (e)–(h) investigates the corresponding cumulative power generation cost for these 4 weather conditions, respectively.

Proof. Notice that in our designed game, all the SPE coincide with the maximizer of the potential function. Based on Theorem 3, the designed mechanism will lead to one SPE of *CSGM*. Therefore, any cheating will only deviate the aggregated strategy profile from SPE and cannot lead to a better payoff for any user. In particular, the shared cost for each user is based on the actual energy one consumes during the day, instead of the amount of energy each user announces in the mechanism. ■

We note that Theorem 4 is *not* a general conclusion for every OPG, as in general, the players' payoff functions may not always coincide with the OPG's potential function.

5 Simulation Results

The numerical study considers a one-day energy consumption scheduling in a microgrid with $N = 1,000$ users. For each user, the daily load is selected randomly between 1 kWh to 5 kWh. We evaluate the performance of our proposed algorithm in terms of generation cost under different weather conditions. Specifically, we compare three approaches. First, we consider the case without any demand-side management. In this case, each user n arbitrarily schedules its energy consumption within interval $[\alpha_n, \beta_n]$. We implement our proposed distributed dynamic game-theoretic algorithm in the second case based on the Markov Chain model developed in Sect. 2.1. Third, we employ the same approach as in the second case except assuming we now have access to the perfect wind power prediction. Note that this last case is a very good benchmark. This benchmark provides an upper bound for the overall system performance.

We consider the following weather conditions: light/gentle breeze (wind speed less than 6 m/s), moderate/fresh breeze (wind speed between 6 m/s and 10.6 m/s), strong wind (wind speed between 10.7 m/s and 13.6 m/s), and (moderate) gale (wind speed between 13.7 m/s and 20.6 m/s). The results for these conditions in terms of the aggregate load schedule are shown in Fig. 2(a)–(d), respectively. The corresponding cumulative power generation costs for four considered weather conditions are illustrated in Fig. 2(e)–(h), respectively. For the case of a light breeze, our proposed algorithm reduces the total daily generation cost by 11% at the equilibrium compared with the case when no demand side management program is implemented. Improving the wind power prediction can further reduce the total power generation cost up to 17%. For the case of a moderate breeze, our algorithm reduces the generation cost by 40% at the equilibrium. One can further reduce the cost by 21% by improving the prediction accuracy. For the case of a strong wind, the saving in the generation cost is 77%. Finally, for the case of a moderate gale, our proposed algorithm works very well and can save up to 91% in the cost of generation at the equilibrium of *CSGM* compared with the scenario where no demand side management strategy is used. From the simulation results in Figs. 2, we can conclude the following remarks:

- The proportion of the reduced generation cost increases as the available wind power increases. This is intuitive and verifies the suitability of our design.
- Comparing the results when our design uses Markov Chain-based wind power prediction versus perfect wind power prediction, we can see that the curves converge when high wind power is available. This suggests that our proposed algorithm is particularly efficient in places such as West Texas, where wind speed is high in several days every year. Based on the six-month field data in West Texas, our simulation results show that on average, our algorithm can reduce the generation cost by 25%. By deploying more accurate wind power prediction models, one can further reduce the generation cost by 18%.

6 Concluding Remarks

This paper considers an isolated microgrid. The microgrid consists of N users, and these users obtain energy from two sources: a renewable power generator and a backup conventional power plant. We review a dynamic scenario of users' interactions in which these N users share the total energy cost. Note that such a cost is due to the use of the traditional power plant to balance supply and demand. This approach can effectively minimize the total generation cost. Furthermore, we assess its performance via simulation.

References

1. Alternative Energy Institute, West Texas A&M University. https://www.windenergy.org/

2. Cui, J., Wu, C.: On the consumer behavior management in tier price. In: 2021 IEEE Power & Energy Society Innovative Smart Grid Technologies Conference (ISGT), p. 1. IEEE (2021)
3. Cui, J., Gu, N., Wu, C.: Blockchain enabled data transmission for energy imbalance market. IEEE Trans. Sustain. Energy **13**(2), 1254–1266 (2022). https://doi.org/10.1109/TSTE.2021.3108170
4. Cui, J., Gu, N., Zhao, T., Wu, C., Chen, M.: Forecast competition in energy imbalance market. IEEE Trans. Power Syst. **37**(3), 2397–2413 (2022). https://doi.org/10.1109/TPWRS.2021.3117967
5. Cui, J., Wang, H., Wu, C., Yu, Y.: Vulnerability analysis for data driven pricing schemes. In: 2020 IEEE Power Energy Society General Meeting (PESGM), pp. 1–5 (2020). https://doi.org/10.1109/PESGM41954.2020.9281848
6. Cui, J., Wang, H., Wu, C., Yu, Y.: Robust data-driven profile-based pricing schemes. In: 2021 IEEE Power & Energy Society Innovative Smart Grid Technologies Conference (ISGT), pp. 1–5. IEEE (2021)
7. Filar, J., Vrieze, K.: Competitive Markov Decision Processes. Springer, Heidelberg (1997). https://doi.org/10.1007/978-1-4612-4054-9
8. Fudenberg, D., Tirole, J.: Game Theory. MIT Press, Cambridge (1991)
9. Gu, N., Cui, J., Wu, C.: Power-electronics-enabled transactive energy market design for distribution networks. IEEE Trans. Smart Grid 1 (2021). https://doi.org/10.1109/TSG.2021.3127544
10. Hatziargyriou, N., Asano, H., Iravani, R., Marnay, C.: Microgrids. IEEE Power Energ. Mag. **5**(4), 78–94 (2007)
11. Jiang, G., Cui, J., Wu, C.: Role of prediction in data-driven pricing schemes. In: 2021 5th International Conference on Smart Grid and Smart Cities (ICSGSC), pp. 125–129 (2021). https://doi.org/10.1109/ICSGSC52434.2021.9490484
12. Lu, C., Jiang, W., Wu, C.: Effective end-to-end learning framework for economic dispatch. IEEE Trans. Netw. Sci. Eng. 1 (2022). https://doi.org/10.1109/TNSE.2022.3168845
13. Lu, C., Wang, Z., Wu, C.: Storage-aided service surcharge design for EV charging stations. In: 2021 60th IEEE Conference on Decision and Control (CDC), pp. 5653–5658 (2021). https://doi.org/10.1109/CDC45484.2021.9683047
14. Mohsenian-Rad, A.H., Leon-Garcia, A.: Optimal residential load control with price prediction in real-time electricity pricing environments. IEEE Trans. Smart Grid **1**(2), 120–133 (2010). https://doi.org/10.1109/TSG.2010.2055903
15. Monderer, D., Shapley, L.S.: Potential games. Games Econom. Behav. **14**(1), 124–143 (1996). https://doi.org/10.1006/game.1996.0044
16. Rebours, Y.G., Kirschen, D.S., Trotignon, M., Rossignol, S.: A survey of frequency and voltage control ancillary services mdash; part I: technical features. IEEE Trans. Power Syst. **22**(1), 350–357 (2007). https://doi.org/10.1109/TPWRS.2006.888963
17. van de Wekken, T.: Distributed generation and renewables: wind farm case study. Power Quality and Utilisation Guide (2007)
18. Wood, A.J., Wollenberg, B.F.: Power Generation, Operation, and Control. Wiley-Interscience (1996)
19. Wu, J., Lu, C., Wu, C.: Learning-aided framework for storage control facing renewable energy. IEEE Syst. J. 1–12 (2022). https://doi.org/10.1109/JSYST.2022.3154389

Residential Energy Consumption Prediction Based on Encoder-Decoder LSTM

Junni Su, Lide Zhou, Fengchao Chen(✉), and Zejian Qiu

Dongguan Power Supply Bureau, Guangdong Power Grid Corporation,
Dongguan 523000, Guangdong, China
csgcfc@126.com

Abstract. Accurate forecast of load profile is of great benefit to electricity dispatch and power grid management. Recently, the widespread of smart meters enable the power system to collect fine-grained data from massive users. Also, the development of deep learning techniques allow the load forecasting to have better performance. However, the hyperparameter tuning in neural networks is a laborious but ineluctable part to achieve higher accuracy. Combing with huge information concealed in the fine-grained data, data mining is a significant process to accelerate hyperparameter tuning. In this paper, we first explore the metadata to help filter the data, compare the performances with different input and output by varying granularities, and evaluate predictability on various aggregation levels. Numerical studies suggest that on filtered data, accuracy has a higher correlations with predictability, and granularity of 1 h is the most appropriate.

Keywords: Load Forecast · LSTM · encoder-decoder

1 Introduction

The deployment of smart meters and other intelligent terminals enables the frequent interactions between power companies and customers. Collecting and analyzing the load profile from user ends facilitate the load monitoring [16], appliance control [17], power grid management [11], and electricity price [22]. As a time series dataset, load profiles mainly refer to the users' electricity demand over time. And intuitively, choosing short-term forecasting generally has less training time and have quick adaptability. However, the procedure of increasing forecasting accuracy should follow the framework of data mining and include data preprocessing, feature selection, model selection and evaluation. Therefore, data libraries and supporting dataset (metadata) are recommended to help clean the main dataset. But in recent years, deep learning techniques such as recurrent neural network (RNN) are widely applied to tackle time series forecast problems instead of traditional times series models such as ARIMA model.

This work was supported in part by the science and technology study of China Southern Power Grid Cooperation (No. GDKJXM20200475).

H. Yang et al. (Eds.): SmartGIFT 2022, LNICST 483, pp. 319–330, 2023.
https://doi.org/10.1007/978-3-031-31733-0_27

1.1 Related Work

Short term load forecast is a challenging task due to the data uncertainty [14] and nonsmooth and nonlinear behaviors in load profiles [1]. Ding *et al.* [4] has shown that neural network based predictions outperforms time series models and the model design affects the generality abilities. Aowabin Rahman *et al.* [10] has demonstrated that RNN model has a high performance on forecasting tasks but fine tuning issues cannot be avoiding when training the model. In deep learning theory, we can generally increase the width to make the loss landscape smooth [8,13] and the depth to strengthen the representation power [2]. This insight is feasible in RNN model and deeper RNN model like including encoder-decoder framework is able to improve the performance [3]. Evaluation steps previously focus on measuring the distance between target and predictions. Instead, the evaluation of the input are generally ignored. Hence, predictability is adopted to help answer the question "when the input is most predictable" [18].

1.2 Our Research Contribution

In this report, we conduct the demand forecasting on Pecan Street Dataset. The principal contributions are:

- *Understanding the Dataset*: Any dataset must have an underlying background. By analyzing the metadata and weather data in Sect. 2, we filter the whole data into a certain group with same location and same building type as well as focus on a certain period of time without large weather changes.
- *Model Selection*: Instead of applying LSTM model directly, we discuss the effect of the input and output length on the prediction accuracy evaluated by MAPE and MPE. Also, we introduce encoder-decoder LSTM framework to increase the representation power and capacity of the neural network.
- *Predictability and Prediction Performance*: We define the predictability of a time series using the entropy of time and load level. After examining the predictability of different granularity and aggregation level, we find that small aggregation level has a positive effect on predicting the time series.

1.3 Paper Organization

The remainder of the paper is organized as follows. Section 2 presents the data overview and explores the metadata to filter users in the main dataset. Section 3 introduces the encoder-decoder LSTM framework and predictability definition. Section 4 presents the experiments design and corresponding results. Section 5 concludes and discuss future directions.

2 Understanding the Dataset

Pecan Street Dataport [12] is the world's largest residential energy and water research database. Data is organized into schemas by type of data (electricity, water, gas, static data) rather than by geographic location. Residential data is available as Time-series datasets (1-second energy, 1-minute energy, ISO data, water data, and natural gas data). Non-time series datasets (audits, surveys, and others) are available through Direct Database Access. Each home is linked to a unique Data ID.

To ensure the dataset is valuable and applicable, it is necessary to consider the background of dataset and explore the topic we want. Ideally, each user tend to be independent with others when the source is unique. But External factors such as the weather and economic currents inevitably influence users' behaviors. Hence, the data mining methods have to be time efficient and compatible with feature correlations.

2.1 Dataset Overview

Provided Pecan Street Dataset has three columns - "localminute", "Dataid" and "use". The "localminute" ranges from Jan 01, 2016 to Feb 22, 2016 recorded at 1 min level. In total, we have 339 unique data ID. After examining the missing value of each user, we found that data of user "1718", "2510", "3719", "7017", "7731" is not complete from its beginning time to its end time. Moreover, the "use" column represents the load of a certain user at 1 min level. Clearly, the type of data is a time series and the straightforward prediction on this series can be easily achieved by deep learning models. But the challenge is to seek for strategic or practical meanings of this dataset. What feasible direction can be discussed and utilized in companies?

2.2 Exploring the Metadata

For "localminute", the time can represent the local weather or even economic and political environments. Compared to the weather data, the latter one is hard to be quantified and likely to increase the model complexity tremendously if included. For now, we only consider the weather data in Austin (provided by [5]) and start from a short term forecasting to control the weather in a uniform level.

For "dataid", the identity of a user includes the information of location and the type, total area, construction year of user's building. Among all 339 users, we follow the rule of selecting the majority to reduce the variance. After examining the distribution and correlation of selected variables, we found that the relationship between them are not straight to be discovered. Therefore, we only select users from Austin with building type "Single-Family Home 001 (Master)".

In contrast to the data downloaded from the website, the "use" column is clearly an artificially modified feature. Except "localminute" and "Dataid", the raw dataset has 77 features. Searching through the metadata description, we found that the use column is close to the "grid" column, which presents measuring power drawn from or fed to the electrical grid. Though metadata provides the information about a large set of appliance that appears in users' houses, the sum of all appliance in table is not equal to the "grid" value. In other words, not all appliances in each user's home is monitored or recorded. Hence, only the "grid" column, the total amount of data can be valuable to this project. Due to incompleteness of appliance information, we cannot decompose it into the sum of all appliances in the home.

In fact, the information in the metadata is much more than what we mentioned before. For example, we may be interested in exploring whether the house total area and house construction year may have an effect on the load. However, Fig. 1 and 2 suggested that the correlation is unclear.

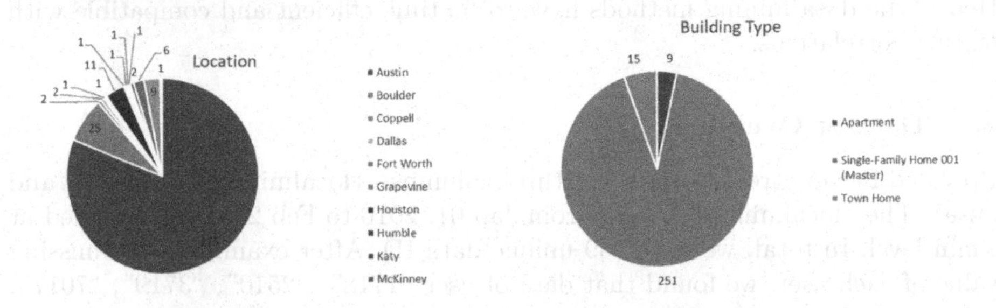

Fig. 1. Location **Fig. 2.** Building Type

3 Model Selection and Evaluation

With the support of metadata and weather data, it is suggested to start from a short term load forecasting on selected users (218 in total). In this section, we will specify the goal of this paper and discuss how to select and evaluate the model. Empirically, the goal of predicting resident electric load varies by the project context. In other words, the input and output of a prediction depends on the feature selection. Since prior knowledge about the length of input and output is unknown, we begin by thinking about what prediction is meaningful.

3.1 Defining the Input and Output

If the input and output are both time series, then each represents a time interval. Equivalently, the question becomes given a certain time interval $\hat{\mathcal{T}}$ with length l_1, what length l_2 of time interval $\mathcal{T}$ before $\hat{\mathcal{T}}$ is most likely to be considered. With sufficient computation power and model capacity, the values of l_1 and l_2 are negligible since the prediction accuracy can be improved through trial and error, or fine-tuning. From the perspective of a electric power company, 1 min exact prediction with high accuracy are not necessary and in fact hard to achieve. To relax the strict requirements, we adopt the following steps:

1. sequence with small granularity → sequence with small granularity
2. sequence with small granularity → scalar with large granularity
3. sequence with small granularity → sequence with large granularity

Typically, using the predictions of "sequence to sequence" is the most straightforward and intuitive way. But the prediction accuracy is generally not satisfying. With the above steps, one may discover the prediction pattern with variation of accuracy. With high accuracy, it further provides insights for demand forecasting and user behavior analysis.

3.2 Modelling Method

The recent researches show a tendency to choose RNN models, especially LSTM model in the prediction task. Traditional time series methods and machine learning methods are fast to train, but the performance and the statistical properties (e.g., stationary sequence) impede their popularity in practice. Hence, in this section, we focus on how to improve the performance of LSTM model by modifying its structures.

In terms of the performance of a deep neural network, there is current belief that increasing the depth of a neural network will increase the representation power of and increasing the width of a layer will increase the smoothness of neural network landscape [2,8,13]. Note that one dimension of the input in LSTM models includes the parameter the number of features selected for a single user. Therefore, to increase the width, we introduce more features into the LSTM model such as the difference sequence or second difference sequence. Also, we increase the layer of the LSTM model. To increase the depth, modifying hidden layer in a single LSTM model cell is not the focus of this project. Hence, we propose to connect LSTM cells with other neural networks including encoder-decoder framework to form a hybrid model (encoder-decoder LSTM). The encoder-decoder LSTM consists of two LSTMs. The first LSTM, or the encoder, processes an input sequence and generates an encoded state. The encoded state summarizes the information in the input sequence. The second LSTM, or the decoder, uses the encoded state to produce an output sequence. Note that the input and output sequences can have different lengths [9]. We will build a encoder-decoder LSTM using PyTorch to make sequence-to-sequence predictions for time series data.

3.3 Evaluation Metric Extension

For sequence prediction, the evaluation metric is ususally Mean Absolute Percentage Error (MAPE) or Symmetric Mean Absolute Percentage Error (SMAPE). For scalar prediction, the evaluation metric is Mean Sqaured Error (MSE) or Mean Absolute Error (MAE). All the previous evaluation methods are aimed at measuring the performance of the output. In this section, we propose to extend the evaluation metric by adding predictability as defined in [18], a metric to evaluate the quality of input.

Intuitively, a model is most predictable over time if it follows an underlying function or a deterministic model while it is most unpredictable over time if it has largest uncertainty with respect to the load level. Therefore, the predictability are negatively correlated with conditional uncertainty of load over time.

Now, we present the calculation in detail. Given a frequency table with c rows of load level and t columns of time slots, every entry N_{ij} denotes the frequency of a sequence lying in the load level within certain time slot. Then the entropy of time $H(T)$ and load level $H(C)$ is defined as follows:

$$
\begin{aligned}
Z &= \sum_{1}^{c}\sum_{1}^{t} N_{ij} \\
\mathbb{P}(C_i) &= \sum_{1}^{t} N_{ij}/Z \\
\mathbb{P}(T_i) &= \sum_{1}^{c} N_{ij}/Z \\
H(C) &= -\sum_{1}^{c} \mathbb{P}(C_i)\log(\mathbb{P}(C_i)) \\
H(T) &= -\sum_{1}^{t} \mathbb{P}(T_i)\log(\mathbb{P}(T_i))
\end{aligned}
$$

The property of entropy gives the result that $H(C)$ and $H(T)$ reaches the maximum $\log(c)$ and $\log(t)$ when each sum of row and sum of column are the same. Then, by the definition, the formula of calculating predictability $\mathcal{P}$ is given by:

$$
\begin{aligned}
\mathcal{P} &= 1 - \frac{H(CT) - H(T)}{\log c} = 1 - \frac{H(C|T)}{\log c} \\
H(CT) &= -\sum_{1}^{c}\sum_{1}^{t} \frac{N_{ij}}{Z}\log\left(\frac{N_{ij}}{Z}\right)
\end{aligned}
$$

Note that after dividing by $\log c$, we can actually scale the predictability into $[0, 1]$. Before we interpret the predictability, we first give the definition of constancy $\mathcal{C}$ and contingency $\mathcal{M}$ as below:

$$
\begin{aligned}
\mathcal{C} &= 1 - \frac{H(C)}{\log c} \\
\mathcal{M} &= \frac{I(CT)}{\log c} = \frac{H(C) + H(T) - H(CT)}{\log c}
\end{aligned}
$$

Now, from all the formula above, the following observations naturally follow:

1. $\mathcal{P} = \mathcal{C} + \mathcal{M}$: the predictability can be decomposed by the sum of constancy $\mathcal{C}$ and $\mathcal{M}$.
2. The contingency $\mathcal{M}$ measures the interaction between the load level and the time. The contingency reaches the maximal $\log(\min\{c, t\})$ means the load level completely depends on the time. In the meantime, the predictability equals to 0 if $c < t$, which is consistent with our intuition.

3. As in each time slot, there are same number of records, then $H(T) = \log(t)$ naturally follows in any situations.
4. The predictability actually measures how much does $H(C)$ lie in the whole load level entropy space. We illustrate this observation in the Fig. 3. Therefore, the predictability is a well defined metric.

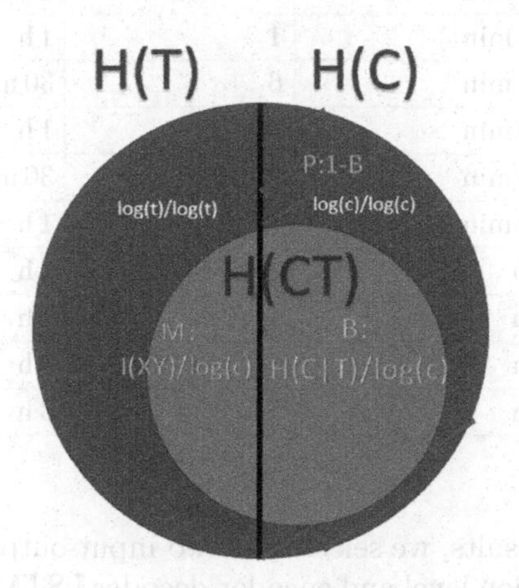

Fig. 3. The whole space denotes the maximum of $H(CT)$, which is reached when the mutual information is 0 and both $H(C)$ and $H(T)$ reach their maixmums respectively. According to the figure, high predictability implies the area B is small. Also, area $P - M$ denotes the constancy.

Having investigated the property of predictability, we now design the experiment setup to verify its effect. There are mainly two key parameters of predictability - granularity and aggregation level. Following Sect. 3.1, we conform the granularity steps and add one more prediction group. In previous method, we aim at predicting the results of each users while in the additional group, we first take an increasing sequence of subsets, sum up all inputs and outputs for each subset and evaluate their performance.

4 Experiment and Results

4.1 Experiment Design

In Sect. 3.1 and 3.3, the basic steps are outlined without specifying the parameters. The first part will not include the aggregation level and encoder-decoder LSTM. The purpose of this part is mainly to explore how LSTM performs on different input-output pairs. For granularity less than 3 h, we select time interval from Jan. 1st to Jan. 2nd. For granularity 3 h, we need to enlarge the time period since the input is not sufficient (Table 1).

Table 1. Experiment Setups

Input Length	Input Granularity	Output Length	Output Granularity
1440	1 min	60	1 min
1440	1 min	1	1 h
96	15 min	60	1 min
96	15 min	1	1 h
48	30 min	6	30 min
48	30 min	3	1 h
48	30 min	2	30 min
48	30 min	1	1 h
24	1 h	3	1 h
24	1 h	1	1 h
24	3 h	4	3 h
24	3 h	1	3 h

According to the results, we select best two input-output pairs and try them with different aggregation level and encoder-decoder LSTM model. In particular, the aggregation levels corresponds to the 2% to 100% of the all Austin Single Family users with stride 2%. The order of the users are randomized rather than sorted by "Dataid".

4.2 Results and Analysis

After trying the different input and output length pairs, we conclude that the input granularity 1 min and 3 h are not suitable for prediction, as shown in Fig. 4. The former one leads to a lengthy input and it is hard to train even after fine tuning and batch normalization. The latter one leads to a large data variance. If we treat each user as a single batch, then the variance among users can be large and a uniform learning rate with training techinques such as Xavier Normal, Stochastic Gradient Descent and weight decay still cannot achieve satisfying results. The prediction are almost same for different users. Therefore, we prefer using granularity 15 min and 30 min as our inputs, and the output can be a sequence of data with granularity 1 h or even 3 h. Figure 5 shows the results with input of different granularities. The results also suggest that LSTM generally performs well for a sequence-to-sequence prediction and there is no implication suggesting a sequence-to-scalar prediction is much better than a sequence-to-sequence prediction. Figure 5 present the value of predictability, constancy and contigency of different aggregation levels. Predictability sharply decreases when the aggregating level increases and keep at a low level later on. According to the

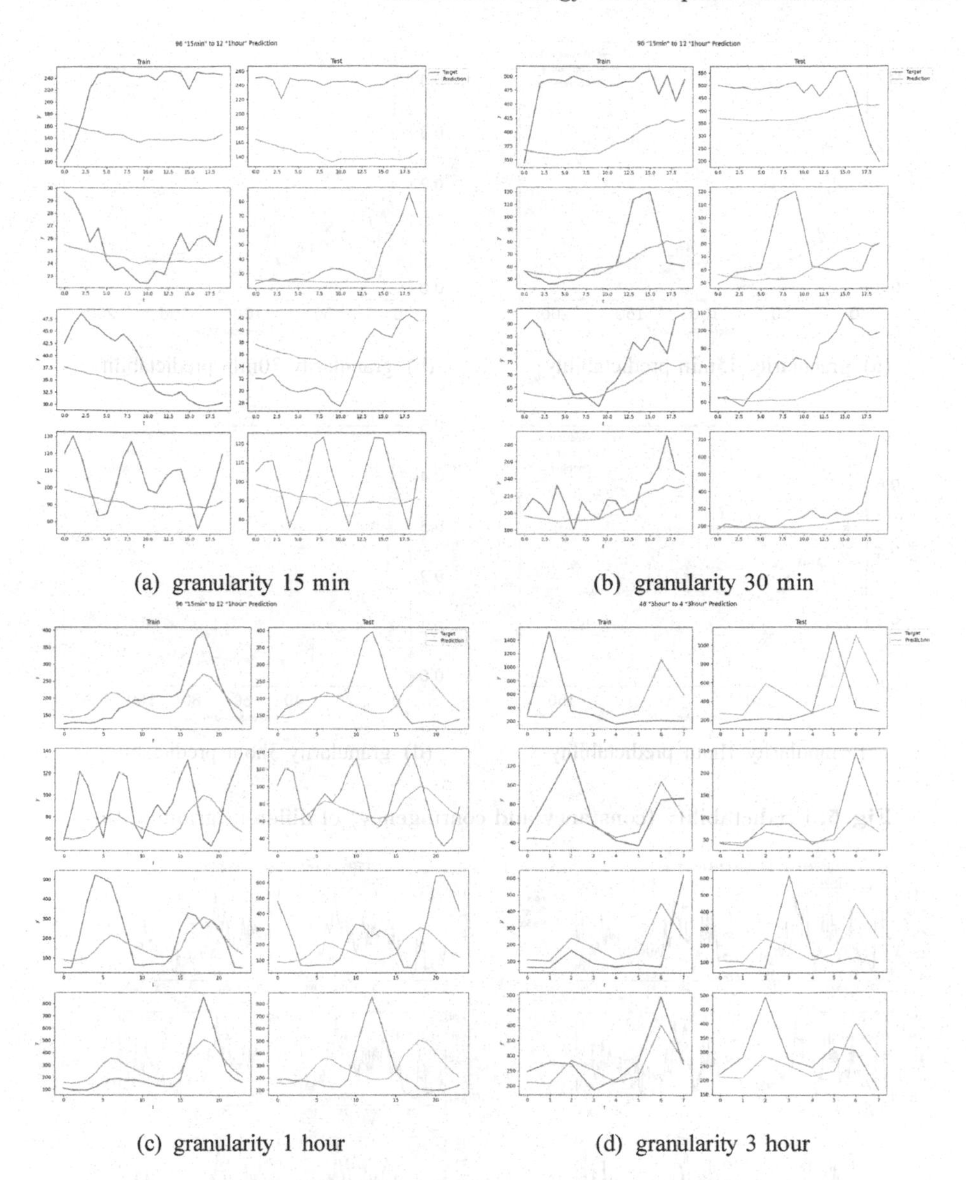

(a) granularity 15 min

(b) granularity 30 min

(c) granularity 1 hour

(d) granularity 3 hour

Fig. 4. Sequence-to-sequence predictions of different granularities

results, we run the proposed encoder-decoder LSTM model with granularity of 15 min and aggregation level 10 and 21 to assess how the aggregation level affect the prediction results. Figure 6 shows that increasing aggregation level may be of little benefit for prediction accuracy, which also implies that predictability has a high positive correlation with the performance of prediction model.

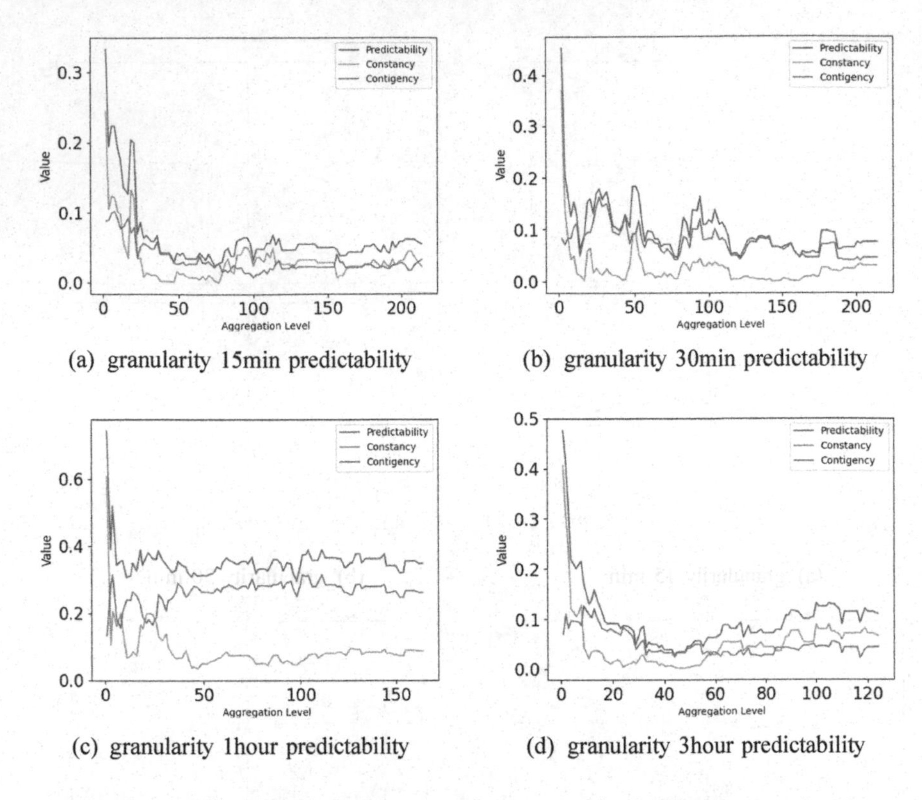

(a) granularity 15min predictability (b) granularity 30min predictability

(c) granularity 1hour predictability (d) granularity 3hour predictability

Fig. 5. Predictability (constancy and contingency) of different granularities

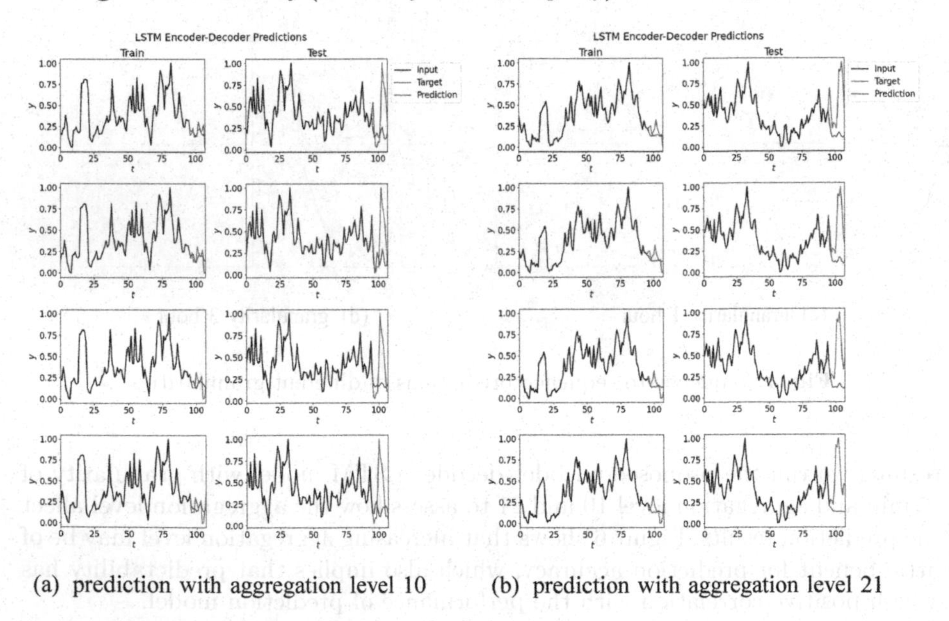

(a) prediction with aggregation level 10 (b) prediction with aggregation level 21

Fig. 6. Sequence-to-sequence prediction of different aggregation levels

5 Conclusions

Data mining techniques can extract technical framework in smart grid topics to facilitate generation dispatches and electricity management. In this project, we seek to forecast load based on Pecan Street individual load dataset. We include metadata and weather data to explore apt preprocessing procedure. Due to the limited size of dataset, we only focus on a certain group and select short term to alleviate the effect of weather. Compared with standard LSTM model, encoder-decoder LSTM model achieves better performance in the sense of MSE and MAE. The result of granularity selection shows that both small and large granularity are not suitable for prediction. After including predictability of data, the results suggest that aggregating data from a subset of users that has higher predictability provides more accurate predictions. Our experiments also have some limitations. From the supply end, filtering may lead to large bias of prediction. In other words, the generalization performance should be discussed and improved. Also, including random forest and AdaBoost may help reduce the performance variance. The encoder-decoder LSTM model is a very powerful learning framework, which can also be applied to many other learning tasks in the electricity sector, e.g., user profiling [15,19], learning-aided storage control [20,21], LMP prediction [6,7], etc.

References

1. Amjady, N., Keynia, F., Zareipour, H.: Short-term load forecast of microgrids by a new bilevel prediction strategy. IEEE Trans. Smart Grid **1**(3), 286–294 (2010)
2. Chatziafratis, V., Nagarajan, S.G., Panageas, I., Wang, X.: Depth-width trade-offs for Relu networks via Sharkovsky's theorem. arXiv preprint arXiv:1912.04378 (2019)
3. Cho, K., et al.: Learning phrase representations using RNN encoder-decoder for statistical machine translation. arXiv preprint arXiv:1406.1078 (2014)
4. Ding, N., Benoit, C., Foggia, G., Besanger, Y., Wurtz, F.: Neural network-based model design for short-term load forecast in distribution systems. IEEE Trans. Power Syst. **31**(1), 72–81 (2015)
5. Apple Inc.: Dark sky. Website (2022). https://darksky.net/forecast/40.7127,-74.0059/us12/en
6. Jiang, G., Cui, J., Wu, C.: Role of prediction in data-driven pricing schemes. In: 2021 5th International Conference on Smart Grid and Smart Cities (ICSGSC), pp. 125–129. IEEE (2021)
7. Jiang, W.J., Cao, S., Wu, C.: LMP prediction with incomplete information. In: 2022 IEEE Power & Energy Society General Meeting, pp. 1–5. IEEE (2022)
8. Li, H., Xu, Z., Taylor, G., Studer, C., Goldstein, T.: Visualizing the loss landscape of neural nets. Adv. Neural Inf. Process. Syst. **31** (2018)
9. lkulowski: Building a LSTM encoder-decoder using PyTorch to make sequence-to-sequence predictions. https://github.com/lkulowski/LSTM_encoder_decoder. Accessed 20 Nov 2020
10. Rahman, A., Srikumar, V., Smith, A.D.: Predicting electricity consumption for commercial and residential buildings using deep recurrent neural networks. Appl. Energy **212**, 372–385 (2018)

11. Raza, M.Q., Khosravi, A.: A review on artificial intelligence based load demand forecasting techniques for smart grid and buildings. Renew. Sustain. Energy Rev. **50**, 1352–1372 (2015)
12. Street, P.: Pecan street dataport. Website (2016). https://dataport.pecanstreet.org
13. Sun, R., Li, D., Liang, S., Ding, T., Srikant, R.: The global landscape of neural networks: an overview. IEEE Signal Process. Mag. **37**(5), 95–108 (2020)
14. Tian, C., Ma, J., Zhang, C., Zhan, P.: A deep neural network model for short-term load forecast based on long short-term memory network and convolutional neural network. Energies **11**(12), 3493 (2018)
15. Wang, H., Luo, X., Wu, C.: Differential privacy in consumer behavior analysis. In: 2021 IEEE Power & Energy Society General Meeting (PESGM), pp. 1–5. IEEE (2021)
16. Wang, H., Zhang, J., Lu, C., Wu, C.: Privacy preserving in non-intrusive load monitoring: a differential privacy perspective. IEEE Trans. Smart Grid **12**(3), 2529–2543 (2020)
17. Wang, Y., et al.: Tracking states of massive electrical appliances by lightweight metering and sequence decoding. In: Proceedings of the Sixth International Workshop on Knowledge Discovery from Sensor Data, pp. 34–42 (2012)
18. Wu, C., Tang, W., Poolla, K., Rajagopal, R.: Predictability, constancy and contingency in electric load profiles. In: 2016 IEEE International Conference on Smart Grid Communications (SmartGridComm), pp. 662–667 (2016). https://doi.org/10.1109/SmartGridComm.2016.7778837
19. Wu, C., Tang, W., Poolla, K., Rajagopal, R.: Predictability, constancy and contingency in electric load profiles. In: 2016 IEEE International Conference on Smart Grid Communications (SmartGridComm), pp. 662–667. IEEE (2016)
20. Wu, J., Lu, C., Wu, C.: Learning-aided framework for storage control facing renewable energy. IEEE Syst. J. (2022)
21. Wu, J., Wang, Z., Wu, C., Wang, K., Yu, Y.: A data-driven storage control framework for dynamic pricing. IEEE Trans. Smart Grid **12**(1), 737–750 (2020)
22. Yue, S., Chen, J., Gu, Y., Wu, C., Shi, Y.: Dual-pricing policy for controller-side strategies in demand side management. In: 2011 IEEE International Conference on Smart Grid Communications (SmartGridComm), pp. 357–362. IEEE (2011)

Pattern-Preserved Normalization Enabled User Profiling

Fengchao Chen(✉), Lide Zhou, Junni Su, and Xin Zhang

Dongguan Power Supply Bureau, Guangdong Power Grid Corporation, Dongguan 523000, Guangdong, China
csgcfc@126.com

Abstract. The legacy power grid is evolving into a more intelligent grid, and the classical preventive control paradigm is also evolving into a more modern data-driven control paradigm. However, the massive data also poses challenges on the data-driven techniques. In this paper, we focus on the clustering problem in the residential energy sector based on long-term energy consumption data. We employ the classical k-means clustering algorithm and analyze the drawbacks of Min-Max normalization and the disadvantages of utilizing Euclidean distance. We further provide a potential solution, PP-normalization, to solve these issues to achieve a better performance in residential consumption data clustering.

Keywords: Clustering · data-driven · Consumer Analysis

1 Introduction

Data analytic methods are changing every aspect of our daily life. This is also true for the power grid. Thanks to the pervasive sensing technology, the system operator gathers vast amounts of data daily, enabling the smart grid's data-driven control paradigm. However, like many other application domains, the transition from the classical preventive control paradigm to a data-driven control paradigm in the electricity sector is not very smooth. The major drawback is that data-driven methods suffer from data pre-processing problems. In this paper, we take the clustering problem at the end-user level as an example, to explore pattern-preserved-normalization (PP-normalization) enabled clustering method based on long-term energy consumption habits.

1.1 Related Works

We identify two lines of research related to our work. The first is about residential energy consumption clustering in power system, and the other focuses on energy consumption data analysis.

Carmo *et al.* put forward the cluster analysis for residential heat load profiles in [6]. Cui *et al.* propose a clustering oriented pricing scheme based on consumer's

This work was supported in part by the science and technology study of China Southern Power Grid Cooperation (No. GDKJXM20200475).

H. Yang et al. (Eds.): SmartGIFT 2022, LNICST 483, pp. 331–341, 2023.
https://doi.org/10.1007/978-3-031-31733-0_28

load profile [5]. Maqsood *et al.* propose STFT cluster analysis for DC pulsed load monitoring in [10]. Wakeel *et al.* explore K-means based cluster analysis for residential smart meter measurements [2]. Wu *et al.* define a novel predictability matrix from an information theoretic perspective to cluster different kinds of loads [23]. References [3,11,26] give detailed reviews of the clustering approach to electricity load profile characterisation using consumption data. Wang *et al.* utilize the historical load profile data from existing users to conduct effective clustering, which contributes to the load forecasting for a new user in the power system [19]. Clustering for the electric load is one of the most classic tasks in power system, and thus is well investigated. Our paper focuses on the preprocessing analysis before clustering, and includes PP-normalization to improve the clustering performance.

Another research focuses on the energy consumption data processing methods. Pavlo *et al.* provides a review for the approaches to large-scale data analysis [13]. Vandijk reviews some statistical load data processing methods in [18]. Noussan *et al.* give the data analysis on district heating load patterns in [12]. Cui *et al.* examine how data quantity and data quality affect the online dispatch efficiency in [4]. Jin *et al.* put forward a load modeling by finding support vectors of load data from field measurements in [8]. Wu *et al.* propose a data mining approach for spatial modeling in small area load forecast in [24]. Afshar *et al.* make data analysis and short term load forecasting for Iran electricity market in [1]. This line of research pays more attention to general data processing techniques. However, in our paper, we seek to design efficient data processing method, i.e., PP-normalization, for load profile clustering.

1.2 Paper Organization

The remainder of the paper is organized as follows. Section 2 discusses the fundamental features of the data and the idea of preprocessing. We also explain the dropping majority of data and the primary process of clustering detection. Then after preprocessing, Sect. 3 introduces how to employ the classical K-means clustering algorithm to accomplish the task. Furthermore, Sect. 4 attempts to improve the performance of K-means clustering using PP normalization. Section 5 conducts a numerical study to highlight the proposed improved k-means clustering performance and the proposed method's limitations. Finally, concluding remarks are delivered in Sect. 6.

2 Overview of the Dataset and Preprocessing

In this section, we first introduce some basic features of the dataset, which could be used to suggest how to conduct valid data preprocessing. In particular, given the data of 1-minute granularity, we check the monthly and seasonal patterns inherent in the data. We believe such information will help us choose the strategy to deal with missing values, select or drop out samples, and determine the efficient period for modeling and analysis.

2.1 Dataset Overview

The dataset used in this paper is the Pecan Street energy consumption dataset [14]. We regard continuous "0" observations (say more than two days) and negative observations as ineffective. To this end, only 182 out of 342 samples have complete effective data (the number standard is effective observations should be larger than 170000). Another 62 samples contain effective observations of 3 months. For the remaining 98 samples, four total samples do not contain any observation (all 0's) and are thus being removed from the analysis. For the remaining data, we regard the samples containing continuous "0" observations for more than seven days. We will propose a strategy to deal with these missing values based on the other fundamental features of the dataset.

2.2 Seasonality Check

We conduct the daily and weekly seasonality using the QS-test, a variant of the Ljung-Box test that computes the test statistic based on seasonal lags of the series. The QS-test requires that the samples are independently distributed and can be modeled using the SARIMA model with a period of l. Therefore, the partial auto-correlation between samples with lag l should be rather large. That is, the null hypothesis of non-seasonality of l will be rejected under a sufficiently large QS value.

Note that if the data sequence has significant daily seasonality, it should also have significant weekly seasonality since a week is an integer multiple of days. Therefore, time series decomposition with daily seasonality is required to capture the actual weekly seasonality. All the samples are tested with all the effective observation data. The empirical results are consistent with common sense: Most samples show significant daily and weekly seasonality. A few samples fail to pass the daily seasonality test and are removed from further analysis.

Most of the samples with daily seasonality will also appear to have weekly seasonality after removing the daily seasonality term. However, the weekly seasonality property is less robust. The weekly seasonality may fail if the QS test is only applied on a partition of the effective observations - say, two continuous months. Therefore, in this study, we will mainly focus on the day seasonality, and the word seasonality will be used instead for convenience.

Since clustering discussed in this study is mainly for providing support to long-term abnormal energy consumer detection. This relatively robust daily seasonality property will allow us to use the aggregate daily consumption profile to represent the consumption profile of the consumer.

2.3 Monthly Trend

Many other factors will affect the energy consumption profile, e.g., outside temperature. To form an effective strategy to fill in the missing data, it will be better if sample trends are straightforward. To detect the monthly trend of the samples, we adopt simple linear regression models for each household and each month.

We can also test whether this linear regression model is a good candidate. A simple approach is to treat the parameter estimation as constant (the actual parameter value) and then apply the t-test. From the empirical test result on the dataset, we observe that the monthly trends are different even for the same household for other months. Therefore, using the sample of the current month to extrapolate data from other months may be unreasonable.

2.4 Preprocessing Strategy

Based on the features discussed above, we choose not to fill in the missing data due to the different trends between months, which means the observations of the current month may not be a good estimation start point for another month. Also, samples without daily seasonality are removed from analysis due to the relatively small sample size. It will be hard to get a reliable result based on about ten samples. Instead, observations from 1-31 18:01 to 3-04 01:18 are selected to be used in this study since almost all the samples have continuous and complete observations over this time interval. Then by kicking out another four samples due to the lack of data over this period, we finally selected 317 samples, each with more than 40,000 observations. Though we remove many observations from the analysis, the remaining observations are still sufficient to construct a robust analysis. However, since we only do clustering over generally one month (February), the difference between the consumption profile of months should not be neglected.

The aggregate data of each day is used to simulate the consumption profile of consumers. Moreover, due to the limitation of computational power, we select only to use the aggregate time on each hour. Therefore, we begin with using a vector $v \in \mathbb{R}^{24}$ to capture the consumption profile of each sample, and we will use the word feature vector to represent this vector.

3 Classical K-Means Clustering

To cluster the consumption profiles, the measurement of similarity should be declared. Distance-based measurements could be reasonable approaches since we expect similar consumption profiles to simultaneously have minor differences between the consumption volumes. A considerable distance between feature vectors generally means significant differences exist in each element. Though this argument may not be valid sometimes, since a considerable distance may also cause a significant difference in some specific element pairs, distance measurement can provide insight into determining the similarity. Thus, we choose to use Euclidean distance as the starting point, and it will be natural first to try K-means, one of the popular distance-based clustering methods.

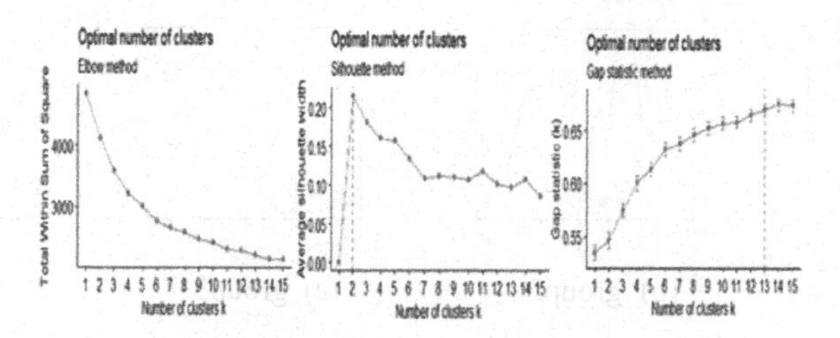

Fig. 1. Cluster number selection base on three different methods.

3.1 Initial Attempts

Recall the goal that we want to form a clustering model to help improve long-term abnormal energy consumer detection. This drives us to do clustering only based on the pattern of sample consumption profile but not the consumption volume of the samples. Therefore, a suitable normalization method should be applied to preserve the pattern and scale the samples in the same range. We will first try Min-Max normalization in the range 0 to 1. This is generally a promising approach for normalization tasks but still has some disadvantages that we will discuss later. At this point, we will directly try Min-Max normalization and then turn to K-means++ clustering, which is just a modified K-means that spreads out the k initial points as much as possible to obtain a more robust clustering outcome compared with the traditional K-means algorithm. In this study, K-means is the same as K-means++ for convenience of report writing.

Since K-means clustering requires an initial assignment of the number of clusters, the Elbow, Silhouette, and gap statistic methods are applied and serve as a reference to the final cluster number selection (see Fig. 1 for a comparison). The reason for applying these three methods is because the Silhouette method focuses more on the distance between clusters but not the difference between clusters; the gap statistic method cares more about the in-cluster performance, and the Elbow method generally performs better on considering both in-cluster and out-cluster performance. We can depend on all the results of these methods to get a better decision on the number of clusters.

For this simple attempt, we can find these methods provide different suggestions on the cluster number selection. Moreover, though the default function result suggests 13 clusters for the gap statistic curve, there is no significant global maximum with $k \leq 15$. The result of the gap statistic method remains doubtful. For the Silhouette method, which suggests 2 clusters are the best, its result is counter-intuition. Since it is hard for the result of these three methods to reach an agreement, we decide to try from $k = 13$. The idea of this decision is based on the intuition that if the K-means algorithm cannot perform well on a large number of k, then it will even perform worse when the k is small. Thus, choosing a relatively large k at the beginning is reasonable. This simple attempt's cluster centers are shown in Fig. 2.

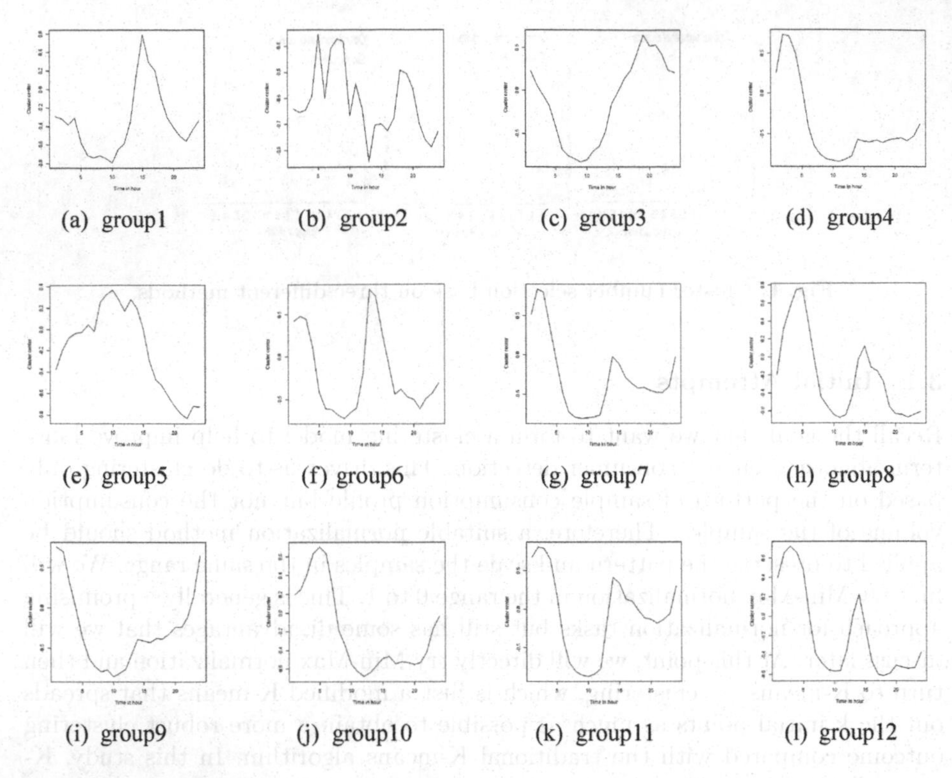

(a) group1 (b) group2 (c) group3 (d) group4

(e) group5 (f) group6 (g) group7 (h) group8

(i) group9 (j) group10 (k) group11 (l) group12

Fig. 2. Cluster centers of Min-Max + K-means approach. Cannot find significantly different between center of group 5 and center of group 10.

3.2 Drawbacks of Classical K-Means Clustering

By looking into the cluster centers shown in Fig. 2, it can be found that the center of group 5 is close to the center of group 9. The Euclidean distance between these two centers is even less than some of the distance between samples in groups 5 and 9 and their centers. We doubt whether these two groups show no significant difference from each other. However, if we carefully check the in-cluster samples, more than one possible pattern has been grouped into the same cluster. This phenomenon suggests increasing the number of clusters. However, if we change the number of clusters from k = 13 to k = 17, we can still find samples with possible different patterns within the same cluster, but some clusters will only contain a few samples (less than or equal to 3) at this time. Therefore, this phenomenon is not caused by the excessive or insufficient number of clusters.

As mentioned in the introduction paragraph of Sect. 3.1, the value of Euclidean distance cannot guarantee the number of significant different elements between two vectors. In other words, the relatively small Euclidean distance does not mean the two feature vectors are the same but only close to each other in high dimensional space. For example, consider a consumption pattern only with one peak at 19:00–20:00. If there is another consumption pattern whose consumption peaks appear at 7:00–8:00 and 19:00–20:00, and these two consumption patterns are almost the same except 7:00–8:00. By intuition, samples with these two consumption patterns should not be grouped. However, the difference in Euclidean distance caused by the "morning consumption peak" may not be significant enough to separate these two samples.

4 Proposed Improvements

One possible solution to the problem is to make a dimensional reduction. Unfortunately, traditional dimensional reduction methods like PCA and T-SNE do not help much. We want to improve the in-cluster performance from other approaches. Another problem that needs to be concern is the Min-Max normalization. Though Min-Max normalization is an excellent approach to maintaining the consumption pattern of samples, it cannot remove noises in the feature vector. The noises discussed here are small random fluctuations within a relatively constant consumption period. These noises may cause extra distance between two series with the same pattern. Besides, Min-Max normalization probably will enlarge the within-sample difference of relatively flat samples since it will always normalize the curve to a pre-defined region. To avoid the drawbacks of Min-Max normalization, we constructed a modified Min-Max method so-called Pattern-Preserved normalization (PP-normalization).

4.1 PP-Normalization

The basic idea behind the PP-normalization is that: We can consider the PP-normalization as a mapping function f,

$$f(\mathbf{x}) = \mathbf{y} \tag{1}$$

where $\mathbf{x}, \mathbf{y} \in \mathbb{R}^n$, and each element in $\mathbf{y}$ is bounded by $[L, U]$ which is determined by input vector $\mathbf{x}$.

To determine the in-sample fluctuation level of the data $\mathbf{x}$, we set uniform distribution as reference. Let $\mathbf{x}_i, i = 1, 2, \cdots, n$ be the original series data and $\mathbf{x}_{(i)}$ is the ordered data and $\mathbf{x}'_{(i)}$ be series of ordered data from uniform distribution. Assume $\mathbf{x}_{(i)}$ follows uniform distribution, then $\mathbf{x}_{(1)}$ and $\mathbf{x}_{(n)}$ can be estimated as:

$$\hat{\mathbf{x}}_{(1)} = q_{0.5} - (q_{0.75} - q_{0.25}) \tag{2}$$

$$\hat{\mathbf{x}}_{(n)} = q_{0.5} + (q_{0.75} - q_{0.25}) \tag{3}$$

where q_p is p quantile of series data $\mathbf{x}_{(i)}$. If the series has significant consumption peak time and consumption valley time, the whole series will be more compact to the median compare to series $\mathbf{x}'_{(i)}$. Therefore, pick control parameter as θ, general range parameter α, β, L, U are defined as:

$$L = \begin{cases} \alpha, & \min(\mathbf{x}_{(1)}, \theta\hat{\mathbf{x}}_{(1)}) = \mathbf{x}_{(1)} \\ MinMax(\mathbf{x}_{(i)}, \alpha, \beta), & \min(\mathbf{x}_{(1)}, \theta\hat{\mathbf{x}}_{(1)}) = \theta\hat{\mathbf{x}}_{(1)} \end{cases} \quad (4)$$

$$U = \begin{cases} \beta, & \min(\mathbf{x}_{(n)}, \theta\hat{\mathbf{x}}_{(n)}) = \mathbf{x}_{(n)} \\ MinMax(\mathbf{x}_{(n)}, \alpha, \beta), & \min(\mathbf{x}_{(n)}, \theta\hat{\mathbf{x}}_{(n)}) = \theta\hat{\mathbf{x}}_{(n)} \end{cases} \quad (5)$$

4.2 Noise Removing

Let $\bar{x}$ to be the average of the sample $\mathbf{x}$. After choosing an reference example denoted as $\tilde{x}$, we want to remove the sample noise by applying the following idea,

$$\mathbf{x} = \begin{cases} MinMax(\tilde{x}, \alpha, \beta), & |\mathbf{x} - \tilde{x}| \leq \gamma\bar{x} \\ MinMax(\mathbf{x}, \alpha, \beta), & Otherwise \end{cases} \quad (6)$$

That means, if the difference between the real sample and the reference sample is less than the predefined threshold $\gamma\bar{x}$, we will utilize the reference value to substitute the original value. Otherwise, we will keep the original value. Clearly, through this processing, it is easily to remove the useless noisy information, and will contribute to the subsequent clustering.

5 Numerical Studies

Select the number of clusters to be 12 and apply K-means clustering directly. The examples of normalization are shown in Fig. 3.

Indeed, the result of K-means based on PP-normalization is only slightly improved from the simple attempt. Compared to the K-means based on Min-Max normalization, PP-normalization improves the in-sample performance of K-means. By looking into each cluster, the number of samples without obvious different patterns decreases, though such a phenomenon still exists. However, PP-normalization cannot solve the problem that the cluster center of Group 4 and Group 9 are two close to each other. However, decreasing the number of clusters will result in a worse performance.

Moreover, it can be found obviously in the sample plot of Group 0 and Group 10 that one of the samples with a consumption peak more than 5 h apart from another one has been grouped into the same cluster. Intuitively speaking, if the difference in consumption peaks of two samples is only 1 h, their consumption pattern is probably the same. However, if their consumption peak is 5 h apart, it will be hopeless that they hold the same consumption pattern.

This miss-clustering result is also due to the Euclidean distance-based similarity measurement. No matter what kind of distance and L_p norm for any P, this problem will still exist since the traditional distance calculation only focuses on the difference between two corresponding elements in the vector but does not care about the difference between a specific element and its front and back.

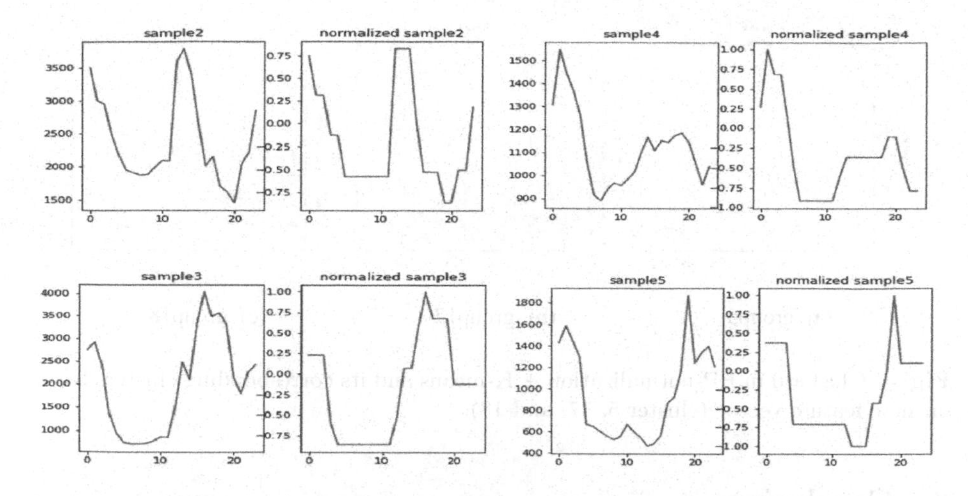

Fig. 3. PP-normalization result.

We are solving the problem caused by using Euclidean distance as a similarity measurement. We could use the alignment distance for K-mean clustering. Through numerical studies, we found that alignment distance provides a solution to cluster two samples with small peak shifts together. Now a method to separate samples with large peak shifts is needed. For simplicity, we will start by trying directly give a penalty on the large peak shift based on the Euclidean distance. By the intuition of patterns of the samples, no more than two significant consumption peaks occur in each sample. Also, no more than two consumption valleys for each sample. Let p_1, p_2 denote the index (time) of the peaks, and v_1, v_2 denote the index of valleys. The feature vector v is modified to a new feature vector $v' \in \mathbb{R}^{28}$. Since $v \in [-1, 1]$, it automatically assigns a high penalty on different peak and valley times. By applying K-means clustering on the new feature vector v', the result of several distinct groups discussed above are shown as follows:

By applying K-means based on the new feature vector, the gap statistic method and Elbow method both suggest a large number of clusters. After parameter selection, we finally choose k = 25 to obtain a relatively robust result. Different from the previous attempt, increasing the number of clusters will cause several clusters only to contain 1 sample. By selecting k = 25, we do not observe this phenomenon for K-means based on the new feature vector. For the in-cluster performance, K-means clustering based on new feature vectors is sensitive to the peak shift of samples. As shown in Fig. 4, cluster 0 discussed in Sect. 3.3 is generally separated into three clusters with close peaks.

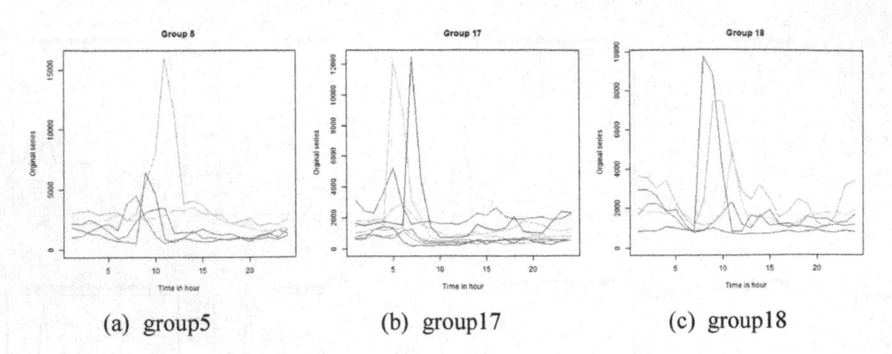

(a) group5 (b) group17 (c) group18

Fig. 4. Cluster 0 in PP-normalization + K-means and its corresponding clusters based on new feature vector (cluster 5, 17, and 18).

6 Conclusions

This paper takes the clustering task for long-term energy consumption data as an example to explore the preprocessing techniques in data-driven methods. Through analyzing the disadvantages of classic Min-Max normalization using Euclidean distance in consumption clustering, we propose a novel PP-normalization idea to improve the clustering performance. Numerical studies shows that our PP-normalization is effective in energy consumption clustering task. We believe PP-normalization is a very promising data pre-processing technique, which could enable many other data-driven tasks, such as LMP prediction [7], convex hull pricing analysis [15,16], demand response program design [21,22], and storage control [9,17,20,25].

References

1. Afshar, K., Bigdeli, N.: Data analysis and short term load forecasting in Iran electricity market using singular spectral analysis (SSA). Energy **36**(5), 2620–2627 (2011)
2. Al-Wakeel, A., Wu, J.: K-means based cluster analysis of residential smart meter measurements. Energy Proc. **88**, 754–760 (2016)
3. Chicco, G.: Overview and performance assessment of the clustering methods for electrical load pattern grouping. Energy **42**(1), 68–80 (2012)
4. Cui, J., Gu, N., Wu, C.: Quantity or quality? Data enabled online energy dispatch. In: Adjunct Proceedings of the 2021 ACM International Joint Conference on Pervasive and Ubiquitous Computing and Proceedings of the 2021 ACM International Symposium on Wearable Computers, pp. 606–612 (2021)
5. Cui, J., Wang, H., Wu, C., Yu, Y.: Vulnerability analysis for data driven pricing schemes. In: 2020 IEEE Power & Energy Society General Meeting (PESGM), pp. 1–5. IEEE (2020)
6. Do Carmo, C.M.R., Christensen, T.H.: Cluster analysis of residential heat load profiles and the role of technical and household characteristics. Energy Build. **125**, 171–180 (2016)

7. Jiang, W.J., Cao, S., Wu, C.: LMP prediction with incomplete information. In: 2022 IEEE Power & Energy Society General Meeting, pp. 1–5. IEEE (2022)
8. Jin, M., Renmu, H., Hill, D.J.: Load modeling by finding support vectors of load data from field measurements. IEEE Trans. Power Syst. **21**(2), 726–735 (2006)
9. Kalathil, D., Wu, C., Poolla, K., Varaiya, P.: The sharing economy for the electricity storage. IEEE Trans. Smart Grid **10**(1), 556–567 (2017)
10. Maqsood, A., Oslebo, D., Corzine, K., Parsa, L., Ma, Y.: STFT cluster analysis for DC pulsed load monitoring and fault detection on naval shipboard power systems. IEEE Trans. Transp. Electrif. **6**(2), 821–831 (2020)
11. McLoughlin, F., Duffy, A., Conlon, M.: A clustering approach to domestic electricity load profile characterisation using smart metering data. Appl. Energy **141**, 190–199 (2015)
12. Noussan, M., Jarre, M., Poggio, A.: Real operation data analysis on district heating load patterns. Energy **129**, 70–78 (2017)
13. Pavlo, A., et al.: A comparison of approaches to large-scale data analysis. In: Proceedings of the 2009 ACM SIGMOD International Conference on Management of Data, pp. 165–178 (2009)
14. Street, P.: Pecan street dataport. Website (2016). https://dataport.pecanstreet.org
15. Sun, J., Gu, N., Wu, C.: Market power in convex hull pricing. In: Proceedings of the Eleventh ACM International Conference on Future Energy Systems, pp. 398–400 (2020)
16. Sun, J., Wu, C.: Temporal vulnerability assessment for convex hull pricing. In: Proceedings of the Twelfth ACM International Conference on Future Energy Systems, pp. 124–136 (2021)
17. Sun, J., Zhang, Y., Yu, Y., Wu, C.: Storage control for carbon emission reduction: opportunities and challenges. In: 2020 IEEE Power & Energy Society General Meeting (PESGM), pp. 1–5. IEEE (2020)
18. Vandijk, G.: Statistical load data processing. NASA. Langley Res. Center Advanced Approaches to Fatigue Evaluation (1972)
19. Wang, Q., Chen, Z., Wu, C.: Clustering enabled few-shot load forecasting. In: 2021 IEEE Sustainable Power and Energy Conference (iSPEC), pp. 2417–2424. IEEE (2021)
20. Wu, C., Kalathil, D., Poolla, K., Varaiya, P.: Sharing electricity storage. In: 2016 IEEE 55th Conference on Decision and Control (CDC), pp. 813–820. IEEE (2016)
21. Wu, C., Mohsenian-Rad, H., Huang, J.: Vehicle-to-grid systems: ancillary services and communications. José MR Gonçalves **129** (2012)
22. Wu, C., Mohsenian-Rad, H., Huang, J., Wang, A.Y.: Demand side management for wind power integration in microgrid using dynamic potential game theory. In: 2011 IEEE GLOBECOM Workshops (GC Wkshps), pp. 1199–1204. IEEE (2011)
23. Wu, C., Tang, W., Poolla, K., Rajagopal, R.: Predictability, constancy and contingency in electric load profiles. In: 2016 IEEE International Conference on Smart Grid Communications (SmartGridComm), pp. 662–667. IEEE (2016)
24. Wu, H.C., Lu, C.N.: A data mining approach for spatial modeling in small area load forecast. IEEE Trans. Power Syst. **17**(2), 516–521 (2002)
25. Wu, J., Wang, Z., Wu, C., Wang, K., Yu, Y.: A data-driven storage control framework for dynamic pricing. IEEE Trans. Smart Grid **12**(1), 737–750 (2020)
26. Yang, S.L., Shen, C., et al.: A review of electric load classification in smart grid environment. Renew. Sustain. Energy Rev. **24**, 103–110 (2013)

Multi-energy Coordinated Dispatch of Integrated Transportation Hub During Peak-Period Transactions

Zhiyun Sun[1], Qizhen Wei[1], Hewei Chen[1], Yuancheng Tang[1], Junyu Li[1], Xiaolong Lu[1], Conglin Fang[2](✉), and Qiang Luo[3]

[1] China Energy Engineering Group Hunan Electric Power Design Institute Co., LTD, Changsha 410000, Hunan, China

[2] Changsha University of Science and Technology, Changsha 410114, Hunan, China
929645237@qq.com

[3] Huazhong University of Science and Technology, Wuhan 430074, Hubei, China

Abstract. The integrated transportation hub is the intersection of the transportation network lines of multiple modes of transportation, and is a whole composed of a variety of fixed devices and mobile devices. With the sharp increase in electricity load and insufficient energy supply, the production and use of electricity has been seriously affected. In order to solve the problem of imbalance between supply and demand during peak load hours, in the gradually opening user-side market, the integrated transportation hub participates in the special transaction of peak demand response as a market entity, and controls the end users under its jurisdiction to reduce the controllable load and obtain compensation costs by signing a contract. This paper first defines the integrated transportation hub considering the flexible load response, and analyzes the function of the integrated transportation hub in the power trading market from the two aspects of market and technology. On this basis, the adjustable potential of various terminal flexible loads of integrated transportation hubs is analyzed and modeled. Finally, the process of the integrated transportation hub's participation in the spike demand response special transaction is analyzed, and the market clearance model for the integrated transportation hub to participate in the spike transaction special session is constructed with the goal of maximizing social welfare, optimizing the transaction price and response amount of the market entity, and realizing the peak load reduction of the power system.

Keywords: Integrated Transportation Hub · Demand Response · Peak Load Period

1 Introduction

With the adjustment of industrial structure, social and economic development and the improvement of residents' living standards, the demand for electricity on the user side continues to grow; a high proportion of clean energy is connected to the grid, the grid

H. Yang et al. (Eds.): SmartGIFT 2022, LNICST 483, pp. 342–353, 2023.
https://doi.org/10.1007/978-3-031-31733-0_29

load shows obvious seasonality and time period, and the social electricity load shows double peaks in winter and summer characteristic, the problem of peak regulation is becoming more and more obvious.

In view of the shortcomings of the traditional supply-demand balance method, under the support of demand response technology, the load aggregator, as an intermediary institution coordinating large industrial users, general industrial and commercial users, residential users and power grid dispatching and trading centers [1], can integrate load resources through professional technical means and participate in the medium and long-term market or demand response market. Taking the implementation measures for power demand response in a province as an example, it is clear that the participants in the power demand response market are direct demand users and load aggregators. Aggregate and disperse small and medium-sized adjustable resources to participate in electricity market transactions, and jointly reduce the load during peak hours and promote clean energy consumption through market-oriented means of demand response; Guide users to transfer noon/evening peak power consumption, which can effectively reduce peak load.

As a passenger and cargo transshipment center connecting a variety of modes of transportation and radiating a certain area, the comprehensive transportation hub builds a convenient, safe and efficient comprehensive transportation system with intensive use of resources, energy conservation and environmental protection, which is of strategic significance for supporting national economic and social development, facilitating the travel of the broad masses of the people, and enhancing national competitiveness. Compared with traditional energy storage power supply, the integrated transportation junction has a variety of adjustable loads, fast response speed and strong climbing ability. A large number of decentralized end users form a flexible energy storage system through the control of load aggregators, so as to integrate the transportation hub, which is a stakeholder to participate in the power trading market, and output power to the power grid to obtain market benefits [2].

Based on the above, this paper proposes a peak transaction clearing model based on integrated transportation junctions. First of all, the comprehensive transportation hub is defined, and from the two aspects of market and technology, the function of the integrated transportation hub in the electricity market is studied to be different from other market entities, and its responsibilities in power trading are clarified. Then, the adjustable potential analysis of various end-user loads at the integrated transportation hub is performed; Finally, the process of the integrated transportation hub's participation in the peak demand response special transaction is analyzed, and on this basis, with the goal of maximizing social welfare, the market clearance model of the integrated transportation hub participating in the peak transaction is constructed, the transaction price and response electricity of the market entities are optimized, and the peak load reduction of the power system is realized.

2 Definition of Integrated Transportation Hub with Demand Response

2.1 Basic Concepts

The integrated transportation hub is a comprehensive transportation and travel service place integrating buses, taxis, long-distance passenger transport, subways and other means of transportation, and is an area with a high degree of distribution of people and traffic, as well as an integrated energy system. It is mainly composed of energy supply networks (such as power supply, gas supply, cooling / heat supply and other networks), energy exchange links (such as CCHP units, generator sets, boilers, air conditioners, heat pumps, etc.), energy storage links (power storage, gas storage, heat storage, cold storage, etc.), terminal integrated energy supply units (such as microgrids) and a large number of end users [3].

The integrated transportation hub refers to the market transaction contract for the market transaction contract of the integrated transportation hub under its jurisdiction that meets the requirements by aggregating the dispersed end users of small and medium-sized flexible resources with load regulation potential, and arranging the charging and discharging plan of the terminal equipment under its jurisdiction by aggregating the dispersed end users of small and medium-sized capacity flexible resources with load regulation potential. The integrated transportation hub shall have the ability to obtain the adjustable capacity of the end-user equipment of the integrated transportation hub under its jurisdiction, the longest and shortest continuous charge and discharge time and other physical parameters, and meet the technical support means of controllable load aggregation and its charge and discharge control.

2.2 Features of the Electricity Market

Under the background of the "plan plus market" dual-track operation [4], power users are divided into non-market-oriented users and market-oriented users, of which non-market-oriented users are mainly residential users who cannot participate in electricity market transactions, and the load aggregator purchases the planned electricity on behalf of the operator, and settles the electricity fee according to the on-grid benchmark electricity price; Market-oriented users are mainly large-scale industrial users and general industrial and commercial users, who can participate in the auction transaction of the electricity market and settle according to the clearing price.

Usually, the electricity trading center will organize the electricity wholesale market and the electricity retail market in the electricity market on time according to the rules of the electricity market, and large industrial users can directly participate in the wholesale market to purchase electricity, or participate in the power purchase transaction represented by the load aggregator, while the general industrial and commercial users must purchase electricity through the load aggregator in the retail market.

In the electricity wholesale market, power trading activities carried out by power generation and integrated transportation hubs through market-oriented methods include medium- and long-term monthly electric energy market transactions, spot electric energy market transactions, and special peak demand response transactions unique to some regions.

Among them, the peak demand response special transaction is the power trading center predicts the next day's power supply and demand balance and determines whether to start the power transaction after the end of the medium and long-term electric energy market, and the integrated transportation hub can participate in the auction and provide interruptible end user load capacity and transferable load capacity as agreed, cut and suspend the electricity demand during the peak period of the power system power supply load, or transfer the peak time electricity demand to the low time of the whole society's electricity demand, and obtain response compensation.

In the electricity retail market, integrated transportation hubs act as electricity sales companies to power users or purchase demand response resources from power users. First, the integrated transportation hub signs demand response agency agreements and electricity sales contracts with end users through bilateral negotiations; Then, on the day of the implementation day, the integrated transportation hub provides power supply services for users, organizes and supervises the neutralization of end users to adjust the load through the load management system, and performs the response duties; Finally, the integrated transportation hub collects the electricity sales fee according to the electricity sales contract and pays the compensation fee to the user according to the demand response agency agreement.

2.3 Technical Features

On the day of operation of the transaction result, under the supervision of the power dispatching center, each market entity will generate and use electricity according to the transaction result. Among them, the centralized control method is generally adopted for demand response resources, that is, the power dispatching center issues dispatching instructions to each load aggregator on the operation day, and then each load aggregator uniformly dispatches and controls the controllable load controlled by itself. Therefore, in order to dispatch and control all kinds of adjustable loads at any time, the integrated transportation hub needs to install a real-time monitoring system of intelligent terminals on the user side, which can monitor the changes in grid voltage and frequency at any time, and make load adjustment according to the power changes of the power grid and the system control instructions.

In the actual operation of the power system, the aggregation and management system of the integrated transportation hub can use the ubiquitous Internet of Things, based on network situation awareness, edge computing and cloud edge integrated control [5], to assist users to achieve metering transformation, collect the user's power, temperature, start-stop control signal, demand response willingness and other information, tap and evaluate the demand response potential contained in the information, and upload the summary information to the power trading center. At the same time, the dynamic optimization control strategy is adopted to realize the real-time optimization of user energy consumption and reduce the energy consumption of electrical equipment. After signing the demand response agreement, the response requirements of the power system are issued to the power users, and the users are helped to perform the responsc to achieve peak migration and valley filling.

3 Analysis of Demand Response Potential of the Transportation Hub

The integrated transportation hub covers three kinds of loads: cooling, heating and electricity: the electric load is provided by the CHP and the power grid, and the excess electricity is sold to the higher-level power grid; The cooling load is provided by absorption chillers and electric chillers; The heat load is supplied by a combination of CHP and gas-fired boilers. Most of the terminal loads are regarded as constant, but in the integrated transportation hub system, the cold, hot and point loads have good flexible and adjustable characteristics, and through the implementation of demand response, the peak-to-valley difference can be effectively reduced, and the system operation and investment costs can be reduced.

3.1 Flexible Loads

Cooling Load. For the air conditioning system, its load size is related to the outside temperature and the room temperature that needs to be maintained, under the premise of ensuring the user's human comfort, the air conditioning load is adjusted by changing the air conditioning temperature, that is, it has flexible control capabilities.

Assuming that the temperature control equipment in the building has been in a stable operating state, that is, the temperature control assumes that the temperature control equipment in the building has been in a stable operating state, that is, the cooling capacity of the temperature control equipment matches the cooling consumption of the building, based on the basic parameters of the building heating area and the average floor height, according to the current indoor temperature and the maximum temperature allowed by the user, the temperature control equipment can reduce the active power. When the duration is determined, the maximum reduction of the active power can be obtained:

$$P^1_{DR,decreased} \times t^1_{DR} \times EER = c \times S \times H \times \rho \times (T_{\lim it} - T_{set}) \tag{1}$$

wherein: $P^1_{DR,decreased}$ is the active power that can be cut by the temperature control equipment; t^1_{DR} is the duration of load reduction; EER for refrigeration energy efficiency ratio for temperature control equipment; t^1_{DR} refrigeration temperature set for the user; T_{limit} is the highest temperature that a building user can tolerate, which is higher than the refrigeration temperature set by the user.

Heating Load. This article assumes that in order to save electricity costs, general industrial and commercial users use energy-saving mode for the use of lighting equipment, that is, the lighting load is already in its lowest load state, and the adjustable potential is small and negligible.

Assuming that the temperature control equipment is already in a stable operating state, that is, the equipment heat production and building heat consumption match, based on the basic parameters of the building heating area and the average floor height, according to the current indoor temperature and the minimum temperature allowed by the user, the active power of the temperature control equipment can be reduced. When the duration is determined, the maximum available active power reduction is:

$$P^1_{DR,decreased} \times t^1_{DR} \times COP = c \times S \times H \times \rho \times (T_{set} - T_{\lim it}) \quad (2)$$

wherein: $P^1_{DR,decreased}$ is the active power that can be cut by the temperature control device; t^1_{DR} for the duration of the cut; COP is the heating energy efficiency ratio of temperature control equipment; c is the specific heat capacity of the air, generally the constant pressure specific heat capacity of the air when the temperature is 300K, the value is 1.005kJ/(kg*K); S is the heating area of the building; H is the average floor height of the building; ρ is the density of air, generally select the density of dry air at a temperature of 300K, the value is 1.177kg/m3; T_{set} the heating temperature set for the user; T_{limit} is the minimum temperature allowed by the user, which is lower than the heating temperature set by the user.

3.2 Traffic Loads

Traffic loads, typically electric vehicles and energy storage. However, the cost of energy storage configuration is large, and this paper mainly considers electric vehicles in the integrated transportation hub.

The usable capacity of single electric vehicles is limited, and the capacity of cluster electric vehicles is very considerable. Taking the 110,000 electric vehicles in Hunan Province as an example, according to the average configuration of 40kWh of energy storage batteries per electric vehicle, the mobile energy storage capacity of the province is about equal to 36 Hunan power grid energy storage power stations, which contains huge peak regulation potential [6].

Compared with traditional energy storage power sources, electric vehicles are fast response, strong climbing ability, and 90–95% of the time idle in public parking lots, office buildings and residential areas. Cluster electric vehicles form a mobile energy storage system through the control of load aggregators, and their grid-connected nodes change dynamically at different times, and the grid-connected power state (power generation power or load power) is dynamically switched through the bidirectional converter of the supply facility to realize the two-way interaction between the energy in the electric vehicle and the power system. Electric vehicles are moved to meet their own travel needs, charged as a load, and discharged as a power source to the grid [7].

The integrated transportation hub collects the travel and power information of electric vehicles located in the same area, including activity trajectory, travel location, power consumption, etc., and integrates this information through the energy management center, and then combines vehicle-to-grid (V2G) technology to regulate dispersed electric vehicle users, as shown in Fig. 1:

The usable capacity of an electric vehicle is equivalent to the power range output to the grid, i.e. by equipping the loads that can be increased with the amount of power generation that can be reduced, resulting in a usable down-regulation power range; By equating discharge or reduced charging to an increased amount of power generation, a usable upregulation power range is generated. Based on the charge and discharge

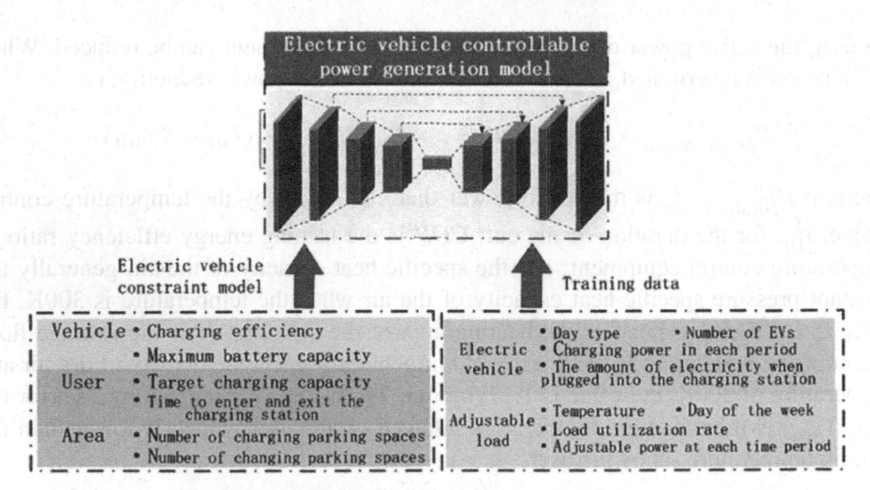

Fig. 1. Electric vehicle load perception mode

boundary between the previous discussions, the usable capacity of the electric vehicle at each moment is as:

$$\Delta\overline{p}_{n,t}^{e} = \frac{(S_{n,t}^{e} - \underline{S}_{n,t+1}^{e})Q_{E}^{e}}{\Delta t} \tag{3}$$

$$\Delta\underline{P}_{n,t}^{e} = \frac{(\overline{S}_{n,t+1}^{e} - S_{n,t}^{e})Q_{E}^{e}}{\Delta T} \tag{4}$$

In the formula, $\Delta\overline{p}_{n,t}^{e}$ and $\Delta\underline{P}_{n,t}^{e}$ represent the up-regulation and down-regulation of the usable capacity of the electric vehicle, $\overline{S}_{n,t+1}^{e}$ and $\underline{S}_{n,t+1}^{e}$ are the charging and discharging boundaries, and $S_{n,t}^{e}$ represents the charge state of the electric vehicle t at the n node at any time.

4 Integrated Transportation Hub Participates in the Special Transaction Process During Peak Periods

The distribution characteristics of peak load are similar to the electricity consumption habits of power users, and their occurrence time is mainly concentrated in the afternoon peak period and evening peak period of user electricity consumption. If the flexible load of industrial and commercial users of the integrated transportation hub is aggregated through the load aggregator, and the user is guided to transfer the electricity consumption of the noon/evening peak, the peak load can be effectively reduced.

The peak demand response session is a special session for the peak load period, using the user's side of the unilateral centralized auction transaction, unified clearing algorithm for clearance, with "spread priority, time priority, environmental protection priority" as the clearing calculation principle [8].

4.1 Special Launch Conditions and Transaction Targets

The power trading center predicts the load curve $p(t)$ of the next day, and determines whether to start the peak demand response session in combination with the peak over-limit δ and over-limit duration threshold ε. Using the peak load exceeding the limit value to determine whether there is a starting period so that the load curve $p(t)$ is greater than δ, that is, a peak period occurs, and the determination method is as follows:

$$p(t_1 - 1) \leqslant \delta, p(t_1 + 1) > \delta \tag{5}$$

$$p(t_2 - 1) > \delta, p(t_2 + 1) \leqslant \delta \tag{6}$$

When the period (t_1, t_2) satisfies the formulas (2) and (2), it can be determined to be a peak period.

The power trading center can set the threshold ε for the over-limit duration according to the opening degree of the special session and the trading time scale, and can determine whether the peak period meets the minimum limit of the opening duration of the special session:

$$t_2 - t_1 \geqslant \varepsilon \tag{7}$$

When the time period (t_1, t_2) satisfies the formula (3), the peak period meets the minimum limit of the opening time of the special session, and the power trading center can start the special session of peak demand response and announce the special transaction target.

The special transaction targets for peak demand response include the response demand Q_{DR} during the transaction period and the upper $\pi_{ds,max}$ and lower limit $\pi_{ds,min}$ of the compensation electricity price. If the power trading center takes the period (t_1, t_2) as a special trading period, the response demand can be calculated:

$$Q_{DR} = \int_{t_1}^{t_2} p(t)dt \tag{8}$$

At 8:00 a few days ago, the Electric Power Trading Center announced the trading information of the special trading session, that is, the trading session, the response demand and the upper and lower limits of the compensation electricity price, and organized the responding subjects to participate in the special trading.

4.2 Unilateral Bidding on the Demand Side

The integrated transportation hub declares the compensatory electricity price that can respond to the capacity and the expectation through the power trading center platform.

4.3 Special Clearing

The electric power trading center sorts according to the declared price of electric vehicle load aggregators from low to high, the declared value of responsive capacity from high to low, and the declaration time from early to late, until the responsive capacity reaches or exceeds the response demand, forming an unconstrained transaction As a result, the clearing price is the declared price of the winning bidder. The electric power trading center calculates the special declaration information to form the unconstrained trading result of unilateral centralized bidding.

4.4 Safety Check

Submit to the power dispatching agency for safety verification, and form a constrained transaction result.

Among them, the compensation point price constraint:

$$\pi_{ds,min} \leqslant \pi_{ds,bd,k} \leqslant \pi_{ds,max} \quad (9)$$

5 Market Clearance

5.1 Objective Function

The power grid company predicts the supply gap curve $P_{d,gap}(t)$ of the next day on $d - 1$, and sends an invitation to the demand response resource pool through the power trading center:

$$P_{d,gap}(t) = \max\{(P_{d,l}(t) - P_{d,s}(t) - P_{d,f}(t) - P_{d,g}(t) - P_{d,t,h,max}), 0\} \quad (10)$$

In the formula: $P_{d,gap}(t)$ is the supply gap curve of the power system on the d day; $P_{d,l}(t)$ is the load curve on the d day; $P_{d,s}(t)$ (t) is the first The hydropower output curve of day d; $P_{d,f}(t)$ is the wind power output curve of the d day; $P_{d,g}(t)$ is the photovoltaic output curve of the d day; $P_{d,t,h,max}$ is the maximum technical output of the thermal power unit on the d day, which is a constant.

The invited load aggregators can query their baseline load standard $P_{l,base}$ through the power trading center and choose whether to be invited. According to the invitation situation, the adjustable load of the resource pool on the d day can be calculated by the following formula:

$$P_d = \sum_{l=1}^{L^*} l^* P_{1,mon}, l^* \in L^* \quad (11)$$

In the formula: P_d represents the adjustable load of the demand response resource library on the d day; l^* represents the invitation status of the l th load aggregator, if it is invited, $l^* = 1$, if it is rejected, then $l^* = 0$.

When there is a period (t_1, t_2) such that $P_{d,gap}(t) > P_d$, the power trading center organizes bidding and listing transactions, and the load aggregators who still have spare capacity after being invited and the load aggregators who failed to delist in the previous stage can participate. According to the order of the declared electricity price from low to high, the power trading center sorts the various levels of the load-electricity price curve declared by the above load aggregators, and also builds a clearing model with the objective function of maximizing social welfare. The objective function can be expressed as follows:

$$\max F(P) = \sum_{l=1}^{L**} \int_{0}^{P_{l,win}} [r_l - \lambda_l(P_l)]dP_l \tag{12}$$

$$L^{**} = L^{-} + \sum_{l=1}^{L*} l^{*} \tag{13}$$

In the formula: L^{**} is the total number of load aggregators that can participate in the bidding and listing transaction; $P_{l,win}$ is the winning load of the l load aggregators.

5.2 Constraints

Supply and demand balance constraints

$$P_d + \sum_{l=1}^{L**} [P_{l,win}(t)] = P_{d,gap}(t), t \in (t_1, t_2) \tag{14}$$

integrated transportation hubs can regulate potential constraints

$$\begin{cases} 0 < P_{l,win}(t) + P_{l,mon} \leqslant P_{l,pub}, l \in L* \\ 0 < P_{l,win}(t) \leqslant P_{l,pub}, l \in L^{-1} \end{cases} \tag{15}$$

For the load aggregator in the R library, the adjustable load that participated in the pricing listing in the previous stage and the bidding in this stage should be less than its public value.

For the load aggregator in the R^{-} library, the adjustable load of the bid winning bid should be less than its public value.

Genset down ramp rate constraint

$$-v_{n*,down,\max} \leqslant P'_{n*}(t) \leqslant 0, n* \in N*, t \in (t_1, t_2) \tag{16}$$

In the formula: $P'_{n*}(t)$ is the derivative of the output function of the unit $n*$ in the time period (t_1, t_2).

5.3 Compensation Fee Settlement

As a market entity, load aggregators may announce or declare their adjustable loads and compensatory electricity prices according to their own wishes。However, in the actual transaction process, there may be the following phenomenon: in the information publicity stage, the integrated transportation hub declares its adjustable load and compensated electricity price according to its actual response cost; According to the market publicity information in the previous stage, the monthly pricing listing is deliberately dropped; In the recent auction listing stage, the strategic quotation method is adopted to raise the price of electricity and increase its own income. In view of this phenomenon, the strategic quotation of load aggregators can be suppressed through a reasonable and effective VCG allocation mechanism.

The settlement process of the day-ahead bidding listing special transaction is shown in Fig. 2:

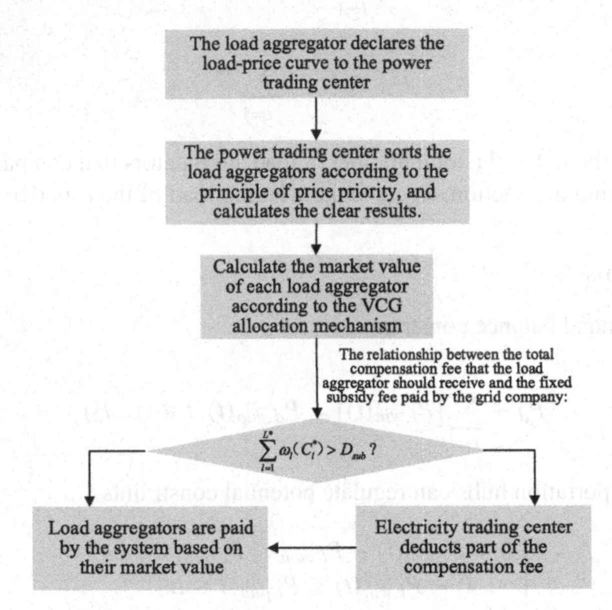

Fig. 2. Peak demand response special transaction process.

6 Conclusion

The peaking potential of integrated transportation hubs is considerable, providing dispatchable capacity for the power system and reducing peak loads. This paper first defines the integrated transportation junction, and studies the function of the integrated transportation hub in the electricity market that is different from other market players from both market and technical aspects, and clarifies its responsibilities in power trading. Then, the adjustable potential analysis of various end-user loads at the integrated transportation hub is performed; On this basis, the process of comprehensive transportation hubs participating in the peak demand response special transaction is elaborated, and on this basis, with the goal of maximizing social welfare, the market clearance model of the comprehensive transportation hub participating in the peak transaction is constructed, the transaction price and response electricity of the market entities are optimized, the theoretical feasibility of the comprehensive transportation hub to participate in the power transaction in response to the demand is provided, and the idea is provided for effectively improving the enthusiasm of the integrated transportation hub to participate in the market independently and promoting the peak shaving of the power grid.

References

1. Yan, Q., Xing, C., Zhang, N., et al.: Dynamic multistage spatio-temporal coordination method for ordered electricity consumption considering power saving loss. Power grid technology **40**(02), 425–432 (2016)
2. Hadley, S.W., Tsvetkova, A.A.: Potential impacts of plug-in hybrid electric vehicles on regional power generation. Electr. J. **22**(10), 56–68 (2009)
3. Jia, H., Wang, D., et al.: Research on several issues of integrated regional energy systems. Automation Of Electric Power Systems **39**(7), 198–207 (2015)
4. Padmanabhan, N., Ahmed, M., Bhattacharya, K.: Simultaneous procurement of demand response provisions in energy and spinning reserve markets. IEEE Trans. Power Syst. **33**(5), 4667–4682 (2018)
5. Bruninx, K., Pandi, H., Le Cadre, H., et al.: On the interaction between aggregators, electricity markets and residential demand response providers. IEEE Trans. Power Syst. **35**(2), 840–853 (2019)
6. Science Daily: http://www.sciencedaily.com/releases/. Last accessed 10 August 2022
7. Chen, Z., Ming, O., et al.: Self-organized droop frequency regulation method for EV aggregator. Electric Power Engineering Technology **38**(6), 77–83 (2019)
8. Zhang, X., Wang, X., Song, Y.H.: Modeling and pricing of block flexible electricity contracts. IEEE Transactions on Power systems **33**(5), 4667–4682 (2018)

Frequency Regulation with Mileage Payments: Is a Competitive Market Always the Winner?

Ran Zhang[1], Chen Zhao[1], Dan Zheng[1], and Wenqian Jang[2,3](✉)

[1] Electric Dispatch and Control Center, Guangdong Power Grid Company Ltd, Guangzhou, Guangdong, China

[2] School of Science and Engineering, The Chinese University of Hong Kong, Shenzhen, China
wenqianjiang@link.cuhk.edu.cn

[3] Shenzhen Institute of Artificial Intelligence and Robotics for Society, Shenzhen, Guangdong, China

Abstract. The advancement in distributed generation units and storage systems is stimulating a vigorous market for frequency regulation. Nevertheless, as identified by the Federal Energy Regulatory Commission, the un-paced payment structure in use may not well recognize the frequency regulation providers' performance, which warrants incorporating the "mileage payment" into the structure. Surprisingly, our theoretical analysis illustrates that such a new form of payment, if not designed carefully, may further prevent the independent system operators from achieving cost-effective frequency regulation. We compare two scenarios to support this argument - a competitive market and a regulated one. Counter-intuitively, due to the difficulty in the concise short-term load prediction in a reasonably large window, the competitive market is not the winner. We further establish the performance guarantee for the regulated market. Extensive simulation results confirm our theoretical analysis and demonstrate our approach's feasibility in the current AGC framework.

Keywords: Frequency regulation · Mileage payment · Model predictive control · Optimization

1 Introduction

Automatic Generation Control (AGC) for frequency regulation has served to balance generation and load and ensure that the frequency is kept close to its nominal value well in the past. However, the advancement in distributed generation units and storage systems, in combination with the increased variability introduced by a higher penetration of renewable resources has led to how to more fairly compensate the resources participating in frequency regulation for their services. As required by the recent Federal Energy Regulatory Commission (FREC) Order 755 [1], the independent system operators (ISOs) need to incorporate mileage payments to recognize the performance of the resources in frequency regulation. The mileage payment intends to "reward those resources that perform more regulation service instead of simply netting the total amount

H. Yang et al. (Eds.): SmartGIFT 2022, LNICST 483, pp. 354–367, 2023.
https://doi.org/10.1007/978-3-031-31733-0_30

of energy injected by the resource" [2], which is not captured by the existing capacity payment (which is used to compensate the lost opportunity cost) and the net energy payment/charge. If a cost-effective AGC is pursued, the limited ramping capacities of the resources render the decision-making at each time slot depends on the past decisions and possibly the future. The introduction of mileage payments is expected to further such coupling in time.

The classic approach to tackling optimization with time coupling constraints and the objective function is to perform model predictive control (MPC) [3]. Unfortunately, implementing MPC requires the prediction of the disturbances in the system, which in the case of AGC is captured by the area control error (ACE) signal. This signal is tough to predict reliably. In this paper, we consider a simplified steady-state linear model between the frequency deviation, the generation outputs and the load variations. Luckily, the generation outputs are the control variables, and recent works on concise short-term (1-min resolution) load prediction [4] shed light on the way to perform the challenging prediction. The proposed algorithm constantly achieves an error between 1 and 7% for 1-min resolution prediction. This warrants the MPC scheme to perform frequency regulation with all the three kinds of payments.

Albeit classic and promising, the cost-effectiveness of MPC in the power system is less concerned. After all, performance and cost-effectiveness both matter. In this paper, we compare two scenarios:

- a competitive market where each resource submits bids for the mileage payment,
- a regulated market where the ISO provides a fixed price for mileage payment.

The theoretical analysis suggests that, due to the difficulty in the very short-term load prediction in a reasonably large window, only the regulated market can provide the necessary, cost-effective guarantee, whereas, surprisingly, the competitive market can be manipulated by the market players. The counterintuitive conclusion seems consistent with market power manipulation [5–7] in the conventional real-time market.

2 Related Work and Contributions

Unlike voltage control [8] and conventional frequency regulation schemes, the understanding of mileage payments started only recently. For example, Papalexopoulos et al. proposed a comprehensive analysis of frequency regulation's performance-based pricing (including mileage payment) in [9]. In [10], Taylor et al. introduced a price and capacity competition with the imbalance fee, conceptually similar to mileage payments. Besides rising interests in the market design with mileage payment, empirical studies to understand the impact of different auxiliary regulation services also emerged: e.g. Lu et al. evaluated the flywheel potential for providing regulation service considering the mileage payment in [11]. Wu et al. explored using a risk-limiting economic dispatch scheme to optimize the dispatch and provision of flexible ramping products in [12], and the impact of flexible ramping products on a bid-based market is further analyzed in [13, 14]. Different from the existing works, which were mostly based on the single time slot optimization, our paper attempts to understand how the mileage payment affects the cost-effective frequency regulation in a dynamic setting and employs an MPC approach to tackle the challenge.

Our work also fits into the growing body of research on utilizing MPC for frequency regulation. Atic et al. presented a decentralized MPC approach to performing regulation in [15]. Gao et al. investigated the impact of introducing the corresponding mileage cost to the renewables for causing fluctuations in the system by the MPC method in [16]. Venkat et al. extensively compared various MPC frameworks and proposed a cooperation-based MPC for the current AGC system in [17]. With the popularity of plug-in electric vehicles, interesting MPC-based frequency regulation frameworks with time-varying resources (the PHEVs) were discussed in [18, 19]. In contrast, our work is motivated by the introduction of mileage payment to frequency regulation, making the theoretical analysis more challenging.

This paper seeks to answer the following key question: *is it possible to design a performance guaranteed market for frequency regulation with mileage payment?*

Towards answering the question, in Section III, we first propose the problem formulation using the MPC approach and identify the analytical difficulty in a straightforward formulation. Then, in Section IV, we compare the competitive market design and the regulated one. After that, we perform extensive case studies for the two kinds of markets in both the linearized simplified model and the swing dynamic model in Section V. Finally, our concluding remarks and directions for future work are discussed in Section VI.

3 Problem Formulation

3.1 Steady-State Linear Model

While swing dynamics can efficiently capture the system evolution, it becomes hard to develop effective control strategies when considering the ramping constraints. A more complicated cost function will make the control strategy design even harder. To better understand the mileage payment's impact on the cost-effective frequency regulation, we consider a simplified steady-state linear model, where we take advantage of the fact that primary frequency control is in place to stabilize the frequency. Denote the set of frequency regulation resources by $\mathcal{N}$, and resource n's regulation contribution at time t by g_n^t. Then, in steady state, the frequency deviation $\Delta f(t)$ from its nominal value is linear in the load deviation from the load prediction used in the energy dispatch, denoted by $\hat{d}^t$. Mathematically, $\Delta f(t)$ will stabilize at

$$\Delta f(t) = \frac{\sum_{n\in\mathcal{N}} g_n^{t-1} - \hat{d}^t}{\gamma} \tag{1}$$

where

$$\gamma = \sum_{p\in\Omega_P} \frac{1}{R_p} \cdot \frac{P_{p,r}}{f_r} \tag{2}$$

and Ω_P is the set of entities participating in primary frequency control [20], R_p is the speed droop and $P_{p,r}$ the nominal power of entity p and f_r is the nominal frequency (here 60 Hz).

3.2 MPC Formulation

Since frequency regulation aims at dealing with minor fluctuations in the power system, in contrast to the energy dispatch problem, it is reasonable to consider frequency regulation in an electricity pool model. Most deregulated electricity markets have separate markets for regulation-up and regulation-down services. Here, to better differentiate the two services, we explicitly define the frequency regulation contribution as the difference between the frequency regulation resource's actual power output and its nominal power decided by the energy dispatch. If such difference (denoted by g_n^t in this paper) is positive, we consider the resource is offering regulation up service, whereas negative regulation contribution leads to regulation down service. We take the regulation-up service market as an example for our analysis. All the discussions can be applied to the regulation-down service market similarly by replacing the non-negative constraint on g_n^t with the non-positive constraint.

At time slot h, assume we could obtain the load deviation prediction $\hat{d}^t$ in a window of size W, i.e., $t \in \mathcal{W}^{\rm h} = \{\rm h, h+1, \cdots h+W-1\}$. The length of one time slot could be 15 s or even less. Thus, if a cost-effective control is pursued, then the ISO seeks to solve the following problem:

$$\min \sum_{t\in\mathcal{W}^{\rm h}} \sum_{n\in\mathcal{N}} (c_n g_n^t + \beta_n |g_n^t - g_n^{t-1}|) \tag{3}$$

$$s.t. \left| g_n^t - g_n^{t-1} \right| \leqslant \Delta g_n, \forall n \in \mathcal{N}, \forall \rm t \in \mathcal{W}^{\rm h}, \tag{4}$$

$$0 \leqslant g_n^t \leqslant \overline{g}_n, \forall n \in \mathcal{N}, \forall \rm t \in \mathcal{W}^{\rm h}, \tag{5}$$

$$\sum_{n\in\mathcal{N}} g_n^t = \hat{d}^t, \forall t \in \mathcal{W}^{\rm h}, \tag{6}$$

The decision variables in the optimization problem (3)-(6) are g_n^t's: frequency regulation resource n's regulation contribution [MW] at time t. The parameters, on the other hand, are.

- c_n: net energy bid [\$/MW] of regulation resource n;
- $\hat{d}^t$: demand deviation from demand prediction value used in the energy dispatch [MW] at time t;
- $\overline{g}_n$: resource n's maximal regulation up capacity [MW];
- Δg_n: resource n's ramping limit [MW/15 s].

Note that g_n^0's are considered as given values. Constraint (4) enforces each regulation resource's ramping limit. Constraint (5) ensures the capacity constraints are met, and the last constraint represents the power balance condition at each time slot. We do not consider the co-optimization determines it with the energy bids in the real time energy dispatch market. Thus, the capacity payment is simply a constant in this optimization stage.

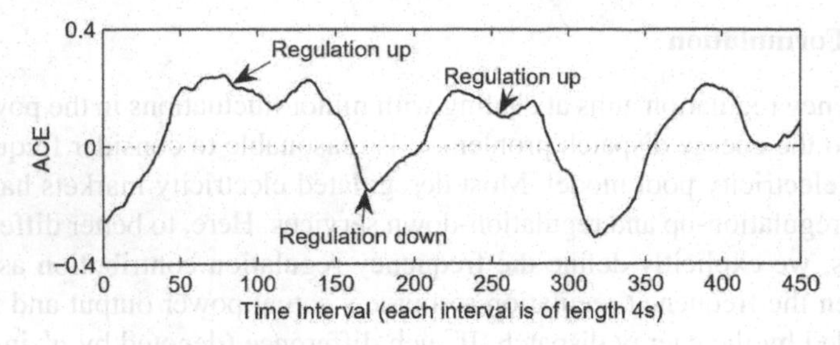

Fig. 1. The ACE signal in PJM [22]

3.3 Relaxation

Though straightforward, the performance analysis (e.g., comparing with the offline optimal) of such a 1-norm MPC formulation is very challenging: even in the unconstrained case, due to the lack of an explicit closed-form expression for the control law [21]. Figure 1 shows the 30-min actual ACE signal in PJM. If the regulation resources accurately follow the control signal, their generation outputs ought to follow this trace. Note that the regulation up and regulation down services switch over time frequently. This implies that during each course of regulation up/down period, the total mileage of ramping up equals that of ramping down. This motivates considering the following alternative formulation to (3) - (6):

$$\min \sum_{t\in\mathcal{W}^{\mathrm{h}}}\sum_{n\in\mathcal{N}}(c_n g_n^t + 2\beta_n[g_n^t - g_n^{t-1}]^+)$$

$$s.t.\ \text{Constraints (4)} - \text{(6)} \tag{7}$$

where $[x]^+ \doteq \max\{0, x\}$. We can only consider the mileage payment when regulation resources ramp up and neglect the ramp down. By doubling the mileage payment, the overall payment for each regulation resource over the long run remains the same.

Another issue is that constraint (6) may be too strict. The ramping constraints may often render the optimization problem infeasible. Thus, we consider the following relaxation:

$$\min f\left(g_n^t, \forall n, \forall t\right) + M \sum_{t\in\mathcal{W}^{\mathrm{h}}} |\sum_{n\in\mathcal{N}} g_n - \hat{d}^t|$$

$$s.t.\ \text{Constraints (4) and (5)} \tag{8}$$

where

$$f\left(g_n^t, \forall n, \forall t\right) = \sum_{t\in\mathcal{W}^{\mathrm{h}}}\sum_{n\in\mathcal{N}}(c_n g_n^t + 2\beta_n[g_n^t - g_n^{t-1}]^+) \tag{9}$$

and M is a large number to trade-off between cost-effectiveness and system performance. When $M \to \infty$, optimization (8) will essentially schedule the power outputs to minimize the mismatch in the system. On the other hand, when M is reasonably large, it reflects the ISO's interest in having a cost-effective solution.

3.4 Illustrative Prototype

Before moving to the performance assessment, we want first to observe how M affects the optimal solution's structure and illustratively exemplify the trade-off with a simple prototype. We use a window size of 3 and assume perfect load deviation prediction.

Table 1. Generator information for the prototype system

	c_n[\$/MW]	β_n[\$/MW]	Δg_n [MW/15 s]	g_u[MW]
Gen 1	50	20	2	20
Gen 2	70	15	3	20
Gen 3	120	10	5	30

The prototype system has three generators as frequency regulation resources. Table 1 shows their parameters. When experiencing a 50 MW step load increase, all the three generators are expected to contribute to compensate for such mismatch. When M is relatively small ($M = 140$), since ramping up the third generator is too expensive (at the cost of $120 + 10 \times 2 = 140$), the MPC approach will not schedule it to perform regulation, as shown in Fig. 2(b). This leads to a supply–demand mismatch of 10 MW, as shown in Fig. 2(a). This case intuitively demonstrates the critical point when selecting M: if

$$M \leqslant \max\{c_n + 2\beta_n\} \tag{10}$$

the system reliability, in terms of utilizing all the resources to recover the mismatch, is not guaranteed. As long as $M > \max\{c_n + 2\beta_n\}$, the MPC approach ensures system reliability, as illustrated in the other two cases. However, a larger M ($M = 180$) will compensate for the mismatch faster, whereas a smaller M ($M = 160$) will perform the regulation in a more cost-effective way, though the final generation output profiles (after 225 s, i.e., $h \geqslant 15$) for the two cases are the same. We will return to this prototype in the case study to better understand our approach.

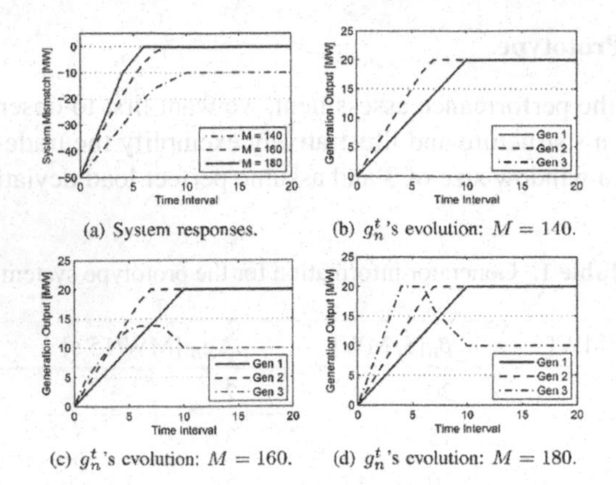

(a) System responses. (b) g_n^t's evolution: $M = 140$.
(c) g_n^t's evolution: $M = 160$. (d) g_n^t's evolution: $M = 180$.

Fig. 2. Prototype system to highlight the impact of M

4 Performance Assessment

Following (8), we compare the competitive market design and the regulated one. We differentiate these two cases by how the β_n's are set. If the resources are allowed to bid their own β_n's, we term such case the competitive one. On the contrary, if the ISO directly sets the same β_n for all resources, we term such case the regulated one.

4.1 Competitive Case

We first consider a competitive scenario. It is seemingly trustworthy that if we allow a competitive market, then by selecting the most efficient regulation resources, the market will achieve maximal efficiency. Let us consider the following simple counterexample, where there are only two regulation resources, A and B, and the ramping and generation capacity constraints are not the primary concerns. Resource A submits a bid consisting of its net energy bid c_a, and mileage bid β_a. Resource B, the more cost-efficient one, tries to manipulate the mechanism by submitting its actual net energy bid $c_b < c_a$, and an extremely high $\beta_b \gg \beta_a$. Thus, when encountering a step load change, the ISO using the MPC approach, with a limited size of prediction window, will be reluctant to choose B due to the high mileage payment, which will lead to an average cost of c_a. However, suppose the ISO knows all the future information (i.e., the load disturbance is a step change). In that case. it will instead choose B regardless of the high mileage payment since such "capital cost" will amortize over time and eventually lead to an average cost of c_b.

This example highlights the daunting part of the MPC design. Indeed, as popular as it is, MPC has limited abilities. The malicious resource can choose to report false information about the mileage cost and directly affect the net energy payment. This might be tackled if the ISO does not select these malicious market players in the first place. However, the current practice - a co-optimization between the energy and frequency regulation bids - does not consider mileage bids. This is large because there are still no mileage bids. The deeper reason is that it is hard to foresee the fluctuations for the entire

15 min (or even one hour) when performing the co-optimization in the real-time energy dispatch.

To this end, alarmingly to the ISOs, it is not wise to design a competitive market for the frequency regulation with mileage payment. In the example, regulation resource B risks losing profits when reporting the wrong information, but this can be rational and reasonable if the two regulation resources collude together to achieve a better total payoff. Though a detailed discussion is beyond the scope of this paper, we want to stress that such a circumstance is not a purely theoretical fantasy, which will never happen in practice.

4.2 Regulated Case

In a regulated scenario, where all the β_n's are the same, the ISO is neutral in selecting different resources to perform frequency regulation in mileage payments. Thus, the performance of MPC, in this case, is almost the same as the performance where there is no mileage payment and enjoys a $(1 + O(1/W))$ competitive ratio, which is the ratio between our approach's performance and the offline (with $W = \infty$) approach's performance [23].

Theorem 1: The regulated MPC is $1 + \frac{2\beta}{W \min c_n}$ competitive.

This is a direct result of [24]. We want to stress that, Theorem 1, in no way, implies that the competitive market cannot perform as well as the regulated one (in fact, it is often better); rather, since we cannot obtain the load deviation over a long time horizon, the competitive market is easier to manipulate and thus does not enjoy the performance guarantee. To this end, if the ISO were to employ an MPC approach to achieve the cost-effective dispatch, the theoretical analysis suggests a regulated market for mileage payment.

5 Case Study

In this section, we test our MPC approach for 200-time slots. The regulation demand profile is the scaled PJM's AGC signal [22], as shown in Fig. 3.

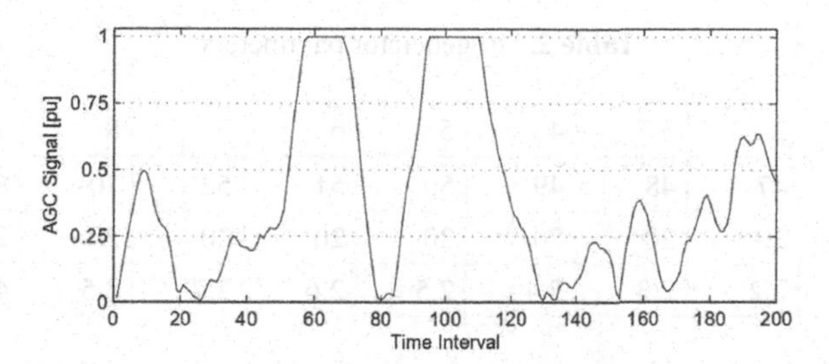

Fig. 3. PJM sample AGC signal

5.1 Competitive Market: Price Manipulation

First, we consider the prototype system. Now, generator 1, the most cost-effective one, tries to manipulate the regulation service market by submitting an extremely high mileage bid of \$50/MW. The peak demand deviation is scaled to 45 MW. With a window size of 3, Fig. 4 shows the three generators' output traces, which confirm our theoretical discussion: the ISO is reluctant to schedule generator 1.

No surprise, in the optimal off-line dispatch ($W = \infty$), generator 1 provides more regulation contribution because of its low net energy cost. It is worth noting that the manipulation can be relieved by increasing the window size, as demonstrated in Fig. 4, where we use a slightly larger window size, $W = 5$, and the generation output traces change dramatically.

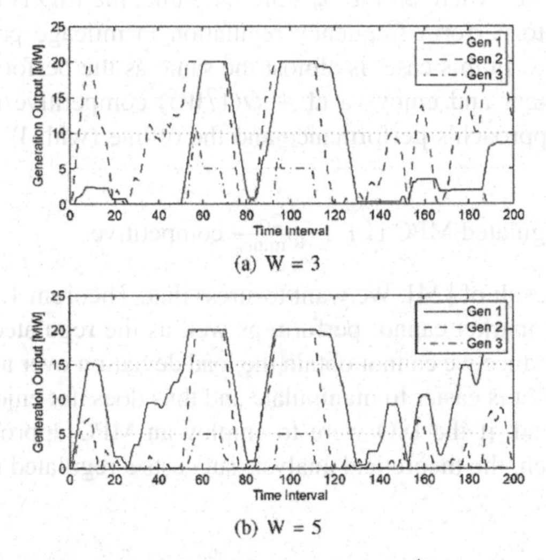

(a) W = 3

(b) W = 5

Fig. 4. Manipulation evolution of g_n^t's output

5.2 Competitive *v.s.* Regulated Market

Table 2. 10 generator parameters

n	1	2	3	4	5	6	7	8	9	10
c_n	46	47	48	49	50	51	52	70	80	120
$\overline{g}_n$	20	20	20	20	20	20	20	20	20	20
Δg_n	2.1	2.2	2.3	2.4	2.5	2.6	2.7	3.5	4	6

Next, we extensively compare the two kinds of markets. We extend the simulations to a 10 generators system. Table 2 shows the generators' parameters. We consider three

Table 3. Mileage bids for 10 generators

n	1	2	3	4	5	6	7	8	9	10
Case R	20	20	20	20	20	20	20	20	20	20
Case M	40	40	15	15	15	15	15	15	15	15
Case C	12	13	14	15	16	17	18	20	30	45

cases of mileage bidding mechanisms shown in Table 3: Case R represents the regulated case; Case M is the competitive case with manipulation; and Case C is the truthful competitive case. Note that the mileage bids summation over all generators again remains the same for different cases ($200/MW). Trade-off M is set to be 140. Figure 5 displays the trend of total payments with the increasing window size W. From the results we can tell that:

- The total payment decreases as the window size increases.
- Case R is better than Case M but is worse than Case C. Again; this shows that if we can ensure a truthful competitive market, then the competitive market can perform very well.

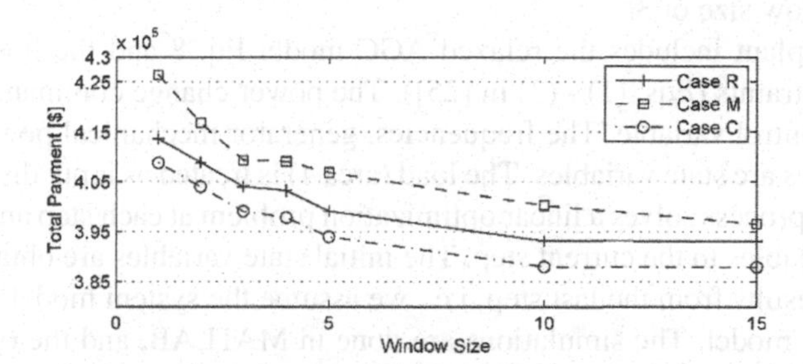

Fig. 5. Total payments for different cases

5.3 Swing Dynamics

Next, we study our MPC approach's performance on an interconnected system with swing dynamics. This demonstrates that, though our analysis is focused on the linearized model, our approach is feasible in the AGC framework and performs well. A 4-area system, as in Fig. 6 is considered. The parameters for the generators are listed in Table 4, where M_j, D_j, and $|V_j|$ stand for generator inertia, damping constant, and voltage magnitude at each area; the others are constant parameters corresponding to generator governor control and ACE-based AGC.

The mileage bids for all generators are 30$/pu, and we do not compare the net energy payment/charge here. All the generators' outputs are bounded from -0.5 to 2.5pu and

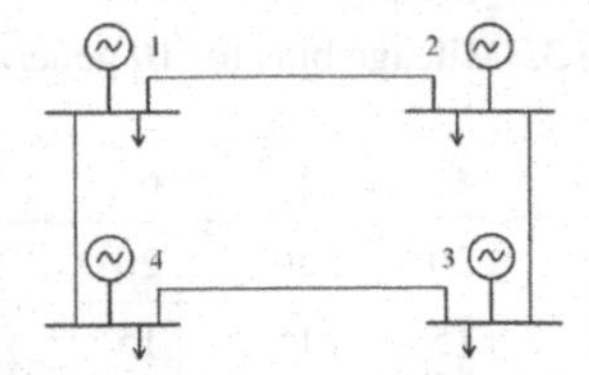

Fig. 6. Diagram for 4-areas Interconnected System

Table 4. Generator parameters for swing dynamic analysis [25]

Area	M_j	D_j	$\|V_j\|$	T_j	R_j	B_j
1	3	1	1.045	4	0.05	2
2	2.5	1.5	0.98	4	0.05	3
3	4	1.2	1.033	4	0.05	2
4	3.5	1.4	0.997	4	0.05	3

have a maximum ramp rate of 0.5pu. The nominal values for generation and load of all areas are set as 1pu, and a step change of load occurs at area 4. The time interval for the simulation is 0.01 s, and the tradeoff for MPC approach is chosen as $M = 140$. We employ a window size of 3.

The MPC plant includes the relaxed AGC model Eq. 8 and the linearized swing dynamics constraints (Eqs. (1) - (3) in [25]). The power change command at each generator is the control variable. The frequencies, generator mechanical power output and line power flows are state variables. The load (area 4) is treated as input disturbance. The MPC decision process solves a linear optimization problem at each step and then applies the control variables to the current step. The initial state variables are obtained from the optimization results from the last step, i.e., we assume the system model is the same as the MPC plant model. The simulations are done in MATLAB, and the optimization is optimal for every time step according to the solver *linprog*.

The dynamics of the frequencies, power change command, and mechanical power outputs for the four areas using ACE-based AGC (left) and MPC-based AGC (right) are displayed in Fig. 7. The mileage payment for these two approaches is compared in Table 5. From the results, we can tell that the MPC approach can smooth the frequency dynamics with much less regulation mileage.

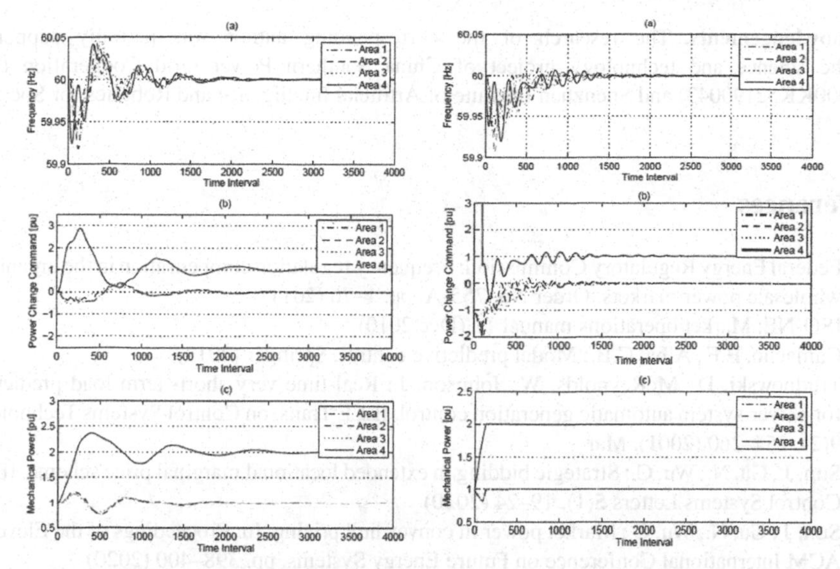

Fig. 7. The ACE-based (left) and MPC-based (right) AGC: (a) System Frequencies, (b) Power Change Command, (c) Mechanical Power Output

Table 5. Mileage payment for interconnected system [$]

Area	1	2	3	4
ACE-based	15.55	16.00	13.91	40.93
MPC-based	4.67	4.56	4.70	29.85

6 Conclusions and Future Work

The impact of mileage payments on the frequency regulation system design may be far-reaching. This paper compares the two kinds of potential markets for frequency regulation with mileage payments: the competitive and regulated markets. Theoretical analysis and simulation results suggest that the competitive market may not be the winner in the near future. This is not a denial of the competitive market. A suitable mechanism in practice is not about having the perfect plan. Instead, it involves working out the advantages of different options. Thus, we reckon that a capped bidding mechanism, the most commonly used in the electricity market, might again be the most desirable option for the mileage bidding.

This paper can be extended in various directions. For instance, we have not included the swing dynamics in the theoretical analysis, which will make our results more practical. Also, we would like to consider the decentralized or distributed MPC for frequency regulation with mileage payments. Such an approach may better suit the future power system with the large volume of participating regulation resources.

Acknowledgements. The research of the corresponding author was partially supported by the science and technology project of China Southern Power Grid Cooperation (No. 036000KK52190043) and Shenzhen Institute of Artificial Intelligence and Robotics for Society.

References

1. Federal Energy Regulatory Commission: Frequency regulation compensation in the organized wholesale power markets. Order No. 755-A, pp. 1–76 (2011)
2. ISO-NE: Market operations manual 11 (Dec 2010)
3. Camacho, E.F., Alba, C.B.: Model predictive control. Springer (2013)
4. Trudnowski, D., McReynolds, W., Johnson, J.: Real-time very short- term load prediction for power-system automatic generation control. IEEE Trans. on Control Systems Technology **9**(2), 254–260 (2001). Mar
5. Sun, J., Gu, N., Wu, C.: Strategic bidding in extended locational marginal price scheme. IEEE Control Systems Letters **5**(1), 19–24 (2020)
6. Sun, J., Gu, N., Wu, C.: Market power in convex hull pricing. In: Proceedings of the Eleventh ACM International Conference on Future Energy Systems, pp. 398–400 (2020)
7. Wu, C., Bose, S., Wierman, A., et al.: A unifying approach to assessing market power in deregulated electricity markets. In: 2013 IEEE Power & Energy Society General Meeting. IEEE, pp. 1–5 (2013)
8. Wu, C., Mohsenian-Rad, H., Huang, J., et al.: PEV-based combined frequency and voltage regulation for smart grid. In: 2012 IEEE PES Innovative Smart Grid Technologies (ISGT). IEEE, pp. 1–6 (2012)
9. Papalexopoulos, A.D., Andrianesis, P.E.: Performance-based pricing of frequency regulation in electricity markets. IEEE Trans. on Power Systems **29**(1), 441–449 (2014)
10. Taylor, J.A., Mathieu, J.L., Callaway, D.S., Poolla, K.: Price and capacity competition in zero-mean storage and demand response markets. In: Proc. of the 50th Allerton. IEEE, pp. 1316–1323 (2012)
11. Lu, N., et al.: Evaluation of the flywheel potential for providing regulation service in California. In: Proc. of IEEE PES General Meeting 2010. IEEE, pp. 1–6 (2010)
12. Wu, C., Hug, G., Kar, S.: Risk-limiting economic dispatch for electricity markets with flexible ramping products. IEEE Trans. Power Syst. **31**(3), 1990–2003 (2015)
13. Chen, Q., Zou, P., Wu, C., et al.: A Nash-Cournot approach to assessing flexible ramping products. Appl. Energy **206**, 42–50 (2017)
14. Wu, C., Hug, G., Kar, S.: A functional approach to assessing flexible ramping products' impact on electricity market. In: 2015 IEEE Power & Energy Society Innovative Smart Grid Technologies Conference (ISGT). IEEE, pp. 1–5 (2015).
15. Atic, N., Rerkpreedapong, D., Hasanovic, A., Feliachi, A.: Nerc compliant decentralized load frequency control design using model predictive control. In: Proc. of IEEE PES General Meeting 2003, vol. 2, pp. 559 (July 2003)
16. Gao, X., Wang, K., Wu, C.: Who should pay for the mileage payment?. In: 2018 IEEE International Conference on Communications, Control, and Computing Technologies for Smart Grids (SmartGridComm). IEEE, pp. 1–6 (2018)
17. Venkat, A., Hiskens, I., Rawlings, J., Wright, S.: Distributed mpc strategies with application to power system automatic generation control. IEEE Trans. on Control Systems Technology **16**(6), 1192–1206 (2008). Nov
18. Hiskens, I., Callaway, D.: Achieving controllability of plug-in electric vehicles. In: Proc. of IEEE VPPC 2009, pp. 1215–1220 (Sept 2009)

19. Ulbig, A., Galus, M.D., Chatzivasileiadis, S., Andersson, G.: General frequency control with aggregated control reserve capacity from time-varying sources: The case of phevs. In: Proc. of 2010 iREP Symposium, pp. 1–14 (Aug 2010)
20. Bergen, A., Vittal, V.: Power systems analysis. Prentice Hall (1999)
21. Garcia, A.E., Prett, D.M., Morari, M.: Model predictive control: theory and practicea survey. Automatica **25**(3), 335–348 (1989)
22. PJM: The PJM fast response regulation signal (Jan 2013). [Online]. Available: http://www.pjm.com/markets-and-operations/ancillary-services/mkt-based-regulation/fast-response-regulation-signal.aspx
23. Borodin, A., El-Yaniv, R.: Online computation and competitive analysis. Cambridge university press (1998)
24. Lin, M., Liu, Z., Wierman, A., Andrew, L.L.: Online algorithms for geographical load balancing. In: Proc. of IGCC 2012. IEEE, pp. 1–10 (2012)
25. Li, N., Chen, L., Zhao, C., Low, S.: Connecting automatic generation control and economic dispatch from an optimization view. to appear in Proc. of the American Control Conference (ACC) (2014)

Smart Control and Diagnosis of Distributed Power System

Hybrid Single-Line-to-Ground Fault Arc Suppression Method in Distribution Networks

Qiong Liu(✉), Wen Wang, Qinze Chen, Chaofeng Zhang, and Xiao Ding

Changsha University of Science and Technology, Changsha, China
1424623598@qq.com

Abstract. Existing voltage-type arc suppression method compensates fault current without considering line impedance. When metallic single line-to-ground (SLG) fault occurs, residual current of fault location rises instead of falling with conventional method, resulting in the failure of arc suppression. To solve this problem, combined current-type and voltage-type arc suppression method, a hybrid method is proposed in this paper. The distribution network is analyzed when considering line impedance and load. According to this, the current and voltage references for active arc suppression device (ASD) are derived for accurate arc suppression. The grounding resistance is estimated by zero-sequence current and voltage of the system. When it is larger than a setting threshold, voltage-type arc suppression method is adopted. Otherwise, current-type method is adopted. The proposed method can reduce fault current to almost zero. The correctness of the proposed method is validated and comparison is presented by simulation in the MATLAB/Simulink environment.

Keywords: Distribution Network · Single-phase-to-ground Fault · Arc Suppression

1 Introduction

SLG (single line-to-ground) faults are the most common fault type and shound be paid attention to [1, 2]. With the the extensive use of power cables, the fault current increases sharply. The resulted ground-fault arc is difficult to extinguish itself, which may cause overvoltage and interphase short circuit [3, 4].

The passive method adopts Petersen coil to acchive capacitive current compensation [5–7]. The active method uses power electronics converters to inject a specific zero-sequence current for full ground-fault current compensation. Z. Zheng [8] presented a three-phase arc suppression device and backstepping control. However, the accuracy of the ground-fault current limits its arc suppression performance. The conventional method [4] achieve arc suppression by setting neutral voltage to the inverse of supply voltage of faulty phase.

However, line impedance is ignored. To address this problem, [9, 10] proposed an arc suppression method by limiting the neutral voltage to a regulated reference. The effect

H. Yang et al. (Eds.): SmartGIFT 2022, LNICST 483, pp. 371–385, 2023.
https://doi.org/10.1007/978-3-031-31733-0_31

of line impedance and load are taken into account [10]. However, the simulation was performed when grounding resistance is set to 30,50 and 100Ω. It ignores the conditions of low grounding resistance and metallic SLG faults. When low-resistance SLG fault occurs at the beginning of faulty feeder, the actual value of neutral voltage is close to the reference, which may leads to the failure of arc suppression.

In this paper, a hybrid method is proposed in Sect. 2. In Sect. 3, the limitations of conventional method and the impact factors of residual current are analyzed. Then, the injection current reference and neutral voltage reference are presented along with the related parameters calculation. The complete implementation process of the hybrid arc suppression method is presented. Finally, simulation results are provided in Sect. 4 to study arc suppression performance.

2 Performance Analysis of Conventional Arc Suppression Method

Conventional arc suppression method works by regulating the neutral voltage to the supply voltage of faulty phase. However, conventional arc suppression method ignores line impedance and load, which leads to an issue that the voltage of fault location is the same as bus. The residual voltage cannot be restricted to zero even bus voltage maintains zero.

2.1 Residual Current Calculation at Fault Location

Figure 1 shows a 10kV distribution network including line impedance and load. The feeder lines length is m km long and the fault feeder is l km long. α is the fault location ratio, i.e., the division of the length from the busbar to the fault point over the total length of the fault feeder. Z_{lX} and Z_{load} are the line impedance and load impedance, respectively. The load is in triangular connection.

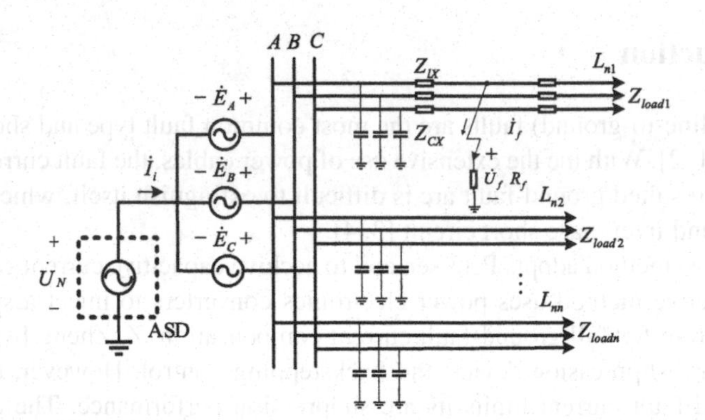

Fig. 1. 10kV distribution network considering line impedance.

The boundary conditions is

$$\begin{cases} \dot{U}_{f1} + \dot{U}_{f2} + \dot{U}_{f0} = \dot{U}_f \\ \dot{I}_{f1} = \dot{I}_{f2} = \dot{I}_{f0} = \frac{1}{3}\dot{I}_f \end{cases} \tag{1}$$

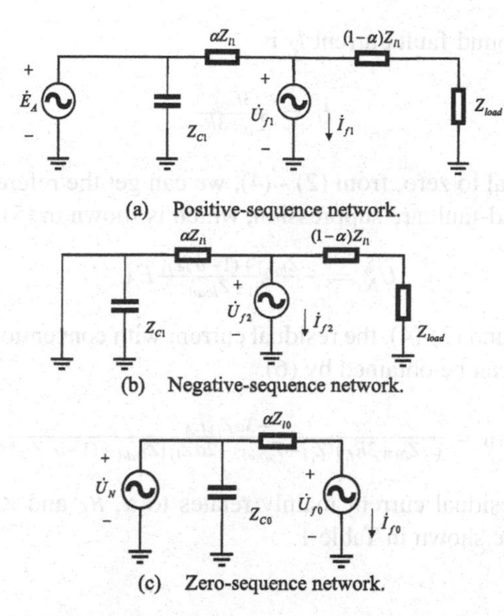

Fig. 2. The sequence networks considering line impedance.

From (1) and Fig. 2, the simplified circuit is shown as Fig. 3, where $Z_{LD} = Z_{load} + (1 - \alpha)Z_{l1}$.

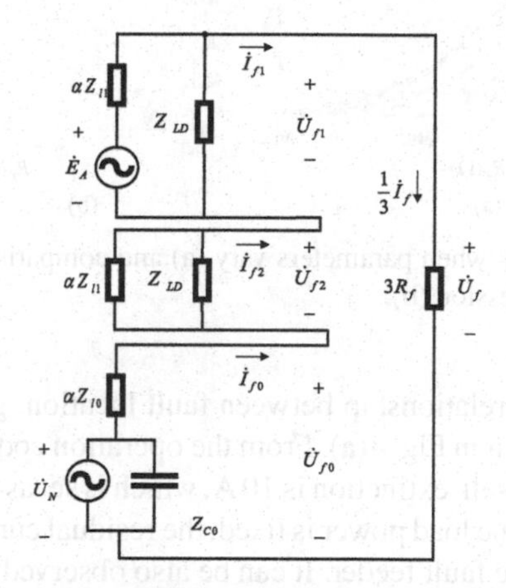

Fig. 3. The simplified composite sequence network.

$\dot{E}_{eq}$ and Z_{eq} are the equivalent voltage source and impedance, shown as (2) and (3).

$$\dot{E}_{eq} = \frac{Z_{load}+(1-\alpha)Z_{l1}}{Z_{l1}+Z_{load}}\dot{E}_A + \dot{U}_N \tag{2}$$

$$Z_{eq} = \frac{2\alpha Z_{l1}[Z_{load}+(1-\alpha)Z_{l1}]}{Z_{l1}+Z_{load}} + \alpha Z_{l0} \tag{3}$$

Therefore, the ground-fault current $\dot{I}_f$ is

$$\dot{I}_f = \frac{3\dot{E}_{eq}}{Z_{eq}+3R_f} \tag{4}$$

Assume $\dot{I}_f$ is equal to zero, from (2) - (4), we can get the reference neutral voltage of the ASD for ground-fault arc suppression, which is shown in (5).

$$\dot{U}_N^* = -\frac{Z_{load}+(1-\alpha)Z_{l1}}{Z_{l1}+Z_{load}}\dot{E}_A \tag{5}$$

According to (1) and (2)-(4), the residual current with conventional voltage-type arc suppression method can be obtained by (6).

$$\dot{I}_{r0} = \frac{-3\alpha Z_{l1}\dot{E}_A}{(\alpha Z_{l0}+3R_f)(Z_{l1}+Z_{load})+2\alpha Z_{l1}[Z_{load}+(1-\alpha)Z_{l1}]} \tag{6}$$

Obviously, the residual current mainly relates to α, R_f and Z_{load}. Typical power system parameters are shown in Table 1.

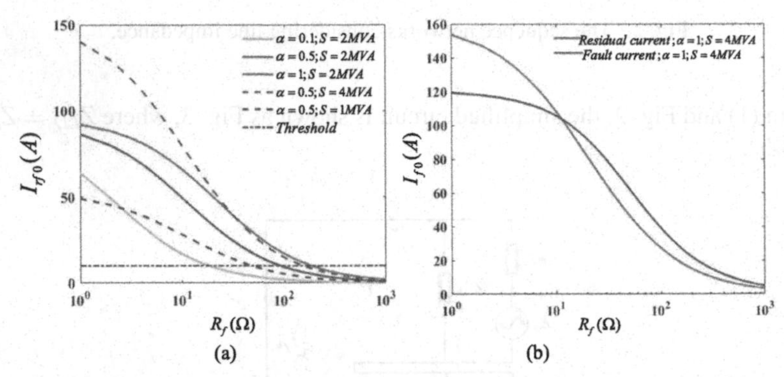

Fig. 4. The residual currents when parameters vary (a) and comparison fault current before and after conventional arc suppression (b).

According to (6), the relationship between fault location, grounding resistance and residual currents are shown in Fig. 4(a). From the operation code, the maximum residual current to ensure fault arc self-extinction is 10 A, which is set as the threshold in Fig. 4(a).

It is shown that when the load power is fixed, the residual current increases as the fault gets close to the end of the fault feeder. It can be also observed that with the decrease of grounding resistance, the residual current increases. Only when the grounding resistance is larger than about 200 Ω, the arc can be suppressed.

Figure 4(b) shows the comparison fault currents before and after conventional arc suppression when $\alpha = 1$ and $S = 4MVA$. The red curve is the residual current after arc suppression. The blue curve is the fault current before arc suppression. We can see that the residual current is even larger than the fault current before SLG fault. In the worst case, the fault current reaches 130% of the capacitive current when grounding resistance is zero.

Table 1. System parameters.

Parameters	Value
Positive-sequence impedances Z_{l1}	$0.27 + j0.07\ \Omega/km$
Positive-sequence impedances Z_{c1}	$9.4e3\ \Omega/km$
Zero-sequence impedances Z_{l0}	$2.7 + j0.32\ \Omega/km$
Zero-sequence impedances Z_{c0}	$1.14e4\ \Omega/km$
Nominal power	1 MVA
Line voltage E_X	10 kV
Total length of feeder lines m	100 km
Total length of fault line l	20 km

3 Hybrid Arc Suppression Method

Current-type arc suppression method needs the distributed parameters. Their detection may be affected by the fluctuation and asymmetry of the distribution network. These factors will lead to measurement errors of grounding parameters, so that the reference injected current is not accurate enough, and it is difficult to restrict fault current to zero. Voltage-type method needs no measurement of grounding parameters, but it has poor performance when low resistance SLG fault occurs. To solve this problem, a hybrid arc suppression method is proposed.

3.1 Principle of Hybrid Arc Suppression Method

The proposed method is shown as follows. When the estimated grounding resistance is larger than a set threshold, voltage-type arc suppression method is adopted. Otherwise, the current-type method will be adopted. Through the complementary advantages of the two methods, the arc suppression performance is maximized.

According to (6), the critical resistance of voltage-type arc suppression failure R_{cr} can be obtained from (7).

$$R_{cr} = \left| \frac{0.3Z_{l1}\dot{E}_A - 20\alpha Z_{l1}[Z_{load} + (1-\alpha)Z_{l1}]}{30(Z_{l1} + Z_{load})} - \frac{\alpha Z_{l0}}{3} \right| \tag{7}$$

Thus, the switching conditions of voltage-type and current-type arc suppression methods are as follow:

1) When $R_f \geqslant R_{cr}$, voltage-type arc suppression method is adopted.
2) When $R_f < R_{cr}$, current-type arc suppression method is adopted.

3.2 Neutral Voltage and Injected Current for Arc Suppression

From circuit theory, the composite sequence network considering the line impedance, fault location and the load impedance can be deduced from Fig. 3 as shown in

Fig. 5, where Z_a is the equivalent impedance, i.e., $Z_a = \alpha Z_{l1}//Z_{LD} = \alpha Z_{l1}[Z_{load} + (1-\alpha)Z_{l1}]/(Z_{l1} + Z_{load})$.

If the current-type ASD is used, the equivalent voltage source and impedance can be obtained from Fig. 5(a), as shown in (8) and (9).

$$\dot{E}_{eq} = \frac{Z_{load}+(1-\alpha)Z_{l1}}{Z_{l1}+Z_{load}}\dot{E}_A + \frac{Z_{C0}\dot{I}_i}{3} \tag{8}$$

$$Z_{eq} = \frac{2\alpha Z_{l1}[Z_{load} + (1-\alpha)Z_{l1}]}{Z_{l1} + Z_{load}} + \alpha Z_{l0} + Z_{C0} \tag{9}$$

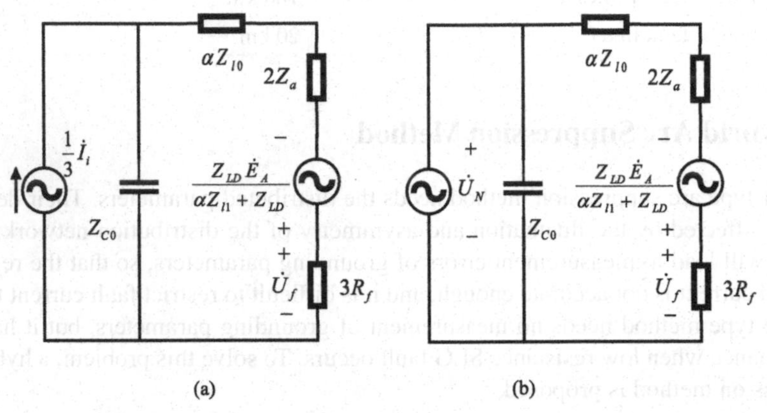

Fig. 5. Simplified composite sequence network when the line impedance is considered (a: with current-type ASD; b: with voltage-type ASD).

Assume $\dot{I}_f$ is equal to zero, from (8) and (9), we can get the reference injected current of the ASD for arc suppression,

$$\dot{I}_i^* = -\frac{3[Z_{load}+(1-\alpha)Z_{l1}]}{(Z_{l1}+Z_{load})Z_{C0}}\dot{E}_A \tag{10}$$

If the reference current $\dot{I}_i^*$ is injected to the neutral, the ground fault current can be restricted to zero. Take notice that (10) is related to fault location, line impedance, load impedance and phase-to-ground impedance. Both of fault location and load impedance need to be measured in real-time, and the distributed capacitance should be estimated in advance.

For the voltage-type ASD, the reference neutral voltage of the ASD can be deduced by setting $\dot{U}_f = 0$ in Fig. 5(b),

$$\dot{U}_N^* = -\frac{Z_{load}+(1-\alpha)Z_{l1}}{Z_{l1}+Z_{load}}\dot{E}_A \tag{11}$$

Voltage-type arc suppression method brings the advantage that it needs no measurement distributed parameters of the feeder line. To implement the proposed method, the grounding resistance should be know.

Assume Y_X is the phase-to-ground admittance. $\dot{I}_0$ is the zero-sequence current of after SLG fault, which can be expressed as (12)

$$\dot{I}_0 = \dot{U}_0\left(Y_A + Y_B + Y_C + \frac{1}{R_f}\right) \tag{12}$$

where $\dot{U}_0$ is the zero-sequence voltage. The expression of ground-fault resistance is as follow:

$$R_f = \frac{\dot{U}_0}{\dot{I}_0 - \dot{U}_0(Y_A + Y_B + Y_C)} \tag{13}$$

There are many methods for fault location [14]-[17], it is not discussed in this paper.

The load impedance to the distribution network transformer is equivalent to Y-type impedance Z_{load}. It is assumed that load current is basically unchanged before and after the fault. During normal operation, the load impedance meets (14).

$$\dot{E}_A\left(\frac{\dot{E}_A}{Z_{load}}\right)^* = \frac{P_L + jQ_L}{3} \tag{14}$$

where P_L and Q_L are the active and reactive power of fault feeder, respectively. Thus the expression of Z_{load} is (15).

$$Z_{load} = \frac{3E_A^2}{P_L - jQ_L} \tag{15}$$

Therefore, the injection current reference and neutral voltage reference can be expressed as follows, respectively, according to (9), (10) and (15).

$$\dot{I}_{ref} = 3\left[\frac{\alpha Z_{l1}(P_L - jQ_L)}{3\left|\dot{E}_A\right|^2 + Z_{l1}(P_L - jQ_L)} - 1\right]\frac{\dot{E}_A}{Z_{C0}} \tag{16}$$

$$\dot{U}_{ref} = \left[\frac{\alpha Z_{l1}(P_L - jQ_L)}{3\left|\dot{E}_A\right|^2 + Z_{l1}(P_L - jQ_L)} - 1\right]\dot{E}_A \tag{17}$$

3.3 Implementation

Figure 6 shows the implementation of the proposed method. When SLG fault occurs. The fault phase and feeder will be identified immediately. The grounding resistance, load impedance and fault location can be calculated according to (13), (15), respectively. If $R_f \geqslant R_{cr}$, the voltage-type method is chosen and the ASD controls the neutral voltage to the reference value according to (17). Otherwise, the current-type method is chosen to inject reference current to the neutral point according to (16).

After a delay, we reduce the injected current and judge whether the zero-sequence voltage changes in proportion to make sure the fault status. When the neutral voltage decreases with the decrease of injection current, it means the fault disappears and remove the injected current. Otherwise, it will be judged as permanent fault and line selection and protection device should be triggered.

3.4 Arc Suppression Accuracy of the Proposed Hybrid Method

By controlling the injected current as (9) or neutral voltage as (10), the residual current can be reduced to zero. According to (9) and (10), the fault location must be known in advance. However, the fault location is very difficult to measure accurately. It is necessary to further analyze the residual current when estimated fault location varies.

It is assumed that the estimated fault location ratio is α_{es}. The existing fault location method can limit $|\alpha_{es} - \alpha|$ to less than 10%. According to (7)-(9), the residual current with current-type arc suppression method can be obtained from (17).

$$\dot{I}_{rc} = \frac{3(\alpha_{es}-\alpha)Z_{l1}\dot{E}_A}{(\alpha Z_{l0}+Z_{C0}+3R_f)(Z_{l1}+Z_{load})+2\alpha Z_{l1}[Z_{load}+(1-\alpha)Z_{l1}]} \tag{18}$$

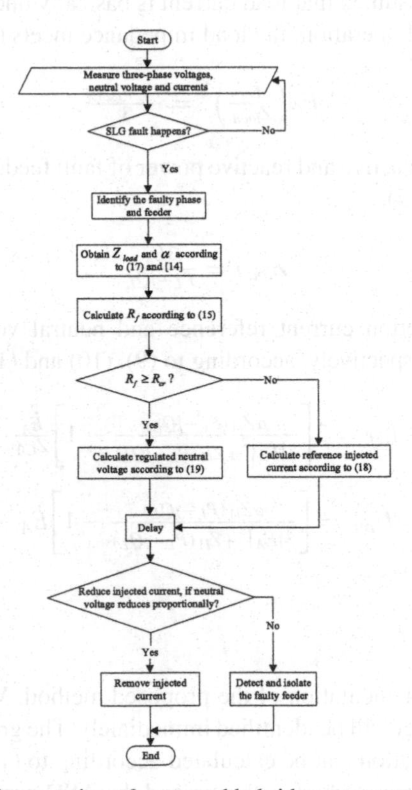

Fig. 6. Implementation of proposed hybrid arc suppression method.

Set $|\alpha_{es} - \alpha| = 10\%$, the relationships between fault location, grounding resistance and residual current with proposed current-type arc suppression are shown in Fig. 7. The residual current decreases with the increase of grounding resistance. With the proposed current-type arc suppression method, the residual current can be limited to a low value within 7A, which has better performance than conventional method.

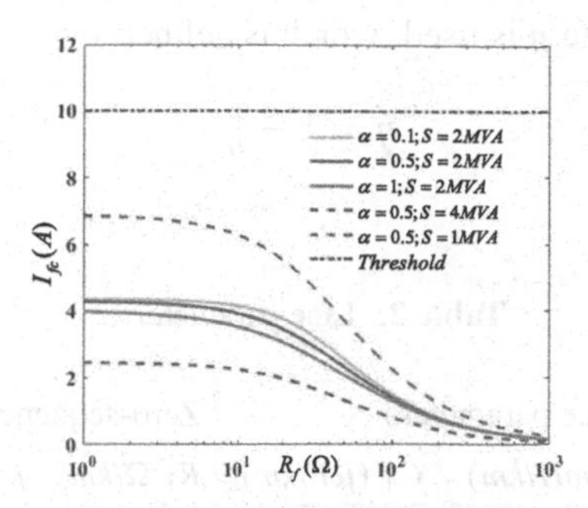

Fig. 7. The residual current with proposed current-type arc suppression.

According to (10) and Fig. 6(b), the residual current with voltage arc suppression method is shown as (19).

$$\dot{I}_{rv} = \frac{3(\alpha_{es} - \alpha)Z_{l1}\dot{E}_A}{(\alpha Z_{l0} + 3R_f)(Z_{l1} + Z_{load}) + 2\alpha Z_{l1}[Z_{load} + (1 - \alpha)Z_{l1}]} \tag{19}$$

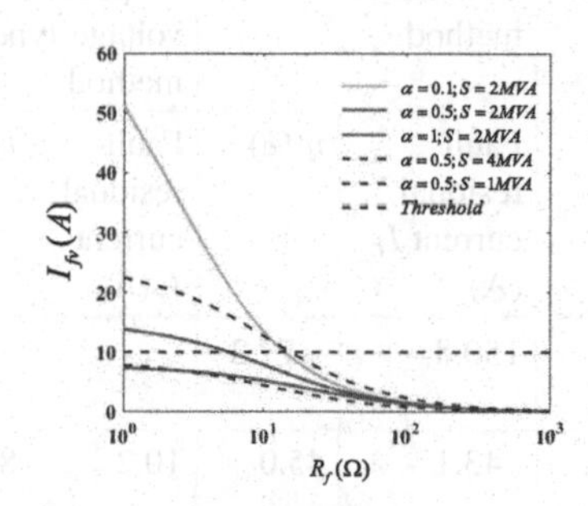

Fig. 8. The residual current with proposed voltage-type arc suppression.

When the proposed method is adopted, the relationships between fault location, grounding resistance and residual current are shown in Fig. 8. With the decrease of grounding resistance and α, the residual current increase. When grounding resistance is low, the residual current is over 10A and arc suppression fails. The failure in case of low resistance SLG fault with voltage-type method should be considered (Fig. 9).

4 Simulation Results

MATLAB/Simulink is used to testify the arc suppression performance of hybrid method and conventional method. A $10kV$ distribution network is built, as shown in Fig. 10. C1, C2 and C3 are cables, the other feeders are overhead lines with the parameters in Table 2. In the simulation, the SLG fault occurs at phase A. K1, K2, K3 and K4 are the fault locations. The error of fault location method is assumed as 10%. The comparative performance waveforms with conventional and proposed method under different α, R_f and Z_{load} are as shown in Figs. 10, 11, 12 and 13.

The arc suppression rate η is used, which is defined by

$$\eta = 1 - \frac{I_r}{I_f} \tag{20}$$

Table 2. Line parameters.

Types	Positive-sequence parameters			Zero-sequence parameters		
	$R_1\ \Omega/km$	$L_1\ (mH/km)$	$C_1\ (\mu F/km)$	$R_1\ \Omega/km$	$L_1\ (mH/km)$	$C_1\ (\mu F/km)$
Overhead line	0.17	1.21	0.011	0.23	5.48	0.008
Cable	0.27	0.255	0.339	2.7	1.019	0.28

Table 3. Simulation results for Arc suppression methods in different grounding resistance.

Fault location	$R_f\ (\Omega)$	I_f (A)	Conventional method		Proposed voltage-type method		Proposed current-type method	
			Fault residual current I_r (A)	$\eta(\%)$	Fault residual current I_r(A)	$\eta(\%)$	Fault residual current I_r (A)	$\eta(\%)$
K3	0 ($R_f < R_{cr}$)	85.1	150.8	−77.2			3.9	95.4
K3	27 ($R_f = R_{cr}$)	78.3	43.1	45.0	10.2	87.0	3.6	95.4
K3	100 ($R_f > R_{cr}$)	50.8	14.7	71.1	3.7	92.7		

Table 4. Simulation results for Arc suppression methods in different load.

Fault location	$R_f\ (\Omega)$	I_{load} (A)	I_f (A)	Conventional method		Proposed method	
				Fault residual current I_r (A)	$\eta(\%)$	Fault residual current I_r (A)	$\eta(\%)$
K2	100	112.5	46.7	5.79	87.6	2.0	95.7
K3	100	248.4	50.8	14.7	71.1	3.7	92.7

Table 5. Simulation results for Arc suppression methods in different fault location.

Fault location	R_f (Ω)	I_f (A)	Conventional method		Proposed method	
			Fault residual current I_r (A)	η(%)	Fault residual current I_r (A)	η(%)
K1	100	54.1	12.2	77.4	4.5	91.7
K3	100	50.8	14.7	71.1	3.7	92.7
K4	100	40.4	23.8	41.1	3.9	90.3

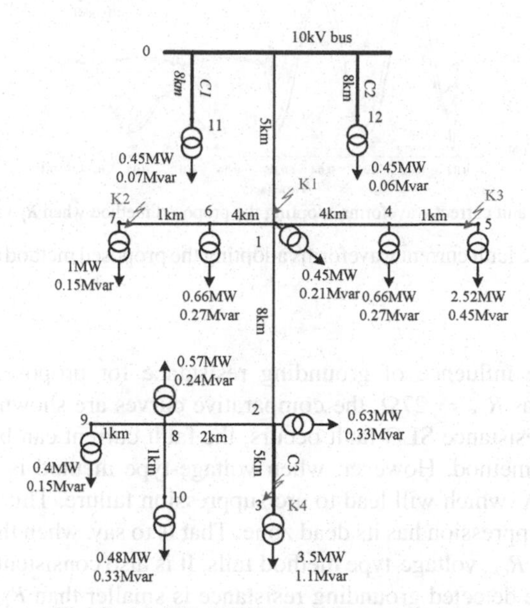

Fig. 9. Modified IEEE 13-node test system.

4.1 Case 1

To compare the arc suppression performance in different grounding resistance, the fault location is set at K3 with the grounding resistances 0Ω, 27Ω and 100Ω. When SLG fault occurs at K3, R_{cr} is 27Ω which is calculated by (13). The comparative fault current waveforms are shown in Fig. 10 and the simulation results are shown in Table 3.

As shown in Fig. 10(a), when metallic SLG fault occurs, the fault current after conventional arc suppression is even larger than before, which has no arc suppression performance. When grounding resistance increases, the fault current will decrease. When the fault location is K3 and R_f is 100Ω, the fault current is 14.7A, which is higher than the threshold 10A and is affected by grounding resistance.

However, proposed method can reduce the residual current to a lower value and is not affected by grounding resistance. When metallic SLG fault occurs, the arc suppression rate is 95.4%.

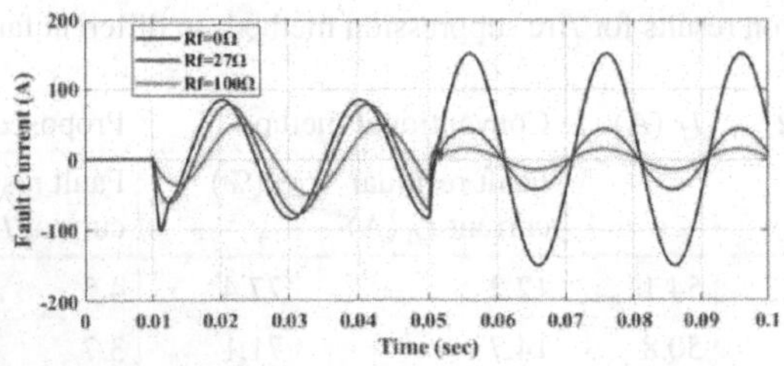

(a) Fault current waveforms adopting the conventional method when R_f varies.

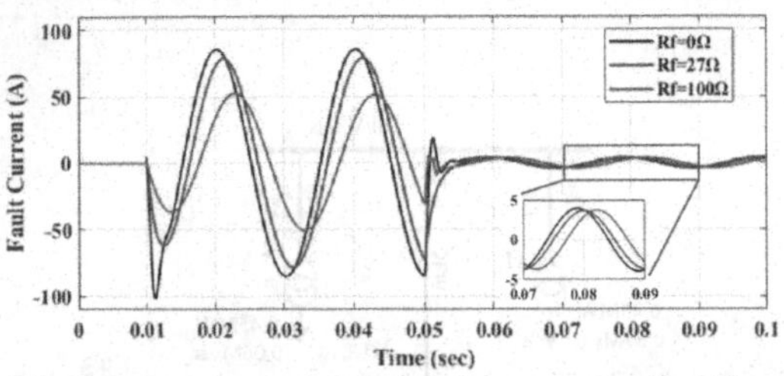

(b) Fault current waveforms adopting the proposed method when R_f varies.

Fig. 10. Comparative fault current waveforms adopting the proposed method and the conventional one when R_f varies.

To explain the influence of grounding resistance for proposed arc suppression method, R_f is set as $R_{cr} = 27\Omega$, the comparative curves are shown in Fig. 11. Obviously, when low resistance SLG fault occurs, the fault current can be reduced to 3.6A with current-type method. However, when voltage-type method is adopted, the fault current is over 10A, which will lead to arc suppression failure. This is mainly because voltage-type arc suppression has its dead zone. That is to say, when the grounding resistance is lower than R_{cr}, voltage-type method fails. It is also consistent with the previous analysis. When the detected grounding resistance is smaller than R_{cr}, the current-type arc suppression strategy is adopted in proposed hybrid method. The proposed hybrid method can solve this problem.

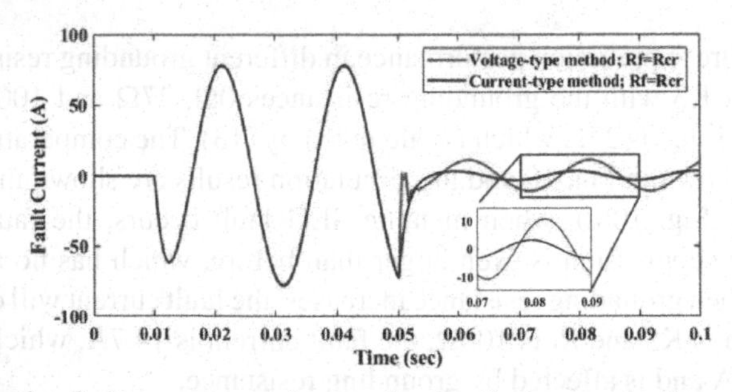

Fig. 11. Comparative fault current waveforms adopting the proposed voltage-type and current-type methods.

4.2 Case 2

The performance comparison of different load is performed, and the comparative waveforms are shown in Fig. 12 and the simulation results are shown in Table 4. It is obvious that conventional method has a large residual current, which may lead to the failure of arc suppression and is affected by load. Moreover, according to the black curve and blue curve, with the increase of load power, the residual current with conventional method will increase too. This is mainly because the line impedance and load impedance are parallel and when load impedance is smaller, the influence of line impedance is relatively obvious. We can also see that proposed method always performs better than conventional method, the residual current is < 4A.

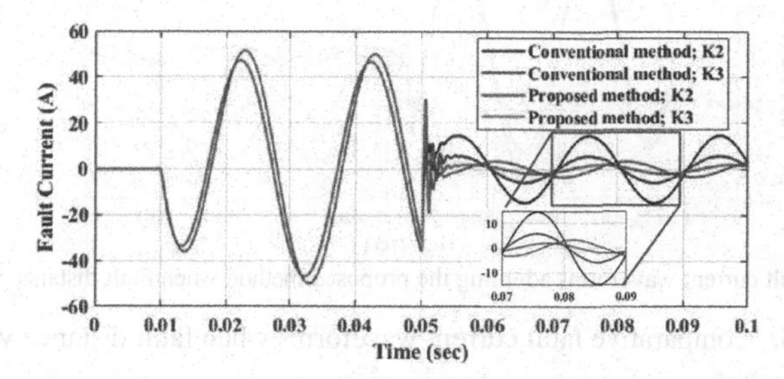

Fig. 12. Comparative fault current waveforms adopting the proposed voltage-type and current-type meth-ods when load varies.

4.3 Case 3

Figure 16 shows the comparative waveforms adopting the proposed method and conventional method when fault distance varies. Table 5 shows the simulation dates. K1 is close to the busbar. K3 is adjacent to the end of fault feeder. According to Fig. 13(a), conventional method can hardly reduce fault current less than 10A. We can see that the residual current at K3 is higher than at K1. This is mainly because when α is small, the series inductive line impedance partly compensates the phase-to-ground capacitance.

Figure 13(b) indicates that the residual currents of proposed method are < 5A and is not influenced by fault location. In addition, when SLG fault occurs at K4, the fault feeder is a mixture of overhead lines and cables. The proposed method still works, and which is also not affected by line structure.

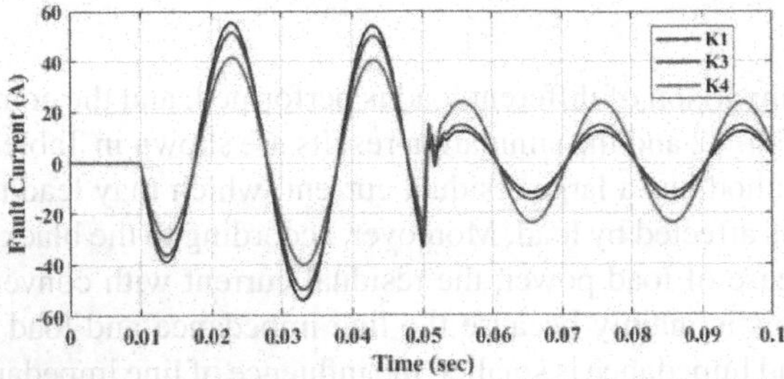

(a) Fault current waveforms adopting the conventional method when fault distance varies.

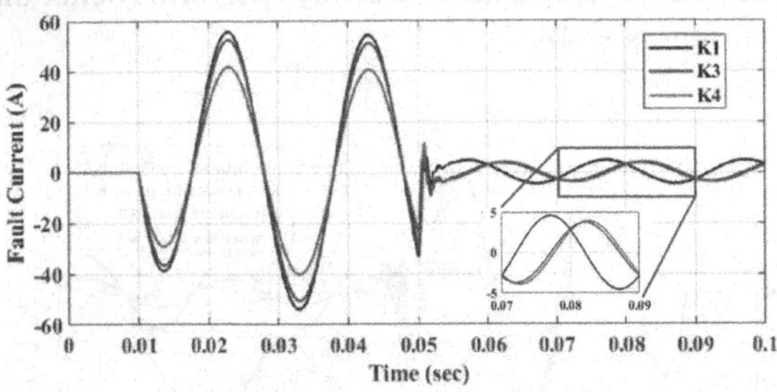

(b) Fault current waveforms adopting the proposed method when fault distance varies.

Fig. 13. Comparative fault current waveforms when fault distance varies.

5 Conclusions

The conventional voltage-type arc suppression method cannot effectively extinguish arc especially when low resistance SLG fault occurs. To solve the issue, this paper proposes a hybrid arc suppression method. Combine with voltage-type method, which need no measurement grounding parameters, and a current-type method, which is effective for low resistance SLG fault, and the residual current can be almost restricted to zero. Compare to conventional method, the proposed ones can effectively achieve arc suppression rate over 90% in spite of influence of line impedances, grounding resistances and loads.

References

1. Burgess, R.: Minimising the risk of cross-country faults in systems using arc suppression coils. Iet Generation Transmission & Distribution **5**(7), 703–711 (2011)
2. Vaziri, M.: Grounding of primary system for LV networks. IEEE Transactions on Power Delivery **31**(2), 419–427 (2016)
3. Guo, M.: Deep-learning-based earth fault detection using continuous wavelet transform and convolutional neural network in resonant grounding distribution systems. IEEE Sensors Journal (2017)
4. Wang, W.: Principle and design of a single-phase inverter-based grounding system for neutral-to-ground voltage compensation in distribution networks. IEEE Transactions on Industrial Electronics **64**(2), 1204–1213 (2017)
5. Ouyang, S.: Control strategy for Arc-suppression-coil-grounded star-connected power electronic transformers. IEEE Transactions on Power Electronics **6**(34), 5294–5311 (2019)

6. Brenna, M.: Petersen coil regulators analysis using a real-time digital simulator. IEEE Transactions on Power Delivery **26**(3), 1479–1488 (2011)
7. Zeng, X.: Some novel techniques for insulation parameters measurement and petersen-coil control in distribution systems. IEEE Transactions on Industrial Electronics **57**(4), 1445–1451 (2010)
8. Ze, Z.: FASD based on BSC method for distribution networks. IET Generation **24**(13), 5487–5494 (2019)
9. Wang, W.: Principle and control design of active ground-fault arc suppression device for full compensation of ground current. IEEE Transactions on Industrial Electronics **64**(6), 4561–4570 (2017)
10. Chen, K.: Terminal open circuit voltage controller for Arc suppression in distribution network. IET Generation Transmission & Distribution **14**(3) (2020)

SE Block-Assisted ResNet for Channel Estimation in OFDM System

Yuanhai Liang and Zhengfa Zhu(✉)

Changsha University of Science and Technology, Changsha, China
1054575560@qq.com, zhuzhengfa@csust.edu.cn

Abstract. Channel estimation (CE) is an important part of wireless communication system, which has a significant impact on the quality of wireless communication. Considering a single-input single-output (SISO) downlink scenario, this paper proposes a "squeeze and excitation" (SE) block combined with residual neural network (SE-ResNet) method to improve the CE performance of the orthogonal frequency division multiplexing (OFDM) system. The SE-ResNet is inputted into a CSI matrix of the pilot position obtained by the least squares (LS) method, and a raw feature matrix is learned by the convolutional layer and a partial residual layer. And the global information of the original feature matrix in each channel is compressed into a descriptor through the squeeze operation in the "SE" block. Then attention map is obtained from information aggregated in the descriptors by an excitation operation which fully captures channel-wise dependencies. The attention map is multiplied by the original feature matrix to get a new feature matrix, which is resized by an interpolation layer to obtain CSI of entire frame. New feature matrix is helpful for interpolation layer to get more accurate complete CSI. To further improve CE performance and optimize network model, this paper adopts methods of network tailoring and Concrete Autoencoder (Concrete AE) for pilot design. Simulation results show that the proposed SE-ResNet is superior to the traditional LS and minimum mean squared error (MMSE) methods in various practical wireless environments. Network pruning will reduce the number of parameters of the network within an acceptable loss range, which will reduce computational costs. Using the pilot scheme designed by Concrete AE for CE will have better performance.

Keywords: Channel Estimation · Squeeze and Excitation Block · Residual Convolutional neural network · Concrete Autoencoder

1 Introduction

With the popularization of 5G technology, fresh challenges such as massive connectivity and ultra reliability has raised and need to be met [1]. Subsequently, CE, as one of the key technologies in wireless communication system, also needs to meet higher accuracy requirement. Among conventional CE methods, LS method is easily implemented and widely adopted in practical communication systems, which is an interpolation-based

H. Yang et al. (Eds.): SmartGIFT 2022, LNICST 483, pp. 386–396, 2023.
https://doi.org/10.1007/978-3-031-31733-0_32

approach and requires no information about the statistics of the channel. However, it cannot obtain satisfactory performance in some scenarios that require higher accuracy. In order to obtain more accurate CSI, MMSE method was proposed to refine CSI, but it is difficult to implement in practical scenarios because of complete channel statistics requirement and high computational complexity.

With the rapid development in computer vision, natural language processing, semantic recognition, and so on, deep learning (DL) has also been introduced into wireless communication system to estimate CSI. At present, DL is divided into two categories to realize CE, namely data-driven and model-driven. In data-driven method, the receiver in wireless communication system is considered as a black box, and wireless signals from transmitter can be accurately recovered at the receiver. For example, in 2, the receiver is instead of a simple designed five-layer deep neural network (DNN) for signal detection and CE. It is shown the DNN based approach, via training with a large amount of data, can achieve the performance comparable to the MMSE estimator. The data-driven scheme proposed above do not rely on channel statistical knowledge, so they may be a promising candidate when channel model is unknown or difficult to model analytically, for example, in high mobility vehicular communications, chemical communications, underwater communications, and so on [3]. Although data-driven method is relatively simple and effective, it requires a large amount of training data, which limiting its application. The model-driven CE approach, which improves neural network by characteristics of the model structure and then trains a large amount of data, is more powerful and has wider applications. For example, in 4 the authors apply DL to estimate the uplink channel of a hybrid analog-to-digital converter massive multiple-input multiple-output (MIMO) system. The received signals of all antennas are used by DNN to estimate the channel, and to eliminate the adverse effects of coarsely quantized signals, a selective input prediction DNN (SIP-DNN) is developed. Signals received by the high-resolution analog-to-digital converter antennas are utilized in SIP-DNN to predict the channels of other antennas as well as to estimate their own channels.

Recently, many DL-based CE approaches have been proposed. In [5], the authors introduced an attention-aided DL framework for massive MIMO systems. By integrating attention mechanism into fully connected network, they improve CE performance significantly at the cost of small complexity overhead. In [6], the author takes the time-frequency response of the fast fading channel as a low-resolution image, and then proposes a ChannelNet network to use super-resolution method to obtain unknown channel response. Inspired by this, a residual learning based deep neural network, called ReEsNet, is designed and optimized for CE in [7], in which the up-sampling function is implemented as transposed convolution layer in order to scale up image height and width. However, the hyperparameters of the transposed convolution and subsequent convolution layers need to be modified according to different pilot patterns. Therefore, in [8], instead of the transposed convolutional layer, bilinear interpolation is proposed to interpolate CSI of pilot position to obtain the CSI of the entire frame, which improves the performance and reduces complexity by 82%. In [9] and [10], after the pilot design of Concrete AE, ChannelNet and a generative adversarial network are cascaded for CE respectively. The simulation results show that the performance of the networks cascaded with Concrete AE are better than original networks. Although the performance of CE has been improved, it is not enough for high-precision communication requirements.

Motivated by the above papers, in this paper we propose a residual neural network combined with a SE block to improve CE accuracy. The full CSI is recovered by self-attention learning on the pilot CSI. Simulation results demonstrate that the presented SE-ResNet can achieve art-of-state performance and outperform other DL based estimation method. On this basis, we use Concrete AE to select the position with the most channel information in the time-frequency resource grid as pilot position, and cascade SE-ResNet for channel estimation. Finally, we will use network clipping to reduce parameters within the acceptable loss range. We conducted experiments and the results show that these methods are effective to improve the performance of CE. The rest of the paper is organized as follows: Sect. 2 introduces traditional CE methods, SE-ResNet is introduced in Sect. 3, followed by Sect. 4 with simulation results and a conclusion at the end.

2 Channel Estimation Based on Traditional Methods

OFDM technology is a multi-carrier modulation method that can make full use of spectrum resources, effectively resist frequency-selective interference and have a simple transmit and receive signal structure. In the frequency domain, the relationship between the transmit signal and the receive signal can be expressed as:

$$Y = H \circ X + W \tag{1}$$

where $X, Y \in \mathbb{C}^{N_c \times N_s}$ denotes the transmit and receive signals in the OFDM system, $H \in \mathbb{C}^{N_c \times N_s}$ denotes the channel coefficients, and $W \in \mathbb{C}^{N_c \times N_s}$ denotes the additive Gaussian white noise (AWGN). $\circ$ denotes the element-wise multiplication operation. And N_C, N_S represent the number of subcarriers and the number of OFDM symbols, respectively.

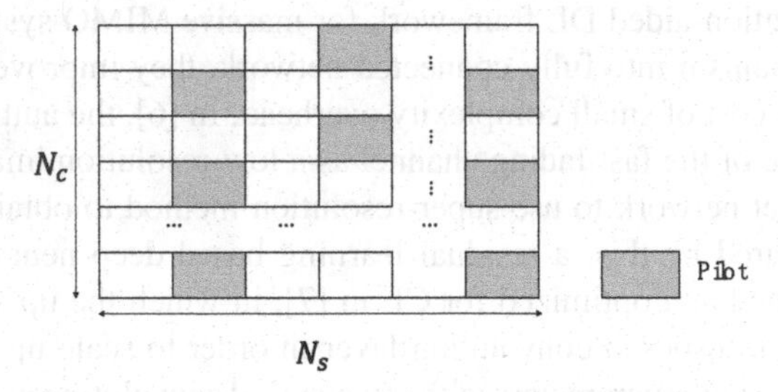

Fig. 1. Pilot and data symbols of one frame.

The frame structure is shown in Fig. 1. For each pilot OFDM symbol, some specific subcarriers are selected as the pilot carriers while the rest of the subcarriers are set to zero, while for the data OFDM symbols all subcarriers are used to transmit the modulated signal. The frequency domain channel estimation is performed based on the pilot OFDM symbols, and the channel coefficients of the whole frame are predicted based on this. The following two methods, LS and MMSE, are described.

2.1 LS Method

By neglecting the noise, the estimated channel gain matrix at the pilot position is derived and expressed as follows.

$$H_{LS} = \frac{Y_P}{X_p} \tag{2}$$

where Y_P, X_p denote the received and transmitted pilot signals, respectively, and the predicted channel gain of the whole frame is obtained by linear interpolation, because the noise calculation is ignored nor is the channel statistical information required, so the LS method is not ideal.

2.2 MMSE Method

By further processing the H_{LS} obtained by the LS method using priori information of the channel, the channel gain matrix of the pilot position can be expressed as follows.

$$H_{MMSE} = R_{HH_P}(R_{H_PH_P} + I\frac{\sigma_N^2}{\sigma_X^2})^{-1}H_{LS} \tag{3}$$

where H denotes the channel gain matrix of the pilot symbol, and H_P is the actual measured channel gain matrix of the pilot subcarrier. $\frac{\sigma_N^2}{\sigma_X^2}$ is the numerical inverse of the signal-to-noise ratio, while σ_X^2, σ_N^2 denote the average power of AWGN noise and transmit signal, respectively. R_{HH_P} and $R_{H_PH_P}$ are the inter-correlation matrix of H and H_P and the autocorrelation matrix of H_P.

Although the MMSE method increases the accuracy of CE by using the a priori information of the channel, it also increases the computational complexity and the difficulty to implementation as well.

3 Deep Learning Based Channel Estimation

Compared with the traditional CE methods mentioned above, although DL methods have advantages, neural network schemes may have gradient disappearance problem, and ResNet are designed to mitigate gradient disappearance. Therefore, researchers proposed many CE methods based on ResNet, such as 3.1 Interpolation-ResNet, and achieved good results. This section details the ResNet-based method proposed in this paper.

3.1 Interpolation-ResNet

The Interpolation-ResNet is an improved network model based on ResNet. The channel gain matrix of the pilot part obtained by LS method is used as the input of Interpolation-ResNet. Since the existing DL framework does not support complex number operations. The input of Interpolation-ResNet is divided into two parts: the real part, and the imaginary part, which are inputted into the network as two channels. Interpolation-ResNet consists of 4 neural blocks, 3 convolutional layers, and an interpolation layer. Neural blocks and convolutional layers learn the features of pilot channel gain. Then, the channel gain matrix of pilot is interpolated by the interpolation layer to the channel gain matrix of the whole frame.

3.2 SE-ResNet

We keep the network structure of Interpolation-ResNet but introduce the SE attention module after the last neural block of the network. The SE-ResNet network structure is shown in Fig. 2, and the overall architecture of this network is divided into three parts.

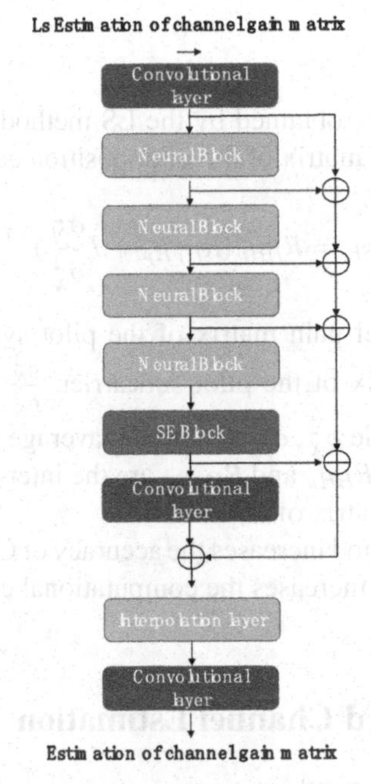

Fig. 2. SE-ResNet.

The first part is a convolutional layer, which has N convolution kernels, and the size of the convolution kernel is $3 \times 3 \times 2$. The second part is connected to the residual block composed of 4 neural blocks, an SE block, and a convolutional layer. Each neural block has two convolutional layers and a Relu layer in the middle. Each convolutional layer consists of N convolution kernels, and each convolution kernel is $3 \times 3 \times N$ in size. The last part consists of an interpolation layer and a convolutional layer, which has two convolution kernels with size is $36 \times 7 \times N$.

Input is divided into two parts: the real part, and the imaginary part, which are inputted to the first convolutional layer. In each neural block, the input of each neural block goes through two convolutional layers and a Relu layer, then the output of the Relu layer is added by the input, which is called residual operation, and summation is used as input of next layer. Output of all the layers before interpolation layer are summed together and the result is forwarded to the interpolation layer, and then resized by bilinear interpolation. The resized data is input to the last convolutional layer to obtain the final output.

The original CNN uses all features with equal importance for all data, while in fact, some features will be more important to some data. Therefore, the introduced SE module can learn these features will play a more important role. The SE module is shown in Fig. 3.

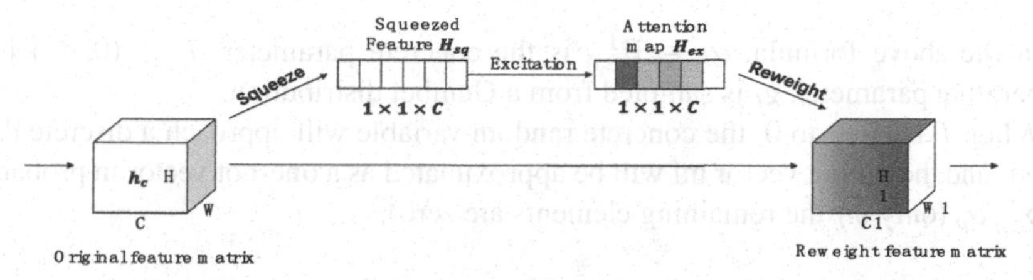

Fig. 3. SE Block.

A three-dimensional original feature matrix compressed according to dimension C, each two-dimensional feature matrix of size $W \times H$ is compressed into a descriptor. Each compressed descriptor represents global information of the corresponding two-dimensional matrix, and the final result is $1 \times 1 \times C$. The above compression process is the squeeze operation, which is implemented in global average pooling. The specific formula is as follows:

$$H_{sq} = \frac{1}{W \times H} \sum_{i=1}^{W} \sum_{j=1}^{H} h_c(i,j) \tag{4}$$

The next two fully connected layers are taken as excitation operations. The first fully connected layer followed by a Relu layer, and the second one followed by a sigmoid layer, as in Eq. 5:

$$H_{ex} = \sigma(W_2 \delta(W_1 H_{sq})) \tag{5}$$

Multiplying the result obtained in (4) by W_1 whose dimension is $C/r \times C$, the reduction ratio r is a hyperparameter, which play an import role on SE block capacity and computational cost and in this paper it equals 1. The dimension of $W_1 H_{sq}$ is $1 \times 1 \times C$, and after a Relu layer. Similarly, after a fully connected layer with a weight of W_2 and a Sigmoid layer, the final dimension of H_{ex} is still $1 \times 1 \times C$. These two fully connected layers are used to generate weights for each feature attention map. Finally, the attention-based original features are recalibrated by multiplying the attention feature map and the original feature matrix.

3.3 Pilot Design Based on Concrete AE Network

Concrete AE will look for a feature subset that effectively identifies the largest amount of channel information. There is a selection layer in this network, which has I neurons to select input features. Specifically, a noisy time-frequency grid h_n is selected as the noise channel input, and the grid size is $N_C \times N_S$. Flatten h_n to get $h_n = h_1, h_2 \ldots h_j$, where $J = N_C \times N_S$ is the length of the vector. The selection layer obtains the result by selecting features, that is, $h_{p,I} = h_n m_I$. Where $h_{p,I} = [h_{p,1}, h_{p,2} \ldots h_{p,I}]$ is the most informative feature subset and m_I is a J-dimensional random variable sampled from a concrete distribution, the elements are defined as:

$$m_I = \frac{\exp((\log \alpha_I + g_I)/T)}{\sum_{j=1}^{J} \exp((\log \alpha_j + g_j)/T)} \tag{6}$$

In the above formula, $\alpha_l \in \mathbb{R}^{J}_{>0}$ is the concrete parameter, $T \in (0, \infty)$ is the temperature parameter, g_l is sampled from a Gumbel distribution.

When T is close to 0, the concrete random variable will approach a discrete distribution, and the output vector ml will be approximated as a one-hot vector in probability $\alpha_l / \sum_p \alpha_p$ (only m_I the remaining elements are zero).

4 Simulation Results

Consider the downlink scenario in the SISO system. The deployed channel models are extended pedestrian a model (EPA), extended vehicle a model (EVA) and extended typical urban model (ETU) in 3GPP. It is worth mentioning that all simulations were performed under the same conditions. The settings of the OFDM system are shown in Table 1.

Table 1. Baseband Parameters

Parameter	Value
Pilot Subcarriers	24
Total number of subcarriers	72
Pilot Symbols	2
Number of OFDM symbols per slot	14
CP length	16
Bandwidth	1.08 MHz
Carrier Frequency	2.1 GHz
Subcarrier Spacing	15 kHz
Frames per slot	1

4.1 Model Training

Training data is collected from the EPA channel model. A total of 100,000 samples were collected, and 20,000 data were collected every 5 dB from a signal-to-noise ratio (SNR) ranging from 0 dB to 20 dB (maximum Doppler shift from 0 Hz to 97 Hz, corresponding to 0 km/h ~ 50 km/h). The training set occupy 95% of the total data set, and the remaining 5% of the data set is validation data set. The training parameters are shown in Table 2.

Table 2. Train Parameters

Parameter	Value
Optimizer	Adam
Maximum epoch	100
Initial learning rate	0.001
Loss function	Mean Squared Error (MSE)
Drop period for learning rate	20
Drop factor for learning rate	0.5
Minibatch size	128
L2 regularization	0.001

We compare the MSE of SE-ResNet network by setting different number of convolution kernels (2, 4, 6, 8, 10) of convolutional layers. The network performance of different convolution kernels is shown in Fig. 4. Considering the space limitation of this paper and the increased computational cost of convolution kernels, we select 8 convolution kernels for subsequent experiments.

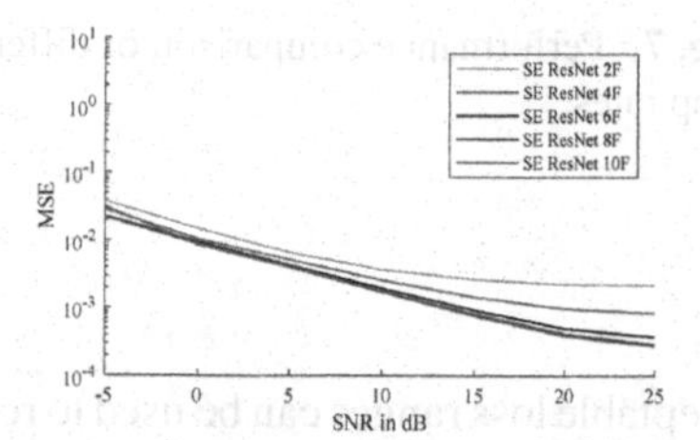

Fig. 4. SE-ResNet performance.

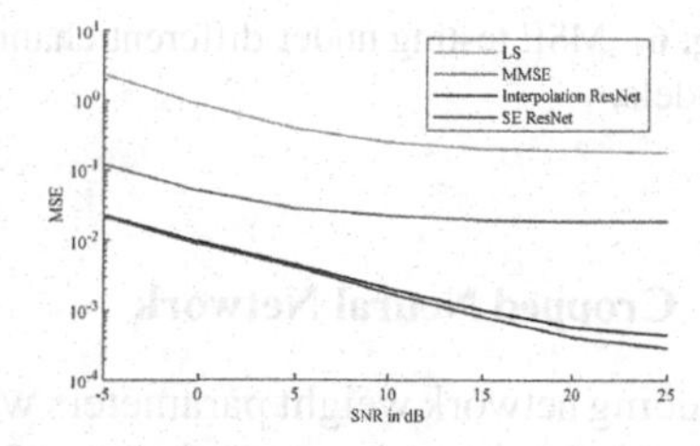

Fig. 5. MSE of estimation for the EPA channel.

4.2 MSE Performance

This paper uses MSE to evaluate the error between the estimated channel and the real channel. To verify that the proposed model is effective under extended range, the SNR is extended from –5 dB to 25 dB in test dataset, and the maximum Doppler shift is still from 0 Hz to 97 Hz. 5000 channel data are collected every 5 dB to form a test data set with a total capacity of 35000.

Figure 5 shows the MSE results of the traditional method, Interpolation-ResNet and SE-ResNet tested under the EPA channel model. It can be observed that Interpolation-ResNet and SE-ResNet have significant advantages over traditional methods. SE-ResNet does not have much improvement over Interpolation-ResNet at lower SNR but has better performance at high SNR, which shows that the proposed model with the SE module can learn the characteristics of channel coefficients with high SNR more easily.

4.3 Generalization Performance

The EPA data described above is used to train the network model as well. The test data set of the network is collected using EPA, EVA and ETU models respectively. Each channel model collects SNR from –20 dB to 25 dB, maximum doppler shift from 0 Hz to 97 Hz, and a total of 50000 (5000 × 10) channel data for testing. The results are shown in Fig. 6.

Figure 6 shows the result that the EPA-trained network being tested on different channels. It can be seen that when the test channel and trained channel are the same, both SE-ResNet and Interpolation-ResNet can have higher performance, while SE-ResNet is superior. But when testing EVA and ETU channels, SE-ResNet will perform better in low SNR range of –20 dB ~5 dB. This means that SE-ResNet has better performance at low SNR when testing non-training channels.

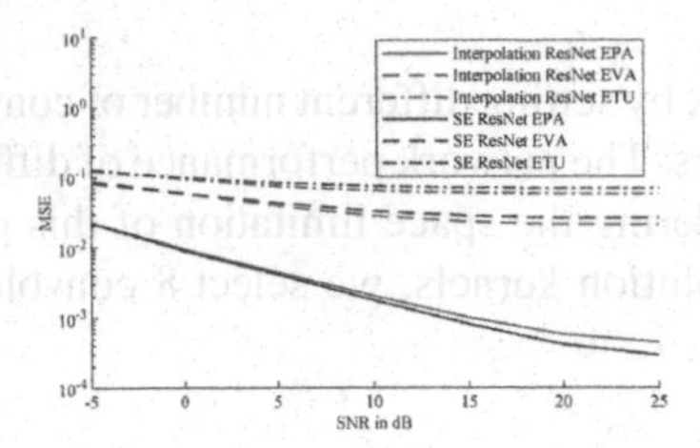

Fig. 6. MSE testing under different channel models.

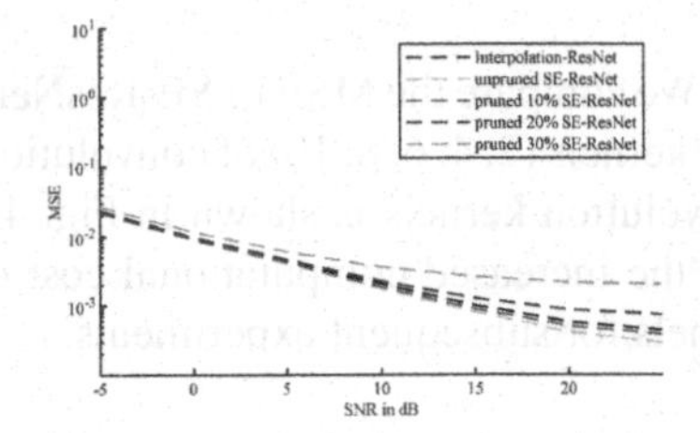

Fig. 7. Performance comparison of different crop rates.

4.4 Cropped Neural Network

Reducing network weight parameters within acceptable loss ranges can be used to reduce SE-ResNet redundancy calculations. Specifically, we try to sort weights by numerical value, and reset some of the weights to 0 according to a certain proportion, there are three cropping results shown in Fig. 7. SE-ResNet performance degrades significantly, even worse than Interpolation-ResNet, when clipping rate is above 10%. On the contrary, when the cropping rate is below 10%, the performance of SE-ResNet is still better than Interpolation-ResNet although there is a certain loss. This proves that SE-ResNet is a low-complexity network.

4.5 Performance of Concrete AE

In order to clearly reflect the performance improvement of SE-ResNet by pilot design of Concrete AE, we adopt two schemes for simulation. In the first scheme, we use 48 pilots and uniform distribution pilot design method, while the second scheme uses 8 pilots and Concrete AE pilot design method, the rest of the conditions are completely identical. Figure 8 shows the performance of the above two schemes, when SNR is less than 19, the Concrete AE cascaded SE-ResNet still shows extremely good performance although it has only 8 pilots. While SE-ResNet has better performance when SNR is greater than 19, it has higher complexity and computational cost.

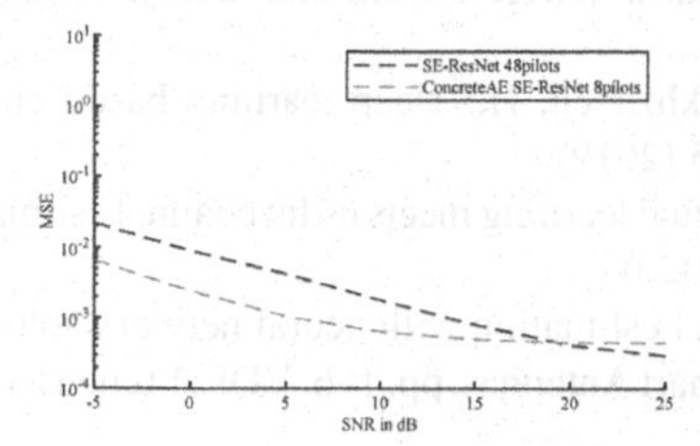

Fig. 8. Performance of concrete AE.

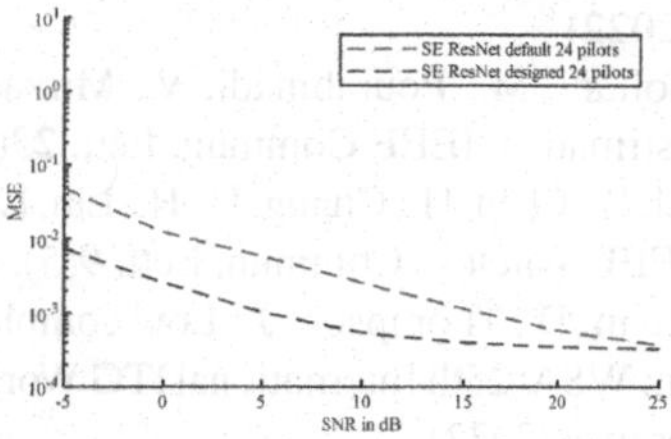

Fig. 9. Comparison of network performance under different SNR.

To comparatively highlight the power of concrete AE, we simultaneously take 24 pilots to train SE-ResNet and SE-ResNet cascaded with concrete AE. Taking the same channel conditions, the training results are shown in Fig. 9. Although the number of pilots is different, Fig. 9 shows that SE-ResNet cascade concrete AE has better performance than single SE-ResNet. This subsection proves that concrete AE can find the most informative points of channel information in the resource grid, and neural networks assisted by it can achieve better results in CE.

5 Conclusion

In this paper, ResNet with a SE block learns the distribution features of channels with weights, thereby improving the accuracy of CE. The traditional method, Interpolation-ResNet and SE-ResNet are compared, and the results show that SE-ResNet outperforms the other approaches in MSE. Regarding generalization performance, SE-ResNet has an advantage at low SNR. To further enhance the quality of CE, the position with the most channel information is selected as the pilot position by Concrete AE and used to replace the traditional pilot schemes in this paper. The simulation experiments prove that SE-ResNet cascaded with concrete AE has better performance than single SE-ResNet. In the future, we will consider using more channel model data to train SE-ResNet, so that the generalization ability of the model becomes better in the high SNR range.

References

1. Xiaohu, Y., Zhiwen, P., Xiqi, G., ShuMin, C.A.O., HeQuan, W.U.: The 5G mobile communication: the development trends and its emerging key techniques. Science China Inf. Sci. **44**(5), 551–553 (2014)
2. Hao, Y., Geoffrey Ye, L., Biing-Hwang, J.: Power of deep learning for channel estimation and signal detection in OFDM systems. IEEE Wireless Commun. Lett. **7**(1), 114–117 (2017)

3. Yang, Y., Gao, F., Ma, Xiaoli, M., Shun, Z.: Deep Learning-Based Channel Estimation for Doubly Selective Fading Channels. IEEE Access 7, 36579–36589 (2019)
4. Shen, G., Peihao, D., Zhiwen, P., Geoffrey Ye, L.: Deep Learning based Channel Estimation for Massive MIMO with Mixed-Resolution ADCs. IEEE Commun. Lett. **23**(11), 1989–1993 (2019)
5. Gao, J., Hu, M., Zhong, C., Li, G.Y., Zhang, Z.: An attention-aided deep learning framework for massive mimo channel estimation. IEEE Trans. Wireless Commun. **21**(3), 1823–1835 (2022)
6. Soltani, M., Pourahmadi, V., Mirzaei, A., Sheikhzadeh, H.: Deep learning-based channel estimation. IEEE Commun. Lett. **23**(4), 652–655 (2019)
7. Li, L., Chen, H., Chang, H.-H., Liu, L.: Deep residual learning meets ofdm channel estimation. IEEE Wireless Commun. Lett. **9**(5), 615–618 (2020)
8. Luan, D., Thompson, J.: Low complexity channel estimation with neural network solutions. In: WSA: 25th International ITG Workshop on Smart Antennas, pp. 1–6. VDE, French Riviera, France (2022)
9. Soltani, M., Pourahmadi, V., Sheikhzadeh, H.: Pilot pattern design for deep learning-based channel estimation in OFDM systems. IEEE Wireless Commun. Lett. **9**(12), 2173–2176 (2020)
10. Kang, X.-F., Liu, Z.-H., Yao, M.: Deep learning for joint pilot design and channel estimation in MIMO-OFDM systems. Sensors **22**(11), 4188 (2022)

Experimental Study on the Influence of Defect Characteristics of XLPE Cable on the Initial Voltage of Electrical Tree

Hengyi Zhou[1], Wan Dai[1](✉), Miao Zhao[1], Xujin Duan[1], Jinliang Li[1], Linjun Liu[2], and Jiang Han[3]

[1] State Grid Hunan Electric Power Company Limited Research Institute, Changsha 410007, China
280241509@qq.com

[2] Qingdao Topscomm Communication Company Limited, Qingdao 266000, China

[3] State Grid Changde Power Supply Company, Changde 415000, China

Abstract. Experimental Study on the Influence of Defect Characteristics of XLPE Cable on the Initial Voltage of Electrical Tree Cross linked polyethylene (XLPE) has excellent electrical insulation performance. Cross linked polyethylene is widely used as the insulating material of 10 kV power cables. With the acceleration of urbanization, a large number of cable entry projects have started. XLPE cables are widely used in medium and low voltage power grids. However, due to the lax production process and other problems, some defects or impurities will inevitably appear in the cable insulation. These problems accelerate the deterioration of cable insulation and lead to the generation of electrical tree, which further leads to the overall Breakdown Failure of the cable. These problems greatly affect the power supply reliability of the whole transmission system. In view of the above problems, this paper carried out an experimental study on the influence of the defect characteristics of XLPE cable on the starting voltage of electrical tree. First, the test platform of needle electrode short cable is built. Then the growth law of electrical tree under different defects is simulated by using this test platform. This research work is of great significance for constructing the numerical model of XLPE cable defects and analyzing the mechanism of the influence of XLPE cable defect characteristics on the starting voltage of electrical tree.

Keywords: Cross Linked Polyethylene · Cable · Electric Tree Branch · Test Platform

1 Introduction

In recent years, power cables are more and more widely used. As a large number of cables gradually approach the full life cycle, related cable discharge faults cause large-scale power outages one after another [1]. In view of the above problems, domestic and foreign scholars have carried out relevant research work on the development law

H. Yang et al. (Eds.): SmartGIFT 2022, LNICST 483, pp. 397–402, 2023.
https://doi.org/10.1007/978-3-031-31733-0_33

of electrical branches in XLPE cables under different defects. Reference [2] carried out the electrical tree aging test of silicone rubber materials under different curvature radii of needle tips, measured the starting voltage of electrical branch and its morphology under different conditions, and analyzed the influence characteristics of different needle tip curvature on the initiation of electrical tree; Reference [3] used ANSYS software to simulate and theoretically analyze the internal needle tip defects of XLPE cables, and compared with the on-site measured cable compressive strength. At present, most studies focus on the structure, growth features and contributing factor of electric branches and so on [4–6], only a few researchers have studied the effect of internal defects of XLPE cables on the generation and growth of electrical branches. The existing studies select a single object, and do not fully and systematically consider the influence of diverse defect characteristics on the generation of electrical tree.

Therefore, this paper uses the actual project short cable as the object, and first builds a pin electrode short cable test platform. Then the growth law of electrical tree under different defects is simulated by using this test platform. This research work is of great significance for constructing the numerical model of XLPE cable defects and analyzing the mechanism of the influence of defect characteristics of XLPE cable on the starting voltage of electrical branch.

2 Test Samples and Test Platform

Because the initiation of electrical branch in the real cable is mainly related to the internal air interval and the bulge defects of the internal and external semiconductor layers, both of them induce the generation and development of electrical tree from the aspects of partial discharge damage and local electric field distortion [7–9]. In this paper, in order to simulate the bulge and air interval joint defects on the semiconductor layer, the needle electrode is repeatedly inserted into the insulation layer of the short cable to introduce the tip and air interval defects. The simulation test platform is shown in Fig. 1. Type and medium voltage cables are selected for the test samples to reflect the actual cable characteristics more accurately and avoid the test impact caused by insufficient technology when making samples. The specific steps of making the test sample: first, uncover the outer sheath of the cable and the shielding copper tape; Steel needles with diverse curvature radius are inserted into the insulation of the cable along the radial direction, and the thickness of the remaining insulation is 2.0 mm. During the insertion process, select the method of repeated insertion to promote the production of air interval at the tip of the needle, the combined defect models of bulge and air interval on semiconductor layers with diverse size were established.

Because the generation and development of electrical tree are accompanied by strong partial discharge signals, and show some differences in different stages. Based on the partial discharge signal features of electrical branch, the initiation time and development of electrical tree are determined. When the partial discharge frequency is mainly distributed in the interval, which can be characterized as the initial stage of electrical branch. The partial discharge signal is observed and collected by Luo coil and oscilloscope. The overall experimental schematic diagram is shown in Fig. 2.

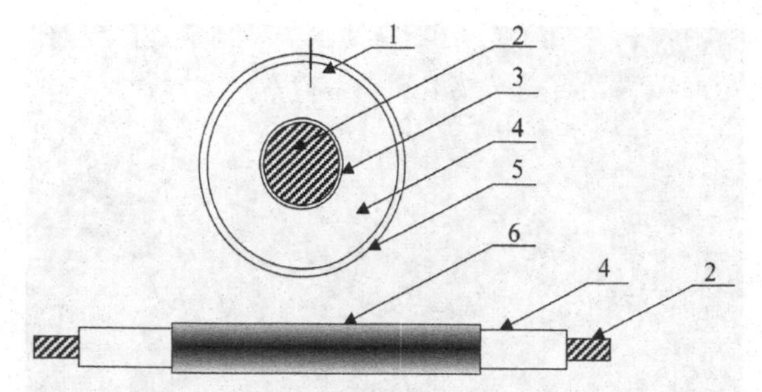

1—Needle defect, 2—Cable core, 3—Inner semiconducting layer, 4—Insulating layer, 5—Outer Semiconducting Layer, 6—Copper shielding tape

Fig. 1. Structure of test sample

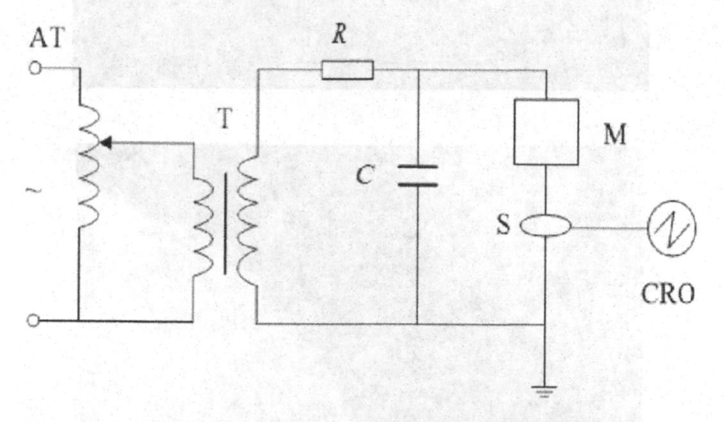

AT—Voltage regulator, T—Test transformer, R—Protective resistance, C—Coupling capacitance, M—Testing system, S—sensor, CRO—Oscilloscope

Fig. 2. Experimental wiring diagram

3 Test Result

In this work, the voltage rises at a rate of 5 kV/min and the frequency of the collected stable local discharge is analyzed, and the electric branch is observed by sectioning. Among them, the initial morphology of electrical tree is mainly filiform carbonization (Fig. 3.a) and gradually develops into a centralized carbonization channel shape (Fig. 3.b).

The time node of generation of the electrical tree is confirmed and the voltage rising at the corresponding time is recorded, which is the starting voltage of the electrical branch of the cable. By sorting out the data of several electrical treeing initiation tests, the correlation between the curvature radius of the needle tip and the treeing voltage of XLPE cable is determined. The mean value and error of the initial voltage under different needle tip curvature are shown in the curve in Fig. 4.

Fig. 3. Initial morphology and channelization growth of electrical tree

According to the experimental results, there is a positive correlation between the radius of curvature of the needle tip and the voltage caused by the electrical tree, that is, with the increase (decrease) of the curvature of the needle tip, the initial voltage of the electrical tree increases (decreases).

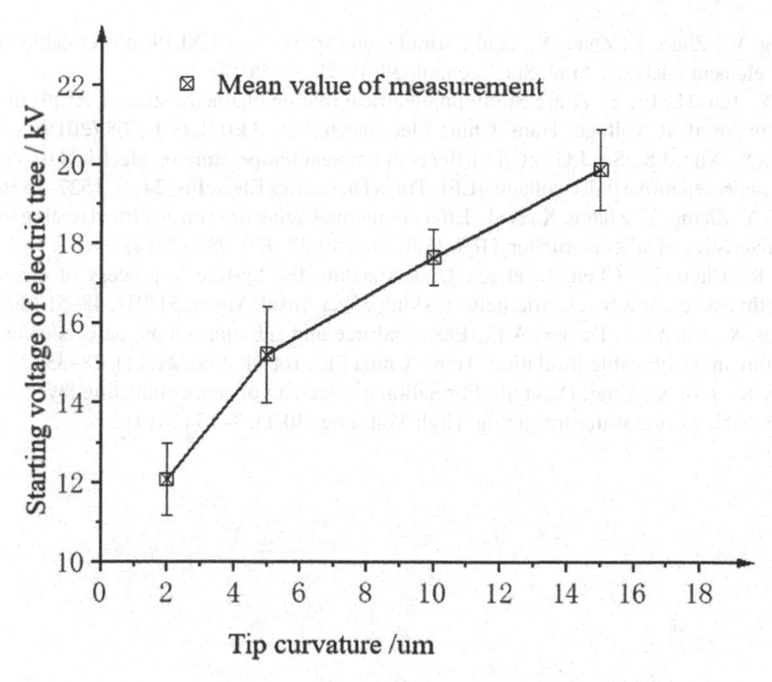

Fig. 4. Correlation between curvature of needle tip and starting voltage of electrical tree.

4 Conclusion

In this paper, a pin electrode short cable test platform is established. Using this test platform, the growth law of electrical tree under different defects is simulated.

(1) The initial morphology of electrical tree is mainly filiform carbonization, and then gradually develops into the shape of centralized carbonization channel.
(2) There is a positive correlation between the radius of curvature of internal defects in cable insulation and the voltage caused by electrical tree, that is, with the increase of the radius of curvature of defects, the initial voltage of electrical tree increases.

Acknowledgement. This work was financially supported by the science and technology project of State Grid Hunan Electric Power Company Limited (5216A520000H).

References

1. Yang, Y., You, J., Zhang, Y., et al.: Evaluation and analysis of 10kV XLPE cable operation state. High Volt. Eng. **43**(05), 1684–1692 (2017)
2. Zhou, Y., Lie, Q., Jiang, L., et al.: Effect of tip curvature radius on aging characteristics of silicone rubber electrical tree. Proc. CSEE **28**(34), 27–32 (2008)

3. Zhang, W., Zhao, S., Zhao, X., et al.: Simulation experiment of XLPE power cable based on finite element analysis. Appl. Sci. Technol. **39**(4), 51–54 (2012)
4. Liu, Y., Liu, H., Li, Y., et al.: Study on electrical treeing characteristics of XLPE under DC superimposed AC voltage. Trans. China Electrotech. Soc. **33**(03), 601–608 (2018)
5. Du, B.X., Xue, J.S., Su, J.G., et al.: Effects of ambient temperature on electrical tree in epoxy resin under repetitive pulse voltage. IEEE Trans Dielectrics Elect. Ins. **24**(3), 1527–1536 (2017)
6. Zhou, Y., Zhang, Y., Zhang, X., et al.: Effect of thermal aging time on electrical treeing initiation characteristics of silicone rubber. High Volt. Eng. 40(4), 979–986 (2014)
7. Wei, R., Chen, X., Chen, J., et al.: Understanding the hysteresis process of cross linked polyethylene clumps by electric field masking effect. Insul. Mater. **51**(01), 48–51 (2018)
8. Zheng, X., Chen, G., Davies, A.E.: Electrical tree and submicroscopic defects of insulation structure in XLPE cable insulation. Trans. China Electrotech. Soc. **21**(11), 28–33 (2006)
9. Zhou, K., Tao, X., Yang, D., et al.: Formation mechanism of semiconducting layer defects in XLPE cable during water tree aging. High Volt. Eng. **40**(1), 7–13 (2014)

Study on the Influence of Defect Characteristics of XLPE Cable on Electrical Tree Deterioration

Xujin Duan[1], Dai Wan[1](✉), Miao Zhao[1], Hengyi Zhou[1], Min Yi[1], Jiang Han[2], and Linjun Liu[3]

[1] State Grid Hunan Electric Power Company Limited Research Institute, Changsha 410007, China
280241509@qq.com

[2] State Grid Changde Power Supply Company, Changde 415000, China

[3] Qingdao Topscomm Communication Company Limited, Qingdao 266000, China

Abstract. With the acceleration of urbanization, the use of power cables is increasing. However, unlike overhead lines, power cables are laid in underground pipe galleries. It is difficult for power grid operation and maintenance personnel to carry out patrol inspection of power cable lines through intuitive detection means. Therefore, many defects of power cables are difficult to be found in time. During the operation of power cables, the influence of insulation electrical treeing is very large. Electrical treeing is an irreversible insulation damage. Electrical treeing can easily lead to penetrating discharge channels in cable insulation, thus affecting the reliability of the entire transmission system. In response to the above problems, the project team carried out an experimental study on the influence of the defect characteristics of XLPE insulated cables on the initial voltage of electrical tree. Based on the experimental results, this paper deeply analyzes the influence mechanism of cable defect characteristics on electrical tree. The numerical model of cable defects is constructed, and the influence of various factors on the generation of electrical tree is analyzed. Finally, the technical measures to weaken the deterioration of electrical tree in cable insulation are put forward. This research work has guiding significance for optimizing the performance and quality of power cables and improving the operation level of cables.

Keywords: Cross Linked Polyethylene · Cable · Electric Tree Branch · Test Platform

1 Introduction

Cross linked polyethylene (XLPE) insulated cables are diffusely applied in power grids with medium and low voltage because of the outstanding insulating property and the characteristics of safe and reliable. With the proposal of the grounding plan of urban power grid, the application of XLPE cables has been further expanded. However, due to the shortcomings of the current production and installation process, some defects or impurities will inevitably appear in the cable insulation, which accelerates the deterioration of the cable insulation and leads to the generation of electrical branches, further

H. Yang et al. (Eds.): SmartGIFT 2022, LNICST 483, pp. 403–411, 2023.
https://doi.org/10.1007/978-3-031-31733-0_34

causing the overall Breakdown Failure of the cable, thus affecting the reliability of the entire transmission system [1]. Therefore, it is of high industrial and engineering value to explore the influence law of defects on the development of electric branches in cable and put forward efficient methods and measures to prevent the generation of electrical tree.

For the analysis of the generation and development of electrical branches in XLPE insulated cable under different defects, domestic and foreign scholars have carried out relevant research in the fields of actual engineering, experimental simulation and model building based on theory. In reference [2, 3], J.H. Mason introduced the formula of maximum field strength of extremely uneven electric field in the needle plate electrode model into the study of branch discharge of organic polymers, revealing the effect of needle tip curvature on the voltage level of branch development, however the effect of the actual material properties on the initiation of the electrical branch was not analyzed. Reference [4] has built a test platform for the simulation of needle plate electrode defects. Based on the simulation results, the influence law of defect dimension in cables on the reliability of electrical branches initiation has been explored, but the corresponding mechanism explanation has not been made. At present, most studies focus on the structure, growth features and contributing factor of electric branches [5–7], only a few researchers have studied the effect of internal defects of XLPE cables on the generation and growth of electrical branches. The existing studies select a single object, and do not fully and systematically consider the influence of disparate defect characteristics on the generation of electrical branches.

Consequently, based on the preliminary test results of the project team, this paper constructs a numerical model of cable defects and analyzes the influence of various factors on the generation of electrical tree. And the technical measures to weaken the deterioration of electrical tree in cable insulation are put forward. It can effectively guide the production, operation and maintenance of power cables.

2 Numerical Model of Cable Defects

To study the correlation between tip curvature and the initial voltage of electric tree, the influence of various factors on the generation of electrotree was analyzed, and the numerical analysis model between the curvature radius of needle electrode and the initial voltage of electrotree was established.

Based on the allocation rule of the internal electric field in the AC electric field, the electric field strength decreases with the increase of dielectric constant. When the air gap inside the cable is introduced, the voltage in the micropore is larger because its dielectric constant is smaller than that of cross-linked polyethylene. According to the electromagnetic distribution model under spherical pores:

$$E_v = \frac{3\varepsilon}{1+2\varepsilon}E_0 \quad (1)$$

where: E_v is the electric strength in themicrovoid. E_0 is the electric field strength in XLPE. Since the dielectric constant ε of XLPE is approximately 2.2, the above formula can be reduced to:

$$E_v = 1.2\, E_0 \quad (2)$$

According to the above formula, the electric strength in the microvoid is about 1.2 times that of crosslinked polyethylene. When the electric field strength raises, local breakdown and discharge will occur in the air interval, and the defects in the microvoid will became worse.

According to the electron collision theory, the energy obtained by charged particles under the acceleration of electric field is:

$$\Delta W = \frac{e^2E^2}{2m}\overline{\tau} \quad (3)$$

where: m is the mass of charged particles. $\overline{\tau}$ is the time of mean free path.

Because the initiation of electrical treeing is determined by the energy of the particles injected into the material, the polymer will undergo molecular fracture and electric corrosion reaction under the action of high-energy particles, and the form of multi carbonization path will further develop. The maximum withstand energy threshold of XLPE under single electron impact is set as ΔW_0, which depends on is related to the properties of XLPE and other factors. When the charged particle energy is higher than the maximum withstand energy threshold, that is, $\Delta W \geq \Delta W_0$, the electrical tree has caused and further deterioration.

To identify the initial voltage of the electrical branch, let $\Delta W = \frac{e^2E^2}{2m}\overline{t} = \Delta W_0$.

Since the combined fault model of bulge and air interval on the semiconductor layer can be approximately equivalent to the needle plate electrode model, based on the Mason formula of the maximum field strength under the needle plate electrode model, the maximum field strength of the cross-linked polyethylene layer can be derived as follows:

$$E_{\max} = \frac{2U_0\sqrt{(1+\frac{d}{r})\frac{d}{r}}}{\ln(\frac{2d}{r}+1+2\sqrt{(1+\frac{d}{r})\frac{d}{r}})d} \quad (4)$$

where r is the radius of curvature of the needle electrode. U_0 is the test voltage. d is the distance between plate electrodes and needle.

When the cross-linked polyethylene at the front end of the air gap is carbonized, that is, the generation of electric branches, the corresponding voltage U_i can be recognized as the starting voltage of electric branches, and the relationship with the internal electric field strength of the material is as follows:

$$U_i = \frac{E_0 \times \ln(\frac{2d}{r}+1+2\sqrt{(1+\frac{d}{r})\frac{d}{r}})d}{2\sqrt{(1+\frac{d}{r})\frac{d}{r}}} \quad (5)$$

Since the electric field in the small space at the front of the air gap is continuous, it can be assumed that the electric field intensity E_0 in the tip region remains the same at the initial stage, and the charged particles accelerate in the electric field and impact the air gap XLPE interface. Combining Eqs. (2), (3) and (5), the following simultaneous equations can be obtained:

$$\begin{cases} U_i = \dfrac{E_0 \times \ln(\frac{2d}{r} + 1 + 2\sqrt{(1+\frac{d}{r})\frac{d}{r}})d}{2\sqrt{(1+\frac{d}{r})\frac{d}{r}}} \\ E_v = 1.2\,E_0 \\ \Delta W_0 = \dfrac{e^2 E_v^2}{2m}\overline{\tau} \end{cases} \tag{6}$$

After converting the above relationship, the starting voltage U_i of the electric branche is:

$$U_i = \frac{d \times \ln(\frac{2d}{r} + 1 + 2\sqrt{(1+\frac{d}{r})\frac{d}{r}})r}{2.4 \times \sqrt{(1+\frac{d}{r})\frac{d}{r}}e}\sqrt{2\Delta W_0}\sqrt{\frac{m}{\tau}} \tag{7}$$

As for the same kind of materials, the maximum withstand energy ΔW_0 can be considered as a constant. The constructed coefficient A is:

$$A = \frac{d \times \ln(\frac{2d}{r} + 1 + 2\sqrt{(1+\frac{d}{r})\frac{d}{r}})r}{2.4 \times \sqrt{(1+\frac{d}{r})\frac{d}{r}}e}\sqrt{2\Delta W_0} \tag{8}$$

Then the starting voltage U_i of the electrical tree can be calculated as follows:

$$U_i = A\sqrt{\frac{m}{\tau}} \tag{9}$$

When the internal space of the micropore is fixed, the average free path of the charged particles can be calculated as follows:

$$\overline{\lambda} = \frac{KT}{\pi r^{\cdot 2} P} = \frac{B}{P} \tag{10}$$

Where, T is the absolute temperature. K is Boltzmann constant. P is the pressure in the micropore. r is the radius of charged particles. Under the same electric field, the velocity obtained by charged particles is almost the same. The average free path time will maintain a positive correlation with the average free path of particles. Therefore, the average free travel can be calculated as follows:

$$\overline{\tau} = \frac{C}{P} \tag{11}$$

Where, C is a constant. Bring expression (8) and expression (11) into expression (7) to get:

$$U_i = \sqrt{\frac{Pm}{C}}A = \frac{d \times \ln(\frac{2d}{r} + 1 + 2\sqrt{(1 + \frac{d}{r})\frac{d}{r}})r}{2.4 \times \sqrt{(1 + \frac{d}{r})\frac{d}{r}}e}\sqrt{2\Delta W_0}\sqrt{\frac{Pm}{C}} \quad (12)$$

From the above formula, it can be seen that the initial voltage of electric treeing is affected by factors such as the radius of curvature of the needle tip, the initial initiation energy of electric treeing, the type of precipitation particles and the pressure of millipore. Assuming that micro pore pressure and the grains colliding with the electrical tree remain unchanged in the experiment, the initialization voltage of the electrical branche is a function of the change of needle curvature. Using the method of experimental test and literature review, determine the parameter size in the relationship, and compare the obtained function image with the test result image, as shown in Fig. 1, it can be analyzed that the test and numerical research results are consistent, identifying that the numerical model is practical, and the needle tip curvature meets a certain positive correlation with the starting voltage of electrical branche.

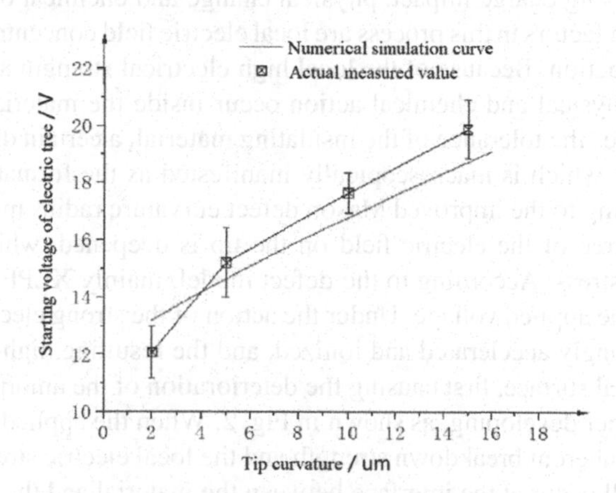

Fig. 1. Comparison between numerical simulation curve and tip curve

According to the established numerical model, when the curvature of the needle tip and the material doesn't change, the initialization voltage of the electrical branche is related to the microporous pressure, and also shows a positive correlation. With the increase (decrease) of the microporous pressure, the higher (decrease) the initial voltage of the electrical branche. Because the test and actual temperature did not exceed the glass transition temperature of XLPE, the material properties remained unchanged. The elastic modulus of cross-linked polyethylene in glass state was large, and the effect of mechanical stress caused by air pressure was small. Air pressure further affected the starting voltage of electrical tree mainly by influencing the process of partial discharge.

The ΔW_0 value mainly represents the energy threshold required for generating branches. This parameter is related to the characteristics, structure and microporous interface of insulating materials. As the process of manufacturing and the curvature of the needle keep the same, the initialization voltage of the electrical branche shows a positive correlation with ΔW_0. The larger the value of ΔW_0, the higher the energy required to generate power branches, and the larger the starting voltage required to generate power branches.

3 Mechanism Research and Analysis

The initiation of electrical branche involves complicated physical and chemical processes, which are affected by external contributor and related to the complex characteristics of insulating materials. As a semi crystalline polymer, cross-linked polyethylene has a high degree of dispersion in the fixed and amorphous regions, and the electrical treeing characteristics have a high dispersion due to the local tensile stress, micropores and inhomogeneous crystallization generated during production. Through experimental simulation and numerical model analysis, this work analyzes the influence of diverse defect characteristics on the starting voltage of electrical tree, and the corresponding influence mechanisms are as follows.

The production of electrical branche involves a variety of physical and chemical phenomena, including charge impact, physical change and chemical oxidation decomposition. The main factors in this process are local electric field concentration and charge injection and extraction. Because of the local high electrical strength and the impact of charged grains, physical and chemical action occur inside the material. As the action intensity overcomes the tolerance of the insulating material, a certain discharge channel will be generated, which is macroscopically manifested as the formation of electrical branches. According to the improved Mason defect curvature radius model established, the distortion degree of the electric field on the tip is deepened, which will enhance the local electric stress. According to the defect model, mainly XLPE and air void are mainly acted by the applied voltage. Under the action of the strong electric field, the gas molecules are strongly accelerated and ionized, and the resulting high-energy particles will hit the material surface, first causing the deterioration of the amorphous area of the material, and further developing, as shown in Fig. 2. When the applied electric strength is lower than the inherent breakdown strength and the local electric stress rises a certain degree, cracks will occur at the interface between the material and the defect. The high temperature generated by the collision will further promote the thermal decomposition, accelerating the initiation of the electric tree and reducing the initial voltage value of the electric branche. Thus, in practice, we can increase the starting voltage of electrical branches by enhancing the curvature of synapses in the semiconductor layer and reducing the number of synapses. For instance, for the actual cable extrusion process, we can set the optimal screw speed based on the material characteristics to improve the extrusion mode of cable insulation layer and semiconductor layer, so as to avoid the problems of material surface roughness and extrusion instability caused by pre crosslinking, so as to produce small bulges and insulation air gaps.

From the mechanism analysis, the influence of micropore pressure on electrical branche initiation is mainly embodied in two aspects: mechanical force stretching and free path of charged grains. The effect of needle tip air pressure makes the interface of cross-linked polyethylene layer bear the effect of radial mechanical stress F_1, and its action diagram is exhibited in Fig. 3. The radial mechanical force will lead to the internal compression of the weak region of the material, which will further cause the generation of tangential stress f_τ, resulting in tangential tensile damage in XLPE, and the crack will develop forward. But due to the fact that the normal operating temperature is lower than 90 °C (the glass transition temperature of XLPE), the movement space of the cross-linked polyethylene chain segment is very small, its own tensile strength is large, and it appears as hard plastic externally. The air void pressure has little influence on the inner wall of the insulation material, and the tensile damage caused by the stress is very small.

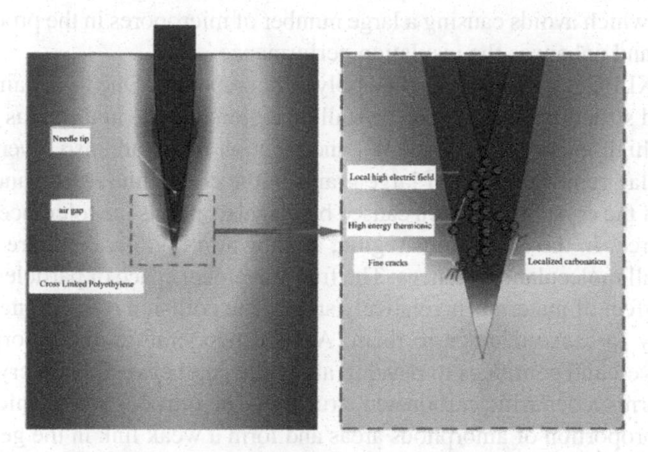

Fig. 2. Hot electron acceleration and material damage under local electric field concentration

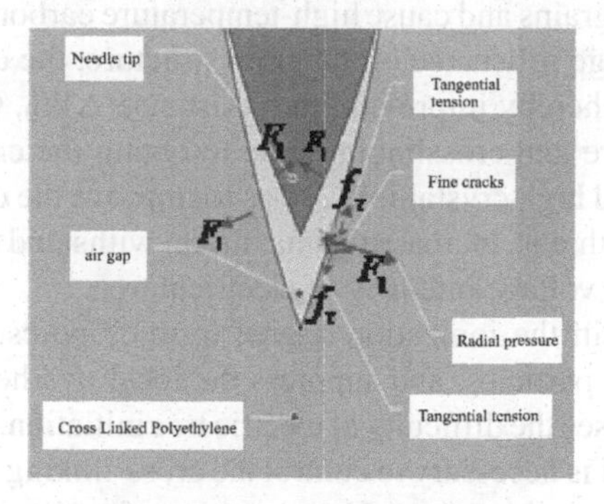

Fig. 3. Stress effect of air gap

From the perspective of particle collision, due to the small micropore gap and pressure of the cable, and the small spacing between particles, the accumulation of energy cannot be completed even under the action of local strong electric field, so sufficient internal electrical stress cannot be generated, and there is no internal discharge, material decomposition and molecular chain fracture in the insulation. By changing the internal pressure of microporous defects to increase the starting voltage of electrical tree, which is mainly carried out from two aspects: ①There are more microholes in cable insulation because of the thermal expansion properties of the material, the non-uniform crystallinity, and the way the material is cross-linked, which mainly reflects that the internal pressure of the micropores in the processing process does not reach the standard value, and the gas cannot be extruded, Improve the extrusion method to reduce the volume of micropores, and increase the pressure of remaining micropores to increase the starting voltage of electric branche; ② The thinner the insulation thickness, the more uniform and concentrated the stress on the material in the pressurization process, and the number of micropores will be reduced, increasing the internal pressure; ③ The dry crosslinking method is selected to replace the wet crosslinking method for polyethylene crosslinking, which avoids causing a large number of micropores in the process of water vaporization and enhances the insulation performance.

Because XLPE is a semi-crystalline polymer compound. Due to certain differences in density and structure between the crystalline region and the amorphous region, their resistance to high-energy particles ΔW_0 and reaction mode are also diverse, and considering the slag removal effect of large grains in the crystalline region and the uneven distribution of the crystalline region caused by it, it also affects the tolerance of materials to electrical tree. In the amorphous region, as shown in Fig. 4a, there are some magazines and small molecular substances. The free movement space of particles is large and the binding effect of materials is relatively small. The collision of high-energy particles is more likely to cause damage to them. At high temperature, the amorphous structure is destroyed and continues to develop along the gap between large crystal regions, and finally forms a dendritic carbonated structure. The introduction of micropores will increase the proportion of amorphous areas and form a weak link in the generation and development of electrical branches. Under the condition of uniform grain distribution (as shown in Fig. 4b), the volume of the amorphous region is small, and the electrons mainly collide with the grains and cause high-temperature carbonization of the interface. Due to the strong damage resistance of the grain structure, the downward development of defects is hindered, thereby improving the resistance ΔW_0. Control the appropriate crosslinking temperature and crosslinking time to obtain the crystal morphology with uniform distribution and high crystallinity, so as to improve the electrical tree resistance of insulating materials, that is, increase the maximum withstand energy value ΔW_0, and then improve the initial voltage intensity of electrical tree.

Inert gas can restrain the ionization degree in micropores, reduce the number of local energetic charged particles, and suppress the local overheating caused by partial discharge, which increases the difficulty of electric tree initiation. At the same time, when manufacturing cables, it is necessary to control the cross-linking process not to occur too early, so as to prevent impurities caused by scorching after the oxidation of the polymer during the early cross-linking, which affect its combination with the normal insulation interface, thus forming bubbles, and reducing the product quality of XLPE. Therefore, changing the crystalline morphology of insulating materials, filling micropores with inert gas and controlling the optimal crosslinking time can improve the size of ΔW_0 and further increase the starting voltage of electrical branche.

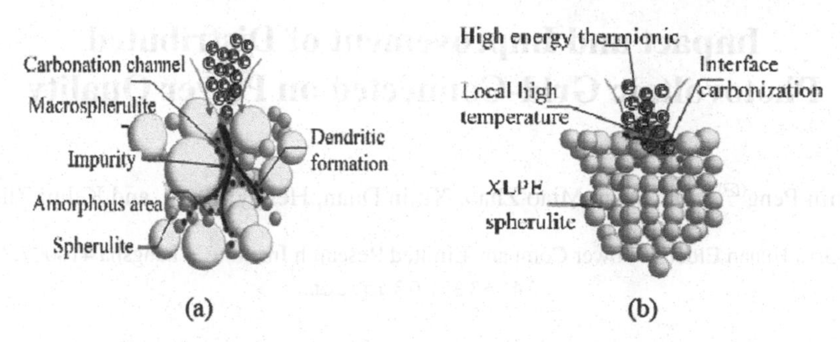

Fig. 4. Target tracking process

4 Conclusion

In this paper, a pin electrode short cable test platform is established. Using this test platform, the growth law of electrical tree under different defects is simulated.

(1) The initial morphology of electrical tree is mainly filiform carbonization, and then gradually develops into the shape of centralized carbonization channel.
(2) There is a positive correlation between the radius of curvature of internal defects in cable insulation and the voltage caused by electrical tree, that is, with the increase of the radius of curvature of defects, the initial voltage of electrical tree increases.

Acknowledgement. This work was financially supported by the science and technology project of State Grid Hunan Electric Power Company Limited (5216A520000H).

References

1. Yang, Y., You, J., Zhang, Y., et al.: Evaluation and analysis of 10kV XLPE cable operation state. High Voltage Eng. **43**(05), 1684–1692 (2017)
2. Mason, J.H.: The deterioration and breakdown of dielectrics resulting from internal dis-charges. Proc. IEE-part I: gen. **98**(109), 44–59 (1951)
3. Zeng, J., Song, J., Lei, Z., et al.: Study on the law of electrical tree growth in XLPE cable insulation under needle plate electrode. High Voltage Apparatus **55**(02), 156–163 (2019)
4. Wu, J., Chen, S.: Study on the mechanism of electrical treeing inhibition in polymer blends. J. Xi'an Jiaotong Univ. **01**, 82–92 (1983)
5. Liu, Y., Liu, H., Li, Y., et al.: Study on electrical treeing characteristics of XLPE under DC superimposed AC voltage. Trans. China Electrotechnical Soc. **33**(03), 601–608 (2018)
6. Du, B.X., Xue, J.S., Su, J.G., et al.: Effects of ambient temperature on electrical tree in epoxy resin under repetitive pulse voltage. IEEE Trans. Dielectr. Electr. Insul. **24**(3), 1527–1536 (2017)
7. Zhou, Y., Zhang, Y., Zhang, X., et al.: Effect of thermal aging time on electrical treeing initiation characteristics of silicone rubber. High Voltage Eng. **40**(04), 979–986 (2014)

Impact and Improvement of Distributed Photovoltaic Grid-Connected on Power Quality

Simin Peng(✉), Dai Wan, Miao Zhao, Xujin Duan, Hengyi Zhou, and Kehui Zhou

State Grid Hunan Electric Power Company Limited Research Institute, Changsha 410007, China
240639880@qq.com

Abstract. With the large-scale access of distributed photovoltaics to the distribution network, its intermittent and random characteristics bring power quality problems such as voltage exceeding the upper limit, broadband oscillation, and three-phase unbalance to the distribution network. The grid connection method and related standards and specifications of distributed photovoltaic grid connection, analyze the main impact of distributed photovoltaic grid connection on the power quality of distribution network, and propose countermeasures.

Keywords: Large-scale distributed PV · Distribution network · Power quality

1 Introduction

With the access of large-scale distributed photovoltaics, the network structure and power supply mode of the distribution network have undergone great changes, and the distribution network has evolved from a one-way passive network to an active network that interacts with supply and demand. The output fluctuation, intermittency, randomness and other characteristics of photovoltaic power generation may lead to the problems of voltage bidirectional over-limit, voltage fluctuation and flicker, three-phase unbalance and harmonic over-standard. In this paper, based on the current main grid-connected methods of distributed photovoltaics and related standards and specifications of distributed photovoltaics, selected practical cases, analyzed the main impact of distributed photovoltaics on the power quality of distribution grids, and proposed countermeasures.

2 Status of Distributed Photovoltaics

2.1 Distributed Photovoltaic Grid Connection Method

At present, the domestic distributed photovoltaic access to the distribution network is divided into four methods: 220 V low-voltage single-phase access, 380 V low-voltage three-phase access, 10 kV access and 35 kV/110 kV centralized access. Distributed photovoltaics with a capacity of 8 kW and below generally use low-voltage 220 V single-phase access. Distributed photovoltaics with a capacity of 8 kW-400 kW generally use

H. Yang et al. (Eds.): SmartGIFT 2022, LNICST 483, pp. 412–422, 2023.
https://doi.org/10.1007/978-3-031-31733-0_35

low-voltage 380V three-phase access, as shown in Fig. 1. Distributed photovoltaics with a capacity of 400 kW–6 MW are generally connected by 10 kV, and the schematic diagram is shown in Fig. 3. Distributed photovoltaics with a capacity of 6 MW–50 MW are centrally connected with a voltage level of 35 kV/110 kV. The schematic diagram is shown in Fig. 4. (Fig. 2)

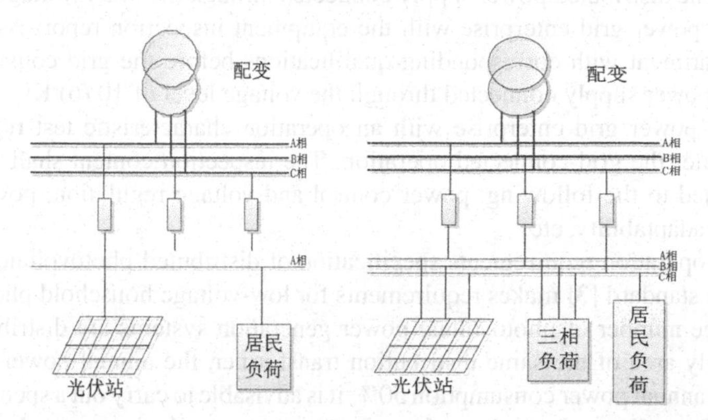

Fig. 1. Schematic diagram of photovoltaic low-voltage single-phase and three-phase connection

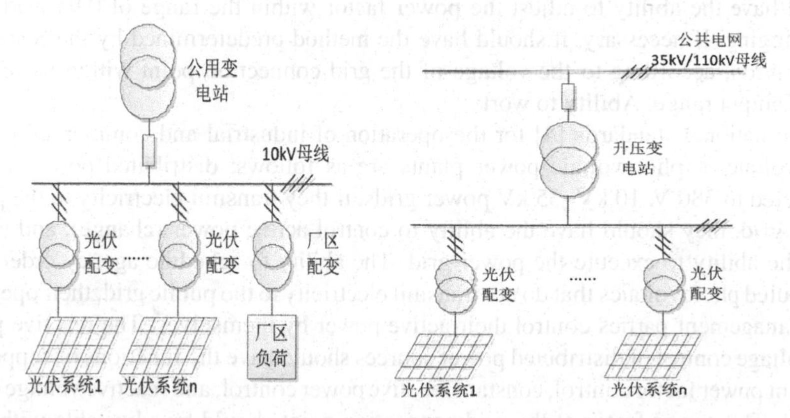

Fig. 2. Schematic diagram of photovoltaic 10kV distributed and centralized access

2.2 Standards and Specifications Related to Distributed Photovoltaic Grid-Connection

In terms of standards and specifications for access to the distribution network, industry standards [1] stipulate that it is necessary to carry out an evaluation of the carrying capacity of distributed power generation access to the power grid to provide a basis for distributed power and power grid planning, design, construction, and operation to ensure the safe and stable operation of the power grid and promote distribution. The healthy and orderly development of the power supply. The evaluation of the carrying capacity of the distributed power grid connected to the power grid includes thermal stability evaluation, short-circuit current check, voltage deviation check, and harmonic check. The national standard [2] stipulates the quality of the power generated by the distributed power source, and the indicators include harmonics, voltage deviation, voltage unbalance, voltage fluctuation and flicker, etc., which should meet the relevant national standards. The distributed power supply connected through the 380V voltage level shall provide the power grid enterprise with the equipment inspection report issued by the unit or department with corresponding qualifications before the grid connection. The distributed power supply connected through the voltage level of 10 (6) Kv–35 kV shall provide the power grid enterprise with an operation characteristic test report within 6 months after the grid-connected operation. The inspection content shall include but not be limited to the following: power control and voltage regulation, power quality, operational adaptability, etc.

For the operation requirements specification of distributed photovoltaic operation, the national standard [3] makes requirements for low-voltage household photovoltaics: when a large number of photovoltaic power generation systems are distributed in the power supply area of the same distribution transformer, the annual power generation exceeds the annual power consumption 50%, it is advisable to carry out a special research on the power quality and reactive voltage in the power supply area as a whole from the perspective of the system. The inverter of the photovoltaic power generation system should have the ability to adjust the power factor within the range of 0.95 leading to 0.95 lagging. If necessary, it should have the method predetermined by the State Grid Corporation, according to the voltage of the grid connection point within its reactive power output range. Ability to work.

The national standards [4] for the operation of industrial and commercial rooftop photovoltaic or photovoltaic power plants are as follows: distributed power sources connected to 380 V, 10 kV–35 kV power grids, if they transmit electricity to the public power grid, they should have the ability to control active power (change), and should have the ability to execute the power grid. The ability to schedule agency orders. For distributed photovoltaics that do not transmit electricity to the public grid, their operation and management parties control their active power by themselves. The reactive power and voltage control of distributed power sources should have the functions of supporting constant power factor control, constant reactive power control, and reactive voltage droop control. The power factor at the grid connection point should be adjustable within the range of 0.95 (leading) to 0.95 (lag) when it is connected to a 380 V distributed power supply connected to the grid via a converter. The distributed power supply connected to the grid of 10 kV–35 kV through the converter should have the ability to ensure that the power factor at the grid-connected point is continuously adjustable within the range of 0.98 (leading) to 0.98 (lag); within the range of its reactive power output It should have the ability to adjust reactive power output and participate in grid voltage regulation according to the voltage level of the grid connection point. Its adjustment method, reference voltage, voltage adjustment rate and other parameters can be set by the grid dispatching agency.

For grid-connected inverters [5], the industry standard stipulates that when the inverter is running, the total harmonic distortion rate of the current injected into the grid is limited to 5%. Under normal operating conditions of the inverter, when the output active power of the inverter is greater than 50% of its rated power, the power factor should not be less than 0.98 (leading or lagging), and when the output active power is between 20% and 50%, the power The factor should not be less than 0.95 (lead or lag). When the inverter is in normal operation, the negative sequence three-phase current unbalance should not exceed 2%, and should not exceed 4% in a short time. When the inverter is in normal operation, the DC current component fed to the grid should not exceed 0.5% of its output current rating.

3 The Main Influence of Distributed Photovoltaics on Power Quality of Distribution Network

With the large-scale access of distributed photovoltaics to the distribution network, its intermittent and random characteristics mainly bring power quality problems such as voltage exceeding the upper limit, broadband oscillation, and three-phase unbalance to the distribution network.

3.1 High Voltage Problem

In the distribution network that is not connected to distributed photovoltaics, the voltage distribution is only affected by load fluctuations, and the voltage of the distribution line gradually decreases with the direction of the power flow. After the distributed photovoltaic is connected, the load is balanced on the spot, so that the power flow of the distribution network changes. When a large number of distributed photovoltaics are connected, the phenomenon of power flow return may occur, raising the back-end voltage of the line. Especially when the line is lightly loaded, the voltage of the distribution line is basically close to the upper limit, and the distributed photovoltaic cannot be absorbed locally, and the back-end voltage of the line may exceed the upper limit. In addition, in order to ensure that low voltage does not occur at the end users of peak loads, some lines have high voltage problems even without distributed photovoltaics at light loads. After distributed photovoltaic power generation, the high voltage problem will be particularly aggravated, and in serious cases, users' household appliances will be damaged. At present, most distributed photovoltaics themselves do not have reactive power-voltage control capability, and the problem of voltage exceeding the upper limit is more difficult to control.

Case 1: A commercial photovoltaic user with a total installed capacity of 1.9 MW is connected to the power grid through a 10 kV dedicated line, and the voltage and power of the grid-connected point are tested. The test waveform is shown in Fig. 1. It can be seen from the figure that the larger the photovoltaic power, the higher the corresponding grid-connected point voltage, and the smaller the safety margin of the voltage. This photovoltaic inverter has a reactive power adjustment mode. Under the premise of not affecting the active power of photovoltaic power generation, that is, within the allowable range of the photovoltaic inverter capacity, by adjusting the reactive power (absorption) of the photovoltaic inverter, it can effectively reduce The voltage level of the photovoltaic 10 kV side, so that the voltage safety margin on the distribution grid side is guaranteed within an appropriate range.

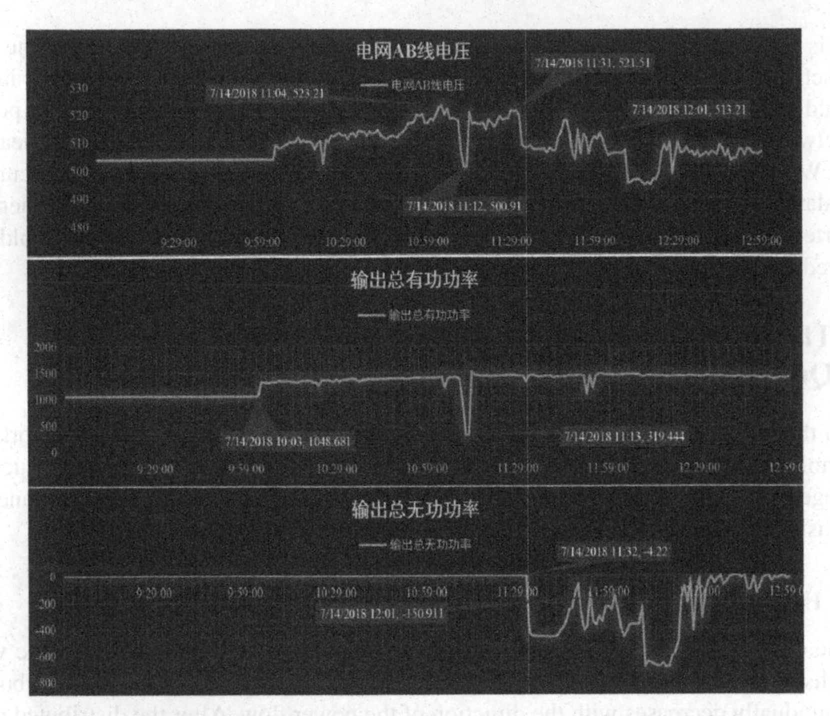

Fig. 3. Test waveform of voltage and power of a commercial photovoltaic user

3.2 Harmonic Problem

The harmonics of distributed photovoltaics are mainly caused by the modulation of inverter PWM switching and the dead zone effect of switching devices. According to the working principle of power electronic switching devices, the harmonic frequency generated by PWM switching modulation is related to the modulation carrier frequency (switching frequency), and is mainly distributed in the vicinity of the multiplication frequency of the carrier frequency, which is a high-frequency harmonic. The sub-harmonics are mainly 19th, 23rd, 41st and 43rd; the switching frequency is 2000 Hz, and the higher harmonics are mainly 38th, 42nd, 79th and 81st. The harmonic frequencies generated by the dead-time effect of the device are mainly low-order harmonics such as the 3rd, 5th, and 7th. The harmonic spectrum generated by distributed photovoltaics is relatively wide, and the potential risk of broadband oscillation with the distribution network is relatively large, especially in the scenario where multiple distributed photovoltaic inverters are connected to the grid, the grid-connected line is a cable line, and the diameter of the grid-connected line is large. Small and distant scenes.

Case 2: A village poverty alleviation photovoltaic power station is a joint establishment model of 4 villages, including 4 sets of 60 kW photovoltaic units with a total installed capacity of 240 kW, which are connected to the grid through a 400 kVA distribution transformer.

Since the village's photovoltaic poverty alleviation power station has been connected to the grid, it has basically operated normally, and faults have occasionally occurred,

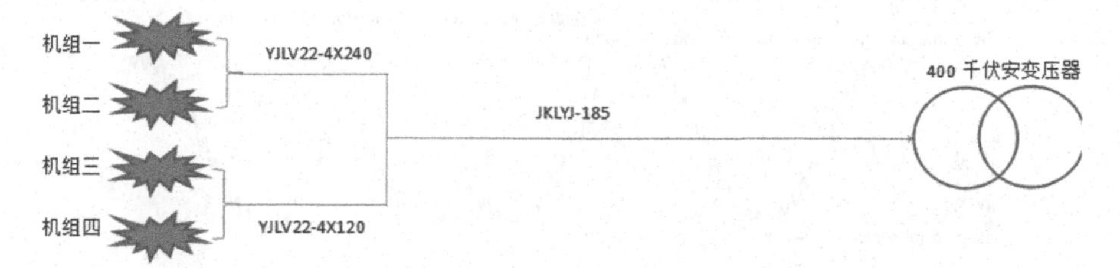

Fig. 4. Schematic diagram of village poverty alleviation photovoltaic power station

but it is within the controllable range. After the transformation of the rural grid, the grid connection of the power station was abnormal. When the power of a single inverter increased to 40 kW, 2 inverters out of the 4 inverters were automatically disconnected from the grid and could not generate full-load power. Through the on-site power quality test, it is found that the output voltage of a single inverter is normal, the power quality is good, and it meets the requirements of grid connection; when two inverters are connected to the grid, harmonic resonance occurs with the grid, and the power quality of the common connection point is poor. The harmonics were seriously exceeded, causing another inverter to be disconnected from the grid (Fig. 5).

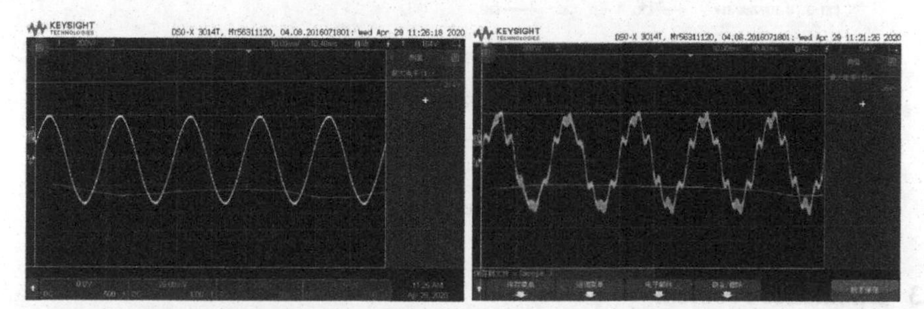

Fig. 5. The voltage waveform when one inverter is connected to the grid and the voltage waveform when two inverters are connected to the grid

Case 3: A 49 MW photovoltaic power station has 98 500 kW photovoltaic inverters, consisting of 49 10 kV distribution transformers (1 distribution transformer with 2 inverters). During the operation of the photovoltaic power station, the inverter will occasionally trip abnormally under certain working conditions, and the noise of the 110 kV grid main transformer is too large. After on-site testing, it was found that the total harmonic distortion rate of 110 kV voltage when all inverters were connected to the grid was seriously exceeding the standard (the maximum was 12.1%, and the national standard limit was 2%). The impedance of the grid-connected line resonates, generating a large 23rd harmonic voltage (7.87 kV), causing multiple inverters to be disconnected from the grid and increasing the noise of the main transformer (Figs. 6 and 7).

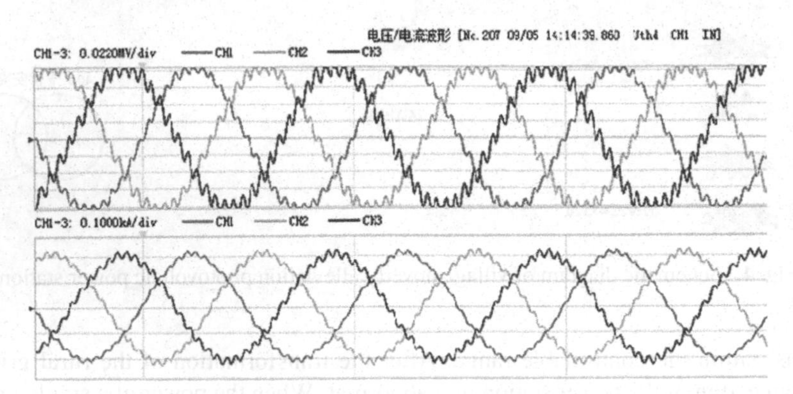

Fig. 6. Grid voltage and current waveforms when all inverters are connected to the grid

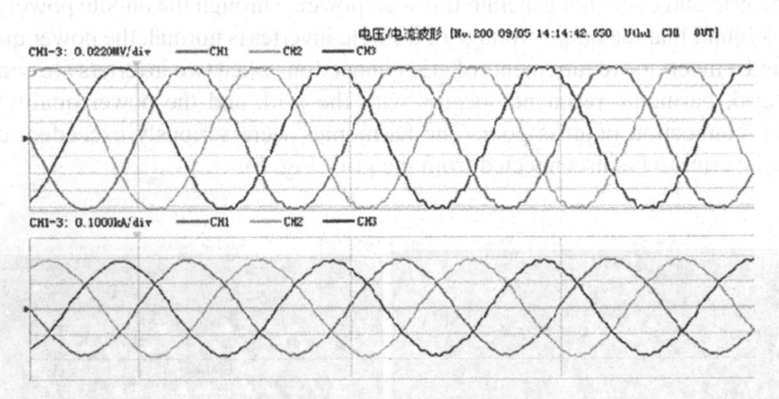

Fig. 7. Grid voltage and current waveforms after abnormal inverter off-grid

3.3 Imbalance Problem

After a large number of single-phase household photovoltaics are randomly connected to the station area, the power flow of the power grid flows in both directions, and the load and power supply in the station area will have randomness and volatility, which will further increase the problem of unbalanced three-phase load in the station area.

Case 3: The capacity of a distributed poverty alleviation photovoltaic distribution transformer is 200 kVA, and the electricity load is mainly household appliances. The annual maximum power consumption is about 120 kW. A total of 78 kW of single-phase poverty alleviation distributed photovoltaics are connected to the Taiwan area. After on-site testing, the unbalance of three-phase current in the platform area exceeded 50% when the poverty alleviation photovoltaics were launched.

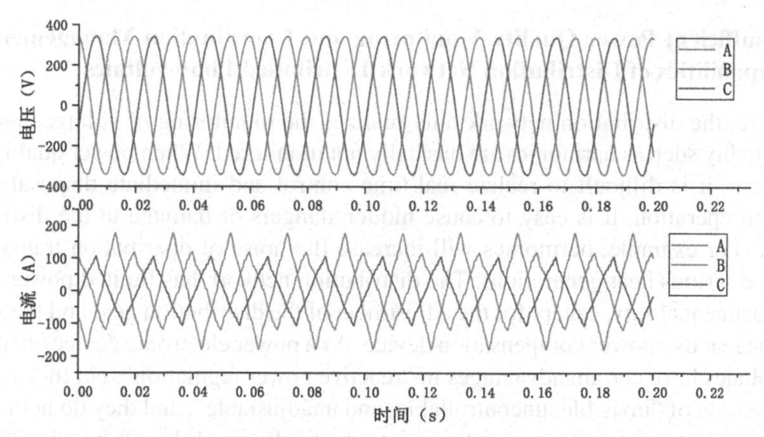

Fig. 8. The voltage and current waveforms of the low-voltage side of a distributed poverty alleviation photovoltaic station area

4 The Main Influence of Distributed Photovoltaics on Power Quality of Distribution Network

4.1 Distributed Photovoltaic Access Does not Fully Consider the Carrying Capacity of the Distribution Network

At present, the calculation of the carrying capacity of distributed photovoltaics by the power grid basically only conducts regional consumption analysis from the aspect of photovoltaic output and load level matching. For small-capacity rooftop photovoltaics, poverty alleviation photovoltaics, household photovoltaics, etc., it is basically in the state of "connecting all connections" and "disorderly control", and does not fully consider the carrying capacity of a single distribution line (including short-circuit current, voltage deviation, harmonics, etc.). Carrying capacity check), especially for lines with weak grids and poor power quality, the connection of distributed photovoltaics will further deteriorate the power quality of the lines. Typical problems include high voltage and harmonics of photovoltaic power distribution lines. Wave resonance amplification, etc.

4.2 The Unreasonable Selection of Distributed Photovoltaic Inverters Has Insufficient Adaptability to the Distribution Network

The selection of equipment such as distributed photovoltaic inverters (such as inverter withstand voltage range, inverter adaptive control strategy) basically does not consider the actual operation of the connected distribution network, and most of them are standardized and unified selection., The adaptability of photovoltaic inverters to the power grid is insufficient, mainly manifested in problems such as high-voltage inverter off-grid, broadband resonant inverter off-grid and even damage. For example, in Shaoyang area, poverty alleviation photovoltaics on small hydropower grid-connected lines were disconnected from the grid due to high voltage problems, and in Hengyang area, severe harmonic distortion occurred, resulting in limited photovoltaic output.

4.3 Insufficient Power Quality Monitoring and Coordination Management Capabilities of Distribution Network-Distributed Photovoltaics

At present, the distribution network only realizes the monitoring of voltage, and other power quality such as harmonics are basically not monitored. When power quality problems occur, it is difficult to realize real-time control and immediate disposal. Under long-term operation, it is easy to cause hidden dangers or damage to the distribution network (For example, harmonics will increase the noise of distribution transformers and cause serious heat generation). The distribution network has limited power quality self-adjustment ability, except for the adjustment of the distribution gear and the switching of the reactive power compensation device. As a power electronic device, distributed photovoltaics have certain advantages in "reactive power regulation", but they are basically in a state of "invisible, uncontrollable, and unadjustable", and they do not have the ability to adjust reactive power and voltage adaptively, much less It has the ability to coordinate and control with the distribution network.

4.4 Insufficient Acceptance Management of Distributed Photovoltaic Access to Distribution Network

Most of the distributed photovoltaics connected to the 380V voltage level did not provide equipment inspection reports to power grid companies in accordance with the standard requirements before grid connection, and the power grid companies did not carry out equipment sampling inspections; distributed photovoltaics connected to the 10 kV voltage level are currently The testing of grid-connected operation characteristics such as reactive power voltage and power quality has not been carried out, which also does not meet the relevant standards. Therefore, it may lead to the connection of photovoltaic inverters that do not meet the standard requirements, such as excessive harmonic generation levels and insufficient reactive power regulation capabilities, to the distribution network.

5 Main Measures

5.1 Carry Out Special Research on Power Quality Problems of High-Proportion Distributed Photovoltaic Distribution Networks and Pilot Projects

For the same distribution network line or station area, when the annual photovoltaic power generation exceeds a certain proportion of the annual electricity consumption (the national standard is 50%), a special study on the power quality and reactive voltage in typical regions is carried out. Strengthen the governance of power quality problems in high-proportion distributed photovoltaic areas, and comprehensively consider the technical and economic characteristics of measures such as on-load voltage regulating transformers, capacitors/reactors/SVG, energy storage devices or photovoltaic inverter reactive power regulation. Copy the economical and practical solutions that can be promoted to further improve the flexibility of the distribution network, which not only improves the acceptance capacity of distributed photovoltaics, but also ensures the safe and reliable operation of the distribution network. It is recommended to give priority to the extreme scenarios of high probability full-time reverse transmission of photovoltaic power generation at the station level and substation level, and carry out an overall research on the qualitative and quantitative comprehensive evaluation of the influence of the reactive voltage and power quality operation of the distribution network.

5.2 Improve the Power Quality Coordination Control Level of the Distribution Network and Distributed Photovoltaics

At present, the level of informatization and automation of the distribution network is rapidly improving year by year, and the reactive voltage and power quality control methods in the distribution network are increasingly abundant (such as distribution transformers, smart capacitors, line voltage regulators, and SVG, etc.). At the same time, the new loads represented by distributed energy, energy storage and electric vehicles can have the technical ability to participate in the reactive power and voltage regulation of the distribution network through functional transformation, which can effectively enhance the flexibility and interactivity of the operation of the distribution network. Therefore, various controllable resources such as distributed energy, distribution network, new loads, and energy storage ("source-grid-load-storage") should be coordinated to overcome the multi-time-scale reactive voltage and power quality of complex distribution networks with source-grid-load-storage coordination. Active control technology achieves multi-level coordination of vertical high-voltage-medium-voltage-low-voltage distribution network, horizontal day-a-day-real-time distribution network multi-time scale coordination, and realizes economical, efficient and reliable operation of distribution network and maximizes distributed energy. Digestion.

5.3 Strengthen the Whole Process Management of Distributed Photovoltaic Access to the Distribution Network

In terms of grid access evaluation, equipment performance sampling inspection, grid connection inspection and acceptance, operation and maintenance, etc., the process and whole-process management of distributed photovoltaic access to the distribution network shall be strengthened. In particular, strengthen the early source control of distributed photovoltaic access, establish an access distribution network evaluation method that fully considers factors such as voltage, harmonics, line loss, and heavy overload, and refine access capacity, matching equipment selection, etc. Establish a sampling inspection platform for power electronic equipment such as photovoltaic inverters, and improve the quality inspection and acceptance of grid-connected 10 kV distributed photovoltaic power.

6 Conclusion

This paper comprehensively analyzes the main grid-connected methods of distributed photovoltaics and the relevant standards and specifications of distributed photovoltaics in the country and the industry, selects actual cases on site, analyzes the main impact of distributed photovoltaics on the power quality of the distribution network, and discusses the current Problems existing after distributed photovoltaics are connected to the distribution network, and targeted solutions are proposed.

Acknowledgment. This work was financially supported by the science and technology project of State Grid Hunan Electric Power Company Limited (5216A5210035).

References

1. DL/T 2041–2019,Technical guideline for evaluating power grid bearing capability of distributed resources connected to network (2019)
2. GB/T 33593–2017,Technical requirements for grid connection of distributed resources (2017)
3. GB/T 33342–2016,Technical specification of utility interface of residential distributed photovoltaic power system (2017)
4. GB/T 33592–2017,Specification of operation and controlling for distributed resources connected to power grid (2017)
5. NBT 32004–2018,Technical specification of PV grid-connected inverter (2018)

Research on the Influence of Distributed Photovoltaic Grid-Connected on the Operation Characteristics of Wide Range OLTC Transformer

Simin Peng(✉), Xujin Duan, Dai Wan, Miao Zhao, Hengyi Zhou, and Kehui Zhou

State Grid Hunan Electric Power Company Limited Research Institute, Changsha 410007, China
240639880@qq.com

Abstract. After the distributed photovoltaic is connected to the distribution network, its power supply characteristics change the load characteristics of the traditional distribution network, so that the power flow of the distribution network begins to change in two directions. Terminal voltage, which puts forward higher requirements for the bidirectional voltage regulation of the wide-width on-load voltage regulating transformer. At present, there are still no authoritative and directly related technical standards for the voltage regulating part and its control part of the wide-width on-load voltage regulating transformer for reference. The relevant suggestions are put forward for the application of wide-width on-load voltage regulating transformers under grid conditions.

Keywords: Distributed PV · OLTC · Distribution network

1 Introduction

After the distributed photovoltaic is connected to the distribution network, its power supply characteristics change the load characteristics of the traditional distribution network [1]. When a large number of distributed photovoltaics are connected, the phenomenon of power flow return may occur and the back-end voltage of the line may be raised [2]. Especially when the line is lightly loaded, the voltage of the distribution line is basically close to the upper limit, and the distributed photovoltaic cannot be absorbed locally, and the back-end voltage of the line may exceed the upper limit [3]. Therefore, higher requirements are put forward for the bidirectional voltage regulation of the wide-width on-load voltage regulating transformer [4].However, there is still a lack of authoritative and directly related technical standards for the 10 kV wide on-load voltage regulation part and its control [5]. In practical application, it is necessary to clarify requirements in terms of wide width, on-load voltage regulation, and control to guide the configuration of equipment control parameters and on-site application [6].

This paper mainly conducts experimental analysis on wide-width on-load voltage regulating transformers, and puts forward relevant suggestions for the application of wide-width on-load voltage regulating transformers under the condition of distributed photovoltaic grid connection.

H. Yang et al. (Eds.): SmartGIFT 2022, LNICST 483, pp. 423–431, 2023.
https://doi.org/10.1007/978-3-031-31733-0_36

2 Test Situation

In this paper, performance tests such as temperature rise, lightning impulse, short-circuit resistance, no-load, load, and overload voltage regulation are carried out on 13 on-load voltage regulation and distribution transformers. Among them, 8 sets of closed three-dimensional wound core amorphous alloy width change, 3 sets of stacked iron core silicon steel sheet width change, 2 sets of traditional amorphous alloy width change.

2.1 Routine Experiment

The routine routine and insulation tests carried out are all qualified, and the items include insulation resistance, winding resistance measurement, voltage ratio measurement and connection group label verification, no-load loss and no-load current detection, short-circuit impedance and load loss measurement, and external withstand voltage test, Induction withstand voltage test, insulating liquid test, temperature rise test, lightning impulse test, zero sequence impedance measurement.

2.2 Short-Circuit Resistance Test

In the short-circuit resistance test of distribution transformers, 3 distribution transformers failed the short-circuit resistance ability, and 1 distribution transformer failed the oil withstand voltage test. In terms of core material, among the unqualified samples, the width of 2 sets of closed three-dimensional wound core amorphous alloys changed, the width of 1 set of stacked iron core silicon steel sheets changed, and the width of 1 set of traditional amorphous alloys changed. On the whole, the failure rate of amorphous alloy distribution test is higher.

2.3 On-Load Voltage Regulator Power Supply Voltage Characteristic Test

For the power supply voltage characteristic test of the on-load voltage regulation controller, all the on-load voltage regulation and variable voltage regulation control systems can be displayed and adjusted normally within the range of −30% to +20% of the rated working voltage. Some samples can work normally within the range of −50% to +30%. The 7 stepper motor samples can work normally in the range of −50% to +30%. The permanent magnet switch does not support working at lower voltage due to the limitation of capacitor charging voltage.

2.4 On-Load Voltage Regulation Automatic Voltage Regulation Test

By manually adjusting the voltage of the high-voltage side of the distribution transformer, the output voltage of the low-voltage side and the shifting action are monitored. The test results show that all samples can be downshifted when the low-voltage side voltage exceeds 235 V and upshifted when the voltage is lower than 20 5V (the delay of gear shifting detection for each sample varies from 10–60 s) (Figs. 1 and 2).

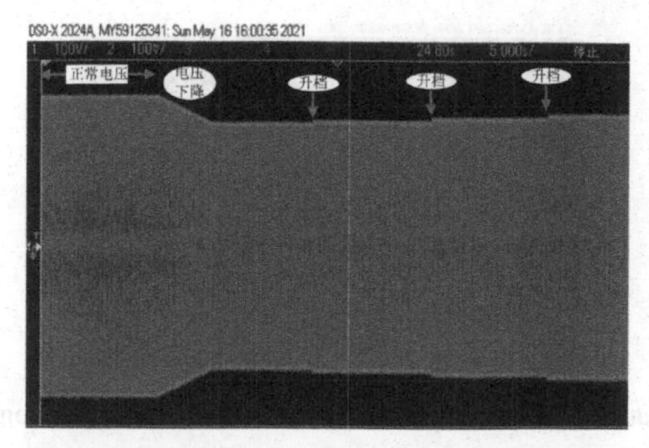

Fig. 1. Test results of automatic voltage regulation of wide-width on-load transformers (automatic downshift)

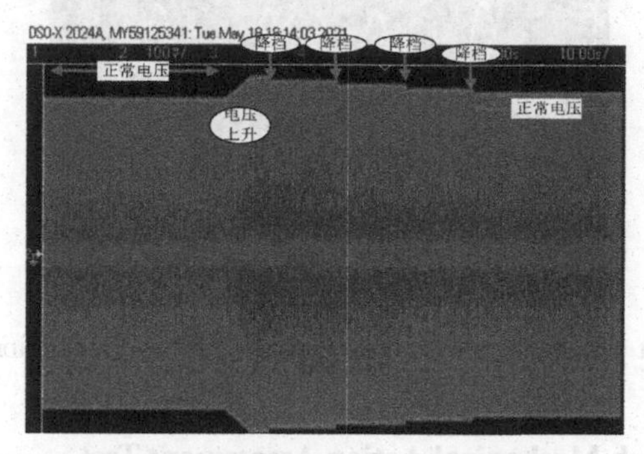

Fig. 2. Test results of automatic voltage regulation of wide-width on-load transformers (automatic upshift)

2.5 Voltage Transient Waveform Under No-Load Condition

Shifting under no-load conditions, and detecting the output voltage waveform of the low-voltage side, it is found that the shifting process can be completed within 1–3 fundamental wave cycles (different sample times are slightly different). There is no obvious voltage dip, swell or voltage interruption during the shifting process, but the output voltage has a us-level glitch during the switching process (Figs. 3 and 4).

2.6 Voltage Transient Waveform Under No-Load Condition

In the test, the output side of each transformer sample is connected to a three-phase balanced constant resistance load (up to 200 kVA). Under the load condition, the samples are switched in the order of rated gear → lowest gear → highest gear → rated gear. Carry out 10 rounds On-load voltage regulation, there is no abnormality after the on-load switch operates.

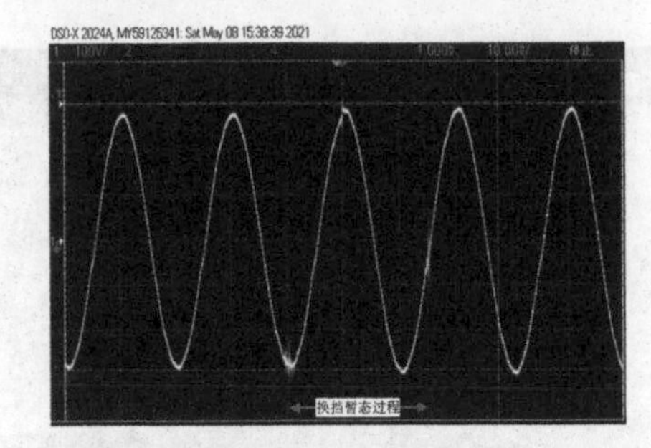

Fig. 3. Output voltage waveform during on-load voltage regulation shifting (a)

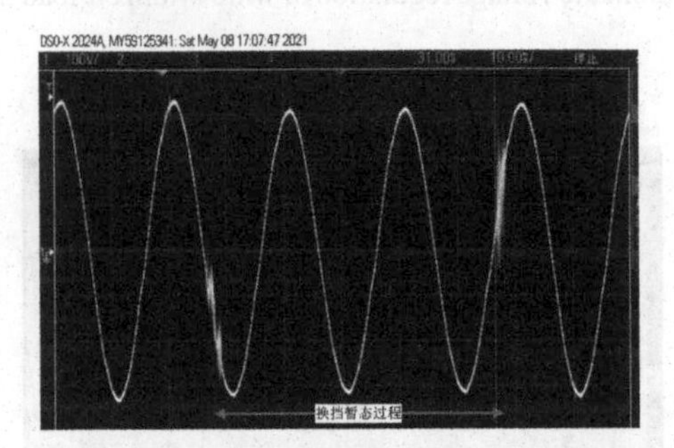

Fig. 4. Output voltage waveform during on-load voltage regulation shifting (b)

2.7 On-Load Switch Mechanical Action Assessment Test

Under the condition that the transformer body is not powered and the control box is powered by an external 220 V power supply, let the on-load switch automatically cycle and adjust the gear every certain time (interval 20–80 s, the specific time refers to the recommended value of each sample manufacturer), and the on-load voltage regulating switch is carried out. Mechanical life test. At present, the maximum number of actions in each sample has reached 50,000 times, and no failure of the on-load voltage regulator body has been found (Table 1).

Table 1. On-load tap changer mechanical life test situation

Sample serial number	1	2	3	4	5	6	7	8	9
Mechanical life (10,000 times)	≥50	≥10	≥50	≥50	≥50	≥50	≥50	≥50	≥50
The number of actions (times)	320	21918	50776	15000	32664	44831	31383	29007	206

2.8 Oil Sample Detection Before and After On-Load Pressure Regulation

Before carrying out the frequent electrified gear shifting assessment test of on-load switches, the oil samples of 5 wide-width on-load voltage regulating transformers were tested, and acetylene (0.15–0.30 uL/L) was detected in 3 of them. The acetylene content in each sample did not change significantly after the gear check (continuous on-load switch on and off). Judging from the influence of the existing adjustment times, it has not been found that the vacuum on-load voltage regulating switch has polluted the oil quality of the transformer.

3 Test Analysis

3.1 Low Pass Rate Resistance to Short Circuit

The overall pass rate of the short-circuit resistance of the voltage regulating transformer is 42.86%, which is lower than the sampling inspection level of full-caliber distribution transformers (the pass rate is 48%). In particular, the unqualified rate of amorphous alloy distribution transformers accounts for as high as 75%.The hanging core inspection was carried out on two closed three-dimensional coil amorphous alloy samples with unqualified short-circuit resistance, as shown in the Figs. 5 and 6.

Fig. 5. Output voltage waveform during on-load voltage regulation shifting (a)

It can be seen from the above figure that the radial direction of the low-voltage coil of the distribution transformer is deformed after the short circuit, and the low-voltage coil (copper foil) is sunk inward, resulting in the change of reactance exceeding the standard. The main reason is that the overall rigidity of the coil is not enough. When the low-voltage coil flows through the short-circuit current, under the action of the electromotive force of the amplitude inward and the tangent circle, it forms an inward extrusion force and a rotation force around the center of the circular section, resulting in separation of high and low voltage windings and Deformation of the low voltage winding.

Fig. 6. Output voltage waveform during on-load voltage regulation shifting (b)

3.2 Controller Problem

During the test, it was found that 4 samples had faults such as controller crash and unreliable measurement control system. After the control system is abnormal, it will directly lead to the loss of the expected function of the on-load voltage regulating transformer.

3.3 Magnetic Circuit Saturation and Waveform Distortion Appear Under High Voltage and High Gear

Among the 9 transformer samples tested, in the process of inputting 7–11 kV on the high-voltage side and manually adjusting the low-voltage side from the lowest gear to the highest gear, some cases were detected (when the input voltage is 10.5–11 kV and the transformer gear is high), causing the secondary side voltage to exceed 265 V) the phenomenon of low-voltage side output voltage waveform distortion and abnormal increase in transformer noise.

The main reason is that the conventional distribution transformer has a narrow voltage regulation range (±5%), and the distribution network transformer core is generally designed with a 10–15% margin, so even if the input voltage is high and it is in a non-rated gear, the core will not will be saturated. However, in the wide-width on-load voltage regulating transformer, the transformer is generally designed according to the steady-state operating conditions of low-speed operation (with a large number of input turns) when the primary voltage is high. In theory, when the input voltage is high, it should be input more in the low gear, the magnetic circuit will not be saturated at this time. However, during the operation of the transformer, if the voltage on the high-voltage side of the distribution transformer changes abruptly due to the load and grid voltage, the magnetic circuit saturation and Conditions that cause waveform distortion (Fig. 7).

3.4 Voltage Dip

During the test, it was found that when a 120 kW resistive load was directly added to the low-voltage side load of the on-load voltage regulation distribution transformer from no-load, the output voltage dropped to zero within 1–2 ms. In actual operation, a sudden increase in load may cause the control system to lose power and crash (Fig. 8).

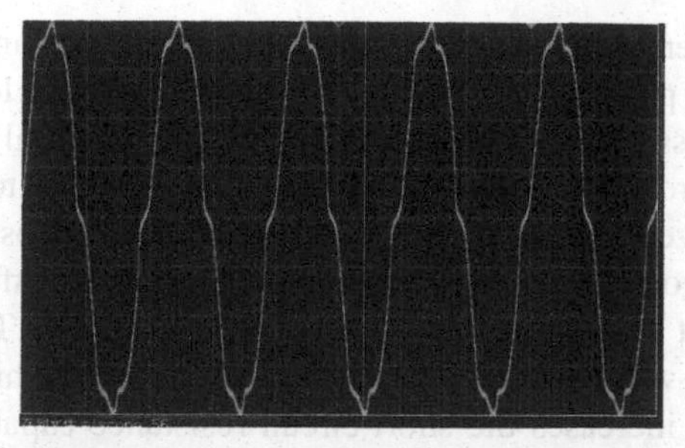

Fig. 7. Distorted waveform when the output voltage is high (high voltage side voltage 10.6 kV, low voltage side 272 V, 8 gears)

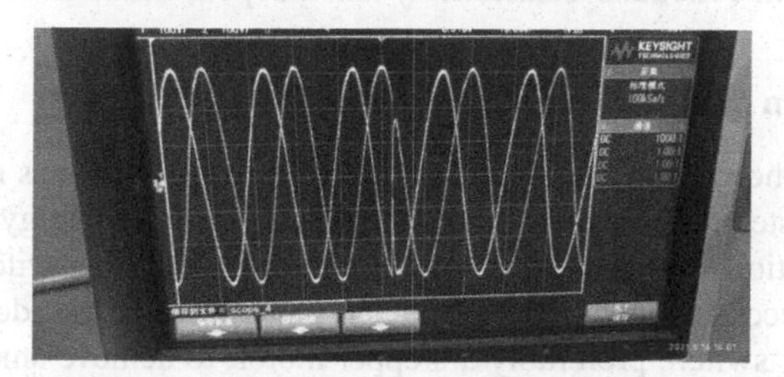

Fig. 8. Output voltage dips briefly to zero during sudden heavy load

3.5 Transformer Oil Problem

The oil samples of 5 wide-width on-load voltage regulating transformers were tested, and it was found that acetylene was detected in 3 samples, and the oil withstand voltage of 1 distribution transformer failed after the short-circuit resistance test. The reliability of the equipment of the wide-amplitude voltage regulating transformer is high, and the quality of the insulating oil directly affects the performance of the body, and it is necessary to increase the quality control.

In order to avoid the magnetic circuit saturation affecting the power quality and user equipment, when selecting equipment parameters, it is necessary to increase the magnetic density margin of the core according to the short-term overvoltage condition; at the same time, the controller needs to differentiate the parameters and logic under the sudden change condition.

4 Application Suggestions for Wide OLTC Transformers

4.1 Core Material and Structure Selection Suggestion

Taking into account the inherent inability to withstand force and strong brittleness of amorphous alloy iron cores, its short-circuit resistance is generally poor. Although the closed three-dimensional wound core amorphous alloy adopts technologies such as magnetic circuit symmetry, the loss performance is greatly improved, but it does not fundamentally change the material characteristics of the amorphous alloy. Short circuit performance. However, when the on-load voltage regulator distribution transformer superimposes high overload performance (the overload performance is mainly achieved by increasing the oil passage, increasing the diameter of the low-voltage wire, and improving the thickness and parameters of the insulating material), the internal space of the fuel tank is more crowded (the on-load voltage regulating switch itself). A part of the space has been squeezed, and the number of leads and gear taps has increased, which makes the internal layout design and manufacturing of the transformer more difficult), and it is more difficult to guarantee the short-circuit resistance. Therefore, it is recommended that the wide-width variable does not superimpose the high overload function, and at the same time increases the short-circuit resistance capability verification and random inspection after the tender to ensure that its short-circuit resistance performance meets the standard requirements. At the same time, the on-load voltage regulating switch preferably can realize modular disassembly and independent maintenance.

4.2 Transmission Mechanism Selection Suggestion

Considering that the vacuum permanent magnet on-load switch has many problems in the company's system, such as the capacity attenuation of the energy storage capacitor under harsh conditions, and the failure of the control system, the switch cannot operate. Therefore, it is recommended that the transmission mechanism adopts a mechanical voltage regulating switch, preferably a stepper motor, to achieve smooth gear shifting and reduce the failure rate of the tap changer. And the switching life is not less than 300,000 times, and provide a type test report.

4.3 Suggestion for Selection of Arc Extinguishing Medium

Referring to the electric power industry standard "DL/T 1853–2018 10kV On-load Capacity-regulating Transformer Technical Specification" and "T/CEC 163–2018 10 kV Low-Maintenance On-load Voltage-regulating Distribution Transformer", it is recommended that the on-load tap-changer should be selected. The vacuum arc extinguishing switch avoids the influence of the arc on the insulating oil and realizes maintenance-free.

4.4 Suggestion for the Selection of Voltage Regulation Range and Gear Range

Two factors are considered comprehensively: one is to avoid the unreliable factors caused by frequent gear shifting in the use of the wide-range variable; the other is to avoid the magnetic saturation problem when the wide-range variable is in low gear. It is recommended that the wide-amplitude variable voltage regulation range is +5% to −15%. Generally, a range of 5% is used, and 5 gears are used, and the distortion rate of the output voltage waveform at any gear should not be greater than 3% (standard required value).); for specific areas with high requirements on power quality and fine voltage regulation, you can choose 2.5% gear adjustment, 9 gears.

4.5 Controller Selection Recommendations

In order to avoid the abnormal voltage regulation caused by the problem of the controller, it is recommended that the controller should have the following functions when selecting the model: First, it has the function of self-starting in abnormal conditions. Second, the control strategy is adjustable. In principle, the completion time of a single command (including the delay) is not more than 1 min, and the blocking time between two shifts is 10 min. The third is that the controller has the function of hot swap, and the normal power supply of the transformer should not be affected during replacement.

4.6 Transformer Oil Quality Selection Recommendation

Considering the reliability of the pressure regulating process, it is suggested that the oil quality of the wide-amplitude pressure regulating transformer should strictly meet the requirements of DL/T 1094 in the technical specification, and the detection requirements for the gas in the oil should be added.

5 Conclusion

Wide-width distribution transformers are preferentially used to solve the problem of low voltage at scattered outlets at the end of the line. In the context of large-scale photovoltaics connected to the distribution network, areas with large load fluctuations and small hydropower grids that lead to drastic voltage changes can be considered for use. The annual low-voltage days at Taiwan's exports shall not be less than 5 days (excluding the influence of voltage imbalance), and the minimum value of the outlet voltage shall not be less than 160 V, which shall be preferentially applied to the range beyond the ordinary on-load voltage regulation and voltage regulation range (±5%, the minimum voltage value about 190 V). In this paper, the relevant test analysis is carried out on the wide-width on-load voltage regulating transformer, and a series of suggestions for the popularization and application of the wide-width on-load voltage regulating transformer are put forward.

Acknowledgment. This work was financially supported by the science and technology project of State Grid Hunan Electric Power Company Limited (5216A5210035).

References

1. Song, D.: The research on grid-connected control of photovoltaic power generation system and its transient process. Tianjin University of Technology, Tianjin (2010)
2. Yang, T.: Introduction to New Energy. Chemical Industry Press, Beijing (2013)
3. Xu, Z., Lang, Z., Su, H.: Impact and improvement of distributed photovoltaic on distribution network voltage. In: China University of Electric Power Systems and Automation Academic Annual Conference
4. Lu, B., Chen, X., Zhang, J., Wang, X., Ding, C.: Experiment and analysis of measurement error of a wide range current transformer. In: 2021 IEEE International Conference on Power Electronics, Computer Applications (ICPECA), pp. 161–164 (2021)
5. Li, X., Wang, W., Zhang, S.: An arcless OLTC model based on arm-bridge structure. Autom. Electr. Power Syst. **30**(7), 55–59 (2006)
6. Zhao, G., Shi, W.: Study on arcless on-load tap changer. High Voltage Eng. **30**(4), 49–51 (2004)

Research on Fast Access Technology Based on Shared Energy Storage of Electric Vehicles

Jin-liang Li[1(✉)], Miao Yang[1], Dai Wan[1], Miao Zhao[1], Jie Tao[2], Shuo Jin[3], and Huisong Ren[4]

[1] State Grid Joint Laboratory for Intelligent Application and Key Equipment in Distribution Network (Hunan), State Grid Hunan Electric Power Company Limted Research Institute, Changsha 410007, Hunan, China
gold921@qq.com

[2] State Grid Changde Power Supply Company, Changde 415000, Hunan, China

[3] Hubei University of Technology, Wuhan 430000, Hubei, China

[4] Hunan Industry Polytechnic, Changsha 410006, Hunan, China

Abstract. Under the background of comprehensively promoting the "dual carbon" strategy, the potential of multiple applications of massive electric vehicles will be fully tapped to carry out electricity protection work with electric vehicles as energy storage medium. At present, users would have short power outage when having access to electric vehicles to restore power supply. In view of this, the fast access technology of electric vehicles and the automatic switching method are presented in this paper, and the corresponding device has been developed. The temperature field simulation analysis and verification of the model were carried out, and the temperature rise test of the device was carried out simultaneously. The method and device has the certain reference value for further research on quick power recovery technology.

Keywords: Electric Vehicles · Fast Access · Emergency Power Supply · Shared Energy Storage · Temperature Field

1 Introduction

At the same time, all kinds of emergency repair tasks are more and more heavy, and a variety of complex electricity consumption scenarios pose great challenges to the emergency power protection work. Especially in towns and other densely populated areas, the traditional single mode of emergency power supply with emergency generator vehicles and diesel generator power protection equipment can no longer meet the reliability, economy and safety requirements of emergency power supply in critical scenarios. This problem can be effectively solved by using electric vehicles instead of traditional electric generators. However, when using electric vehicles to restore power supply, users would have short power outage. The integrated distribution box of the pole-type transformer does not have the function of quick power connection. When the user needs to ensure

H. Yang et al. (Eds.): SmartGIFT 2022, LNICST 483, pp. 432–438, 2023.
https://doi.org/10.1007/978-3-031-31733-0_37

power supply in line maintenance and power failure, a series of preparation work such as power failure, electricity test and grounding need to be completed, and then the bolt fixing method is used to connect the integrated distribution box[1–4]. In view of this problem, this paper puts forward an fast access method of electric vehicles, and the corresponding device is developed that is established on the temperature field simulation analysis and temperature rise test verification.

2 Device Model

The fast access technology of electric vehicles for "quick power recovery" is designed, which includes quick coupling of electric vehicles power, quick switch of ATS dual power supply. It can realize the switch between the main and electric vehicles power at millisecond level (non-inductive). The working principle and structure of the device are shown in Fig. 1.

The design idea of the whole device is as follows:

1) the 380 V main power supply and stand-by power are connected to the outgoing lines through the automatic transfer switch and current transformer. If the main power supply fails, the electric vehicles power will be quickly switched to the low-voltage power supply side through the automatic transfer switch. And the user has no perception in the whole conversion process.
2) The input side of the electric vehicles power of the device adopts the quick coupling. The connection time only needs 2–3 min to realize the fast access of electric vehicles power, which can greatly improve the efficiency of quick power recovery.
3) In order to ensure better waterproof performance, the quick coupling is set at the bottom of the device.
4) To ensure the safety of mains and electric vehicles power inlet side, fuse type isolating switches are set at both mains and electric vehicles power inlet positions.
5) In order to prevent the risk of insulation damage and interphase short circuit of the bus bar on the same horizontal line, the bus bar of the inlet side is set with cross arrangement.

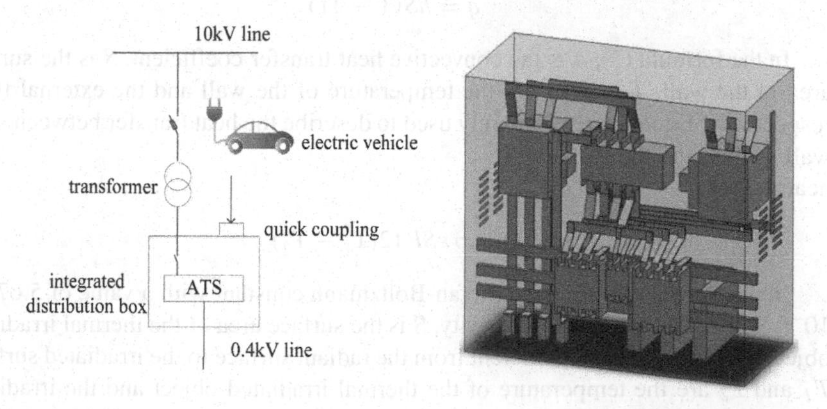

Fig. 1. Schematic diagram of working principle and overall structure drawing of the device

3 Device Model

The temperature rise test is an important test of the integrated distribution box (the corresponding device). The following is a simulation analysis of temperature rise test based on the temperature field.

3.1 Temperature Field Governing Equation

Based on the principle of heat transfer, there are three main forms of heat transfer mechanism between objects: heat conduction, heat convection and heat radiation, and their mathematical description is as follows [5–7]:

1) heat conduction

$$q = -kS\frac{\partial T}{\partial x} \tag{1}$$

In the formula (1), Q is the heat flow per unit area, K is the thermal conductivity, S is the area in the vertical direction of the heat flow density, ∂T/∂X is the temperature gradient in the heat flow direction, and the negative sign indicates that the heat flow direction is always opposite to the positive direction of the temperature gradient.

For a heat transfer system whose temperature does not change with time, that is, a steady-state system, Eq. (1) can be used to describe it. For a heat transfer system whose temperature changes with time, a complete heat conduction equation must be used to describe it. The mathematical expression of the three-dimensional heat conduction equation in the Cartesian coordinate system is as follows:

$$\frac{\partial}{\partial x}\left(k\frac{\partial T}{\partial x}\right)+\frac{\partial}{\partial y}\left(k\frac{\partial T}{\partial y}\right)+\frac{\partial}{\partial z}\left(k\frac{\partial T}{\partial z}\right)+q' = \rho c\frac{\partial T}{\partial t} \tag{2}$$

In the formula (2), q' is heating rate per unit volume, ρ and C are density and specific heat capacity of the material, respectively.

2) heat convection

$$q = hS(\mathrm{T} - \mathrm{Tf}) \tag{3}$$

In the formula (3), h is the convective heat transfer coefficient, S is the surface area of the wall, T and T_f are the temperature of the wall and the external fluid, respectively. Equation (3) is mainly used to describe the heat transfer between solid wall surface and fluid.

3) heat radiation

$$q = \sigma\varepsilon SF12(\mathrm{T}_1^4 - \mathrm{T}_2^4) \tag{4}$$

In the formula (4), σ is the Stefan-Boltzmann constant with a value of 5.670×10^{-8} W m^{-2} K^{-4}, ε is the emissivity, S is the surface area of the thermal irradiated object, F_{12} is the shape coefficient from the radiant surface to the irradiated surface, T_1 and T_2 are the temperature of the thermal irradiated object and the irradiated object respectively.

3.2 Boundary Conditions

For transient thermal analysis, the setting of boundary conditions and initial conditions is an inevitable requirement for the solution of thermal field and the uniqueness of solution results. The mathematical description of three types of boundary conditions and initial conditions is as follows [8, 9]:

1) the first kind boundary condition

$$T|_{\Gamma} = T(x, y, z, t) \tag{5}$$

In the formula (5), Γ is the boundary of the object. T(x, y, z, t) is the known temperature at any point in the boundary of the object, which can be a constant or a temperature function that varies with the space and time.

2) the second kind boundary condition

$$-k\frac{\partial T}{\partial n}\bigg|_{\Gamma} = q(x, y, z, t) \tag{6}$$

In the formula (6), k is the thermal conductivity coefficient, q (x, y, z, t) is the known heat flux function, also can be a constant. Equation (6) means that the heat flux at the boundary of the object is known.

3) the third kind boundary condition

$$-k\frac{\partial T}{\partial n}\bigg|_{\Gamma} = h(T - T_f)|_{\Gamma} \tag{7}$$

In the formula (7), h and T_f are the convective heat transfer coefficient and temperature of the fluid in contact with the object boundary respectively, which can be a constant or a function that varies with space. Equation (7) means that the heat transfer between the boundary of the body and the fluid is known.

4) the initial condition

$$T|_{t=0} = T0(x, y, z) \tag{8}$$

In the formula (8), T_0(x,y,z,t) is the temperature distribution of the object at the initial moment. If it is a constant, it means the temperature distribution of the object is uniform; if it is a known temperature distribution function, it means the temperature distribution is not uniform.

Consider that when the device is running, the current is only distributed inside the current-carrying conductor. The current carrying conductor is the main heat source of device heating. The conductor material is copper, and the resistivity is set to 1.67 × 10^{-8} Ω m. In addition, to simulate the contact resistance of the device joint, a contact resistance layer of 0.5 mm is set at joints. The resistivity of the contact resistance layer is set to 1 × 10^{-6} Ω m. The ambient temperature is set to 20 °C. The current of the inlet line side is set to 630 A. The current of the one outlet line side is set to 630 A, and the current of the other outlet line side is set to 0 A.

The convective heat transfer coefficient h of each face of the cabinet is calculated as follows:

$$h = \frac{kN_u}{L} \tag{9}$$

$$Nu = aR_a^b \tag{10}$$

The practical calculation formula of the constant a and b is shown in Table 1.

Table 1. The practical calculation formula of the convection heat transfer in a natural convection system

Surface shape, relative position and direction of heat flow	a	b	Range of application
Vertical cylinder and panel	0.59	1/4	$Ra = 10^4$ --10^9
	0.10	1/3	$Ra = 10^9$-10^{18}
Horizontal cylinder	0.53	1/4	$Ra = 10^4$-10^9
	0.13	1/3	$Ra = 10^9$-10^{12}
Horizontal panel of hot face up	0.54	1/4	$Ra = 10^5$-2×10^7
	0.14	1/3	$Ra = 2 \times 10^7$-3×10^{10}
Horizontal panel of hot face down	0.27	1/4	$Ra = 3 \times 10^5$-3×10^{10}

After calculation, the convective heat transfer coefficient of the top panel is 4.78 W/(m^2 °C), the convective heat transfer coefficient of the side panel is 3.41 W/(m^2 °C), the convective heat transfer coefficient of the bottom panel is 1.74 W/(m^2 °C).

3.3 Simulation Results

According to the above settings, the surface temperature of the equipment inside the device is shown as Fig. 2. The maximum temperature inside the device reaches 89.44 °C, and the maximum temperature rise reaches 69.44 °C. The maximum temperature rise occurs at the B phase inlet line side of the fuse type disconnecting switch.

4 Field Test and Validation

The temperature rise test was carried out on the developed device, and the layout of temperature measuring points of the field temperature rise test is shown in Fig. 3. The measured results of temperature rise test are shown in Table 2. The maximum temperature rise reaches 79.9 °C, and the maximum temperature rise occurs at the B phase inlet line side of the fuse type disconnecting switch similarly. After carrying out the temperature rise test, the electric vehicle access method is simulated and verified.

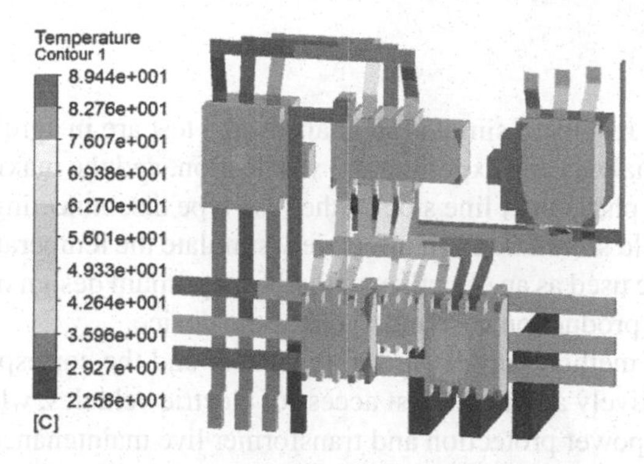

Fig. 2. Simulation results of device surface temperature

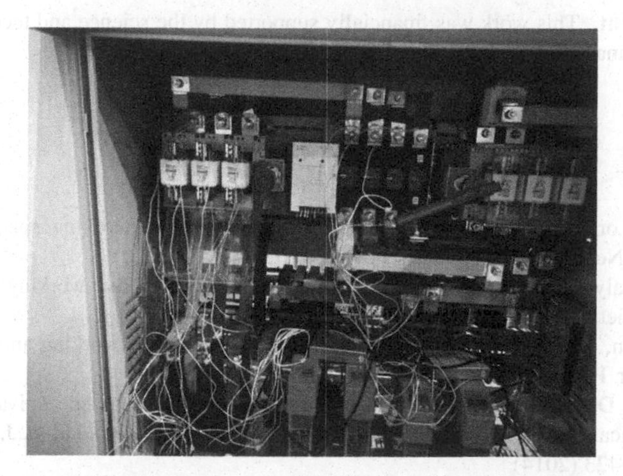

Fig. 3. Layouts of temperature measuring points of the field temperature rise test

Table 2. Temperature rise test results

Position	Temperature rise test results (K)		
	A phase	B phase	C phase
The inlet line side of the fuse type disconnecting switch	74.0	79.9	75.6
The outlet line side of the fuse type disconnecting switch	68.3	69.4	67.4
The inlet line side of 630 A circuit breaker	66.9	67.0	64.1
The outlet line side of 630 A circuit breaker	54.0	49.8	52.3
The joint fastening the busbar	39.0	42.5	41.4
The operating handle of the fuse type disconnecting switch	18.7		
The body shell	7.2		

5 Conclusion

It is known that the results of simulation analysis and test are in agreement through the above simulation analysis and experimental verification, and the maximum temperature rise occurs at the B phase inlet line side of the fuse type disconnecting switch similarly. The temperature field simulation can effectively simulate the temperature rise test of the device, and it can be used as an effective method for optimum design of device structure, which can save the production cost and cycle of the device.

The fast access method put forward in this paper and the corresponding developed device can be effectively applied in fast access of electric vehicles, which can be widely used in emergency power protection and transformer live maintenance and replacement scenarios, and users do not have short power outages.

Acknowledgment. This work was financially supported by the science and technology project of State Grid Hunan Electric Power Company Limited (5216A5220003).

References

1. Yang, M., Long, C., Zhou, H.: Development ideas of live working specialty in Hunan Distribution Network. Hunan Electr. Power **40**(03), 42–47 (2020)
2. Fang, J.: Analysis on risk factors and preventive measures of live working management in distribution network. Enterp. Reform Manag. (04), 43–44 (2019)
3. Jiang, Y., Fan, S., Chen, J.: New intelligent technology for live working and its application. Hunan Electr. Power **38**(05), 1–4 (2018)
4. Seaman, A., Dao, T.S., Mcphee, J.: A survey of mathematics-based equivalent-circuit and electrochemical battery models for hybrid and electric vehicle simulation. J. Power Sources **256**(3), 410–423 (2014)
5. Shi, P., Xia, X., Chen, C.: Temperature field of permanent magnet synchronous motor based on coupled field-circuit. J. Nanjing Univ. Aeronaut. Astronaut. **53**(03), 425–434 (2021)
6. Zhou, X., Sun, L., Wang, J.: Temperature rise calculation of permanent magnet synchronous motor based on equivalent heat network method. Micromotors **52**(11), 21–26 (2019)
7. Xu, Y., Ai, M., Yang, Y.: Heat transfer characteristic research based on thermal network method in submersible motor. Int. Trans. Electr. Energy Syst. **28**(3), e2507 (2018)
8. Wang, D., Liang, Y., Li, C., et al.: Thermal equivalent network method for calculating stator temperature of a shielding induction motor. Int. J. Thermal Sci. **147**, 106149 (2020)
9. Li, T., Sun, X.-W., Du, X.-P.: Simulation analysis of transformer flow field and temperature field based on finite element method. Autom. Instrum. **35**(05), 1–6 (2020)

Simulation Research on the Ground Resistance Measurement of the Tower with Clamp Meter Considering the Influence of the Tower Foundation

Zoujun Wang[1](✉), Wenbo Li[1], Huashi Wu[2], Jiafeng Chen[3], and Hailiang Lu[3]

[1] StateGrid Hunan Electric Power Company Limited Research Institute, Changsha 410007, China
513474070@qq.com
[2] Guangdong Power Grid Corporation, Guangzhou 510200, China
[3] School of Electrical and Automation, Wuhan University, Wuhan 4130072, China

Abstract. The grounding resistance of the tower is the main parameter to measure the grounding safety performance of the tower. As a commonly used method of measuring the grounding resistance of the tower, the clamp meter method has certain errors in the measurement principle. Based on the measurement principle of the clamp meter method, the artificial grounding device, tower foundation, transmission line tower and lightning protection wire are modeled and simulated, and the influence of different factors on the error of the clamp meter method measurement of the ground resistance of the tower is studied. The calculation results show that the change of soil resistivity has the most obvious influence on the calculation results. The higher the soil resistivity is, the coefficient of transformation between the measurement results of clamp tab. Method and the actual value gradually decreases. In the case of multi base tower grounding, the measured transformation ratio coefficient will be smaller than that in the case of single base tower grounding due to the shunt of tower lightning line parallel branch; The shorter the span between towers or the lower the height of towers, the smaller the parallel equivalent impedance of tower lightning line branches and the smaller the transformation ratio coefficient.

Keywords: Clamp meter method · Tower foundation · p ground resistance

1 Introduction

The grounding safety performance of transmission line towers is an important factor affecting the reliability of power system operation. Therefore, it is necessary to accurately measure its grounding resistance to judge whether it meets the requirements of the regulations [1, 2]. The traditional three pole method used for tower grounding resistance measurement is time-consuming and laborious, while the clamp meter method does not

H. Yang et al. (Eds.): SmartGIFT 2022, LNICST 483, pp. 439–451, 2023.
https://doi.org/10.1007/978-3-031-31733-0_38

need to arrange auxiliary electrodes, which greatly reduces the working intensity of the measuring personnel [3–5].

However, the clamp meter method actually measures the total loop impedance of the current flow path [6, 7]. Previous studies [8–11] usually only considered the current flow circuit formed by the parallel grounding of multi base towers. However, the grounding system of each base tower includes two parts: artificial grounding device and natural grounding electrode of the tower foundation, which can also form a series circuit [12, 13]. Even if the tower is grounded on multiple bases, the tower foundation will still have a certain shunt.

Therefore, it is necessary to build a tower grounding model considering both tower foundation and artificial grounding device, calculate and analyze to find out the influence law of relevant factors on the measurement error of clamp meter method.

2 Measuring Principle of Clamp Method

When the clamp meter method is used to measure the tower grounding resistance, the clamp meter is clamped around the grounding downlead, and the measurement result is the total impedance value of the circuit where the grounding downlead is located. The measuring circuit formed can be divided into two parts: the first part of the current flows through the path formed by the measuring tower artificial grounding device, grounding downlead, tower foot main materials, foundation bolts, tower foundation and soil; The second part of the current flows through the artificial grounding device of the measuring tower, the grounding downlead, the measuring tower body, the lightning wire, the tower body and grounding body near the multi base, and the path formed by the soil, as shown in Fig. 1. For single base towers without lightning wires, the measuring circuit will only include the first part.

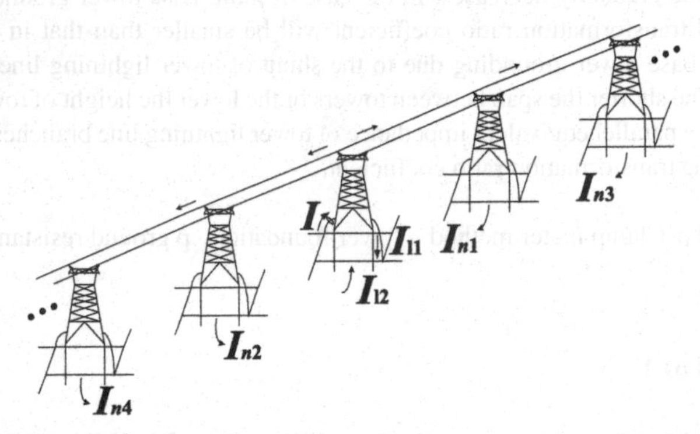

Fig. 1. Schematic diagram of tower grounding resistance measurement by clamp meter method.

2.1 Theoretical Calculation Principle of Tower Grounding Resistance

The tower grounding body includes two parts: artificial grounding device and tower foundation. When the current flows into the ground through two parts of the grounding body, the corresponding potential and current relationship [14,15] on the two parts of the grounding body are:

$$\begin{cases} V_1 = R_{11}I_1 + R_{12}I_2 \\ V_2 = R_{21}I_1 + R_{22}I_2 \end{cases} \tag{1}$$

where, V_1 and V_2 are the potentials of the artificial grounding device and the basic grounding body respectively, I_1 and I_2 are the potentials of the artificial grounding device and the basic grounding body respectively, R_{11} and R_{22} are the potentials of the artificial grounding device and the basic grounding body respectively, and R_{12} and R_{21} are the potentials of the artificial grounding device and the basic grounding body respectively.

For the two connected grounding bodies, if the voltage drop on the connecting conductor between them is ignored, then the potential of the two is equal. If the total incoming current is I, then there are:

$$\begin{cases} V_1 = V_2 = V \\ I = I_1 + I_2 \\ R_{12} = R_{21} \end{cases} \tag{2}$$

The actual value of tower grounding resistance can be obtained by combining formula (1) and formula (2):

$$R = \frac{V}{I} = \frac{R_{11}R_{22} - R_{12}^2}{R_{11} + R_{22} - 2R_{12}} \tag{3}$$

2.2 Measurement Principle of Clamp Meter Method in the Case of Single Tower Grounding

When testing the single base grounding of the tower, the measured current will only flow through the artificial grounding device of the test tower and the circuit where the tower foundation is located. For the artificial grounding device and foundation grounding body in the series circuit, considering the induced potential E generated by the pincer meter on the grounding downlead, there are:

$$\begin{cases} V_1 = V_2 + E \\ I_1 = -I_2 = I' \\ R_{12} = R_{21} \end{cases} \tag{4}$$

where, $I'$is the current flowing on the grounding down lead.

Simultaneous Eqs. (1) and (4) can be used to obtain the actual grounding resistance measured by clamp meter method when a single tower is grounded:

$$R' = \frac{E}{I'} = R_{11} + R_{22} - 2R_{12} \tag{5}$$

With simultaneous Eqs. (3) and (5), the transformation coefficient between the measured value and the actual value of the clamp meter method at this time can be obtained η Is:

$$\eta = \frac{(R_{11} + R_{22} - 2R_{12})^2 + R_{12}^2 - R_{11}R_{22}}{R_{11}R_{22} - R_{12}^2} + 1 \tag{6}$$

From Eq. (6), it can be seen that the error increment between the measured value of clamp meter method and the actual value is related to the self resistance of the artificial device and the basic grounding body and the mutual resistance between them.

2.3 Measurement Principle of Clamp Meter Method in the Case of Multi Base Tower Grounding

When testing the multi base grounding of towers and using the clamp meter method to verify its grounding performance, it is equivalent to adding other towers and lightning wires on the basis of the single base tower grounding. For the current flowing into the ground through multiple grounding bodies, the corresponding potential and current relationship on the two grounding bodies of the test tower are as follows:

$$\begin{cases} V_1 = R_{11}I_1 + R_{12}I_2 + R_{13}I_3 + \cdots + R_{1n}I_n \\ V_2 = R_{21}I_1 + R_{22}I_2 + R_{23}I_3 + \cdots + R_{2n}I_n \end{cases} \tag{7}$$

where, $R_{12}, R_{13}, \ldots, R_{1n}$are the mutual resistance between the artificial grounding device of the test tower and other tower grounding bodies, andR_{22}, R_{23}, ..., R_{2n} are the mutual resistance between the foundation grounding body of the test tower and other tower grounding bodies.

Since there is at least one span distance between the grounding body of other towers and the grounding body of the test tower, the mutual resistance between the grounding body and the grounding body of the test tower is very small and can be ignored, so formula (7) can be simplified to formula (8).

$$\begin{cases} V_1 = R_{11}I_1 + R_{12}I_2 = (R_{11} - R_{12})I_1 + R_{12}(I_1 + I_2) \\ V_2 = R_{12}I_1 + R_{22}I_2 = (R_{22} - R_{12})I_2 + R_{12}(I_1 + I_2) \end{cases} \tag{8}$$

Similarly, the grounding bodies of other connected towers can be converted into similar forms, so the equivalent circuit diagram of clamp meter method measurement in the case of multi base tower grounding is shown in Fig. 2.

3 Simulation Calculation of Single Tower Grounding

3.1 Simulation Model

Because in the case of single base tower grounding, the self resistance and mutual resistance of the artificial device and tower foundation will have an error impact on the measurement results, so it is necessary to model the two parts of grounding body carefully. The international general Grounding Calculation Software CDEGS is used to build a single base tower grounding model, as shown in Fig. 3. The specific parameters of the model are as follows.

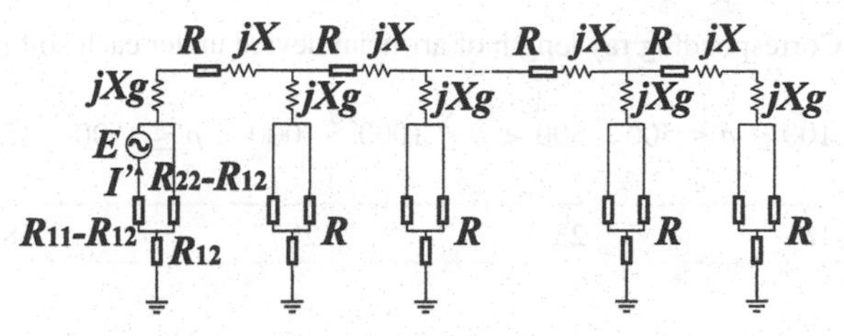

Fig. 2. Equivalent circuit diagram of tower grounding resistance measured by clamp meter method.

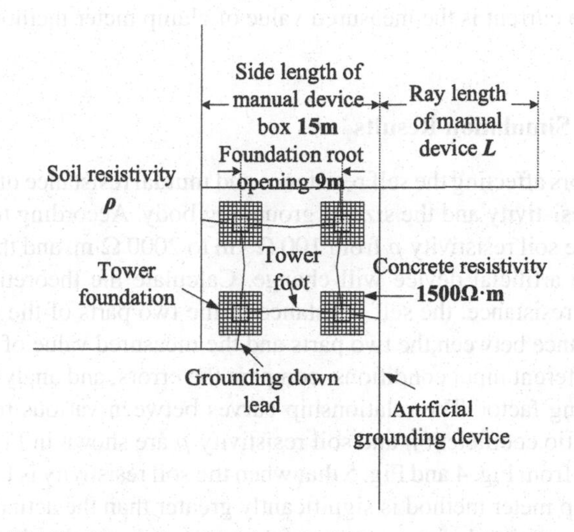

Fig. 3. Simulation model of single base tower grounding.

Tower Foundation Model. Straight column slab foundation is a commonly used type of tower foundation [16]. In this paper, straight column reinforced concrete slab foundation is used for modeling. There are 24 bars with a length of 3.8 m in the straight column φ 16 main bars and 16 pieces of 2.8 m long φ 8 hoops of steel bars, 48 steel bars with a length of 3.9 m for the plate type part φ 48 base plate reinforcement. The height of the foundation above the ground is 0.9 m. Each tower foundation is located in a concrete module with a wall thickness of 0.1 m, and the concrete resistivity is 1500 Ω m.

Artificial Grounding Device Model. The artificial grounding device adopts the form of closed box with rays, and the material is φ 12 round steel, the side length of the box is 15 m. The value of ray length *L* of artificial device under different soil resistivity of a project is shown in Table 1.

Tower Foot Connection Part Model. The grounding down lead is 50 mm × 5 mm flat steel, 75 mm main material of tower foot × 40 mm × 40 mm angle steel [14, 15]. Each foundation adopts 4 1.2 m long φ 42 anchor bolts.

Incentive Model. By applying current excitation, the theoretical value of tower grounding resistance, the self resistance of artificial device and tower foundation are calculated

Table 1. Corresponding ray length of artificial device under each soil resistivity.

Soil resistivity $\rho/\Omega{\cdot}$m	$100 \leq \rho \leq 500$	$500 < \rho \leq 1000$	$1000 < \rho \leq 1500$	$1500 < \rho \leq 2000$
Ray length L/m	18	23	28	38

respectively. Apply voltage excitation to a certain section of the grounding down lead, and measure the axial current through the excitation conductor at the same time. The ratio of voltage to current is the measured value of clamp meter method.

3.2 Analysis of Simulation Results

The relevant factors affecting the self resistance and mutual resistance of grounding body are mainly soil resistivity and the size of grounding body. According to the calculation model, change the soil resistivity ρ from 100 Ω · m to 2000 Ω·m, and the corresponding ray length of the artificial device will change. Calculate the theoretical value of the tower grounding resistance, the self resistance of the two parts of the grounding body, the mutual resistance between the two parts and the measured value of the clamp meter method under different input conditions, compare the errors, and analyze the sensitivity of each influencing factor. The relationship curves between various resistance values, transformation ratio coefficient η and soil resistivity ρ are shown in Fig. 4 and Fig. 5.

It can be seen from Fig. 4 and Fig. 5 that when the soil resistivity is low, the measured value of the clamp meter method is significantly greater than the actual value. With the increase of soil resistivity, the increase rate of the measured value by clamp meter method is less than the actual value, and the transformation coefficient will gradually decrease.

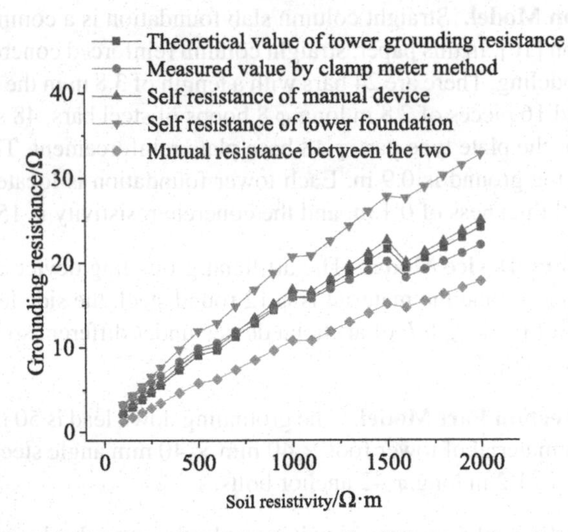

Fig. 4. Various resistance values under different soil resistivity.

From the comparison of curve size relationship in Fig. 4, it can be seen that the reason for this trend is: the existence of high resistivity concrete module makes the self resistance R_{22} of tower foundation much larger than the self resistance R_{11} of artificial device and the mutual resistance R_{12} between them under the condition of low soil resistivity, which makes the transformation coefficient η In formula (6), the first term $(R_{11} + R_{22} - 2R_{12})^2$ of the error increment numerator is much larger than the third term $R_{11}R_{22}$, so the error increment part is also positive. Therefore, in the range of low soil resistivity, the simulation value of clamp meter method is higher than the actual value. The self resistance of tower foundation and artificial device increases faster with the increase of soil resistivity than that of mutual resistance and clamp meter method. Therefore, with the increase of soil resistivity, the error increment changes from positive to negative. In general, the impact of the increase in soil resistivity plays a leading role.

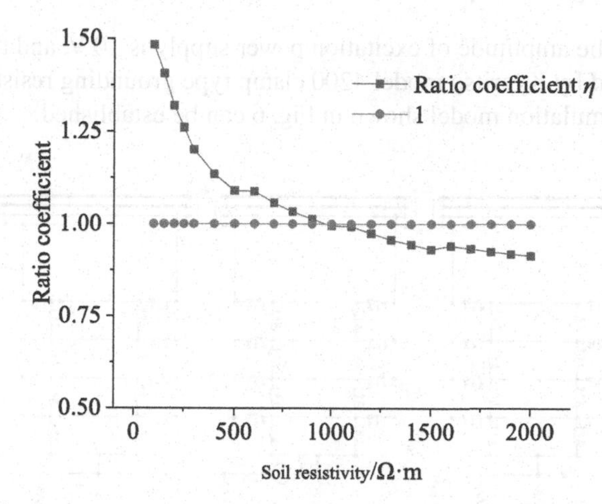

Fig. 5. Transformation coefficient under different soil resistivity.

4 Simulation Calculation of Multi Base Tower Grounding

4.1 Simulation Model

For the measurement under the condition of multi base tower grounding, compared with the measurement of single base tower, the test tower body, lightning wire, and the parallel branches of other towers and their grounding bodies are added. Therefore, it is necessary to model the adjacent towers and lines. The tower grounding resistance model is equivalent according to the equivalent circuit diagram in Fig. 2 and the calculation results under the condition of single base tower grounding. The specific parameters are as follows.

Line and Tower Model. The transmission line adopts Jmarti model, the DC resistance of lightning conductor is 2.86 Ω/km, the height of tower is 45 m, and the span of tower is 200 m. The tower model is simulated by using the segmented wave impedance model

[17–20], which is divided into main materials, inclined materials and cross arms. The wave impedance of each section is taken as the conventional value, in which the wave impedance Z_{Tk} of the main material is taken as 150 Ω; The wave impedance of the inclined material $Z_{Lk} = 9Z_{Tk} = 1350$ Ω, and the length of the inclined material is set to 1.5 times the length of the corresponding main material; The cross arm wave impedance Z_{Ak} is taken as 200 Ω; The propagation speed of shock wave in the tower is 0.85 times the speed of light, that is2.55 × 10^8 m/s.

Tower Grounding Resistance Model. According to the calculation results of single base tower grounding, the self resistance and mutual resistance of the corresponding artificial grounding device and tower foundation grounding body under different soil resistivity can be obtained, and the tower grounding parameters in the simulation model can be set according to the equivalent circuit diagram in Fig. 2.

Power Model. The amplitude of excitation power supply is 10 V, and the frequency is 2400 Hz measured by Kyoritsu model 4200 clamp type grounding resistance tester.

Finally, the simulation model shown in Fig. 6 can be established.

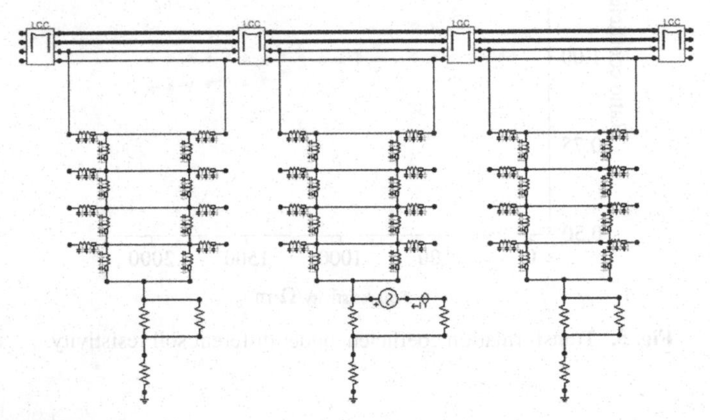

Fig. 6. Partial diagram of multi base tower clamp Table measurement simulation model.

4.2 Analysis of Simulation Results

The main factors affecting the impedance of this new parallel branch are the tower and lightning conductor. The effects of tower span, tower height, DC resistance of lightning conductor and soil resistivity on the measurement results are simulated.

Influence of the Number of Surrounding Parallel Towers. Firstly, the influence of the number of tower circuits on the measurement results is studied, and the number of towers on both sides of the measured tower is changed in the simulation model to study the change of the measurement results. In the simulation, various resistance values are set as the calculation data when the soil resistivity is 500 Ω·m. The grounding resistance of the tower artificial device is 9.587 Ω, the foundation grounding resistance is 11.929 Ω, the mutual resistance is 5.805 Ω, and the theoretical value is 9.089Ω. The relationship between the transformation ratio coefficient and the number of unilateral towers can be obtained by measuring the loop current, as shown in Table 2.

Table 2. Calculation results under different numbers of parallel towers.

Number of single pole and tower	Measuring current/A	Measured value by clamp meter method/Ω	Ratio coefficient η
1	1.284	7.788	0.857
2	1.299	7.698	0.847
3	1.312	7.622	0.839
4	1.318	7.587	0.835
5	1.319	7.582	0.834

According to the calculation results in Table 2, the more towers are connected in parallel, the more parallel circuits are formed, and the smaller the equivalent impedance is, the smaller the transformation ratio coefficient is. In addition, after the number of unilateral towers exceeds 4, the trend of reduction of transformation ratio coefficient tends to be saturated. It can be seen that the measuring current mainly forms a loop through the towers within 800 m from both sides of the measuring tower, and the influence of other towers at a longer distance on the resistance is negligible. Therefore, the later simulation research is slightly simplified, using the model of four towers on both sides, which helps to speed up the calculation speed, and has little impact on the results.

Influence of Tower Span. Within the range of 800 m from the measured tower, if the distance between the towers is changed, the number of towers will change, that is, the number of circuits formed by lightning wires is different. Since the circuits can be regarded as parallel relationship, the parallel equivalent resistance of circuit resistance will also change. The relationship between the ratio coefficient and the span of the tower can be obtained, as shown in Table 3.

Table 3. Calculation results under different tower spans.

Tower span/m	Measuring current/A	Measured value by clamp meter method/Ω	Ratio coefficient η
100	1.360	7.353	0.809
160	1.333	7.502	0.825
200	1.318	7.587	0.835
400	1.262	7.924	0.872

According to the calculation results in Table 3, the shorter the span between towers is, the more parallel circuits will be formed within a certain distance. Therefore, the smaller the parallel equivalent impedance of tower lightning line branch is, the smaller the measured loop impedance is and the smaller the transformation ratio coefficient is.

Influence of Tower Height. By changing the height of the tower and correspondingly changing the sectional wave impedance of the tower, the relationship between the transformation ratio coefficient and the height of the tower can be obtained, as shown in Table 4.

Table 4. Calculation results under different tower heights.

Tower height/m	Measuring current/A	Measured value by clamp meter method/Ω	Ratio coefficient η
35	1.328	7.530	0.828
45	1.318	7.587	0.835
55	1.307	7.651	0.842
65	1.304	7.669	0.844

According to the calculation results in Table 4, the lower the tower height is, the smaller the equivalent wave impedance is, the smaller the transformation ratio coefficient is. Because at this time, the smaller the tower impedance makes the reduction effect of parallel branches on the total loop impedance more obvious.

Influence of DC Resistance of Lightning Conductor. By changing the DC resistance of the lightning conductor, the relationship between the transformation ratio coefficient and the DC resistance of the lightning conductor can be obtained, as shown in Table 5.

Table 5. Calculation results under different DC resistance of lightning conductor.

DC resistance of lightning conductor/Ω	Measuring current/A	Measured value by clamp meter method/Ω	Ratio coefficient η
0.18	1.321	7.570	0.833
0.36	1.320	7.576	0.834
0.72	1.320	7.576	0.834
1.43	1.319	7.582	0.834
2.86	1.318	7.587	0.835

It can be seen from the calculation results in Table 5 that when using the lightning conductor with better conductivity and smaller outer diameter, the DC resistance of the lightning conductor is smaller, and the transformation ratio coefficient is smaller.

At this time, the smaller lightning conductor impedance makes the reduction effect of parallel branches on the total loop impedance more obvious. However, since the measured current propagation range is mainly within 800 m, the total DC resistance of the lightning conductor changes little when the distance is short, and the influence on the transformation ratio coefficient is small, which can be ignored.

Influence of Soil Resistivity. Various resistance values are taken according to the calculation results of different soil resistivity in Fig. 4. Changing various resistance values can obtain the relationship between transformation coefficient and soil resistivity, as shown in Table 6.

Table 6. Calculation results under different soil resistivity.

Soil resistivity/Ω·m	Theoretical value/Ω	Measuring current/A	Measured value by clamp meter method/Ω	Ratio coefficient η
100	2.163	3.557	2.811	1.300
150	2.924	2.900	3.448	1.179
200	3.803	2.444	4.092	1.076
250	4.665	2.138	4.677	1.003
300	5.566	1.906	5.247	0.943
400	7.329	1.528	6.545	0.893
500	9.089	1.318	7.587	0.835
800	12.830	1.001	9.990	0.779
1100	15.911	0.846	11.820	0.743
1400	20.169	0.697	14.347	0.711
1700	20.559	0.719	13.908	0.677
2000	24.124	0.621	16.103	0.668

According to the calculation results in Table 6, the transformation ratio coefficient will still decrease with the increase of soil resistivity in the case of multi base tower grounding, but due to the shunt of tower and lightning wire, the measurement result at this time is smaller than that in the case of single base tower grounding. When the soil resistivity is 100 Ω·m, the transformation ratio coefficient is 1.300. When the soil resistivity exceeds 300 Ω·m, the transformation coefficient will fall below 1.

5 Conclusion

In this paper, the following conclusions are obtained by establishing the simulation models of measuring the tower grounding resistance with clamp meter method under the conditions of single base tower grounding and multi base tower grounding respectively:

1) In the case of single tower grounding, when the soil resistivity is low, the measured value of clamp meter method is significantly greater than the actual value. With the increase of soil resistivity, the measured value of clamp meter method will show a trend of decreasing to a large extent, even smaller than the actual value.
2) In the case of multi base tower grounding, the measurement result of clamp meter method is smaller than that of single base tower grounding due to the shunt of tower and lightning wire.
3) The shorter the span between towers is, or the lower the height of towers is, the smaller the parallel equivalent impedance of tower lightning line branches is, the smaller the transformation ratio coefficient is.
4) In the measurement of tower grounding resistance, multiple error factors affect together, and different factors will play a leading role in different situations. Combined with the above simulation results and actual conditions, corresponding calculations can be carried out.

Acknowledgment. This work was financially supported by the science and technology project of State Grid Hunan Electric Power Company Limited (5216A5220005).

References

1. Wang, D., Li, Q., He, Z., et al.: Guide for Measurement of Grounding Connection Parameters. China Electric Power Press, Beijing (2017)
2. Du, S., Lu, J., He, J., et al.: Code for Design of AC Electrical Installations Earthing. China Electric Power Press, Beijing (2011)
3. Zeng, H., Ma, X., Xu, K., et al.: Measurement method and applicability analysis of transmission line tower power frequency grounding resistance in mountainous area. Hunan Electr. Power **39**(03), 66–69 (2019)
4. Zhang, B., Hu, Z., Zhang, K.: Influence of ground wire shunting on tower grounding resistance measurement. Electr. Power Constr. **37**(04), 70–75 (2016)
5. Lin, J.: Analysis of grounding resistance of tower in transmission line measured by three pole method and clamp meter method. Mech. Electron. Inform. **30**, 1–2 (2016)
6. Chen, R., Lan, B., Wang, Y., et al.: Research on new measurement technology of tower grounding resistance. Electrotechnical (05), 103–104 (2017)
7. Luo, C., He, M.Z., Zhou, W.: Feasibility study on grounding properties messurement of transimission lines and towers by clamp ampere meters. Hunan Electr. Power **31**(05), 1–7 (2011)
8. Zhang, K., Hu, Z., Zhang, B.: Method for measuring grounding resistance of grounding grid considering the influence of earth wire coupling. Electr. Meas. Instrum. **54**(12), 77–82 (2017)
9. Wu, H.: Research on Measurement Method and Experiment of Tower Grounding Resistance. Chongqing University, Chongqing (2016)
10. Zhang, Z., Xu, X., Liu, C., et al.: A multi-frequency sweeping method of measuring tower grounding resistance. Proc. CSEE **35**(19), 5078–5086 (2015)
11. Li, H., Wang, J., Liang, Y., et al.: Calculation of error of tower grounding resistance measurement using clamp meter. High Voltage Eng. (06), 48–49+52 (2002)
12. Wang, J.: Research on Grounding Impedance Testing Technology of Live Tower. Xi'an University of Science and Technology, Xi'an (2019)

13. Zhou, H.: Error simulation analysis of transmission line tower ground resistance measurement by clamp meter method. Hunan Electr. Power **33**(03), 18–22 (2013)
14. He, J.: Grounding Technology of Power System. Science press, Beijing (2007)
15. Xie, G.: Grounding Technology of Power System. China electric power press, Beijing (1991)
16. Tong, X., Dong, X., Gu, B.: Independent grounding performance simulation analysis of UHV transmission line tower footings. High Voltage Eng. **38**(12), 3323–3330 (2012)
17. Xiao, B., Ni, M., Yue, S., et al.: Lightning withstand performance analysis and enhancement method of high-altitude landscape tower. Electr. Meas. Instrum. **57**(23), 9–16 (2020)
18. Zhang, Y., Liu, J., Huang, X., et al.: Modeling and simulation for insulation performance analysis of composite transmission line tower underlightning overvoltage. Electric Power **51**(05), 68–74 (2018)
19. Long, Y., Yao, C., Wu, H., et al.: Simulation study on lightning distribution coefficient with different direct lightning fault types. Electr. Meas. Instrum. **53**(03), 12–17+31 (2016)
20. Huang, W., Xiao, M., Yang, X., et al.: Research on transmission tower models for lightning flashover analysis. High Voltage Apparatus **51**(06), 166–172 (2015)

Control and Operation of UAV

Research on a Fuzzy Adaptive PID Control Method for Four Rotor UAV Control System

Dai Wan[1(✉)], Simin Peng[1], Miao Zhao[1], Liang Peng[2], Yingying Yi[3], and Hengyi Zhou[1]

[1] State Grid Hunan Electric Power Company Limited Research Institute, Changsha 410007, China
280241509@qq.com
[2] Changsha University of Science & Technology, Changsha 410000, China
[3] Changsha Tax Service, Changsha 410000, China

Abstract. Research on A Fuzzy Adaptive PID Control Method for Four Rotor UAV Control System With the continuous improvement of national living standards, people have higher and higher requirements for the reliability of power supply. The emergence of unmanned aerial vehicle inspection technology provides a new idea to solve the contradiction between the increasing equipment scale and the increasing inspection requirements. However, at present, the stability of the traditional proportion integration differentiation (PID) control system of the four rotor unmanned aerial vehicle (UAV) is not high enough. During the inspection, there are accidents of drones hitting power equipment from time to time. In view of the above problems, this paper studies the fuzzy adaptive PID control method to support the stable flight of four rotor UAV. The principle of fuzzy control is analyzed. The fuzzy control method and PID control method are deeply integrated. A fuzzy adaptive PID control system is designed. The universe and membership function of the relevant control parameters of the system are formulated. The tuning rules of fuzzy adaptive PID control system are formulated. Finally, the improved control system is simulated. The simulation results show that the fuzzy adaptive PID control algorithm can effectively improve the stability, reliability and emergency ability of UAV. This method can effectively improve the adaptability of UAV to perform complex missions in complex environments. The research results have guiding significance for expanding the application field of UAV.

Keywords: Four Rotor Unmanned Aerial Vehicle · Fuzzy Control · Proportion Integration Differentiation

1 Introduction

Four rotor UAV has the characteristics of light and compact, rich flight posture, simple operation and so on [1]. At present, it has been widely used in many fields. Especially in the power industry, the application scale of four rotor UAV is growing [2]. However,

H. Yang et al. (Eds.): SmartGIFT 2022, LNICST 483, pp. 455–465, 2023.
https://doi.org/10.1007/978-3-031-31733-0_39

with the large number of UAV patrol inspection of power equipment, accidents of UAV impacting power equipment occur from time to time [3]. This is mainly because the four rotor UAV is a strongly coupled underactuated system. At present, the commonly used traditional UAV PID control system has low control accuracy and slow response speed [4]. When the UAV performs a simple flight mission, the defect of low stability of the control system has not been shown. When unmanned aerial vehicles perform complex flight tasks or deal with complex application scenarios, the defects of low stability of the control system are undoubtedly exposed [5]. At present, the state has very strict requirements on power supply reliability. Once a foreign object touches the power equipment, it is very likely to cause a power failure. Therefore, the stability of UAV control system must be improved to adapt the needs of power inspection application scenarios [3].

Aim at the above-mentioned problems, this paper improves the traditional proportion integration differentiation control method. Fuzzy control method is deeply integrated into the control system of four rotor UAV. On this basis, incomplete differential and anti integral saturation modules are introduced. Finally, the simulation experiment of the improved fuzzy adaptive PID control system of four rotor UAV is carried out. The research results have guiding significance for improving the stability of UAV control system.

2 Principle of Fuzzy Control

Fuzzy control logic can use simple language to describe the specified intelligent logic algorithm. Although the fuzzy control method has nonlinear characteristics, it can fully integrate the advantages of the two by introducing the fuzzy control theory into the traditional proportion integration differentiation control system. After the deep integration of fuzzy control theory, the safety and reliability of proportion integration differentiation control system will be greatly improved.

The input of fuzzy control needs to meet the needs of system design. Many factors such as external input, system output and UAV system status will affect the effect of fuzzy control. So the input information should be within a reasonable range. Then, the input signal is transformed into fuzzy vector by using proportional conversion.

Database and rule base together constitute the knowledge base of fuzzy control. The input signals, Output information and all fuzzy subsets are stored in the database. These fuzzy control rules come from the long-term experience of experts.

In short, fuzzy theory is to use the corresponding fuzzification rules and logic summarized by experts to constantly modify the system parameters.

In the process of fuzzy control, the fuzzy set is obtained by fuzzy reasoning. Fuzzy sets cannot be used directly. Only accurate values can be applied to the control system. Defuzzification is the process of solving fuzzy sets into exact values.

Figure 1 is the schematic of One dimensional fuzzy proportion integration differentiation control system. First, fuzzy inference is carried out on the initial data. Convert the input signal into fuzzy quantity. Then the fuzzy set is deduced according to the fuzzy rules of experts. Finally, the precise output value is calculated through the anti fuzzification operation. The following is the structure introduction of three fuzzy control systems with different dimensions.

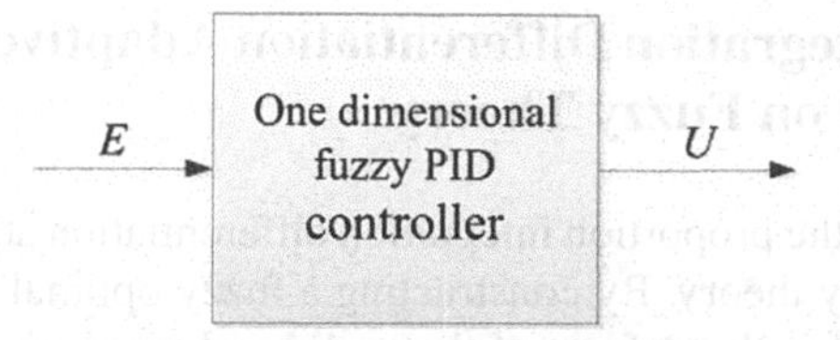

Fig. 1. One dimensional fuzzy proportion integration differentiation controller

The structure of this control system is very simple. Because the system only uses error as input, it is often difficult to reflect the real dynamic characteristics of the controlled object, and the control effect is not ideal. One dimensional fuzzy control system is rarely used in engineering applications. In the figure, e is the error. U is the error value fed back by the control structure.

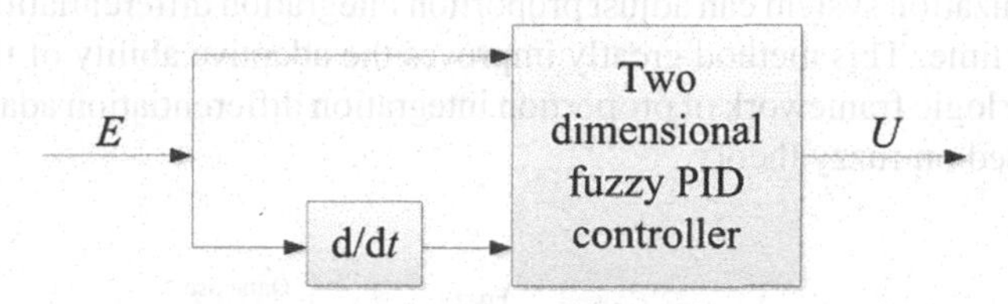

Fig. 2. Second order fuzzy optimal proportion integration differentiation controller

Figure 2 is Second order fuzzy optimal proportion integration differentiation control system. The input signal of two-dimensional control system includes error and error rate after differential processing. The two-dimensional control system can accurately image the output dynamic performance of the controlled object in the controlled process. In practical engineering applications, two-dimensional control system is widely used.

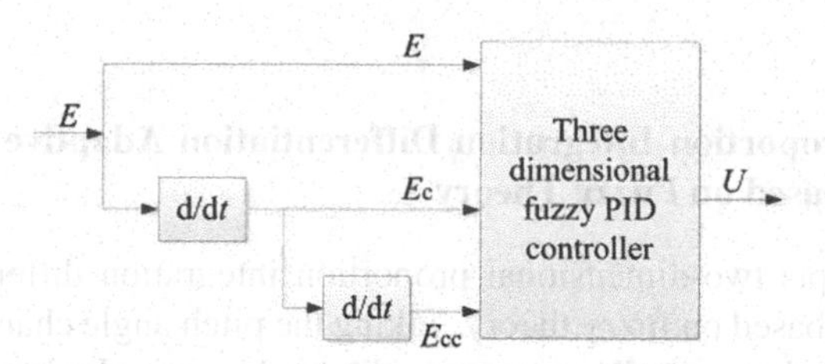

Fig. 3. Three dimensional fuzzy optimal proportion integration differentiation controller

Figure 3 is three-dimensional fuzzy optimal proportion integration differentiation controller. There are three inputs of three-dimensional fuzzy optimal proportion integration differentiation controller, which are error, the variety rate of error and change rate of error change. The structure of three-dimensional fuzzy optimal proportion integration differentiation controller is very complex. This kind of controller is generally only used in the field where the control accuracy is very high.

3 Proportion Integration Differentiation Adaptive Optimal Control Method Based on Fuzzy Theory

This paper introduces the proportion integration differentiation adaptive optimal control method based on fuzzy theory. By constructing a fuzzy optimal proportion integration differentiation controller, the defects of the traditional proportion integration differentiation control system are made up. The proportion integration differentiation adaptive optimal control method based on fuzzy theory can enhance the accuracy, timeliness and robustness of the control system. In theory, the fuzzy optimal proportion integration differentiation controller is far better than that of traditional proportion integration differentiation controller.

The fuzzy optimal proportion integration differentiation controller has two important components. They are fuzzy inference and proportion integration differentiation controller respectively.

The optimization system can adjust proportion integration differentiation parameters online in real time. This method greatly improves the adaptive ability of the controller. Figure 4 is the logic framework of proportion integration differentiation adaptive optimal controller based on fuzzy theory.

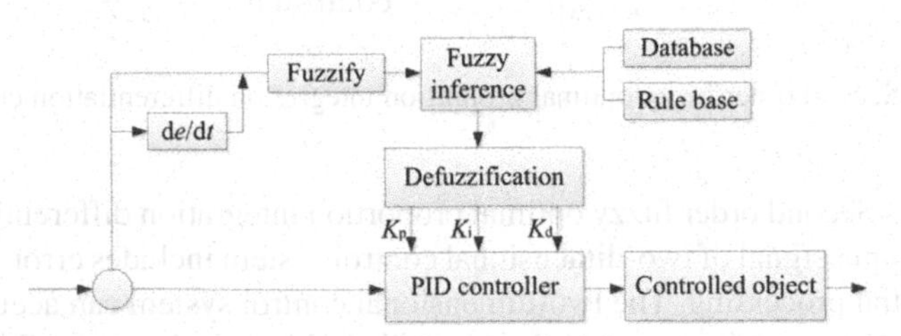

Fig. 4. The logic framework of proportion integration differentiation adaptive optimal controller based on fuzzy theory

3.1 Design of Proportion Integration Differentiation Adaptive Optimal Controller Based on Fuzzy Theory

This research adopts two-dimensional proportion integration differentiation adaptive optimal controller based on fuzzy theory. Taking the pitch angle channel as an example, the input signal of the controller system is the angle error obtained by feedback and the error rate after differential processing. Firstly, the input quantity is subjected to fuzzy reasoning, and the fuzzy vector is output. Then, according to the logic rules and membership function in the knowledge base, the fuzzy vector is calculated, and the fuzzy set is output. Finally, the fuzzy combination is defuzzified. Finally, the control variation of the three arguments, namely ΔK_{p}, ΔK_{i} and ΔK_{d}, can be obtained. Figure 5 is the fuzzy adaptive control system simulation model (Fig. 6).

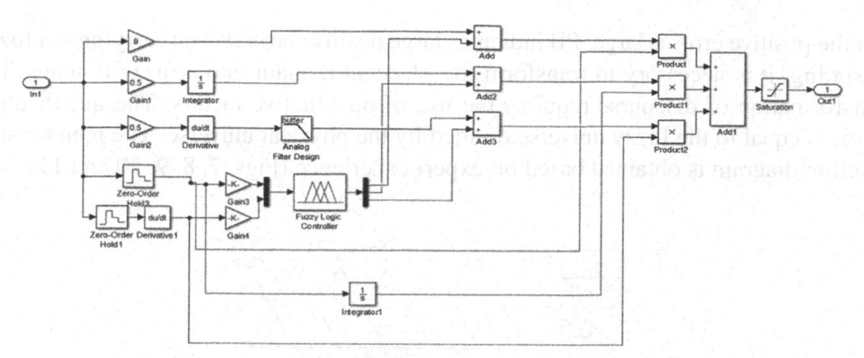

Fig. 5. Simulation model of proportion integration differentiation adaptive optimal controller based on fuzzy theory

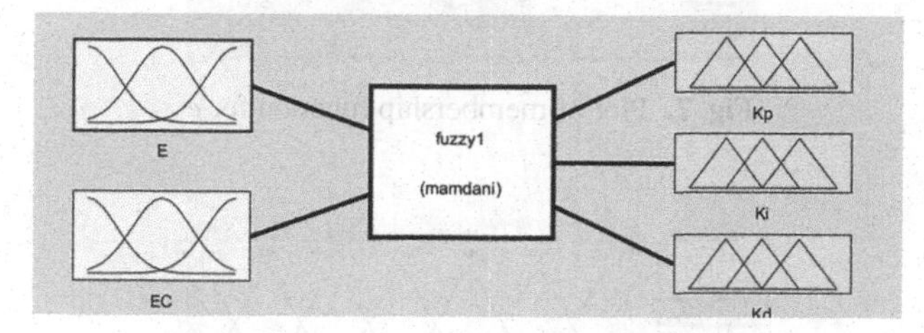

Fig. 6. Fuzzy reasoning structure diagram

3.2 The Choice of Universe and the Graph of Membership Function

The inputs of the two-dimensional proportion integration differentiation adaptive optimal controller based on fuzzy theory constructed in this paper are error e and error rate e_c. The output of two-dimensional proportion integration differentiation adaptive optimal controller based on fuzzy theory is the control variation of three parameters, namely ΔK_d, ΔK_i and ΔK_p. The whole process of fuzzy method such as fuzzy reasoning and anti fuzzy solution is carried out in the fuzzy module of MATLAB. The domain of input and change rate of Y is [−3, 3]. The domain of input variables and rate of change of attitude angle is [−3, 3]. The universe of the proportional coefficient between Y and attitude angle is [−1, 1]. The universe of the integral coefficient between Y and attitude angle is [−0.01, 0.01]. The universe of the differential coefficient between Y and attitude angle is [−1, 1]. The domain of the proportional coefficient of the body height Z is [−5, 5]. The domain of the differential coefficient of Z is [−0.01, 0.01]. The domain range of the integral coefficient of Z is [−5, 5]. In order to optimize the effect of proportion integration differentiation adaptive optimal controller based on fuzzy theory method, a large fuzzy universe is selected in this paper for the larger proportion coefficient and differential coefficient of Z channel.

Fuzzy sets are represented by [N-BS, N-MS, N-SS, Z-OS, P-SS, P-MS, P-BS]. Taking the output variable ΔK_p as an example, N-BS indicates that the negative error is large. N-MS indicates that the negative error is large. N-SS means small negative error. Z-OS means the error is 0. P-SS means that the positive error is small. P-MS indicates that the positive error is large. PB indicates large positive error. When carrying out fuzzy reasoning, it is necessary to transform the physical domain into a fuzzy domain. The transformation of discourse requires the use of quantitative factors. The quantization factor is equal to the fuzzy universe divided by the physical universe. The membership function diagram is obtained based on expert experience (Figs. 7, 8, 9, 10 and 11).

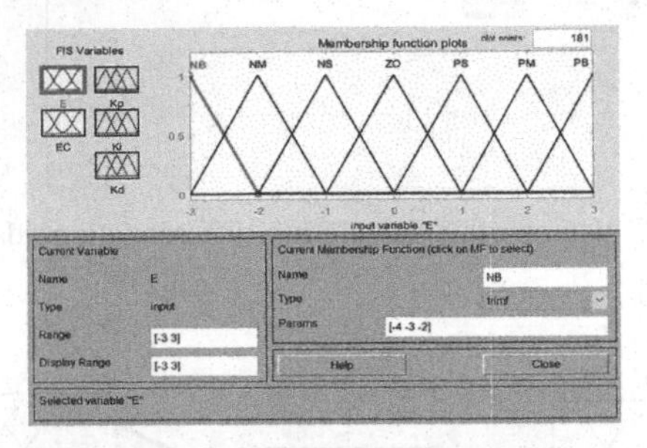

Fig. 7. Plot of membership function for e

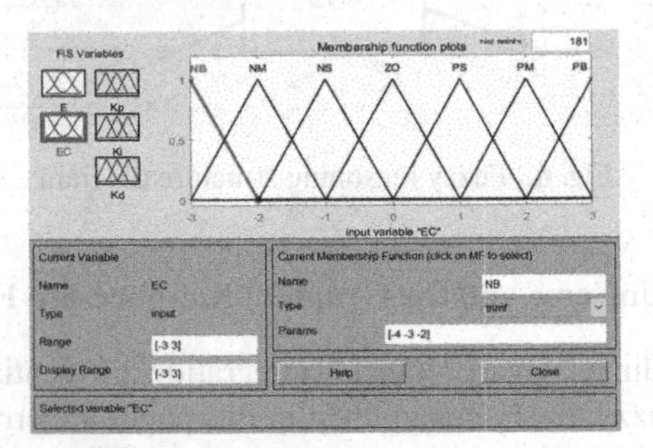

Fig. 8. Plot of membership function for e_c

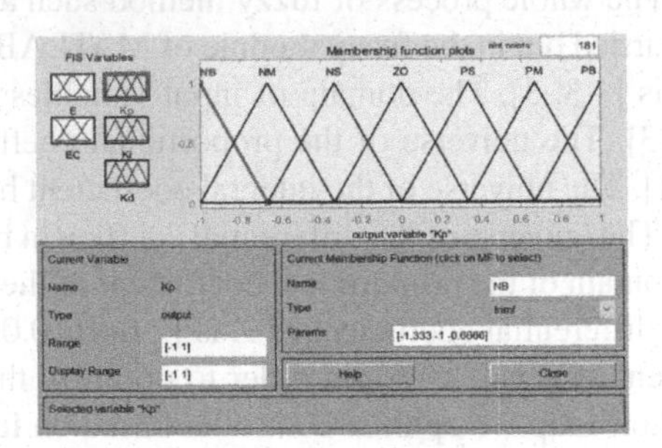

Fig. 9. Plot of membership function for ΔK_p

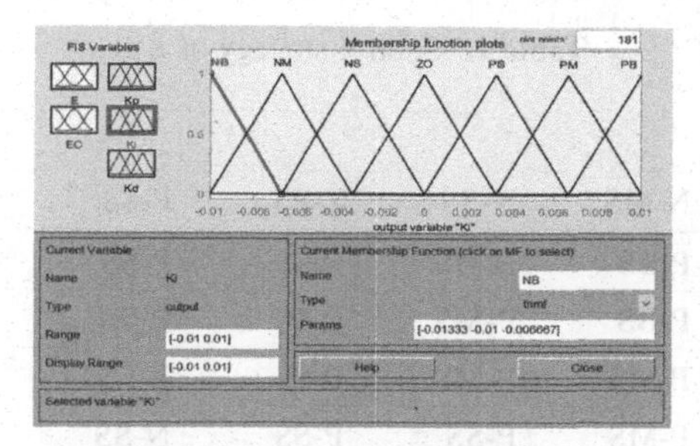

Fig. 10. Plot of membership function for ΔK_{i}

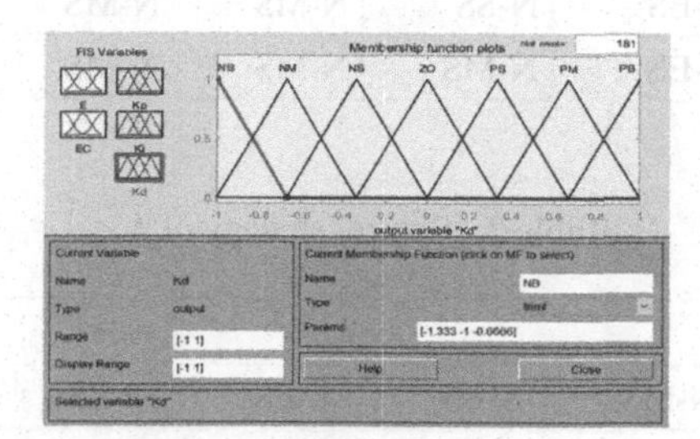

Fig. 11. Plot of membership function for ΔK_{d}

3.3 Confirm Fuzzy Rules

The proportion integration differentiation adaptive optimal controller based on fuzzy theory can modify the parameters of the UAV control system in real time according to the feedback error e and error change rate e_{c}.

The proportion integration differentiation adaptive optimal control method based on fuzzy theory can enhance the dynamic response performance and make the UAV fly smoothly all the time. The tuning rules are as follows.

(1) When the deviation is large, the system needs to quickly adjust the deviation. First, you should increase the value of the scale parameter. However, the value of error change rate will increase under the action of proportional link. Larger error will cause integral saturation. Therefore, smaller integration parameters should be selected.
(2) When the values of error and error rate are moderate. If the scale coefficient is too large, the system will have overshoot. Therefore, we should reduce the size of the proportional parameter and choose a smaller integral coefficient. In addition, in order to improve the stability and the system response speed, appropriate differential coefficients should be selected.
(3) When the error value is small, a larger proportion coefficient and integral coefficient should be selected. When the error change rate is small, a larger differential coefficient should be selected (Tables 1, 2 and 3).

Table 1. Control strategy of Kp

ΔK_{p}	e_{c}						
e	N-BS	N-MS	N-SS	Z-ES	P-SS	P-MS	P-BS
N-BS	P-BS	P-BS	P-MS	P-MS	P-SS	Z-ES	Z-ES
N-MS	P-BS	P-BS	P-MS	P-SS	P-SS	Z-ES	N-SS
N-SS	P-MS	P-MS	P-MS	P-SS	Z-ES	N-SS	N-SS
Z-ES	P-MS	P-MS	P-SS	P-SS	N-SS	N-MS	N-MS
P-SS	P-SS	P-SS	Z-ES	N-SS	N-SS	N-MS	N-MS
P-MS	P-SS	Z-ES	N-SS	N-MS	N-MS	N-MS	N-BS
P-BS	Z-ES	Z-ES	N-MS	N-MS	N-MS	N-MS	N-BS

Table 2. Control strategy of Ki

ΔK_{i}	e_{c}						
e	N-BS	N-MS	N-SS	Z-ES	P-SS	P-MS	P-BS
N-BS	N-BS	N-BS	N-MS	N-MS	N-SS	Z-ES	Z-ES
N-MS	N-BS	N-BS	N-MS	N-SS	N-SS	Z-ES	N-SS
N-SS	N-BS	N-SS	N-SS	N-SS	Z-ES	P-SS	P-SS
Z-ES	N-MS	N-SS	N-SS	Z-ES	P-SS	P-MS	P-MS
P-SS	N-MS	N-SS	Z-ES	P-SS	P-SS	P-MS	P-BS
P-MS	Z-ES	Z-ES	P-SS	P-SS	P-MS	P-BS	P-BS
P-BS	Z-ES	Z-ES	P-SS	P-MS	P-MS	P-BS	P-BS

Table 3. Control strategy of Kd

ΔK_{d}	e_{c}						
e	N-BS	N-MS	N-SS	Z-ES	P-SS	P-MS	P-BS
N-BS	P-SS	N-SS	N-BS	N-BS	N-BS	N-MS	P-SS
N-MS	P-SS	N-SS	N-BS	N-MS	N-MS	N-SS	Z-ES
N-SS	Z-ES	N-MS	N-MS	N-MS	N-SS	N-SS	Z-ES
Z-ES	Z-ES	N-SS	N-SS	N-SS	N-SS	N-SS	Z-ES
P-SS	Z-ES	Z-ES	Z-ES	Z-ES	Z-ES	Z-ES	Z-ES
P-MS	P-BS	N-SS	P-SS	P-SS	P-SS	P-SS	P-BS
P-BS	P-BS	P-MS	P-MS	P-MS	P-SS	P-SS	P-BS

3.4 Defuzzification Solution

After fuzzy reasoning, the subcollection can be achieved. An numerical value can be obtained by defuzzifying the fuzzy set. Using this value, the actuator can be accurately controlled. There are three ways to defuzzify.

The first method is the maximum membership method. This method has the advantages of simple operation and strong real-time performance. However, due to the need to choose the number with the largest membership as the control quantity, the accuracy of the results obtained by using this method is also very low.

The second method is the central number method. The disadvantage of this method is the large amount of calculation and poor real-time performance. However, because this method uses all the data in the fuzzy set, the result obtained has the highest accuracy.

The third method is the barycenter method. In this method, the center of the closed shape formed by the function curve and parameter coordinate axis in the fuzzy rule base is taken as the fuzzy output. After fuzzy reasoning, the changes of three parameters are obtained, namely ΔK_{p}, ΔK_{i} and ΔK_{d}.

4 Comparison and Analysis of Simulation Results

The sake of this paper is to improve the flight control effect of UAV, so we will improve the decoupled attitude control loop separately. The fuzzy control method is deeply integrated in the PID control system. Figure 12 is the simulation diagram of pitch angle. Figure 13 shows the simulation diagram of of rolling angle. The simulation diagram of z channel is shown in Fig. 14. Figure 15 is the simulation diagram of of yaw angle.

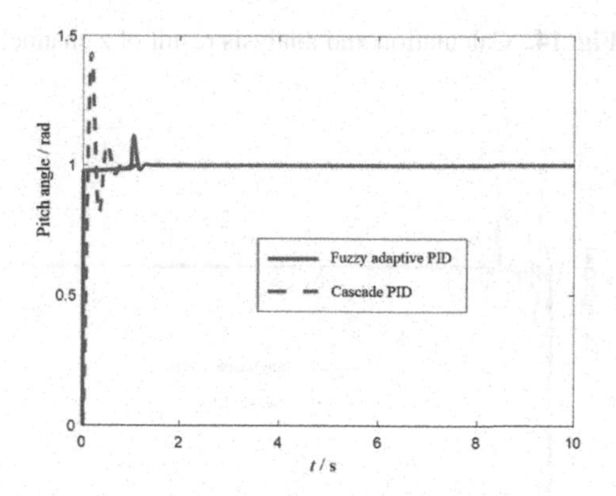

Fig. 12. Calculation and analysis result of pitch angle

In Figs. 12, 13, 14 and 15, the horizontal axis is the time axis. The vertical coordinate axis represents the radian of pitch angle, roll angle, yaw angle and the value of Z channel respectively. According to the simulation results, compared with the traditional cascade proportion integration differentiation controller the proportion integration differentiation adaptive optimal controller based on fuzzy theory completes the online tuning of four

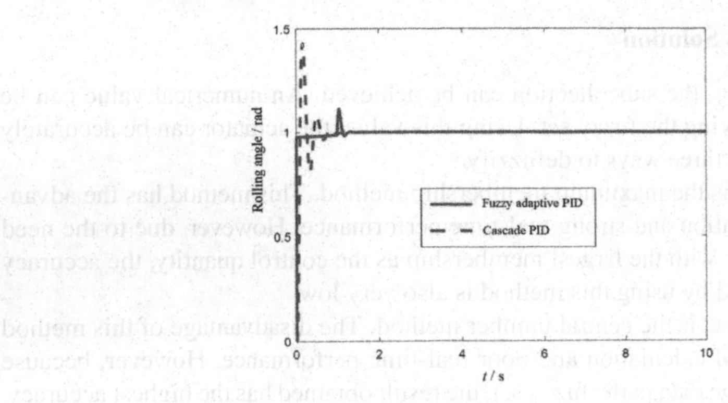

Fig. 13. Calculation and analysis result of rolling angle

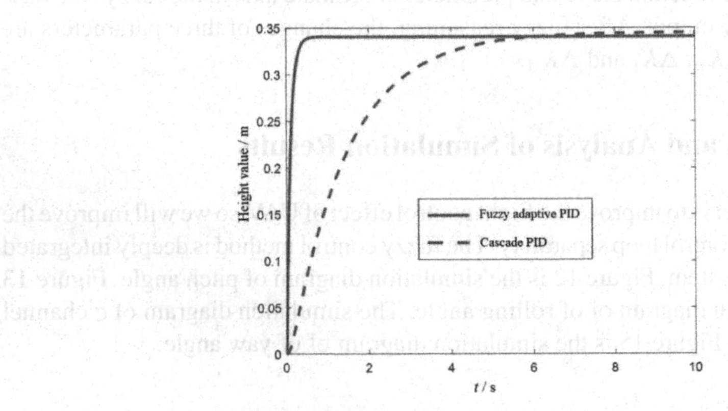

Fig. 14. Calculation and analysis result of z channel

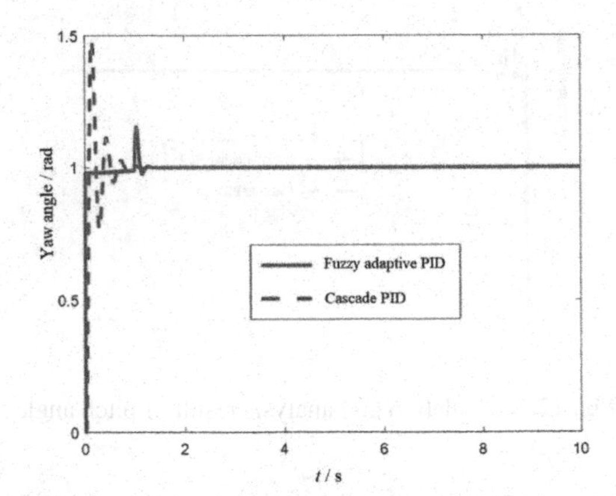

Fig. 15. Calculation and analysis result of yaw angle

control parameters in a very short time. The response curve of the parameters of the proportion integration differentiation adaptive optimal controller based on fuzzy theory is relatively smooth without violent fluctuations. In general, after the fuzzy adaptive improvement, the overshoot and oscillation of the system are greatly reduced, and the system response speed is greatly improved.

5 Conclusion

The proportion integration differentiation adaptive optimal control method based on fuzzy theory suitable for the control system of four rotor UAV is studied in this pape. The proportion integration differentiation adaptive optimal controller based on fuzzy theory is designed. The universe and membership function of the relevant control parameters of the system are formulated. The tuning rules of fuzzy adaptive PID control system are formulated. Through simulation analysis, it is found that the stability and the system response speed are greatly improved after the fuzzy adaptive improvement. Therefore, the fuzzy adaptive PID control algorithm can effectively improve the stability, reliability and emergency ability of UAV. This method can effectively improve the adaptability of UAV to perform complex missions in complex environments.

Acknowledgment. This research work is supported by State Grid Hunan Electric Power Company Limited. The number of the science and technology project is 5216A521001J.

References

1. Rau, J.Y., Hsiao, K.W., Jhan, J.P., et al.: Bridge crack detection using multi-rotary UAV and object-base image analysis. The Int. Archiv. Photogrammetry, Remote Sens. Spatial Inform. Sci. **42**(01), 311 (2017)
2. Deng, C., Wang, S., Huang, Z., et al.: Unmanned aerial vehicles for power line inspection: a cooperative way in platforms and communications. J. Commun. **9**(09), 687–692 (2014)
3. Liu, C., Liu, Y., Wu, H., et al.: A safe flight approach of the UAV in the electrical line inspection. Int. J. Emerg. Electr. Power Syst. **16**(05), 503–515 (2015)
4. Han, J.: From PID to active disturbance rejection control. IEEE Trans. Industr. Electron. **56**(03), 900–906 (2009)
5. Shah, P., Agashe, S.: Review of fractional PID controller. Mechatronics **38**(01), 29–41 (2016)

An Auto Disturbance Rejection Control Method for Four Rotor UAV Flight Operation

Dai Wan[1(✉)], Simin Peng[1], Jinliang Li[1], Liang Peng[2], Yingying Yi[3], and Zoujun Wang[1]

[1] State Grid Hunan Electric Power Company Limited Research Institute, Changsha 410007, China
280241509@qq.com
[2] Changsha University of Science and Technology, Changsha 410000, China
[3] Changsha Tax Service, Changsha 410000, China

Abstract. The four rotor unmanned aerial vehicle (UAV) can carry out all-round and efficient inspection of power equipment. At present, the four rotor UAV has become an essential equipment in the inspection of transmission lines. However, the support of UAV for distribution line inspection is far less than that for transmission line inspection. This is mainly because the operating environment of distribution lines is much more complex and harsh than that of transmission lines. In the process of power distribution line inspection, all kinds of environmental interference are far more than transmission lines. The existing four rotor UAV control methods have poor resistance to external interference. Aiming at the above problems, the research on ADRC method of four rotor UAV is carried out in this paper. The principle of active disturbance rejection is analyzed. A linear active disturbance rejection scheme is proposed. The attitude control module of UAV is designed. The simulation model of ADRC system of four rotor UAV is constructed. The simulation results show that the ADRC method can effectively alleviate the influence of random interference on the flight state of UAV. For the UAV operating in complex environment, it is necessary to optimize the anti-interference of its control system. The research results have guiding significance for improving the anti-interference ability of UAV in the process of distribution line inspection.

Keywords: Four Rotor Unmanned Aerial Vehicle · Auto Disturbance Rejection Control · Control Method

1 Introduction

With the continuous improvement of national living standards, people have higher and higher requirements for the reliability of power supply. However, in recent years, the scale of distribution lines and equipment has become larger and larger. The traditional manual inspection mode has been unable to cope with the large-scale inspection objects and the requirements of lean inspection work. The emergence of unmanned aerial vehicle inspection technology provides new technical means for power grid operation and

H. Yang et al. (Eds.): SmartGIFT 2022, LNICST 483, pp. 466–477, 2023.
https://doi.org/10.1007/978-3-031-31733-0_40

maintenance personnel [1]. At present, unmanned aerial vehicle inspection technology has been widely used in the field of power grid, and has achieved good application results. Especially in the field of power transmission, UAV Patrol has become a very mature operation mode [2]. However, UAV inspection technology is still in its infancy in the field of power distribution. Because the operating environment of distribution lines is far more complex and harsh than that of transmission lines, UAV will face a lot of environmental interference during patrol inspection. The existing flight state control system of four rotor UAV is difficult to adapt to the complex operating environment of distribution network [3].

At present, most of the multi rotor UAV use proportional integral derivative (PID) control system. PID control technology is a relatively mature technology. The PID control system can adjust the output response of the system according to the error signal of the feedback loop, so as to reduce the error with the expected input [4]. In the current mainstream engineering control, PID is still a very excellent solution. However, the performance of PID control method is not satisfactory in the face of complex systems. In the face of multiple disturbances, the control effect of PID is seriously affected by the disturbance [5]. With the continuous development of control technology, there are many modern control technology theories that pursue high-precision control effect. However, these modern control theories, which strongly rely on accurate models, are difficult to realize in practical engineering applications. In view of the above problems, academia has proposed an active disturbance rejection control (ADRC) method. Active disturbance rejection control method is evolved from PID control method. Suppose that there is a total disturbance consisting of internal disturbance and external disturbance in the control system. After assuming this uncertain fuzzy model, extended state observer (ESO) is used for observation. The result of ESO observation can be regarded as the total disturbance of the system. Therefore, we can build this system into a series integral system through ESO. Then create an nonlinear state error feedback control law (NSEF) to realize the interference suppression of the total disturbance of the system, which can make the system obtain better control effect and system stability [4].

This paper deeply analyzes the principle of ADRC. Tracking differential controller (TD), extended state observer (ESO) and nonlinear state error feedback control law (NSEF) are designed. A linear active disturbance rejection control method is proposed. The active disturbance rejection control model of four rotor UAV is constructed. The simulation test is carried out. The research results have guiding significance for improving the anti-interference ability and environmental adaptability of UAV.

2 Analysis of Active Disturbance Rejection Algorithm

2.1 Active Disturbance Rejection Principle

The core of active disturbance rejection control method is to regard the controlled object as a standard system with integral series connection. The ESO is used to estimate it. The estimation results are used to dynamically compensate the total disturbance of the system. ADRC is generally composed of three parts.

(1) Tracking differentiator
TD can track signals with random noise or discrete discontinuous signals. Its function is to improve the control quality of the system and simplify the structure of the control system. The TD can output two signals. They are the tracking signal and its differential signal. Among them, the tracking signal can be output through the fastest control synthesis function. Based on the above two signals, a transition process can be set in the closed-loop system. This transition process can not only reduce the overshoot of the control system, but also quickly respond to the control requirements of the system.
(2) Extended state observer
The ESO is the decision-making and observation mechanism of the control system. The ESO can not only observe the state of the controlled object, but also compensate the disturbance in the control system. The ESO does not need an accurate model when observing the state of the controlled object.
(3) Nonlinear state error feedback control law
The NSEF is similar to the control rule of PID. By calculating the tracking signal and differential signal output by the TD, corresponding groups of error signals can be generated. NSEF can be formed by nonlinear combination of error signals.

2.2 Analysis of Nonlinear Active Disturbance Rejection Algorithm

In the nonlinear ADRC method, the ESO is designed by using fal function. The control system is designed by using the nonlinear combination of fal function and the fastest control synthesis function fhan. The control system needs to meet two rules. First, large gain corresponds to small system error state. Second, small gain corresponds to large system error state. This design scheme can effectively eliminate the disturbance in the uncertain model. The problem of overshooting and system response speed can be solved simultaneously with only a set of parameters. The structure of the nonlinear ADRC system is shown in Fig. 1.

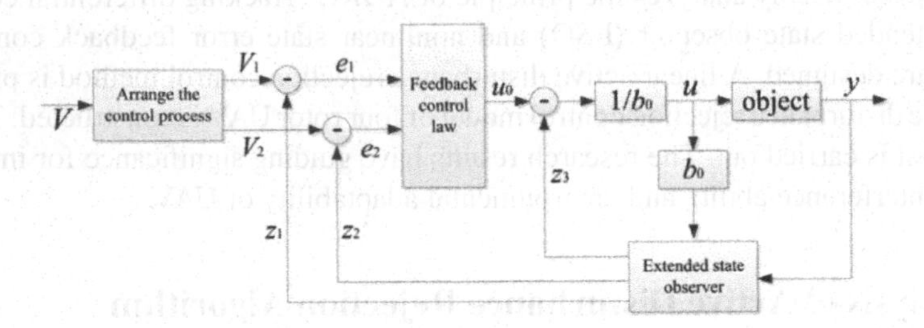

Fig. 1. Structure diagram of nonlinear ADRC system

First, the TD is designed. Suppose a second-order uncertain controlled object is $x^{(n)}$.

$$x^{(n)} = f(x, \dot{x}, \cdots, x^{(n-1)}, t) + w(t) + b(t)u(t) \tag{1}$$

where, $f(x, \dot{x}, \cdots, x^{(n-1)}, t)$ and $b(t)$ represent unknown functions. $u(t)$ represents the input control quantity. $w(t)$ represents the unknown disturbance function.

In order to make the system input smooth and not affected by sudden change interference, a transition process is designed in the system control flow. This transition process can make the system track the input signal quickly and reduce sudden change interference. Suppose the input signal of the TD is *u(t)*. It will output two signals, $x_1(t)$ and $x_2(t)$. $x_1(t)$ is the tracking signal of *u(t)*. $x_2(t)$ is the differential signal of the tracking signal $x_1(t)$. Similarly, $x_1(t)$ can be regarded as the differential signal of the input signal *u(t)*.

The expression of the second-order system is as follows.

$$\begin{cases} x_1(k+1) = x_1(k) + h \times x_2(k) \\ x_2(k+1) = x_2(k) + h \times u \, |u| \leqslant r \end{cases} \tag{2}$$

The second-order discrete system expression of the TD is as follows.

$$\begin{cases} x_1(k+1) = x_1(k) + h \times x_2(k) \\ x_2(k+1) = x_2(k) + h \times fst(x_1(k) - v(k), x_2(k), r, h) \, |u| \leqslant r \end{cases} \tag{3}$$

where *fst*(•) is the fastest control synthesis function. *fst*(•) is defined as follows.

$$\begin{aligned} & d = rd \\ & d_0 = hd \\ & y = (x_1(k) - v(k) + hx_2(k)) \\ & a_0 = \sqrt{d^2 + 8r|y|} \\ & a = \begin{bmatrix} x_2(k) + \frac{(a_0 - d)}{2} \operatorname{sgn} y \; |y| < d_0 \\ x_2(k) + \frac{y}{h} \qquad |y| \leqslant d_0 \end{bmatrix} \\ & fhan = -\begin{bmatrix} r \operatorname{sgn} a \; |a| > d \\ r\frac{a}{d} \quad |a| \leqslant d \end{bmatrix} \end{aligned} \tag{4}$$

where, *h* is the integration step factor. *r* is the tracking speed factor. R determines the speed of the tracking system. The larger *r* is, the faster the tracking input *u*(*t*) of $x_1(t)$ is. *h* is the filter factor. *h* can eliminate the strong noise pollution in the input signal. However, if the value of *h* is too large, the tracking signal will be distorted and the tracking effect will become worse. Appropriate values of *h* and *r* should be selected.

Next, an ESO is designed. ESO is the most important module in NADRC system. The ESO is mainly responsible for real-time estimation of the current state of the control system and compensation of the disturbance of the control system. The disturbance estimated by ESO is called the expansion state of the total disturbance of the system. The expression of third-order ESO is as follows.

$$\begin{cases} \varepsilon_1 = z_1 - x_1 \\ \dot{z}_1 = z_2 - \beta_1 \varepsilon_1 \\ \dot{z}_2 = z_3 - \beta_2 fal(\varepsilon_1, \alpha_1, \delta) + bu \\ \dot{z}_3 = -\beta_3 fal(\varepsilon_1, \alpha_1, \delta) \end{cases} \tag{5}$$

where, $\beta_1, \beta_2, \beta_3$ and α_1 is greater than 0. α_2 is less than 1. The function expression of *fal*(•) is as follows.

$$fal(\varepsilon, \alpha, \delta) = \begin{cases} |\varepsilon|^{\alpha} sign(\varepsilon), |\varepsilon| > \delta \\ \varepsilon/\delta^{1-\alpha}, |\varepsilon| \leqslant \delta \end{cases} \tag{6}$$

Changing each variable in expression (7) can better observe the control system, so as to estimate the expanded state variables in real time.

Finally, the ESF is designed.

Finally, the NSEF is designed. NSEF can output a virtual control quantity u_0. u_0 can be used to control approximate integral series system. NSEF takes many forms. In general, the expression composed of U0 and disturbance estimator is as follows.

$$u = u_0 - z_3/b \tag{7}$$

where, *b* is the control gain of the uncertain object. *b* is an adjustable parameter.

2.3 Design of Linear Active Disturbance Rejection Control Method

The nonlinear auto disturbance rejection control (NADRC) system is simplified. Omit the TD module in the original scheme. The extended state observer and error feedback control law in the original scheme are optimized. A linear active disturbance rejection control (LADRC) system can be formed. The basic structure of linear auto disturbance rejection control system is shown in Fig. 2.

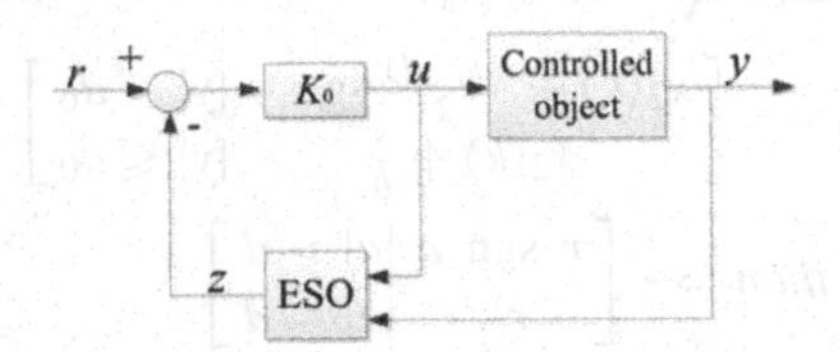

Fig. 2. Structure diagram of linear active disturbance rejection control system

When the control system meets any of the following three conditions, the linear extended state observer can be used. The first condition is that the system running time $t < T$. The second condition is that the tracking error of ESO is greater than 1. That is, $|e| > 1$. The third condition is that the total disturbance value of the system is greater than *M*. That is, $|z_{n+1}(k)| > M$. Where, *M* is an adjustable parameter. Assume that the general controlled object model is as follows.

$$\ddot{y} = bu(t) + f(x(t), u(t), d(t)) \tag{8}$$

where, f($x(t)$,$u(t)$,$d(t)$) is the total disturbance. B is the gain of the control channel. Therefore, the state space equation of the system is expressed as follows.

$$\begin{cases} \dot{x}_1 = x_2 \\ \dot{x}_2 = x_3 + bu \\ \dot{x}_3 = h \\ y = x_1 \end{cases} \tag{9}$$

Assume $z_1 = x_1, z_2 = \dot{x}_1 \cdots, z_n = x_1^{(n+1)}, z_{n+1} = f$. f is a differentiable function. The following expression can be obtained by further calculation.

$$\begin{cases} \dot{z} = A_e z + B_e u + \dot{f} E_e \\ x_1 = C_e u \end{cases} \tag{10}$$

where, the expression of each parameter is as follows.

$$z = \begin{bmatrix} z_1 \ z_2 \ z_3 \end{bmatrix}^T A_e = \begin{bmatrix} 0\,1\,0 \\ 0\,0\,1 \\ 0\,0\,0 \end{bmatrix}, B_e = \begin{bmatrix} 0 \\ b \\ 0 \end{bmatrix}, E_e = \begin{bmatrix} 0 \\ 0 \\ 1 \end{bmatrix}, C_e = \begin{bmatrix} 1\,0\,0 \end{bmatrix} \tag{11}$$

The expression of LADRC can be obtained as follows.

$$\begin{cases} \dot{z} = A_e z + B_e u + L(y - \dot{y}) \\ y = C_e z \end{cases} \tag{12}$$

$$L = \begin{bmatrix} \beta_1 \ \beta_2 \ \beta_3 \end{bmatrix}^T \tag{13}$$

where, L is the gain of the observer.

Take the derivatives of each order of the given input signal as v_i ($i = 1,2,\ldots, n$).

$$u = \frac{-z_3 + u_0}{b} \tag{14}$$

where, u_0 represents the linear control law.

$$u_0 = \sum_{i=1}^{n} k_i(v_i - z_i) \tag{15}$$

At present, most industrial controls use PID controllers. LADRC can be obtained through the parameters of PID controller. The parameters obtained in this way can ensure that the system can realize a smooth transition from PID controller to LADRC system. In addition, nadrc parameters are difficult to adjust. Once the control parameters are improperly selected, it is very likely to lead to the unsatisfactory control effect of the system. LADRC can adjust parameters online based on bandwidth. According to the parameters of the existing PID controller, the initial value of LADRC can be selected, and then fine-tuning can achieve good control effect.

The conversion process from PID controller parameters to LADRC system control parameters is as follows.

The parameter expression of the known PID controller is as follows.

$$K_P(1 + \frac{1}{T_I S} + T_D S) = K_P + \frac{K_I}{S} + K_D S \tag{16}$$

$$K_I = \frac{K_P}{T_I}, K_D = K_P T_D \tag{17}$$

Suppose that the adjustable parameters K and L can be controlled by the controller bandwidth ω_c and observer bandwidth ω_0.

$$L = [\beta_1, \beta_2, \beta_3]^T, \beta_1 = 3\omega_0, \beta_2 = 3\omega_0^2, \beta_3 = \omega_0^3 \tag{18}$$

$$K = [K_1, K_2, 1]/b, K_1 = \omega_c^2, K_2 = 2\xi\omega_c^2 \tag{19}$$

First select α. α satisfy the following equation.

$$\omega_0^5 - \alpha K_d \omega_0^2 + 3\alpha K_P \omega_0 - 6\alpha K_i = 0 \tag{20}$$

The equation has at least five solutions, and there is at least one real solution. Hypothesis α If the value of is large enough, the equation can have a positive real solution. After the positive real solution is obtained, it can be set as the observer bandwidth.

In the second step, the bandwidth of the controller can be obtained through the following equation expression.

$$\omega_c = \sqrt{\frac{\alpha K_i}{\beta_3}}$$
$$\xi = \frac{\alpha K_p - \alpha K_i \beta_2/\beta_3}{2\omega_c \beta_3} \tag{21}$$

Third, after obtaining the solution of β_1, β_2 and β_3, the gain b_0 can be obtained by the following equation expression.

$$b_0 = \frac{\alpha}{\beta_2 + K_P + \beta_1 K_d} \tag{22}$$

Through the above three steps, the parameters of LADRC and two bandwidth values can be obtained.

2.4 Comparative Simulation and Analysis

This paper simulates the linear active disturbance rejection control system. Suppose a controlled object is G_s.

$$G_s = \frac{1}{s^2 + 2s + 1} \tag{23}$$

PID parameters are adjusted through experience. The parameters of the three links are $k_p = 0.83$, $k_i = 0.33$, $k_d = 0.5$. Next, select $\alpha = 10000$. Therefore, the parameters of LADRC controller can be obtained according to the expression provided in the previous section as follows.

$$\omega_c = 0.98, \omega_0 = 15.09, b_0 = 12.74, \xi = 1.13 \tag{24}$$

This paper designs a comparative simulation experiment of PID system and LADRC system, as shown in Fig. 3.

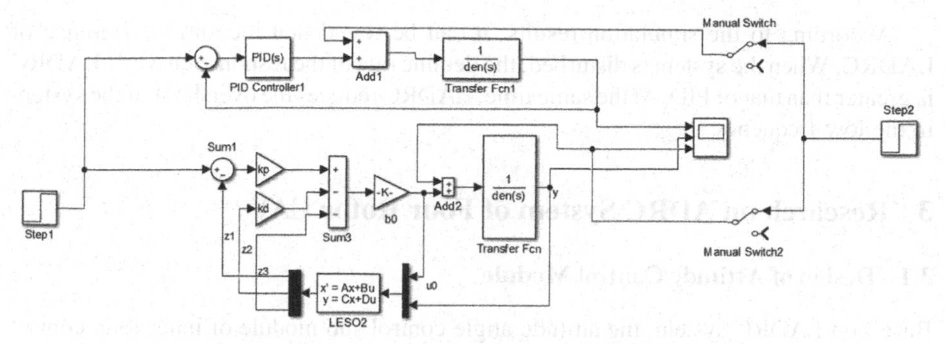

Fig. 3. Simulation diagram of PID and LADRC comparison

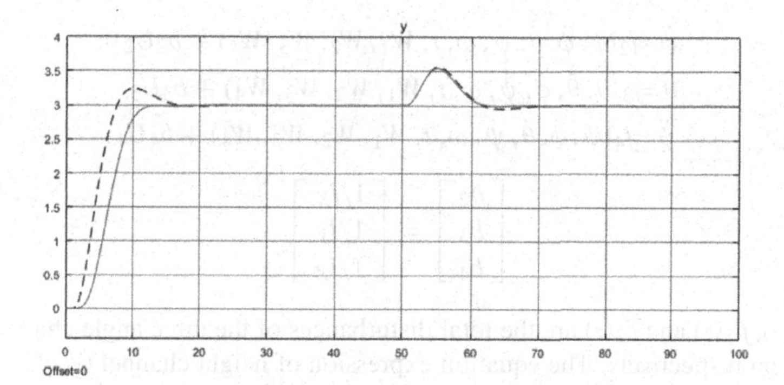

Fig. 4. Simulation result

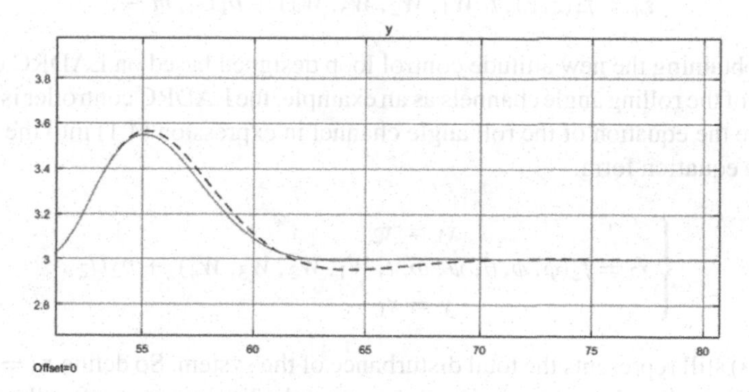

Fig. 5. Comparison curve of anti disturbance ability of two control systems in disturbance stage

Step2 module in Fig. 3 is a step response module. When the system runs to 50 s, the module will give the system a step response with a value of 1. The simulation results are as follows.

In Fig. 4, the black dotted line represents the response curve of PID. The red solid line represents the response curve of LADRC (Fig. 5).

According to the simulation results, it can be found that the anti-interference of LADRC. When the system is disturbed, the decline rate of the response curve of LADRC is greater than that of PID. At the same time, LADRC reduces the overshoot of the system in the low-frequency stage.

3 Research on ADRC System of Four Rotor UAV

3.1 Design of Attitude Control Module

Based on LADRC system, the attitude angle control sub module of inner loop control is improved again in this paper. The expression of UAV attitude angle control loop is as follows.

$$\begin{aligned} \ddot{\phi} &= f_2(\phi, \dot{\phi}, \dot{\theta}, \dot{\psi}, \omega, t, W_1, W_2, W_3, W_4) + b_2 U_2 \\ \ddot{\theta} &= f_3(\theta, \dot{\theta}, \dot{\phi}, \dot{\psi}, \omega, t, W_1, W_2, W_3, W_4) + b_3 U_3 \\ \ddot{\psi} &= f_4(\psi, \dot{\phi}, \dot{\theta}, \dot{\psi}, \omega, t, W_1, W_2, W_3, W_4) + b_4 U_4 \end{aligned} \tag{25}$$

$$\begin{bmatrix} b_2 \\ b_3 \\ b_4 \end{bmatrix} = \begin{bmatrix} 1/I_X \\ 1/I_Y \\ 1/I_Z \end{bmatrix} \tag{26}$$

where $f_1(\bullet)$, $f_2(\bullet)$ and $f_3(\bullet)$ are the total disturbances of the three angle channels of the UAV system respectively. The equation expression of height channel (Z channel) is as follows.

$$\ddot{z}_d = f_4(z, \dot{z}_d, t, W_1, W_2, W_3, W_4) + b_1 U_1/m - g \tag{27}$$

After obtaining the new attitude control loop designed based on LADRC controller, taking one of the rolling angle channels as an example, the LADRC controller is designed.

Rewrite the equation of the roll angle channel in expression (4.1) into the following state space equation form.

$$\begin{cases} \dot{x}_1 = x_2 \\ \dot{x}_2 = f_2(\phi, \dot{\phi}, \dot{\theta}, \dot{\psi}, \omega, t, W_1, W_2, W_3, W_4) + b_2 U_2 \\ y = x_1 \end{cases} \tag{28}$$

where, $f_2(\bullet)$ still represents the total disturbance of the system. So define $x_3 = f_2(\bullet)$, and $\dot{x}_3 = a(t)$. From the above expression, we can get the linear system after the expansion of expression (29).

$$\begin{cases} \dot{x}_1 = x_2 \\ \dot{x}_2 = x_3 + b_2 U_2 \\ \dot{x}_3 = a(t) \\ y = x_1 \end{cases} \tag{29}$$

So as to establish a new leso.

$$\begin{cases} e_l = z_1 - y \\ \dot{z}_1 = z_2 - \beta_1(e_l) \\ \dot{z}_2 = z_3 - \beta_2 e_l + b_2 u \\ \dot{z}_3 = -\beta_3 e_l \end{cases} \tag{30}$$

Let $z_1(t)$, $z_2(t)$ and $z_3(t)$ satisfy the following expressions.

$$\begin{aligned} z_1(t) &\to x_1(t) \\ z_2(t) &\to x_2(t) \\ z_3(t) &\to x_3(t) \end{aligned} \tag{31}$$

The expression of the control quantity U_2 is as follows.

$$U_2 = u_0 - z_3/b \tag{32}$$

The linear system expression can be obtained as follows.

$$\begin{cases} \dot{x}_1 = x_2 \\ \dot{x}_2 = bu_0 \\ y = x_1 \end{cases} \tag{33}$$

where, $u_0 = k_p(v_c - z_1) - k_d z_2$.

After calculating the attitude angle control equation and height control equation, a new attitude angle control module based on LADRC controller can be designed (Fig. 6).

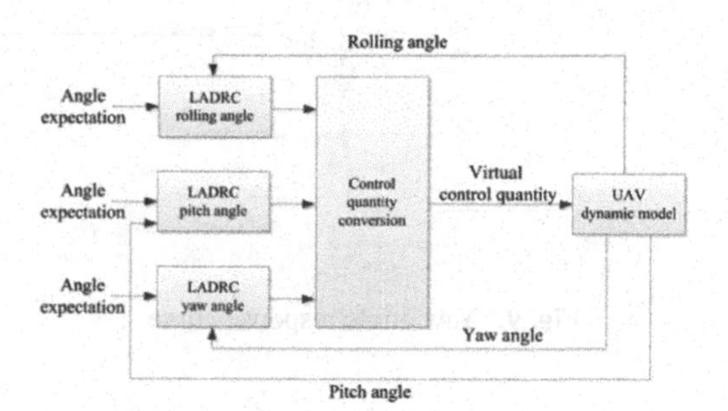

Fig. 6. Attitude angle control module

3.2 Simulation Results and Analysis

This paper uses four control parameters of PID to adjust the parameters of LADRC. The four control parameters are roll angle, pitch angle, yaw angle and Z-channel height. On this basis, the system is simulated. The simulation results are shown in the Figs. 7, 8, 9 and 10 below.

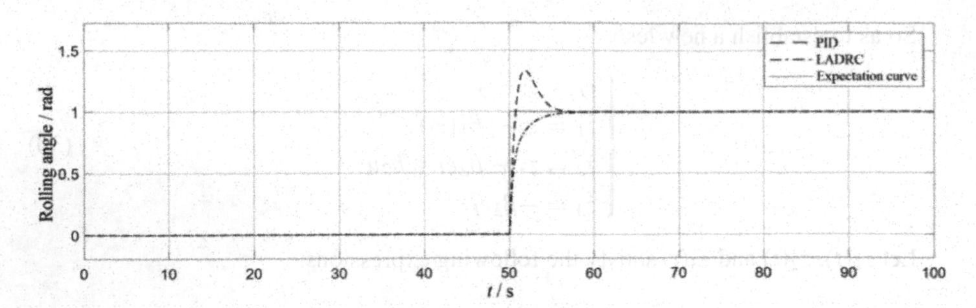

Fig. 7. Roll angle response curve

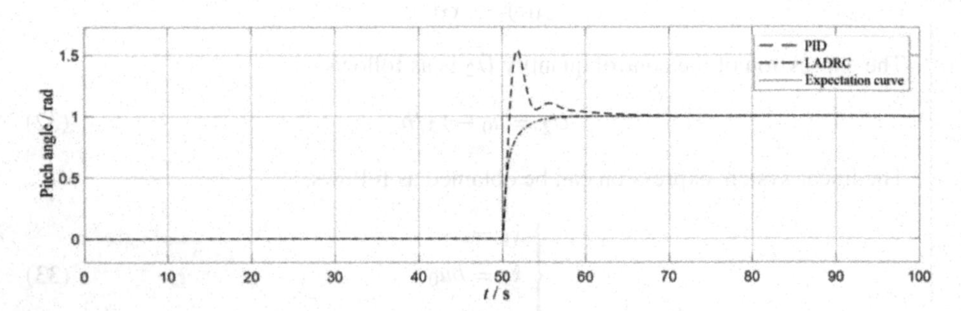

Fig. 8. Pitch angle response curve

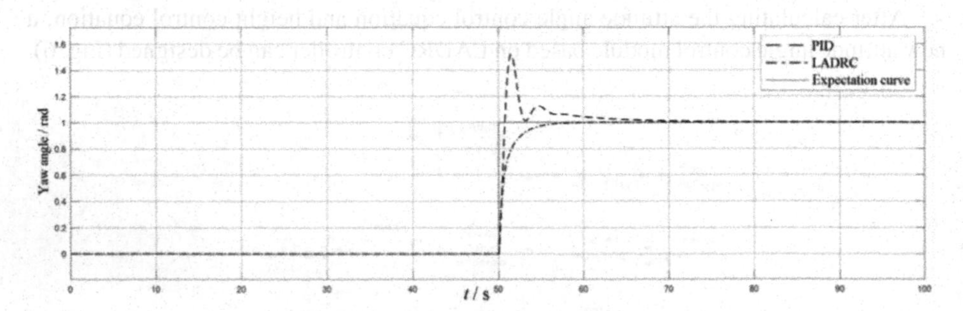

Fig. 9. Yaw angle response curve

At the moment of 50 s, sudden change interference is added to the angle control parameters. From the response curves of roll angle and pitch angle, it can be seen that the PID control system has a large overshoot, while the LADRC system changes smoothly. It can be seen that the small four rotor UAV system is an underactuated and strongly coupled system, and the disturbance inside the system can not be ignored. When using PID control system, PID is easy to cause imbalance in the face of system internal disturbance, and even cause instability of UAV flight control system. When LADRC system is used, overshoot caused by the system can be effectively suppressed.

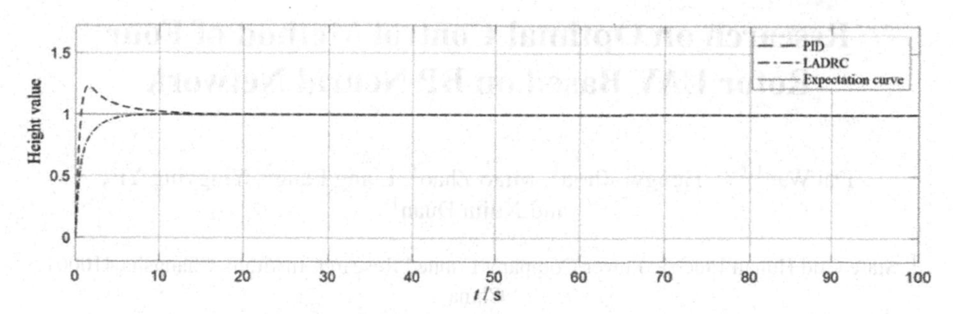

Fig. 10. z-channel response curve

4 Conclusion

This paper studies the effect of active disturbance rejection control method on the flight attitude of four rotor UAV. Firstly, the nonlinear active disturbance rejection algorithm is analyzed. Then a linear ADRC system model is designed. LADRC system and traditional PID control system are used to simulate the running state of the control object, and the differences between them are compared synchronously. The advantages and characteristics of LADRC system are verified. Finally, a LADRC scheme which can be used for flight attitude control of four rotor UAV is designed. The stability and effectiveness of the scheme are verified by simulation experiments. The research results have guiding significance for the flight control technology of multi rotor UAV.

Acknowledgment. This work was financially supported by the science and technology project of State Grid Hunan Electric Power Company Limited (5216A521001J).

References

1. Deng, C., Wang, S., Huang, Z., et al.: Unmanned aerial vehicles for power line inspection: a cooperative way in platforms and communications. J. Commun. **9**(09), 687–692 (2014)
2. Park, J., Kim, S., Lee, J., et al.: Method of operating a GIS-based autopilot drone to inspect ultrahigh voltage power lines and its field tests. J. Field Robot. **37**(03), 345–361 (2020)
3. Liu, C., Liu, Y., Wu, H., et al.: A safe flight approach of the UAV in the electrical line inspection. Int. J. Emerg. Electr. Power Syst. **16**(05), 503–515 (2015)
4. Shah, P., Agashe, S.: Review of fractional PID controller. Mechatronics **38**(01), 29–41 (2016)
5. Han, J.: From PID to active disturbance rejection control. IEEE Trans. Industr. Electron. **56**(03), 900–906 (2009)

Research on Optimal Control Method of Four Rotor UAV Based on BP Neural Network

Dai Wan[1(✉)], Hengyi Zhou[1], Miao Zhao[1], Liang Peng[2], Yingying Yi[3], and Xujin Duan[1]

[1] State Grid Hunan Electric Power Company Limited Research Institute, Changsha 410007, China
280241509@qq.com
[2] Changsha University of Science & Technology, Changsha 410000, China
[3] Changsha Tax Service, Changsha 410000, China

Abstract. With the development of related technical fields, the application scenarios of four rotor unmanned aerial vehicle (UAV) is becoming wider and wider. Especially in the field of power inspection, UAV inspection has gradually replaced manual inspection, forming a new working mode. At present, the unmanned aerial vehicle inspection technology applied to transmission lines has become increasingly mature. However, UAV technology has only been gradually applied to the patrol inspection of overhead power distribution network in recent years. The traditional proportional integral derivative (PID) control method of unmanned aerial vehicle (UAV) is difficult to meet the needs of UAV patrol inspection work in terms of control accuracy and response speed. To solve this problem, this paper uses back propagation neural net to optimize the traditional control method. Appropriate control parameters are trained by online learning. The improved control core unit has the function of automatic setting of control parameters. This enables the UAV to adapt to the changing flight environment and fly more smoothly. Finally, the improved back propagation neural net PID controller is used to simulate the system model. The research results have a positive role in promoting the development of unmanned aerial vehicle inspection technology for distribution lines.

Keywords: Four Rotor Unmanned Aerial Vehicle · BP Neural net · Proportional Integral Derivative · Control Method

1 Introduction

Four rotor UAV has outstanding advantages such as small size, easy to carry, high quality and low price. In recent years, four rotor unmanned aerial vehicles have attracted more and more attention. Especially in the field of power inspection, unmanned aerial vehicle inspection has gradually replaced manual inspection, forming a new working mode [1, 2]. The performance of the control core unit directly determines the flight state of the four rotor UAV [3]. The control core unit of the four rotor UAV has four input signals, but it controls six outputs. The six outputs of the control core unit include three position

H. Yang et al. (Eds.): SmartGIFT 2022, LNICST 483, pp. 478–486, 2023.
https://doi.org/10.1007/978-3-031-31733-0_41

motion control signals and three attitude angle motion control signals [4]. Therefore, the four rotor UAV has the characteristics of underdrive. At the same time, the mechanical structure of the four rotor UAV is relatively complex. Its control core unit is a nonlinear system. When it controls the attitude angle, it will also affect the position state of the UAV [5]. However, the control accuracy of classical PID control core unit is not high and the response speed is slow. When UAV needs to perform complex work tasks, its control method needs to be further optimized [6]. For example, in the daily inspection work scene of transmission lines, only drones need to fly and take photos at a constant speed along the smooth line channel. Classical PID control core unit can be used to perform such a simple task. However, the working scenario of lean inspection of distribution lines requires that UAVs can shuttle freely in rugged and complex line channels, and that UAVs can quickly avoid obstacles. When performing such complex tasks, it is necessary to improve the control accuracy and response speed of the four rotor UAV control core unit.

This paper studies the performance optimization of the flight control core unit of a four rotor UAV. Back propagation neural net is introduced into the PID control core unit of four rotor UAV. A self-tuning method of UAV flight control parameters is proposed. The improved four rotor UAV control core unit is simulated. The research results have a guiding role in improving the operation ability of UAV and expanding the application field of UAV.

2 Operation Principle of PID Control Core Unit Based on BP Neural Net

BP neural net has three levels from the perspective of structure, namely, input level, output level and hidden level. BP neural net is a network structure of forward feedback error. For a simple control core unit, only one hidden level is usually used. For complex system structures, multiple hidden levels may be used. Each hidden level can have multiple neurons. Figure 1 is the typical levels of BP neural net.

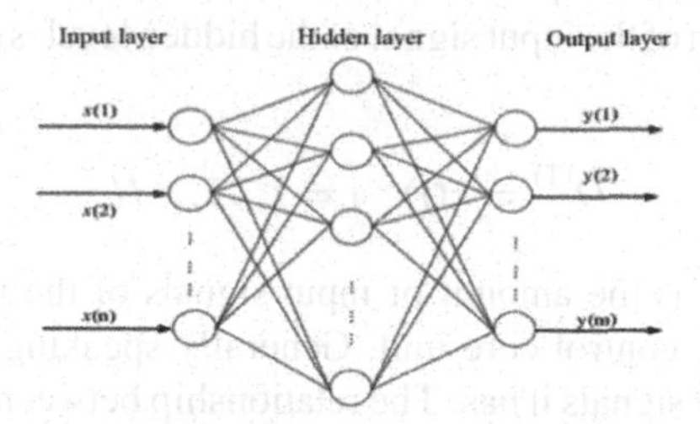

Fig. 1. Typical level of BP neural net

As shown in Fig. 1, the input signal is input through the input level. The signal is multiplied by the corresponding weight as the independent variable of the input activation function. Relevant variables are calculated in the hidden level. The signal enters the output level after being processed by the hidden level. At this time, the signal is multiplied by the corresponding weight as the independent variable of the output activation function. This variable is compared with the desired value. If there is a deviation between the two, the deviation signal of the two is fed back to the lower input level. The weight of each neuron is calculated by gradient descent method. When the deviation does not reach the set range, or the training times do not reach the set range, repeat the above process. By continuously training the above process, the appropriate weights of each neuron can be matched.

The PID control core unit of four rotor UAV is a nonlinear system. If you want to obtain good control effect, you must adjust the appropriate control parameters. Relevant control parameters include proportional constant KP, differential time constant Ki and integral time constant KD. The training method can be optimized by BP neural net to match the three parameters of proportional constant KP, differential time constant Ki and integral time constant KD. The UAV controller optimized by BP neural net is mainly divided into PID control core unit and BP neural net. Figure 2 is BP neural net optimization control core unit.

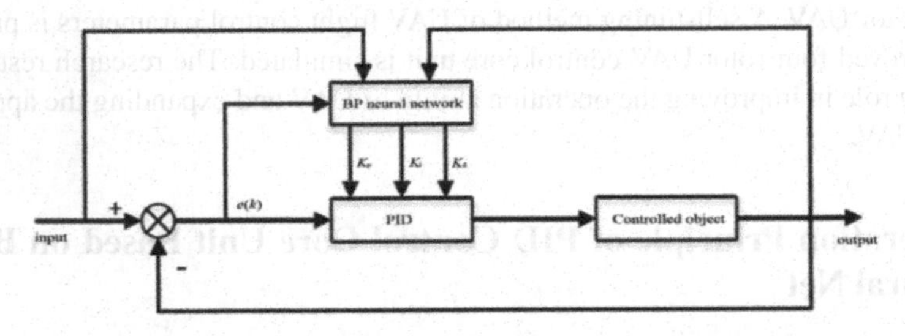

Fig. 2. BP neural net optimization control core unit

BP neural net is a network structure with multi-level forward feedback and error back propagation. The process of reverse calculation of weights between neurons in each level during Back propagation neural net training is as follows.

The output signal of the input level of the control core unit is the input signal. Therefore, the expression of the input signal of the hidden level is described by expression (1).

$$O_{\mathrm{j}}^{(1)} = x(j) \quad j = 1 \ldots\ldots N \tag{1}$$

In expression (1), N is the amount of input signals of the input level. N is related to the complexity of the control core unit. Generally speaking, the more complex the system is, the more input signals it has. The relationship between output signal and input signal of the hidden level is described by expression (2).

$$net_i^{(2)}(k) = \sum_{j=1}^{N} w_{ij}^{(2)} \mathrm{O}_{\mathrm{j}}^{(1)}(\mathrm{k}) \tag{2}$$

$$O_{\mathrm{i}}^{(2)}(k) = f(\mathrm{net}_i^{(2)}(k)) \quad k = 1 \ldots\ldots Q \tag{3}$$

In expression (2) and expression (3), Q is the amount of neurons. The corner mark of the input level is (1). The corner mark of the hidden level is (1). The corner mark of the output level is (3). f (*) is the activation function. Sigmoid activation function can accurately fit any nonlinear function. Therefore, sigmoid function is described by expression (4) in this paper.

$$f(x) = \frac{e^x - e^{-x}}{e^x - e^{-x}} \tag{4}$$

The expression of input signal and output signal of BP neural net output level is described by expression (5).

$$net_i^{(3)}(k) = \sum_{i=1}^{Q} w_{ij}^{(3)} \mathrm{O}_\mathrm{i}^{(1)}(\mathrm{k}) \tag{5}$$

$$o_l^{(3)}(k) = g(net_l^{(3)}(k)), l = 1, 2, 3 \tag{6}$$

In expression (5), The output level designed in this paper consists of three neurons. The output signals of these three neurons correspond to K_p, K_i and K_d respectively. The sigmoid functions of output level are described by expression (7), expression (8), expression (9) and expression (10).

$$g(x) = \frac{1}{1 + e^{-x}} \tag{7}$$

$$o_i^{(3)}(k) = K_\mathrm{p} \tag{8}$$

$$o_2^{(3)}(k) = K_\mathrm{i} \tag{9}$$

$$o_3^{(3)}(k) = K_\mathrm{d} \tag{10}$$

3 UAV Control Algorithm Based on BP Neural Net Optimization

This paper mainly studies the training weight through online training. The loss function expression of BP neural net is described by expression (11).

$$E = \frac{1}{2}[(r - \mathrm{y})(k + 1)]^2 \tag{11}$$

The corresponding weights of each neuron are continuously adjusted by the method of gradient descent. Adjust the weight coefficient according to the direction in which the derivative of the loss function is less than zero. The expression of this process is as follows.

$$\Delta w_{li}^{(3)}(k + 1) = -\eta \frac{\partial E}{\partial w_{li}^{(3)}} \tag{12}$$

In expression (12), η is the rate of learning of the optimization algorithm in this paper. The control parameters of incremental PID can be calculated by chain rule.

$$u(k) = \Delta^2 e(k) + K_P \Delta e(k) + K_i e(k) + u(k-1) \quad (13)$$

Take K_{i}, K_{p} and K_{p} in the above formula as input variables. The expression (13) can be rewritten again.

$$u(k) = f\left[\Delta^2 e(k), \Delta e(k), K_i, K_p, K_d, u(k-1)\right] \quad (14)$$

The main purpose of BP neural net is to find the most suitable mapping relationship between output and input through learning and training. $\partial u(k)/\partial O_l^{(3)}(k)$ in expression (12) can be derived from the above expression.

$$\frac{\partial u(k)}{\partial O_1^{(3)}(k)} = -e(k-1) + e(k) \quad (15)$$

$$\frac{\partial u(k)}{\partial O_2^{(3)}(k)} = e(k) \quad (16)$$

$$\frac{\partial u(k)}{\partial O_3^{(3)}(k)} = e(k-2) - 2e(k-1) + e(k) \quad (17)$$

The weight adjustment expression of the channel between the output level and the hidden level is described by expression (18).

$$\frac{\partial E}{\partial w_{li}^{(3)}} = -\delta_l^{(3)} * O_i^{(2)}(k) \quad (18)$$

Bring expression (18) into expression (12). It can calculate the weight calculation expression from hidden level to output level.

$$\Delta w_{li}^{(3)}(k+1) = \eta \delta_l^{(3)} O_i^{(2)}(k) \quad (19)$$

The weight calculation expression of neurons from the input level to the hidden level is described by expression (20).

$$\begin{cases} \Delta w_{ij}^{(2)}(k+1) = \eta \delta_{\mathrm{i}}^{(2)} O_j^{(1)}(k) \\ \delta_i^{(2)} = f'(net_i^{(2)}(k)) \times \sum_{l=1}^{3} \delta_l^{(3)} w_{li}^{(3)}(k), i = 1, 2, ..., Q \end{cases} \quad (20)$$

Expression (18) and expression (20) are the weight coefficient expressions of each neuron in the optimal control algorithm.

4 Simulation Experiment of UAV Control Core Unit Based on BP Neural Net Optimization

4.1 Proportional Integral Derivative Controller

This paper constructs a Proportional Integral Derivative control core unit model based on BP neural net in Simulink environment. Firstly, the neural net with 3–5–3 structure is written by using S-Function in S-function module. Then the neural net is coupled with PID controller. This neural net can use the real-time feedback information of PID control core unit for online learning and training. By adjusting the weight between the neurons of each level, three appropriate PID control parameters can be matched. Figure 3 shows the logic structure of the optimized control core unit. Figure 4 shows the internal structure of S-function module input.

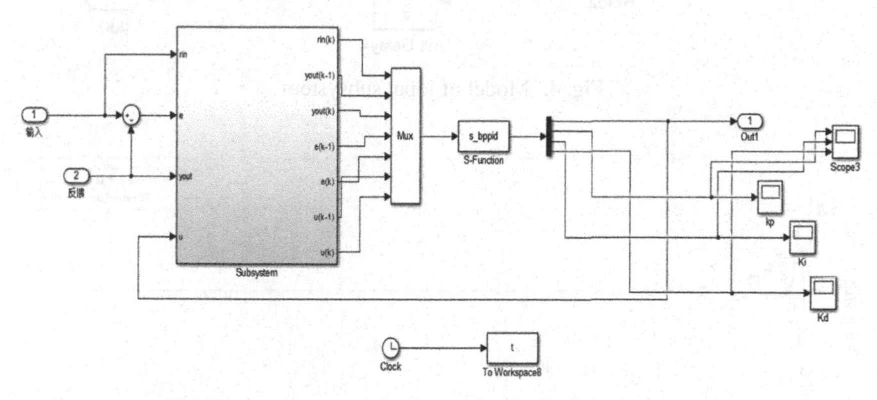

Fig. 3. Logic structure of the optimized control core unit

4.2 Simulation Analysis

The flight attitude is the most important control object. The four axis vehicle model is decoupled. The simulation of each attitude angle is carried out in Simulink. Figure 8 shows the changes of three control parameters of the PID control core unit when selecting the pitch angle control simulation (Fig. 5 , Fig. 6, Fig. 7).

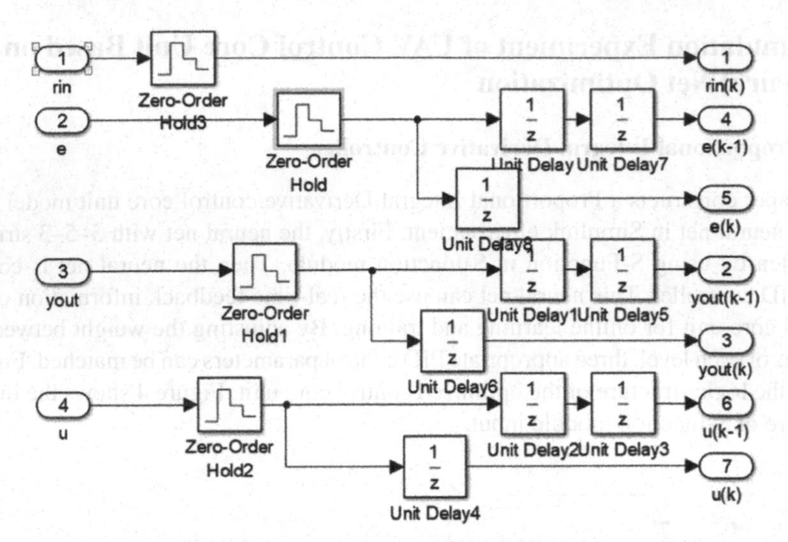

Fig. 4. Model of input subsystem

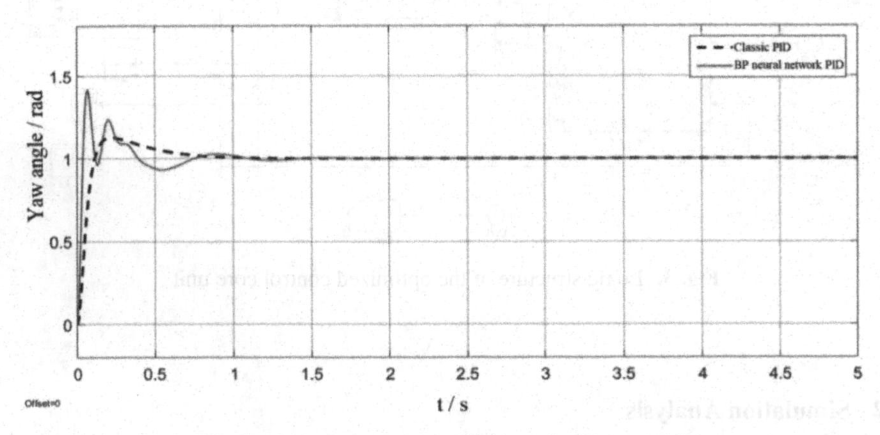

Fig. 5. Calculation and analysis result of yaw angle

The simulation results show that the optimization control method proposed in this research has good control effect on three attitude angles. The response speed and stability of the new method are obviously superior to the traditional PID control method. On the other hand, the three attitude angles fluctuated violently within one second of starting the control process. This is mainly because the neural net is constantly on-line training and learning, changing PID control parameters, resulting in the curve is not smooth.

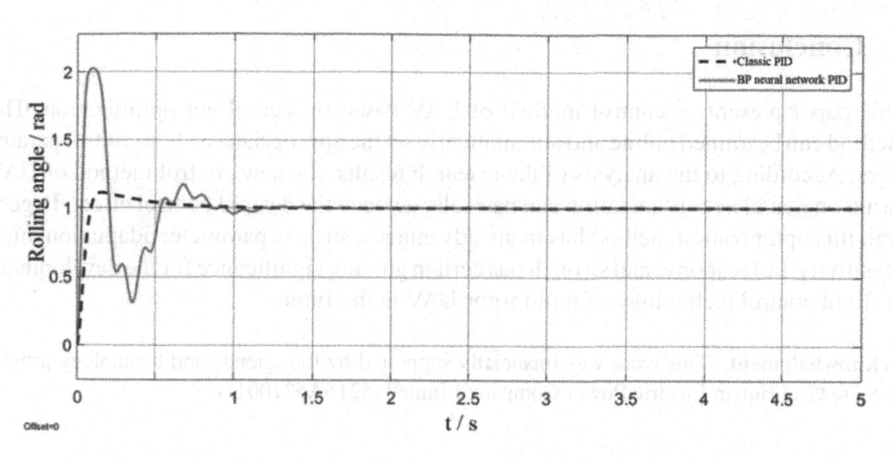

Fig. 6. Calculation and analysis result of rolling angle

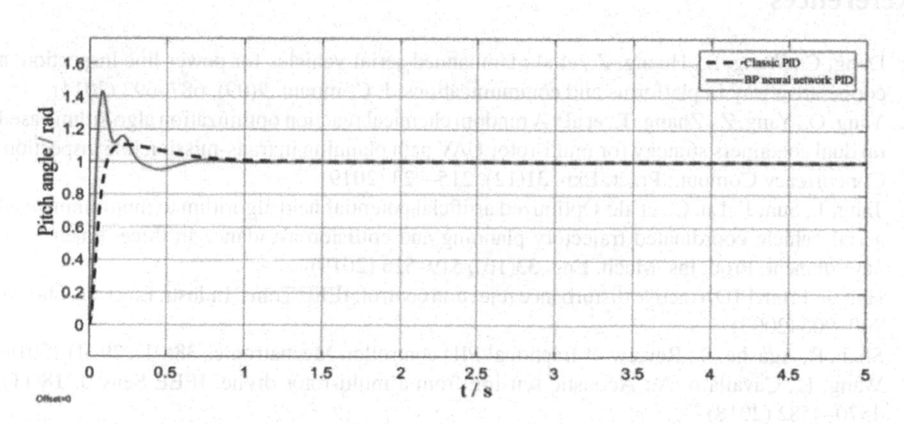

Fig. 7. Calculation and analysis result of pitch angle

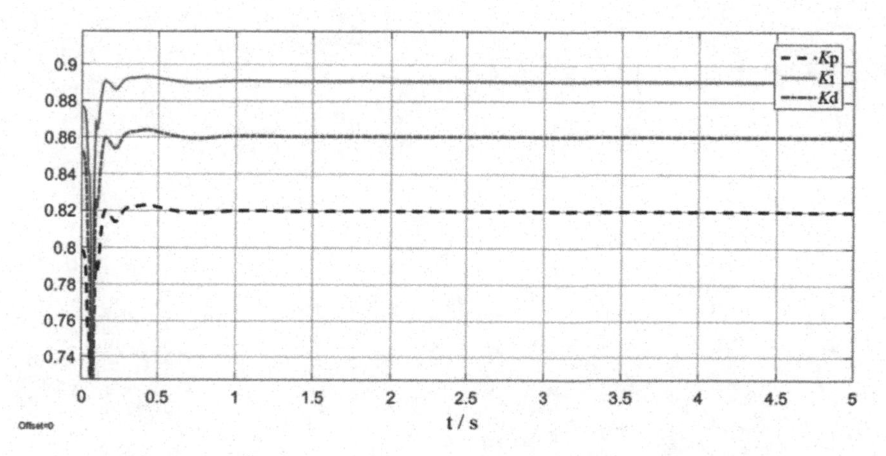

Fig. 8. Calculation and analysis result of three PID control parameters

5 Conclusion

This paper presents a control method of UAV based on neural net optimization. The method can be trained online and automatically set the appropriate system control parameters. According to the analysis of the research results, the new control method of UAV based on neural net optimization can basically achieve the desired control effect. In general, this optimization method has many advantages, such as parameter adaptation, high sensitivity, fast response and so on. It has certain guiding significance for the development of flight control technology of multi rotor UAV in the future.

Acknowledgment. This work was financially supported by the science and technology project of State Grid Hunan Electric Power Company Limited (5216A521001J).

References

1. Deng, C., Wang, S., Huang, Z., et al.: Unmanned aerial vehicles for power line inspection: a cooperative way in platforms and communications. J. Commun. **9**(09), 687–692 (2014)
2. Yang, Q., Yang, Z., Zhang, T., et al.: A random chemical reaction optimization algo-rithm based on dual containers strategy for multi-rotor UAV path planning in trans-mission line inspection. Concurrency Comput.: Pract. Exp. **31**(12), 215–223 (2019)
3. Tang, J., Sun, J., Lu, C., et al.: Optimized artificial potential field algorithm to multi-unmanned aerial vehicle coordinated trajectory planning and collision avoidance in three-dimensional environment. Proc. Ins. Mech. Eng. **33**(16), 519–526 (2019)
4. Han, J.: From PID to active disturbance rejection control. IEEE Trans. Industr. Electron. **56**(03), 900–906 (2009)
5. Shah, P., Agashe, S.: Review of fractional PID controller. Mechatronics **38**(01), 29–41 (2016)
6. Wang, L., Cavallaro, A.: Acoustic sensing from a multi-rotor drone. IEEE Sens. J. **18**(11), 4570–4582 (2018)

Dynamic Modeling and Simulation Analysis of Four Rotor UAV

Miao Zhao[1], Dai Wan[1(✉)], Simin Peng[1], Xujin Duan[1], WenHui Mo[1], and Jiang Han[2]

[1] State Grid Hunan Electric Power Company Limited Research Institute, Changsha 410007, China

280241509@qq.com

[2] State Grid Changde Power Supply Company, Changde 415000, China

Abstract. With the development of unmanned aerial vehicle (UAV) technology, its application field is more and more extensive. At present, UAV inspection has become an indispensable part of the production and operation of distribution network. Most of the UAVs used in the field of distribution line inspection are four rotor UAVs. Because the control system of the four rotor UAV has the characteristics of underdrive, it is difficult to control it accurately. In view of the above problems, this paper has carried out the research on Dynamic Modeling and simulation analysis of four rotor UAV. The working mechanism of four rotor UAV is analyzed. The dynamic model of four rotor UAV is constructed. Taking the cascade proportion integration differentiation (PID) control method as an example, the control system framework of four rotor UAV is established. The relationship between the position and attitude of UAV in the process of motion is analyzed in depth. The attitude control sub module and position control sub module of UAV are designed. The simulation model of four rotor UAV control system is built. The simulation results show that the four rotor UAV has high requirements for the setting rate and accuracy of control parameters. The traditional PID control scheme is suitable for low-speed UAV. However, for the high-speed UAV, the control method needs to be further optimized. The research results of this paper have certain guiding significance for the research of four rotor UAV control system.

Keywords: Four Rotor Unmanned Aerial Vehicle · Dynamics · Modeling · Simulation

1 Introduction

UAV technology has been developed for more than 80 years. It involves many cutting-edge technology fields such as aviation, electronics, power, flight control, communication, image recognition and so on [1]. In recent years, the emergence of multi rotor UAV has further reduced the manufacturing cost of UAV and greatly improved the economy of related products. The most common multi rotor UAV is the four rotor UAV. Four rotors have outstanding advantages of light weight, small size and low cost. Therefore, the four rotor UAV has become a research hotspot in the field of UAV and has received more

H. Yang et al. (Eds.): SmartGIFT 2022, LNICST 483, pp. 487–501, 2023.
https://doi.org/10.1007/978-3-031-31733-0_42

and more attention [2]. By carrying visible light, infrared detection and other equipment, the four rotor UAV can carry out efficient, non-contact and all-round inspection of power equipment. Therefore, UAV has been widely used in the field of distribution line inspection [3, 4].

The control system is the most important module in the four rotor UAV. The performance of the control system directly determines the flight state of the four rotor UAV [5]. However, the mechanical structure of the four rotor UAV is relatively complex. Its control system is a nonlinear system. When it controls the attitude angle, it will also affect the position state of the UAV. In addition, the control system of the four rotor UAV has four input signals, but controls six outputs. The six outputs of the control system include three position motion control signals and three attitude angle motion control signals [6]. Therefore, the four rotor UAV also has the characteristics of underdrive. The above problems make the research of UAV control system more difficult. Therefore, in-depth analysis and Research on the dynamic characteristics of UAV in the process of motion is the basis of optimizing the UAV control system and improving its control ability.

This paper focuses on the small four rotor UAV. The relationship between position subsystem and attitude subsystem is deeply analyzed. Then the dynamic model of four rotor UAV is constructed by Newton Euler method. Finally, the position sub module and attitude sub module of the UAV control system are designed respectively, and the simulation experiments are carried out on the matlab/simulink platform. Relevant research has laid a foundation for the research of the control system of four rotor UAV.

2 Control Principle of Four Rotor UAV

At present, there are mainly two kinds of attitude control schemes for small or micro four rotor UAV in the market, namely "X" control scheme and cross control scheme. The two control schemes are distinguished by the UAV itself. The "X" control scheme takes the forward direction of the UAV as the X axis. Determine the motion coordinate system according to the right-hand rule. Put the connecting lines of the two rotors of the UAV on the x-axis, and the connecting lines of the remaining two rotors will be plumb on the -x-axis at the same time. The cross control scheme takes the two connecting rods of the UAV used to connect the rotor as the coordinate axis. One of them is the x-axis and the other is the y-axis.

Although there are two flight postures of the four rotor UAV, both of them control the forward and overturn of the UAV by adjusting the speed of the four motors, which affects the direction of the UAV's lift force.

This paper uses the "X" structure to explain the specific control mode.

(1) Vertical motion

The speed change of the four rotors of the four rotor aircraft will change the lift. As long as the lift of the four rotors is increased or reduced synchronously, the height of the UAV can be changed.

Pitching motion (fore-and-aft motion): increase the rotation speed of the two motors M1 and M2 at the same time, and decrease the rotation speed of the two motors M3 and M4 at the same time. In this way, the lifting force on the body becomes backward and upward, and the body will fly backward under the action of gravity, and the same is true for flying forward.

(2) Rolling motion (left and right rolling motion)
In order to make the lift force direction of the body incline to the upper right, it is only necessary to increase the rotation speed of two motors M1 and M3 at the same time, and reduce the motors of the other two motors at the same time, so that the attitude flight of the UAV can fly to the right. Fly to the left in the same way, just adjust the rotation speed adjustment sequence of the four motors.

(3) Yaw motion (left and right turn in place)
The need for the UAV to turn in place is that the two motors on the diagonal increase the speed at the same time, and the other two motors slow down. This operation can make our body turn in place.

The value ranges of pitch angle, roll angle and yaw angle of three angles are specified here.

(1) Pitch angle
Take the body motion coordinate system as the benchmark, take the forward direction of the body as the nose, and if the nose is raised, it is regarded as a positive angle. The rest are negative values.

(2) Roll angle
The UAV body rolls to the right as a positive value. The rest are negative values.

(3) Yaw angle
The UAV body yaw to the right is positive. The rest are negative values.

3 Dynamic Modeling of Four Rotor UAV

To model a small four rotor UAV, the position information of the body needs to be obtained through the transformation between coordinate systems. In order to accurately and completely describe the motion attitude of small four rotor UAV, it is necessary to establish a reasonable UAV dynamic model. This model can lay a good foundation for the later motion attitude control of UAV

(1) Ground coordinate system
The most important parameters in the ground coordinate system are the three coordinate axes of origin *O* and *XYZ*. You can choose any point in earth space as the origin *O*. With the origin *O* as the starting point, any direction can be specified as the *X* axis. The *Y* axis is perpendicular to the *X* axis. The direction of *Z* axis and its relationship with *X* axis and *Y* axis can be determined by the right-hand rule. The origin *O* coincides with the starting points of the three coordinate axes *XYZ* (Fig. 1).

(2) Body coordinate system
The body coordinate system (*oxzy* coordinate system) also conforms to the right-hand rule. The origin *o* of the coordinate system is at the centroid of the rigid body

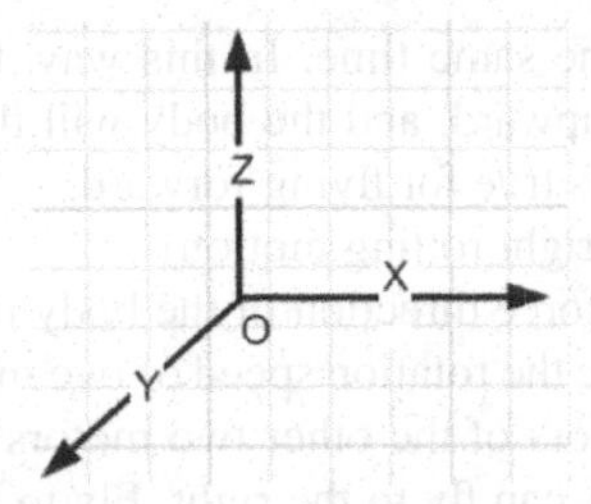

Fig. 1. Ground coordinate system

of the UAV. The *x*-axis is in the same horizontal plane as the rigid body of the UAV. The *x*-axis is located on the symmetry axis of the UAV and points to the forward direction of the body. The *y*-axis is perpendicular to the *x*-axis and is located in the same horizontal plane as the rigid body of the UAV. The *z*-axis is perpendicular to the *oxy* plane and in the upward direction. The origin o coincides with the starting points of the three coordinate axes *xyz* (Fig. 2).

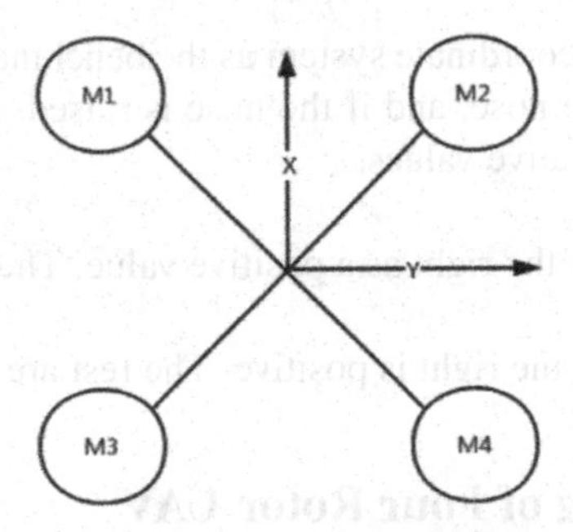

Fig. 2. Body coordinate system

(3) Coordinate conversion
After specifying the ground coordinate system and the body coordinate system, it is necessary to convert the body coordinate and the ground coordinate. If you want to convert, you can specify three Euler angles to represent the converted coordinates. The specified pitch angle is θ. Roll angle is Φ. Yaw angle is ψ.

It is assumed that the following relationship exists between the ground coordinate and the body coordinate system.

$$\begin{bmatrix} X \\ Y \\ Z \end{bmatrix} = R_B \begin{bmatrix} x \\ y \\ z \end{bmatrix} \tag{1}$$

The specific form of rotation matrix is as follows.

$$R_1 = \begin{bmatrix} \cos\theta\cos\psi & \sin\phi\sin\theta\cos\psi - \sin\phi\cos\psi & \cos\phi\sin\theta\cos\psi + \sin\phi\sin\psi \\ \cos\theta\sin\psi & \sin\phi\sin\theta\sin\psi + \cos\phi\cos\psi & \cos\phi\sin\theta\sin\psi - \cos\phi\sin\psi \\ -\sin\theta & \sin\phi\cos\theta & \cos\phi\cos\theta \end{bmatrix} \tag{2}$$

The expression of UAV attitude control quantity is as follows.

$$\begin{bmatrix} U_1 = b(\Omega_1^2 + \Omega_2^2 + \Omega_3^2 + \Omega_4^2) \\ U_2 = lb(\Omega_4^2 - \Omega_2^2) \\ U_3 = lb(\Omega_3^2 - \Omega_1^2) \\ U_4 = d(\Omega_2^2 + \Omega_4^2 - \Omega_1^2 - \Omega_3^2) \end{bmatrix} \tag{3}$$

where, U_1 is the total lift of the four rotors. U_2 is the rolling torque of UAV. U_3 is the pitching moment of UAV. U_4 is the yaw moment of the UAV. When the micro four rotor UAV moves at low speed, it can be assumed that the structure of the four axis UAV is completely symmetrical, and the influence of air resistance is ignored.

After obtaining the expression of lift, the displacement equation can be obtained by Newton's second law.

$$\begin{aligned} \ddot{x} &= (\cos\phi\sin\theta\cos\psi + \sin\phi\sin\psi)U_1/m \\ \ddot{y} &= (\cos\phi\sin\theta\sin\psi - \cos\phi\sin\psi)U_1/m \\ \ddot{z} &= (\cos\phi\cos\theta)U_1/m - g \end{aligned} \tag{4}$$

Because the four rotor UAV model is based on dynamic coordinates. According to Euler equation, the following expression can be obtained.

$$M = I\dot{A} + A \times (IA) \tag{5}$$

where, M is the moment. I is the moment of inertia. $\dot{A}$ AB is angular acceleration. A is the angular velocity.

The expression of moment of inertia is as follows.

$$I = \begin{bmatrix} I_X & & \\ & I_Y & \\ & & I_Z \end{bmatrix} \tag{6}$$

Using Newton Euler equation, the angular velocities of three coordinate axes can be derived.

$$\begin{bmatrix} p \\ q \\ r \end{bmatrix} = \begin{bmatrix} \dot{\phi} - \dot{\psi}\sin\theta \\ \dot{\theta}\cos\phi + \dot{\psi}\sin\phi\cos\theta \\ -\dot{\theta}\sin\phi + \dot{\psi}\cos\phi\cos\theta \end{bmatrix} \tag{7}$$

When the four rotor UAV moves in a small range, the attitude angular displacement is very small.

$$\begin{cases} \sin\theta \approx \sin\phi \approx \sin\psi \approx 0 \\ \cos\phi \approx \cos\theta \approx \cos\psi \approx 1 \end{cases} \tag{8}$$

Further, the following expression can be obtained.

$$\begin{bmatrix} p \\ q \\ r \end{bmatrix} = \begin{bmatrix} \dot{\phi} \\ \dot{\theta} \\ \dot{\psi} \end{bmatrix} \tag{9}$$

Therefore, the UAV dynamic model is defined as follows.

$$\begin{aligned} \ddot{x} &= (\cos\phi \sin\theta \cos\psi + \sin\phi \sin\psi)U_1/m \\ \ddot{y} &= (\cos\phi \sin\theta \sin\psi - \cos\phi \sin\psi)U_1/m \\ \ddot{z} &= (\cos\phi \cos\theta)U_1/m - g \\ \ddot{\phi} &= \frac{(I_Y - I_Z)}{I_X}\dot{\theta}\dot{\psi} + \frac{U_2}{I_X} \\ \ddot{\theta} &= \frac{(I_Z - I_X)}{I_Y}\dot{\phi}\dot{\psi} + \frac{U_3}{I_Y} \\ \ddot{\psi} &= \frac{(I_X - I_Y)}{I_Z}\dot{\theta}\dot{\phi} + \frac{U_4}{I_Z} \end{aligned} \tag{10}$$

4 PID Control Method of UAV

According to the four rotor UAV dynamic model constructed above, it can be determined that there are four inputs and six outputs of UAV. The four inputs are the speed of the four motors respectively. The six outputs are the three-dimensional actual coordinates and three attitude angles of the UAV. Therefore, the four rotor UAV is a complex nonlinear system. The traditional single loop proportion integration differentiation (PID) control scheme can not meet the dynamic response requirements of the UAV system. Using single loop PID will cause problems such as slow response and unstable operation of UAV. To solve this problem, this paper adopts cascade PID control method.

4.1 PID Controller

PID control scheme refers to subtracting the actual output from the expected input to obtain the error value. The error value is obtained by linear superposition of three links. So as to eliminate systematic errors. The traditional PID controller generally includes three main links: proportion, integral and differential. At present, PID control scheme or derivative control scheme of traditional PID controller is still mainly used in engineering. Because PID controller has the characteristics of easy realization, low cost and simple structure, PID control technology is widely used. In addition, PID controller has good compatibility, which can expand the application field of PID control method by integrating relevant cutting-edge technologies. Figure 3 is the schematic diagram of PID controller.

In the figure, K_p is the proportion link. K_i is the integral coefficient. $1/S$ is the integral link. K_d is the differential coefficient. S is the differential link.

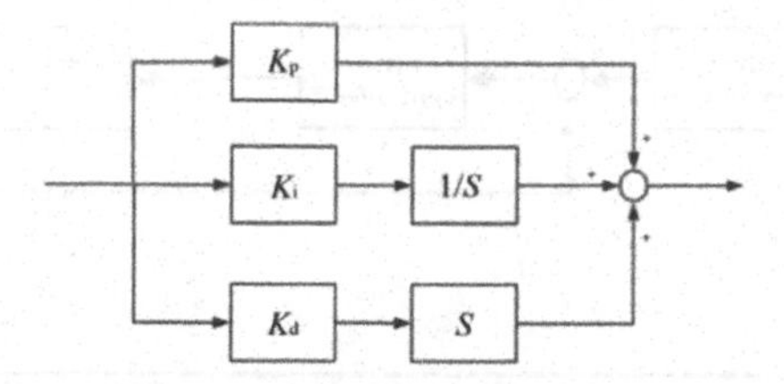

Fig. 3. Schematic diagram of PID controller

When the input is error *e* (*t*), the expression of PID controller can be derived.

$$u(t) = k_p e(t) + k_i \int e(t)dt + k_d \frac{d}{dt} e(t) \tag{11}$$

PID can achieve different control effects according to the change of three coefficients. The proportional link can change the speed of system response. However, too large scale coefficient may lead to system imbalance. Too small proportion coefficient will lead to slow adjustment speed of the system and affect the response speed. Therefore, selecting the appropriate proportion link can make the system run stably and quickly.

The integration link is mainly used to adjust the system error. Proper integral effect can eliminate the static error of the system and improve the control effect of the system. The integration link is the accumulation of past state errors. Excessive integral adjustment may lead to integral saturation effect in the system. The integral saturation effect will cause serious overshoot of a system, which will greatly affect the stability of the system.

The differential link has certain prediction function. The differential link can reflect the change rate of the current error signal and predict the future change trend. The differential link can make the controller produce advanced control effect, so that the system can quickly reduce overshoot. In addition, the differential link can also indirectly improve the lag caused by the integral link. However, excessive differential action will make the system adjustment time longer and the system response slower. The most important thing is that it will seriously affect the anti-interference ability of the system.

There are many ways to adjust the three parameters. Generally, the parameter value of PID controller is set through the test data in engineering. In addition, the control parameters can also be adjusted according to the trial and error method and the critical proportional band method. As long as the appropriate control parameters can be set, a good control effect can be achieved through the PID controller.

4.2 Cascade PID Controller Principle

Cascade PID control method is an effective means to improve control quality. Unlike single loop PID, cascade PID adopts two controllers to form the control system. The output of the outer loop control loop is the input of the inner loop control loop. The output of the inner loop control loop controls the actuator. This method can make the control effect of the system better. Figure 4 is the schematic diagram of cascade PID control.

According to the cascade PID control principle, the cascade PID control method of four rotor UAV can be obtained. Take the position signal as the control object of the main

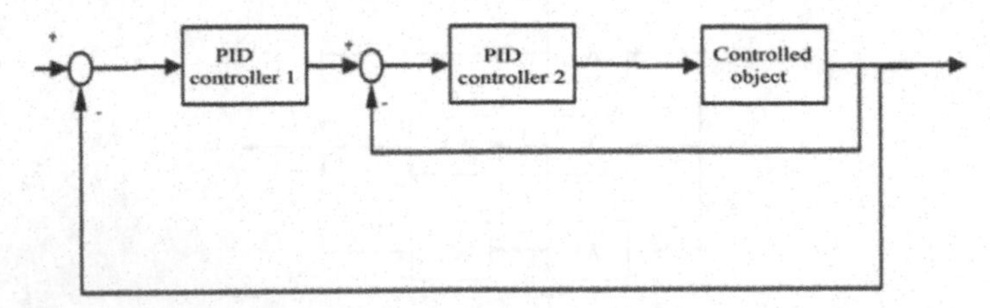

Fig. 4. Cascade PID control schematic diagram

circuit of the control system. The angle signal is the control object of the secondary loop of the control system. The output value of the position signal between the two is the input value of the attitude signal.

The four rotor UAV is a front drive system. It cannot track the six degrees of freedom of the system at the same time. Therefore, three attitude angles and an altitude value of the system can be used as control quantities. These four control quantities can be converted into the rotational speed of four rotor motors through calculation. The rotational speed of the four rotor motors is the input of the controlled object of the system. Therefore, the coordinates [x, y, z] and yaw angle of the UAV trajectory can be controlled ψ To control the attitude of UAV. Figure 5 is the flight control schematic diagram of a small four rotor UAV.

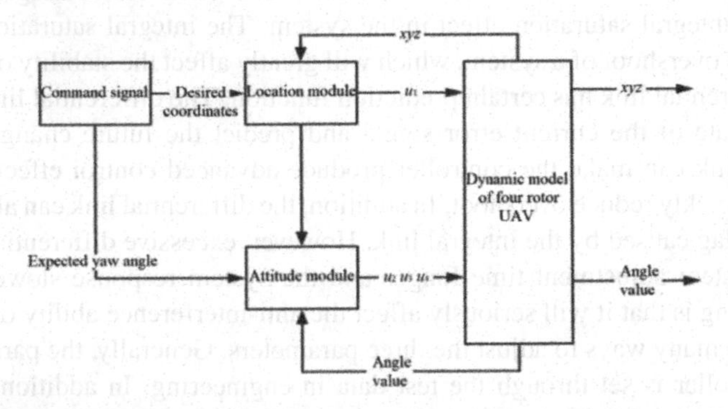

Fig. 5. Flight control schematic diagram of small four rotor UAV

As shown in the figure, the flight control system of the small four rotor UAV consists of two parts. One part is the outer loop control loop used to control the position parameters. The input of the outer loop control loop is the desired position signals x_d, y_d and z_d. Calculate the difference between these three signals and the actual position signal *xyz* fed back by the system. The difference generates intermediate variables through the position subsystem φ_d. Another part of the system is the inner loop control loop for attitude control. The control parameters of the attitude controller are θ_d and U_1. The input of the inner loop control loop is the intermediate variable generated by the position subsystem φ_d, θ_d and yaw angle ψ. Calculate the difference between these three angles and the actual angle signal fed back by the system. Then the calculation results are transmitted to U_2, U_3 and U_4 of the attitude subsystem. By taking U_1, U_2, U_3, U_4

and other relevant parameters into the UAV dynamic model, the actual coordinate value and attitude angle of the UAV can be calculated.

4.3 UAV Attitude Control Sub Module

To make the attitude angle at $t \to \infty$, the angle error is 0. It is suitable to use PID control law to design attitude angle control.

set up φ_e, θ_e and ψ_e are the errors of three attitude angles respectively. φ, θ and ψ are the current angles of the UAV.

$$\begin{cases} \phi_e = \phi_d - \phi \\ \theta_e = \theta_d - \theta \\ \psi_e = \psi_d - \psi \end{cases} \tag{12}$$

The attitude control law of roll angle is as follows.

$$\ddot{\phi} = k_p\phi_e + k_i \int \phi_e dt + k_d \frac{d}{dt}\phi_e \tag{13}$$

The pitch angle control law is as follows.

$$\ddot{\theta} = k_p\theta_e + k_i \int \theta_e dt + k_d \frac{d}{dt}\theta_e \tag{14}$$

The yaw angle control law is as follows.

$$\ddot{\psi} = k_p\psi_e + k_i \int \psi_e dt + k_d \frac{d}{dt}\psi_e \tag{15}$$

It can be derived from the dynamic model.

$$\begin{cases} \ddot{\phi} = \dfrac{(I_Y - I_Z)}{I_X}\dot{\theta}\dot{\psi} + \dfrac{U_2}{I_X} \\ \ddot{\theta} = \dfrac{(I_Z - I_X)}{I_Y}\dot{\phi}\dot{\psi} + \dfrac{U_3}{I_Y} \\ \ddot{\psi} = \dfrac{(I_X - I_Y)}{I_Z}\dot{\theta}\dot{\phi} + \dfrac{U_4}{I_Z} \end{cases} \tag{16}$$

The calculation expression of the moment is as follows.

$$M = I \times \ddot{A} \tag{17}$$

where, M is the moment. I is the moment of inertia. $\ddot{A}$ is angular acceleration.

$$\ddot{\phi} = U_2/I_X$$
$$\ddot{\theta} = U_3/I_Y$$

$$\ddot{\psi} = U_4/I_Z \tag{18}$$

The control law of the attitude control sub module is as follows.

$$\begin{aligned}
\ddot{\phi} &= k_p\phi_e + k_i\int \phi_e dt + k_d\frac{d}{dt}\phi_e \\
\ddot{\theta} &= k_p\theta_e + k_i\int \theta_e dt + k_d\frac{d}{dt}\theta_e \\
\ddot{\psi} &= k_p\psi_e + k_i\int \psi_e dt + k_d\frac{d}{dt}\psi_e \\
U_2 &= \ddot{\phi} \times I_X \\
U_3 &= \ddot{\theta} \times I_Y \\
U_4 &= \ddot{\psi} \times I_Z
\end{aligned} \tag{19}$$

4.4 UAV Position Control Sub Module

In order to make the position error tend to 0 at $t \to \infty$, it is necessary to use PID control law for the position module. *Xyz* are the current coordinate values. x_d, y_d and z_d are the expected coordinate values entered. x_e, y_e and z_e are three error values.

$$\begin{aligned}
x_e &= x_d - x \\
y_e &= y_d - y \\
z_e &= z_d - z
\end{aligned} \tag{20}$$

It is assumed that the three virtual control quantities u_x, u_y and u_z represent the following meanings respectively.

$$\begin{aligned}
u_x &= k_{p1}x_e + k_{i1}\int x_e dt + k_{d1}\frac{d}{dt}x_e \\
u_y &= k_{p1}y_e + k_{i1}\int y_e dt + k_{d1}\frac{d}{dt}y_e \\
u_z &= k_{p1}z_e + k_{i1}\int z_e dt + k_{d1}\frac{d}{dt}z_e
\end{aligned} \tag{21}$$

Then the position control law can be obtained according to the dynamic model.

$$\begin{cases}
T = m\sqrt{(u_x^2 + u_y^2 + (u_z + g)^2)} \\
\phi_d = ac\sin((\sin\psi_d u_x - \cos\psi_d u_y)m/T) \\
\theta_d = ac\sin((u_x m - T\sin\psi_d \sin\phi_d)/(T\cos\psi_d\cos\phi_d))
\end{cases} \tag{22}$$

There is an anti sinusoidal trigonometric function in this expression. Define it again. $AC = (\sin\psi_d u_x - \cos\psi_d u_y)m/T$. $AB = (u_x\, m - T\sin\psi_d \sin\varphi_d)/(T\cos\psi_d\cos\varphi_d)$.

When the value of *AC* and *AB* are greater than 1, the expression (22) will not have a solution. Therefore, when *AC* and *AB* are greater than 1, $\varphi_d = \pi/3$, $\theta_d = \pi/3$. When the absolute value of *AC* and *AB* are not greater than 1, set $\varphi_d = \text{acsin}(AC)$, $\theta_d = \text{acsin}(\boldsymbol{AB})$. When the value of *AC* and *AB* are less than 1, set $\varphi_d = \theta_d = -\pi/3$.

5 Design of UAV Flight Control System

After obtaining the control laws of the position sub module and the attitude sub module, the UAV control system can be simulated according to these equations. The simulation of flight control system of four rotor UAV is mainly realized by matlab simulink. The design idea of four rotor unmanned flight control system mainly includes six processes. The first step is to enter the desired coordinate value. The second step is to compare the coordinate value calculated by the system with the current actual coordinate value of the UAV, and generate an error value through operation. The third step is to transmit the generated error value to the position controller. A virtual control quantity will be generated, together with the pitch angle and roll angle calculated by the system. The fourth step is to compare the pitch angle and roll angle calculated by the system with the current actual angle of the UAV, and generate an error signal through calculation. The fifth step is to transmit the error signal to the attitude control module and generate three virtual control quantities U2, U3 and U4. The sixth step is to transmit the above virtual control quantity to the UAV dynamic model module, and generate six outputs through operation. The six outputs are three coordinate values and three angle values respectively. Then the six outputs are fed back to the control system. Repeat the above operation steps until the output value of the control system is consistent with the set expected value.

The MATLAB Simulink simulation diagram of UAV flight control system built in this paper is shown in Fig. 6.

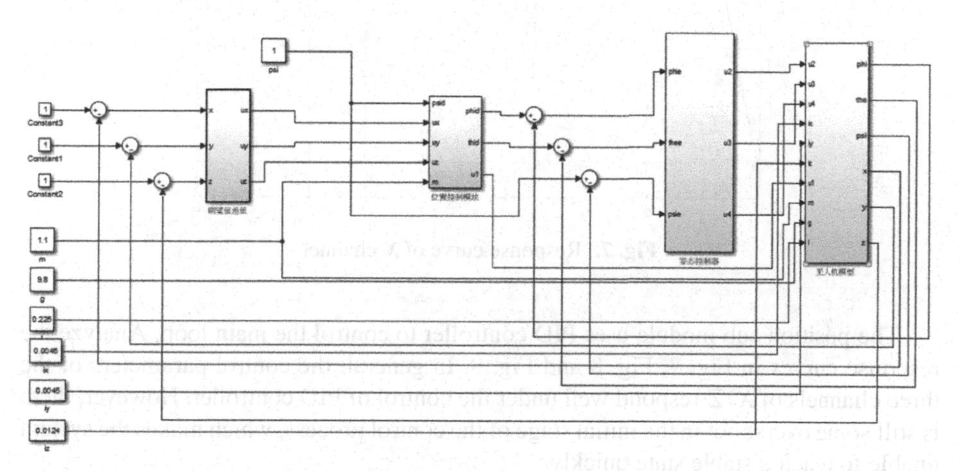

Fig. 6. Simulation diagram of UAV flight control system

6 Simulation Analysis

According to the simulation system shown in Fig. 6, the flight control system of UAV built with cascade PID controller is simulated. Before the simulation test, the parameters in the UAV flight control system are assigned (Table 1).

Table 1. Parameters of four rotor UAV

Parameters	value
K	0.75
L/m	0.225
m/kg	1.1
I_x/(kg•m^2)	0.0045
I_y/(kg•m^2)	0.0045
I_z/(kg•m^2)	0.0045
g/(m•s^{-2})	

Assume that the expected coordinate value of the system is (4, 4, 4). Set the yaw angle to 1. The simulation results are shown in the figure below.

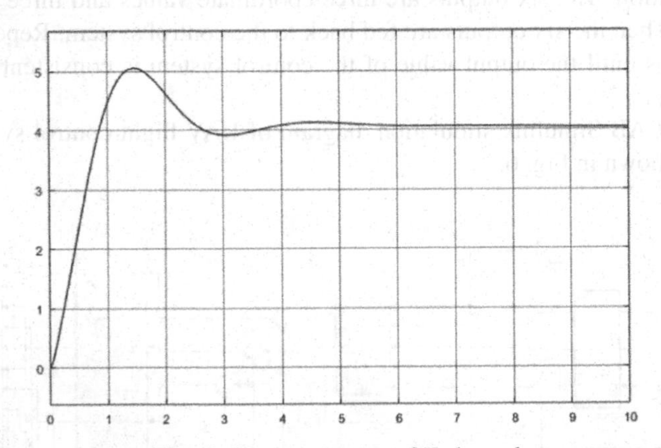

Fig. 7. Response curve of *X* channel

The position sub module uses PID controller to control the main loop. Analyze the response curves in Fig. 7, Fig. 8 and Fig. 9. In general, the control parameters of the three channels of *XYZ* respond well under the control of PID controller. However, there is still some overshoot in the initial stage of the control process, which makes the system unable to reach a stable state quickly.

Analyze the response curves in Figs. 10 and 11. In the initial stage, the roll angle and pitch angle will change rapidly. The final roll angle and pitch angle approach 0. When unmanned flight reaches the desired position, there will be no error value. The input of the final position controller is 0. The following roll angle and pitch angle will also make the error equal to 0 under the control of the controller. Thereafter, the control quantity transmitted to the control system model is also 0. The production angle calculated by the model also becomes 0. In this way, all the operation processes of the control system are basically completed (Fig. 12).

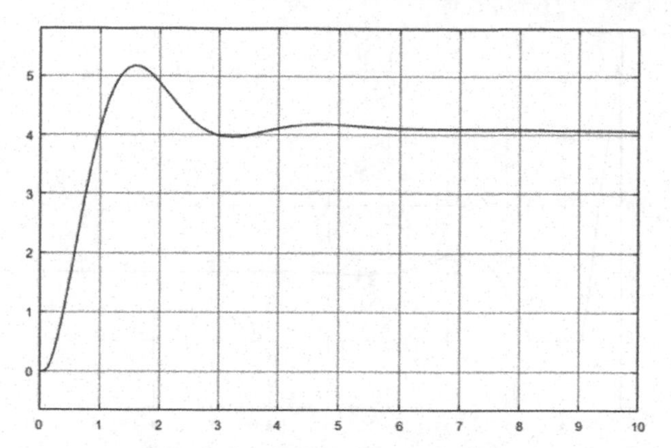

Fig. 8. Response curve of *Y* channel

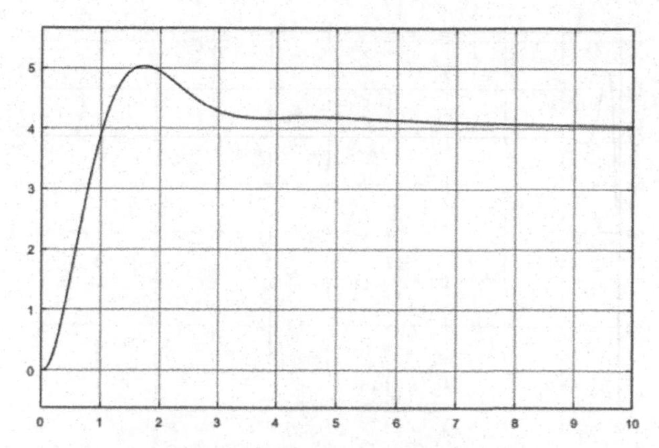

Fig. 9. Response curve of *Z* channel

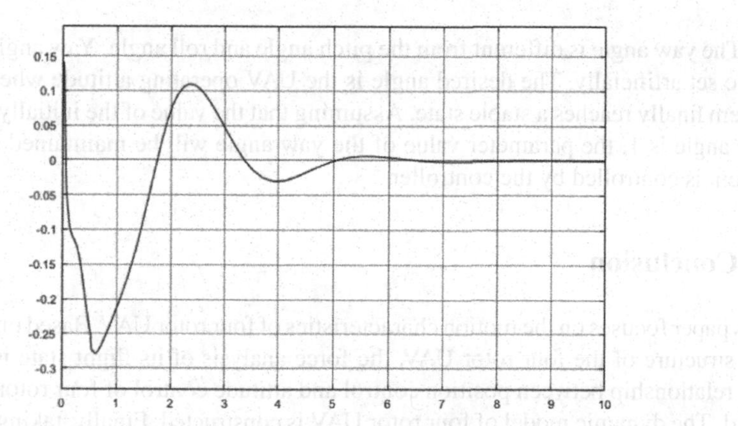

Fig. 10. Response curve of rolling angle

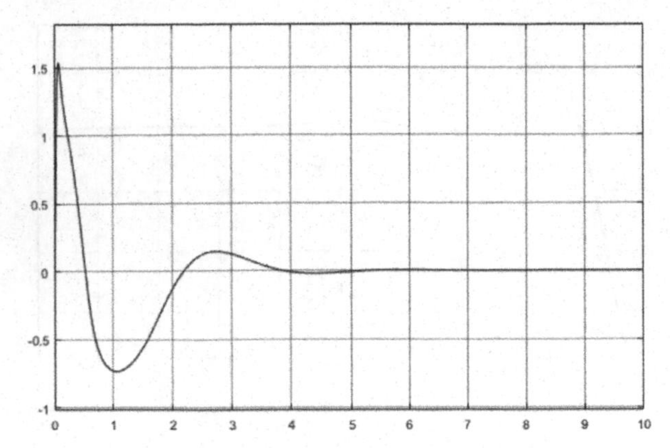

Fig. 11. Response curve of rolling angle

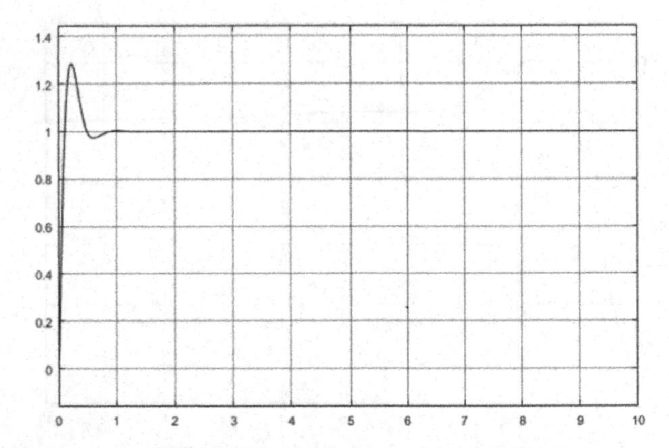

Fig. 12. Response curve of yaw angle

The yaw angle is different from the pitch angle and roll angle. Yaw angle is a desired angle set artificially. The desired angle is the UAV operating attitude when the control system finally reaches a stable state. Assuming that the value of the initially set expected yaw angle is 1, the parameter value of the yaw angle will be maintained at 1 after the system is controlled by the controller.

7 Conclusion

This paper focuses on the motion characteristics of four rotor UAV. Based on the mechanical structure of the four rotor UAV, the force analysis of its flight state is carried out. The relationship between position control and attitude control of four rotor UAV is analyzed. The dynamic model of four rotor UAV is constructed. Finally, taking the classical cascade PID control method as an example, the simulation experiment is carried out by using matlab/simulink platform. The simulation results show that the traditional PID control method can well control the four rotor UAV in low-speed operation. However, it is still difficult to control the underactuated system of the four rotor UAV in high-speed flight. We need to find a more advanced control method to achieve precise control of the four rotor UAV flying at high speed.

Acknowledgment. This work was financially supported by the science and technology project of State Grid Hunan Electric Power Company Limited (5216A521001J).

References

1. Rau, J.Y., Hsiao, K.W., Jhan, J.P., et al.: Bridge crack detection using multi-rotary UAV and object-base image analysis. Int. Arch. Photogr. Remote Sens. Spat. Inf. Sci. **42**(01), 311 (2017)
2. Deng, C., Wang, S., Huang, Z., et al.: Unmanned aerial vehicles for power line inspection: a cooperative way in platforms and communications. J. Commun. **9**(09), 687–692 (2014)
3. Liu, C., Liu, Y., Wu, H., et al.: A safe flight approach of the UAV in the electrical line inspection. Int. J. Emerg. Electr. Power Syst. **16**(05), 503–515 (2015)
4. Yang, Q., Yang, Z., Zhang, T., et al.: A random chemical reaction optimization algorithm based on dual containers strategy for multi-rotor UAV path planning in transmission line inspection. Concurr. Comput.: Pract. Exp. **31**(12), 215–223 (2019)
5. Tang, J., Sun, J., Lu, C., et al.: Optimized artificial potential field algorithm to multi-unmanned aerial vehicle coordinated trajectory planning and collision avoidance in three-dimensional environment. Proc. Inst. Mech. Eng. **33**(16), 519–526 (2019)
6. Han, J.: From PID to active disturbance rejection control. IEEE Trans. Industr. Electron. **56**(03), 900–906 (2009)

Research on Control Method of Four Rotor UAV Based on Classical PID Control System

Dai Wan[1](✉), Miao Zhao[1], WenHui Mo[1], Liang Peng[2], Jingyang Wang[3], and Guanxuan Liang[1]

[1] State Grid Hunan Electric Power Company Limited Research Institute, Changsha 410007, China
280241509@qq.com
[2] Changsha University of Science and Technology, Changsha 410000, China
[3] China Three Gorges University, Yichang 443000, China

Abstract. In recent years, four rotor unmanned aerial vehicle (UAV) has been widely used in the field of power inspection. The four rotor UAV has the characteristics of small size, low manufacturing cost, fast moving speed and so on. It is very convenient to use in various complex and inaccessible places. With the increasing strength of related control technology, the stability, functionality and safety performance of four rotor UAV have been significantly improved. In order to further verify the adaptability of the four rotor UAV to the field of power inspection. In this paper, the flight state control method of multi rotor UAV is studied. The principle of proportion integration differentiation (PID) control is analyzed. The position controller and attitude controller in the PID control system are designed. On this basis, a four rotor UAV Control System based on classical PID control method is constructed. Finally, the designed control system is simulated. The results show that the position control parameters and attitude angle control parameters in the PID control system are the key to ensure the stable operation of the system. The classical PID control system can meet the needs of UAV for simple flight tasks. However, for the application scenarios that require UAV to perform complex actions, the control method of four rotor UAV needs to be further improved. The research results play a guiding role in expanding the application field of UAV.

Keywords: Four Rotor Unmanned Aerial Vehicle · Proportional Integral Derivative · Attitude Control · Position Control

1 Introduction

In recent years, with the rapid development of UAV technology, UAV inspection mode is becoming more and more popular, and its application is also becoming more and more extensive [1]. There are many kinds of power equipment, which are scattered all over the country. Especially in the distribution network, most of the rural distribution network equipment is located in remote areas, and the operating conditions are poor

H. Yang et al. (Eds.): SmartGIFT 2022, LNICST 483, pp. 502–512, 2023.
https://doi.org/10.1007/978-3-031-31733-0_43

[2]. The length of overhead distribution lines in Hunan power grid is more than 200000 km, and the scale of equipment is still growing rapidly every year. At present, the distribution network inspection of Hunan power grid mainly adopts manual inspection, that is, relying on the operation and maintenance personnel to find the line defects and hidden dangers through ground inspection, pole climbing inspection and other methods. With the rapid growth of the scale of distribution network equipment, the timeliness and accuracy of distribution network inspection requirements continue to improve. The traditional manual inspection mode can no longer meet the current operation inspection requirements [3].

Compared with the traditional manual inspection method, UAV inspection has the characteristics of high efficiency, high quality and high security. It is an important means for the development of distribution network line management in a more safe, efficient, refined and economic direction [1]. At present, four rotor UAV is widely used to carry out the inspection of distribution line UAV. Because the operating environment of distribution lines is very complex and harsh. In order to make the UAV fly safely and reliably in a space full of obstacles, scholars at home and abroad have carried out a lot of research in the field of four rotor UAV flight control technology [4, 5]. This paper focuses on the four rotor UAV, and designs a multi rotor UAV Control System Based on classical PID controller. The designed control system is simulated and analyzed. The results of this paper have a guiding role in expanding the application field of UAV.

2 Analysis of PID System Control Structure

Classical PID control system is divided into inner loop control system and outer loop control system. The inner loop control system is the attitude control system. The attitude control system has the characteristics of fast response and wide frequency band. The outer loop control system is a position control system. The position control system mainly realizes the position control of the aircraft on the X, y and Z axes by changing the size of U. Make certain changes to the control variables according to the real-time feedback parameters and the desired attitude angle of the aircraft, and enable the aircraft to fly to the desired place and fly along the preset route [6]. The whole system has four inputs: X, Y, Z and an angle, and the output is three position coordinates and three Euler angles. Figure 2 below shows the simulation diagram of the whole system, and Table 1 shows the parameters used in the simulation of four rotor UAV (Fig. 1).

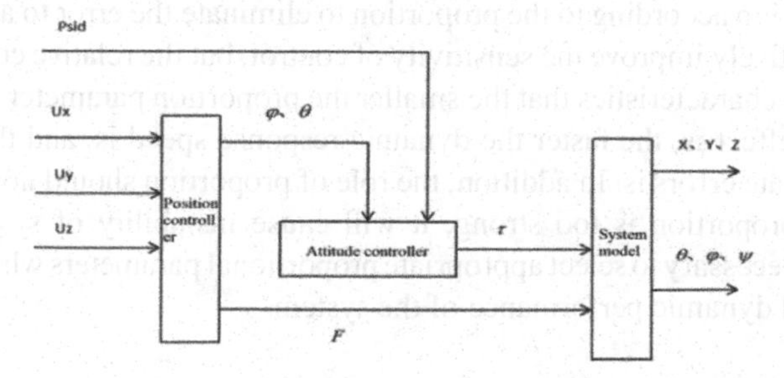

Fig. 1. Schematic diagram of classical PID control system

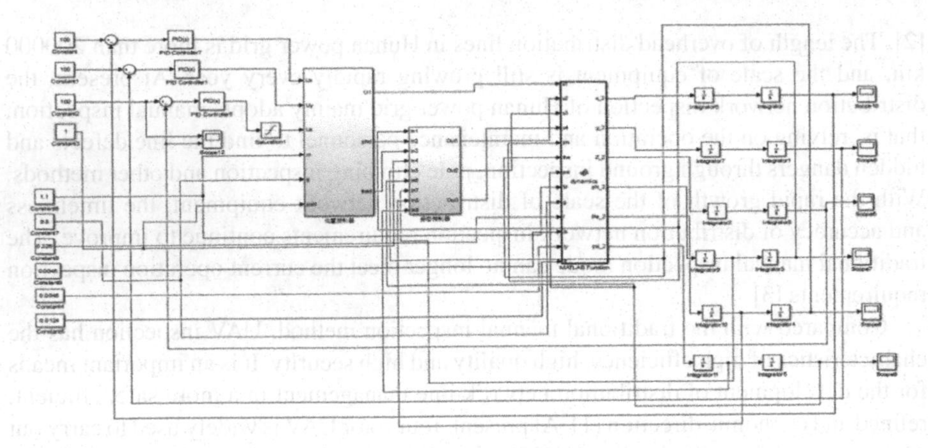

Fig. 2. Simulation diagram of classical PID control system

Table 1. Parameters of four rotor UAV

Parameters	value
m/kg	1.1
L/m	0.225
K	0.75
τ	0.1
$I_x/(\mathrm{kg}\cdot \mathrm{m}^2)$	0.0045
$I_y/(\mathrm{kg}\cdot \mathrm{m}^2)$	0.0045
$I_z/(\mathrm{kg}\cdot \mathrm{m}^2)$	0.0124

3 PID Control Principle

The PID system structure is shown in Fig. 3. The three parameters of proportion, integral and differential can be adjusted respectively, and one or two control laws can also be used. In short, the functions of each unit of the PID controller are as follows.

The proportional control unit can respond to the deviation quickly and timely, and adjust the deviation according to the proportion to eliminate the error to a certain extent, which can effectively improve the sensitivity of control, but the relative control accuracy is low. It has the characteristics that the smaller the proportion parameter is, the stronger the proportion effect is, the faster the dynamic response speed is, and the stronger the ability to eliminate errors is. In addition, the role of proportion should not be too strong. If the role of proportion is too strong, it will cause instability of system vibration. Therefore, it is necessary to select appropriate proportional parameters while maintaining the stability and dynamic performance of the system.

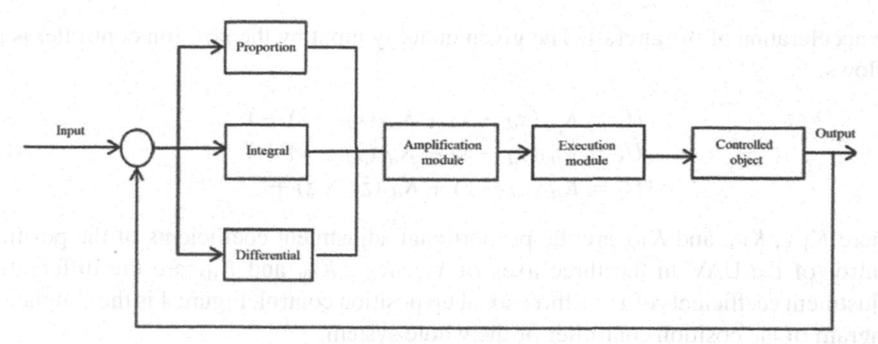

Fig. 3. PID system structure

The main function of the integrating element is to eliminate the steady-state error. The strength of the integration link depends on the size of the time constant. If the integral action is too strong, the phenomenon of superharmonic oscillation will occur.

The function of the differential link is to prevent the deviation signal from becoming too large. If the deviation signal produces large fluctuations, the differential link is equivalent to an early correction signal to avoid oscillation of the system. In short, the differential function is to find the trend of error before the system produces error, and make certain adjustment actions to solve the adverse consequences of error.

The function of traditional PID controller is based on the difference of feedback, and K_P, K_i and K_D are used to eliminate errors and reduce errors, so as to stabilize the system and reduce interference. Therefore, in order to make the stability of the whole system better and make the whole system reach the best state, it is necessary to properly adjust and optimize K_P, K_i and K_D. By constantly adjusting the parameters and judging by the effect, whether the parameters at this time meet the requirements. There are many methods to adjust the parameters of PID controller, including two examples. One is to calculate the most appropriate parameters according to the theoretical formula. The other is to constantly carry out experiments and modify them according to the experimental results, and finally find the most suitable K_P, K_i and K_D. The second method is more commonly used.

4 Position Controller Design

Due to the input of attitude controller φ_d and θ_d and other parameters need to be determined according to the output of the position controller. Therefore, it is necessary to establish a position controller. According to the control variables of three positions of U_x, U_y and U_z fed back by the position control loop. Then, the desired attitude angle is calculated, and the command is issued to establish a corresponding relationship between the input of the attitude controller and the output of the position controller. Finally, the attitude controller constantly modifies the feedback attitude angle according to our preset position, and finally realizes the real-time control of the aircraft. Set $[x_d\ y_d\ z_d]$ to the desired position. $[x\ y\ z]$ is the actual position of the aircraft. $\left[\dot{x}d\ \dot{y}d\ \dot{z}d\right]$ is the expected linear velocity signal. $\left[\dot{x}\ \dot{y}\ \dot{z}\right]$ is the linear velocity of the aircraft. $\left[\ddot{x}\ \ddot{y}\ \ddot{z}\right]$ is the acceleration of the aircraft. The given quantity input by the position controller is as follows.

$$\begin{aligned} U_x &= K_{px}(x_d - x) + K_{dx}(\dot{x}_d - \dot{x}) + \ddot{x} \\ U_y &= K_{py}(y_d - y) + K_{dy}(\dot{y}_d - \dot{y}) + \ddot{y} \\ U_z &= K_{pz}(z_d - z) + K_{dz}(\dot{z}_d - \dot{z}) + \ddot{z} \end{aligned} \tag{1}$$

where K_{PX}, K_{PY} and K_{PZ} are the proportional adjustment coefficients of the position control of the UAV in the three axes of *xyz*. K_{dx}, K_{dy} and K_{dz} are the differential adjustment coefficients of *xyz*'s three axial up position control. Figure 4 is the simulation diagram of the position controller of the whole system.

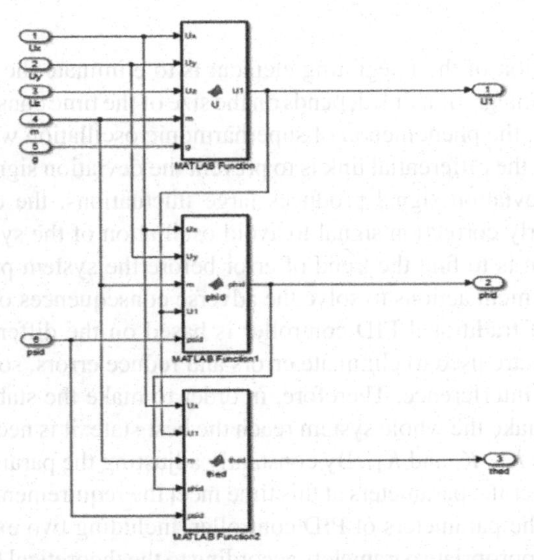

Fig. 4. Simulation diagram of position controller

The altitude channel control quantity U_1 is defined as T_{x}, T_{y} and T_{z} based on the triaxial components of the ground coordinate system.

$$\begin{aligned} T_x &= (\cos\varphi \sin\theta \cos\psi + \sin\varphi \sin\psi)U_1 \\ T_y &= (\cos\varphi \sin\theta \sin\psi - \sin\varphi \cos\psi)U_1 \\ T_z &= (\cos\varphi \cos\theta)U_1 \end{aligned} \tag{2}$$

It can be seen from the above formula that the inputs U_{x}, U_{y} and U_{z} of the position controller are approximately equal to the component of the acceleration of the aircraft decomposed into the ground coordinate system. Ignoring the effect of aerodynamic force, the following relationship can be obtained.

$$\begin{aligned} U_x &= \frac{1}{\mathrm{m}} T_x \\ U_y &= \frac{1}{\mathrm{m}} T_y \end{aligned}$$

$$U_z = \frac{1}{\mathrm{m}} T_z - g \tag{3}$$

Input signal of attitude control loop ψ_{d} is the given value of the system. φ_{d} and θ_{d} can be obtained by formula.

$$\begin{aligned} U_1 &= m\sqrt{U_x^2 + U_y^2 + (U_z + g)^2} \\ \varphi_d &= \arcsin\left((U_x sin\psi_d - U_y \cos \psi_d) \frac{m}{U_1} \right) \\ \theta_d &= \frac{\arcsin(U_x m - U_1 \sin \psi_d \sin \varphi_d)}{(U_1 \cos \psi_d \cos \varphi_d)} \end{aligned} \tag{4}$$

From the above formula, the input of the aircraft attitude controller can be calculated φ_{d} and θ_{d}.

5 Attitude Controller Design

If you want the UAV to reach the specified position and form the specified attitude, you need to constantly adjust the attitude angle. The input of the attitude controller is three attitude angles. After passing through the cascade PID controller, the angular acceleration is obtained, and then multiplied by the corresponding kinematic inertia to obtain three torques, which are used as the input of the system model. Finally, through the feedback of attitude angle sensor, the feedback adjustment is carried out to realize the dynamic adjustment of pitch angle, roll angle and yaw angle. Figure 5 is the schematic diagram of the attitude controller.

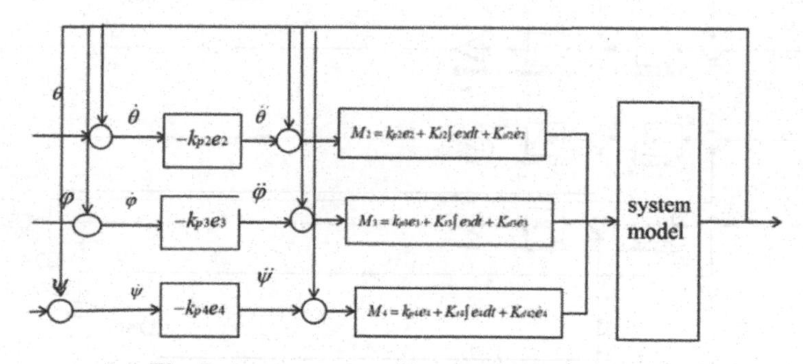

Fig. 5. Loop structure diagram of attitude control

Considering that the coupling and nonlinear relationship are ignored when the attitude angle is small, the control torque and angular acceleration have the following relationship.

$$\begin{aligned} U_2 &= J\ddot{\theta} \\ U_3 &= J\ddot{\varphi} \end{aligned}$$

$$U_4 = J\ddot{\psi} \tag{5}$$

Set the given attitude angle signal as $[\theta\ \varphi\ \psi]$. The actual attitude angle signal is $[\theta_3\ \varphi_3\ \psi_3]$. The expression of the control quantity is as follows.

$$\begin{aligned} M_2 &= k_{p2}e_2 + K_{i2}\int e_2 dt + K_{d2}\dot{e}_2 \\ M_3 &= k_{p3}e_3 + K_{i3}\int e_3 dt + K_{d3}\dot{e}_3 \\ M_4 &= k_{p4}e_4 + K_{i4}\int e_4 dt + K_{d42}\dot{e}_4 \end{aligned} \tag{6}$$

where:

$$\begin{aligned} e_2 &= \theta_3 - \theta, \quad \dot{e}_3 = \dot{\varphi}_3 - \dot{\varphi} \\ e_3 &= \varphi_3 - \varphi, \quad \dot{e}_2 = \dot{\theta}_3 - \dot{\theta} \\ e_4 &= \psi_3 - \psi, \quad \dot{e}_4 = \dot{\psi}_3 - \dot{\psi} \end{aligned} \tag{7}$$

Based on PID controller control, the following expression can be obtained.

$$\begin{aligned} U_2 &= JM_2 \\ U_3 &= JM_3 \\ U_4 &= JM_4 \end{aligned} \tag{8}$$

The simulation diagram of attitude control is shown in Fig. 6.

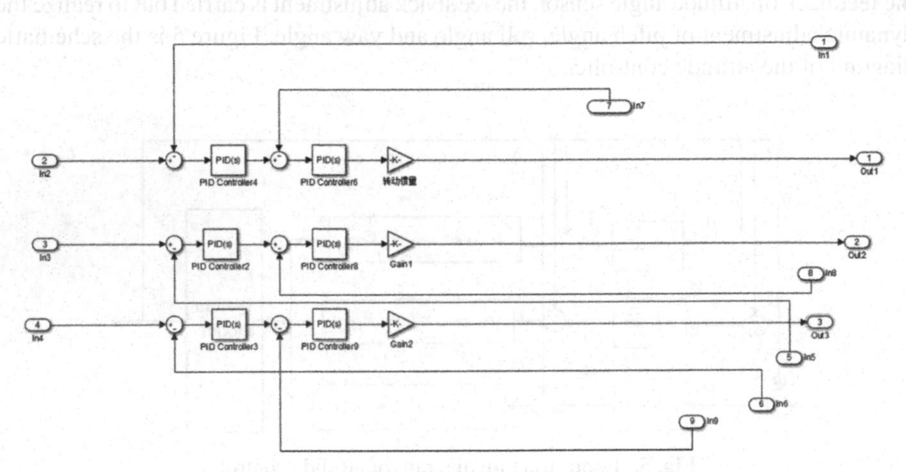

Fig. 6. Simulation diagram of attitude controller

6 Simulation Analysis of Control System Based on Classical PID

Based on the above research content, the classical PID control system is simulated and analyzed. The simulation results are shown in the figure below (Figs. 7, 8, 9, 10, 11 and 12).

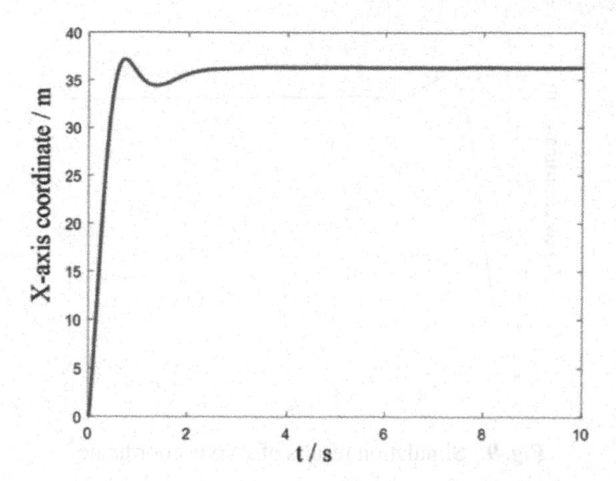

Fig. 7. Simulation results of X-axis coordinate

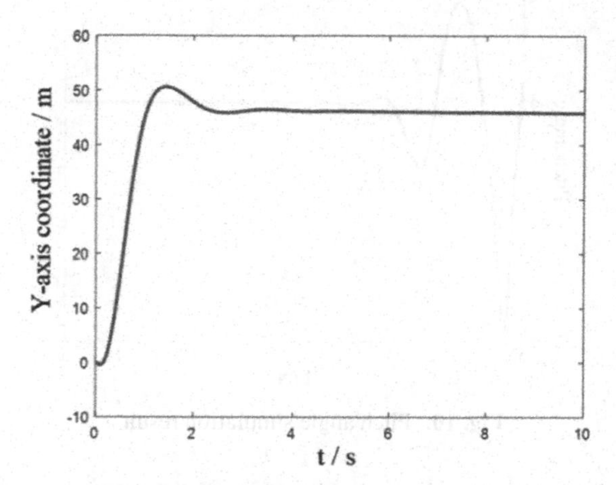

Fig. 8. Simulation results of Y-axis coordinate

The simulation results are shown in the figure above. It can be seen from the oscilloscope display graph that the oscilloscope display curve is relatively stable. However, there are certain overshoot and fluctuations, and the steady state can be reached in about 3S. In addition, the system has only four inputs, so the pitch angle and roll angle return to the origin after fluctuation.

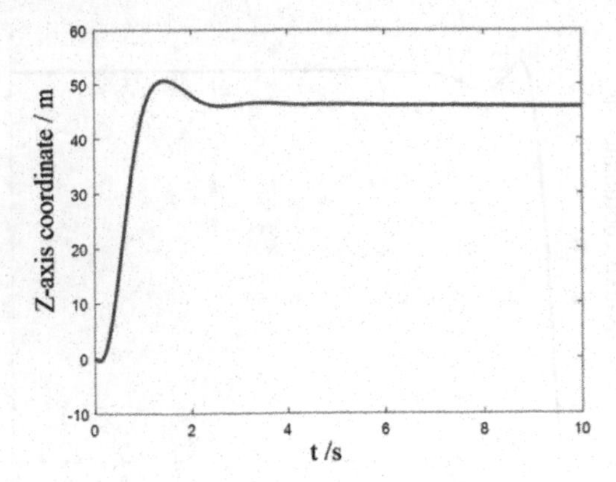

Fig. 9. Simulation results of Z-axis coordinate

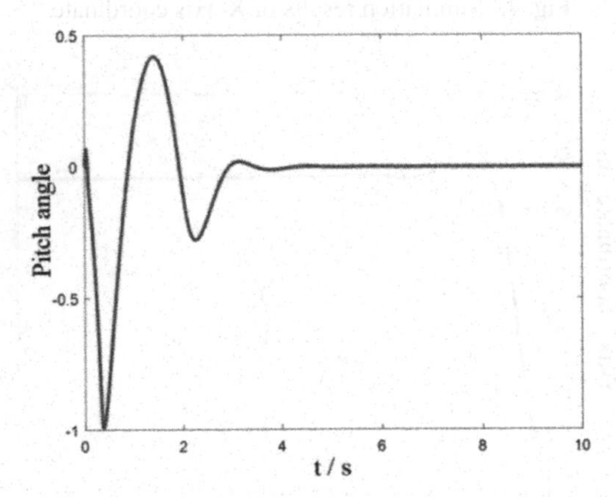

Fig. 10. Pitch angle simulation result

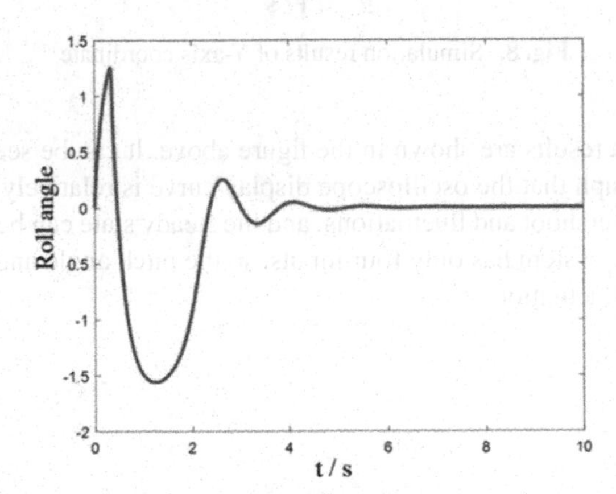

Fig. 11. Roll angle simulation result

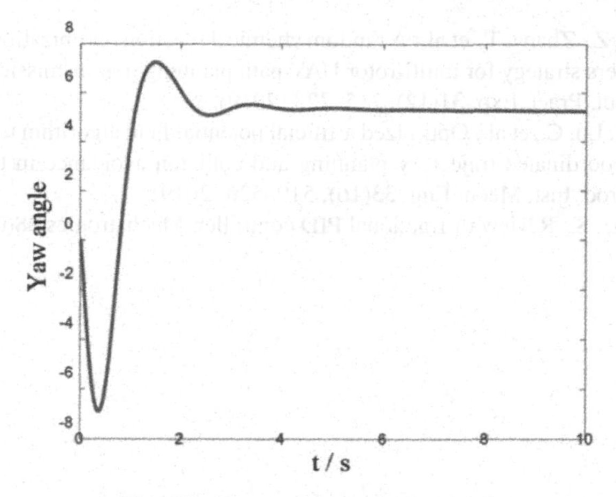

Fig. 12. Yaw angle simulation result

7 Conclusion

This paper takes the motion state control method of four rotor UAV as the research object. The control system of UAV running state based on classical PID controller is designed. The inner loop control model to realize the flight attitude control of UAV and the outer loop control model to realize the space position control of UAV are constructed. The simulation experiment of UAV operation state control system is carried out.

The research results show that the classical PID control system meets the needs of UAV for simple flight tasks. For example, in the daily inspection work scene of transmission lines, only drones need to fly and take photos at a constant speed along the smooth line channel. Classical PID control system can be used to perform such a simple task.

The working scenario of lean inspection of distribution lines requires that unmanned aerial vehicles can shuttle freely in rugged and complex line channels, and that unmanned aerial vehicles can quickly avoid obstacles. When performing such complex tasks, it is necessary to further improve the control method of four rotor UAV.

Acknowledgment. This work was financially supported by the science and technology project of State Grid Hunan Electric Power Company Limited (5216A521001J).

References

1. Deng, C., Wang, S., Huang, Z., et al.: Unmanned aerial vehicles for power line inspection: a cooperative way in platforms and communications. J. Commun. **9**(09), 687–692 (2014)
2. Liu, C., Liu, Y., Wu, H., et al.: A safe flight approach of the UAV in the electrical line inspection. Int. J. Emerg. Electr. Power Syst. **16**(05), 503–515 (2015)
3. Chen, Y., Yu, J., Mei, Y., et al.: Modified central force optimization (MCFO) algorithm for 3D UAV path planning. Neurocomputing **71**(14), 878–888 (2016)

4. Yang, Q., Yang, Z., Zhang, T., et al.: A random chemical reaction optimization algorithm based on dual containers strategy for multi-rotor UAV path planning in transmission line inspection. Concurr. Comput. Pract. Exp. **31**(12), 215–223 (2019)
5. Tang, J., Sun, J., Lu, C., et al.: Optimized artificial potential field algorithm to multi-unmanned aerial vehicle coordinated trajectory planning and collision avoidance in three-dimensional environment. Proc. Inst. Mech. Eng. **33**(16), 519–526 (2019)
6. Shah, P., Agashe, S.: Review of fractional PID controller. Mechatronics **38**(01), 29–41 (2016)

Research on Target Tracking Technology of UAV in Distribution Network Based on Deep Learning

Dai Wan[1](✉), Simin Peng[1], Miao Zhao[1], Yingying Yi[2], Hengyi Zhou[1], WenHui Mo[1], and Jingyang Wang[3]

[1] State Grid Hunan Electric Power Company Limited Research Institute, Changsha 410007, China
280241509@qq.com

[2] Changsha Tax Service, Changsha 410000, China

[3] China Three Gorges University, Yichang 443000, China

Abstract. With the rapid development of unmanned aerial vehicle (UAV) technology, the application of UAV patrol inspection in the power grid side is becoming more and more popular. At present, the application of UAV inspection technology in the power transmission profession has become increasingly mature. However, there are still many problems in the application of UAV inspection technology in power distribution specialty. First, the operation environment of distribution lines is complex, and there are many vegetation and obstacles around the lines. In this case, the UAV is easy to touch foreign objects by mistake during flight, resulting in aircraft explosion. Second, the volume of distribution equipment is much smaller than that of transmission equipment. In this case, it is very difficult for UAV to identify the defects of distribution equipment. The above characteristics of distribution lines and equipment put forward higher requirements for the performance of UAV front-end target tracking and environmental recognition. In order to reduce the risk of blowing up and hanging up in the process of distribution line UAV inspection and improve the efficiency of UAV inspection, this paper carried out the research on the front-end target tracking and intelligent recognition technology of distribution network UAV Based on deep learning. The research results have guiding significance for improving the applicability of UAV patrol technology in the field of power distribution.

Keywords: Distribution Network · Unmanned Aerial Vehicle · Target Tracking · Deep Learning

1 Introduction

Recently, UAV patrol technology is more and more widely used in the field of power distribution network. This new technology has greatly improved the patrol efficiency of the power distribution discipline [1]. However, the complex operating environment of distribution network and the small volume of distribution equipment put forward higher requirements for UAV target tracking technology [2].

H. Yang et al. (Eds.): SmartGIFT 2022, LNICST 483, pp. 513–518, 2023.
https://doi.org/10.1007/978-3-031-31733-0_44

This paper first analyzes the single target tracking process of UAV, and then further analyzes the twin network target tracking technology based on model compression in the complex operation environment of distribution network. The target tracking algorithm for the traditional twin network consumes a lot of computation, which can not be used on the UAV platform; And due to the small target of distribution equipment, it is necessary to make more efficient use of the characteristics of different layers. In this paper, the geometric median method is used to compress the feature extraction network RESNET to improve the operation efficiency of the model, so that the model can run on the UAV platform, and the tracking accuracy is controlled within an acceptable range. In view of the shortcomings of the twin network tracking algorithm siamrpn + + in multi-layer feature fusion, an improved depth feature fusion weighting method is proposed, and the convolution neural network is used for training the weights to make the algorithm more accurate for classification and regression results.

2 UAV Single Target Tracking Process

After decades of development, visual tracking technology has made great progress, and the execution steps of visual tracking methods have been studied thoroughly [3]. First, initialize the model parameters. That is, the current frame state of the image target to be tracked is taken as the initial state of future tracking. The second step is to analyze the characteristic parameters and establish the target model. The second step is to analyze the image feature parameters and establish a feature model. The third step is to apply the final target strategy to the image feature model of the previous step. In this way, a new image feature model can be obtained. Finally, repeat the above steps [4, 5]. Figure 1 is the basic flow chart.

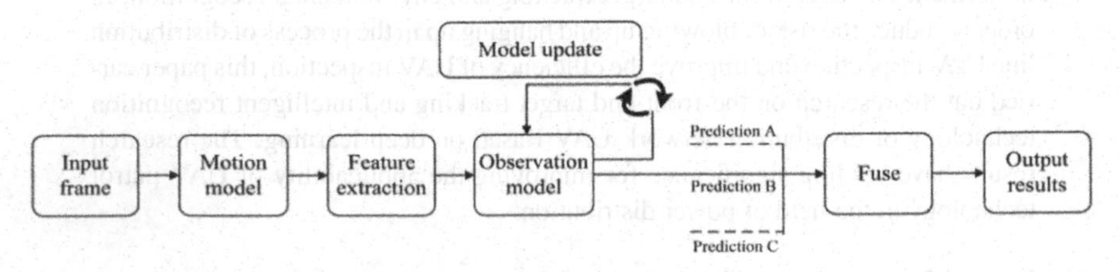

Fig. 1. Target tracking process

The target tracking strategy can adopt generation method. The first step is to learn the global information of the image and extract the feature parameters. The second step is to classify various characteristic parameters. The third step is to analyze the area close to the target features. The fourth step is to compare the template with similar areas. Finally, find the area with the highest similarity (Fig. 2).

In addition to the generation method, the target tracking strategy can also use the discriminant method. The discriminant method directly learns the target model through data samples. In target tracking, the discriminant method directly trains a model through sample distribution for tracking targets. The specific step is to give a series of samples, train a model through the sample data, and output the probability value. When there

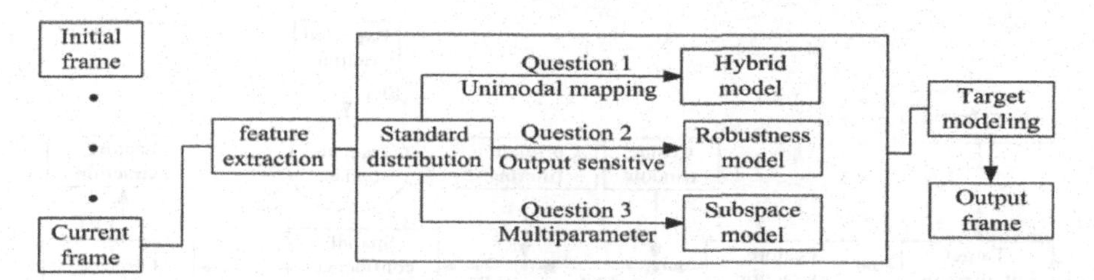

Fig. 2. Target tracking process

are new samples next time, the classification can be judged by the discriminant model. Therefore, the difference between the discriminant method and the generation method is that the discriminant method directly studies the prediction model and then predicts. After the initialization of the target, the feature is extracted and the model is established. The foreground target and the background are divided by the classifier. The tracker tracks the foreground target and updates the window until the next frame. At the same time, the background information is added in the next frame to increase the interference of the background, which improves the robustness of the classifier. The flow of discrimination class tracking method is shown in Fig. 3.

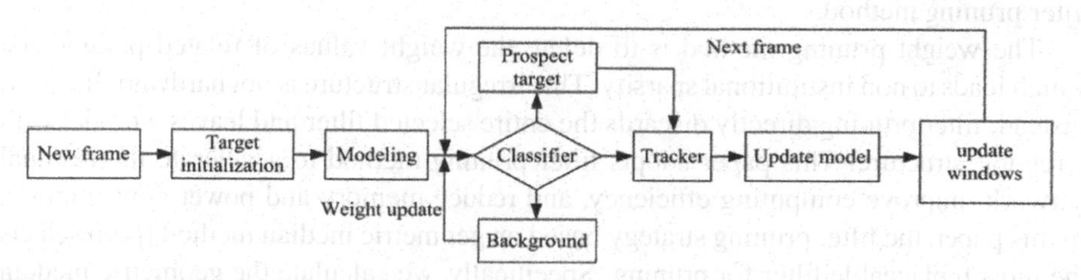

Fig. 3. Target tracking process

As shown in Fig. 4, the first step is to initialize the first frame. The second step is to use the initialized prediction target as the input signal of the second frame. The third step is to extract different visual features to better describe the input. The fourth step is to convolve and correlate the FFT converted signal with the correlation filter, where FFT is the fast Fourier transform. The fifth step is to invert the operation result of the fourth step to obtain the spatial confidence graph. The sixth step is to extract new feature parameters from the spatial confidence graph. The seventh step is to train the data processing strategy and update it with the expected output.

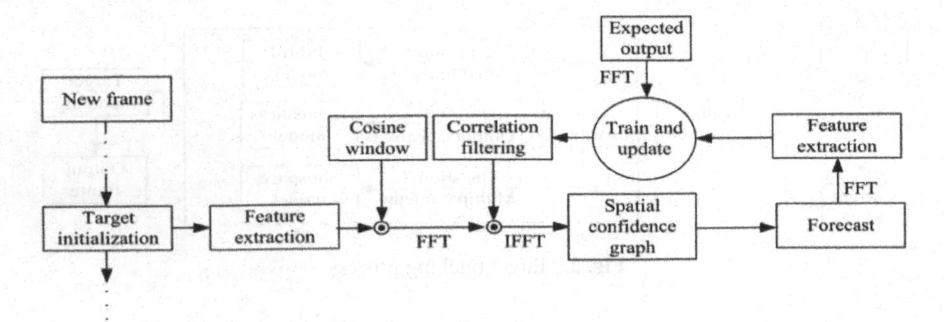

Fig. 4. Target tracking process

3 Twin Network Target Tracking Based on Model Compression

The siamrpn++ model used in this paper uses the residual network structure. Although the performance is very strong, this high computational cost is very expensive to deploy on UAV. A low computational cost deep convolution neural network can be obtained by model compression to optimize the model. One method of model compression is pruning. There are two main pruning methods. They are weight pruning method and filter pruning method.

The weight pruning method is to delete the weight values of related parameters, which leads to non institutional sparsity. This irregular structure is not hardware friendly. Instead, filter pruning directly discards the entire selected filter and leaves a model with a regular structure. This paper adopts filter pruning method to accelerate the residual network, improve computing efficiency, and reduce memory and power consumption. In this paper, the filter pruning strategy based on geometric median method fpgm selects the most replaceable filter for pruning. Specifically, we calculate the geometric median of the filter in the same layer. According to the characteristics of geometric median, the filter near it can be represented by residual filter. Therefore, pruning these filters will not have a substantial negative impact on the performance of the model. Fpgm is used to prune the most replaceable filter containing redundant information, so that it can still maintain good performance when the norm based criterion fails.

The twin network model siamrpn++ mainly solves the problem of how to apply deep networks such as RESNET and inception to the tracking network based on twin networks. After siamfc algorithm, although there have been many tracking algorithms based on twin networks, most of these networks use shallow networks as feature extractors. In previous attempts, directly using the pre trained deep network will lead to the decline of the accuracy of the tracking algorithm. Therefore, a key problem to be solved for the tracker based on twin network is how to use the deeper network for tracking. The relevant operations in siamfc can be regarded as calculating the similarity of each position in the form of sliding window, so it needs to have translation invariance, and the filling in the depth network will destroy this translation invariance, because according to the training method of siamfc, the positive samples are in the positive center, and the network will gradually learn this statistical characteristic, and learn the distribution of positive samples in the samples, that is, the central position is a positive sample, and the edge position is a negative sample, The filling method will change the original edge position to the center position, resulting in performance degradation. Therefore, when training, let the target not focus on the central position, but let it be in different positions of the image, offset a certain distance from the central point, so as to alleviate the problem of shallow network caused by unable to fill. Figure 5 is Siamrpn++ architecture.

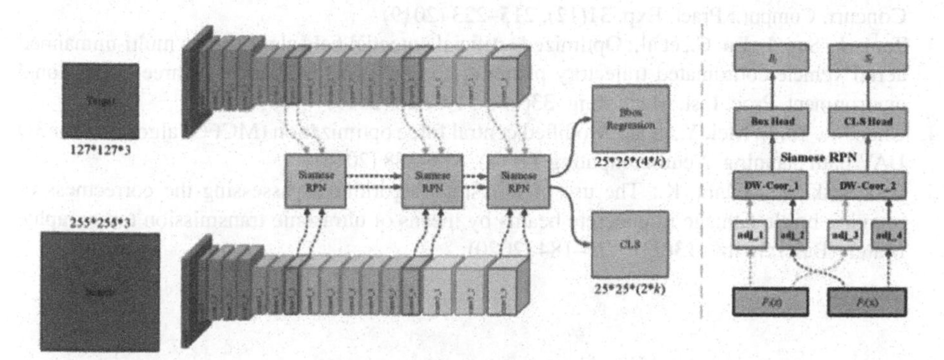

Fig. 5. Target tracking process

The output of multiple Siamese region suggestion blocks can be fused to improve the operation effect. The siamrpn block is shown on the right. Siamrpn++ uses resnet-50 as the backbone. Each block output is appended with a 1×1 to keep the number of characteristic image channels 256. By uniformly sampling and processing samples, the filling operation is added to the network characteristic graph, and the parameters of the filled characteristic graph will increase after convolution, which brings a certain amount of computational consumption. Siamrpn++ cuts the central area of the image as a template, and makes the target distributed in the image template. By reducing image pixels, the amount of calculation is reduced. Siamrpn++ also improves the cross-correlation layer in the previous twin network, uses the deep correlation layer to achieve more efficient information correlation, reduces the amount of parameters, increases the fine-tuning of resnet-50 backbone network, and improves the performance of the feature extractor. After adopting the new sampling strategy in the training process, RESNET can be successfully trained and the video can be tracked.

4 Conclusion

Aiming at the complex operating environment of distribution network and the small size of distribution equipment, this paper deeply analyzes the more applicable target tracking technology of UAV. The deep convolution neural network with low computational cost and high accuracy is obtained by model compression. At the same time, the depth feature fusion weighting method is improved, and the convolution neural network is used to train the weights, so as to obtain an efficient and high-precision target tracking method.

Acknowledgment. This research work is supported by State Grid Hunan Electric Power Company Limited. The number of the science and technology project is 5216A521001J.

References

1. Wang, Y.: Research on track planning of electric patrol rotor UAV. Lanzhou Jiaotong University, Lanzhou (2020)
2. Yang, Q., Yang, Z., Zhang, T., et al.: A random chemical reaction optimization algorithm based on dual containers strategy for multi-rotor UAV path planning in transmission line inspection. Concurr. Comput.: Pract. Exp. **31**(12), 215–223 (2019)
3. Tang, J., Sun, J., Lu, C., et al.: Optimized artificial potential field algorithm to multi-unmanned aerial vehicle coordinated trajectory planning and collision avoidance in three-dimensional environment. Proc. Inst. Mech. Eng. **33**(16), 519–526 (2019)
4. Chen, Y., Yu, J., Mei, Y., et al.: Modified central force optimization (MCFO) algorithm for 3D UAV path planning. Neurocomputing **71**(14), 878–888 (2016)
5. Perkowski, Z., Tatara, K.: The use of Dijkstra's algorithm in assessing the correctness of imaging brittle damage in concrete beams by means of ultrasonic transmission tomography. Mater. (Basel Switz.) **13**(03), 175–184 (2020)

Author Index

H. Yang et al. (Eds.): SmartGIFT 2022, LNICST 483, pp. 519–521, 2023.
https://doi.org/10.1007/978-3-031-31733-0

Printed in the United States
by Baker & Taylor Publisher Services

Printed in the United States
by Baker & Taylor Publisher Services